THE KANTIAN MIND

The thought of Immanuel Kant is fundamental to understanding Western philosophy. Spanning epistemology, metaphysics, ethics, and religion, the sheer scope and originality of Kant's ideas have decisively shaped the history of modern philosophy.

The Kantian Mind is an outstanding reference source and guide to Kant's thought and a major new publication in Kant scholarship. Comprising forty-five chapters by a stellar team of contributors, the collection is divided into four clear parts:

- Background to the Critical Philosophy
- Transcendental Philosophy (Critique and Doctrine)
- Posthumous Writings and Lectures
- Kant and Contemporary Kantians

In addition to coverage of Kant's main works, the volume contains chapters on a broad range of topics including Kant's views on logic, mathematics, the natural sciences, anthropology, religion, politics, and education. The concluding chapters cover the influence of Kant's thought on contemporary analytic and continental philosophy.

Including suggestions for further reading at the end of each chapter, *The Kantian Mind* is essential reading for all students and scholars of Kant and contemporary Kantian thought. It will also be extremely helpful to those in related humanities and social sciences disciplines such as religion, history, politics, and literature.

Sorin Baiasu is Professor of Philosophy at Keele University, UK. He is the author of *Kant and Sartre* (2011), and co-editor (with Mark Timmons) of *Kant on Practical Justification* (2013), and (with Alberto Vanzo) of *Kant and the Continental Tradition* (2020).

Mark Timmons is Professor of Philosophy at the University of Arizona, USA. He is the author of *Kant's* Doctrine of Virtue: *A Guide* (2021), and editor of *Kant's* Metaphysics of Morals: *Interpretative Essays* (2002) and of the annual *Oxford Studies in Normative Ethics*.

ROUTLEDGE PHILOSOPHICAL MINDS

In philosophy past and present there are some philosophers who tower over the intellectual landscape and have shaped it in indelible ways. So significant is their impact that it is difficult to capture it in one place. The Routledge Philosophical Minds series presents a comprehensive survey of all aspects of a major philosopher's work, from analysis and criticism of their major texts and arguments to the way their ideas are taken up in contemporary philosophy and beyond. Edited by leading figures in their fields and with an outstanding international roster of contributors the series offers a magisterial and unrivalled picture of a great philosophical mind.

THE LOCKEAN MIND
Edited by Jessica Gordon-Roth and Shelley Weinberg

THE ANSCOMBEAN MIND
Edited by Adrian Haddock and Rachael Wiseman

THE BERGSONIAN MIND
Edited by Mark Sinclair and Yaron Wolf

THE JAMESIAN MIND
Edited by Sarin Marchetti

THE MURDOCHIAN MIND
Edited by Silvia Caprioglio Panizza and Mark Hopwood

THE PROUSTIAN MIND
Edited by Anna Elsner and Thomas Stern

THE KANTIAN MIND
Sorin Baiasu and Mark Timmons

For more information on this series, please visit: www.routledge.com/Routledge-Philosophical-Minds/book-series/RPM

THE KANTIAN MIND

Edited by Sorin Baiasu and Mark Timmons

LONDON AND NEW YORK

Cover image: Getty Images

First published 2024
by Routledge
4 Park Square, Milton Park, Abingdon, Oxon OX14 4RN

and by Routledge
605 Third Avenue, New York, NY 10158

Routledge is an imprint of the Taylor & Francis Group, an informa business

British Library Cataloguing-in-Publication Data
A catalogue record for this book is available from the British Library

Library of Congress Cataloging-in-Publication Data
Names: Baiasu, Sorin, editor. | Timmons, Mark, 1951– editor.
Title: The Kantian mind / edited by Sorin Baiasu and Mark Timmons.
Description: Abingdon, Oxon ; New York, NY : Routledge, 2023. |
Series: Routledge philosophical minds | Includes bibliographical references and index.
Identifiers: LCCN 2022061825 (print) | LCCN 2022061826 (ebook)
Subjects: LCSH: Kant, Immanuel, 1724–1804. | Knowledge, Theory of. |
Thought and thinking.
Classification: LCC B2798 .K22557 2023 (print) | LCC B2798 (ebook) |
DDC 193—dc23/eng/20230421
LC record available at https://lccn.loc.gov/2022061825
LC ebook record available at https://lccn.loc.gov/2022061826

ISBN: 978-1-138-82748-6 (hbk)
ISBN: 978-1-032-52425-2 (pbk)
ISBN: 978-1-003-40661-7 (ebk)

DOI: 10.4324/9781003406617

Typeset in Bembo
by Apex CoVantage, LLC

CONTENTS

NOTE ON ABBREVIATIONS

In citing Kant's works, the following abbreviations are used throughout this book. Pagination references in the text and footnotes are to the volume, page number, and (in some cases) section and/or line numbers in the German edition of Kant's works, *Kants gesammelte Schriften*, edited by the Königlich Preußischen Akademie der Wissenschaft, subsequently Deutsche, now Berlin-Brandenburg Akademie der Wissenschaften (originally under the editorship of Wilhelm Dilthey) (Berlin: Georg Reimer, subsequently Walter de Gruyter, 1902–). References to the *Critique of Pure Reason* (*KrV*) follow the A (first edition), B (second edition) convention. When not stated otherwise or specified in the References section of the respective chapters, translations are from Kant (1992–2016) *The Cambridge Edition of the Works of Immanuel Kant in English Translation*. P. Guyer and A.W. Wood (eds). 16 Vols, Cambridge: Cambridge University Press. Abbreviations for texts other than Kant's are specified in the respective chapters, usually under References.

AA	Kants gesammelte Schriften
Anth	Anthropologie in pragmatischer Hinsicht (AA 07)
AP	Aufsätze, das Philantropin betreffend (AA 02)
BBM	Bestimmung des Begriffs einer Menschenrace (AA 08)
BDG	Der einzig mögliche Beweisgrund zu einer Demonstration des Daseins Gottes (AA 02)
Bem	Bemerkungen zu den Beobachtungen über das Gefühl des Schönen und Erhabenen (AA 20)
Br	Briefe (AA10–13)
DI	Meditationum quarundam de igne succincta delineatio (AA 01)
EaD	Das Ende Aller Dinge (AA 08)
EACG	Entwurf und Ankündigung eines Collegii der physischen Geographie (AA 02)
EKZA	Erläuterung Kants zu G. Achenwalls *Iuris naturalis Pars posterior*
EEKU	Erste Einleitung in die Kritik der Urteilskraft (AA 20)
FBZE	Fortgesetzte Betrachtung der seit einiger Zeit wahrgenommenen Erderschütterungen (AA 01)
FEV	Die Frage, ob die Erde veralte, physikalisch erwogen (AA 01)

FM	Welches sind die wirklichen Fortschritte, die die Metaphysik seit Leibnitzens und Wolf's Zeiten in Deutschland gemacht hat? (AA 20)
GMS	Grundlegung zur Metaphysik der Sitten (AA 04)
GNVE	Geschichte und Naturbeschreibung der Merkwürdigen Vorfälle des Erdbebens, welches an dem Ende des 1755sten Jahres einen großen Theil der Erde erschüttert hat (AA 01)
GSE	Beobachtungen über das Gefühl des Schönen und Erhabenen (AA 02)
GSK	Gedanken von der wahren Schätzung der lebendigen Kräfte (AA 01)
GUGR	Von dem ersten Grunde des Unterschiedes der Gegenden im Raume (AA 02)
HN	Handschriftlicher Nachlass (AA 14–23)
IaG	Idee zu einer allgemeinen Geschichte in weltbürgerlicher Absicht (AA 08)
KpV	Kritik der praktischen Vernunft (AA 05)
KU	Kritik der Urteilskraft (AA 05)
Log	Logik (AA 09)
MAM	Mutmaßlicher Anfang der Menschheitsgeschichte (AA 08)
MAN	Metaphysische Anfangsgründe der Naturwissenschaft (AA 04)
MoPh	Metaphysicae cum geometria iunctae usus in philosophia naturali, cuius specimen I. continent monadologiam physicam (AA 01)
MpVT	Über das Mißlingen aller philosophischen Versuche in der Theodicee (AA 08)
MS	Die Metaphysik der Sitten (AA 06)
RL	Metaphysische Anfangsgründe der Rechtslehre (AA 06)
TL	Metaphysische Anfangsgründe der Tugendlehre (AA 06)
MSI	De mundi sensibilis atque intelligibilis forma et principiis (AA 02)
NEV	Nachricht von der Einrichtung seiner Vorlesungen in dem Winterhalbjahre von 1765–1766 (AA 02)
NLBR	Neuer Lehrbegriff der Bewegung und Ruhe und der damit verknüpften Folgerungen in den ersten Gründen der Naturwissenschaft (AA 02)
NTH	Allgemeine Naturgeschichte und Theorie des Himmels (AA 01)
OP	Opus Postumum (AA 21 and 22)
Päd	Pädagogik (AA 09)
PG	Physische Geographie (AA 09)
PND	Principiorum Primorum cognitionis metaphysicae nova dilucidatio (AA 01)
Prol	Prolegomena zu einer jeden künftigen Metaphysik (AA 04)
Refl	Reflexion (AA 14–19)
RezHerder	Recensionen von J.G. Herders Ideen zur Philosophie der Geschichte der Menschheit (AA 08)
RGV	Die Religion innerhalb der Grenzen der bloßen Vernunft (AA 06)
SF	Der Streit der Fakultäten (AA 07)
TG	Träume eines Geistersehers, erläutert durch die Träume der Metaphysik (AA 02)
TP	Über den Gemeinspruch: Das mag in der Theorie richtig sein, taugt aber nicht für die Praxis (AA 08)
TW	Neue Anmerkungen zur Erläuterung der Theorie der Winde (AA 01)
UD	Untersuchung über die Deutlichkeit der Grundsätze der natürlichen Theologie und der Moral (AA 02)
UFE	Untersuchung der Frage, ob die Erde in ihrer Umdrehung um die Achse, wodurch sie die Abwechselung des Tages und der Nacht hervorbringt,

	einige Veränderung seit den ersten Zeiten ihres Ursprungs erlitten habe (AA 01)
ÜE	Über eine Entdeckung, nach der alle neue Kritik der reinen Vernunft durch eine ältere entbehrlich gemacht werden soll (AA 08)
ÜGTP	Über den Gebrauch teleologischer Principien in der Philosophie (AA 08)
VAMS	Vorarbeit zur Metaphysik der Sitten (AA 23)
V-Anth/Busolt	Vorlesungen Wintersemester 1788/1789 Busolt (AA 25)
V-Anth/Collins	Vorlesungen Wintersemester 1772/1773 Collins (AA 25)
V-Anth/Fried	Vorlesungen Wintersemester 1775/1776 Friedländer (AA 25)
V-Anth/Mensch	Vorlesungen Wintersemester 1781/1782 Menschenkunde, Petersburg (AA 25)
V-Anth/Mron	Vorlesungen Wintersemester 1784/1785 Mrongovius (AA 25)
V-Anth/Parow	Vorlesungen Wintersemester 1772/1773 Parow (AA 25)
V-Anth/Pillau	Vorlesungen Wintersemester 1777/1778 Pillau (AA 25)
V-Lo/Blomberg	Logik Blomberg (AA 24)
V-Lo/Busolt	Logik Busolt (AA 24)
V-Lo/Dohna	Logik Dohna-Wundlacken (AA 24)
V-Lo/Philippi	Logik Philippi (AA 24)
V-Lo/Pölitz	Logik Pölitz (AA 24)
V-Lo/Wiener	Wiener Logik (AA 24)
V-Met/Dohna	Kant Metaphysik Dohna (AA 28)
V-Met/Heinze	Metaphysik L1 (Heinze) (AA 28)
V-Met-L1/Pölitz	Metaphysik L1 (Pölitz) (AA 28)
V-Met-L2/Pölitz	Metaphysik L2 (Pölitz, Original) (AA 28)
V-Met/Mron	Metaphysik Mrongovius (AA 29)
V-Met/Schön	Metaphysik von Schön, Ontologie (AA 28)
V-Met/Volckmann	Metaphysik Volckmann (AA 28)
V-Mo/Collins	Moralphilosophie Collins (AA 27)
V-Mo/Mron II	Moral Mrongovius II (AA 29)
V-MS/Vigil	Die Metaphysik der Sitten Vigilantius (AA 27)
V-NR/Feyerabend	Naturrecht Feyerabend (AA 27)
V-PG	Vorlesungen über Physische Geographie (AA 26)
V-Phil -Th/Pölitz	Philosophische Religionslehre nach Pölitz (AA 28)
VRML	Über ein vermeintes Recht, aus Menschenliebe zu lügen (AA 08)
VT	Von einem neuerdings erhobenen vornehmen Ton in der Philosophie (AA 08)
V-Th/Volckmann	Natürliche Theologie Volckmann nach Baumbach (AA 28)
VUE	Von den Ursachen der Erdenschütterungen bei Gelegenheit des Unglücks, welches die westliche Länder von Europa gegen das Ende des vorigen Jahres betroffen hat (AA 01)
VvRM	Von den verschiedenen Racen der Menschen (AA 02)
WA	Beantwortung der Frage: Was ist Aufklärung (AA 08)
WDO	Was heißt sich im Denken orientiren? (AA 08)
ZeF	Zum ewigen Frieden (AA 08)
ZREM	Zur Rezension von Eberhards Magazin (AA 20)

V-Lo/Bauch	Logik Bauch, in *Logik-Vorlesung Unveröffentlichte Schriften* I, ed. T. Binder, Hamburg: Felix Meiner (VL 1)
V-Lo/Hechsel	Logik Hechsel, in *Logik-Vorlesung Unveröffentlichte Schriften* II, ed. T. Binder, Hamburg: Felix Meiner (VL 2)
V-Lo/Warschauer	Warschauer Logik, in *Logik-Vorlesung Unveröffentlichte Schriften* II, ed. T. Binder, Hamburg: Felix Meiner (VL 2)

NOTES ON CONTRIBUTORS

Sorin Baiasu is Professor of Philosophy at Keele University. He is co-editor (with Mark Timmons) of *Kant on Practical Justification* (2013) and (with Alberto Vanzo) of *Kant and the Continental Tradition: Sensibility, Nature and Religion* (2020). He published work on Kant (in metaphysics, metaethics, and political philosophy) in, among others, *Kant-Studien*, *Kantian Review*, and *Studi Kantiani*. He is currently working on a monograph entitled: *Kantian Justice: A Responsibility-enhancing Desert-centred Theory of Justice*.

Giovanni Pietro Basile studied physics, theology, and philosophy. He did his PhD in philosophy at the Ludwig-Maximilians-Universität Munich. He has recently been appointed as associate professor at Boston College. Among his main publications are two books as author – *Transcendance et finitude. La synthèse transcendantale dans la* Critique de la raison pure *de Kant* (2005) and *Kants Opus postumum und seine Rezeption* (2013) – and several papers on Kant, Karl Jaspers, and Paul Ricœur.

Alyssa R. Bernstein is Associate Professor of Philosophy at Ohio University. She has received both a Fulbright Fellowship and a Mellon Fellowship, and was a Graduate Fellow at the Harvard Center for Ethics, prior to receiving her PhD in Philosophy from Harvard University (where she both took and helped to teach courses taught by John Rawls, who advised her dissertation together with T. M. Scanlon and Hilary Putnam). Bernstein has been a post-doctoral Fellow of the Carr Center for Human Rights Policy at Harvard University's Kennedy School of Government (2000–2002), the Nancy Schaenen Visiting Scholar at DePauw University's Prindle Institute for Ethics (2007–2008), and the Director of Ohio University's Institute for Applied and Professional Ethics (2011–2016). She has published a number of articles on Kant and Rawls in academic journals, including *Kantian Review*, *Jarbuch für Recht und Ethik*, and *Philosophia*, as well as in several edited volumes.

Graham Bird, after graduating from Oxford, held a senior scholarship and temporary fellowship at Magdalen College. He was appointed to lectureships at Aberdeen and St. Andrews universities and was a professor at Stirling and Manchester universities. He has published many articles and books on Kant's philosophy and more general philosophical problems, including *Kant's Theory of Knowledge*, *William James*, and *The Revolutionary Kant*. He was instrumental in starting up the UK Kant Society and, with Howard Williams, the journal *Kantian Review*.

Andrew Chignell is Professor in the University Center for Human Values at Princeton, with appointments in the Religion and Philosophy departments. From 2020 to 2023, he served as the president of the North American Kant Society. Together with Lara Buchak, he directs the new Princeton Project in Philosophy and Religion. His research focuses mostly on Immanuel Kant and other early modern philosophers, as well as on philosophy of religion, the ethics of belief, and certain issues in aesthetics and moral psychology (especially hope and despair). He is also developing a scholarly-activist interest in food ethics.

Alix Cohen is Professor of Philosophy at the University of Edinburgh. She is the author of *Kant and the Human Sciences: Biology, Anthropology and History* (2009) and the editor of *Kant's Lectures on Anthropology: A Critical Guide* (2014) and *Kant on Emotion and Value* (2014). She is currently co-editor of the *British Journal for the History of Philosophy*.

Katherine Dunlop is Associate Professor of Philosophy at the University of Texas at Austin. She has published numerous articles on the history and philosophy of mathematics, especially in relation to physical science, in the early modern period. She is co-editor, with Samuel Levey, of *From Leibniz to Kant* (*Logical Analysis and History of Philosophy*, volume 21).

Gabriele Gava is Associate Professor of Theoretical Philosophy at the University of Turin. He has published articles in leading philosophical journals on Peirce, Kant, pragmatism, and epistemology. He is the author of *Peirce's Account of Purposefulness: A Kantian Perspective* (Routledge 2014) and *Kant's Critique of Pure Reason and the Method of Metaphysics* (Cambridge University Press 2023). He is also co-editor with Robert Stern of *Pragmatism, Kant and Transcendental Philosophy* (Routledge 2016) and assistant editor of *Studi Kantiani*.

Ido Geiger is Professor of Philosophy at Ben-Gurion University of the Negev, Israel. His main research interests are German idealism (principally, Kant and Hegel) and aesthetics. He is the author of *The Founding Act of Modern Ethical Life: Hegel's Critique of Kant's Moral and Political Philosophy* (Stanford University Press, 2007), *Kant and the Claims of the Empirical World: A Transcendental Reading of the 'Critique of the Power of Judgment'* (Cambridge University Press, 2022) and papers on Kant's and Hegel's theoretical philosophy, practical philosophy, and aesthetics.

Anil Gomes is Fellow and Tutor in Philosophy at Trinity College, Oxford, and Professor in Philosophy at the University of Oxford. He has published in *Mind, Philosophical Perspectives, The Philosophical Quarterly, Philosophical Studies, European Journal of Philosophy, Kant-Studien,* and *Kantian Review*. He is the editor, with Andrew Stephenson, of *Kant and the Philosophy of Mind: Perception, Reason, and the Self* (2017) and the *Oxford Handbook of Kant* (forthcoming).

Michelle Grier is Professor of Philosophy at the University of San Diego. Grier's publications to date have centered on the philosophy of Immanuel Kant, especially his theoretical philosophy (the *Critique of Pure Reason*). In addition to numerous articles, chapters, and presentations, she is the author of *Kant's Doctrine of Transcendental Illusion* (Cambridge University Press, 2001). She has also been working on Kant's theory of the sublime, and has recently begun a manuscript on Nietzsche's Conception of Autonomy.

Paul Guyer received his AB and PhD from Harvard University. He taught at the University of Pennsylvania for thirty years before becoming the Jonathan Nelson Professor of Humanities and Philosophy at Brown in 2012. He was General Co-Editor of the *Cambridge Edition of the Works of*

Immanuel Kant, in which he worked on the *Critique of Pure Reason*, the *Critique of the Power of Judgment*, and Kant's *Notes and Fragments*. He is the author of more than a dozen books on Kant and of *A History of Modern Aesthetics* in three volumes (2014). His most recent book is *Reason and Experience in Mendelssohn and Kant* (Oxford, 2020).

John E. Hare is Noah Porter Professor of Philosophical Theology at Yale Divinity School. He published several books, including *The Moral Gap* (1996), *God's' Call* (2001), *God and Morality* (2009), *God's Command* (2015), *Unity and the Holy Spirit* (2023), His interests extend to ancient philosophy, medieval Franciscan philosophy, Kant, Kierkegaard, contemporary ethical theory, the theory of the atonement, medical ethics, international relations (he has worked in a teaching hospital and for the Foreign Affairs Committee of the U.S. House of Representatives), and aesthetics (he is a published composer of church music).

Thomas E. Hill, Jr. is Kenan Professor of Philosophy, Emeritus, at the University of North Carolina at Chapel Hill. Previously he taught at UCLA, Pomona College, and Johns Hopkins University. His essays are collected in *Autonomy and Self-Respect* (1991); *Dignity and Practical Reason in Kant's Moral Theory* (1992); *Respect, Pluralism, and Justice* (2000); *Human Welfare and Moral Worth* (2002); *Virtue Rules and Justice* (2012); and *Beyond Duty: Kantian Ideas of Respect, Beneficence, and Appreciation* (2022). He co-edited *Kant's Groundwork* (2002) and edited *A Blackwell Guide to Kant's Ethics* (2009).

Otfried Höffe is Professor em. of Philosophy and Director of the Research Centre for Political Philosophy at the Eberhard Karls University of Tübingen, and Professor of Practical Philosophy at the Tsinghua University in Beiking. He is the author of numerous books on moral and political philosophy, including *Political Justice, Democracy in the Age of Globalization* and commentaries on Kant's *Critique of Pure Reason* and Kant's *Critique of Practical Reason*. He is a member of the Heidelberg Academy of Sciences and Humanities, and of the German National Academy of Sciences Leopoldina.

Fiona Hughes is Senior Lecturer in Philosophy in the School of Philosophy and Art History at the University of Essex. She has taught at the universities of Oxford, Edinburgh, and York. She works on inter-relations between Kant's Aesthetics and Epistemology, Phenomenology and the Philosophy of the Arts, including prehistoric art. She is author of *Kant's Aesthetic Epistemology: Form and World* (2007) and *Readers' Guide to Kant's Critique of Aesthetic Judgement* (2010). She has published papers in several Kant handbooks (de Gruyter and Palgrave) and articles in journals including: *British Journal for the History of Philosophy*, *Études phénoménologiques, Inquiry, Kantian Review, Journal of Aesthetics and Art Criticism, Journal of the British Society for Phenomenology* and *Mind*.

Robert Johnson is Professor of Philosophy at the University of Missouri. He is the author of *Self-Improvement: An Essay in Kantian Ethics* and papers in ethical theory and Kant's ethics in journals such as *Ethics, Philosophical Quarterly,* and *Philosophical Studies*.

Frode Kjosavik is Professor of Philosophy at the School of Economics and Business, Norwegian University of Life Sciences. He was group leader for a metaphysics and science project at the Centre for Advanced Study at the Norwegian Academy of Science and Letters, 2015–16. He has published papers on Kant's views of logic, mathematics, and metaphysics.

Katharina T. Kraus is Associate Professor of Philosophy at Johns Hopkins University, Maryland, USA. She is the author of *Kant on Self-Knowledge and Self-formation* (Cambridge University Press,

2020) and has published numerous articles on Kant's theoretical philosophy in journals such as *Studies in History and Philosophy of Science, European Journal of Philosophy*, and *Noûs*.

Marguerite La Caze is Associate Professor of Philosophy at the University of Queensland. Her publications include *Ethical Restoration After Communal Violence: The Grieving and the Unrepentant* (2018); *Wonder and Generosity: Their Role in Ethics and Politics* (2013); *The Analytic Imaginary* (2002); *Integrity and the Fragile Self*, with Damian Cox and Michael Levine (2003); and the edited collections *On What Cannot Be Touched: Contemporary Perspectives on Vladimir Jankélévitch*, with Magdalena Zolkos (2019), and *Phenomenology and Forgiveness* (2018).

Robert B. Louden is Distinguished Professor of Philosophy at the University of Southern Maine. His publications include *Anthropology from a Kantian Point of View* (Cambridge University Press, 2021), *Johann Bernhard Basedow and the Transformation of Modern Education: Educational Reform in the German Enlightenment* (Bloomsbury, 2021), *Kant's Human Being* (Oxford University Press, 2011), *The World We Want* (OUP, 2007), *Kant's Impure Ethics* (OUP, 2000), and *Morality and Moral Theory* (OUP, 1992). A former president of the North American Kant Society (NAKS), Louden is also co-editor and translator of two volumes in *The Cambridge Edition of the Works of Immanuel Kant*.

Huaping Lu-Adler is Associate Professor of Philosophy at Georgetown University. She is the author of *Kant and the Science of Logic* (Oxford University Press, 2018) and numerous articles on Kant's metaphysics, logic, and philosophy of science. As her 2018 book can attest, her interest in history of logic is extensive, covering philosophers from Aristotle all the way to Frege.

G. Felicitas Munzel is Professor in the Program of Liberal Studies and the Department of Philosophy at the University of Notre Dame. She is the author of *Kant's Conception of Moral Character: The "Critical" Link of Morality, Anthropology, and Reflective Judgment* and of *Kant's Conception of Pedagogy: Toward Education for Freedom*, and translator of "Anthropology Friedländer (1775–1776)" in *Lectures on Anthropology* (Cambridge Edition of the Works of Immanuel Kant).

Valentin Mureşan was Emeritus Professor of Moral Philosophy in the Faculty of Philosophy at the University of Bucharest, and a distinguished research fellow of the Oxford Uehiro Centre for Practical Ethics. His research interests covered various topics, from praxeology and philosophy of science to ethical theories and ethics management. He published extensive commentaries on some basic works by Plato, Aristotle, Kant, and Mill, as well as studies on analytical moral philosophy and ethics management. He translated and edited Mill's *Utilitarianism* and a volume of Millian essays, as well Kant's *Groundwork of the Metaphysics of Morals*.

Steve Naragon is Emeritus Professor of Philosophy at Manchester University (Indiana, USA). He co-edited and translated (with Karl Ameriks) *Kant's Lectures on Metaphysics* (Cambridge University Press, 1997), maintains the *Kant in the Classroom* website, is co-editor (with Werner Stark) of *The Herder Notes from Immanuel Kant's Lectures* (De Gruyter, forthcoming), and the editor of *Portraits of Kant* (Bloomsbury, forthcoming).

Christian Onof is Honorary Research Fellow at Birkbeck College, London, and Reader at Imperial College London. He has published papers in the *Philosophical Review, Philosophy and Phenomenological Research, Kantian Review, Kant-Studien, Kant Yearbook*, and the *Journal of Mind and Behavior*. His publications deal with Kant's theoretical and practical philosophy, existentialism, the hard problem of consciousness, and social epistemology.

James O'Shea, Professor of Philosophy at University College Dublin (UCD), received his PhD in 1992 from the University of North Carolina at Chapel Hill, on Hume and Kant on substance. His books include (ed.) *Kant's Critique of Pure Reason: A Critical Guide* (Cambridge University Press, 2017), (ed.) *Sellars and His Legacy* (Oxford University Press, 2016), *Kant's* Critique of Pure Reason: *An Introduction and Interpretation* (Routledge, 2014), and *Wilfrid Sellars: Naturalism With a Normative Turn* (Wiley/Polity, 2007).

Tanehisa Otabe is Professor of Aesthetics at the University of Tokyo. His areas of interest cover 18th-century German aesthetics as well as intercultural aesthetics. He is a board member of the International Schelling-Society (2010–), former executive member of the International Society for Eighteenth-Century Studies (2011–15), and former assistant secretary general of the International Association for Aesthetics (2016–2019).

Stephen R. Palmquist (DPhil, Oxford) was Professor of Religion and Philosophy at Hong Kong Baptist University, where he taught for 34 years before retiring to Los Angeles in 2021. His 210+ publications include 120+ refereed articles/chapters and 12 books, most recently, *Comprehensive Commentary on Kant's Religion* (2016), *Kant on Intuition* (2019), and *Kant and Mysticism: Critique as the Experience of Baring All in Reason's Light* (2019).

Andrews Reath is Professor of Philosophy at the University of California, Riverside. He is the author of *Agency and Autonomy in Kant's Moral Theory* (Oxford, 2006) and editor (with Jens Timmermann) of *Kant's 'Critique of Practical Reason': A Critical Guide* (Cambridge, 2010).

Kenneth F. Rogerson is Professor Emeritus at Florida International University. He has published extensively on various aspects of Kant's philosophy (as well as other philosophical issues); however, Kant's aesthetics has been his most enduring research area. In addition to the monographs *Kant's Aesthetics: The Roles of Form and Expression* and *The Problem of Free Harmony in Kant's Aesthetics*, he has published several journal articles on Kant's aesthetics.

Alexander Rueger is Professor Emeritus at the University of Alberta. He has published widely on the history and philosophy of science and on Kant's aesthetics. His study *Kant on Pleasure and Judgement* is forthcoming from Cambridge University Press.

Martin Schönfeld was Professor of Philosophy at the University of South Florida, where he taught comparative philosophy, history of ideas, and environmental thought. At the time of his unexpected death, he was completing a book entitled *Philosophy of Climate Change: A Kantian Approach*.

Dennis Schulting is an independent philosopher and has published widely on Kant and German Idealism. Among his books are *Kantian Nonconceptualism* (Palgrave, 2016), *Kant's Deduction From Apperception. An Essay on the Transcendental Deduction of the Categories* (de Gruyter, 2018), *Apperception and Self-Consciousness in Kant and German Idealism* (Bloomsbury, 2021), and *The Bounds of Transcendental Logic* (Palgrave Macmillan, 2021).

Oliver Sensen is Associate Professor of Philosophy at Tulane University, USA. He is the author of *Human Dignity* (Cambridge, forthcoming), *Kant on Human Dignity* (de Gruyter, 2011), as well as the editor or co-editor of six essay collections, including *Kant on Moral Autonomy* (Cambridge, 2012) and *Respect* (Oxford, 2021). Sensen is the author of around 60 articles on Kant's Moral Philosophy.

Camilla Serck-Hanssen is Professor of Philosophy at the University of Oslo and Scientific Director at the Centre for Advanced Study, Oslo. Her publications include articles on Kant's logic, Kant's meta-metaphysics, Heidegger's reading of the *Critique of Pure Reason*, and the *Ethics of War*.

Susan Shell is Professor of Political Science at Boston College. Her books include *The Rights of Reason: A Study of Kant's Philosophy and Politics* (1980); *The Embodiment of Reason: Kant on Generation, Spirit and Community* (1996); and *Kant and the Limits of Autonomy* (Harvard University Press, 2009). She is the co-editor (with Richard Velkley) of the Cambridge Critical Guide to *Kant's Observations and Remarks* (Cambridge University Press, 2012), and editor of *The Strauss-Krüger Correspondence: Returning to Plato Through Kant* (Palgrave, 2017). She has also authored numerous essays on Kant, Rousseau, Fichte, Hobbes, and contemporary political issues.

Houston Smit is Associate Professor of Philosophy at the University of Arizona. His publications focus mainly on Kant's critical philosophy, theoretical and practical, but he has also published articles on Aquinas and Hume.

Andrew Stephenson is a lecturer in philosophy at the University of Southampton. He has published on Kant in *Philosophical Review*, *The Philosophical Quarterly*, *Philosophers' Imprint*, *Synthese*, and *Kantian Review*. He is the editor, with Anil Gomes, of *Kant and the Philosophy of Mind: Perception, Reason, and the Self* (2017) and the *Oxford Handbook of Kant* (forthcoming).

Thomas Teufel is Associate Professor of Philosophy at the City University of New York (Baruch College | The Graduate Center). He is the author of the forthcoming *Kant and Teleology* (Cambridge University Press).

Mark Timmons is Professor of Philosophy at the University of Arizona specializing in metaethics, normative moral theory, and Kant's ethics – topics on which he has published extensively. He is the author of *Kant's* Doctrine of Virtue: *A Guide* (2021), and editor of *Kant's* Metaphysics of Morals: *Interpretative Essays* (2002) and of the annual *Oxford Studies in Normative Ethics*.

Gabriele Tomasi is Professor of Aesthetics at the University of Padua. His principal areas of research are Kant, the history of modern aesthetics, Wittgenstein, and, more recently, the philosophy of literature.

Helga Varden is Professor of Philosophy, of Gender and Women Studies, and of Political Science at the University of Illinois at Urbana-Champaign. Her main research interests are Kant's practical philosophy, legal-political philosophy and its history, feminist philosophy, and the philosophy of sex and love. In addition to her *Sex, Love, and Gender: A Kantian Theory* (Oxford University Press, 2020), Varden has published many articles on a range of classical philosophical issues, including Kant's answer to the murderer at the door, private property, care relations, political obligations, and political legitimacy, as well as on applied issues such as privacy, poverty, non-human animals, and terrorism.

Ralph Walker was educated at McGill and Oxford, and was Fellow and Tutor at Magdalen College Oxford from 1972 to 2011; he has continued to teach there since retiring. He has written various articles, mostly on the concept of truth or the work of Kant (or both). He has written three books, and edited two others, as well as spending a number of years in the administration of Oxford University. He has recently added a fourth book, *Objective Imperatives – An Exploration of Kant's Moral Philosophy* (Oxford University Press, 2022).

Wayne Waxman is the author of five books and numerous papers on Kant and British empiricism. His current projects include a short book on transcendental synthesis, another on convention language and thought, and a third on democracy.

Kenneth R. Westphal is a lifetime member of *Academia Europaea*, elected in 2020. He held two professorships in England, and recently retired from Boğaziçi Üniversitesi (İstanbul). His monographs include *Kant's Transcendental Proof of Realism* (Cambridge, 2004); *How Hume and Kant Reconstruct Natural Law: Justifying Strict Objectivity Without Debating Moral Realism* (Clarendon, 2016); *Grounds of Pragmatic Realism: Hegel's Internal Critique and Transformation of Kant's Critical Philosophy* (Brill, 2018); *Hegel's Civic Republicanism: Integrating Natural Law With Kant's Moral Constructivsm* (Routledge, 2020); *Kant's Critical Epistemology: Why Epistemology Must Consider Judgment First* (Routledge, 2020); and *Kant's Transcendental Deduction of the Categories: Critical Re-Examination, Elucidation & Corroboration* (Helsinki U.P., 2021).

Marcus Willaschek is Professor of Philosophy at the University of Frankfurt. His publications include *Praktische Vernunft. Handlungstheorie und Moralbegründung bei Kant* (Stuttgart/Weimar: Metzler 1992); *Der mentale Zugang zur Welt. Realismus, Skeptizismus und Intentionalität* (Frankfurt: Klostermann 2003); *Kant on the Sources of Metaphysics* (Cambridge/New York: Cambridge University Press, 2018); *Kant-Lexikon* (3 vols, ed. with J. Stolzenberg, G. Mohr, and S. Bacin) (Berlin/Boston, 2015).

Howard Williams is the author of three books on Kant: *Kant's Political Philosophy* (1983); *Kant's Critique of Hobbes: Sovereignty and Cosmopolitanism* (2003); *Kant and the End of War* (2012). He is Honorary Distinguished Professor at Cardiff University, and editor of *Kantian Review*.

Allen W. Wood is Ruth Norman Halls Professor, Indiana University, and Ward W. and Priscilla B. Woods Professor Emeritus, Stanford University. He is the author of a dozen books, about half of them on Kant, and co-general editor with Paul Guyer of the Cambridge edition of Kant's writings in English translation.

INTRODUCTION

Sorin Baiasu and Mark Timmons

★★★

Immanuel Kant's work continues to be a main focus of attention in almost all areas of philosophy.[1] Not only are there interesting interpretive issues, which continue to spark new debates, but his thought has proved to be a rich source of innovative views in theoretical, practical, and teleological philosophy, at metaphilosophical, normative, or applied levels. In designing this volume, we aimed to reflect the comprehensiveness of Kant's thought[2] and its relevance for some of our current significant theoretical predicaments. The volume has not been conceived of as exclusively (or even primarily) an introduction and overview of Kant's philosophy, but as a contribution through new specialized research to the most important debates in the broad area of Kantian studies. Each chapter includes an accessible presentation of some of the most relevant debates in the area, but also takes the discussion further with important contributions to Kantian studies and philosophy more generally. All of the chapters in this volume have been especially written for this collection. Each of them focuses on a particular important topic in Kant's philosophy, presents the state-of-play in research, and suggests the likely course of future directions of research in the respective area. The contributors represent an international cast of well-known authors, and we attempted to combine best expertise with good global geographical spread.

In what follows, we will explain the reasons behind the way the volume is structured. We will introduce the main distinctions that determine the domains within which the various chapters of this volume have been placed. For several reasons, we have decided not to attempt a traditional introduction, which would present briefly each chapter and how they link to each other. First, with a volume of this size, introducing each of the forty-five chapters would have resulted in a text too long to be a proper introduction. Second, even as part of a longer introduction, all we would have been able to include would have been only very short presentations of the contributions, which would have been as useful as the already existing abstracts. Furthermore, any attempt to draw the connections between the chapters would not have been able, within our self-imposed space constraints, to say something of sufficient significance to justify inclusion here. Finally, the presentation and justification of the volume's structure will by itself offer an overview of the main connections between the various parts of the book.[3]

DOI: 10.4324/9781003406617-1

Chapter 1 is biographical, and aims to offer an overview of Kant's life and work. With progress made by commentators in the exploration of historical aspects of Kant's life and work, several shifts in the received view of Kant have been taking place during the last few decades. Given that Kant's life is so much connected with his work, this biographical part is equally well philosophical in character, since it is linked to an account of Kant's thinking, from the early views and writings to his posthumous work.

The remaining chapters are structured into four parts. The first two parts can easily be identified by reference to the standard distinction between Kant's pre-Critical and Critical philosophy. Part of what motivates this distinction is Kant's claim, in the third *Critique* (1790), that he completed the critical part of his system, a part that he had begun with the first *Critique* (first edition, 1781). Given that before the publication of the first edition of the first *Critique*, for eleven years (the 'silent decade'), Kant had published almost nothing, commentators distinguish between his pre-Critical and his Critical works, and consider as pre-Critical everything Kant published before 1781.

Recent scholarship has revealed that the distinction between Kant's pre-Critical and Critical writings is not as sharp as it is suggested by the eleven-year gap of the 'silent decade'. Moreover, since in Kant there is a distinction between critique and doctrine, the pre-Critical/Critical distinction can be confusing, since some writings following the third *Critique* are Critical, in the sense that they belong to the Critical system, without being critical, in the sense that they have a doctrinal character (they are related to doctrine, rather than critique in Kant's distinction between critique and doctrine). For this reason, we distinguish between the background to the Critical philosophy (including writings before the first *Critique*) (Part 1) and his transcendental philosophy (which includes both critique and doctrine – Part 2), rather than using the standard pre-Critical/Critical distinction.

Part 3 includes discussions related to writings that, for several reasons, are not clearly connected to Kant's transcendental philosophy. These include the *Opus Postumum*, the *Nachlass*, the philosophical correspondence, and the lecture notes taken by his students during the forty-one years of Kant's university teaching. To be sure, it is not possible to include here chapters on all these writings, so a focus on the *Opus Postumum* and a general chapter on the lecture notes seemed a good choice, given the important clarificatory role of the latter and the significance of the former as what we might call Kant's 'post-Critical' work. Indeed, the *Opus Postumum* is interesting from the perspective of Kant's distinction between critique and doctrine, since here Kant returns to some of the key topics of his transcendental philosophy and sometimes clearly with a different view.

Part 4 examines some of the crucial developments in philosophy that are indebted to Kant. Given the revival of Kantian studies during the last fifty-sixty years, a considerable amount of 'Kantian' work has been produced – from textual commentaries to accounts that are Kantian in spirit but do not claim to represent accurate interpretations of Kant. The focus will be on those authors and works that are Kantian in some important sense; that is, those authors and works that aim to begin from some of Kant's insights and to develop them further – either better than Kant did or more explicitly or because Kant did not attempt to develop them in that particular direction.

We have already mentioned Kant's distinction between critique and doctrine. Not much has been written on this distinction in the literature. What has been written and what Kant himself says (among others, in the third *Critique*, in the *Groundwork*, and *The Metaphysics of Morals*) suggest the following picture: the critical part of Kant's transcendental philosophy examines the conditions that make possible judgment; these conditions represent *necessary* conditions of judgment and, hence, a source of metaphysics, a source of claims which are a priori. It remains to be seen, however, how these a priori claims contribute to judgment concerning particulars, and it is the doctrinal part of transcendental philosophy that is in charge of formulating the first principles for the application of a priori claims.

Part 4 examines the influence of Kant's thought on contemporary philosophy. This influence exerts itself from all areas of Kant's philosophy – hence the distinction between theoretical, practical, and teleological philosophy, a distinction that follows that between the areas of the three *Critiques*. Given that the systematic ambitions of Kant's philosophy were challenged early on, and given that systematic philosophy (in the Kantian sense) has recently fallen out of favor more generally, a distinction between critique and doctrine does not survive in contemporary philosophy, if not simply as a remotely similar distinction between a justification of principles and their application. But even this distinction between justification and application is sometimes challenged today. Hence, no further distinction between critique and doctrine was necessary in this part of the volume, where the main focus is on Kantian contemporary philosophy.

In Part 2, section A, subsections i, ii, and iii have to do with the critical part of Kant's transcendental philosophy and can be easily presented. They correspond to the three *Critiques*. Commentators sometimes claim that additional *Critiques* can be found in other of Kant's works, for instance, a *Critique of Political Reason*, in *Towards Perpetual Peace*, or a *Critique of Religious Reason* in some arguments of *Religion Within the Boundaries of Mere Reason*. After all, numerous such works have been written by post-Kantian philosophers, for instance, Sartre's *Critique of Dialectical Reason*, Gorz's *Critique of Economic Reason*, or Sloterdijk's *Critique of Cynical Reason*. Nevertheless, claims to the discovery of new *Critiques* in Kant are controversial. So, subsection i refers to Kant's first *Critique*, where the emphasis is on theoretical philosophy; subsection ii, to Kant's second *Critique*, where he talks about practical philosophy; and subsection iii, to the *Critique of Judgment*, where teleology plays a very important role.

Part 2, section B includes subsections i through vi. They focus on some of Kant's texts where he attempts to derive first principles for the application to particulars of theoretical and practical judgments. Hence, these subsections will include chapters on specific natural and social sciences that Kant examines explicitly in his works. Several criteria guided us in making the selection. First, we put emphasis primarily on those areas on which Kant has worked and published more extensively, for instance, political theory, religion, history, anthropology, education, and several natural sciences. Second, we have chosen chapter topics on which commentators have either published considerably (for instance, physics, mathematics, religion, politics) or have recently started to publish more (e.g., anthropology, education) or have suggested as particularly interesting topics to pursue (among others, physics or biology).

In making the selection and in organizing this section, we had also to ignore some issues with which we could only have dealt elsewhere. As an illustration, consider Kant's claim in the third *Critique* that there is no doctrinal counterpart for the critical work undertaken in his third *Critique*; and, yet, biology seems to be a good example of a natural science for which we need teleology in order to make sense of how it functions. As such, philosophy of biology seems to be part of the doctrine corresponding to the third *Critique*, which, however, Kant says does not exist.

Finally, we combined chapters that look at disciplines as a whole (for example, anthropology or education) with chapters that focus on problems that have been perceived as particularly threatening for the Kantian system (for instance, the issue of universality and accommodating differences, in particular those differences that are the topic of some of Kant's most problematic claims, or the issue of moral education). The aim has therefore been to go beyond the articulation of first principles for the judgment of particulars, and to approach more concrete issues concerning the status of women, the propertyless, or the role moral education can have (given that, according to Kant, we need no special education to judge what is right or wrong).

The final part of this Introduction concerns the chapters themselves. As we have already mentioned, it is appropriate at this stage to present only the main areas of Kantian studies that chapters focus on and to note their complementarity. Chapter 1 (Paul Guyer's "Kant's Life and Work") will focus on philosophically relevant aspects related to Kant's biography and work. Chapter 2 ("Physics" by Martin Schönfeld) examines Kant's important contribution to physics in the works preceding the first *Critique*. Chapters 3 and 4 ("Kant and the Rationalist Tradition" by Ralph Walker and "Kant and the Empiricist Tradition" by Wayne Waxman, respectively) present the main issues in the relations between Kant's transcendental philosophy and the two main traditions at that time – the rationalist and empiricist directions in epistemology. These bio-bibliographical and foundational chapters – Chapters 1 through 4 – offer the background for the discussion of Kant's transcendental philosophy, in Part 2, which will occupy the main part of the volume.

Eighteen chapters of Part 2, section A focus on the main parts of Kant's most important critical writings – the three *Critiques*. For instance, for the *Critique of Pure Reason*, Graham Bird wrote on "The First *Critique*: Prefaces and Introduction"; Sorin Baiasu, on "Transcendental Aesthetic"; Anil Gomes and Andrew Stephenson, on "The Analytic of Concepts"; Kenneth R. Westphal, on "The Analytic of Principles"; Camilla Serck-Hanssen and Houston Smit, on "The Schematism"; and Michelle Grier, on "The Transcendental Dialectic" (the additional chapter on methodology will be mentioned shortly). The *Groundwork*, which is a very significant but shorter work, will be discussed in one chapter (by Thomas E. Hill Jr.: "The *Groundwork*"). For the three *Critiques*, chapters will focus on the main parts of each text. We have already seen the chapters for the first *Critique*. For the second *Critique*, Valentin Mureşan authored the piece on Preface and Introduction; Andrews Reath, on "The Analytic of Pure Practical Reason"; and Oliver Sensen, "Dialectic of Pure Practical Reason". Whereas for the third *Critique*, we have Gabriele Tomasi on Preface and Introductions; Fiona Hughes, on "Analytic of the Beautiful"; Alexander Rueger, "Analytic of the Sublime"; Tanehisa Otabe, "Dialectic of the Aesthetic Power of Judgment"; Christian Onof and Dennis Schulting, "Analytic of Teleological Judgement"; and Thomas Teufel, "Teleological Power of Judgment – Dialectic" – two other chapters on the methodologies of these *Critiques* will be mentioned next. Thus, the final part of each of subsections i–iii will examine the methodological discussions in the three *Critiques* (in, respectively, the chapters on "Method" by Gabriele Gava and Marcus Willaschek, Robert Johnson, and Ido Geiger). Apart from the fact that these are usually neglected parts of the *Critiques*, they are also good starting points for a consideration of the unity of the Kantian system. If transcendental philosophy has unity, given that its various parts are concerned with different aspects of our cognitive capacities, what must give these parts unity is the way in which transcendental philosophy develops its methodology, rather than specific common topics.

The next fourteen chapters that constitute section B of Part 2 examine aspects of the doctrinal part of Kant's transcendental philosophy. Some chapters focus on important texts that define the first principles for the application of judgment to particulars, for instance, the *Metaphysics of Morals* (to which three chapters are devoted by Otfried Höffe, on the "Introduction"; Howard Williams, "Doctrine of Right"; and Mark Timmons, "The Doctrine of Virtue"), *Anthropology* (by Robert B. Louden), and *Religion* (Steven R. Palmquist). Other chapters focus on particular natural or social sciences ("Mathematics" – authored by Frode Kjosavic; "Biology" – by Alix Cohen; "Physics" – by Katherine Dunlop) or more foundational disciplines (such as logic, on which Huaping Lu-Adler wrote her chapter), which although Kant does not devote specific texts to, he, nevertheless, discusses at length. Finally, we selected a few topics that seemed important in their own right and for

Kant's thought – in particular, religion and theology (with a chapter by John E. Hare), universality and differences (by Helga Varden), and moral education (by G. Felicitas Munzel). These are topics that are both philosophically important and on which Kantian scholars have argued more extensively. It may perhaps seem too much to allocate two chapters to Kant's views on history and politics in his essays (by Allen Wood and Susan Shell), especially given a perceived lack of interest in the philosophy of history during the last few years; nevertheless, this is a way to encourage more debate and analysis in this particular area, which, in Kant but also more generally, has implications for politics, education, and morality more generally.

Part 3 consists of two chapters by Giovanni Pietro Basile and Steve Naragon. The first looks at Kant's important *Opus Postumum*, where significant aspects of his transcendental philosophy are discussed. The second examines the relation between Kant's thought and his teaching. Some of the set of lecture notes that Kant's students took have been used extensively by scholars to clarify his views and to develop aspects that remain underdeveloped in Kant's published work. Some sets of lectures were in fact published during Kant's lifetime and under Kant's direction, although it is likely they were regarded as useful teaching tools, rather than useful guides into his philosophy.

Finally, Part 4 examines the heritage of Kant's work. Although in general we regard the distinction between the analytic and continental traditions as unhelpful at best and detrimental in many cases, we use it to distinguish between two different traditions that sometimes may share much in common, although they are pursued mostly independently. Thus, on the one hand, philosophers such as Husserl, Heidegger, Sartre, Levinas, or Derrida discuss, criticize, and transform some elements of Kant's thought; their followers tend to pursue the same line (with natural variations and exceptions, of course – Luc Ferry and Alain Renaut, for instance, are less critical of Kant and the Kantian tradition). On the other hand, philosophers such as P.F. Strawson, Gareth Evans, Quassim Cassam, or Galen Strawson discuss Kant or engage with Kantian themes independently from their continental colleagues. This explains the need for two distinct chapters on the 'continental' and 'analytic' traditions in contemporary Kantian philosophy by, respectively, Marguerite La Caze and James O'Shea.

By contrast, most contemporary or recent Kantian philosophers working on Kant's practical philosophy tend to belong to the Anglo-American tradition. This, we think, is mainly due to the fact that, with very few exceptions (a notable one, for instance, being Sartre, but also Ferry and Renaut), authors engaging with Kant in the phenomenological and post-phenomenological tradition have tended to draw mainly on Kant's theoretical philosophy and teleology, sometimes for good systematic reasons. As a result, we made room for two chapters on contemporary Kantian practical philosophy – one on "Kantian Philosophies of Hope, History, and the Anthropocene" by Andrew Chignell and one on "Rawlsians and Other Kantians" by Alyssa R. Bernstein.

The situation is again different as far as the heritage of the third *Critique* is concerned. This is mainly due to the structure of the third *Critique*, in particular the division of this work into the Critique of the Aesthetic Power of Judgement and the Critique of the Teleological Power of Judgement. In both these areas the distinction between a 'continental' and 'analytic' tradition is no longer so visible, so we only assigned one chapter for those developments in Kantian aesthetics ("Contemporary Kantian Philosophy of Art", authored by Kenneth F. Rogerson) and philosophy of science ("Contemporary Kantian Philosophy of Science", written by Katharina Kraus). The latter is a more controversial topic, since it has only recently emerged, but it is worth exploring. Our hope is that it will provide a teleological account of explanation in science, an alternative to the classical nomological account that can also be found in Kant's first *Critique*, as well as in the doctrinal work, *Metaphysical Foundations of Natural Science*.

Scholarly interest in the philosophical work of Kant is becoming increasingly stronger. The situation is remarkable, given that the beginning of this revival goes back to the 1960s: over fifty years of discussion, interpretation, development, and re-evaluation that is being pursued as if Kant were one of our contemporaries. It will not be surprising therefore that publication of scholarly work on Kant, of Kant's own texts, and of writings by Kantian authors seems to undergo a similar revival. For instance, only within the last few years, we have learned about the foundation of more academic journals that are devoted to Kantian Studies. This happened although there were already several established journals in the area. Moreover, more and more research grants are offered for projects on Kant.

The context is therefore very apposite for the publication of this volume, since it responds to what seems to be a real need for a comprehensive and thorough examination of the Kantian corpus. Given the combination of scope, novelty, and significance, it will be of benefit for a large part of the potential audience, both academic and the general public.

Notes

1 The size of this volume is four times the size of a standard edited collection, but the delays we encountered probably exceed those of a standard collective volume (even considering the extraordinary years at the beginning of the pandemic). We are first of all grateful to all contributors, especially to those who delivered their work early on and had the patience to wait for the volume to be published, as well as to those who agreed to step in when an initially commissioned author had to pull out. We are also very grateful for the support of the series editor, Adam Johnson, who offered invaluable help at every stage of the process. Thanks are due also for editorial help to Zachary Vereb and Emilian Mihailov in relation to the chapters by Martin Schönfeld and Valentin Mureşan. For Sorin Baiasu, work on this volume was made possible by three periods of institutional leave from Keele University, as well as funding from the European Research Council Project 'Distortions of Normativity', at the University of Vienna, and the British Academy Newton Advanced Grant 'Ethics and Conflicts Between Deep Commitments' (initially held by Ruhi Demiray and Sorin Baiasu at Keele University and the University of Kocaeli, but then moved from Kocaeli to University of Siegen and the Free University in Berlin, after Demiray was arrested and dismissed from Kocaeli for signing the second petition of the 'Academics for Peace'). He is grateful to the PIs of the grants and the respective institutions for enabling research on this project. For help during the crucial production process, we would like to thank Aruna Rajendran and her team for working with us to prepare the manuscript for the printer – their responsiveness and professionalism have been greatly appreciated. We started work on this volume more than ten years ago; sadly, during these years, three of our contributors passed away: Martin Schönfeld (1963–2020), Valentin Mureşan (1951–2020), and Graham Bird (1930–2021) – this volume is dedicated to their memory.
2 The volume includes forty-five chapters, which make it the most comprehensive volume on Kant's philosophy to have been published so far. The only other existing volume that gets close to this expanse is the *Blackwell Companion to Kant* (2006), which consists of thirty-three chapters. The *Continuum Companion to Kant* (2012) is impressive in terms of thematic coverage, but includes relatively short contributions to specific works or to discrete issues and topics – the same goes for the excellent three-volume *Kant-Lexikon* and the associated *Kant-Lexikon: Studienausgabe* published by De Gruyter (2015, 2017). This volume offers both relatively thorough accounts of the main works of Kant and informed discussion of research on specific important themes and areas in Kantian studies.
3 To heed to Kant's suggestion not to avoid being candid whenever possible, we can confess that time constraints played a significant role too.

References

Banham, G., Schulting, D. and Hems, N. (eds.) (2012) *The Continuum Companion to Kant*, London: Continuum.
Bird, G. (ed.) (2006) *A Companion to Kant*, London: Blackwell.
Willaschek, M., Stolzenberg, J., Mohr, G. and Bacin, S. (eds.) (2015) *Kant-Lexikon*, Berlin: Walter de Gruyter.
Willaschek, M., Stolzenberg, J., Mohr, G. and Bacin, S. (eds.) (2017) *Kant-Lexikon: Studienausgabe*, Berlin: Walter de Gruyter.

Further Reading

P. Guyer (ed.), *The Cambridge Companions to Kant* (Cambridge: Cambridge University Press, 1992) is a great overview of Kant's philosophy in fourteen chapters. P. Guyer (ed.), *The Cambridge Companion to Kant and Modern Philosophy* (Cambridge: Cambridge University Press, 2006) represents a more comprehensive (eighteen chapters) discussion of Kant in the general context of modern philosophy. P. Guyer (ed.), *The Cambridge Companion to the Critique of Pure Reason* (Cambridge: Cambridge University Press, 2010) is another comprehensive overview (seventeen chapters divided into three sections: background, arguments, impact). An excellent and more detailed critical discussion (eleven chapters, but on a much shorter text than the first *Critique*) on the *Groundwork* can be found in J. Timmermann (ed.), *Kant's Groundwork of the Metaphysics of Morals: A Critical Guide* (Cambridge: Cambridge University Press, 2009); A. Reath and J. Timmermann (eds.), *Kant's Critique of Practical Reason: A Critical Guide* (Cambridge: Cambridge University Press, 2012) offers a great discussion, in nine chapters of Kant's second *Critique*.

1

KANT'S LIFE AND WORK

Paul Guyer

★★★

In the *Groundwork for the Metaphysics of Morals* (1785), Kant states that the moral law applies to the human being because it is only as "intelligence" that the human being is his "proper self" (*GMS* 4: 457). Kant derives the moral law not from any authority that is outside of us, such as God, nor from mere nature, including our own sensible nature, but from something that he identifies as essential rather than accidental to our selves. And this is Kant's strategy throughout his mature philosophy. Not only does he derive the moral law, to which the world *ought* to conform insofar as we must make it into a moral world, from ourselves; he also derives the fundamental forms of the world as it *is*, the world of experience and scientific knowledge, from the structure of our own sensibility and understanding; and he derives the regulative principles that we apply to nature in all its concrete detail, such as the maxim that nature makes no leaps, from the structure of our own reason. Beyond that, Kant argues that the beauty that we attribute to nature is only its suitability for the free play of our own cognitive powers of imagination and understanding; that the sublimity that we "subreptively" ascribe to nature is actually an aesthetic experience of the power of our own theoretical and practical reason; and that the purposiveness that we ascribe to organisms in nature and even to nature as a whole is a projection of our own way of understanding things, culminating in a conception of nature as a system aimed at our own moral development. In other words, Kant's philosophy is as extreme a development of anthropomorphism and anthropocentrism as has ever been developed. Even the idea of God, Kant wrote in his uncompleted drafts for a final statement of his philosophy, is nothing but an image of our own power to give both theoretical and moral form to the world: "God and the world are the two objects of transcendental philosophy: thinking *man* is the subject, predicate, and copula" (*OP* 21: 37).

Kant himself puts the point I have just made by means of his term "autonomy." He introduces this term in his moral philosophy. But in the published Introduction to the *Critique of the Power of Judgment*, his third great critique, Kant uses the term more generally:

> In regard to the faculties of the soul in general, insofar as they are considered as higher facul-
> ties, i.e., as ones that contain an autonomy, the understanding is the one that contains the
> **constitutive** principles *a priori* for the **faculty of cognition** (the theoretical cognition of

nature); for the **feeling of pleasure and displeasure** it is the power of judgment, independent of concepts and sensations that are related to the determination of the faculty of desire and could thereby be immediately practical; for the **faculty of desire** it is reason, which is practical without the mediation of any sort of pleasure, wherever it might come from, and determines for this faculty, as a higher faculty, the final end, which at the same time brings with it the pure intellectual satisfaction in the object.

(*KU* Introduction, section IX, 5: 196–7)

Here the distinction between our "proper self" and the implied "improper" self becomes the distinction between the "higher" faculties of the soul or mind and the implied "lower" faculties: in all cases, we require inputs to which we must be receptive, and which are supplied through our "lower" faculties, but which we must then form and govern by our "higher" faculties. Thus our senses deliver sensations to our cognitive powers of imagination, understanding, and reason, which can either form them into a representation of a law-governed nature in accordance with the *a priori* forms of intuition and rules of conceptualization and inference or else freely play with them and thus experience such nature as beautiful or sublime; and our lower faculty of desire – our inclinations – suggests possible courses of action to us, which our pure practical reason, through maxims grounded in the moral law, must transform into an intra- and interpersonally consistent exercise of freedom (*V-Mo/Collins* 27: 344–6) leading in turn to a "realm of ends" (*GMS* 4: 433). Kant does not conceive of the human mind as a windowless monad, unaffected by sensory influences from outside; but form, whether the lawful form of nature, moral order, or the aesthetic beauty or sublimity of nature or art, must always be imparted by the human mind.

It will hardly be possible to provide the details of this ambitious model of anthropocentric autonomy, in which the human mind gives the law to nature, even to human nature, in this chapter. It will take the rest of this volume to do so. The remainder of this chapter will merely outline the stages of Kant's life and work to be filled in by what follows.

Kant may have been a modern Prometheus, but he was hardly a modern Athena, springing full-grown from the brow of Zeus. Kant developed his mature philosophical system slowly: it took two decades, from 1755 to 1775, before he formulated the main ideas of his first great work, the *Critique of Pure Reason*, and then another quarter-century for him to work out his whole system of philosophy. Even after he had stopped teaching and publishing, by 1798, he continued to rethink his system, but had not completed a restatement of it by the time of his death in 1804.

Kant was born in Königsberg, the capital of East Prussia and an important Baltic port, on April 22, 1724. His parents were devout Pietists, members of a reform movement within Lutheranism that stressed "independent Bible study, personal devotion, the priesthood the laity, and a practical faith issuing in acts of charity" (Kuehn 2001: 34). Although Kant's eventual argument that we have grounds to believe in only so much theology as is necessary to make our practice of morality rational would push far beyond the limits of any conventional form of religiosity, Pietism's emphasis on individual responsibility would certainly be decisive for Kant's own conception of autonomy. After attending the Pietist school in Königsberg, the *Collegium Fridericianum*, Kant entered the *Albertina*, the local university. Instead of passing on to one of the "higher" or professional faculties of theology, medicine, or law, Kant remained within the philosophical faculty, focusing on philosophy and natural science. However, he left the university at twenty-three (1747) without a degree. He did publish a book that year, the *True Estimation of Living Forces*, but it was in German rather than Latin, thus not eligible as a dissertation, and it defended a versions of the Leibnizian metaphysics of pre-established harmony rather than the theory of physical influx favored by the philosophy professor

Martin Knutzen and other Pietists at the *Albertina*. Kant may have left the university because he knew he had no chance of earning a degree given this departure from the orthodoxy that by this point Pietism itself had become.[1]

Kant spent the next half-dozen years (1748–54) as a tutor in a succession of households in the vicinity of Königsberg. This occupation left Kant time for his own studies, and when he returned to Königsberg in 1754 he rapidly completed three short Latin treatises that earned him his master's degree, the *venia legendi* or right to teach as a private lecturer (*Privatdozent*), and the right to be considered for a salaried professorship. The first of these was a scientific work, *De Igne* ("On Fire," 1755), the second a philosophical treatise, *Principiorum primorum cognitionis metaphysicae nova dilucidatio* ("A New Elucidation of the First Principles of Metaphysical Cognition," 1755), and the last a work straddling science and philosophy, *Monadologium Physicam* ("Physical Monadology," 1756). In 1755, Kant also published a longer book in German, the *Universal Natural History and Theory of the Heavens, or Essay on the Constitution and the Mechanical Origin of the Whole Universe according to Newtonian Principles*, in which he showed how the solar system could have evolved out of an original nebula of dust in a purely mechanical way, without divine intervention. Unfortunately the copies of the book were impounded when the publisher went bankrupt, and Kant's anticipation of a similar argument offered by the French astronomer Pierre-Simon Laplace in 1796 did not become widely known until later (Kuehn 2001: 105). These publications did not in fact earn him a professorship, so Kant spent the next fifteen years as a *Privatdozent* dependent on fees paid by the students who attended his lectures. Consequently he lectured on a wide range of subjects, including logic, metaphysics, mathematics, physics, geography, ethics, and even on the principles of military fortification, a leading branch of engineering at that time. When Kant was finally appointed at professor of logic and metaphysics in 1770, he lectured on those subjects but continued the lectures on ethics and geography and added courses on natural right and anthropology, all of which continued to be popular and lucrative for him.

In the "New Elucidation," Kant took a step away from Leibnizianism by arguing that since everything contained in a subject must be present in it from the start, there can only be "succession" or change in substances if they are acted on from without; ironically he thereby comes closer to the position of his teachers such as Knuzten. Kant also offered a first version of his famous critique of the ontological argument for the existence of God on the ground that even if (necessary) existence is included in the idea of God, that is still only an "existence in ideas" (*PND* 1: 395), not in reality; he instead proposed an argument for the existence of God as the ground of all *possibility* that he would continue to affirm for some years but ultimately reject in the *Critique of Pure Reason*. Finally, Kant rejected the libertarian conception of freedom as *undetermined* choice advocated by Christian August Crusius (another Pietist) in favor of a Leibnizian position that freedom is choice determined by an agent's internal principles rather than by any external principle (Kant would ultimately reconcile the two positions he contrasted in 1755 by combining a Leibnizian model of the source of the moral law in *Wille* as pure practical reason with a Crusian model of *Willkür* as the inscrutable choice between the moral law and self-love). Kant's argument in the "Physical Monadology" that the infinite divisibility of space can be reconciled with the existence of indivisible physical monads points the way toward his eventual theory that matter must consist of attractive and repulsive forces that are centered in points in space no matter how finely divided, although it would be fifteen more years before Kant would add the claim that space and time themselves are nothing but our own forms of intuition, thus that particular regions of space are nothing but our own representations also, and that they are thus indefinitely extendable or divisible but never actually infinitely extended or divided.

Kant's next publications fall between 1762 and 1770. During this period he took many steps toward his mature philosophy, although his most characteristic – and controversial – doctrine, transcendental idealism, would emerge only in the final year of this period. From 1762 to 1764 Kant published four especially significant works. In the fall of 1762, he submitted an essay to the Berlin Academy of Sciences competition on the question of whether philosophy had the same prospects for certitude that mathematics does. The Wolffian Academy awarded first prize to an elegant essay by Moses Mendelssohn, but thought well enough of Kant's contribution, the *Inquiry concerning the Distinctness of the Principles of Natural Theology and Morality*, to publish it alongside Mendelssohn's essay "On Evidence in Metaphysical Sciences" in 1764 (Mendelssohn 1997: 253–306). Mendelssohn argued for the characteristic Wolffian synthesis of rationalism and empiricism, defending an account of mathematics as a formal system anchored to reality by experience, an *a priori* argument for the existence of God anchored in our experience of our own existence, and a morality aimed at the perfection of the "intrinsic" and "extrinsic" human condition as we are empirically acquainted with it. Kant's entire subsequent career can be seen as his attempt to refute this version of Wolffianism.[2] In particular, he argued that philosophy cannot use the same method as mathematics, because the latter can begin with definitions but the former must begin with common concepts and can only end with proper definitions. Kant also argued against a purely formalistic approach to morality, holding that "formal first principles" (such as "perform the most perfect action in your power") must be supplemented by "indemonstrable material principles of practical cognition" to tell us what the most perfect actions in our power are. Kant alluded to Francis Hutcheson's moral sense, our approbation of benevolent intentions, as a promising avenue toward a material first principle for morality. Kant subsequently repudiated Hutcheson's moral feeling as the source of the fundamental *principle* of morality (e.g., *KpV* 5: 40), and is commonly thought to have rejected the idea of any material first principle for morality altogether. But his eventual argument in *GMS* that the categorical imperative must be "grounded" in the existence of rational being or humanity as an end in itself suggests that he retained the thought that a formal first principle must be complemented by a material one, although not an empirical one, while his later theory of the feeling of respect as at least part of any account of moral *motivation* shows an enduring influence of the moral sense school on his own philosophy.

Two other key works published in 1763 were an "Attempt to Introduce the Concept of Negative Magnitudes into Philosophy" and *The Only Possible Basis for a Demonstration of the Existence of God*. In the former, Kant distinguished between logical and real relations, for example between the logical relation of contradiction and the physical relation of an opposition of forces; this prepared the way for his subsequent distinction between logical relations that can be established analytically and real relations like causality that must be established by other means, and perhaps more generally for his eventual distinction between analytic and synthetic (*a priori*) cognitions. In the *Only Possible Basis*, Kant renewed his attack upon the ontological argument, further developed his alternative argument for the necessity of the existence of God as the ground of all possibility, and then proposed a "Revised Method of Physico-Theology," in which he argued that "great regularity and the harmoniousness of a complex harmony is [. . .] inconceivable in the absence of an Intelligent Author" (*BDG* 2: 165), although such an author must be conceived as responsible for and achieving his ends through the laws of nature rather than ever interfering with them. Kant would always remain attracted to such a teleology, and employed teleological assumptions throughout his philosophy, although he would eventually insist that *we must conceive* of a harmonious system of natural laws and of nature itself and of its intelligence authorship regulatively, not constitutively.

The last of Kant's major works of the period 1762–64 was a more popular essay, *Observations on the Feeling of the Beautiful and Sublime*. The most significant aspect of the work is the step towards Kant's mature moral philosophy represented in his statement that

> true virtue can only be grafted upon principles, and it will become the more sublime and noble the more general they are. These principles are not speculative rules, but the consciousness

of a feeling that lives in every human breast . . . the **feeling of the beauty and the dignity of human nature**. The first is a ground of universal affection, the second of universal respect, and if this feeling had the greatest perfection in any human heart then this human being would certainly love and value even himself, but only in so far as he is one among all to whom his widespread and noble feeling extends itself.

(GSE 2: 217)

Kant still uses the language of both perfection and feeling here, but hints at his later position that morality consists in acting on universally valid principles. In notes written in his own copy of the book Kant further develops his emerging moral theory, anticipating his later distinction between hypothetical and categorical imperatives, intimating that adherence to universalizable principles is necessary to ensure one's own freedom and that of all others, and suggesting that the reason why we must place unconditional value on the freedom of all is that freedom is the very essence of the human will, which it would be a contradiction to deny (e.g., HN 20: 161, 155–6, 67, and 93). Here was the germ of Kant's conception of the human being's proper self.

In 1766 Kant published *Dreams of a Spirit-Seer Elucidated by Dreams of Metaphysics*. Its ostensible target was the claim of the Swedish mystic Emmanuel Swedenborg to be able to communicate with human spirits without any physical intermediary. This led to a more general argument against metaphysical hypotheses without empirical confirmation, which Kant would later express by saying that through pure reason alone we can *conceive of* but not *cognize* objects. But just as Kant would later argue that reason alone can give us no theoretical cognition but can and does give us essential moral ideas, so in this work he argues that Swedenborg's idea of a community of souls is not useless if understood as a *moral* ideal, of the regulation of our will "in accordance with the will of another [. . .] in strong opposition to our selfish inclination" (TG, 2: 334).

In 1768 Kant took a further step toward his mature philosophy in an essay on "The Differentiation of Regions of Space." Here he argued that the difference between "incongruent counterparts," such as left- and right-handed gloves and screws, cannot be captured by any conceptual representation of relations among their parts but only by their different situation in absolute space. Thus he argued in behalf of Newtonian absolute space rather than a Leibnizian theory of space as generated by relations among objects.

Two years later this argument underwent a momentous revision. In 1770 Kant was finally offered the chair in logic and metaphysics. Appointment as a professor required the presentation and defense of an inaugural dissertation. Kant's work was entitled *De mundi sensibilis atque intelligibilis forma et principiis* ("On the form and principles of the sensible and the intelligible world"), and he designated as his respondent for the event Marcus Herz, a Jewish medical student. Kant introduced the doctrine that he came to call transcendental idealism in this inaugural dissertation. Transcendental idealism combined the physics of Newton, the metaphysics of Leibniz, and the first part of a new epistemology of Kant's own. That is, Kant continued to hold that the difference between incongruent counterparts can only be explained by their situation in absolute space, but that our knowledge of the necessity of the structure of space and of time as well cannot be grounded in mere abstraction from either experience of absolute space as an entity independent of us or from empirically known relations among independent objects, but can only be grounded in our acquaintance with "internal principles in the mind" (MSI §4, 2: 393). Thus space and time can only be the "formal principle[s] of our intuition" of particular objects, and are the conditions under which anything can be "the object of our senses" (§10, 2: 396). This in turn, Kant argued, means that space and time are the ways in which objects *appear* to us but not the way they *are* in themselves (§3, 2: 392). Kant borrowed the Leibnizian distinction between "phenomena" and "noumena" to make this point, although his argument that space and time are only *phaenomena bene fundata* was based on his own claim that our knowledge of them is *a priori*. Thus Newton's absolute space and time were transformed into the forms of our own intuition, while Leibniz's treatment of space and time as phenomena was derived from Kant's epistemology rather than from Leibniz's metaphysics. This would become the basis for Kant's theory of our cognitive autonomy.

Kant's retention of the Leibnizian term "noumena" for things as they are in themselves was telling, however, for at this stage Kant still entertained the thought that core "intellectual" concepts such as "possibility, existence, necessity, substance, cause, etc." "never enter into sensory representations as parts" but do give us knowledge of things as they are in themselves – thus such things can be called noumena, literally, things known by *nous* or intellect. Kant mentioned in passing that the "*first principles of judgment*" in "*moral philosophy*" can only be "cognized by the pure understanding" (*MSI* §9, 2: 396) or reason, a decisive break with his earlier attraction to the idea of a moral feeling as the source of the fundamental *principle* of morality and a premise for his subsequent conception of our moral autonomy. And Kant's promise that he would soon follow the inaugural dissertation with a work to be entitled "The Bounds of Sensibility and of Reason," which would "work out in some detail the foundational principles and laws that determine the sensible world together with an outline of what is essential to the Doctrine of Taste, of Metaphysics, and of Moral Philosophy" (letter to Herz of June 7, 1771) became hostage, not to the objections to his new theory of space and especially time as mere forms of intuition that had been made by Mendelssohn, Sulzer, and Lambert (*see Br* 10: 103–16), but to his own realization that representations of the spatial and temporal properties of objects are not sufficient to give us knowledge of them, that these representations also have to be organized by "pure concepts of the understanding," but that such concepts in turn give us knowledge of objects only when supplemented with spatio-temporal representations of them and thus cannot give us knowledge of things as they are in themselves after all. When Kant first voiced this concern to Herz in a second letter in February, 1772 (*Br* 10: 129–35), he remained confident that he would still be able to publish the first part of his new book within three months, but in fact work on what Kant began to call "a critique of pure reason" in a third letter to Herz took the rest of the 1770s. (Major steps toward the emerging work are recorded in one set of notes from 1774–75 known as the *Duisburg Nachlaß*, especially *Refl* 4672–84, and sketches from 1776–79 such as *Refl* 4849, 4851, 5552, and 5553.)

The *Critique of Pure Reason* was finally published in the spring of 1781. This book, which as Kant's letters to Herz had indicated was originally intended to be the sole foundation for his further systematic work in metaphysics, moral philosophy, and even aesthetics, was monumental as well as momentous. Its 851 pages were divided into a "Doctrine of Elements" and a "Doctrine of Method," the first part laying out Kant's own theory of the principles of knowledge and their limits as well as his critique of all previous metaphysics, and the latter clarifying the relation of Kant's method – now called "transcendental" to connote that it concerns the condition of the possibility of "synthetic *a priori* cognition" (B40), that is, knowledge of the properties of objects that goes beyond the tautologies that can be derived from mere analysis of their concepts but yet can be known to be universally and necessarily true, and thus must be known *a priori* – to rationalism, which can yield only analytic results, empiricism, which yields only contingent and restricted results, and skepticism, which yields no knowledge at all.

The Doctrine of Elements is in turn divided into a "Transcendental Aesthetic" and a "Transcendental Logic." In the former Kant reprises his argument that space and time are *nothing but* the forms of our representation of outer objects and inner states, thus universal and necessary features of the appearances of objects but *not* features of things in themselves at all (see A26/B42, A32–3/B49–50). Kant's key argument for what he now names transcendental idealism is that if space and time were properties of things in themselves we could only know them to be so contingently, but that we do know that space and time are universal and necessary features of their proper objects, so they cannot be properties of things in themselves at all (see A 46–9/B 64–6, as well as *Prol*, §13, Note I, 4: 287–8) – a debatable application of *modus tollens*!

The Transcendental Logic is then divided into two parts, the "Transcendental Analytic" and "Transcendental Dialectic": the logic of truth and the critique of metaphysical illusion. In the Transcendental Analytic, Kant establishes the conceptual rather than intuitional conditions of the possibility of knowledge of objects. Kant argues that the pure concepts of the understanding, the "categories," are necessary conditions for all knowledge of objects and indeed for all self-consciousness, or "apperception," but that they yield knowledge only when applied to intuitions – representations of states of objects in space and time – and so also yield knowledge only of appearances, not things in themselves. First, in what he calls (in the second edition of the *Critique*) the "metaphysical deduction," Kant argues that since judgments in general have certain "functions" – every judgment has some quantity (e.g., is universal or singular) and some quality (e.g., is affirmative or negative), and expresses some relation (e.g., that between subject and predicate or ground and consequence) and some modality (asserts a possibility, actuality, or necessity) – so concepts of objects must also have quantity, quality, relation, and modality if we are to be able to make judgments about them by means of judgments with those functions. These necessary features of concepts of objects, what we might think of as the forms of more concrete, for example, empirical concepts of objects, just as space and time are the forms of particular intuitions, are the categories. Thus far Kant has established that when we make judgments about objects we must use the categories. In the "transcendental deduction," Kant then argues that we must be able to make objective judgments about any representations of which we are self-conscious at all, or that we can ascribe representations to ourselves ("apperception") only if we also ascribe them to objects, thus that the categories must apply to all representations that can be included in our "transcendental unity of apperception" (e.g., A 107–8, A 113, A 116–18, B 132, B 143).

Kant next points out that the categories, derived from the logical structure of judgments, must be given a spatio-temporal interpretation if they are to be applied to spatio-temporal interpretations (the "schematism"), for example, the logical relation of ground-and-consequence must be interpreted as the spatio-temporal relation of causality, and then argues that the necessity of certain principles of judgment, including those that the quantum of substance is unchanging, that every event has a cause, and that all substance in space must interact, are necessary conditions for determinate knowledge of the relations of states of objects in time. This is the heart of Kant's argument with David Hume, who had held that the principle of causality, although the basis of our knowledge of the external world, can only be known inductively and therefore contingently. Kant's defense of the necessity of interaction among substances can also be seen as a response to Leibniz's replacement of "physical influx" with "pre-established harmony," although Kant's confinement of causality to the relations among appearances suggests that the difference between his position and Leibniz's is not as great as first appears. The difference is that Leibniz argues that causality can only be a feature of experience, while Kant argues that it is a necessary feature of appearance, that is, of our experience.

The Transcendental Analytic concludes with a chapter on "The Distinction between Phenomena and Noumena" in which Kant both affirms the existence of things in themselves but denies that we can have any determinate knowledge of their properties through the application of the categories to spatio-temporal intuition: he will thus allow noumena in a "negative sense," that is, things that we can conceive and even know to exist but about which we can know nothing else by means of concepts alone – that would be to know noumena in a "positive sense" (A 252–3, A 256/B 311–12). This is the basis for the critique of traditional metaphysics that Kant expounds in the Transcendental Dialectic. Here Kant explains how the faculty of reason generates "ideas" of the immortal soul, the world-whole, and God by applying its characteristic notion of the "unconditioned" to ideas of the self, world, and ground without regard to the limits of sensibility – that is, without regard to the requirement that intuitions as well as concepts are needed for knowledge, and that our intuitions of space and time in particular are always indefinitely extendable or divisible but never completed. On this basis he criticizes the "paralogisms" of rational psychology, the "antinomies" of rational cosmology, and the *a priori* arguments for the existence of God of rational theology. Kant takes these names from Baumgarten's version of Wolff's "special" metaphysics, but presents his critique of historical metaphysics as a critique of a natural human illusion. However, he also argues that the ideas of pure reason have an indispensable heuristic and regulative use in an Appendix to the Transcendental Dialectic, an argument he will reprise in the later *Third Critique*. This completes Kant's account of our cognitive autonomy. Finally, the Doctrine of Method, in a section entitled the "Canon of Pure Reason," argues that pure reason has a constitutive use in the practical sphere, where it yields the moral law and the ideal of a moral world to which we *ought* to make the natural world conform (A 809–10/B 837–8). Here Kant first introduces his conception of the "highest good" as a "system of happiness proportionality combined with morality" and first argues that we can believe in personal immortality and the existence of God not on theoretical grounds but as the conditions of the rationality of striving to achieve these moral goals. Thus Kant replaces "rational theology" with "moral theology" (A 819/B 847). This commences his statement of our moral autonomy.

Kant intended to proceed directly from the *Critique of Pure Reason* to a more concrete "system" comprising "metaphysical foundations of natural science" and a "metaphysics of morals," but more foundational work became necessary. Having next begun what he intended as a popularization of the *Critique*, Kant took the occasion to respond to the charge that his "transcendental idealism" was nothing but the "subjective idealism" of Berkeley under a new name made in the first review of his book (by Christian Garve, heavily edited by J.H. Feder). Thus when the *Prolegomena to Any Future Metaphysics that Would Come Forth as Science* appeared in 1783, Kant proposed that his idealism would better be called "critical" idealism because it had "never entered his mind" to doubt the *existence* of objects distinct from our representations of them (*Prol*, §13, 4: 293). In this introductory work, Kant also proposed to use an "analytic" rather than "synthetic" method, that is, to "ascend to the sources" of mathematical and scientific knowledge "already known to be dependable" and then descend to the general truths of metaphysics, rather than "inquiring within pure reason itself" for the synthetic *a priori* principles of knowledge (§4, 4: 274). Whether there is really a difference in method between the two works is debatable, both because the general principles of metaphysics to which Kant wishes to descend in the *Prolegomena* once having ascended to the sources of the synthetic *a priori* cognition in "pure physics" do not obviously differ from the latter, and because the *Critique* too ascends to the sources of a synthetic *a priori* cognition, namely that of the transcendental unity of apperception itself (see A 117n, B 133–4), then to descend to the principles of judgment that Kant will soon argue are the foundations of physics. Nevertheless the *Prolegomena*'s distinction between analytic and synthetic methods is important because two years later it would structure Kant's argument in the *Groundwork for the Metaphysics of Morals*.

The *Groundwork* also seems to have been at least in part a response to Christian Garve, who in 1784 had published a translation of Cicero's *De Officiis* with a lengthy commentary. Although Kant felt closer to Stoicism than to any other form of ancient ethics, the *Groundwork*'s opening argument that virtues such as prudence and courage are not intrinsically good but are good only if governed by an unconditionally good will is intended as a rejection of all antecedent approaches to moral philosophy. The *Groundwork* is then structured around the distinction between analytic and synthetic methods in the following way: Kant first analyzes the common conceptions of good will and duty and then the philosophical concept of a rational agent to arrive at his formulation(s) of the fundamental principle of morality applicable to all rational agents, and then, in the synthetic phase of the argument, argues that this principle is binding on us human beings. Thus, in an analysis of common moral notions, Kant first argues that a good will is the only unconditionally good thing, but that the human duty to achieve a good will requires that our courses of action ("maxims") be determined independently of mere inclinations and their objects, to which the only alternative is that we choose maxims solely on the basis of their formal property of universalizability – that one could still act on a maxim even if everyone else also did. Next, more philosophically, Kant argues that only rational beings act on their own representations of laws, and that purely rational beings would select their maxims only on account of their lawfulness, thus arriving at the same conclusion as before; but now he adds that rational *agents* or *wills* must also have *ends* for their actions, and if their laws are to be *necessary* they must have a *necessary* end. He then "postulates" (*GMS* 4: 429n) that this end can be nothing other than "rational being" or "humanity" itself, thus that the fundamental principle of morality must be always to treat rational being whether in one's own person or any other person as an end and never merely as a means. Indeed, he states that this formulation supplies the "ground" of a "possible categorical imperative," thus is the most fundamental formulation in the order of demonstration even if the requirement of universalizability remains fundamental in application (see *GMS* 4: 436–7). But what does Kant mean by "rational being" or "humanity"? Kant explains that "rational nature" is simply an agent's capacity "to set itself an end" (*GMS* 4: 437; see also *MS* 6: 387, 392), which means that the fundamental requirement of morality is to preserve and promote the capacity – or freedom – of each to set his or her own ends. This is reflected in Kant's final formulation of the categorical imperative as the requirement to act towards a "realm of ends," that is, "a whole both of rational beings as ends in themselves and of the ends of his own that each may set himself" (*GMS* 4: 433).

All of this is just an analysis of what follows from the concept of a rational agent. In the synthetic phase of the argument, Kant must prove that this analysis applies to and binds *us*. If it were a fallacy to infer an "ought" from an "is," this would seem to require an argument from some strictly normative premise. But that is not the strategy that Kant follows. Instead, he argues that reason is what distinguishes us not only from all other things in the world but even from ourselves as mere appearance, thus that reason characterizes our real and proper selves, and that reason is *self-activity*, so that we liberate ourselves from the *passivity* of being determined by mere inclination only by adherence to the moral law (*GMS* 4: 451–2). This is an argument that our real selves *are* self-active and determined by the moral law, and might be called normative essentialism: Kant does not try to prove that we *ought* to follow the moral law, rather he argues that our proper selves just *are* rational and thereby moral.

Momentarily satisfied that he had established the foundation of morality, Kant thought that he could at last turn to the metaphysical "system" that he intended to ground upon his critique, and in 1786 published the *Metaphysical Foundations of Natural Science*. Here he argued that if we add to the synthetic *a priori* principles of judgment established in the *Critique of Pure Reason* the sole empirical assumption that we humans detect the presence of matter by its motion, then Newtonian physics can be derived. This suggests that in the corresponding *Metaphysics of Morals* the particular duties of human beings would be derived by adding one or several key empirical assumptions about the human condition to the *a priori* principle of morality valid for all rational beings. That is what Kant would eventually do – but only after another dozen years had passed. For once again intervening events required further foundational work.

The first event that intervened was the need for a second edition of the *Critique of Pure Reason*. Kant prepared this in 1786 and published it in 1787. Substantive changes in the first half of the work including a new version of the transcendental deduction of the categories and an entirely new "Refutation of Idealism," which built on the clarification of his transcendental idealism that Kant had achieved in the *Prolegomena*. But Kant's revisions stopped at the Antinomies, where he had discussed freedom, and did not further develop his doctrine of rational belief in immortality and God based on practical rather than theoretical grounds. This seems to have been because he decided that his treatment of both freedom and what he would now call the postulates of pure practical reason needed more space than he could give them in a mere revision of the previous book, and so in 1788 Kant published a previously unforeseen second critique, the *Critique of Practical Reason*. In particular, Kant seems to have formed reservations about the style of the synthetic argument in the third section of the *Groundwork*, and to have decided that rather than the application of the moral law to us being inferred from the self-activity of reason, the normative force of the moral law should simply be accepted as a "fact of reason" (*KpV* 5: 31, 42, 47), from which the reality of our freedom to act in accordance with it could in turn be derived. But in fact Kant's argument still turns on the assumption that the purity of our faculty of reason immediately implies the purity of our will (5: 30).

Kant's reiteration of this key premise quickly triggered the objection, first raised by J.A.H. Ulrich in his *Eleutheriology or on Freedom and Necessity*, also in 1788, that if the moral law is really the law of our "proper" self, that is, *the causal law of our noumenal will*, as Kant asserted (*GMS* 4: 446 and *KrV* 5: 47), then an *immoral* act cannot be the product of our real will, thus we cannot really be responsible for it. Kant did not respond to this objection immediately, for while he was finishing the second critique the idea for yet another had occurred to him. This was the *Critique of the Power of Judgment*, published in 1790, only two years after the *Critique of Practical Reason* (preceded by an essay "On the Use of Teleological Principles in Philosophy" also published in 1788). Having submitted the theoretical use of pure reason and the practical use of reason to their critiques, the first having shown that a purely theoretical use of reason leads only to illusion, the second that a purely empirical practical use of reason does not lead to morality but that morality is founded on a pure practical use of reason, Kant then decided that the faculty of judgment, specifically the "reflecting" use of judgment, in which it seeks universals for given particulars, also needs a critique. This is divided into two parts, the critique of aesthetic and that of teleological judgment. The first of these argues that at its core aesthetic judgment is universally valid judgment about the pleasure induced by particular objects, but "disinterested" pleasure, independent from the physiological pleasure of the "agreeable" and the practical or moral pleasure of the "good." Our pleasure in a beautiful object is instead grounded in the "free play" of imagination within the boundary of "lawfulness" imposed by the understanding that is triggered by an object, and the judgment of taste is the claim that under optimal conditions everyone would be pleased by that object because the pleasure in it has such a foundation in shared cognitive capacities. But even though "pure" or simple cases of beauty, such as the beauty of a flower or decorative border, are independent of moral concerns in this way, all of the more complex cases of aesthetic response and judgment turn out to have important connections to morality without sacrifice of their own autonomy. Our mixed but ultimately pleasurable experience of the sublime, which is not a species of beauty at all although artistic representations of the sublime must also be beautiful (*Anth* §68, 7: 243), is an aesthetic intimation of the power of our own theoretical or practical reason triggered by vast or powerful scenes in nature. The adherent beauty of artifacts, such as buildings, depends upon the free play of the imagination within the constraints entailed by the purpose of the object (*KU* §16). Beauty in the fine arts depends upon free play between the sensory form and matter of the work on the one hand and its content on the other, which Kant argues must ultimately be a moral idea if the work is to be of enduring attraction (§§49–50). Further, once we have become familiar with art, it is inevitable that we will read moral significance into natural beauty (§§42, 51) and, because our experience of beauty is an experience of the freedom of the imagination, we will use beauty as a symbol of morality because that is also founded upon our freedom. Because of the centrality of morality in our lives, in other words, we will find moral interest even in the very disinterestedness of aesthetic experience (§59). Aesthetic autonomy interacts with moral autonomy.

In the second half of the third *Critique*, Kant offered a qualified defense of the kind of teleological thinking, that is, finding purposiveness in nature and a designer at the bottom of such purposiveness, that had been discredited by thinkers from Spinoza to Hume. Kant argues that even though we have no theoretical justification for attributing purposiveness either to individual organisms or to nature as a whole, it is nevertheless both natural and valuable for us to read purposiveness into nature. This is because our conception of both organisms and nature as a whole as purposive systems guides us in our theoretical inquiry into these systems and also leads us to posit a final end for the system of nature as a whole which, because it must be unconditionally valuable, can only be our own moral development. Such a conception of nature is not theoretically "constitutive," that is, it is not to be included within our scientific representation of the world, but it is both theoretically and practically "regulative," that is, it guides us in the conduct of both science and morality. Kant calls this form of autonomy "heautonomy."

This vision of how to bridge the great "gulf" between the "legislation of nature" and the "legislation of freedom" (*KU* 5: 175) is the culmination of Kant's Critical philosophy. But work remained to be done. For one, Kant had to answer the question about the possibility of immorality. He did this in *Religion within the Boundaries of Mere Reason* (Part One was published as an article in 1792 and all four parts were published as a book in 1793). This work has a complex agenda, arguing on the one hand that humans need symbols for the central concepts of the "religion of reason" and that the central symbols of Christianity are better than any others in this role, but on the other hand that the practices and especially the priesthood of organized religion are unnecessary and even injurious to the moral development of human beings. But the original part of the book, on "The Radical Evil in Human Nature," answers Ulrich by distinguishing between *Wille*, the source of the moral law, which is identical with pure practical reason, and *Willkür*, our power of choice, which is nothing less than the power to choose between good, that is, subordinating self-love to morality, and evil, that is, subordinating morality to self-love (*RGV*, 6: 36). Evil is "radical" in the sense that it concerns an agent's *fundamental* maxim, the basic choice to subordinate morality to self-love, which infects all of the agent's more particular maxims, but also because the possibility of evil is rooted in the very nature of free choice itself, which is nothing other than the power to choose between good and evil. And then Kant can argue that because evil is rooted in freedom, even the evil person can still choose to be good, although since freedom is really noumenal, we cannot really represent the possibility of such moral conversion in temporal terms. In temporal terms we can only represent the possibility of progress toward complete moral conversion (6: 67). Nevertheless, the possibility of complete conversion at the noumenal level undercuts Kant's original argument for the postulate of immortality.

Kant had flourished under Friedrich II ("the Great"), but his attack upon organized religion in the *Religion* earned him a prohibition of further publication upon the subject from the conservative regime of Friedrich Wilhelm II. So Kant turned to a defense of republican principles of government that should have been at least as objectionable to the regime. Kant promulgated his republicanism, on which the only true sovereign is a people represented by a parliament and any executive is merely their agent, in an essay "On the common saying: That may be right in theory but it is of no use in practice," also published in 1793, and in his pamphlet *Towards Perpetual Peace*, published in 1795. The latter argues that the only prospect for world peace lies in the worldwide conversion of governments into republics that will not undertake war for dynastic aggrandizement, although because Kant proscribes both internal rebellions and external interventions the only prospect for this worldwide conversion lies in "moral politicians," that is, in hereditary rulers motivated by their own respect for the moral law converting their own monarchies into republics. The possibility of political conversion thus not only mirrors but also depends upon the possibility of moral conversion.

That government must be grounded in morality is also a central message of the last part of Kant's system, namely the *Metaphysics of Morals* finally published in 1797 to complement the metaphysics of nature published in 1786. Just as the latter work had applied the *a priori* principles of knowledge to the perception of matter, so on the definition that Kant now uses a metaphysics of morals takes as its "object the particular *nature* of human beings, which is cognized only by experience, in order to *show* in it what can be inferred from universal moral principles" (*MS*, 6: 217). That is, the metaphysics of morals shows what duties follow for *human* beings from the fundamental principle of morality that is valid for all *rational* beings. The *a priori* principle is that morality requires the preservation and promotion of the freedom of all to set their own ends; the empirical assumption is that human beings are rational beings embodied in the kinds of bodies that we have and living on the finite surface of a sphere that is not naturally divided into regions assigned to individuals or individual nations, any part of which may be reached from any other. This combination of principle and fact requires that the innate right of each to equal freedom with every other, which itself rests upon the *obligation* of each to treat the humanity of all as an end and never merely as a means, be secured, and that the right of each to acquire property on equal terms with others be made determinate as well as secure, all of which requires government, which humans are thus morally obligated to institute. This is the foundation of *Recht*, or "right," that subset of moral duties that can be coercively enforced insofar as coercion is a hindrance to the hindering of freedom (*MS* 6: 231). "Ethics" proper concerns instead all those duties that cannot be coercively enforced, including such self-regarding perfect duties as the prohibition of suicide, but especially the "duties of virtue," that is, the imperfect or wide duties to promote the ends of self-perfection and the happiness of others. These duties arise from the combination of the fundamental requirement to treat humanity in all persons as an end and never merely as a means with the empirical fact that human beings are not born, and never are, entirely self-sufficient, but must develop their physical, mental, and moral powers and even then must rely on the assistance of others to achieve their ends and thus to enjoy maximal freedom in setting their ends (since a rational being cannot rationally set an end for which it does not have possible means).

The *Metaphysics of Morals* completed Kant's systematic philosophy, although in 1798 he published *Anthropology from a Pragmatic Point of View*, a handbook for the lectures on anthropology (which he had given for the last time in the previous year), as well as *The Conflict of the Faculties*, three essays in which he argues that the philosophical faculty of the university is distinguished from the other three faculties (theology, law, and medicine) by its duty to search for the truth free from all external constraints, even though like the other faculties it is supported by the state. This is a path-breaking argument for academic freedom. Under Kant's supervision, textbooks on logic, physical geography, and pedagogy were also published. These completed Kant's work, for he was not able to finish his final project, which began as an attempt to make the transition "from the metaphysical foundations of natural science to physics" but was developing into a restatement of transcendental idealism as a whole. Kant was incapacitated by what appears to have been a stroke in October 1803, and died on February 12, 1804. But his philosophy of the "proper self" or human autonomy in all its forms had fundamentally transformed Western philosophy.

Notes

1 See Kuehn (2001: 86–95).
2 See Guyer (1991: 119–52), reprinted in Guyer (2000: 17–59, 2020).

References

Guyer, P. (1991) "Mendelssohn and Kant: One Source of the Critical Philosophy," *Philosophical Topics* 19: 119–52.
Guyer, P. (2000) *Kant on Freedom, Law, and Happiness*, Cambridge: Cambridge University Press, pp. 17–59.
Guyer, P. (2020) *Reason and Experience in Mendelssohn and Kant*, Cambridge: Cambridge University Press.
Kuehn, M. (2001) *Kant: A Biography*, Cambridge: Cambridge University Press.
Mendelssohn, M. (1997) *Philosophical Writings*, D.O. Dahlstrom (ed.), Cambridge: Cambridge University Press.

Further Reading

L.W. Beck, *Early German Philosophy: Kant and His Predecessors* (Cambridge, MA: Harvard University Press, 1969) is highly readable account of the development of German philosophy before and into Kant that provides the most accessible introduction to Kant's philosophical milieu in English. H.-J. de Vleeschauwer, *The Development of Kantian Thought* (London: T. Nelson and Sons, 1962) is an older but still valuable work that emphasizes the development of Kant's "transcendental method" and its application to the several areas of his philosophy, originally published in French in 1939; it is a summary of the author's monumental three-volume work in French, *Le déduction transcendentale dans l'oeuvre de Kant* (The Hague: Martinus Nijhoff, 1936–39). P. Guyer, *Kant*, 2nd ed. (London: Routledge, 2014) is a survey of all aspects of Kant's work from the point of view represented in the present article. M. Kuehn, *Kant: A Biography* (Cambridge: Cambridge University Press, 2001) is an eminently readable biography of Kant that both sets his work firmly in his immediate historical context and emphasizes the development of the moral vision at the heart of Kant's philosophy. J.B. Schneewind, *The Invention of Autonomy: A History of Modern Moral Philosophy* (Cambridge: Cambridge University Press, 1998): this work does for Kant's moral philosophy specifically what Beck's did for Kant's philosophy as a whole, presenting to the development of the conception of autonomy in modern moral philosophy – British, German, and French – as the background for the approach to Kant's moral philosophy sketched in its final chapters. M. Schönfeld, *The Young Kant: The Pre-Critical Project* (New York: Oxford University Press, 2000) is an intellectual biography of Kant from 1746 to 1766; this work emphasizes Kant's developing effort to reconcile his commitment to the truth of Newtonian physics with his conception of the necessity of a libertarian conception of freedom as the condition of moral responsibility.

PART 1

Background to the Critical Philosophy

2

PHYSICS

Martin Schönfeld

★★★

What we now call physics was part of *philosophy of nature* in early modernity. It included all topics of natural science, not just those of material nature, and its methods involved a range of approaches. Newton, for example, adopted an empirical, quantitative, and analytic methodology in works such as *Principia* (1687), whose full title is *Mathematical Principles of Philosophy of Nature*. Kant, on the other hand, favored a conjectural, qualitative, and synthetic approach in his early, pre-critical contributions to philosophy of nature. Kant did not rely on experimentation and quantification, but proceeded in non-mathematical form by critiquing experimental results and empirical findings, and by connecting pieces of information into larger syntheses, always searching for deeper causal patterns of reality.

In the 1740s and 1750s, Kant investigated the energetic and elementary aspects of nature – force, space, matter, as well as fire, storms, and earthquakes. Philosophy of nature was his sole focus from 1744 to 1755, his main focus from 1756 to 1763, and a side-interest thereafter. He wrote the last tract on the topic in 1768. The leitmotif of his inquiries is *evolution*: the origin of space and matter, the emergence of order and complexity, and the self-organization and dissolution of nature. In his day, however, such inquiries were not well received. They collided with the creationist dogma of the Christian belief-systems that dominated Germany in early modernity before the completion of the Enlightenment. Evolutionary lines of inquiry drew accusations of atheism, freethought (*Freigeisterei*) and 'Spinozism,' a label that denoted Spinoza's pantheism but also Chinese metaphysics, especially Daoism (Cf. *EaD* 8: 335.25–36; "Lao-Kiun," in Kant's spelling, is Laozi 老子).

As a consequence of his early physics, Kant was marginalized and failed to advance. Only after he abandoned these interests and assumed the guise of a skeptic – with *TG* (1766), which could be read as a critique of conjecture, and *MSI* (1770), with its cognitive distinction between conceptual patterns and empirical structures – was it possible for him to become a professor of logic and metaphysics. In the 1780s, in the critical period, his interest in physics returned, but instead of investigating nature, he now examined the investigation itself. His focus shifted from first-order to second-order concerns, or from questions on nature to questions on science.

This critical philosophy of science deserves an account of its own, but can be treated here only in passing, since our concern is Kant's actual philosophy of nature. Yet interesting about Kant's

DOI: 10.4324/9781003406617-4

eventual return to physics is its importance for the critical project. In *KrV* (1781/1787), physics is the benchmark for investigations. It serves as marker of what it means for a research program to "travel the secure course of a science" (B viii).[1] The ideal of an investigation is science; the ideal of science is physics; and the ideal of physics is Newtonian physics (Friedman 1992: 136). At the end of *KrV*, Kant sees future philosophers systematically embracing a scientific method, whose adoption, he hopes, would let philosophy answer all the questions of human reason (A855/B883).

Despite its indirect role, physics is the engine that propels the critical project forward and serves as the yardstick for its completion. The critical elevation of physics in *KrV* is certainly in need of proof. It committed Kant to a series of demonstrations, which shed light on his trajectory in the 1780s and 1790s. In this idealized characterization, and as the quote of the "secure course" already suggests, an inquiry qualifies as a science only if it has certainty. But certainty is not given empirically; it can only be demonstrated a priori. Since physics is the ideal science, the certainty of its foundations needs to be shown.

The general object of physics is matter, and in *MAN* (1786), Kant constructs a groundwork for Newtonian physics aimed at the identification of the a priori in matter. This theory of matter derives from the categories in *KrV*. *MAN* applies quantity, quality, relation, and modality to determine matter, quantitatively, as "the moveable in space"; qualitatively, as "the moveable insofar as it fills a space"; relationally, as "the movable insofar as it, as such a thing, has moving force"; and concerning its mode of knowability, as "the movable insofar as it, as such a thing, can be an object of experience" (4: 480, 496, 536, 554). In Kant's mind, the categorical demonstrations of *MAN* yield a transition from the critical philosophy to the metaphysical foundations of natural science.

Believing that *MAN* had discharged the burden of proof, he thought that the critical project was reaching completion and regarded the third Critique, *KU* (1790), as the work that "brings [his] entire critical enterprise to an end" (5: 170). But certainty happens to be just one of two traits in need of demonstration. A set of propositions can be certain and yet fail to be scientific if they lack interconnections and a theoretical center. In Kant's critical project, science possesses unity next to certainty. Unity expresses itself in propositional coherence. Like certainty, unity can only be shown a priori. But since certainty is about the foundations, while unity is about the propositional edifice, proving certainty does not prove unity. Another and separate demonstration is needed.

In letters to Christian Garve and Johann Kiesewetter in 1798, Kant conceded that there is still a hole in his project, right between the foundations of physics, and physics itself (Förster 1993: xvi, *Br* 12: 257, *Br* 12: 258). Without filling this second gap, the critical project would not be complete. To close this gap and show the unity of science, a "transition from the metaphysical foundations of natural science to physics" (to Kiesewetter, *Br* 12: 258) needed to be done. He worked on this project until his health started failing in 1801. The unfinished result is the *OP*. It does not give us the promised demonstration of the unity of physics. Instead, its argumentation oscillates between second- and first-order questions and shows Kant returning, in a way, to his pre-critical roots. Once more he engages in conjecture about nature, and like Einstein and others after him, he seeks the ontological unity of the physical world in the hypothesis of a self-organizing energy-field, the ether.

Fascinating about the pre-critical conjectures of the young Kant is their controversial character to this day. Scholars, by and large, dismiss them as misguided and obsolete (e.g. Lalla 2003: 453). This is the interpretive standard, and as a result, the scholarly literature is scant. On the other hand, scientists praise pre-critical conjectures such as the Nebular Hypothesis as "the essence of modern models" (Coles 2001: 240), and they find anticipations of modern physics even in Kant's earliest work, *GSK* (Barrow 2002: 203–5). This disagreement is not entirely due to faulty communication across disciplinary boundaries (although it surely plays a part), for both sides do have a point. Scholarly skepticism is appropriate in that the concepts Kant uses for the phenomena investigated – matter, force, or space – differ from their definitions today. But scientific praise is appropriate, too, because discrepancies do not constitute discontinuities from Kant's physics to the Standard Model. There are links between the ideas in the former and the information in the latter. When Kant examines 'living force' or *vis viva* and 'dead force' or *vis mortua* in *GSK*, for example, he works with concepts that are now obsolete. Also, Kant's scientific context – Leibnizian dynamics and Cartesian kinematics – lacks the definition of mass that would be found in Newtonian mechanics. Nonetheless, the dynamic phenomena denoted by these concepts are real enough and have quantitative correlates (the product of mass and velocity squared, and the product of mass and velocity, respectively). Leibnizian *vis viva* and Cartesian *vis mortua* are fuzzy on 'mass,' but their approximations such as 'quantity of matter' worked well enough in experimental setups. So, there are scholarly reasons to regard 'living force' and 'dead force' as antiquated notions, and there are scientific reasons to consider them as legitimate and meaningful precursors to their modern equivalents, *energy* and *momentum*.

Recent scientific progress has made it easier to make sense of Kant's obscure early physics. As we know more about nature now, we can also see the pre-critical conjectures in clearer light. Findings in physics, chemistry, and complexity theory have made possible readings of Kant's conjectures that simply had not been possible a generation ago. As this chapter will describe, it appears Kant not only anticipated isolated aspects of the Standard Model but also got the overall story of natural evolution right. In light of these progressions, scholarly misgivings appear increasingly dated. Today, scientific praise has the last word.

1. Liabilities and Kant's Retreat

However, before the early physics became obscure, it had been rather provocative. Continuously working on its central claims would prove to be an academic liability and eventually forced Kant to retreat. His actual investigations of material nature are wide and varied. He examined the nature of force (in his first book, *GSK*, written 1745–47); the history and future of the Earth (in two articles, *FEV* and *UFE*, 1754); the nature of fire (in his Magisterial Dissertation, *DI*, 1754); the fate of the cosmos (in his anonymous second book, *NTH*, 1755); the origin of solar systems and the structure of star clusters (also in his second book, and in his third, *BDG*, 1763); the ultimate elements of matter and space (in his Professorial Dissertation, *MoPh*, 1756); the mechanics of earthquakes, winds, and the monsoon (a series of articles, *VUE*, *GNVE*, *FBZE*, *TW*, and *EACG*, 1756–57); the concept of mass (a tract, *NLBR*, 1758), and the structure of space (a short tract, *GUGR*, 1768). All these investigations interlock with one another, collectively casting light on a systematic conception of nature (Schönfeld 2000: 3–4).

Over time, Kant's conception of nature underwent shifts. It did so not, as one might expect, from a theoretical need to revise his conclusions, but rather as rhetorical attempts at damage control. His early conclusions – the positions advanced from 1745 to 1756 – had created a problem, preventing him from filling the vacant professorship of metaphysics and logic that he applied for. He secured employment as an assistant librarian and adjunct instructor, but his application in April 1756 for the position was denied, despite his degrees – promotion to *Magister* in June 1755 with *DI*, permission to lecture (*venia legendi*) in September 1755 with *PND*, and defense in April 1756 of *MoPh*.

In order to teach physics, philosophy of nature, or metaphysics at a Prussian university in the mid-eighteenth century, the successful candidate need possess not only the requisite credentials (which Kant had), but must also abide by a certain political correctness. By the 1750s, the ongoing Enlightenment was sufficiently advanced so that it was not necessary anymore to profess one's piety at every turn. But the division of Church and State had not yet progressed to the point so as to free teaching from the authority of faith. According to Biblical doctrine, nature was created in a limited time by a supernatural God, who also created humans in his own image, with supernatural, immortal souls. This was dogma. It entailed three constraints on propositions about nature:

- First, since creation, nature underwent variations *but no constitutive changes*. All constitutive changes had been wielded by God during creation. None happened afterwards.
- Second, because God is the creator, creative activity is in God. Nature's activity follows lawful processes, and its parts can reproduce and procreate, *but the whole is devoid of creative power*.
- Third, nature is a composite of physical nature, living creatures, and humans with souls. Physical nature and living creatures are of the same stuff, matter. Supernatural, immortal souls are of another kind, mind. Matter and mind are mutually exclusive. Matter is extended but does not think, and minds think but are not extended. Ontologically, they have nothing to do with one another. *Their interaction cannot be accounted for by physical means.*

These constraints meant that a professor of philosophy had to acknowledge that nature is static; that it is mechanical and passive; that its ontology is dualistic, and that the problem of mind-body interaction can only have a theological solution. If one chooses to deny any of this and state the opposite – that nature is dynamic, that it has power to evolve on its own, that it is a coherent whole in which mind and matter are surface aspects whose interaction is energetic – then one cannot teach. At best, one's career will not advance, and one will risk being branded as an atheist, Spinozist, or 'freethinker' (*Freigeist*).

This was no different in Königsberg than anywhere else in Prussia, if not Europe. The former chair of metaphysics and logic, Martin Knutzen, belonged to the Pietist congregation and fit administrative expectations (Kuehn 2001a: 76–86). However, the former holder of the (discontinued) chair in natural philosophy, the sinologist Christian Gabriel Fischer, had chosen to challenge the dogma. He was expelled from the university, banished from the city, and forcibly exiled from Prussia in 1725 (Kuehn 2001b: 12).

Freethinkers were not always persecuted in Germany, but if they were tolerated at all, then only outside academia. Christian Wolff (1679–1754) defended Chinese philosophy at Halle, which led to accusations of Spinozism and to his exile in 1723 (Albrecht 1985: XLVI–LIII). Georg Bilfinger (1693–1750), a scholar of Chinese philosophy, followed Wolff into exile, and moved to Russia to do physics at the St Petersburg Academy of Sciences (Schönfeld 2011: 48–56). Life improved for freethinkers in the 1730s, and markedly got better in Prussia with the coronation of Frederick II in 1740. Bilfinger went back to Swabia in 1734. Fischer received permission to return to Königsberg in 1736. Wolff was allowed to return to Halle in 1740. But Bilfinger resigned from academics, Fischer remained barred from teaching, and Wolff was rehabilitated only because he spent years in exile writing assurances that his views agreed with dogma. The king's secular reach was checked by the clout of the clergy and the power of theology departments at universities. Theologians served as watchdogs on campus, as Fischer, Wolff, Bilfinger, and Kant all had to learn the hard way.

Kant entered the university in 1740 and eventually studied under Knutzen. In 1745 he started working on a topic about the nature and measurement of physical force. But instead of writing up his research as a dissertation in Latin, he wrote a book in German, *GSK*, which disqualified it as an academic document. He completed it in 1747 and then left the university without a degree. *GSK* appeared in 1749. It is an amateurish work, a raw unedited text, stylistically crude, and flawed in its contents. Evidently it is the product of a lone wolf, without a teacher who might otherwise have been willing to proof-read the manuscript and suggest revisions. Apparently, Kant and Knutzen had suffered a fall-out, which was no surprise considering the risky claims in *GSK* (e.g. §§1, 6, 9–10, and see Section 2, paragraphs on *GSK*). Instead of heeding Knutzen's Christian views, Kant followed Fischer's. And, like Fischer, he left school and town, only returning years later.

The three dissertations upon his return, on fire, metaphysical cognition, and physical monads (*DI*, *PND*, and *MoPh*), contained no theologically controversial statements. But just as the freethinker John Toland (1670–1722) had differentiated between exoteric and esoteric statements – the former kowtowing to dogma and for public consumption; the latter frank but just for friends – Kant had dropped hints, in *UFE*, that he had been working on an evolutionary cosmology, or *cosmogony* (*UFE* 1: 191.4–8), which he published anonymously as his second book, *NTH*, in 1755. Only few copies saw the light of day, because the publisher went bankrupt, or was driven into bankruptcy, just when printing the text, and the copies, locked up in a warehouse, fell victim to a fire. Some copies survived, and a bookseller's advertisement offering "*NTH* by Magister Kant," either a casual slip or deliberate sabotage, just when he applied for the position that had been left vacant since Knutzen's death, blew his cover (Rahts 1902 in *NTH* 1: 545).

His third book, *BDG* (1763), is an exercise in contrition and reads as an attempt to make amends. It is a diligent effort in rational theology, and it contains a summary of *NTH* – but only of the parts related to the so-called Nebular Hypothesis (see more on this later in the chapter) and purged of all the former problematic contentions. The conception of nature laid out (*BDG* II.7, 2: 137–51) was perfectly mechanical, beautifully Newtonian, and devoid of any and all conjectures about force before space, cosmogonic self-organization, and cyclic universes. The nebular hypothesis, which details the emergence of complexity out of chaos, is now applied only to the solar system (*BDG* 2: 144–7) and the rings of Saturn (*BDG* 2: 149–50), not to the whole cosmos anymore. By reducing his evolutionary cosmology to historical astrophysics, Kant hoped to demonstrate his desire to stay within the constraint that concedes only non-constitutive changes to variations of nature. The purpose of this summary, he writes, is to show that mechanistic explanations of natural developments harmonize with faith in an omniscient and wise creator-God (*BDG* 2: 147.31–8.13).

Still, it was to no avail. The professorship in metaphysics kept eluding him. In 1764, the university offered him a professorship in poetry. As Voltaire's case illustrates, poetry can take more liberties. Kant would not be allowed to teach philosophy, given his publication record on material nature, but his pre-critical conjectures could be forgiven – as poetic license, as it were – if deemed fiction. Kant rejected this offer. In 1770, he wrote the inaugural dissertation, *MSI*, which could be read as a concession to dualism and skepticism, and thereby as a tacit disavowal of freethought. With this public recanting, he joined academic philosophy full time at last.

2. Evolution of Space

If one wanted to sum up the theological liabilities of Kant's physics in one word, then *evolution* would come to mind. In the preface to *NTH*, he writes:

> I assume the matter of the entire world in a state of general dispersion and render it into complete chaos. I see matter form in accordance with the established laws of attraction and modify its motion through repulsion. [. . .] I enjoy the pleasure to see the generation of a well-ordered whole only guided by established laws of motion [. . .]. This unexpected evolution (*Auswickelung*) of the order of nature on a large scale seems initially suspect to me, since it bases such a composite rightness (*zusammengesetzte Richtigkeit*) on such a mean and simple basis. But [. . .] such an evolution of nature (*Auswickelung der Natur*) is nothing incredible, because nature's essential striving (*wesentliche Bestrebung*) necessarily brings this about, and

[. . .] this is the most magnificent testimony of nature's dependence on that primordial being (*Urwesen*), which contains even the source of beings as such and their first laws of causation.

(*NTH* 1: 225.32–226.15 my translation;
compare Reinhardt's translation in Kant2012a: 197)[2]

Kant's *Auswickelung der Natur* (*NTH* 1: 226.8) is a German rendition of the Latin *evolutio naturae*. The verb *auswickeln* and its noun, *Auswicklung* (in Kant's spelling with an extra 'e'), denotes activities such as unfolding, unfurling, or unwrapping. The root of 'evolution' refers to the opening or unrolling (*e-volvere*) of parchments in libraries. Evolution in Kant is the unrolling of the book of nature. This differs from our understanding. We associate evolution with life, while Kant used it for matter. Evolution, for us, governs organic nature. For Kant, evolution happens to material nature first, and to organic nature only after material nature has gained the requisite level of *composite rightness* (*NTH* 1: 226.6–7). We also associate evolution with a mutability of life against shifting adaptive pressures. For Kant, evolution does not consist in random adaptations, but instead in an irreversible emergence of complex structures. Composite rightness – complexity – emerges by lawful processes from a "mean and simple basis" (*NTH* 1: 226.7). This basis is a chaos of particles subject to laws of motion. Kant's evolution of nature is something we now call emergent evolution or *emergence*, whose study belongs to the systems and complexity theories located in the material sciences between physics and biology. How entropy not only allows for, but also necessitates complexity, was shown by Ilya Prigogine, whose work on dissipative structures was a contribution to non-equilibrium thermodynamics and won him the 1977 Nobel Prize in chemistry (Prigogine 1993: 263–85).

With what does nature's evolution begin? In *NTH*, Kant traces the emergence of complexity from dispersed matter in space. In *GSK*, however, he considers an earlier stage, the emergence of matter *and* space from energy. He begins with praising Leibniz as the first who understood bodies contain essential forces – a force that belongs to matter "even prior to extension" (*GSK* §1; 1: 17.20–3). Extension is the property shared by space and matter. Since force exists prior to extension, there must have been a primordial stage in which there was only force, but neither space nor matter yet. In §4 Kant deduces, "the origin of what we call motion": in a given substance, force is determined to act outwardly, thereby altering the state of other substances (*GSK* 1: 19.2–6). In §7 he deduces "links and relations" emerging from reciprocal effects of energetic activity (*GSK* 1: 21.30–3). This growing web of "connections, situations, and relations" entails the emergence of places (*GSK* 1: 22.5–7). In §9, he remarks:

> It is easy to show that there would be no space and no extension (*Ausdehnung*) if substances had no force to act external to themselves. For without force there is no connection, without connection, no order, and, finally, without order, no space. Yet it is somehow more difficult to see how the plurality of dimensions in space derives from the law according to which this force of substances acts externally.
>
> (*GSK* 1: 23.4–9; translation by Schönfeld and Edwards, in Kant 2012b: 26–7)

The primordial stage of nature consists of undifferentiated energy. But as an aside, it needs to be noted that present-day knowledge of physical phenomena such as 'matter,' 'mass,' 'space,' and 'energy' is qualitatively and quantitatively vastly sharper than it had been in Kant's lifetime. The ongoing revolution in the natural sciences began around 1600, and while Kant's understanding of these phenomena reflects the one-and-a-half century mark of scientific progression, ours has passed the four-century mark. But what Kant's understanding lacks in physical precision is made up by metaphysical imagination. He likens the creative and all-pervading energy to Spinoza's *conatus*, calling it 'force' or 'living force' in *GSK*. In a tract written next, *FEV*, he adds ontological details: this "continuously effective force" (*FEV* 1: 211.24) constitutes life in nature, governs all creation, and should not be understood as a non-material force, like a soul, but rather as

a subtle but universally effective matter, a general world spirit, which serves as the principle of activity in the products of nature, and which is a true Proteus, capable of assuming all shapes and forms.

(FEV 1: 211.24–34; my trans., MS)

This living force, subtle matter, or undifferentiated energy acts outwardly. Energy radiates, and radiation yields a field, which turns out to be a fabric of links, constitutive of places, and thus of space (*GSK* §7 1: 21.30–3; 1: 22.5–7; §9 1: 23.5–9). Radiation creates extension (*GSK* §9 1: 23.5–9). This may sound like a non sequitur in English, but the semantic implication is shared by Latin and German. The Latin *extensio* consists of the preposition *ex* meaning 'out' and the verb *tendere*, 'to stretch.' It is the same with the German *Ausdehnung*, a compound of *aus* and *dehnen*. Extension, in Kant's mind, is a 'stretching-out.' English makes it seem as if extension were a state. German and Latin, however, suggest that extension is an effort, sustained by force. What acts outwardly is radiation (*Ausbreitung*, a 'broadening-out'; *GSK* §10 1: 24.24). By acting outwardly, force broadens and stretches out. Out-stretching is extension. Thus the volume of space stems from the action of force. Radiation is the cause. Extension is the effect.

But something is still missing. Radiation may be simple, but extension is complex. Energy dissipating is one thing, but space extended is three things: length, width, and depth. Where do these new properties come from? In §9, Kant acknowledges that the derivation of dimensions from the activity of force is more difficult, but in §10 he attempts just that:

Because everything found among the properties of a thing must be derivable from what contains within itself the complete ground of the thing itself, the properties of extension, and hence also its three-dimensionality, must also be based on the properties of the force substances possess in respect of the things with which they are connected. The force by which any substance acts in union with other substances cannot be conceived without a certain law that manifests itself in its mode of action. Since the kind of law by which substances act on each other must also determine the kind of union and composition of many substances, the law according to which an entire collection of substances (i.e., a space) is measured, or the dimension of extension, will derive from the laws according to which the substances seek to unite by virtue of their essential forces. [. . .] I am of the opinion that substances [. . .] have essential forces [. . .] such [. . .] that they propagate their effects in union with each other according to the inverse-square relation of the distances; secondly, that the whole to which this gives rise has, by virtue of this law, the property of being three-dimensional; thirdly, that this law is arbitrary, and that God could have chosen another, e.g., the inverse-cube relation; fourthly, and finally, that an extension with different properties and dimensions would also have resulted from a different law.

(GSK 1: 24.2–30; translation by Schönfeld and Edwards, in Kant 2012b: 27–8)

So radiation generates extension, and this creative activity happens in a regular, lawful mode. As a quantity of force stretches out from its source, its intensity – the power per unit area in the direction of travel – gets ever more stretched out the farther it travels. The farther it goes, the thinner it gets. Intensity wanes inversely proportional to the square of the distance from the source. This evokes

Newton's inverse-square law of universal gravitation. But Kant argues for something else. While Newton examines nature in the context of mechanics, Kant examines nature's history in the context of cosmology. For Newton, space is the referential frame for the propagation of gravitational force, and the strength of this force weakens in the inverse-square as it traverses space. But for Kant, space is the structural consequence of the radiation of primordial force, and the density of space weakens in the inverse-square as this space expands from the source. In Newton, force travels across space, and here, the propagation of force is relative to space, while space serves as the absolute backdrop for traveling forces. But, in Kant, *force extends space*. This makes force into the absolute backdrop of space and space into the relational fabric of force. The consequence of Kant's conjecture, relational space, evokes Leibniz, not Newton.

The origin of space is a chain of transformations. As force acts outwardly, it radiates a field. As the field spreads out, it gets thinner. As it decompresses its tightly packed being, it wraps itself out, unfolding along dimensions, unfurling as space. The generative radiation is governed by the inverse-square law. This use of the law evokes Newton's predecessor Johannes Kepler (1571–1630), who found the inverse-square law in light in 1604, as the rate of photometric measurement that governs how luminance wanes when traveling from the source.[3] Combining Leibniz's relational space with Kepler's inverse-square law of radiation, Kant hypothesizes in §10 the emergence of spatial dimensionality from radiated extension.

3. Evolution of Matter

So now nature has evolved space. Where does matter come from? Kant's answer in *GSK* that matter derives from places (*Orte*) in the spatial dimensionality only raises new questions. In the fabric of space, any place is a point. But points are not extended. This is good news insofar as a lack of extension means points are not divisible, suggesting that matter consists of indivisible ultimate elements. But it is bad news, too, since extension-less points do not add up to the volume of a body, suggesting that elements would have to have volume while being indivisible. Geometrically this is a problem. How can matter have elements if they are not points? And how can matter be in space if its elements are points? Kant attacks this problem in *MoPh*.

His approach in *MoPh* hinges on ideas in *GSK* on the nature of force – not so much on what force *does* but rather what it *is*. Following a suggestion by the sinologist and natural philosopher Georg Bilfinger (1693–1750), Kant suspected that the stalemated conflict between Cartesian and Leibnizian theories of force indicates that the truth of the matter *is* the conflict; that force really is captured by both theories (*GSK* §20, 1: 32). The structure of force is a yin-yang 阴阳 of mutually exclusive aspects: Descartes' 'quantity of motion' that anticipated the physical quantity of momentum, *and* Leibniz's 'living force' that anticipated kinetic energy. Force is both. Put in modern terms, Kant's 'true estimation' of force is a combination of Cartesian momentum and Leibnizian energy (*GSK* §163, 1: 181).[4]

Applied to matter, Kant argues in *NTH* that this combination expresses itself in force acting outwardly in two ways, as attraction and repulsion (*NTH* 1: 234). This attractive-repulsive interplay, for Kant, is the "single universal rule" of material nature (*NTH* 1: 306.22). It explains nature's evolution from a simple basis to complex order. The interplay weaves space into a fabric and stitches points into folds. In *PhMo* Kant argues that the two actions of force differ in their reach: attraction acts in the inverse square, repulsion in the inverse cube (*PhMo* 1: 484.32–3). This is the key to Kant's solution of the puzzle of matter.

Consider a point. But assume it nothing to be but power: a source of radiation. This power-point or 'physical monad' acts in a binary way, spreading attraction and repulsion. Further assume that repulsion is stronger than attraction, making the source energetically impenetrable and effectively resistant to division. Repulsion, propagating in the inverse-cube, falls off quicker than attraction, propagating in the inverse-square. The energy field generated by attractive-repellent radiation from the power point thus gains a boundary, at which repulsion (strong but declining quickly) and attraction (weak but declining slowly) are equal (*PhMo* 1: 484–5). Inside the horizon, repulsion prevails, allowing the monad to sustain itself. Outside, attraction prevails, letting other monads coalesce into a matrix.

The geometric problem finds a resolution in dynamics. A point is unextended, but if physical space is energetic, so must ultimately be its points. A point source creates extension by outward activity. The binary radiation creates bubbles, which Kant calls 'activity spheres' (*sphaerae activitatum*; *PhMo* 1: 481.36–9). Its center is a power point. Its volume is a field ruled by repulsion. Equidistant from the center in all directions is an attractive-repulsive equilibrium, the dynamic horizon, or the surface of the bubble.

The trick to this dynamic resolution of the puzzle is to add time. A geometric point is unextended, but a point source produces extension through activity over time. A power point acting outwardly in mutually opposite directions, by attractive pulls and repellent pushes, can do so by successive oscillation, alternating in a dynamic vibration. This binary radiation spawns bubbles whose surface is the energy equilibrium of attraction and repulsion. These activity-spheres are three-dimensional volumes in time. They are the smallest indivisible units of spatial and material extension.

So now nature has evolved matter. According to *MoPh*, the ultimate elements of material particles are energetic vibrations with standing wave-fronts, with physical monads at the centers and oscillating activity-spheres enveloping them. Kant's reasoning anticipates, in philosophical, non-mathematical form, the contemporary view that final elements are strings vibrating in bubbles that lend space to their hidden dimensions. Today Kant's activity-spheres are called Calabi-Yau manifolds, after Eugenio Calabi, whose work on the Kähler metric in differential geometry earned him the Steele Prize in 1991, and Shing-Tung Yau 丘成桐, whose proof of the Calabi conjecture earned him the Fields Medal in 1982. Calabi-Yau manifolds have made string theory into a candidate for the unified final theory.

4. Evolution of Complexity

In *NTH*, Kant shifts perspectives from particle physics to astrophysics and cosmology. Nature's primordial force has generated space and matter. Matter is still tiny, and as yet unordered, dispersed through space. Kant imagines this by envisioning fog. Is it possible to link this imagined archaic state to the present? Nature today consists of planets, stars, and galaxies. Locally it consists of the solar system, with the Sun at the center and the Earth in orbit housing life. How does one get from here to there, from fog to system?

At this juncture, Newtonian mechanics enters the picture. Gravitational force (the macroscopic guise of attractive force) and the laws of motion gain key importance now. Start with a fogbank, then, and imagine a chaos of particles suspended in space (*NTH* 1: 263.16–23). As soon as masses exert gravitational forces, uniform distribution yields local concentrations. The fog lifts in some places and thickens in others (*NTH* 1: 264.20–34). Concentrations pull on one another, until one pull prevails as gravitational center (*NTH* 1: 265.16–19). The fog collapses into itself, leaving clear skies in its wake. *Fog becomes cloud*. The cloud keeps accreting (*NTH* 1: 265.20–4), and the particle streams accelerate toward a center growing crowded. Collisions happen. Crashing particles veer off at odd angles. Repulsion makes itself known. Widening currents of the inbound stream are deflected laterally (*NTH* 1: 265.24–30). The cloud tightens into a sphere, but surges soar this way

31

and that. *The cloud grows tides.* The tides suffer the same fate as the concentrations earlier on (*NTH* 1: 265.30–4). One tide, one deflected current, one lateral vector prevails (*NTH* 1: 265.34–6.8). The tides join and surge in one direction. *The cloud spins.* As rotation gains speed, centrifugal forces check attraction at the equator of spin (*NTH* 1: 266.8–12). Meanwhile accretion pulls in the poles. *The cloud bulges out and flattens into a disk.* Somewhere along this process (*NTH* 1: 266–8) the center grows so hot that it bursts into flame. *A sun is born.* Along the disk spinning around the star, lumps accrete into planets and absorb the last fog shrouds while rotating in one ecliptic plane. *The disk becomes a planetary system* (*NTH* 1: 267).

Nature, Kant thinks, reiterates its patterns across scales, and 'analogies and harmonies' govern them all (*NTH* 1: 235.16). What happens to solar systems is bound to happen to spiral galaxies (*NTH* 1: 250–3). On the planets, meanwhile, complexity keeps unfolding. Planets have a purpose; their *telos* is to evolve conditions that can support organisms and minds (*NTH* 1: 352.34–3.4). Where conditions are best, life flourishes and cultures arise.

Kant's conjecture that stellar and galactic systems evolve from clouds is the Nebular Hypothesis. In 1943, C.F. von Weizsäcker gave Kant's hypothesis its astrophysical form, which included testable predictions (such that the outer regions of the solar system would contain remnants of the cloud; cf. also *NTH* 1: 281.14–19). In 1949, G.P. Kuiper confirmed the Weizsäcker-Kant prediction and found the Kuiper Belt named after him. Astrophysicists predict that even older shrouds of the fog, the conjectured Oort Cloud, will soon be found.

Unfortunately, evolution does not continue for good. The oldest areas, which formed up earliest, are also first to decay. At the heart of expansion, dissolution sets in. Chaos spreads once more (*NTH* 1: 319). Nature expands outwards but its center does not hold, collapsing into itself – thus to face the very conditions that make the process start all over again. For Kant, the universe in eternity is a *phoenix of nature* who burns up only to take wing from the ashes (*NTH* 1: 321.13–14). Today, this remains speculation. But, as it so happens, the 1998 discovery of the acceleration of cosmic expansion, which earned Saul Perlmutter, B.P. Schmidt, and A.G. Riess the Nobel Prize in physics in 2011, lends support to the idea that the Big Bang may actually be part of Kant's larger cosmic cycle.[5] Thus nature evolves. In sum, the freethinker Kant can rightly boast, "*just give me matter, and I shall build you a world with it!*" (*NTH* 1: 229.10–11 and 1: 230.1–2). To make due on his claim, all he needs is energy.

Notes

1 Translations of Kant's works are listed in the References by translator's name and year of publication in the *Cambridge Edition*.

2 Reinhardt translates *Auswickelung* as 'development'; cf. Kant 2012a: 197. This is not quite accurate, because the German for 'development' would be *Entwicklung*, which is not Kant's term.

3 The inverse-square law of force propagation was first formulated as the photometric law in Kepler's *Astronomia Pars Optica* (1604), chapter 1, proposition 9; cf. Kepler (1936ff.: 20ff. 2:19). Kepler was also the first to conjecture that gravitational force is a property of matter, such that bodies are attracted to one another by a force propagating at the inverse-square to their distance; cf. letter to Fabricius, item 4, 11 Oct 1605 (1936ff: 15:241).

4 Kant's momentum-energy conjecture of force makes more sense in Einsteinian relativity than in Newtonian mechanics. In Newtonian mechanics, momentum, energy, and force are three distinct but related quantities: the space integral of force is energy, and its time integral is impulse, which changes an object's momentum. In General Relativity, space-time is relative to mass, and constant in a mass before and after collisions is its total of momentum-energy. Analogous to the contraction *spacetime*, Einstein's student John A. Wheeler suggested *momenergy* for this invariant dynamic quantity.

5 Cf. Bojowald (2008a, 2008b); and Class for Physics (2011).

References

Albrecht, M. (1985) "Einleitung," in M. Albrecht (ed.), *Christian Wolff, Oratio de Sinarum philosophia practica* [1723], Hamburg: Meiner.

Barrow, J.D. (2002) *The Constants of Nature*, New York: Pantheon.

Bojowald, M. (2008a) "Big Bang or Big Bounce? New Theory on the Universe's Birth," *Scientific American* 299(4): 44–51.

Bojowald, M. (2008b) "What Happened Before the Big Bang?" *Nature Physics* 3: 523–5.

Class for Physics of the Royal Swedish Academy of Sciences (2011) *The Accelerating Universe: Scientific Background on the Nobel Prize in Physics 2011*, www.nobelprize.org/nobel_prizes/physics/laureates/2011/advanced-physicsprize2011.pdf (last accessed: 18/7/2020).

Coles, P. (ed.) (2001) *The Routledge Companion to the New Cosmology*, London: Routledge.

Förster, E. (1993) "Introduction," in E. Förster (ed. and trans.), *Opus Postumum: The Cambridge Edition of the Works of Immanuel Kant*, Cambridge: Cambridge University Press.

Friedman, M. (1992) *Kant and the Exact Sciences*, Cambridge, MA: Harvard University Press.

Kant, I. (2012a) "Universal Natural History and Theory of the Heavens," in E. Watkins (ed.) and O. Reinhardt (trans.), *Natural Science: The Cambridge Edition of the Works of Immanuel Kant*, Cambridge: Cambridge University Press.

Kant, I. (2012b) "Thoughts on the True Estimation of Living Forces," in E. Watkins, M. Schönfeld and J. Edwards (eds. and trans.), *Natural Science: The Cambridge Edition of the Works of Immanuel Kant*, Cambridge: Cambridge University Press.

Kepler, J. (1936ff) *Gesammelte Werke*. M. Caspar (ed.), Munich: Beck.

Kepler, J. ([1604] 2000) *Ad Vitellionem paralipomena. Astronomiae pars optica. Optics: Paralipomena to Witelo & Optical Part of Astronomy*, William H. Donahue (trans.), New Mexico: Green Lion Press.

Kuehn, M. (2001a) *Kant: A Biography*, Cambridge: Cambridge University Press.

Kuehn, M. (2001b) "Kant's Teachers in the Exact Sciences," in E. Watkins (ed.), *Kant and the Sciences*, Oxford: Oxford University Press, pp. 11–30.

Lalla, S. (2003) "Kant's 'Allgemeine Naturgeschichte und Theorie des Himmels' (1755)," *Kant-Studien* 94: 425–53.

Newton, I. ([1687] 1999) *The Principia: Mathematical Principles of Natural Philosophy*, B. Cohen and A. Whitman (eds.), Berkeley, CA: University of California Press.

Prigogine, I. (1993) "Time, Structure and Fluctuations, Nobel Lecture 8 Dec 1977," in T. Frängsmyr (ed.), *Nobel Lectures, Chemistry 1971–1980*, Singapore: World Scientific, pp. 263–85.

Rahts, J. (1902) "Anmerkungen zu *Allgemeine Naturgeschichte und Theorie des Himmels*," in *AA 1*, Berlin: Reimer (later DeGruyter), pp. 545–58.

Schönfeld, M. (2000) *The Philosophy of the Young Kant: The Pre-Critical Project*, Oxford: Oxford University Press.

Schönfeld, M. (2011) "Bilfinger, Georg Bernhard," in H. Klemme and M. Kuhn (eds.), *Dictionary of Eighteenth Century German Philosophers*, vol. 1, 3, London: Thoemmes, Oxford Reference, pp. 48–56.

Further Reading

E. Adickes's *Kant als Naturforscher* (Berlin: DeGruyter, 1924) is a comprehensive account of Kant's scientific research, in two volumes, by one of the first editors of the Academy Edition; J. Cañedo-Argüelles's *Commentario*, pp. 311–473 in Cañedo's Spanish translation of *GSK*, *Pensamientos sobra la verdadera estimación de las fuerzas vivas* (Bern: Peter Lang, 1988), is the most detailed commentary with historical backstories about Kant's earliest work; I. Polonoff's *Force, Cosmos, Monads and Other Themes in Kant's Early Thought* (Bonn: Bouvier, 1971) is an in-depth study of Kant's philosophy of nature; G. Tonelli's *Elementi metodologici e metafisici in Kant dal 1747 al 1768* (Torino: Edizione di 'Filosofia', 1959), is a classic of scholarship and an authoritative examination of the metaphysical assumptions and methodological approaches in Kant's pre-critical philosophy.

3

KANT AND THE RATIONALIST TRADITION

Ralph Walker

★★★

Kant does not always signal clearly his most interesting contributions to philosophy. Two of them are closely related, one about the nature of reason, the other about concepts. His predecessors, whether rationalists or empiricists, thought of concepts or "ideas" as inner objects. Leibniz, here in substantial agreement with Locke, defines an idea as "an immediate inner object . . . [which] expresses the nature or qualities of things" (Leibniz 1981: 109). Kant, on the other hand, sees a concept as a rule: a rule for synthesizing, for putting together, the various things we call dogs, or red surfaces, under a single heading (A106, A141/B180).[1] Concepts are not just mental entities, they involve rule-governed activity by the mind. And so does reason. For the rationalists, reason was a kind of insight that yielded us truths about reality independently of experience. For Hume, the most consistent of the empiricists, reason did involve mental activity, but not rule-governed activity, just a habit of thinking that comes naturally to us. For Kant it is neither a habit nor an insight into a priori truth. It is an imperative: an imperative which is objective in its own right, in the sense of being something that is independent of us but also binding upon us. It tells us how we *ought* to think, and it tells us how we *ought* to act. The rationalists had misunderstood its nature. They had also misunderstood its scope.

The rationalist tradition of the 17th and 18th centuries was by no means monolithic, but rationalists agreed in holding that reason was a powerful source of knowledge, independent of sense-experience. Many held that all truths were in principle knowable by reason, though in practice not to us, because our intellects are limited, some more than others. Descartes may not have gone as far as this, but Spinoza did; so did Leibniz and his successor Christian Wolff, the dominant philosopher in Germany when Kant was young. They recognized that in practice much human knowledge must be derived from experience, because of our limitations, and because the senses only provide us with confused and indistinct ideas, which we cannot make fully distinct. Baumgarten, whose work Kant used as the basis for many of his lectures, took the same view. Only God, whose intellect is infinite, can see all truths by reason alone.

Kant's *Critique of Pure Reason* is a critique of the pretensions of reason. Human speculation can range widely, and with the rationalists it ranges too far. It "falls into obscurity and contradictions [. . .]. The battlefield of these endless controversies is called *metaphysics*" (Aviii). The rationalists can frame theories, but they have no way of justifying them, or refuting their opponents. Kant aims to

DOI: 10.4324/9781003406617-5

set out a new metaphysics which will be properly grounded. But to do this the scope of metaphysics must be severely restricted. The empiricists had criticized rationalist claims, and Hume had taken these criticisms to their logical conclusion. But this was at the cost of a scepticism that Kant finds unsatisfactory. It questioned the coherence of fundamental concepts like those of necessity, object, and cause. Kant believes that the use of these concepts can be justified, and that a substantial amount of a priori cognition – *Erkenntnis* – can be justified too, as telling us about the world as we can experience it. But cognition can be justified only when it is deployed within the context of possible experience. Rationalists' metaphysical speculations went well beyond this, making claims about God and the nature of all reality – all reality, not just the world as we can experience it. For Wolff, philosophy is "the science of being as such", a potentially endless field (Wolff 1963: §73).

The rationalists, of course, thought that they could justify their claims perfectly well, by demonstrating them: "inferring [them . . .] by legitimate sequence from certain and immutable principles", which are taken to be logical principles (Wolff 1963: §30). Wolff believed this was a matter of deriving them from the principle of contradiction. Leibniz said that "in every true affirmative proposition [. . .] the predicate is contained in the subject" (Leibniz 1967: 63); it is not entirely clear what he meant by that, but Couturat interpreted him as holding that all truths are analytic (Couturat 1901: xi). That is an anachronistic way to put it, of course, since the analytic/synthetic distinction was first drawn by Kant – though Crusius, an opponent of Wolff who influenced Kant, may have been moving towards it (Crusius 1745). Kant's own account of analyticity is not very precise. He says analytic propositions are those "whose certainty rests on *identity* of concepts" (*Log* 9: 111). Frege clarifies this and captures what must be Kant's intention, defining an analytic truth as one the proof of which depends only on general logical laws and definitions of terms (Frege 1959: §3). But the decisive move was made by Kant.

One of the reasons Wolff said what he did was that he was thoroughly unclear about the nature and scope of logic. The same was true of his followers, like Baumgarten and Meier. Kant was not entirely clear himself. Leibniz had made major advances in the area, but they remained unpublished. Kant's essential contribution lies in his understanding of what a concept is. The rationalists thought of concepts as mental entities which can be scrutinized more or less carefully, so that fuller examination of a concept might enable one to grasp it more distinctly, thus coming to see more and more conceptual relationships with the same clarity and distinctness as "All bachelors are unmarried". In effect, they thought that the field of conceptual analysis was virtually unlimited. For Kant, on the other hand, concepts are rules, rules for collecting items together in synthesis. Moreover, and crucially, the items collected together are, in the basic case, items that are given to us in sense. Sense-experience is not a confused kind of thought. The data of sense are very different from thought. They are given to us, and synthesized under concepts by us, so that with empirical concepts like "dog" or "red" conceptual analysis can tell us nothing except that these are the terms under which we classify those items.

Unlike the rationalists, Kant recognizes a fundamental distinction between the active and receptive faculties of the mind. The mind is active in synthesis, understanding, reason – in thinking generally. It is essentially the same active power that is at work in each of these, and its ways of working have the same rational structure throughout; they can all be called reason in a broad sense of the word (A835/B863). In sensibility, on the other hand, the mind is receptive, and it is sensibility that makes possible our awareness of particular things. "Intuition" (*Anschauung*) is the immediate awareness of particulars (A19/B33). This awareness is only possible because of the spatio-temporal framework which we use to distinguish items from one another and to reidentify them across change. Space and time are themselves intuitions, particular things, but our awareness of other particulars must presuppose our awareness of space and time. Leibniz had argued that space and time are learnt about empirically as systems of relations between individuals, individuals being recognizable as such independently of their spatio-temporal positions (Leibniz 1956: Paper V). That would mean that there could not be two individual things which differed only in spatio-temporal position. There would be nothing to differentiate them, so they could not be two. Kant rejects this as absurd. We can readily distinguish two water drops without finding any difference between them except their position. Thus our awareness of space and time must be presupposed. They are a priori forms of intuition, a priori because our grasp of them is a precondition of our being able to experience things at all.

Kant accepts analytic truths as a priori, but regards them as uninformative: they tell us nothing worthwhile about the world. The fact that our intuition of space and time must itself be a priori opens for him the possibility that reason can take us beyond the merely analytic – reason being "the faculty that provides the principles of cognition a priori" (A11/B24). In the mid-1760s he had been inclined towards empiricism, and it was the discovery that the empirical account of space and time was inadequate that led him to take the first major step towards his Critical philosophy. The point that struck him initially was that there seemed to be an unavoidable difference between a universe containing only a left hand and a universe containing only a right hand, something that could be understood only by supposing that they had different relations to space as a whole, since the internal relations of the parts of the hand would be the same in each case (*GUGR* 2: 378ff). In his *Inaugural Dissertation* of 1770, though, his main argument is the one about the need to presuppose both time and space in order to identify particulars. So they must be a priori forms of intuition, allowing us to know a priori truths about them. Geometrical truths are truths about space, and arithmetical ones are truths about time and space together. He develops this further in the *Critique of Pure Reason*. Mathematical truths are not analytic, as Leibniz had argued, but synthetic and a priori. Mathematics is done by "constructing concepts in pure intuition", which means taking, say, the concept of a triangle, considering whether it is consistent with the spatial order, and if so what its essential features must be given the character of that spatial order. He points out that the concept of a bi-angle – a plane figure bounded by two straight sides – is a perfectly good concept, but we cannot do geometry with it, because a bi-angle cannot be constructed in the space of our pure intuition (A220f/B268). (He was aware that consistent "geometries" could be drawn up for "spaces" different from ours; but geometry, as he understood it, is the geometry that fits with our a priori intuition of space.)

Mathematics constituted just one kind of synthetic a priori cognition for Kant. Many people have thought he is wrong about mathematics, but if that is true it need not affect what he says about other kinds of synthetic a priori cognition. The *Critique* goes on to explore the possibility of such cognition quite generally. Hume had denied that concepts like necessity, object, and cause have an adequate empirical basis; Kant now provides an a priori argument to show that there not only are, but must be, instances of them in the spatio-temporal world of our experience. Certain a priori principles concerning their application must be true, for instance the principle that "All alterations occur in accordance with the law of the connection of cause and effect" (B232). His argument seeks to prove that unless these concepts did apply, and unless these principles were true within the world as we can know it, self-conscious experience would not be possible for us at all. Kant makes much use of arguments of this type, justifying the acceptance of something by showing that it must hold if experience, or self-conscious awareness, is to be possible.

Such arguments (now often called transcendental arguments, though he did not call them that) were new with Kant, and not employed by his predecessors. Wolff has a principle analogous to Kant's causal principle: "Nothing is without a sufficient reason." But he deduced it from the principle of contradiction, by one of the worst arguments in the history of philosophy. If there is something without a sufficient reason, then nothing is its sufficient reason. "But this is absurd, so nothing is without a sufficient reason" (Wolff 1736: §70).

Kant's argument about the need to presuppose space and time is also a transcendental argument. If he is right, experience – which involves an awareness of particulars – would not be possible for us unless we could make use of the spatio-temporal order. A qualification is needed here, though. He admits he cannot exclude the possibility that there might be "finite thinking beings" who did *not* experience things spatio-temporally (B72). Space and time are *our* forms of intuition, but these other beings might be very different from us. However, his argument implies that if they could be aware of particulars at all, as given in experience, they would have to have forms of intuition of some kind. Some alternative locating matrix would be needed, to make identifying and individuating particulars possible (cf. A89/B121; B145).

What Kant's transcendental arguments show, if they are successful, is that certain synthetic a priori truths must hold with respect to our spatio-temporal world, because otherwise experience would not be possible for us. These include his principle about cause, which goes beyond anything we could establish by Humean means; they include a requirement that there be enduring objects, which all stand in a relationship of mutual interaction. This is why Kant feels his position on the synthetic a priori implies transcendental idealism. Space and time are the forms of *our* intuition, and we have no ground for thinking that anything like them belongs to the ultimate reality of things as they are in themselves. Similarly, the way we order the data of experience depends on *our* cognitive capacities, and beings with different cognitive capacities – or different forms of intuition – might experience the same underlying reality in a very different way. But the spatio-temporal world, as experienced by beings with our cognitive capacities, just *is* our world, so it is entirely right for us to claim to know a great many truths about that world and to regard it as real. Kant says it is "empirically real": it has all the reality we need to be concerned about for our normal purposes. But it is also "transcendentally ideal", because it is the world *as* it can be cognized by beings who share our cognitive capacities, our forms of intuition and our forms of thought. What the underlying reality is like we cannot know.

Nevertheless, Kant is not out of sympathy with the pressures that drove the rationalists to seek an overall account of all reality. The latter part of the *Critique of Pure Reason* is concerned with showing how easy and natural it is for us to think in the way they did, raising questions about reality that cannot be answered by any kind of reference to possible experience. For instance, whether the universe is infinite in extent, or alternatively somehow bounded, is a question we cannot help feeling needs an answer, although it takes us beyond the limits of possible experience (A297/B353–4). It is typical of the kind of question that Kant thinks lands the rationalists in "obscurity and contradictions" (Aviii). His transcendental idealism allows him to say that the world as we can know it, the spatio-temporal world, is neither finite nor infinite, spatially or temporally. For it extends only as far as possible human experience, and the limits of that are indeterminate. As to what the underlying reality is like we cannot know anything, and we should not suppose it to be spatially or temporally extended.

Despite this limitation upon human cognition, he argues that there is a positive use to be made of some, at least, of the speculations we so naturally make about what lies beyond the limit. This is of great importance for science. Reason cannot lead us to any final answers in this area, but it can be employed "regulatively", leading us always to *look* for causes, and for causes of those causes, and so on, "*as if* nature were infinite in itself" so that there were always more ultimate causes to be found; and always to *look* for order and unity in nature, *as if* the spatio-temporal world had been the product of "an independent, original, and creative reason", "a most wise cause" (A672/B700). Many people would agree that it is a good idea to look for unitary and simple explanations of things, just because we find it convenient, but that is not what Kant has in mind. Reason requires us to proceed in these ways. They are "*set* us *as a task*" (A498/B526),[2] as something reason demands of us. "For the law of reason to seek unity is necessary, since without it we would have no reason, and without that, no coherent use of the understanding" (A651/B680).

So far, we have been considering what Kant calls theoretical, or speculative, reason. But practical reason is no less important to him. He considers them two species of the same thing. This can seem puzzling, because at first sight they appear very different.

He distinguishes two kinds of "imperative" of practical reason – imperatives being "commands of reason" and "expressed by an *ought*" (*GMS* 4: 413). Hypothetical imperatives tell one what one ought to do in order to achieve some goal that one has: a goal being what one just happens to want, or perhaps a goal that all human beings naturally want, like happiness. Hypothetical imperatives are commands of reason, because reason determines the best way to achieve the goal. As such there is nothing moral about them. The imperatives of morality are categorical imperatives. Categorical imperatives are commands of reason which "represent an action as objectively necessary of itself, without reference to another end" (*GMS* 4: 414). By calling it "necessary of itself" Kant does not mean that the agent will inevitably do the action; she may very well not. He means it is an absolute requirement of morality that she should. But it is always open to us either to obey the commands of morality, or to ignore them and follow our inclinations instead. Famously, the basic imperative of morality is "act only in accordance with that maxim through which you can at the same time will that it become a universal law" (*GMS* 4: 421).

There are important differences from his predecessors here. Hume declared that in practical matters reason could only be "the slave of the passions" (Hume 1888: 415). We can work out how to achieve our ends, and Hume is prepared to call this reasoning, though he considers it just to be a certain kind of habit of thought. So he allows that "reason" can give us hypothetical imperatives. But not categorical ones. Moral requirements are "nothing but a general calm determination of the passions, founded on some distant view or reflexion" (Hume 1888: 583). Reason works things out; it cannot motivate us. Moral judgements do have some sort of motivational force, so they must express "passions" – desires and inclinations – rather than reason.

For the rationalists, of course, moral truths are facts discernible by reason. But as facts they do not have motivating force. If we are motivated by them, it is because we *want* to be moral. For Leibniz and Spinoza, to become morally better is to become more rational, something that they think people naturally want. Wolff fills this out with a metaphysical account of perfection. Kant objects to the rationalists, and also to Hume. Moral requirements are intrinsically motivating, but they are not matters of "passion"; they are requirements of practical reason, but not simply facts. Both sides fail to recognize that there are "motives that, as such, are represented completely a priori by reason alone" (*GMS* 4: 391). Reason itself can motivate us, both in its practical and its theoretical form, for reason lays down rules that tell us what we ought to do. And these rules are fully objective, just as objective as the rationalists took their moral truths to be: objective in the sense of obtaining independently of what we either think or feel about them.

We shall return to this. But we should first notice that there is another way in which Kant differs sharply from the rationalists of his time. Because they thought all truths were in principle accessible to reason, even if not to finite minds like ours, they held that nothing could happen without there being a sufficient reason for it. This committed them to a form of determinism, which found room for freedom only in what is now called "compatibilism", the view that freedom consists in something that is compatible with determinism. Baumgarten puts it by saying, "The faculty of willing or refusing according to one's own preference is FREEDOM (free choice)"; and that is all it is: there are of course antecedent factors determining what one's preference is (Baumgarten 2013 §719).

We do not now associate compatibilism with any form of rationalism, and in Kant's day too it was to be found in other traditions. Many empiricists were compatibilists. They did not rely on the rationalists' argument, but maintained that responsible choice must arise from the nature of the agent, and that the agent's nature is itself determined by factors external to her unconditioned volition. An unconditioned choice would seem no more than chance. Rationalists could use that argument too, of course: "If something happens by pure chance, what has that to do with me?" (Baumgarten 2013: 82). Nevertheless, in Kant's Germany rationalism was often associated with the denial of free will in the strong incompatibilist sense. Determinism was often alleged to be tantamount to fatalism. For that Wolff was dismissed from his post at Halle in 1723, and the same accusation was part of Jacobi's attack on Mendelssohn and Lessing in 1783–5. The more sophisticated defenders of free will in the strong, incompatibilist sense included Crusius. In one of his early writings – well before his Critical period – Kant argued Crusius was wrong: he was at that time a compatibilist himself (*PND* 1: 398ff).

In the Critical period, his stand on free will is uncompromising. He dismisses the compatibilist's conception of freedom as "a wretched subterfuge": "a human being would be a marionette or an automaton" (*KpV* 5: 96, 101). A moral agent must be able to exercise choice that is fully free, free in the strongest sense. Her choice is between doing what the moral law requires, or following her own inclinations instead. All the arguments for morality lie on the one side; all the arguments, and all the power, of inclination and inherited nature lie on the other. She must decide.

This lands Kant in an apparent contradiction. He believes he has shown not only that we must always go on searching for causes, but also that "[a]ll alterations occur in accordance with the law of the connection of cause and effect" (B232). So he has to recognize, and indeed does explicitly recognize, that if we could fully understand the relevant antecedent factors, "we could calculate a human being's conduct for the future with as much certainty as a lunar or solar eclipse" (*KpV* 5: 99, cf. A550/B578). So my choices are fully determined; yet they are free in a sense that is incompatible with their being determined. His way out of the contradiction is to say that we must see ourselves and others in two ways: as belonging to the spatio-temporal "empirically real" world, in which all our choices are determined; but also "as belonging to the intelligible world, under laws which, being independent of nature, are grounded merely in reason" (*GMS* 4: 452). For "the very same subject, being [. . .] conscious of himself as a thing in itself, also views his existence *insofar as it does not stand under conditions of time* and himself as determinable only through laws that he gives himself by reason" (*KpV* 5: 97) – acting, therefore, wholly freely and independently of the determining causes of the empirical world.

Whether this can be understood coherently is not clear. More directly relevant to our present concern is why he thinks himself entitled to assert the freedom of the self "as a thing in itself", or indeed to make claims about morality at all, in view of the limits he has placed on human cognition. Whatever Kant means by saying that one can be "conscious of" oneself as a thing in itself, he has clearly and explicitly ruled out the possibility of any cognition of it. Not only can this self never be an object of possible experience, the same must apply to whatever moral truths there are, for these can neither be discovered by observation nor shown to be required for the possibility of self-conscious experience. Some would say that there is nothing objective about morality at all, and that moral judgements just express people's attitudes; but this is emphatically not Kant's view. Paradoxical though it may seem, he considers moral obligation to be as objective as anything can be, and more objective than the spatio-temporal world around us. For the spatio-temporal world is indeed dependent on us – not on our attitudes, but on our forms of intuition and on the ways in which we must order the data we receive in accordance with the synthetic a priori principles of substance, causality, and so on. The moral law is given by pure reason alone: pure practical reason.

What is given is a *law*: it is not a set of facts, of any kind. It is this that makes Kant's conception of reason so distinctive, and it is this that allows him to avoid the objection that it is just a misuse of words to apply the term "reason" both to theoretical reasoning and to the requirements of morality. The categorical imperative tells us what we *ought* to do, and imperatives are "commands of reason". We cannot simply disregard them. In modern terminology, they are prescriptive. If we are aware of them at all – and Kant considers all rational beings are aware of them – we must be motivated by them. Not necessarily so strongly motivated as to act on them, because our inclinations may motivate us in a different direction, and we may make the choice to follow inclination rather than duty. But it is true of everyone, "even the worst", according to Kant, that he would do what morality requires "if no other incentive were at work against it" – as, of course, selfish incentives very often are (*RGV* 6: 36).

In this respect, the moral law is parallel to the laws of logic, so there is nothing artificial about calling both of them "reason". The same applies to the theoretical reason that requires us to look for unity and simplicity, and to search for ever further explanations, ever further conditions. Reason lays down *imperatives*. Kant generally reserves the term "imperative" for moral imperatives, but this is only a matter of words; he is clear that logic, and reasoning more generally, set us norms that we are motivated to follow, and which we may fail to follow at times. Like the requirements of morality, they are categorical norms, categorical imperatives. It is not that we follow the basic principles of logic because we want to obtain some particular objective (which would make them hypothetical imperatives), we follow them because we see we ought to. Oddly, some people nowadays are inclined to think that logical laws do have that hypothetical character, because students are often introduced to them through the idea that the validity of an argument-form is due to the fact that it will never take us from true premises to a false conclusion. Kant would have pointed out that this gets things backwards. The only way we can know that the argument-form "All A is B, All B is C, therefore All A is C" never yields a false conclusion from true premises is by seeing that it is valid, not by checking instances to see if it regularly works.

Some people will say that these theoretical principles are not really *imperatives*, not really *prescriptive*, because they don't motivate us to *do* things. Kant agrees that they do not motivate the will to action. But they do motivate how we argue, and how we think. They motivate us to accept conclusions (cf. *GMS* 4: 449). And 'motivate' is the right word here, because they don't *compel* us to accept the conclusions that are validly drawn from premises we accept, any more than the imperatives of morality compel us to perform the right actions. We can see what morality requires of us and fail to do it. It is the same with theoretical reason. Setting aside simple mistakes, which are possible in any sphere, one can deliberately reject a logical or inductive conclusion. As is also true in the moral case, we may need some other motivation to do this, a motivation of a different kind, but other motivations there certainly are. Mothers can refuse to believe that their sons have been killed in war despite all the evidence. Kierkegaard believed that for Abraham, about to sacrifice Isaac, faith overrode all reason. And although it is possible to state the doctrine of the Trinity consistently, many people subscribe to it despite believing that for God to be both three and one is a contradiction. In their view there is an authority to be heard that is higher than reason. Kant did not believe that, of course, or anything like it – his view of religion is that it belongs "within the limits of reason alone" (*RGV*). He repudiates firmly the idea that the requirements of morality are commands of God, here agreeing with the rationalists and very much disagreeing with the Pietists of Königsberg (*GMS* 4: 408–9). The imperatives of reason command in their own right. They neither have nor need an author.

These imperatives – both theoretical and practical – are also *objective*. They are not just something that human beings feel, in a way that could be explained in psychological or evolutionary terms.

They apply not just to human beings, but to all rational beings – though if there are rational beings, like perhaps God, who have a "holy will" that never feels any inclination to disobey them, the word "imperative" will not be quite right for them (*GMS* 4: 414). The moral law, and the laws of logic, are objective in the sense that they are independent of what any being thinks or feels about them. They exist in their own right.

In recent years moral philosophers have tended to divide between those who think moral judgements are expressions of attitude, and those who think they are statements of fact. Both sides appeal to something about human psychology. One side holds that our moral judgements really express attitudes that are inherently motivating, but are the product of our psychology. The other side holds that they state facts, but facts to which human beings – or human beings socialized in certain ways – have natural motivational reactions, so that the information that someone is torturing a child connects with a desire to stop that happening. Both approaches make morality dependent on something to do with the peculiarities of human beings, individually or collectively. Both approaches ignore Kant's alternative, which is to hold that morality is a matter of objective imperatives, requirements that necessarily motivate any rational being that is aware of them at all. Properly to defend Kant would be a lengthy matter, but he is at least arguably right in claiming that most people do think of morality in this way, when they reflect on it. And it is very hard seriously to believe that our principles of logic and inductive inference are nothing more than habits of human thought, and that in following them – or in following moral obligations – we are only responding to some internal program which we, like faulty computers, follow a good deal of the time.

This conception of reason is a radical departure from what Kant's predecessors thought, and what many people nowadays still think. For them, the aim is ultimately to achieve the truth. For Kant, truth about ultimate reality can never be attained, and there is no way in which we can aim at it. Instead, theoretical philosophy can tell us what we *ought to cognize* about the spatio-temporal world – following the a priori principles laid down by theoretical reason as applied in ordering and making sense of our experience. We can talk about truth within that spatio-temporal world, but truth within that spatio-temporal world is a matter of coherence: coherence with the formal and material conditions of experience (A218ff/B265ff; *Refl* 5642, 18: 281). It is reason, applied to sense-experience in the form of the understanding, that determines what this coherence amounts to, and our aspirations to find truth in the spatio-temporal world are manifestations of this obligation to seek coherence that is placed on us by theoretical reason.

Theoretical reason also tells us what we *ought to hypothesize*. Here it goes beyond what the understanding can do in ordering our experience, and "sets us as a task" the requirement to go on searching for ever more remote causes and ever more unitary explanations, even though doing so takes us beyond what is needed for coherence with the formal and material conditions of experience. But Kant tries hard to show that in doing this reason is still acting in the same ways, deploying the same twelve concepts that govern all synthesis, no longer as categories for ordering everyday experience, but instead as "ideas of pure reason", determining ways in which we should think about things without providing the same ground for claiming truth within the spatio-temporal world.

Practical reason, of course, tells us what we *ought to do* and what we ought to abstain from doing. Here again he holds that twelve analogous concepts are deployed, "categories of freedom" (*KpV* 5: 65–6), and he insists that it is "one and the same reason which, whether from a theoretical or a practical perspective, judges according to a priori principles" (*KpV* 5: 121). But between theoretical reason and practical reason, it is practical reason that is primary, because "all interest is ultimately practical and even that of speculative reason is complete in practical use alone" (*KpV* 5: 121). And this, given his general approach, should not be surprising. What we ought to believe, and what we ought to hypothesise, are obligations on us not because they help us to find the truth about ultimate reality, but because understanding the spatio-temporal world and making as good sense of it as we can is a precondition of the only thing that really matters: living worthwhile lives.

Practical reason also tells us that we ought to *assume* [*voraussetzen, annehmen*], and thus *hold-as-true* [*fürwahrhalten*], certain things that cannot be established by theoretical means. It cannot motivate us to act morally unless we are free agents, so we must hold-as-true that we – and others – are free, free in the strong incompatibilist sense. Kant argues that rational reflection on what morality requires of us shows that we ought also to hold-as-true that our souls are immortal, so that we can approximate to the moral perfection enjoined upon us, and likewise that there is a God, who can bring about a state of affairs in which happiness is proportionate to morality (*WDO*; *KpV* 5: 122ff; *RGV* 6: 3ff; cf. Crusius 1745: §14).

There is an indication here, perhaps, of how to overcome the apparent contradiction over free will. When we are thinking about the spatio-temporal world and how it works, we must accept, as unqualified fact, the reality of causal determination. It is something that we "cognize". But when we think about our own agency, and that of other rational beings, we must think differently, since practical reason requires us to hold-as-true that we, and they, are free agents. "Holding-as-true" is a form of belief (*Glaube*), though when, as here, it is based in practical and not in theoretical reason, it is not to be described as cognition (cf. A822f/B850f). It is plausible to conclude from this that Kant wants us to recognize that we are *really* free, and that the spatio-temporal world of our experience, which he often calls "the world of appearances", is just that, a world of appearances – of how we must understand things to be, when we are considering how things work and not making moral assessments (cf. *KpV* 5: 114).

I think this must be right. On the other hand, it can be pointed out that Kant does claim, very insistently, that we can have no cognition about the underlying reality of things as they are in themselves, including ourselves as we are in ourselves. So it might be just that reason requires us to think about ourselves in one way under one set of circumstances, and in another way under another. But that will not really do. For the moral law requires us to act in a way that would not be possible without incompatibilist freedom. And "the moral law is given, as it were, as a fact of pure reason of which we are a priori conscious and which is apodictically certain" (*KpV* 5: 47). It is fundamental, too fundamental to be derived from anything else or justified by reference to anything else. In this it is parallel to the principles of theoretical reason, including the logical laws. Any attempt to justify the laws of logic would inevitably be circular, since it would have to rely on logic:

> We can become aware of pure practical laws just as we are aware of pure theoretical principles, by attending to the necessity with which reason prescribes them to us and to the setting aside of all empirical conditions to which reason directs us.
>
> (*KpV* 5: 30)

So it seems that practical reason enables us, though only in a limited way, to enter the territory closed off from us by the *Critique of Pure Reason* as not open to cognition. In any case, it is clear that Kant's rejection of rationalism is by no means complete. He is very far from denying a central place to reason. He started by sharing many of the rationalists' presuppositions; the inadequacy of their arguments led him to reflect deeply on philosophical method and on the nature of reason itself. It seems likely that a major catalyst for his thinking was Leibniz's detailed critique of Locke, written in 1704 but published only in 1765 (Leibniz 1981). But it may be that the greatest influence of this book on Kant was in helping him to see how certain of Locke's empiricist doctrines could be transformed into something he could accommodate. Leibniz's own conception of reason still depended too much on rational insight, an insight which could be justified only by the goodness of God.

Kant sees, more clearly than others, that to ask for a justification is to ask what one *ought* to believe or think or do. So the answer cannot be adequately given by citing facts. It has to be a normative answer. Kant provides this. His radical conception of reason, as taking the form of objective imperatives, does not answer all the questions; but it provides a challenging way to think about it, the implications of which have not yet been fully assimilated.

Notes

1 Translations are from Kant 1992, unless otherwise stated.
2 The translation is from Kant 1929: the word is *aufgegeben*.

References

Baumgarten, A. (2013) *Metaphysics*, C.D. Fugate and J. Hymers (eds. and trans.), London and New York: Bloomsbury.

Couturat, L. (1901) *La logique de Leibniz*, Paris: Félix Alcan.

Crusius, C.A. (1745) *Entwurf der nothwendigen Vernunft-Wahrheiten*, Leipzig: Gleditsch.

Frege, G. (1959) *The Foundations of Arithmetic*, J.L. Austin (trans.), 2nd ed., Oxford: Blackwell.

Hume, D. (1888) *A Treatise of Human Nature*, L. Selby-Bigge (ed.), Oxford: Oxford University Press.

Kant, I. (1929) *Immanuel Kant's Critique of Pure Reason*, N. Kemp Smith (trans.), London: Macmillan.

Kant, I. (1992) *The Cambridge Edition of the Works of Immanuel Kant*, P. Guyer and A.W. Wood (eds.), Cambridge: Cambridge University Press.

Leibniz, G.W. (1956) *The Leibniz-Clarke Correspondence*, H.G. Alexander (ed.), Manchester: Manchester University Press.

Leibniz, G.W. (1967) *The Leibniz-Arnauld Correspondence*, H.T. Mason (ed. and tr.), Manchester: Manchester University Press.

Leibniz, G.W. (1981) *New Essays on Human Understanding*, P. Remnant and J. Bennett (eds. and trans.), Cambridge: Cambridge University Press.

Wolff, C. (1736) *Philosophia Prima sive Ontologia*, new ed., Frankfurt and Leipzig: Renger.

Wolff, C. (1963) *Preliminary Discourse on Philosophy in General*, R.J. Blackwell (trans.), Indianapolis: Bobbs-Merrill.

Further Reading

M. Kuehn, *Kant: A Biography* (Cambridge: Cambridge University Press, 2001) is an excellent guide to Kant's intellectual development as well as to his life. R. Lanier Anderson, *The Poverty of Conceptual Truth* (Oxford: Oxford University Press, 2015) is a thorough examination of the basis of Wolff's philosophy and of Kant's reaction to it. C.D. Fugate and J. Hymers' translation of Baumgarten's *Metaphysics*, listed under References, contains a very helpful introduction and useful notes. E. Watkins, *Kant and the Metaphysics of Causality* (Cambridge: Cambridge University Press, 2005); C.W. Dyck, *Kant and Rational Psychology* (Oxford: Oxford University Press, 2014) explore different aspects of the relationship between Kant and the rationalists.

4

KANT AND THE EMPIRICIST TRADITION

Wayne Waxman

★★★

Kant's critical philosophy is often viewed as falling midway between rationalism and empiricism. Hume roused him from the dogmatic slumber of rationalism by disabusing him of his former confidence in the competency of pure reason to ascertain the ultimate nature and workings of reality. At the same time, Kant remained committed to the philosophical superiority of pure reason over empirical, and so never permitted experience the final say in any question of metaphysics, epistemology, morality, teleology, aesthetics, or philosophy of science. Thus, by employing Humean skepticism to denude rationalism of the last vestiges of Platonic idealism and Scholastic ontology, Kant is portrayed as having transformed a priori philosophy into something fundamentally different: self-critical pure reason.

Is this an accurate depiction of Kant's place in the history of philosophy? Or is his critical philosophy better regarded as continuous with, and so, at bottom, essentially a variant of either rationalism or empiricism? The consensus among scholars, in practice if not always avowedly, is that as soon as one turns from generalities to the detailed exposition of Kant's positions and the reasoning on which he based them, the more evident becomes their essential unity and continuity with the past. For the vast majority, it is the rationalist past. However, in this chapter, I shall argue the contrary: that once one understands the empiricism of Locke, Berkeley, and Hume as prioritizing the sensible as such, without any essential restriction to the a posteriori sort, Kant's critical philosophy reveals itself to be a theory of exactly the same kind as theirs.[1]

1. The Psychological A Priori

Knowledge, for Kant, is essentially propositional. Even considered purely logically, nothing can count as true or false until formed into a proposition; and it is only insofar as a proposition conforms to the transcendental conditions for cognition of objects that it becomes even so much as a candidate for an item of knowledge. Because of this, it is a mistake, albeit a common one, to treat Kant's notion of the a priori as epistemological. For him, being a priori is, first and foremost, a matter of a representation's *origin* in the mind, and so a *psychological* question that has nothing to do with whether it does, or even can, enter into propositions. A representation counts as

DOI: 10.4324/9781003406617-6

psychologically a priori if and only if it can be received or produced in the mind without incorporating the least consciousness of the impressions of outer or inner sense, and is otherwise a posteriori, that is, empirical in origin. A proposition can be a priori in the epistemological sense without being so in the psychological, as evidenced by Kant's metaphysical first principles of natural science, which incorporate empirical concepts and observational data and yet still count as a priori (A171–2/B213, *MAN* 04: 469–70). To qualify as *pure* rather than simply a priori, a proposition must therefore consist exclusively of representations that are a priori *in origin*. Psychologically a priori representations, however, need not be epistemologically a priori since they may be logically incapable of entering into propositions. The pure intuitions, space and time, are a case in point: because they incorporate nothing discursive (logically universal) in their representation (A24–5/B39 and A31–2/B47), they can no more be slotted into the subject or predicate positions of propositions than sensations, feelings of pleasure and pain, emotions, desires, and other non-discursive representations can.

To grasp the critical importance of the psychological a priori for Kant, one must recognize that he derived from Hume not only the problem to which he devoted the *Critique of Pure Reason* – how are synthetic a priori judgments possible? – but the method of solving it as well:

> One cannot, without feeling a certain pain, behold how entirely every one of his opponents – Reid, Oswald, Beattie, and lastly Priestly – missed the point of his problem [. . .]. It was not the question whether the concept of cause is correct, serviceable, and in respect of the whole of our cognition of nature indispensable, for this Hume never doubted. Rather, it was the question whether the concept is thought through reason a priori and in this way has an inner truth independent of all experience and therefore also a far more extended employment, not limited to objects of experience: here is where Hume expected a breakthrough [*Eröffnung*]. It was indeed only the issue of the origin of this concept, not its indispensability in use: if only the former were ascertained, then everything concerning the conditions of its use and the sphere in which it can be valid would already of itself have been given.
>
> (*Prol* 4: 258–9)

Hume and Kant not only did not question the normative indispensability of concepts like cause and effect but emphasized it and sought its basis. However, they did so not by undertaking an epistemological inquiry, much less a logical or metaphysical one, but by endeavoring to discover their origins as representations in the mind. For the chief lesson Kant learned from Hume is that the psychological processes involved in the formation of a representation may contribute essential elements of its content and, if they do, limit the scope of its application to the representations of an appropriately constituted psyche.

Hume's account of the origin of the idea of necessary connection, understood as an essential component of the indispensable concept of cause and effect, is the *locus classicus*. Instead of tracing it either to something present to the senses (outer or inner), intuited by intellect, or inferred by reason, Hume held that the actions and affects incident to the customary transitions of thought whereby causal inferences are formed are themselves the originating impression of the idea. And from this he concluded that its scope is limited to customary associations between perceptions forged by suitably equipped psyches:

> [The] discovery [. . .] that this connexion, tie, or energy lies merely in ourselves, and [. . .] is acquir'd by custom [. . .] not only cuts off all hope of ever attaining satisfaction, but even prevents our very wishes; since it appears, that when we say we desire to know the ultimate and

operating principle, as something, which resides in the external object, we either contradict ourselves, or talk without a meaning.

(*THN* 1.4.7: ¶5)

Here Hume uses psychology to expose the meaninglessness of the claim that *necessary connections* hold between external objects (which he subsequently extended to the objects of internal perception such as volitions) independently of customary association by substituting for "necessary connection" the concept that explicates it, "customary association." He thereby transformed a disguised absurdity into the patent absurdity that *customary associations* between objects may hold independently of customary association.

Hume's influence on Kant is consequently never more unmistakable than when we find him employing precisely the same method to expose the meaninglessness of the notion that relations of space and time may exist between objects independently of the representing subject (as on Leibniz's view), or that space and time themselves may do so (Newton's view):

[S]pace and time, including all the appearances in them, are nothing existent in themselves and outside my representations but themselves only modes of representation, and it is patently contradictory to say that a mere mode of representation also exists outside our representation. The objects of the senses therefore exist only in experience; whereas to accord to them a self-subsistent existence apart from or prior to experience is as much as to represent the actuality of experience apart from or prior to experience.

(*Prol* 4: 341–2)

Having determined that space and time originate as pure intuitions of sensibility and that nothing appearing in them can exist independently of experience, Kant could, in classically Humean style, convert the disguised absurdities that space and time exist apart from or prior to our modes of representing them and that objects experienced in them exist apart from or prior to experience into the patent absurdities that modes of representation exist apart from or prior to modes of representation and that experience exists apart form or prior to experience.

Yet, Kant's primary affinity with empiricism is not his insistence on the need to trace concepts to their origin as representations in the mind but the origin to which he traced them. According to empiricism, the contents of human understanding all either originate in sensibility, are produced (synthesized) from contents originating in sensibility, or are preceded and made possible by such productions. It is only because Locke, Berkeley, Hume, and other early modern empiricists seem never to have considered the possibility that sensibility also supplies a priori representations that their commitment to sensibilism made them empiricists by default. For clearly it is sensibilism, not its restriction to the a posteriori, that most narrowly and fundamentally defines what empiricists were about. Hence, in order to show that Kant is rightly classified as one of them, it suffices to show that his theory of the understanding is as thoroughgoingly sensibilist as theirs.

2.   Rationalizing Kant: How to Make the Problem of Origins Go Away

Pure intuitions of space and time are the lynchpin of Kant's a priori psychology. They are indispensable to the solution of the problem addressed in his critique of pure reason, how are synthetic a priori judgments possible? (B73, *Prol* 4: 377, *ÜE* 8: 245, *Refl* 18: 5552, 5637, 5927, 6353, 6355, and *OP* 22: 4). Without the manifold they precede and make possible, transcendental logic is a nonstarter (A15–6/B29–30, A55/B79–80). Pure concepts of the understanding (categories) in particular can only be given insofar as the synthesis of this manifold in imagination is available to be represented universally (B76–9/B102–5, A321/B378, A401). The same is true of the transcendental schemata that deputize for the categories in the predicate position of transcendental judgment's principles of pure understanding (A181/B223): they are sensible concepts (A146/B186) of the determination of the manifold of pure time conformably to the categories (A138–9/B177–8). Even the most purely intellectual representation of all depends on the manifold made possible by pure space and time. For as explicated by Kant, the I think is the representation of an identity of consciousness that extends to all the manifold a priori, or *analytic unity of apperception*, which in turn is possible only given an original *synthetic unity* of this manifold in one apperception (B133–4) that is in place in intuition a priori, ahead of all thought (B132), that is, all discursivity (representation by means of universals, be they concepts, judgments, or inferences). As an essential component of this synthetic unity, the a priori sensible manifold made possible by pure space and time must be acknowledged as indispensable to what Kant considered the "highest point" and "supreme principle" of both the analytic of the understanding and the possibility of synthetic a priori judgments (A117n, B135, B136, A158/B197), so that even analytic judgment (B131n) and pure general logic (B131, B133–4n) are impossible without it. It therefore seems beyond doubt that Kant was as fully committed to the sensibilist principle that the contents of thought all either originate in sensibility, are produced from contents originating in sensibility, or are essentially preceded and made possible by such productions, as Locke, Berkeley, and Hume.

But if the case for classifying Kant's analytic of the understanding as a philosophy of the same kind as the empiricists is as clear-cut as the foregoing might make it seem, then why is it that virtually every scholar dismisses the notion out of hand and instead treats it as a variant of rationalism? It happens, I believe, because they find themselves stymied when it comes to making sense of the paradoxical seeming coupling of "pure" with "sensible". In virtually any accepted meaning of the term, a representation counts as "sensible" if and only if it incorporates sensation, be it via experience, memory (recollected sensation), or imagination (reproduced sensation). If it is absolutely non-visual, non-tactual, and everything else a representation is required to be if it is to count as pure, how can it possibly still be sensible? To be sure, Kant and the empiricists extended the meaning of "sensible" to include data of inner sense (or senses: Kant sometimes spoke of it in the plural, e.g. *Refl* 15: 224 [1783–4]). But setting aside any misgivings one may have about such an extension, it seems clear that "sense" must here carry the same meaning it has in relation to the outer senses, so that inner sense differs from outer in essentially the same way that vision differs from smell not *qua* sense but as the source of sensations of color rather than odor. But if this is so, then any representation incorporating data (also termed "affections" and "impressions" by Kant) of either the inner or the outer sense is not only sensible but empirical. Conversely, because a *pure* representation must *ipso facto* be absolutely non-visual, non-tactual, and "non-" every other kind of sense affection (including those of inner sense), it seems quite impossible for it to be non-empirical without its also being altogether non-sensible. This is why the notion of a pure yet sensible intuition such as Kant supposed space and time to be is so perplexing. And since the same considerations apply to the I think and other pure representations that he regarded as intellectual in their own right and sensible only by presupposition, is it any wonder that the divide separating Kant's transcendental philosophy from rationalism (non-sensibilist accounts of the origin of these representations) is apt to seem paper-thin and risks disappearing altogether?

While details may differ, all interpretations with which I am familiar deal with the problem by construing one feature of pure sensible representations as essential and the other as merely accidental; and since purity is generally deemed most important, both for Kant and for us, it is the sensible aspect that typically gets downgraded. In practice, this means that instead of being a source of the contents of pure representations, sensibility is treated merely as a source of our consciousness of those contents. Pure space and time thus count as "sensible" because our psychology equips us to represent them as individual intuitions prior to and independently of all discursive representation (concepts, judgments, inferences), whereas the categories, their schemata, and transcendental judgments are "intellectual" insofar as they cannot be brought to awareness until universals are added to the mix. In either case, their *essential* contents (spatial, temporal, and/or categorial) are already fully in place ahead of the psychological operations involved in forming conscious representations of them, so that any contents added by the latter count as merely *accidental* (superficial incrustations that must be stripped away before clear representations can be made distinct). The psychological method that Hume and his predecessors deemed indispensable to identifying the essential contents and demarcating the scope of meaningful application of cause and effect, substance, space, time, and other philosophically significant representations is thus rendered redundant. One must instead suppose that Kant explicated them non-psychologically, which, given the purity of the representations concerned, points back to a rationalist conception of origin and a normativist conception of scope.

As concerns origin, only two basic types of explanation seem possible: we come by pure representations through a special non-sensible, purely intellectual illumination, or they are implanted in us innately (the first is most closely associated with Malebranche but approximates the views of Frege and many mathematicians as well; the second was favored by Descartes and Leibniz; while Plato and Spinoza seem to have drawn on both). To my knowledge, no one takes Kant to have been an intellectual illuminationist. By contrast, implantationism is the fallback position for all interpreters whose *de facto* supposition is that it was not truly possible for Kant to have assigned equal weight to "pure" and "sensible", including those who are aware that Kant, like Locke before him, limited innatism to faculties of the mind and vehemently rejected representational innatism (innate contents of thought) (*ÜE* 8 221–3). For where the psychological a priori is assumed to be logically incoherent, one cannot help agreeing with rationalists like Descartes that, in the case of representations purported to be pure, the distinction between faculties innatism and representational innatism is a distinction without a difference. After all, what other source of content can such representations have than the constitution peculiar to the faculty responsible for producing them? This seems particularly true (as argued, e.g., by Leibniz) of the contents of internal sense perceptions: how can the psychological operations responsible for their formation contribute any content to them that is not already present in the innate constitution of the faculties concerned?

For interpreters who read Kant as a *de facto* rationalist, the point of such considerations is not that one side or the other is right but that the very distinction between innate and acquired cannot get a grip, at least in the case of purportedly pure representations. Since the problem of origins is today generally disregarded, not least in analytic philosophy, this has the signal benefit of enabling them to treat Kant's critical philosophy as more "contemporary" than would otherwise be possible. For insofar as the exclusion of the psychological a priori marginalizes the problem of origins, the way is opened to construing Kantian pure representations as objective in essentially the same sense that Frege and post-Fregeans distinguish the objective sense and meaning (*Sinn und Bedeutung*) of concepts from their subjective character as mental representations (*Vorstellungen*) (which itself can be regarded as a rationalist updating of Descartes's version of the distinction between the objective reality of an idea and its formal reality as the modification of a mind). And this in turn permits interpreters to reframe the question of their scope as a purely normative task of providing a non-psychological justification for their cognitive application in experience (*quid juris*).

3. The Preeminence of the Psychological in Kant

Although the temptation to make Kant relevant to contemporary philosophy is very great, the way of doing so described in the preceding section rests on three tacit suppositions, none of which stand up under scrutiny. The first is the assumption that the problem of representational origins remains unchanged when the psychological a priori of sensibilism is discarded in favor of the rationalist alternative. What happens instead is that Kant's Hume-derived (*KU* 5: 258–9) problem is split in two. On the sensibilist model, a pure representation is discovered to owe essential elements of its content to the psychological operations responsible for forming it so that the explanations of how the representation comes to be in our minds – its origin *in us* – and how the *representation itself* comes to be – its origin *tout court* – are the same. Once the rationalist model is adopted, however, the explanation of the first no longer suffices for the second, and vice versa. As objective in the psyche-independent sense, the contents of pure representations, on a rational analysis, are completely indifferent to whether and how our minds come to form conscious representations of them. Their own (psyche-independent) origin might be physical (part perhaps of the information-theoretic contents of the material universe itself), metaphysical (intelligible realities such as Platonic ideas, Cartesian true and immutable natures, Fregean *Bedeutungen*, Russellian panprotopsychic atoms, etc.), or something comparable (Fregean *Sinne*, Chomskyan UG, language of thought algorithms, etc.). But whatever it may be, the objectivity of their contents makes *their* origin an entirely separate question from how they come to be represented in *us* (being implanted by a beneficent Creator, via our evolved genetic endowment, divinely vouchsafed illumination, etc.). Thus, the shift from the psychological a priori to the psyche-independent kind characteristic of the rationalistic analyses so common among Kant's interpreters surreptitiously changes his original question into a different one entirely. And this obliges one to ask whether their proceeding still qualifies as a reflection of what Kant, the historical personage, thought and why, rather than the sort of "extreme makeover" that genuine interpreters are obliged to avoid.

The second questionable supposition underpinning the rationalization of Kant is the well-nigh universal assumption that the categories are necessary conditions for the unity of apperception and apperception a sufficient condition for the categories. Since apperception (the representation I think, self-consciousness) is quintessentially subjective, were the converse true so that the categories were beholden to apperception for an essential element of their content but not vice versa, the psychological independence distinctive of the sense of objectivity accorded to the categories on rationalistic analyses would straightaway be annulled. The reason, it seems to me, that the supposition is so widely taken for granted, with little if any thought given to proving it, is that interpreters generally fail to distinguish the conditions of the *objectivity* (objective unity) of apperception from the conditions of *apperception as such*. There can be no dispute that Kant deemed the categories to be conditions of the former since, on his theory, no objects or objectivity are possible until necessity is introduced into the synthesis of the manifold and the categories are the unique source of that necessity. But I know of no reason to suppose that such necessity is essential for apperception itself. On the contrary, the evidence suggests that not only this necessity but the categories themselves presuppose apperception, with the implication that the representation I think, together with its pure sensible presuppositions, condition the categories, not vice versa.

Due to limitations of space, I can here provide only a sampling of the evidence:

1. Kant variously referred to apperception as a unity presupposed by and higher than the unity thought in the category and the logical function of judgment (B131), as the supreme principle of intuition in relation to the understanding (B136), the first principle of thought in general

(A117n), the highest point to which all employments of the understanding must be ascribed (B133–4n), the highest principle of the entire sphere of human cognition (B135), and the highest principle of synthetic judgments (A158/B197). But how could apperception merit this preeminence if it were in any way beholden to the categories and logical functions? Wouldn't they then be the higher unity, the more supreme principle of intuition, and so on?

2. "Apperception is itself the ground of the possibility of the categories" and "is therefore the representation of that which is the condition of all unity and yet is itself unconditioned" (A401). The contrary assumption leads inexorably to the illusion that the categories can be applied to apperception to determine it as an object, a subreption that hypostatizes the thinking subject, Cartesian style, as an efficacious substance with qualities and quantitative determinateness. So, once again, the question needs to be addressed of how these concepts can be necessary for apperception if apperception is the "unity of consciousness that underlies the categories" (B421).

3. Insofar as Kant explicated the Cartesian I think as the pure representation of the identity of consciousness in respect to all the manifold, he saw fit to term it the *analytic unity of apperception* (B133–4). It is this unity that warrants Kant's claim that apperception underlies pure general logic no less than transcendental logic (B131, B133–4n). For insofar as the I think must be able to accompany all my representations (B131), it is *ipso facto* a representation logically *common* to them all. As such, it need only be added to a sensation, intuition, or any other non-universal representation to straightaway make "it into a *conceptus communis*" (B133–4n). Hence, the "analytic unity of consciousness attaches to all common concepts as such" (B133–4n); it is "the vehicle of all concepts in general, and so of transcendental concepts as well, and thus is always conceived along with these latter" (A341/B399–400); that is, "the mere apperception I think [. . .] makes possible even all transcendental concepts, in which it means that I think substance, cause, etc." (A342–3/B400–1; also A348/B406). But if the categories are only possible insofar as concepts in general are possible, how can they be supposed to condition apperception when apperception is the *logical* condition of all common concepts as such? Vicious circularity can only be avoided if we suppose that apperception can and does obtain prior to and independently of both the categories and their objectivization of apperception.

4. If the only representational use the understanding can make of concepts is to combine them into judgments (A68/B93), then the analytic unity of apperception whereby alone representations can be converted into concepts must be supplemented by the logical functions that make possible the propositional combination of universals. Conversely, if sensations, feelings, intuited appearances, and other nonconceptual representations are to occupy the slots of subject and predicate in categorical judgments, and so have logical quantity and quality, they must first be converted into concepts by adding the analytic unity of the I think to their representation. Given this essential interdependence, Kant's transcendental explanation of the possibility of general logic (B133–4n) obliges us to re-conceive logical functions of judgment as a priori psychological modes for the combination of representations to which the analytic unity of apperception already attaches. In other words, from a Kantian perspective, the traditional view of logical functions as forms for the combination of universals *tout court*, without reference to apperception, is merely an abstraction and not a true picture of their psychological nature and workings. So, without denying that omitting their a priori psychological nature and workings may be useful, even indispensable, when doing logic, this may never be done when interpreting Kant's transcendental account of the possibility of thought because it risks giving logical functions a falsely objectivist (psyche-independent) cast.

4. Understanding How the Sensible Can Also Be Pure

Once it is conceded that apperception, as the contributor of universal form, enters essentially into the content of the categories as pure concepts of the understanding, the way is opened to making sense of Kant's a priori sensibilism. The analytic unity of apperception constitutive of logical universals analytically entails the original *synthetic* unity of the manifold in one apperception (B133–6). Since the former is constitutive of the logical universals without which judgment (thought itself as such, cognitive or not) is impossible, this original synthetic unity must be in place already in intuition itself, "ahead of all thought" (B132). Since the categories, being concepts, presuppose the analytic unity of apperception, the synthetic unity in question must therefore obtain prior to and independently of them as well.

Now, the only a priori unity present in intuition ahead of all thought (discursivity, representation by means of universals) is the unity that the pure intuitions of the Transcendental Aesthetic, space and time, confer on their manifolds. Although Kant did not state there that it is an original synthetic unity, he made good this want in the Transcendental Deduction of the Categories shortly after distinguishing the synthetic from the analytic unity of apperception:

> Space and time and all their parts are intuitions, hence individual representations with the manifold they contain in them (see the Transcendental Aesthetic), not mere concepts through which one and the same consciousness is contained in many representations but many contained in one and in the consciousness of that one, and thus as composite; consequently, unity of consciousness that is synthetic yet also original is met with in them.
>
> (B136n)

This original synthetic unity is imposed by the understanding via the imagination, yet "does not belong to the concept of understanding" but "to space and time" because "space and time are first *given* as intuitions" (B160–1n) by their means (see also A99–100 and A107). With the exclusion not only of the categories but concepts generally (B160–1n) from the original synthetic unity of pure space and time described in the Transcendental Deduction, there is no difficulty reconciling it with Kant's insistence in the Aesthetic that pure intuitions are in no way discursive (A24–5/B39 and A31–2/B47). For in order for space, time, and the unity of the manifold in (not under) them to count as purely aesthetic and sensible, it is enough that no universals (concepts, judgments, inferences) enter into their representation. Imagination, for Kant, is a purely sensible faculty whose synthesis has to be brought to concepts by the understanding (A78/B103); and the evidence that he believed it to be involved in the production of pure space and time is quite compelling (e.g. A99–100, *ÜE* 8: 203, *Anth* 7: 167, *Refl* 18: 5876, and *OP* 22: 76). The other essential factor, as indicated by texts such as B136n and B160n (cited earlier), is pure apperception. Provided one remembers that the supposition that the categories enter into its content is unfounded (section 3), there is no reason not to suppose that Kant took apperception to function prediscursively as well as discursively, and so enters into the prediscursive unity of the pure intuitions of space and time just as it enters into the discursive unity of the logical functions and the categories (B131).

It is the recognition that the origin of the unity of the manifold in pure space and time is original and synthetic that enables one to resolve the conundrum of how a representation can be at once pure and sensible. Previous to Kant, no one seems to have believed that there was any need to explain what unites the manifold data of the outer and inner senses in sensibility. It was assumed to be passively given, a matter purely of receptivity, so that the philosopher's psychological task concerned only what is subsequent to this unity: how memory, imagination, and other active faculties operate on this manifold to retain it, separate what is met with in it together, combine what is met with separately, compare, relate, associate, abstract, generalize, and so forth. So far as I am aware, the first inkling that this assumption might be problematic was the quandary concerning personal identity that Hume described in an appendix to the second volume of his *Treatise of Human Nature* (1740), where, "having thus loosen'd all our particular perceptions [. . .] all my hopes vanish, when I come to explain the principles, that unite our successive perceptions in our thought or consciousness" (Hume 1978 [1740]: 635). Hume could see no way out except to posit the kind of real substrate or causal connection (in place of ideal fictitious associative ones) that his sensibilist principles precluded. And though unremarked by Hume, it should also be noted that the compresence of sensations poses essentially the same problem as their succession: while blue can be apprehended immediately together with yellow and other colors as a single manifold (the visual field), what can unite a sound, smell, headache, desire, or shift of attention with them? The visual field includes no sounds, the auditory field no smells, and so on. How, without positing a real substrate or cause of precisely the sort Hume's skepticism precludes, can one explain the unity of the data of the outer and inner senses in one and the same consciousness?

Whereas Hume's empiricist brand of sensibilism proved unequal to the challenge of explaining the unity of sensibility, Kant's appropriation of Hume's problem as his own (the possibility of synthetic a priori judgments) and his extension of Hume's psychological method of solving it to include the psychological a priori (section 1) seem to have enabled him to both recognize and overcome Hume's quandary. Receptivity alone, without synthesis, does not suffice for anything like a unified sensibility, but instead leaves "each individual representation [. . .] completely alien, isolated as it were, and separate from other representations" (A97). To make good this want, Kant looked to what he termed "the synthesis of apprehension in intuition" (A99), where "distinct perceptions are met with in the mind scattered and single in themselves" (A120), ahead of all reproduction, comparison, and the relating and ordering operations to which imagination had traditionally been confined. To establish that the imagination extends to so elementary a level of consciousness, and thereby become the first psychologist for whom "the imagination is a necessary ingredient of perception itself" (A120n), he argued that the empirical synthesis of apprehension is preceded and made possible by synthetic unitary pure space and time intuitions (B159–60), which themselves are "first given" (B160–1n) by the imagination's pure synthesis of apprehension (A99–100) and the understanding's prediscursive unity of apperception (B136n and B160–1n). Thus, it is precisely because the unity of sensibility present in bare apprehension, ahead of all higher operations of the mind, depends as much on imagination and apperception as on outer and inner sense that the pure intuitions that make this unity possible can and must be regarded as sensible.

5. Kant's Propositional Subjectivism

The third questionable supposition of Kant's rationalistic minded interpreters is that the objectivist analytic/synthetic distinction targeted by Quine and others is essentially the same as Kant's original distinction. Proponents of an objectivist construal of the distinction hold that the judger's state of knowledge or ignorance is irrelevant to the logical fact of the matter as to whether the predicate of a judgment is or is not analytically related to its subject concept. For example, the predicates "is soluble in acqua regia" and "is atomic number 79" may be deemed analytically related to the subject "gold" even if the judger happens to be ignorant of these facts. Similarly, a rationalist in the Platonic tradition like Descartes or Leibniz would judge the predicate "has its external angle greater than either of its opposing internal angles" to be analytically related to the subject "triangle". A Quinean critic, in turn, might argue that there is not always, or even ever, a clear line of demarcation between analytically related predicates and predicates that are logically, mathematically, or otherwise directly inferable from the subject concept yet not part of its meaning (the contents implicitly contained in the concept, its constituent marks), while nevertheless agreeing that the state of knowledge or ignorance of the judger is irrelevant.

For a subjectivist, by contrast, the subject and predicate concepts contain all and only what the judger represents in them; there is never an independent "logical" or "semantic" fact of the matter; and there can be no objectivist doubt as to whether the predicate is contained in or merely inferable from the subject concept because it is settled by the psychological fact that the judger does or does not *actually* think the predicate when thinking the subject. Sensibilists are always subjectivists because nothing can be combined in a representation unless and until the representing subject brings together (synthesizes) a manifold and considers it as one. Locke is a prime example. Where "having Ideas, and Perception [are] the same thing" (ECHU 2.1.9), the contents of any idea and the contents perceived in it – its reality and its appearance to (sensing, imagining, conceiving) consciousness – are one and indistinguishable (2.29.5). Thus, contrary to rationalists like Descartes, Locke defended subjectivism:

> [T]hat the external Angle of all Triangles, is bigger than either of the opposite internal Angles; which relation of the outward Angle, to either of the opposite internal Angles, making no part of the complex Idea, signified by the name Triangle, this is a real Truth, and conveys with it instructive real Knowledge.
>
> (4.8.8)

Perhaps the simplest, most direct proof of Kant's allegiance to Lockean propositional subjectivism is his insistence that "analysis, which seems to be the opposite of synthesis, yet always presupposes it" (B130; also A77/B103). Because synthesis "is an act of self-activity", it "is the only thing among all representations that cannot be given through objects but only by the subject itself" (B130). Since this is just to say that "we can represent nothing as combined in the object without having ourselves previously combined it", analysis can never reveal anything in a representation not put there by the synthesizing subject. The distinction between analytic and synthetic judgments is simply a case in point: "the question is not what we are *supposed* to join in thought to the given concept but what we *actually* think in it, if only obscurely" (B17 and *Prol* 4: 269). For example, "that I am supposed to think 12 in the addition of 7 and 5 is here beside the point, for in analytic propositions the question is only whether I actually think the predicate in the representation of the subject" (A164/B205; also *FM* 20: 322–3). In other words, because I no more actually think, however obscurely, equality to 12 when I conceive the sum of 7 and 5 than I think equality to the cube root of 1,728, the difference between 14,873,639 and 14,873,627, or anything else, it follows that the a priori judgments expressing these equalities depend on synthesizing acts of the judging subject, and are therefore one and all synthetic.

Indeed, interpreters too often forget or overlook that Kant chose the designations he did for a reason. A synthetic judgment is so-called because it essentially involves a psychological act of synthesis and so depends ultimately on sensible intuition:

> [T]hat something outside the given concept must still be added as substrate which makes it possible to go beyond the concept with my predicates is clearly indicated by the expression 'synthesis,' and consequently investigation is directed toward the possibility of a synthesis of representations for the sake of cognition in general, which must soon turn to intuition, while pure intuition must be acknowledged as the unavoidable condition for a priori cognition.
>
> (*ÜE* 8: 244–5)

Similarly, the expression "analysis" alludes to the process whereby given representations are transformed into concepts (A76/B102 and A78/B104), the ultimate ground of which is the quintessentially subjective psychological representation I think, explicated as analytic unity of apperception (section 3). The latter, together with the synthetic unity of apperception "ahead of all thought" (B132) it presupposes, which I have argued in section 4 is none other than the prediscursive synthetic unity of pure intuition (space and time), are the components of Kant's most fundamental and important analysis-presupposes-synthesis thesis. We therefore need to accept, and cease attempting to evade or palliate in the name of contemporary relevance, that the problem to which the *Critique of Pure Reason* is directed, the possibility of synthetic a priori judgment, is inseparably bound up with three interrelated doctrines that Kant shared with the empiricists: sensibilism, the relevance of psychological origin to conceptual content and scope of application, and propositional subjectivism.

6. Conclusion

In a brief chapter such as this, I could only scratch the surface of Kant's relationship with the empiricist tradition. Discussion of the essential Humean background both to the problem of synthetic a priori judgment and Kant's method of solving it had to be omitted, along with such important topics as causality and freedom, time, idealism, the relation of language to thought, infinite divisibility, the self, morality, and religion. Nevertheless, I hope to have said enough to make clear that Kant's critical philosophy can and should be viewed not only as continuous with but the culmination of the sensibilizing tendency initiated by Locke, advanced by Berkeley, and developed to its empirical outrance by Hume.

Note

1   The ideas presented in this chapter derive from my two-volume work on self and understanding in Kant and British empiricism (Waxman 2005, 2014).

References

Hume, D. (1978 [1740]) *A Treatise of Human Nature*, L.A. Selby-Bigge (ed.), 2nd ed., Revised by P.H. Nidditch. Oxford: Clarendon Press.
Waxman, W. (2005) *Kant and the Empiricists: Understanding Understanding*, New York: Oxford University Press.
Waxman, W. (2014) *Kant's Anatomy of the Intelligent Mind*, New York: Oxford University Press.

Further reading

Interesting considerations of Kant in relation to Hume can be found in Lewis White Beck, *Essays on Kant and Hume* (New Haven: Yale University Press, 1978). More information regarding Kant's relation to Hume is provided in Günter Gawlick and Lother Kreimendahl, *Hume in der deutsche Aufklärung: Umrisse einer Rezeptionsgeschichte* (Stuttgart-Bad Cannstatt: Frommann-Holzboog, 1987); Wolfgang Ertl, *David Hume und die Dissertation von 1770: Einer Entwicklungsgeschichte der Philosophie Immanuel Kants* (Frankfurt am Main: Peter Lang, 1999). Kant's relation to Berkeley is discussed in Eugen Stäbler, *George Berkeley's Auffassung und Wirkung in der Deutschen Philosophie bis Hegel* (Zeulenroda: Bernhard Sporn, 1935). And Kant's relation to the Scottish common sense tradition is considered in Manfred Kuehn, *Scottish Common Sense in Germany, 1768–1800: A Contribution to the History of Critical Philosophy* (Kingston, ON: McGill-Queen's University Press, 1987).

PART 2

Transcendental Philosophy
(Critique and Doctrine)

A. Critical Part

I. THEORETICAL PHILOSOPHY

5

THE FIRST *CRITIQUE*

Prefaces and Introduction

Graham Bird

***

Kant's two prefaces to the *Critique* (Avii–xxii/Bvii–xliv), though expressed sometimes in slightly different terms (see section 1.4 later in this chapter), nevertheless both outline the same revolutionary aims. The Introduction (B1–30) goes further in providing a new technical apparatus, centered on the classification of synthetic a priori judgements, on which those revolutionary aims turn. The connection between these two aspects of the work is this: Kant aims to turn round, to revolutionize (Bxxii), a traditional philosophy, such as empiricism, which assumed that knowledge must conform to objects, in an experiment to test the alternative view that in some way objects must instead conform to our knowledge. Kant believes that the experiment succeeds (Bxviii). Put crudely but forcefully, Kant represents our cognitive powers as actively imposing a structure on experience rather than as reflecting passively a quite independent reality. He classifies that active knowledge as "a priori" (Axvi–xvii/Bxvi–xvii) and accounts for it as what "we ourselves put into things" (Bxviii). It is crucially a priori but not analytic, expressed in principles which are synthetic a priori. Evidently Kant's revolution requires accounts of the technical classifications 'a priori/a posteriori' (of concepts, intuitions, or judgements), and 'synthetic a priori' (of judgements or principles), as well as of the two surrounding and opposed traditional and Kantian views. These requirements begin to be met in the two prefaces and the technical apparatus of the Introduction.

Philosophers before Kant had recognized some forms of the distinction 'a priori/a posteriori', but Kant's use of it is novel. Some earlier philosophers, such as Hume, would regard a priori truth as derived from analytic relations between concepts, and contrast these with bare matters of fact. The former relations might tell us something about words and their meaning, but only the latter express the way things actually are. Other earlier philosophers disputed that exclusive distinction by claiming that their a priori claims inform us about the way things actually are but at a very high level of generality. For them while science may provide us with insight into particular facts only philosophy, with its use of reason, can complete and unify their systems by appealing to those higher level a priori principles. Metaphysics is represented in such an account as continuous with science, both completing and correcting the latter's claims. Kant cites Wolff (Bxxxvi) as subscribing to such views, but Descartes might also have been mentioned.[1] Kant held that both of these earlier views of the 'a priori/a posteriori' distinction were inadequate. Wolff's account needed a discipline to restrain its

DOI: 10.4324/9781003406617-9

exaggeration of the scope of metaphysics (B738), while the Humean view misclassified disciplines such as mathematics, and failed to distinguish legitimate from spurious metaphysics (B20; B792–7). In the prefaces Kant identifies these errors with, respectively, dogmatism and scepticism, and blames the disrepute into which metaphysics has fallen on the endless, and futile, oscillation between these two poles. The dogmatist appeals to high level, a priori principles without considering how they can be justified; (Bxxxv; B790) the sceptic argues that those metaphysical principles cannot be justi-fied, and so leaves science and knowledge generally without any philosophical basis.

Kant's central conclusion in the prefaces is that metaphysics has to be reformed. It has to map out a legitimate program which points in a fruitful direction away from that futile oscillation between dogmatism and scepticism. Central to that aim is an enquiry, to remedy the dogmatist's neglect, into what our cognitive powers can legitimately achieve, with a primary emphasis on what metaphys-ics and reason can properly achieve in their appeal to a priori principles (B23). But, as Kant makes clear, that goal requires also a wider, more technical revision of the 'a priori/posteriori' distinction. Kant holds that all sciences, including philosophy, contain a priori principles which are not merely expressions of trivial relations between concepts. Such principles, and the relations between con-cepts which they express, may also be a priori but not analytic, a priori but also synthetic. In this way his primary aim of reforming metaphysics requires an answer to the question how such synthetic a priori judgements are possible, and it is for this reason that such a technical question is identified as the central issue in the *Critique* (B19).

These points make it clear also why Kant talks of the *Critique* as a "treatise on method" (Bxxii), and why it is useful to read the prefaces in conjunction with the final section of the work, namely the Doctrine of Method.[2] If Kant's central goal is to reform philosophy's method then the concluding Doctrine of Method should, and does, elaborate, more than the prefaces, what the new reformed discipline looks like. In that later section Kant underlines and elaborates the following ideas from the prefaces; first the belief that philosophy's role, like that of the police, is negative and disciplinary, that is, not to engage in social, economic or scientific activities but rather to set aside the obstacles to their pursuit (B26; B738). Second the requirement to be clear about the distinctive character of different sciences, differentiating, for example, the properly dogmatic character of mathematics from the problematic nature of metaphysics (B740ff.). As Kant says: "We do not enlarge but dis-figure sciences if we allow them to trespass on each other's territory" (Bviii–ix; B871).[3] Third the careful formulation of the limitations to legitimate metaphysical principles which go beyond what we can legitimately claim to *know*. Just as, in the prefaces, Kant makes room for the claims of faith, as against knowledge (Bxxx), so in the Doctrine of Method (in the Canon, B803–47), he outlines his 'defensive' advocacy of principles (B803–4) about the greatest good, the ultimate end of pure reason, morality and freedom. In such contexts, he now explains, these cannot be "demonstrated dogmas" but only "necessary postulates" (B846). They cannot be proved dogmatically by metaphys-ics but they can be defended against dogmatic criticism.

Those philosophical aspects of Kant's reforming programme are linked also to his introduction of the synthetic a priori classification of judgements, but his attempt to define and exemplify those judgements has been generally regarded as a failure. The criteria used to identify them are varied and unclear; at least one argument used to identify examples from arithmetic is known to be falla-cious (B15–17). It is not worth rehearsing all the criticisms that might be made of Kant's attempt, and instead I offer a brief account of the classification which has come to be widely accepted even though it is not expressed in these terms by Kant himself. In that account a distinction is drawn between an epistemic 'a priori/a posteriori' contrast for judgements and a semantic division between analytic and synthetic truth.[4] The former provides a classification of two kinds of knowl-edge we may acquire; one (a posteriori) which depends on empirical evidence from the course of

O'Neill, O. (1992) "Vindicating Reason," in P. Guyer (ed.), *The Cambridge Companion to Kant*, Cambridge: Cambridge University Press, pp. 280–308.

Strawson, P.F. (1974) "Imagination and Perception," in *Freedom and Resentment and Other Essays*, London: Methuen, pp. 45–65.

Strawson, P.F. (2011a) "Perception and Its Objects," in G. Strawson and M. Montague (eds.), *Philosophical Writings*, Oxford: Oxford University Press, pp. 125–45.

Strawson, P.F. (2011b) "Sensibility, Understanding, and the Doctrine of Synthesis," in G. Strawson and M. Montague (eds.), *Philosophical Writings*, Oxford: Oxford University Press, pp. 157–65.

Stroud, B. (1994) "Kantian Argument, Conceptual Capacities, and Invulnerability," in P. Parrini (ed.), *Kant and Contemporary Epistemology*, Dordrecht: Kluwer, pp. 231–51.

Tetens, J.N. (1777/1913) *Philosophische Versuche über die menschliche Natur und ihre Entwicklung*, Leipzig: M.G. Weidmanns Erben und Reich; W. Uebele (ed.), Berlin: Reuther & Reichard.

Travis, C. (2008) *Occasion-Sensitivity: Selected Essays*, Oxford: Oxford University Press.

Unger, P. (2014) *Empty Ideas: A Critique of Analytic Philosophy*, Oxford: Oxford University Press.

Westphal, K.R. (2004) *Kant's Transcendental Proof of Realism*, Cambridge: Cambridge University Press.

Westphal, K.R. (2013) "Hume, Empiricism and the Generality of Thought," *Dialogue: Canadian Journal of Philosophy/Revue canadienne de philosophie* 52: 233–70.

Westphal, K.R. (2015) "Conventionalism and the Impoverishment of the Space of Reasons: Carnap, Quine and Sellars," *Journal for the History of Analytic Philosophy* 3(8): 1–66, http://jhaponline.org; doi: 10.15173/jhap.v3i8.42.

Westphal, K.R. (2018) "Epistemology, Cognitive (In)Capacities and Thought Experiments," in J.R. Brown, Y. Fehige and M.T. Stuart (eds.), *The Routledge Companion to Thought Experiments*, New York and London: Routledge, pp. 128–49.

Westphal, K.R. (2020) *Kant's Critical Epistemology: Why Epistemology Must Consider Judgment First*, London: Routledge.

Westphal, K.R. (2021) *Kant's Transcendental Deduction of the Categories: Critical Re-Examination, Elucidation & Corroboration*, Kant's revised 2nd (B) ed. (1787), German Text with Parallel New Translation, Helsinki: Helsinki University Press. doi: 10.33134/HUP-7.

Westphal, K.R. (2023) "The Question Answered: What Is Kant's 'Critical Philosophy'?," in M.F. Bykova (ed.), *The History of Philosophy as Philosophy: The Russian Vocation of Nelly V. Motroshilova*, Leiden: Brill.

Williamson, T. (2015) "Review of Peter Unger, Empty Ideas: A Critique of Analytic Philosophy," *The Times Literary Supplement* 5833: 22–3.

Wittgenstein, L. (1958) *Philosophical Investigations*, G.E.M. Anscombe (trans.), 2nd ed., London: Palgrave Macmillan.

Wolff, C. (1736) *Philosophiae Primae, sive Ontologia*, 2nd ed., Frankfurt a. M. and Leipzig.

Wolff, M. (2017) "How Precise Is Kant's Table of Judgments?" in J. O'Shea (ed.), *Kant's Critique of Pure Reason: A Critical Guide*, Cambridge: Cambridge University Press, pp. 83–105.

Wolff, M. (forthcoming) "Kant's Table of Judgments: Frege's Critique and Kant's Counterargument."

Further Reading

G. Bird, *The Revolutionary Kant: A Commentary on the Critique of Pure Reason* (Chicago: Open Court, 2006) is philosophically sensitive, lucid, exoteric and detailed. A. Brook, *Kand and the Mind* (Cambridge: Cambridge University Press, 1994) remains an important study of Kant's first *Critique* in relation to cognitive psychology. J. Buroker, *Space and Incongruence: The Origins of Kant's Idealism* (Dordrecht: Reidel, 1981) remains highly instructive; her *Kant's Critique of Pure Reason: An Introduction* (Cambridge: Cambridge University Press, 2006) is one of the very best. J. Haag, *Erfahrung und Gegenstand: Das Verhältnis von Sinnlichkeit und Verstand* (Frankfurt am Main: Klostermann, 2007) is a penetrating re-examination of Kant's *Critique* in connection with contemporary epistemology. A. Melnick, *Space, Time, and Thought in Kant* (Dordrecht: Reidel, 1989) is a difficult yet unjustly neglected masterpiece. J. Rosenberg, *Accessing Kant: A Relaxed Introduction to the Critique of Pure Reason* (Oxford: Oxford University Press, 2005) considers topics in the systematic detail they deserve. K. Westphal, *Kant's Critical Epistemology: Why Epistemology Must Consider Judgment First* (London: Routledge, 2020) argues that Kant understood object identification to require perceptual–motor causal discrimination, and that Kant's account holds independently of transcendental idealism. K. Westphal, "The Question Answered: What Is Kant's 'Critical Philosophy'?", in M.F. Bykova (ed.), *The History of Philosophy as Philosophy: The Russian Vocation of Nelly V. Motroshilova* (Leiden: Brill, 2023) details Kant's critical system of philosophy consisting in his critique of the scope, point and use of a system of principles of rational judgment, thus providing Kant's systematic context for the 'Principles' chapter considered herein.

9

THE SCHEMATISM

Camilla Serck-Hanssen and Houston Smit[1]

***

The Critical Kant contends that concepts and sensible intuitions "constitute the elements of all our cognitions, so that neither concepts without intuition corresponding to them in some way nor intuition without concepts can yield a cognition" (A50/B74). In the *Critique of Pure Reason* Kant develops and defends this claim primarily in the service of explaining both why, *pace* rationalists, we cannot apply pure concepts of the understanding to things in themselves in theoretical synthetic a priori cognition of them and why, *pace* empiricists, we can apply these concepts to things as they appear to us in theoretical synthetic a priori cognition of them.[2]

This chapter focuses on "On the Schematism of the Pure Concepts of the Understanding" (hereafter, 'the Schematism'), which is the first of the two chapters that make up the "Transcendental Doctrine of the Power of Judgment." Now, according to Kant, this Doctrine itself consists of rational cognition that exhibits as such all the fundamental conditions that the nature of our capacity of cognition itself sets, purely a priori, on the possibility of our putting the pure concepts of the understanding to use in judgments to subsume sensible representations under them. Since all our theoretical cognition of things consists, in respect of its form, in this use of the pure concepts of the understanding, these conditions are, then, the fundamental conditions that the nature of our capacity of cognition itself sets on the possibility of our having any such cognition. The Schematism concerns a species of these conditions, namely "the sensible condition under which alone pure concepts of the understanding can be used," which condition he introduces as "the schematism of the pure understanding" (A136/B175). The Schematism chapter purports to exhibit this condition in and through identifying what Kant calls "the schemata of the pure concepts of the understanding": certain sensible representations produced by our imagination that correspond to the pure concepts of understanding as what collectively constitute "the formal and pure condition" to which these concepts are "restricted in their use" (A140/B179). What makes this condition *sensible* is that it has its determining ground in the nature of our capacity of sensible representation. What makes it *the* sensible condition to which the pure concepts of the understanding are restricted in *any* use to which we can put them is that it is a condition that is set solely by the form of our inner sense, Time, in which any sensible intuition to which we are to apply these concepts must be given to us.

DOI: 10.4324/9781003406617-13

According to the Schematism, the schema of a concept is the sensible condition under which that concept is applicable to objects. Moreover, the schema of a concept constitutes such a condition as the representation that a subject of a power of judgment can and must use in subsuming sensible intuitions under that concept. And we can subsume an object under a concept, that is, apply the latter to the former, only in subsuming under that concept a sensible intuition in which that object is given to us. This, in outline, is how the schema of a concept is the sensible condition under which that concept is applicable to objects. But just what a schema is, let alone how the schema of a concept is supposed to make possible the subsumption of sensible intuitions and their objects under it, are matters of continuing controversy among Kant scholars. These interpretive challenges have led several scholars to dismiss the chapter as confused and hopelessly obscure – although others have lauded it as a profound and lasting contribution to a fundamental classical question about the nature of universals.

A root cause of this controversy is the failure to see clearly how Kant conceives of the subsumption of an object under a concept.[3] This failure, in turn, has left obscure exactly how Kant distinguishes between the schemata of pure concepts of the understanding – to which he also refers as 'transcendental schemata' – and those of sensible concepts. Regarding the root cause, we will see that he conceives of this subsumption as consisting in one's exercising one's power of judgment to determine that the same marks that are contained, as its logical *essentialia*, in a concept are also contained in these objects themselves, insofar as we are immediately conscious of them in our sensible intuition. Regarding the obscurity, we will begin to see how these schemata are different in kind, and mediate between concepts and sensible intuitions in importantly different ways; appreciating these differences is indispensable to understanding Kant's account of schemata.

Moreover, in clarifying what is distinctive about the schemata of pure concepts of the understanding, it will prove crucial to recognize that Kant identifies these schemata as representations that are required to solve a particular problem, one that has specifically to do with the possibility of subsuming sensible intuitions under *the pure concepts of the understanding*. Indeed, Kant tells us that this problem is what "makes a doctrine of the transcendental power of judgment necessary" (A138/ B177) to begin with.

The opening five paragraphs of the Schematism present this problem regarding subsumption and explain, in brief, how the transcendental schemata solve it. In particular, its fourth paragraph introduces transcendental time determinations of appearances in general as the only representations that, given the nature of our inner sensibility, can and must mediate between the pure concepts of the understanding and appearances that are given to us if these appearances are to be subsumable under these concepts. The present chapter focuses almost exclusively on these paragraphs, because they are essential to understanding Kant's account of how the transcendental schemata can and must mediate between the pure concepts of the understanding and appearances in general, if the subsumption of the latter under the former is to be possible.

1. Subsumption, the Power of Judgment, and the Real Use of a Concept

As mentioned earlier, Kant describes the Schematism as what "deals with the sensible condition under which alone pure concepts of the understanding can be used" (A136/B175). The present section will begin elucidating this description in light of Kant's view that "the understanding can put concepts to no other use than that of judging by means of them" (A68/B93). Toward this end, we explain how the use of the pure concepts of the understanding at issue in the Schematism is their *real* use. What makes this use real is its having as its constitutive aim the subsumption under these concepts of objects themselves: an object, in the relevant sense, is as such a subject of power, and the real use of a concept of an object is one that requires that the subject be warranted in taking what one thinks as an object as really, and not just merely logically, possible.[4] On Kant's account, the only objects that we can subsume under the pure concepts of the understanding in any real use to which we are to put them are appearances that can be given to us in our sensibility. And this subsumption, in turn, consists in one's prescribing to these appearances the conformity to the conditions thought in these concepts in virtue of which they constitute objects of an experience that is possible for us.[5] We also clarify how the power of judgment, in using a pure concept of the understanding to subsume an object under that concept, distinguishes not only whether that object satisfies the conditions of subsumption that the concept itself specifies but also whether it satisfies the sensible condition under which we can put that concept to a real use.

Now, as A68/B93 makes clear, on Kant's view, our capacity to use a concept is the power of judgment. Moreover, he conceives of the power of judgment as the capacity to subsume under universals. For he holds the traditional view that understanding in general (*überhaupt*) consists of three sub-capacities: the capacity to grasp a concept as a universal representation (the understanding in a narrower sense), the power to subsume under universals (the power of judgment), and the power to draw mediate inferences between judgments (reason). For our purposes, it will prove crucial to attend to how Kant conceives of the use of a concept as consisting in subsuming representations under that concept.

Consider, then, how Kant opens the Transcendental Doctrine of the Power of Judgment by recapping how, on his account, the distinctive work of the power of judgment is subsuming under rules:

> If the understanding in general is explained as the capacity of rules, then the power of judgment is the capacity of subsuming under rules, i.e., of distinguishing [*unterscheiden*] whether something stands under a given rule (*casus datae legis*) or not.
>
> (A132/B171)

Now a rule, in Kant's sense of 'rule', is "an assertion under a universal condition [*unter einer allegemeinen Bedingung*]" (Log AA 9: 121). A concept is a species of rule in this sense of 'rule'. Assume, for the sake of illustration, that the concept *ductile* is the assertion that something is ductile under the condition that it can be drawn out into a thin wire. This condition is the *universal* condition under which this assertion is made, in that the assertion (it is ductile) is one advanced as obtaining for all (possible) objects that satisfy this condition. To distinguish "whether something stands under a given rule" is to distinguish whether an object satisfies that rule's universal condition. So, for example, when one judges 'Gold is ductile', one purports to determine that the object one thinks in the concept *gold* satisfies the universal condition (being able to be drawn out into a thin wire) of being ductile represented in the concept *ductile*.

The next point to see is that, in Kant's terminology, 'determine', and thus also 'use' and 'subsume', are success verbs: if in exercising one's power of judgment one is to put a concept to use, and subsume something under that concept, one must thereby not merely purport to determine that it stands under that concept's universal condition; one's assertion that it does must be correct and warranted. Moreover, the requisite warrant consists in one's being able, in principle, to achieve cognition of the principle (Prinzip) of this determination. Appreciating these points puts us in a position to explain Kant's distinction between the logical use and the real use of a concept.

The logical use of a concept has as its principle of subsumption a law of formal general logic – namely, the principle of non-contradiction, the highest principle of analytic judgment. Now any logical use of the understanding in general, because it has a law of formal general logic as its principle of subsumption, cannot determine any object itself, but rather merely the concept under which one subsumes it. For the subsumption of a representation under a concept in the logical use of that concept, is grounded merely in this representation's containing that concept. And this subsumption, properly understood, does not assert anything more than a merely logical connection among different representations. It does not, in particular, assert that there is a really possible object corresponding either to the concept that it puts to this use, or to the representation it subsumes under this concept, let alone an object to which either relates in a cognition.

The real use of a concept, in contrast, consists in the subsumption of given sensible intuitions and, thereby, the objects themselves that are given (if not as actual, as least as really possible) in and through them, under that concept. Kant's understanding of the real use of a concept is a complicated issue but for our purposes it suffices to make the following point. The real use of a concept requires, not just that we have sensible intuitions in which objects corresponding to that concept can be given, but that we can determine these objects themselves – insofar as we are immediately conscious of them in our sensible intuition – as ones that fall under that concept. And this, in turn, requires that we be able to determine these objects, insofar as they are given to us as actually existing and so as really possible subjects of power, as containing the marks that are thought in that concept as its universal condition. And for us to be capable of such determining is for us to be in possession of principles under which we are warranted in putting our concepts of objects to this use. The Schematism aims to explain how our capacity of sensible representation provides the purely a priori sensible condition required for us to be able, in this way, to represent the objects themselves that are given to us as actual in our sensible intuition as containing the universal conditions thought in the pure concepts of the understanding and thereby how this necessary condition of the real use of these concepts is met.

Several commentators have noticed that for Kant the capacity of subsuming under rules, that is, the power of judgment, is also what provides the Minor of a syllogism:

> In every syllogism I think first a rule (the major) through the understanding. Second, I subsume a cognition under the condition of the rule (the minor) by means of the power of judgment. Finally, I determine my cognition through the predicate of the rule (the conclusion), hence a priori through reason.
>
> (A304/B360–1)

His point can be clarified by considering the logical form of a categorical syllogism:

All S are P
R is S
R is P

The Major, as a universal categorical judgment of the understanding, is a rule in Kant's sense of 'rule', the subject term of which (S) is "the condition of the rule" while P is "the predicate of the rule". The Minor is a product of the power of judgment, one that subsumes a cognition (R) under this condition (S) as a particular instance that satisfies this condition. Finally, reason draws the conclusion from the premises a priori and thus determines that R is P.

We believe however that Kant's understanding of the categorical syllogism also contains the clue to understanding how the power of judgment subsumes something under *a concept*. Consider a syllogism that has as its Major an analytic judgment that expresses, as such, what is represented in that concept as the universal condition of something falling under that concept. Such a judgment may be dubbed 'a concept-rule' as it makes explicit in its condition (the subject term) what anything falling under that concept (the predicate term) must satisfy. Now, any concept can in principle be made into a concept-rule, and any use of a concept can be expressed in a categorical syllogism of this sort. The point was already implicit in our earlier example where the concept *ductile* gave rise to the rule "Whatever can be drawn out into a thin wire is ductile." This rule functioned as the Major in a syllogism, in which the Minor read "Gold can be drawn out into a thin wire", and in which is drawn the conclusion "Gold is ductile."

Consider now another example. If my concept of gold is that of a heavy, yellow, and soft metal, the subsumption effected in my judgment 'This ring is gold' can be made explicit in the following categorical syllogism:

Whatever is a heavy, yellow, soft metal is gold.
This ring is a heavy, yellow, soft metal.
This ring is gold.

What this categorical syllogism makes explicit is what is asserted in a particular real, empirical, and singular use to which the empirical concept *gold* is being put in subsuming some individual perceptually presented ring under this concept. That the use of the concept *gold* that this categorical syllogism makes explicit is real is reflected in its having as its Minor a synthetic judgment: the Minor's assertion that the individual perceptually presented ring satisfies the universal condition of the concept *gold* ('heavy, yellow, soft metal') is grounded, not in any relation of conceptual containment, but rather in that object's manifesting in our experience, and so in empirical intuition, its instantiation of this condition.

2. The Homogeneity Requirement, the Problem of the Schematism Chapter, and Transcendental Schemata

We turn now to the body of the Schematism. As we saw, Kant's concern in this chapter is "to deal with the sensible conditions under which alone" we can put the pure concepts of the understanding to real use. As will emerge, these sensible conditions are the schemata of the pure concepts of the understanding, or transcendental schemata, and these schemata meet this description as the sensible conditions under which alone, given the distinctive character of our sensibility, our power of judgment can subsume objects that are, or can be, given to us in sensible intuitions under the pure concepts of the understanding.

Kant opens the Schematism chapter by raising a problem: pure concepts of the understanding and sensible intuitions are entirely unhomogeneous; how then can objects be subsumed under these concepts? The aim of the present section is to explain the nature of this problem and to provide a sketch of how the Schematism chapter identifies the transcendental schemata – characterized as transcendental time-determinations – as the only representations that can solve it. Indeed, it is as the only representations that can solve this problem that these transcendental time-determinations constitute "the sensible conditions under which alone" we can put the pure concepts of the understanding to real use.

The problem with which Kant opens the Schematism is posed by the following requirement, referred to hereafter as 'the homogeneity requirement':

> In any subsumption of an object [*eines Gegenstandes*] under a concept, the representations of the former must be homogenous with the latter, i.e., the concept must contain that which is represented in the object [*Gegenstand*] that is to be subsumed under it, for that is just what is meant by the expression 'an object [*Gegenstand*] is contained under a concept'. Thus the empirical concept of a plate has homogeneity with the pure geometric concept of a circle, for the roundness that is thought in the former can be intuited in the latter.
>
> (A137/B176)

Recall that to subsume an object under a concept is, in an exercise of one's power of judgment, to make a true and warranted assertion that this object is contained under this concept – that is, that this concept contains "that which is represented in the object that is to be subsumed under it". Recall, too, that this last phrase reflects Kant's conception of an object, on which an object is a subject of power, considered insofar as it can be represented in a capacity of representation as the subject of some power. On Kant's account, a subject of power constitutes an object for a conceptual understanding only as what it can represent in its sensibility as the subject of some power. For an object to be contained under a concept, then, just is for that concept to contain what is contained in the sensible representation in relation to which a subject of power constitutes that object. The problem about the possibility of subsuming objects given in sensible intuition under the pure concepts of the understanding arises from the worry that the pure concepts of the understanding do not – indeed, cannot – contain "that which is represented in" these objects because these concepts, unlike sensible concepts, are "entirely unhomogenous" with all sensible intuitions, and so also with empirical intuitions (A137/B176).

Clarifying the nature both of this unhomogeneity and the problem it poses for the possibility of subsuming sensible intuitions under a pure concept of the understanding requires seeing that this problem is one that arises *in part* because such a concept is a pure concept, and thus requires, if it is to be used to subsume objects under it, that we be able to determine *on purely a priori grounds* a manifold given in a (perhaps merely possible) empirical intuition as one that meets, in some particular way, the universal condition specified in that concept. However, the purity of a concept, though necessary, is not *sufficient* to raise a problem about the possibility of subsuming sensible intuitions, and thereby empirical intuitions, under it. Such a problem arises only for the pure concepts of the understanding, and not for pure concepts generally (which include pure sensible concepts), because the former are purely intellectual and thus, of themselves, specify a universal condition of assertion that cannot be represented in any sensible intuition. This is, however, a difficult point, and in the service of clarifying it we do well to attend in some detail to the example Kant offers, immediately after stating the homogeneity requirement, of a concept that clearly meets this requirement. Now most scholars have taken the concept that Kant offers at A137/B176 as one that clearly meets the homogeneity requirement as the empirical concept *plate*. We suggest, however, that what he is offering as such an example is, rather, the geometric, and so pure sensible, concept *circle*. He offers this example in the service of, among other things, bringing out how such a concept, as a pure *sensible* concept, clearly meets the homogeneity requirement, despite being, like the pure concept of the understanding, purely a priori.

What makes a concept sensible is its having a content that derives from an operation of sensibility. As such, a sensible concept is a rule (assertion under a universal condition) with a universal condition the representation of which derives from operations of sensibility. For example, the empirical concept *plate* Kant invokes has as its content a universal condition – being round, flat, used to serve food, and so on – that derives from operations of sensibility that constitute empirical intuitions in and through which we represent these conditions *in concreto*. The geometric concept *circle* is not only sensible, but also pure, because its content derives solely from an operation of pure sensibility, and the universal condition of the concept *circle* – being a two-dimensional shape that can be described by moving a straight line around a fixed point – is represented in this operation, and so in a pure intuition of a circle. Now the concept *round* – which we may suppose is that of what has a two-dimensional shape with a continuous degree of curvature – is also sensible, and its universal condition can be contained in both pure and empirical intuition. This makes it possible to put the geometric concept *circle* to a use that is not only real, but also a priori, to subsume the object of any empirical concept *plate* that has roundness thought in it under this geometric concept, a use that can be expressed in the following categorical syllogism:

Whatever occupies a region of space that can be described by moving a straight line around a fixed point is circular.
Plates, being round, occupy a region of space that can be described . . .
Plates are circular.

Crucially, the Minor is a synthetic a priori cognition that is grounded in geometric insight into roundness as a proprium (i.e., a necessary and uniquely distinguishing accident) of a circle and so in a purely a priori synthetic cognition that any two-dimensional shape with a continuous rate of curvature is a circle. That this mathematical cognition, on Kant's account, is had in and through exhibiting roundness as a proprium of a circle *in pure intuition* explains why he tells us that what justifies us in asserting that the relevant empirical concept *plate* and the geometric concept *circle* are homogenous in the manner required for the subsumption of plates under the latter, is our ability to *intuit* the roundness that is thought in the former in the latter (A137/B176). Notice, too, that on the present reading Kant's example of a plate illustrates nicely his description of the homogeneity between a concept and the representations of an object that he says is required for the subsumption of that object under that concept. What it is for the object of the relevant empirical concept *plate* to be contained under the geometric concept *circle* – as one asserts in subsuming it under that concept – is for the latter concept to contain, synthetically, the mark *roundness* – something that we determine on purely priori grounds in achieving geometric insight. For this mark *roundness* is also contained in the relevant empirical concept *plate*.

Now let us consider in more detail how Kant presents the "entire unhomogeneity" between the pure concepts of the understanding and sensible intuitions, as well as the problem this unhomogeneity poses for subsuming appearances under these concepts. He characterizes this unhomogeneity as follows: "the pure concepts of the understanding are, in comparison with empirical (indeed in general sensible) intuitions, entirely unhomogenous, and can never be encountered in any intuition" (A137/B176). He then claims that this unhomogeneity raises a question about the possibility of the subsumption of empirical intuitions under these concepts:

Now how is the subsumption of the latter [sensible intuitions] under the former [the pure concepts of the understanding], thus the application of the category to appearances possible, since no one would say that the category, e.g., causality, could also be intuited through the senses and is contained in the appearance? This question, so natural and important, is really the cause that makes a transcendental doctrine of the power of judgment necessary, in order, namely, to show the possibility of applying the pure concepts of the understanding to appearances in general.

(A138/B177)

This problem is dire: unless we can solve it, we forfeit the a priori warrant to apply the categories to appearances (the undetermined objects of empirical intuition) that the transcendental deduction of the categories had defeasibly secured for them in the previous book of the Transcendental Analytic.

It is important to see that to assert the entire unhomogeneity between the pure concepts of the understanding and sensible intuition, and the consequent impossibility of encountering these concepts *in* any sensible intuition, is *not* to assert that these concepts cannot, *in any way*, be encountered through what is given to us in our sensible intuitions. Indeed, Kant implies that we *can* encounter the relation of causality in experience – for example, when he writes that the category of causality serves only for recognizing dynamical connection "where it is encountered in experience" (A770/B798).[6] Moreover, to deny that we can intuit the categories *through the senses*, or that the categories are contained in the appearance, is not to deny that we can intuit the categories *at all*. Indeed, on Kant's account, if we could not encounter the categories in experience, and thereby intuit them (if only a posteriori) through given appearances, we could not subsume any objects under them. For any such subsumption requires that we be able to adduce synthetic grounds for judging that an object realizes, in a particular case, the universal conditions that these concepts specify, and such grounds can be given to us only by appealing to a way in which that object is, or could be, given to us in experience.

Here, then, is what we propose to be Kant's line of thought. The categories are purely a priori concepts, so if the subsumption of appearances under them is to be possible, so that they are to be applicable to objects, we must be able to adduce synthetic and purely a priori grounds for this subsumption. But because the categories are purely intellectual, they cannot, as the concept *circle* can, be encountered in any sensible intuition. It follows, a fortiori, that we cannot *intuit* the categories purely a priori, as we can geometric concepts. And this is to say that we cannot adduce the purely a priori and synthetic grounds requisite for the categories to be applicable to the objects of our sensible intuition, in the distinctive way in which we can adduce such ground for geometric concepts. How, then, can we adduce for them the required grounds?

In providing his solution, Kant claims that the transcendental schemata are, given this entire unhomogeneity and the nature of our sensibility, the sole representations that could function as such grounds and thus mediate between the pure concepts of the understanding, on the one hand, and appearance, on the other, so as to make the subsumption of the latter under the former possible.

> Now it is clear that there must a third thing, which must stand in homogeneity with the category on the hand and the appearance on the other, and makes possible the application of the former to the latter. This mediating representation must be pure (without anything empirical) and yet *intellectual* on the one hand and *sensible* on the other. Such a representation is the *transcendental schema*.
>
> The concept of the understanding contains pure synthetic unity of the manifold in general. Time, as the formal condition of the manifold of inner sense, thus of the connection of all representations, contains an a priori manifold in pure intuition. Now a transcendental time-determination is homogeneous with the *category* (which constitutes its unity) insofar as it is *universal* and rests on a rule a priori. But it is on the other hand homogeneous with the *appearance* insofar as *time* is contained in every empirical representation of the manifold. Hence an application of the category to appearances becomes possible by means of the

transcendental time-determination which, as the schema of the concept of the understanding, mediates the subsumption of the latter under the former.

(A138–9/B138–9)

This is the first appearance, not only of the term 'transcendental schema', but of the term 'schema', in the Schematism. And the solution Kant here provides turns on his characterization of a transcendental schema as a transcendental time-determination, for it is as such a determination that a transcendental schema is homogeneous both with a category and with the appearance that corresponds to that category. The schema of substance, for example, is homogeneous with this category as "the persistence of the real in time, i.e., the representation of the real as the substratum of empirical time-determination in general, which therefore endures while everything else changes" (A144/B183). Moreover, Kant specifies that this homogeneity of the category and its schema consists in their both being universal and resting on a rule a priori. Both of these respects of homogeneity stand in need of clarification.

The universality of the transcendental time-determination, unlike that of a category, is one in respect, not of the objects of intuition in general (i.e., regardless of the form of that sensible intuition), but only of any appearance in general that is possible for us given only that we have time as the form of our inner sense. This means that the universal condition for the use of the category that the transcendental schema, as a transcendental time-determination, represents is not the universal condition of its logical use (one that this category itself specifies), but rather a universal (and, at the same time sensible) condition of the only real use to which we can put this category, namely, one that subsumes the manifold of an empirical intuition that can be given to us under this category. Nonetheless, in being universal to all appearances that are possible for us, a transcendental schema differs from the schema of a pure sensible concept, which essentially represents some particular way in which the forms of our sensible intuition can be delimited in an act of pure a priori imagination, and thus is not universal to all appearances that are possible for us. And since it is only insofar as a synthetic unity is a particular way in which the manifold given in the forms of our sensible intuition can be delimited that this unity is one that we can encounter in a sensible intuition, the universality shared by a category and its schema is one that precludes their being encountered in a sensible intuition. This explains Kant's remark that a transcendental schema, unlike the schema of a sensible concept, "can never be brought to any image" (A142/B181).

Consider next Kant's cryptic, but crucial, claim that a transcendental time-determination, like a category, "rests on a rule a priori". We propose that this amounts to the claim that a transcendental time-determination, like a category, derives its objective validity a priori from a rule that specifies it as a universal condition under which a sensible intuition relates, in cognition, to an object. In the case of a transcendental time-determination, the rule in question is the synthetic and purely a priori judgment that asserts that a transcendental time-determination of appearances in general that can be given to us makes them subsumable under the category that constitutes the unity of that transcendental time-determination. Indeed, this rule constitutes the Minor of a categorical syllogism that makes explicit the universal condition or ground of the subsumability of appearances that can be given to us under a category. Take the following case:

What can serve only as subject, and never as predicate, is substance.
The real, as it persists in time and is the substratum of empirical time-determination in general, can serve only as subject, and never as predicate.
The real, as it persists in time . . . is substance.

The Minor asserts that the real, as it constitutes appearance that persists as the substratum of empirical time determination in general, can serve only as subject, and never as predicate – and thus satisfies the universal condition of being subsumable under the category of substance.

But in identifying the transcendental time-determinations that correspond to the categories as their schemata, Kant is asserting more than that they can serve as sensible conditions for any real use to which we can put the categories. He is also claiming that – given the nature of our sensibility – it is necessarily true that *only* they can serve as such conditions. Since appearances can be given to us, as subjects of cognition, only through our inner sense, and time is the form of our inner sense, time, and only time, is a sensible condition common to any and all appearances that can be given to us. The transcendental schemata, then, since they are to have the homogeneity with the categories requisite to mediate the application of these concepts to all possible objects of our sensible intuition, can only be transcendental time-determinations. And Kant is advancing this claim as the content of a synthetic and purely a priori judgment concerning what belongs to the formal possibility of our experience in general.

3. Conclusion

We have examined the case Kant makes, in the first four paragraphs of the Schematism, for identifying transcendental time-determinations as the only representations that, given the nature of our sensibility, can make possible our use of the pure concepts of the understanding to subsume objects under these concepts. This case forms the core of the Schematism's characterization of these representations as the sensible conditions of any real use to which we can put these concepts, that is, their schemata. It would prove instructive to explicate the remainder of the Schematism – especially its distinction between the transcendental schemata and the schemata of sensible concepts – in light of what we have seen. Doing so would help bring into clear relief just how Paragraphs 8–16 provide brief characterizations of the particular schemata of different pure concepts of the understanding, as well as how in light of these characterizations the final three paragraphs expand on the solution provided in the fourth paragraph; these paragraphs serve to elaborate how the transcendental schemata both realize our capacity for theoretical cognition of things and in doing so restrict the scope of this capacity to possible objects of our experience. But providing such an explication is a task that will have to wait for another occasion.

Notes

1 This is a collaborative work; the order of authorship is alphabetical. We thank Lanier Anderson, Christian Beyer, Thomas Christiano, Mirja Hartimo, Frode Kjosavik, Toni Kannisto, Olli Koistinen, and Mark Timmons for helpful discussion and/or comments. This chapter is a product of the research project "The Possibility of Metaphysics in the Age of Science" we pursued at the Center for Advanced Study in Oslo, Norway, during the 2015–16 academic year; we gratefully acknowledge the Center for its support. A note on translations: we started with the Cambridge translation, but in many cases made some revisions.
2 The force of 'theoretical' here is captured by contrast, not with ordinary cognition, but with practical cognition: theoretical cognition is cognition of what is the case, as against cognition of what we are to make the case through our use of our practical reason to determine our capacity of choice.
3 Ernst Robert Curtis (1914), and following him Kemp Smith (1918: 336), read Kant as guilty of conflating the subsumption of a cognition under a rule that is the Major of a categorical syllogism (and so a judgment), with the subsumption of an object under a concept (which they take to be an achievement of the imagination). They thus claim that the sense of 'subsumption' Kant employs at A132/B171 is different from that which he employs in the body of the Schematism. And the charge of this equivocation is a key part of Kemp Smith's scathing, but as we will see entirely unfair, dismissal of Kant's description of the project of

the Schematism in terms of subsumption as "completely misleading," "artificial," and betraying the unfortunate influence his "logical architectonic is constantly exercising on his Critical principles" (p. 334f). Henry Allison thinks that Kant's use of the term 'subsumption' undergoes this shift, but that the shift reflects, not a conflation, but an attempt to bring out a useful analogy between the use of a concept in a syllogism and that in subsuming an object (2004: 212f.). The reading we offer has the virtue of making these uses univocal, and helps make clear the cogency of the way in which Kant frames his critical philosophy within traditional Aristotelian logic.

4 Here, and throughout this chapter, 'object' is used to translate '*Gegenstand*'. As we understand Kant's use of this term, a *Gegenstand* is the subject of a power – and, as such, what is real – considered insofar as it is or can be represented in a capacity of representation as the subject of some power. What makes a subject of power a *Gegenstand*, then, is this relation it bears to some particular capacity of representation as what is suited to being, in this way, represented positively in respect of its reality in an operation of that capacity. Indeed, in the sense in which Kant uses 'real' and 'reality', what makes something real is its being a subject of power, so that the nature and degree of reality is a function of the nature and degree of some power.

5 A real use of the pure concepts of understanding may be one in which we determine an object of an experience that is possible for us only in respect of what belongs to the formal possibility of given appearances constituting an experience that is possible for us. One such use is the use to which we put the category of quantity in pure mathematics: in this use, we determine purely a priori ways in which the forms of our sensibility can be delimited, and thereby the possibility of empirical intuitions with sensible forms that instantiate these delimitations, though only as such; to this extent, pure mathematics determines the objects of the experience we would have were we to subsume the appearances that are the objects of such empirical intuitions under the dynamical categories.

6 One encounters causality in experience when, in making a judgment of experience one is immediately conscious of a succession of token appearances, as they are given in one's empirical intuition as instantiating the relation of cause and effect. This judging is what constitutes the subsuming of an individual object of experience under the category of cause (*Prol* AA 4: 300–1). This act of judging is directed immediately to an object as one is conscious of it in intuition, and thus conjoined with an act of imagination. But, *pace* Kemp Smith (cf. n3), what constitutes this subsumption is the act of judging, not an act of imagination.

References

Allison, H. (2004) *Kant's Transcendental Idealism*, 2nd ed., New Haven: Yale University Press.
Curtis, E.R. (1914) "Das Schematismuskapitel in der Kritik der reinen Vernunft," *Kant-Studien* 19: 338–66.
Kemp Smith, N. (1918) *A Commentary to Kant's Critique of Pure Reason*, London: Palgrave Macmillan. Reprinted 2003, London: Palgrave Macmillan.

Further Reading

Since the appearance of the *Critique of Pure Reason*, its Schematism chapter has received attention well out of proportion to its length, but entirely appropriate in light of its importance. One can get a sense of the range of different treatments it has received, and the remarkable lack of convergence among them, by consulting M. Pendlebury, "Making Sense of Kant's Schematism," *Philosophy and Phenomenological Research* 55(4) (1995): 777–97. For a proposal regarding how the Schematism is to be understood in the context of the larger argument of the Transcendental Analytic that is informed by a deep appreciation of how Kant frames this argument in terms of traditional Aristotelian logic, see B. Longuenesse, *Kant and the Capacity to Judge* (Princeton: Princeton University Press, 1998), especially pp. 243–7. Due to space limitations, we have said nothing about the crucial sixth and seventh paragraphs of the Schematism. Here, again, the aforementioned book by Longuenesse deserves special mention, as much of the best recent work has been inspired by its groundbreaking treatment of the Transcendental Analytic. One recent book that provides a useful entry to many of the interpretative issues posed by Kant's theory of the imagination is R.P. Horstmann's *Kant's Power of Imagination* (New York: Cambridge University Press, 2018). For a helpful recent discussion of Kant's conception of an image, and of images (as against intuitions) as products of imagination, see B. Tracz, "Imagination and the Distinction Between Image and Intuition in Kant," *Ergo* 6(38) (2020): 1087–120. The works to which this article refers make up much of the most useful recent secondary literature that bears directly on the interpretation of Kant's account of schemata.

10

THE TRANSCENDENTAL DIALECTIC

Michelle Grier

***

1. Introduction

In the *Critique of Pure Reason* Kant offers a transitional chapter, "On the Distinction of All Objects in General into Phenomena and Noumena" (A235–59/B294–315). There, Kant cautions the reader to keep in mind the results of the Analytic, those which have secured our entitlement to knowledge:

> We have now not only traveled through the land of the understanding, and carefully inspected each part of it, but we have also surveyed it, and determined the place for each thing in it. But this land is an island, and enclosed in unalterable boundaries by nature itself. It is the land of truth (an enchanting name), surrounded by a broad and stormy ocean, the true seat of illusion, where many a fog bank and rapidly melting iceberg pretend to be new lands and, ceaselessly deceiving with empty hopes the voyager looking around for new discoveries, entwine him in adventures from which he can never escape and yet also never bring to an end.
>
> (A236/B295)

The odd, almost threatening, depiction of our epistemological predicament, its fragility and its vulnerability to deception, illusion, and enchantment, seem inconsonant with the deliberative, authoritative limitations imposed on knowledge throughout the earlier portions of the Doctrine of the Elements. Kant thinks he has already shown that knowledge is limited to possible human experience, that such experience itself is made possible by certain subjective ("transcendental") cognitive conditions, and that these conditions provide the boundaries within which our faculties (here, sensibility and understanding) can be employed. Indeed, throughout the Transcendental Analytic we were repeatedly instructed to accept these limitations of human knowledge. Any attempt to transgress them by judging about Objects in General/things in themselves, any "transcendental use of the understanding," involves a misemployment of concepts.[1] In such cases, according to Kant, we fall victim to judgmental errors, deceptions, subreptions.[2] It was on this account that General Metaphysics, or Ontology, the discipline concerned to make a priori judgments about Objects in General, was shown in the Analytic to be dialectical (A247/B304). Such errors are traced back to

     DOI: 10.4324/9781003406617-14

the methodological standpoint known as Transcendental Realism and its characteristic conflation of appearances and things in themselves. The transcendental distinction between appearances and things in themselves (more generally, transcendental idealism) promised once and for all to provide a tool/method sufficient to avoid deception and judgmental error.

As we read the passage just cited, however, we come to see that our victory is incomplete. Although great effort was successfully expended identifying the conditions and boundaries of *sensibility* and *understanding* (and thus, together, *experience*), reason now poses a unique challenge to itself. For pure reason now has the task of securing its *own* boundaries, even though doing so, as we shall see, is in many ways against its nature. In this reason inevitably comes to learn that it, along with sensibility and understanding, needs a "discipline" (A710/B738). Reason learns this for itself because despite knowing the boundaries of *experience* it finds itself in conflicts "with itself" over *non-experiential issues*:

> Reason is driven by a propensity of its nature to go beyond its use in experience, to venture to the outermost bounds of all cognition by means of mere ideas in a pure use, and to find peace only in the completion of its circle in a self-subsisting systematic whole.

> (A798/B826)

It is this, "pure" reason's lingering brashness, which is at issue in the Dialectic. Whereas the Transcendental Analytic was primarily devoted to curbing the pretensions of the *understanding*, the Transcendental Dialectic will be devoted to curbing the pretensions of *reason* (disciplining it). Thus, Kant will be concerned not simply with Ontology, but with *Special* Metaphysics, those doctrines centering on the specifically rational ideas of allegedly transcendent objects or substances: the Soul, the World, and God. Here, the restriction or self-discipline of pure reason is all the more challenging, since we find ourselves increasingly farther adrift from the "island" of the understanding, and we have now entered waters wherein sensible orientation and appeal to the conditions of experience will be increasingly irrelevant. Accordingly, in the Dialectic Kant suggests that even if one accepts the transcendental distinction between appearances and things in themselves, one still has the unresolved problem of *reason's* pretensions to transcendent knowledge of things in themselves.

2. Reason's Lust and Hope

In the Discipline, Kant suggests that there are two natural forces or passions which attend to human reason's drive to pursue transcendent knowledge: Lust (for knowledge) and Hope (A708–97/B736–822). It is reason's lust for knowledge, its "unquenchable desire" for completeness of knowledge, for a resting place, peace, unconditioned systematic unity, that makes its "discipline" all the more challenging, for "reason does not gladly accept the restraint in the paroxysms of its lust for speculative expansion, to the discipline of abstinence" (A789/B814). This lust for knowledge, the desire for completeness, is attended by the "hope" (the "fantastical hope," the "empty hope") that we shall achieve this (A727/B755, A742/B770, A743/B771). Little wonder, then, that Kant is concerned with such questions as: "What can I know?", "What may I hope?"[3] Together, it is this dogmatic desire for a resting place for thought, and this hope of achieving it, which ceaselessly entrap the unsuspecting voyager in the passage with which we began. This indeed is the "fate of reason" presented in the Preface to the *Critique of Pure Reason* (Cf. Avii-viii). Even given this fateful confluence of hope and desire, Kant is well aware that "reason" in its natural progress is much too self-correcting to take human hopes and desires to *justify*, by themselves alone, the presumption of transcendent insight, let alone to show that the ultimate explanation or ground which we seek and hope for and desire is actually given in itself, independently of us, that it is objectively real. An investigation into the transcendental ground for reason's presumptions is thus in order.

In the Introduction to the Transcendental Dialectic, Kant introduces reason as the third (highest) capacity. Kant links the use of reason up with an impulse to seek ultimate justifications/explanations (A303–5/B360–62). Considered logically, Reason is the formal capacity for making mediate or syllogistic inferences. Kant connects the formal or logical procedure of reason up to a search for "conditions" or explanations. By its own logic, reason proceeds indefinitely in search of ever-expanding knowledge. Kant therefore takes reason to be guided by the demand for the complete set, or totality, of all conditions: the "unconditioned." Kant thus tells us that reason is guided by the following maxim: *Find for the conditioned knowledge given through the understanding the unconditioned whereby its unity is brought to completion* (hereafter P_1).[4] P_1 expresses the demand for a systematic unity of thought, a *unity of reason*. Reason seeks to order, unify systematically, and bring to completion the knowledge given through the understanding. However, in its logical function, this is merely a *maxim* of pure reason, a "subjective law for the orderly management of the possessions of the understanding" (Cf. A306–09/B363.) Kant thus insists that P_1 announces nothing "objective"; it prescribes merely that we *seek* the unconditioned, the complete explanation, the systematic unification of knowledge. Nevertheless, Kant argues that reason's pretensions, its desires and hopes, are grounded in "transcendental illusion," which is endemic to human reason and which leads us to take the preceding subjective maxim to be another, a metaphysical principle. Thus, Kant suggests that in its efforts to undertake the *prescription to seek the* unconditioned, reason assumes that the unconditioned is *given*: *If the Conditioned is given, the entire series of conditions and therewith the absolute totality is also given* (hereafter P_2). Kant calls this the "supreme principle of pure reason." It is also illusory, for the "unconditioned" is not an object which ever could be given to or known by us.

Transcendental illusion is a "natural and unavoidable" illusion which "even after it has ceased to beguile still continues to delude [*tauscht*] though not to deceive [*betrugt*] us, and which though capable of being rendered harmless can never be eradicated (A422/B450). Its unavoidable status involves an allegedly inevitable tendency to hypostatize the subjectively necessary principles and interests of reason and to posit them as objective ends towards which we aspire (A297/B353; A792/B820). As Kant elsewhere puts it, "[t]he transcendental attempts of pure reason [. . .] are all conducted within the real medium of dialectical illusion i.e. the subjective which offers itself to or even forces itself upon reason as objective" (A792/B820). Kant accordingly defines Dialectic as the "Logic of illusion"; its purpose is to "expose the illusion of transcendent judgments" (A298/B355).

The assumption that the unconditioned is given problematically underlies all the arguments of Special Metaphysics. Indeed, the Kantian theory of ideas is essentially linked up with this, for the movement from the formal demand for ultimate explanations to the ideas of the soul, world, and God are said by Kant to be attempts to think the unconditioned in various ways. More specifically, he suggests the idea of the soul is the idea of the unconditioned in relation to thought in general, the idea of world allegedly is that idea in relation to empirical thought, and the Ideal (the idea of God) is a way of thinking the unconditioned in relation to pure thought (A397). For Kant, the ideas are the inevitable products of reason's natural progress towards "complete" knowledge. This progress is aided by the postulation of metaphysical (and not merely logical) grounds/explanations, with the result that the ideas appear to be objects given to reason independently of any experience. Indeed, this is one of Kant's most often repeated complaints, that the ideas are mere "fictions of the brain", "empty thought entities", "pseudo-ideas," ones inextricably bound up with transcendental illusion. Yet, as we shall see, Kant does not ultimately reject the ideas. Instead, he adopts a strategy that involves assigning to the ideas an indispensably necessary "regulative role". For the present, we may simply note that, along with the ideas, Kant subsequently assigns this same indispensably necessary status to P_2. Kant tells us that not only is reason's *prescription to seek* the unconditioned (P_1) unavoidable, and indispensably necessary, but so too is the *transcendental illusion* itself, and with it, the assumption that the unconditioned is given (P_2) (cf. A651/B679).[5]

Why, given the aforementioned and established limitation of knowledge to appearances, should we accept Kant's claim that we *must* assume a principle (P_2) that completely violates those limits, especially given that P_2 is the transcendental ground to which all metaphysical error seems to be traced? One might suggest that P_2 is a kind of application condition for P_1.[6] In this sense the assumption that the unconditioned is given is inseparable from the ongoing (and I take it historical) project of knowledge acquisition. In connection with this, Kant suggests that the idea of the absolutely unconditioned acts as the imaginary focal point towards which our collective ("human") reason aspires.[7] Indeed, if we accept P_1, if we agree, that is, that we ought to follow P_1, and if indeed we are enjoined by reason itself to do this, then we must be assuming that we *can* in some relevant sense actualize our goals. Without P_2, it seems, our theoretical/speculative *hopes* for a complete systematically unified whole of knowledge would have no basis.

Even apart from this, Kant has deep theoretical reasons for "defending" the necessity of the very robust idea of the unconditioned. His reasons for doing so are similar to those offered in the explication of the necessity of the concept of the thing in itself. In the Transcendental Analytic, Kant considers what he takes to be a common dogmatic assumption – that we can use the *understanding alone* (independently of sensibility) to access a noumenal world (A250). Kant's claim is that, because we can think beyond (in abstraction from) sensibility, we can and must form a problematic concept of the thing in itself (noumenon in the negative sense). The problem is that by a certain "*deception [Tauschung]*" we are led to think we thereby have access to non-sensible objects (noumena in the positive sense). This is an error, as we have seen. Kant's view is that I cannot help but "think" the thing in itself, despite the fact that, as a merely problematic concept, there is no object corresponding to it; it is, famously, a concept without intuition, and is thus empty. The unavoidability and necessity that nevertheless attaches to the *thought* of the thing in itself is accounted for by noting that the concept is methodologically entailed by the consideration of things as appearance (B307).[8] Kant tells us that the concept of the thing in itself "is not invented arbitrarily, but is rather connected with the limitation of sensibility" (A255/B311). Even so, as a "boundary concept," its use is merely negative.[9]

The concept of the thing in itself is also essential to Kant's transcendental idealism in another way, for, as a *boundary concept*, it serves a double purpose. First of all, it sets the limits to sensible intuition/sensibility, by circumscribing the sphere of its (sensibility's) proper employment.[10] The results of the Transcendental Aesthetic illuminate these limits of sensibility and their parameters (space and time). The point here, as in the *Dissertation*, is that judgmental error (subreption) arises whenever we attempt to apply, say, spatio-temporal predicates to concepts of non-sensible "objects", as when for example we ask whether the "world in general" has a beginning in time, or find ourselves bedeviled by how many angels can dance on the head of a pin (cf. A256/B312). Second, and perhaps more interestingly, in setting limits to sensibility, the understanding is *at the same time* hitting up against/discovering *its own* limits, for, as we have seen, Kant claims repeatedly throughout the Analytic that the categories, independently of any sensible manifold (the "unschematized categories"), are merely empty forms of thinking and yield by themselves alone, no knowledge. Although the understanding enjoys a standpoint from which we identify the limits of sensibility, in abstracting from the sensible form and content of knowledge, it lacks any object upon which to execute its function; it essentially finds itself in an empty lot. As Kant puts it,

> [n]ow in this way our understanding acquires a negative expansion, i.e. it is not limited by sensibility, but rather limits it by calling things in themselves (not considered as appearances) noumena. But it also immediately sets boundaries for itself, not cognizing these things through categories, hence merely thinking them under the name of an unknown something.
>
> (A256/B312)

Similar considerations apply to the idea of the unconditioned, which is clearly a boundary concept. Just as the thought of appearances methodologically entails the consideration of something that is "not" an appearance (a negative judgment), so too, the thought of something as conditioned methodologically entails the thought of something "not" conditioned – hypostatically, the unconditioned. The problem, analogous to the issue with respect to the understanding/thing in itself, is that by a certain (in this case) *illusion* [*Schein*] reason cannot help but posit the unconditioned as already objective and *given*. Although we can avoid being deceived by it (avoid drawing faulty, subreptive judgments characteristic of metaphysics in general/Ontology), the illusion itself remains, and indeed, enjoys a respectable status as a subjectively necessary guiding principle in relation to the idea of a form of a whole of knowledge, that "self-subsisting systematic whole" (A798/B826). Thus, as with the concept of the thing in itself, the idea of the unconditioned is not an arbitrary or invented idea, but one (in this case) inextricably connected up with the limitation of human experience altogether (sensibility *and* understanding). As with his characterization of the experience of the understanding as it feels itself freed from the constraints of sense, Kant frequently characterizes reason's expansionary propensities in terms of a "freedom" from (not merely sense, as with the understanding) but *experience altogether*. Yet this expansion of reason at the same time involves an element of humiliation: "It is humiliating for human reason that it accomplishes nothing in its pure use, and even requires a discipline to check its extravagances and avoid the deceptions that come from them" (A795/B823; cf. A710/B738). This kind of "phenomenology" of the experience of reason bears some obvious resemblances to the experience of the sublime.[11] Regardless of this, in the *Critique*, the three chapters on the dialectical inferences of pure reason (the Antinomies, the Paralogisms, the Ideal) chronicle reason's experience as it gets humiliated in its transcendent efforts.

3. The Pseudo-Empirical Idea of the World: Rational Cosmology

The cosmological debates concerning the "world" enact the theatrical example of the way in which our faculties seemingly come into conflict with one another when moving beyond experience. Kant argues that each of the historical conflicts in cosmology arises whenever we try to think the sensible "world as a whole," and he thinks that the traditional cosmological debates presuppose this notion of a world, together with the illusory postulation of it as given.[12] According to Kant, all the antinomies are instantiations of the following dialectical syllogism:

1. If the conditioned is given, the entire series of all conditions is likewise given (P_2).
2. Objects of the senses are given as conditioned.
3. Therefore, the *entire series of all conditions of objects of the sense is already given* (A498/B526).

Compelled by the illusory principle that the unconditioned is given (P_2), it is concluded that the *entire series* of all conditions of *appearances* (i.e. the world) is already given. The problem is that there is (A479/B509) no given or givable object that corresponds to this idea. Any attempt to acquire knowledge of such a "pseudo- object" thus proceeds by a transcendental employment of concepts. Insofar as so much has been written on the details relating to the specific antinomial conflicts, in what follows, I shall consider the details of the arguments very generally.

Kant identifies four conflicts in the field of cosmology: (1) the debate about the finitude vs. the infinitude of the world in space and time, (2) the clash between the demand for some necessarily simple being vs. the defense of infinite divisibility, (3) the Freedom vs. Determinism debate, and (4) the arguments for and against Necessary Being. In each of these cases, according to Kant, the thesis arguments opt for intelligible beginnings and express the "dogmatic" hope and desire for a resting place for thought. Towards this, the proponents of the thesis positions deploy intellectual arguments deduced from considerations about the world in general to find the resting place that is demanded by reason's desire for complete knowledge. The antitheses counter that any attempt to think the world whole as *spatio-temporal*, any effort to restrain reason from transgressing the field of experi-ence, requires the denial of the theses' conclusions. What we presumably find in each of these cases is a conflict between pure reason's subjectively necessary demands on the one hand (theses), and the formal conditions of experience on the other (antitheses). In the Antinomies, the clash between different norms for thinking the world-whole is fueled by the uniquely problematic status of the idea itself. Note first that the idea of the world (the totality of all appearances and their connections) can be thought in one of two different ways, as an intelligible or a spatio-temporal object.[13] The antinomial conflicts in each case exploit the ambiguity in this mutually shared idea.

The first two mathematical antinomies concern disputes about the relation between *the world or objects in the world* on the one hand, and *space/time*, on the other. The first antinomy concerns the issue of whether the world is finite or infinite in space and time. The thesis position argues that indeed, the world must have some first beginning and must be limited in space. The antithesis posi-tion opposes this, arguing instead that the world is coextensive with infinite space and time. The second antinomy pits the proponents of simplicity against those for infinite divisibility. The thesis argument defends the necessity of some absolutely simple being, whereas the antithesis position remains within space and time. Both sides are false; they are to be rejected not, however, because of the content of their conclusions, but because both sides to the dispute share assumptions which are groundless and without justification. Kant's own "Critical" objection involves undermining the proofs without making any claims about the constitution of the object under consideration (A389). In the case of the Antinomies it seems clear that each side to the dispute assumes that "There is a world," that it is an object and that it is given as a whole. But even this presupposition is only an instantiation of the more generally shared presupposition by all the metaphysicians, that the "uncon-ditioned is given" (P_2).

The second set of antinomies (conflicts three and four), the so-called dynamical antinomies, provide an interesting transition from the mathematical antinomies to the later more "transcendent" disciplines centering on the soul and God. The third antinomy displays the freedom–determinism debate, that is whether we must posit transcendental freedom in addition to mechanistic causal-ity, or whether we must stay within nature's own resources. The fourth antinomy exhibits the conflict between those who argue for the necessity of some Necessary Being, and those who, on the contrary, argue on behalf of contingency. Operating with the same shared conception of the world, each party to the dispute exploits the ambiguity in the idea. The theses emphasize intellec-tual beginnings (freedom, Necessary Being), and seek empirically unconditioned conditions. The antitheses seek to remain within nature's resources, and reject any appeal to intelligible grounds.

Kant states that here both positions are compatible, that is both positions could be *true* without conflict. This resolution clearly draws on the fact that the *thesis* positions are not (as happened in the mathematical antinomies) really arguing about any kind of empirical object at all. Neither "transcendental freedom" nor a "Necessary Being" is something that presumes to be encountered or given in sensibility (space and time).

In reflecting back on the Antinomies, Kant claims that all of the antinomial conflicts are generated because the rational cosmologists (on both sides) begin (and proceed) from a transcendentally realistic framework. The transcendental distinction between appearances and things in themselves allows Kant to reveal that a conflict seemingly unavoidable was grounded in this misunderstanding. This is particularly true with respect to the mathematical antinomies:

> It is worrisome and depressing that there should be an antithetic of pure reason at all, and that pure reason, though it represents the supreme court of justice for all disputes, should still come into conflict with itself. We had such an apparent antithetic of reason before us [. . .] but it turned out that it rested on a misunderstanding, namely that of taking, in accord with common prejudice, appearances for things in themselves, and then demanding an absolute completeness in their synthesis. [. . .] There was thus in that case no **real contradiction of reason** with itself in the propositions "The series of appearances given in themselves has an absolutely first beginning" and "The series is absolutely and in itself without any beginning".
>
> (A740–1/B768–9)

Kant's final pronouncement was that the antinomial conflicts, at first so vexing, could be resolved by way of the transcendental distinction between things in themselves and appearances, and in such a way as to disclose the fact that all along they were enacting the theatrical spectacle of a mock combat. Although the resolution to the dynamical antinomies clearly depends upon the transcendental distinction between appearances and things in themselves, in this case the distinction provides a refuge for dogmatic reason against the assaults of the skeptics. According to the Critical observer, the proponents are not in intention arguing about the same thing at all. Reason thus reconciles itself to itself by using the distinction between appearances and things in themselves, and providing a space for pure reason.

4.   The Pseudo-Rational Ideas of Soul and God: Rational Psychology and Rational Theology

It is against the background theory of illusion and the ideas that we can consider Kant's assessment of the disciplines of Rational Psychology and Rational Theology. Again, Kant offers objections from the standpoint of the Critical observer, "critical objections" (A389). His aim is to undermine the arguments about the soul and God without asserting anything whatsoever about the alleged objects themselves, that is, to show that in the argument something has been assumed that renders the argument ineffective. I have suggested in connection with the Antinomies that at its most general, the underlying assumption that characterizes all of the disciplines of rationalist metaphysics is the view that the unconditioned is given (P_2).

In the Paralogisms, the syllogistic conclusions have to do with the nature and constitution of the Soul. Here, the dogmatic rationalist argues on behalf of the substantiality, the simplicity, identity, independence, and so on of the Soul, and thus satisfies reason's desire for a final resting place for thought. Its conformity to the maxim (P_1) coincides with a dogmatic presumption to have some purely rational insight into the constitution of the soul, presented to reason a priori as an objectively real object. This generates the assumption that substantive claims can be made a priori about the transcendental subject (the I of apperception). According to Kant, what the rational psychologist is *really* seeking is the "unconditioned unity of the thinking subject itself", the unconditioned which grounds all thought in general (A334/B391). As with the arguments about the world, one problem has to do with the hypostatization of a mere idea, the representation of it as having objective reality. Kant puts the hypostatization of the soul in a number of ways.[14] In so doing, Kant suggests, the metaphysician, beguiled by transcendental illusion, falls victim to dialectical forms of thinking/ judging, that is, the transcendental misemployment of the understanding. Or, as Kant elsewhere puts it, the paralogistic arguments display the "subreption of the hypostatized consciousness [*apperceptionis substantiatae*]" (A402).

Insofar as the Paralogistic arguments are not two-sided disputes, what we find are a group of direct arguments for a set of propositions (e.g. "The soul is a substance"), together with assessments or analyses from the Critical observer behind the scenes. The critical diagnosis is essentially the same as in the Antinomies: reason, in accordance with its inherent illusion seeks to achieve the expansion and completion of knowledge by positing its own subjective interests as objects having objective reality, as theoretical ends towards which we ought to aspire. On the basis of this, the rationalist metaphysician in his efforts to make judgments about the pseudo-object, falls into a transcendental (dialectical) misemployment of concepts. The nest of dialectical errors include here, as in the Antinomies: (1) taking subjective conditions and necessities to be objective, (2) taking the subjectively necessary formal ideas of reason to have objective reality (i.e. to hypostatize them), (3) attempting to acquire a priori knowledge through a misuse of the categories.

Much the same can be said about the fate of Rational Theology. Kant argues that the idea of God is yet another (and the highest and most abstract) way of "thinking" the unconditioned. In Kant's view the idea of God (a supremely real and necessary Being) is a way of thinking the unconditioned condition of all pure thought (A397). The idea of God is obviously even more untethered and distant from experience than is the idea of the Soul. As such, Kant refers to it as an Ideal (A570/B598). The Ideal, albeit a pseudo-rational idea, issues into an exemplar. In this Ideal (the idea of God) is distinct from the idea of the soul insofar as it is the idea of a thoroughly determined (or at least determinable) and completely individuated concept of an object.[15]

Kant famously critiques three traditional arguments for the existence of God: the Ontological, the Cosmological, and the Physico-theological. The general thrust of Kant's criticisms is well known: the Ontological argument generates its conclusion ("God exists") by taking (erroneously) "existence" to be a real, determining predicate. Moreover, insofar as Kant seems to suggest that the Cosmological and Physico-theological arguments presuppose the Ontological one, once the dialectical nature of the Ontological argument is exposed, these latter argumentative types collapse for lack of grounding.[16] Rather than attack the conclusions or propositions (e.g. "God exists"), however, a critical objection merely aims to explain and describe, from an implicit critical standpoint, the argumentative strategies, the hypostatizations and subreptions that are involved, and thus seeks to nullify the success or efficacy of the argument without taking any position whatsoever about whether God exists or does not. Thus, here, as with the soul, Kant's objective is to demonstrate the nest of dialectical errors involved in the arguments. Kant's critical analysis, therefore, never ventures to claim that, for example, "The soul is *not* a substance" or that "God does not exist". Rather, as we have seen, Kant merely takes himself to be demonstrating that the arguments are ill grounded and dialectical.

Given Kant's own critical assessment of the psychological and theological arguments, it might seem that Kant is aligning himself with those who would reject these propositions. Indeed, it does seem here that we have a genuine conflict (either God exists or God does not exist). Interestingly, however, Kant does not take this line of argument. Instead, he claims that even here there may be, ultimately, no true conflict of reason with itself:

> There is no contradiction if, say, it is asserted theistically **There is a highest being** and asserted atheistically on the contrary, **There is no highest being**, or when it is asserted in psychology, "Everything that thinks is of absolutely persistent unity and therefore distinct from a transitory material unity", against which someone else asserts, "The soul is not an immaterial unity and cannot be exempted from all transitoriness." For the object of the question is here free of anything foreign that contradicts its nature, and the understanding is concerned only with things in themselves and not appearances. There would thus certainly be a genuine conflict here, if only pure reason had anything to say on the negative side that would approximate the ground for an assertion.
>
> (A741/B769)

Does pure reason have anything to say on the negative side? Kant's analyses of the metaphysical arguments, his claim that they all rest on a transcendental illusion and the attendant hypostatization of the ideas, his scathing rejection of the "transcendental misemployment of concepts" in the arguments suggest that he eschews the use of the ideas. Note however that although Kant clearly wants to curb the pretensions of reason, and to demonstrate the dialectical nature of the inferences about the soul or God, he does not dismiss these ideas altogether; indeed, he wants to defend (along with P_2), their indispensable nature. The ideas, and especially the Ideal, persist as subjective directives that are essential in a number of ways. The first has to do with the important role of the principles and ideas of reason in theoretical pursuits. In this, the ideas of reason are indispensable in guiding our speculative attempts towards the expansion of knowledge in accordance with reason's theoretical demand for completeness.[17]

However, the ideas also play a defensive role in guarding and protecting reason from skeptical attacks, in neutralizing them. In this connection, Kant defends the use of metaphysical propositions as "transcendental hypotheses," which serve a role both theoretically and practically, in the service of reason's final ends. Although any hypothesis of pure reason (any so-called transcendental hypothesis) has only a very limited and specific ("polemical") use, it is a use essential for protecting reason's rights to honor its demand for the unconditioned. Hypotheses of this sort, Kant tells us, are "allowed in the field of pure reason only as weapons of war, not for grounding a right but only defending it" (A77/B806). Such transcendental hypotheses are weapons of war for pure reason in the sense that they prevent the skeptics from themselves becoming dogmatic. Thus the "two cardinal propositions of pure reason: 'There is a God' and 'There is a future life' can continue to guide us (regulatively) in our efforts towards the speculative ends prescribed and demanded by reason" (A742/B77). Although skepticism does, on Kant's view, mark an advance from dogmatism (rouses us from our dogmatic slumbers), it grants us no alternative rights; it provides us with no ultimate explanations, or resting place. It does not quell reason's desire. Despite his critique of metaphysical dogmatism, such dogmatism, reinterpreted "regulatively," serves a critical purpose in protecting reason from any totalizing humiliation, as it seeks its aims and establishes its rights. The transcendental hypotheses expressing reason's desire for closure/completeness serve as weapons against the attacks of the skeptics. Despite the problematic nature of the ideas of the Soul and God, these cannot be shown to be impossible by the skeptics. Recognizing the "boundaries" here is all the more important, for although the skeptics can draw limits, they cannot draw boundaries.

In illuminating its own boundaries, reason is oddly vindicated, not overthrown, but self-limiting, self-disciplined. Indeed, according to Kant, if reason is given the freedom to follow its own "path" it finds that it is "promoted just as much as by setting limits to its insights as by expanding them" (A744/B772; cf. A 769/B797). What the arguments in the Transcendental Dialectic purport to show is that neither the path of the dogmatists (rationalists) nor that of the skeptics (empiricists) could rescue us from the thorny nest of conflicts and confusions that serve to mislead and impede reason's development. And yet, nevertheless, there is still hope.

> The critical path alone is still open. If the reader has had pleasure and patience in traveling along in my company, then he can now judge, if it pleases him to contribute his part to making this footpath into a highway, whether or not that which many centuries could not accomplish might not be attained even before the end of the present one: namely, to bring human reason to full satisfaction in that which has always, but until now vainly, occupied its lust for knowledge.

> (A855/B883)

Notes

1　See "Phenomena-Noumena" chapter. Cf. B147–B153.
2　Kant defines a subreption as a judgmental error. *See V-Lo/Blomberg* 24:255.
3　Cf. A806/B834, where Kant tells us that the first question ("What can I know?") is *purely speculative*. The question "What ought I to do" is said to be *purely practical*. Whereas the question "What may I hope?" relates to *both the theoretical and the practical interests of reason*.
4　I have previously introduced this manner of referring to the prescription to seek the unconditioned as P_1. As we shall see later, I refer to the related, metaphysical, principle (that the unconditioned is given) as P_2 (see Grier 2001: 117–30). I continue to refer to these as P_1 and P_2, including here, and I do so merely out of habit and convenience.
5　See also A653/B681, A651/B679, A308/B365.
6　See Grier (2001: 117–30). For a discussion of this, see Allison (2004: 329–32). See also Wood (2010).
7　P_2 is a principle or presupposition that is necessary if the merely formal demand for systematic unity (P_1) is to be followed. I argue for this in Grier (2001: esp. 124–6).
8　For a discussion of this, see Allison (2004: Ch. 3, 50–73).
9　Karl Ameriks convincingly argues for a more metaphysical interpretation of the requirement attending to things in themselves. See Ameriks (2006: 269–302).
10　In the *Critique*, as in the *Inaugural Dissertation*, Kant wants first to "curb the pretensions of sensibility." See *Inaugural Dissertation* (*MSI* 2:411–17).
11　I discuss this in an unpublished (work in progress paper) "The Sublimity of Reason."
12　I discuss this in Grier (2001: 175). See Heimsoeth (1967: 199).
13　See Grier (2011: 63–84). See also Wood (2005: 89–98). Indeed, Kant suggests in the *Prolegomena* that the "world" is not a true "idea" at all (*Prol* 4:337–8).
14　The metaphysician's arguments are said to involve taking "the formal condition of thought" (the I) to represent an object (A398; cf. A402). Similarly, Kant charges the argument for taking the unity of apperception to be an object. Elsewhere he claims that the rational psychologist takes "[t]he subjective condition of thinking as being knowledge of the object" (A396/B397).
15　For a full analysis of this issue, see A568–91/B596–619.
16　This is obviously reduced dramatically and is misleading.
17　Kant's position on the positive role of the principles and ideas of reason for theoretical purposes is complex and nuanced. I try to discuss this in Grier (2001: Ch. 8).

References

Ameriks, K. (2006) "The Critique of Metaphysics: The Structure and Fate of Kant's Dialectic," in P. Guyer (ed.), *The Cambridge Companion to Kant and Modern Philosophy*, Cambridge: Cambridge University Press.

Allison, H.E. (2004) *Kant's Transcendental Idealism: An Interpretation and Defense*, rev. and enlarged ed., New Haven: Yale University Press.

Grier, M. (2001) *Kant's Doctrine of Transcendental Illusion*, Cambridge: Cambridge University Press.

Grier, M. (2011) "Reason: Ideas, Syllogisms, Antinomies," in W. Dudley and K. Engelhard (eds.), *Kant's Key Concepts*, London: Acumen.

Heimsoeth, H. (1967) *Tranzendentale Dialectik: Ein Commentar zu Kants Kritik d. reinen Vernunft*, vol. 2, Berlin: Walter de Gruyter.

Kant, I. (1998) *Critique of Pure Reason*, P. Guyer and A. Wood (eds. and trans.), Cambridge: Cambridge University Press.

Kant, I. (1992a) "Prolegomena to Any Future Metaphysics," in D. Walford and R. Meerbote (trans. and eds.), *Theoretical Philosophy, 1755–1770*, Cambridge: Cambridge University Press.

Kant, I. (1992b) "Inaugural Dissertation," in D. Walford and R. Meerbote (eds. and trans.), *Theoretical Philosophy, 1755–1770*, Cambridge: Cambridge University Press.

Kant, I. (1992c) "The Blomberg Logic," in M. Young (trans.), *Lectures on Logic*, Cambridge: Cambridge University Press.

Wood, A. (2005) *Kant*, London: Blackwell.

Wood, A. (2010) "The Antinomies of Pure Reason," in P. Guyer (ed.), *The Cambridge Companion to the Critique of Pure Reason*, Cambridge: Cambridge University Press.

Further Reading

G. Bird, *The Revolutionary Kant* (Chicago: Open Court, 2006) is the most recent commentary of Kant's first *Critique*, which discusses all parts of the *Critique*, including the Dialectic. G. Bird (ed.), *A Companion to Kant* (London: Blackwell, 2006) is a comprehensive edited collection, which includes chapters on the Dialectic. For a great introductory text focusing on Kant's fundamental concepts, including those relevant for the Dialectic, see W. Dudley and K. Engelhard (eds.), *Kant's Key Concepts* (London: Acumen, 2001); P. Guyer, *Kant and the Claims of Knowledge* (Cambridge: Cambridge University Press, 1987); P. Guyer (ed.), *The Cambridge Companion to Kant and Modern Philosophy* (Cambridge: Cambridge University Press, 2006); P. Guyer (ed.), *The Cambridge Companion to Kant's Critique of Pure Reason* (Cambridge: Cambridge University Press, 2010) are all excellent resources for the discussion of Kant's first *Critique* and in particular of the Dialectic. For an excellent discussion of the paralogisms, see P. Kitcher, *Kant's Transcendental Psychology* (Oxford: Oxford University Press, 1990), ch. 7.

11

TRANSCENDENTAL DOCTRINE OF METHOD

Gabriele Gava and Marcus Willaschek

★★★

The Transcendental Doctrine of Method (hereafter TDM) is the second main part of the *Critique of Pure Reason*. Its four chapters make up only 150 original pages of that work, as opposed to the more than 700 pages of the first main part, the Transcendental Doctrine of Elements (hereafter TDE). Given that the theses for which the first *Critique* is most famous (such as transcendental idealism) are all to be found in the TDE, it is unsurprising that the TDM has long received comparatively little attention. In recent years, however, there has been a surge of new studies on different aspects of the TDM that show both its importance to our understanding of Kant's philosophy and its relevance to current philosophical concerns.

In this chapter, we will first briefly discuss how Kant conceives of the tasks of both the TDM as a whole and its individual chapters (section 1). Since it is impossible to cover all of the topics discussed by Kant in the TDM here, we will focus on a cluster of issues that have recently become the focus of intensive scholarly debate. In particular, in section 2, we will consider those aspects of Kant's *account of reason* that are not discussed in the TDE but only come out clearly in the TDM. In section 3, we will analyze Kant's *concept of architectonic unity* as a condition of scientificity and his claim that metaphysics can reach this standard only when it is developed according to the "worldly" concept of philosophy. This will make clear that the interconnection between practical and theoretical reason is a central theme of the *Critique of Pure Reason*. Finally, in section 4, we will discuss Kant's *account of belief*, which is both essential to understanding his views on the unity of philosophy and an important topic independently of its role in Kant's system.

1. The Role and Structure of the Transcendental Doctrine of Method

At the beginning of the TDM, Kant explains its role in the *Critique* by using the traditional analogy of an edifice. If we understand metaphysics as a building that needs to be constructed (A707/B735), the *Critique*, according to Kant, considers the prior question of what kind of edifice we will be able to erect in the first place. In this respect, the TDE and the TDM have two different roles. In the former, Kant has "made an estimate of the building materials and determined for what sort of edifice, with what height and strength, they would suffice" (A707/B735); these "materials" include

DOI: 10.4324/9781003406617-15

the fundamental faculties of our mind (sensibility and understanding), their more specific variants (imagination, power of judgment, reason), and the corresponding kinds of representation (intuition, concept, schema, judgment, and inference), all of which are considered specifically with respect to the possibility of a priori cognition based on pure reason. The TDM, by contrast, is "concerned not so much with the materials as with the plan" (A707/B735). Accordingly, Kant contends that the TDM has to do with the "determination of the *formal* conditions of a complete system of pure reason" (A708/B736), whereas the TDE was concerned with the *material* conditions of such a system.

This description of the role and place of the TDM within Kant's system of philosophy may suggest that the TDM cannot contribute much to our understanding of the TDE. Kant stresses that the TDM can only start working on the "plan" of the system of pure reason after the "building materials" have been catalogued in the TDE. This seems to imply that the TDE is completely independent of the content of the TDM.

Moreover, the metaphor of construction suggests that all we find in the TDM is a preliminary clarification of methodological principles, to be considered before we embark on the project of establishing a scientific metaphysics. This traditional model of the relation between method and science is, for example, suggested when Kant refers to the whole *Critique* as a "treatise on the method, not a system of the science itself" (Bxxii).[1]

On closer inspection, however, the TDM shows itself to be quite important for any adequate understanding of the TDE while also allowing us to problematize the claim that a critique of pure reason is a propaedeutic endeavor that must come before, and is completely independent of, the system of metaphysics that it makes possible. First of all, it must be noted that the distinction between a doctrine of elements and a doctrine of method is not a scholastic legacy (as claimed by Kemp Smith 1918: 563). Rather, it is a novel distinction developed by Kant himself as an alternative to the (in his eyes misguided) distinction between *theoretical* and *practical* logic (A708/B736; *V-Lo/Wiener* 24: 794; Bacin 2010; La Rocca 2015). Accordingly, Kant distinguishes between two senses in which we can speak of a doctrine of method. The doctrine of method can either be what he calls the technical part of *general* logic (as opposed to its dogmatic part, *Log* 9: 18), or it can be the doctrine of method of a *particular* science (*V-Lo/Wiener* 24: 795). According to the former sense, the doctrine of method "has to deal with the form of a science in general" (*Log* 9: 139). However, the doctrine of method of general logic cannot convey any substantive insights. It can only "expound titles for possible methods and technical expressions that are used in regard to that which is systematic in all sorts of sciences" (A708/B736). It is only in the doctrines of method of *particular* sciences that we can find instructive directions on how to integrate the multitude of cognitions belonging to a science into a systematic whole.[2] The TDM of the *Critique of Pure Reason* belongs to this latter group insofar as it is the doctrine of method of *metaphysics* as a science.

If we take into account how Kant describes the relationship between particular sciences and their own doctrines of method, it becomes clear why the TDM could in fact contain relevant insights for understanding both the TDE and, more generally, the relationship between the critique and the system of pure reason. In contrast to the traditional view, Kant stresses that methodological reflection should come *after*, not *before*, the development of the science in question. Thus, in the Vienna Logic, he maintains that the doctrine of method "can only appear at the end of a science, because only then am I acquainted with the nature of the science" (*V-Lo/Wiener* 24: 795; see also *V-Lo/Hechsel* 488, Eng. 416; A52/B76–7). Therefore, if we understand the *Critique of Pure Reason* as a whole as a "treatise on method" (Bxxii),[3] this does not mean that it should be seen as a kind of preparatory consideration that precedes, and is independent of, the development of the science of metaphysics proper. In the Introduction to the first *Critique*, Kant admittedly emphasizes the sharp distinction between critique (as a propaedeutic) and the system of reason's a priori cognitions (as transcendental philosophy), where transcendental philosophy is an integral part of metaphysics proper, according to the Architectonic (A845/B 873).[4] However, he also sometimes contends that the difference between the two is only quantitative, not qualitative (A14/B28). This points to quite an original understanding of the way in which methodological rules and procedures should be identified. According to Kant, the latter can only be identified from within the practice of a particular science. A "methodology of science" thus cannot be developed without first taking into consideration how we are already engaged in gaining particular cognitions belonging to a certain science.

While this emphasizes the self-reflective character of methodological considerations for Kant, it also shows that the TDM is of central importance within Kant's *Critique of Pure Reason* insofar as the latter is a self-reflective investigation of reason, where reason is both the subject and the object of study (Axi–xii). In the Hechsel Logic, Kant defines method as "the unity of the manifold insofar as it rests on principles of reason" (*V-Lo/Hechsel* 488–9, Eng. 416). A doctrine of method must thus display those principles that give unity to a science and make it possible to see it as a self-contained body of knowledge. Therefore, even though doctrines of method come at the end of a science for Kant – in the twofold sense that they come at the end of its *development* and of its *exposition* – this does not mean that they are not integral parts of that science, insofar as they display principles and relations among cognitions that are essential to understanding it. The purpose of providing a self-reflective examination of our attempts to philosophize that shows how metaphysics can become a science (and thus be seen as a unitary and self-sufficient body of cognitions) is of course central to the *Critique of Pure Reason* as a whole (Bxv). In this framework, the TDM is a culmination of the critical self-reflective investigation of reason, where fundamental principles and concepts that have animated transcendental philosophy and metaphysics from the very beginning are finally made explicit and displayed in their systematic relationships.

In sum, we can see that according to Kant, the TDE, the TDM, the first *Critique* as a whole and the science of metaphysis stand in complex relations of mutual dependence. First, the *Critique of Pure Reason* as a whole can be considered the doctrine of method of metaphysics; as such, it differs from other doctrines of method in that it does *not* come at the *end* of this science. Metaphysics cannot await its own establishment as a science in order to clarify the principles that render it a systematic body of knowledge. As Kant emphasizes in both the A and the B preface, self-reflective critical inquiry into the limits of cognition is essential if metaphysics is to *become* a system of cognitions. Second, as we have seen, for Kant self-reflective methodological considerations cannot be carried out if we are not already engaged in the development of the "doctrinal" part of a science. It is for this reason that the *Critique of Pure Reason* must already contain elements that belong to transcendental philosophy and metaphysics proper. Third, insofar as the TDM is the culmination of the *Critique*'s self-reflective investigation, which makes the establishment of metaphysics possible, it is the doctrine of method of metaphysics, which, like the *Critique* as a whole, comes *before* its science has fully been established. But fourth, the TDM is also the doctrine of method of the TDE (or the *Critique of Pure Reason*, respectively); like every doctrine of method, it must rely on cognitions of the corresponding science that have already been established. In this sense, the TDM comes *after* at least *some* parts of metaphysics, that is, the parts that are introduced in the TDE.

The TDM is divided into four chapters: the Discipline of Pure Reason, the Canon of Pure Reason, the Architectonic of Pure Reason, and the History of Pure Reason. Since, as we have seen, the purpose of the TDM is to formulate the principles according to which metaphysics could become a science and a unitary system of cognitions, its first task is to prevent reason from venturing into investigations that result not in science but in fallacies and contradictions. The Discipline of Pure Reason thus has the task of erecting "a system of caution and self-examination out of the nature of reason and the objects of its pure use" (A711/B739). This system of cautions should spring "out of the nature of reason" because what we need is not simply a censure but a "negative legislation" (A711/B739) which puts inescapable restrictions on our attempts to gain speculative knowledge through reason – restrictions that are ultimately based on the uncovering (in the Dialectic) of reason's tendency to succumb to transcendental illusion. In contrast to the negative function of the Discipline, the Canon of Pure Reason provides an outline of a positive use of pure reason in metaphysics, which, according to Kant, cannot be purely theoretical but needs a basis in moral principles, which in turn are intrinsic to pure reason itself. Here, reason is presented as having fundamental ends and interests, which also explain our tendency to go beyond the limits of our knowledge and to seek speculative warrant for the notion that our most fundamental practical ends can be met (A797–800/B825–8). The Canon shows that even though this speculative warrant cannot be achieved, we can nonetheless be justified in believing that the conditions for the attainment of our essential practical ends are satisfied, where this for Kant implies that there is a "source of positive cognitions that belong in the domain of pure reason" (A795/B823).

Finally, while the chapter on the Architectonic of Pure Reason is concerned with the "plan" of metaphysics as a science, the History of Pure Reason emphasizes once again the self-reflective character of the TDM and the first *Critique* in general. On the one hand, it confirms that the critical examination of reason cannot abstract from past attempts to attain metaphysical cognition in philosophy. On the other, it shows that once we have achieved the "critical" standpoint of the *Critique of Pure Reason*, this gives us a new perspective on the history of philosophy (A852–5/B880–3).

With this brief discussion of the tasks of the TDM and its chapters in hand, let us now turn our attention to specific issues that have been much discussed in the recent literature, either because they shed new light on Kant or because they are considered of interest on their own (or both).

2. Kant's Account of Reason in the Doctrine of Method

The task of providing a comprehensive and coherent interpretation of Kant's account of reason is notoriously challenging. For example, Kant scholars have long debated how we should account for the relationship between the theoretical and the practical use of reason (see Timmermann 2009).

In the first *Critique*, Kant defines reason in the wide sense as "the faculty that provides the principles of cognition *a priori*" (A11/B24), or as "the entire higher faculty of cognition" (A835/B864). Reason in the narrow sense is characterized either as the faculty "of drawing consequences mediately" (A299/B355) or, more generally, as "the faculty of principles" (A299/B356; see Willaschek 2013). While these definitions are meant to include practical cognition, inferences, and principles, it can seem as though the *Critique of Pure Reason* is only concerned with the theoretical (or "speculative") use of reason. In fact, this is what Kant himself suggests when, in the *Critique of Practical Reason*, he refers to the first *Critique* as a critique of "speculative reason" (*KpV* 5: 3, 5: 50) or the "theoretical *Critique*" (*KpV* 5: 46).

The TDM (and in particular the Canon) shows that the relationship between practical and theoretical reason is already of central importance in the first *Critique* (see O'Neill 1992). Moreover, in the TDM, Kant discusses aspects of his account of reason that do not come to the fore in the TDE, where this enriches our understanding of Kant's perspective in various ways. In this section, we will focus on three aspects of Kant's account of reason in the TDM. Reason is portrayed as a faculty that (1) has essential ends and interests, (2) is fundamentally public, and (3) has a history.

1. Both the Canon and the Architectonic depict reason as having essential ends and interests (see Kleingeld 1998; Ferrarin 2015: ch. 1). Kant tends to identify *ends* of reason with those states of affairs that would result from the perfect and complete application of our rational faculties. In this sense, ends of reason are both theoretical, as the achievement of complete rational knowledge, and

practical, as the realization of the highest good. By contrast, *interests* of reason are directed towards those states of affairs that are conditions for the realization of reason's ends. In order to see how interests and ends of reason are related to one another, let us focus on practical reason. In the Canon Kant argues that, as rational beings, we are subject to practical laws and, among those, to moral laws, which, as "imperatives, i.e., objective laws of freedom, [. . .] say what ought to happen" (A802/ B830). Since objective moral laws primarily concern the moral quality of the will, and thus imply the idea of moral desert (or "worthiness to be happy"), they lead to the notion of a moral world in which everyone is precisely as happy as they morally deserve to be. This moral world is the object of the idea of the highest good, which for Kant is the idea "of a world into which we must without exception transpose ourselves in accordance with the precepts of pure but practical reason" (A814/ B842). The highest good is thus a necessary end of reason. Kant argues that we must assume the existence of God and the immortality of the soul in order to regard the highest good as possible (A803/B831, A811/B839), and for this reason God's existence and our immortality are part of the essential interests of reason in its practical use. Thus, according to Kant, the search for a theoretical proof of the immortality of the soul and of God's existence is actually grounded in a practical interest of reason (A798–801/B826–9). In this way, the Canon makes clear that the practical use of reason is already of central importance even in the *Critique of Pure Reason*. From the Dialectic, we know that reason has a natural tendency to search for the totality of conditions for a given conditioned. This produces the idea of the unconditioned and the transcendental ideas of the soul, the world and God (A322–3/B378–80). The Canon now shows that the ideas of reason arise not only as a consequence of the natural regress of reason in the series of conditions but also because they are necessary conditions for the realization of the highest good. The purpose of the *Critique of Pure Reason* is thus not simply to determine the limits of our theoretical cognition but also, and most importantly, to find a way to harmonize the different interests and ends of theoretical and practical reason.[5] For, if practical reason requires us to believe in the existence of God and the immortality of the soul, we might think that we need to provide a theoretical proof for them. The TDM instead illustrates that even though we cannot attain theoretical cognition of God and immortality, this does not mean that we must forsake our (and reason's) practical interests in them or regard belief in God and immortality as irrational.

2. In the TDE, Kant discusses reason in terms of its "logical use" (in syllogistic reasoning) and its "real use" (in metaphysical speculation) (A300/B356–7). In both of these 'uses', reason consists in abstract structures of reasoning that hold independently of the subjective attitudes of the individuals who make use of the faculty. Just as syllogistic logic abstracts from the psychological processes of individual thinkers and concentrates on timeless inference patterns, Kant's discussion of metaphysics in the Dialectic abstracts from the arguments of individual philosophers and concentrates on timeless forms of metaphysical speculation. In the Discipline, we find quite a different picture of reason. Here, reason is described as a faculty that each of us shares with others and whose verdicts arise not timelessly but as a result of conflict, discussion, and (ultimately) agreement. Reason "has no dictatorial authority" and does not involve "anything more than the agreement of free citizens, each of whom must be able to express his reservations, indeed even his veto, without holding back" (A738–9/B766–7, see also A752/B780). According to this characterization, reason is essentially a public faculty in which individual voices must play a role, although they must always seek the agreement of others and be ready to respond to their criticisms and counterproposals (see Mauss 1990; O'Neill 1992; Gava 2016; Macarthur 2016).

How do these two descriptions of reason fit together? First of all, we have already seen that reason cannot be identified with theoretical reason even in the first *Critique*. But second, and more importantly, reason is not a faculty that is completely transparent to itself. On the contrary, if left to its own devices, it is often the source of illusion. In the words of the Discipline, it presents "an entire system of delusions and deceptions" (A711/B739). When each of us individually follows the norms of theoretical reason, we cannot be sure that our results are correct and amount to knowledge. Of course, it is not the agreement of others that *makes* our beliefs correct or true. Rather, when our claims are rational and correct, we may expect them to be accepted by others as well. Insofar as the individual use of reason can lead us astray, the agreement of others is an ineludible means of confirming that what we subjectively *take* to be rationally valid really *is* rationally valid (see Gava 2016).

3. For Kant, reason forms a system that gives rise to a series of interconnected cognitions and ideas. This system is fixed and does not change historically. Both the categories and the *a priori* forms of sensibility are necessarily and universally valid. Transcendental ideas are equally necessary, even though they do not amount to cognitions and can only be used as regulative principles of inquiry. This ahistorical characterization of reason and its cognitions notwithstanding, the TDM contains a section dedicated to the History of Pure Reason. In what sense does pure reason have a history? We have just seen that reason is not completely self-transparent. The *Critique of Pure Reason* can be understood as an attempt to make reason perspicuous to itself through an exercise in self-reflection. We have also seen that according to the TDM, transforming a body of isolated cognitions into a science requires the use of principles and procedures that can only be clearly articulated within the practice of the very science in question. Therefore, historical attempts to attain cognition in a particular science must also count as essentially belonging to that practice. This applies equally to the TDM, and to the *Critique of Pure Reason* as a whole, in their attempt to provide a self-examination of reason that is able to display those principles according to which metaphysics can become a science. Accordingly, Kant claims in the Discipline that

> [r]eason also very much needs such a conflict [the historical conflict between opposing metaphysical claims, *our note*], and it is to be wished that it had been undertaken earlier and with unlimited public permission. For then a mature critique would have come about all the earlier.
>
> (A747/B775)

On the one hand, reason has a history because its attainment of self-knowledge through critique can only be understood as an historical achievement (*IaG* 8: 19). On the other hand, once the critical standpoint has been reached, we can regard past conflicts between opposing metaphysical positions as finding an explanation in reason's internal and ahistorical structure (see Yovel 1980; Kleingeld 1995; Willaschek 2018).

To summarize, only the TDM gives us an integrated picture of Kant's account of reason. Here, reason is described as a faculty with fundamental interests and aims, where moral ends play a central role (A816/B844). Moreover, reason is seen as a faculty that is essentially public but not transparent to itself. Finally, the consideration of historical attempts to attain metaphysical cognition are the basis for reason's attaining self-knowledge through critique.

3. How Can Metaphysics Become a Science?

In the first section, we saw that Kant characterizes the task of doctrines of method of specific sciences as that of displaying the principles according to which a science can become a system. Given this description, it is easy to see that the chapter on the Architectonic plays a fundamental role in the TDM, for Kant opens this chapter with the following words:

> By an architectonic I understand the art of systems. Since systematic unity is that which first makes ordinary cognition into science, [. . .] architectonic is the doctrine of that which is scientific in our cognition in general, and therefore necessarily belongs to the doctrine of method.
>
> (A832/B860)[6]

For a body of cognitions to count as a science, the cognitions belonging to it must form a system of interconnected parts. But what distinguishes a mere "aggregate" from a "system"? A system, Kant continues, is "the unity of the manifold cognitions under one idea," which in turn "is the rational concept of the form of a whole." This concept of the form of the whole functions as an "end" of the science itself (A832/B860). When we consider a particular proposition of a science, or a particular sub-division of it, we regard the place of that proposition or of that sub-division in that theory – its theoretical relation to other propositions and parts of the theory – not as arbitrary or accidental but as depending on internal relations that are objective and independent of our individual standpoint. In a science, some propositions are more fundamental than others, and where they stand is not a matter of choice. There are also propositions that clearly do not belong to that science and thus do not contribute to its unity or structure. Thus, Kant's point is that when we develop a particular doctrine as part of a science, we already rely on the idea of a systematic order of cognition, of which the doctrine in question will become a part (see Gava 2014). It is in this sense that the idea of a system is fundamental to our understanding of science. Kant attributes a teleological role to the idea of a whole of cognitions because in every individual contribution to a science, we are already promoting the system of cognitions to which it belongs.

In order to become a science, metaphysics (like all other disciplines) must display a systematic order of cognitions that is traceable back to a unifying idea that provides the form of the whole. According to Kant, metaphysics comprises all discursive cognitions that spring from the nature of pure reason itself (A841/B869).[7] We have seen, however, that reason develops its cognitions by following its fundamental ends and interests, which are both theoretical and practical. Without a clear grasp of those ends and interests and how they relate to the cognitions we seek, it is impossible to obtain a distinct view of the cognitions that are actually within our reach and how they relate to one another. Kant accordingly distinguishes between two different conceptions of philosophy. Philosophy according to the "school concept" is "a system of cognition that is sought only as a science without having as its end anything more than the systematic unity of this knowledge" (A838/B866).[8] It is not clear whether Kant thinks that we can actually obtain a coherent system of metaphysical cognitions by following the school concept alone. In fact, we have seen that when we seek to develop theoretical cognitions about God and the soul independently of their relation to the highest good, we end up in contradictions and unsolvable metaphysical controversies. Accordingly, it is reasonable to think that metaphysics can only become a science by following an alternative concept of philosophy (see Gava 2014). Hence, Kant identifies a "worldly" concept (*Weltbegriff*) of philosophy, according to which philosophy is "the science of the relation of all cognition to the essential ends of human reason" (A839/B867).[9] These essential ends are subordinated to a final end, which Kant describes as the "entire vocation [*Bestimmung*] of human beings," while he specifies that "the philosophy of it is called moral philosophy" (A839/B867).

This account of how metaphysics can become a science highlights why this discipline cannot be a science like any other. It is not simply a collection of determinate cognitions ordered according to a unifying idea. It essentially refers to practical and moral ends which, while they are necessary for rational beings, often cannot be regarded as realizable in the empirical world – such as the highest good, which is a world in which everyone is exactly as happy as they morally deserve to be. At least according to the first *Critique*, the highest good can be realized only by God and in the afterlife, of which we cannot have cognition or knowledge. Therefore, when it is developed according to the worldly concept of philosophy, metaphysics is destined to remain an unaccomplished task (A839/ B867). It must foster our attempts to realize (or at least approximate) the highest good, but at the same time we must admit that we cannot cognize the very conditions of its realization. This, in a sense, places metaphysics at a disadvantage with respect to the other sciences, which can become complete systems of cognition. In another sense, however, metaphysics has a privileged position: scientists who fail to make reference to the ultimate end of philosophy cannot appreciate the relevance of their discoveries for humanity and will thus remain mere "artists of reason" (A839/B867).

4. Kant on Belief

We have seen that Kant portrays reason as having fundamental ends and interests, the most important of which are practical. From this perspective, a central task of the *Critique of Pure Reason* is to show how we can harmonize these interests and ends. On the one hand, there is the speculative end of reason: extending the realm of theoretical cognition as far as possible (while at the same time giving it systematic unity). On the other, there is the practical end of reason: realizing the highest good and the related interests in the existence of God and the immortality of the soul, each of which, according to Kant, is a necessary element of our self-understanding as moral agents. Since the metaphysical claims based on reason's practical interest are beyond the scope of human knowledge and thus cannot be incorporated in a system of speculative cognition, there is a question of how the speculative and practical ends of reason can be reconciled. Accordingly, the Canon dedicates an entire section to the elaboration of a complex account of doxastic attitudes that allows Kant to deny us *knowledge* of God and the soul while insisting that it is rational for us to *believe* in God's existence and the immortality of our souls.[10] We will here focus our attention on the Kantian account of belief in particular.[11]

Kant first defines assent, or taking-to-be-true [*Fürwahrhalten*], as "the subjective validity of judgment" (A822/B850). By this he means the attitude towards a proposition we take to truly represent some state of affairs. Taking-to-be-true is thus similar to what in contemporary philosophy is called "belief." Kant then identifies three "stages" of taking-to-be-true: having an opinion, believing, and knowing.[12] He explains that having an opinion is a taking-to-be-true that is both subjectively and objectively insufficient, whereas believing is subjectively sufficient and objectively insufficient, and knowing is both subjectively and objectively sufficient (A822/B850; see Chignell 2007b: 333–6; Höwing 2016; Stevenson 2003: 82–8; Willaschek 2016).

On one possible reading, while the objectively sufficient taking-to-be-true is based on evidence or "grounds" that guarantee the truth of the proposition in question, subjective sufficiency concerns the degree of confidence in the truth of a proposition. Accordingly, Kant identifies subjective sufficiency with "conviction (for myself)" and objective sufficiency with (objective) "certainty (for everyone)" (A822/B850).[13] The degree of confidence is measured by our willingness to withdraw our taking-to-be-true in light of changes regarding (1) the available evidence and (2) what is at stake (which makes betting an adequate test of subjective sufficiency; A824/B852). The degree of confidence that counts as subjectively *sufficient* is different in cases of knowledge on the one hand and cases of belief on the other. While knowledge for Kant seems to require a uniformly high degree of confidence (something like subjective certainty), the degree of confidence required for belief must only be "enough for action [*genug zum Handeln*]" (*Log* 9: 68) and thus can vary from case to case.

Thus, as a taking-to-be-true that is subjectively sufficient but objectively insufficient, belief for Kant is a propositional attitude that both requires a high degree of confidence in the truth of the proposition we take to be true and is not based on objective grounds (on 'evidence') that actually guarantee the truth of the proposition in question. Moreover, when in a state of belief, we must *recognize* that our grounds are not objectively sufficient. Kant accordingly stresses that in a state of belief our taking-to-be-true, while subjectively sufficient, "is at the same time held to be objectively insufficient" (A822/B850). A taking-to-be-true in which we have the utmost confidence because we *falsely* take it to be based on objective grounds would be a case of *persuasion* (*Überredung*) for Kant (A820/B848), not belief.

But how can we ever be rationally justified in believing something on objectively insufficient grounds? The rational warrant for a state of belief comes not from the evidence in its favor but from the role it plays in rational agency. Provided it is not inconsistent with the overall evidence we have, a belief can be justified insofar as it serves as a basis for action, in the sense that an action that is either categorically or hypothetically necessary would not be rational unless one holds the belief in question. Kant offers the example of a doctor who, for lack of a better alternative, treats a patient for consumption even though she knows that the evidence is inconclusive. Given that the doctor wants (or perhaps is even morally obligated) to help the patient, and the only way to do so is by treating him for consumption, she must, according to Kant, *believe* that the patient suffers from consumption (if that is the only option not ruled out by the evidence), no matter how weak the evidence in favor of that belief.

Kant accordingly claims:

> Once an end is proposed, then the conditions for attaining it are hypothetically necessary. This necessity is subjectively but still only comparatively sufficient if I do not know of any other conditions at all under which the end could be attained; but it is sufficient absolutely and for everyone if I know with certainty that no one else can know of any other conditions that lead to the proposed end.
>
> (A823–4/B851–2)

Kant's basic point can be put briefly as follows: We cannot rationally pursue an aim if we do not believe that the necessary conditions for its attainment are satisfied (see Höwing 2016). Kant makes this point first and foremost with respect to beliefs that concern necessary conditions for the attainment of morally necessary ends. This is what he calls "necessary belief" (A824/B852). Accordingly, we have seen that for Kant, the highest good is an end that we necessarily set for ourselves as addressees of moral obligations. The existence of God and the immortality of the soul are two conditions without which we could not consider the highest good to be realizable, on Kant's view. Kant then concludes that we are rationally justified in believing in the existence of God and the immortality of the soul because otherwise we would not be able to rationally pursue the highest good. It is the rational necessity of the end (the highest good) that accounts for the rationality of the belief (in God and immortality as necessary conditions for realizing the highest good).

To summarize, Kant's account of belief in the Canon is important for at least two reasons. First, it highlights a point on which we have repeatedly insisted in this chapter: The unity of reason and the attempt to harmonize practical and theoretical ends and interests of reason are central themes of the *Critique of Pure Reason*. Second, Kant's account of belief is interesting in its own right insofar as it offers a complex and multifaceted approach to non-evidential justification, that is, to a kind of taking-to-be-true that is rationally justified even though it lacks sufficient (theoretical) evidence.[14] In this respect, Kant's discussion in the Canon foreshadows not only aspects of pragmatism but also Bayesian conceptions of belief and recent debates on so-called pragmatic (and moral) encroachment (see Fantl and McGrath 2007) and the "ethics of belief" (Chignell 2018).

5. Conclusion

Far from being an unimportant appendix to the *Critique of Pure Reason*, the TDM is of central importance to understanding Kant's philosophy. First, it integrates in relevant ways the descriptions of reason that Kant provides in the TDE. Moreover, it gives us a fresh perspective on the project of a critique of pure reason, which can now be understood from the vantage point of Kant's project of a metaphysics developed according to the worldly concept of philosophy, where the attempt to harmonize reason's practical and theoretical ends is central. One aspect of this is Kant's account of non-evidential justification, which prefigures views on doxastic attitudes that have been of philosophical interest in recent decades.[15]

Notes

1 This traditional model can be found in Christian Wolff, who places a *Short Lesson on the Mathematical Method* at the beginning of the *Anfangsgründe aller mathematischen Wissenschaften* (Wolff 1962: div. 1, vol. 12) and a *Preliminary Discourse on Philosophy in General*, which contains a whole chapter on the method of philosophy (Wolff 1962: div. 2, vol. 1.1, § 115*ff.*), at the beginning of his *Latin Logic*.

2 Note that Kant seems to use the expression "doctrine of method" in another sense in the context of his practical philosophy, for example in the *Critique of Practical Reason* and the *Doctrine of Virtue* (see Bacin 2002, 2010).

3 Kant goes so far as to refer to the entire book as a "Doctrine of Method" (A82–3/B 108–9).

4 It is not clear whether Kant's characterizations of transcendental philosophy in the Introduction and the Architectonic are compatible. For example, both the A version of the Introduction and the Architectonic describe transcendental philosophy as having to do with a priori cognitions of objects in general (A11–2, A845/B873). In the B version of the Introduction, however, transcendental philosophy is presented not simply as identifying the pure a priori cognitions of objects in general but also as a "meta-investigation" into the "modes" of our a priori cognitions (B25).

5 As is well-known, Kant claims in the Canon that the interest of reason can be united in the three questions "What can I know?", "What should I do?", and "What may I hope?" (A805/B833).

6 On the Architectonic, see Gava 2014; La Rocca 2003; Manchester 2003, 2008; Ypi 2011.

7 In this way, metaphysics is distinguished from mathematics, which includes all rational cognitions from the construction of concepts (A713/B741, A837/B865), and from philosophy more broadly, which also contains rational cognitions from empirical concepts (A840/B868).

8 We here follow Pluhar's translation of the first *Critique* in rendering *Schulbegriff* as "school concept," whereas we follow Young's translation of the *Lectures on Logic* by rendering *Weltbegriff* as "worldly concept."

9 On the worldly concept of philosophy, see Ferrarin 2015.

10 For different readings of Kant's account of doxastic attitudes in the Canon, see Chignell 2007a, 2007b; Pasternack 2014; Stevenson 2003; Willaschek 2016.

11 For a discussion of the Kantian notion of opinion, see Pasternack 2014. For knowledge see: Gava 2016; Höwing 2016; Willaschek and Watkins 2020.

12 As will become apparent, Kant's notion of belief is much narrower than the current one. Moreover, it often has overtones of "faith."

13 Kant's use of "conviction" is in fact confusing because he also says that conviction is based on objective grounds (A820/B848), which suggests that he may be working with two different concepts of conviction.

14 See, however, Baiasu 2013 for an account of belief that relies on epistemic justification.
15 We would like to thank Stefano Bacin and Sorin Baiasu for helpful comments on previous drafts of this chapter.

References

Bacin, S. (2002) "Sul rapporto tra riflessione e vita morale in Kant: Le dottrine del metodo nella filosofia pratica," *Studi Kantiani* 15: 65–91.

Bacin, S. (2010) "The Meaning of the *Critique of Practical Reason* for Moral Beings: The *Doctrine of Method of Pure Practical Reason*," in A. Reath and J. Timmermann (eds.), *Kant's Critique of Practical Reason: A Critical Guide*, Cambridge: Cambridge University Press.

Baiasu, S. (2013) "Kant's *Rechtfertigung* and the Epistemic Nature of Practical Justification," in S. Baiasu and M. Timmons (eds.), *Kant on Practical Justification: Interpretative Essays*, Oxford: Oxford University Press.

Chignell, A. (2007a) "Kant's Concepts of Justification," *Noûs* 41: 33–63.

Chignell, A. (2007b) "Belief in Kant," *Philosophical Review* 116: 323–60.

Chignell, A. (2018) "The Ethics of Belief," in E.N. Zalta (ed.), *The Stanford Encyclopedia of Philosophy*, spring ed., https://plato.stanford.edu/archives/spr2018/entries/ethics-belief/.

Fantl, J. and McGrath, M. (2007) "On Pragmatic Encroachment in Epistemology," *Philosophy and Phenomenological Research* 75: 558–89.

Ferrarin, A. (2015) *The Powers of Pure Reason: Kant and the Idea of Cosmic Philosophy*, Chicago: University of Chicago Press.

Gava, G. (2014) "Kant's Definition of Science in the *Architectonic of Pure Reason* and the Essential Ends of Reason," *Kant-Studien* 105: 372–93.

Gava, G. (2016) "The Fallibilism of Kant's Architectonic," in G. Gava and R. Stern (eds.), *Pragmatism, Kant and Transcendental Philosophy*, London: Routledge, pp. 46–66.

Höwing, T. (2016) "Kant on Opinion, Belief and Knowledge," in T. Höwing (ed.), *The Highest Good in Kant's Philosophy*, Berlin: Walter de Gruyter.

Kemp Smith, N. (1918) *A Commentary to Kant's Critique of Pure Reason*, London: Macmillan.

Kleingeld, P. (1995) *Fortschritt und Vernunft: Zur Geschichtsphilosophie Kants*, Würzburg: Königshausen & Neumann.

Kleingeld, P. (1998) "The Conative Character of Reason in Kant's Philosophy," *Journal of the History of Philosophy* 36: 77–97.

La Rocca, C. (2003) "Istruzioni per costruire: La Dottrina del metodo della prima Critica," in *Soggetto e mondo. Studi su Kant*, Venezia: Marsilio, pp. 183–215.

La Rocca, C. (2015) "Methodenlehre, transzendentale," in M. Willaschek, J. Stolzenberg, G. Mohr and S. Bacin (eds.), *Kant-Lexikon*, vol. 2, Berlin: Walter de Gruyter, pp. 1573–8.

Macarthur, D. (2016) "A Kant-Inspired Vision of Pragmatism as Democratic Experimentalism," in G. Gava and R. Stern (eds.), *Pragmatism, Kant and Transcendental Philosophy*, London: Routledge, pp. 67–84.

Manchester, P. (2003) "Kant's Conception of Architectonic in its Historical Context," *Journal of the History of Philosophy* 41: 187–207.

Manchester, P. (2008) "Kant's Conception of Architectonic in its Philosophical Context," *Kant-Studien* 99: 133–51.

Mauss, I. (1990) "Zur Theorie der Institutionalisierung bei Kant," in G. Göhler, K. Lenk, H. Münkler and M. Walther (eds.), *Politische Institutionen im gesellschaftlichen Umbruch. Ideengeschichtliche Beiträge zur Theorie politischer Institutionen*, Opladen: Westdeutscher Verlag, pp. 358–85.

O'Neill, O. (1992) "Vindicating Reason," in P. Guyer (ed.), *The Cambridge Companion to Kant*, Cambridge: Cambridge University Press, pp. 280–308.

Pasternack, L. (2014) "Kant on Opinion: Assent, Hypothesis, and the Norms of General Applied Logic," *Kant-Studien* 105: 41–82.

Stevenson, L. (2003) "Opinion, Belief or Faith, and Knowledge," *Kantian Review* 7: 72–100.

Timmermann, J. (2009) "The Unity of Reason: Kantian Perspectives," in S. Robertson (ed.), *Spheres of Reason: New Essays in the Philosophy of Normativity*, Oxford: Oxford University Press, pp. 183–97.

Willaschek, M. (2013) "Kant's Two Conceptions of (Pure) Reason in the *Critique of Pure Reason*," in S. Bacin, A. Ferrarin, C. La Rocca and M. Ruffing (eds.), *Kant und die Philosophie in weltbürgerlicher Absicht: Akten des XI. Internationalen Kant-Kongresses*, vol. 2, Berlin: Walter de Gruyter, pp. 483–92.

Willaschek, M. (2016) "Kant and Peirce on Belief," in G. Gava and R. Stern (eds.), *Pragmatism, Kant and Transcendental Philosophy*, London: Routledge, pp. 133–51.

Willaschek, M. (2018) *Kant on the Sources of Metaphysics: The Dialectic of Pure Reason*, Cambridge: Cambridge University Press.

Willaschek, M. and Watkins, E. (2020) "Kant on Cognition and Knowledge," *Synthese* 197: 3195–213.

Wolff, C. (1962) *Gesammelte Werke*, Hildesheim: Olms.

Yovel, Y. (1980) *Kant and the Philosophy of History*, Princeton: Princeton University Press.

Ypi, L. (2011) "Practical Agency, Teleology and System in Kant's Architectonic of Pure Reason," in S. Baiasu, S. Pihlström and H. Williams (eds.), *Politics and Metaphysics in Kant*, Cardiff: University of Wales Press, pp. 134–52.

Further Reading

A. Chignell, "Knowledge, Discipline, System, Hope: The Fate of Metaphysics in the Doctrine of Method," in J. O'Shea (ed.), *Kant's Critique of Pure Reason: A Critical Guide* (Cambridge: Cambridge University Press, 2017) provides an encompassing account of the contents of the TDM based on the concepts of Knowledge, Hope, and Belief introduced in the Canon. G. Gava's *Kant's* Critique of Pure Reason *and the Method of Metaphysics* (Cambridge: Cambridge University Press, 2023) provides an interpretation of the method(s) of the *Critique of Pure Reason* that contains detailed analyses of the TDM. Vol. 4 (*Die Methodenlehre*) of H. Heimsoeth's *Tranzendentale Dialektik: Ein Kommentar zu Kants Kritik der reinen Vernunft* (Berlin: Walter de Gruyter, 1971) is still the most detailed commentary of the TDM available. G. Mohr and M. Willaschek (eds.), *Immanuel Kant: Kritik der reinen Vernunft* (Berlin: Akademie, 1998) contains four chapters dedicated to the TDM (written respectively by P. Rohs, V. Gerhardt, B. Recki and O. Höffe). G. Tonelli's *Kant's "Critique of Pure Reason" Within the Tradition of Modern Logic* (Hildesheim: Georg Olms, 1994) provides an interpretation of the first *Critique* which relies extensively on the TDM. B.-S. von Wolff-Metternich's *Die Überwindung des mathematischen Erkenntnisideals: Kants Grenzbestimmung von Mathematik und Philosophie* (Berlin: Walter de Gruyter, 1995) discusses the Discipline of Pure Reason in detail. Chignell's *Knowledge and Belief in Kant: Making Room for Practical Metaphysics* (Oxford: Oxford University Press, forthcoming) contains chapters on many of the attitudes and kinds of justification Kant discusses in the Canon of Pure Reason. Lea Ypi's *The Architectonic of Reason: Purposiveness and Systematic Unity in Kant's First Critique* (Oxford: Oxford University Press, 2021) focuses on the Architectonic of Pure Reason, examining the role of teleology in the integration of the practical and speculative uses of reason.

II. PRACTICAL PHILOSOPHY

12

THE *GROUNDWORK*

Thomas E. Hill, Jr.

***

1. Background: From the First Critique to the *Groundwork*

Immanuel Kant's *Groundwork for the Metaphysics of Morals* has been one of the most influential works in the history of moral philosophy. It was also an important step in the development of Kant's critical philosophy. After noting some background themes in Kant's earlier work, this chapter reviews its aims, method, and main conclusions, highlighting some especially influential features, and then calls attention to a few significant points of interpretation on which scholars continue to disagree. The historical Kant has been blessed – or cursed – with generations of commentators who have sought to absorb and explain his monumental works. Different understandings are to be expected. No definitive and comprehensive interpretation has been (or perhaps can even be) given. This chapter is no exception but aims to articulate my understanding of some main ideas before mentioning a few of the many controversies.

Kant's *Groundwork* followed shortly after his groundbreaking *Critique of Pure Reason*, from which he drew ideas to develop for ethics in new and radical ways (Kant 1965 [1781/1787]). Among these were, *first*, his critical methodology that starts with an examination of the powers of reason, *second*, the idea of a Copernican Revolution in philosophy that calls for shifting our attention from the things we know to our perspective as knowers, *third*, his defense of the possibility of agent causation that is not entirely explicable by empirical causal laws, and, *fourth*, his thesis that neither experience nor reason can prove or even allow us to fully comprehend the existence of God, immortality, or freedom of the will. To expand on these points briefly:

First, Kant's methodology was to investigate the powers and limits of *pure* reason, that is, reason insofar as it is not relying on empirical data. The challenging question for mathematics, critical philosophy, and traditional metaphysics was, "How are synthetic a priori propositions possible?" In other words, how is it possible for there to be substantive propositions that are knowable without reliance on empirical evidence and yet are not merely self-contradictory to deny? The same question turns out to be a challenge for ethics as well, though the challenge is hidden at first by Kant's discussion of more familiar moral questions. The problem, to which Kant thought he had a solution, is that common morality presupposes a guiding and constraining supreme principle that

DOI: 10.4324/9781003406617-17

purports to be necessarily rational but is not self-contradictory to deny. Although many earlier philosophers emphasized the importance of reason for ethics, Kant's methodology deviates radically from many of its rivals in the history of ethics. It rejects the Stoic attempt to ground human norms in the nature of the universe, and it rejects theories of Aristotle, Epicurus, and Hume insofar as they attempt in different ways to derive ethics from human nature. It denies the Platonic idea that reason can perceive a realm of independent moral truths, and it also rejects divine command theories that base norms on an arbitrary divine will, though it leaves a place for the Idea of a holy will or God that necessarily conforms to reason.

Second, Kant's *Critique of Pure Reason* aims to bring about a revolution in philosophy that is analogous to the Copernican Revolution in astronomy (Bxvi–xviii). In brief, in the *Critique of Pure Reason* Kant argues that the world as it appears to us, indeed the only world that we can know through science and experience, is not entirely external to our powers of thought and understanding but is deeply dependent upon them. *Moral* judgments, however, do not describe physical and psychological facts about the empirical world, and so they are not beholden in the same way to what is "given" in spatiotemporally structured perception. For ethics, Kant develops an idea that is partly analogous to his Copernican Revolution for theoretical philosophy, namely, the idea that goodness is not to be found simply by observing nature but by applying our rational action-guiding principles to the choices that natural phenomena pose. Analogous to the pure categories of the understanding, which represent necessary features of our take on how the world *is*, the idea of goodness, and related moral ideas, represent how we must think that the world *ought* to be. In the *Groundwork* what we judge good or bad *to do* depends ultimately on what we *will* insofar as we are free and reason-governed. In Kant's view, the foundational principles of ethics do not stem from natural science, public legislation, or individual choice but are principles that every person who has practical reason cannot help but acknowledge, at least when clear-eyed and not self-deceptive.

Third, a significant outcome of the *Critique of Pure Reason* for ethics is that, according to Kant, every phenomenal event has a cause according to which its effects must follow but nevertheless it is *possible* that there is another kind of causality, a spontaneous initiation of a series of events, not explicable by empirical laws of causation (A435–9/B463–7). In the *Critique of Pure Reason*, however, this non-empirical causation remains merely a possibility. It is a task for the *Groundwork* (and the later *Critique of Practical Reason*) to argue that we have compelling grounds to accept that we human beings, as rational agents, have the capacity to be such free causes.

Fourth, the *Critique of Pure Reason* argues that the traditional metaphysical ideas, such as God, a free will, and an immortal soul, cannot be comprehended in empirical terms or grasped by intuition. What we can understand are things that we can experience, or infer from experience, but these are things as they appear to us (phenomena), not things in themselves (noumena). For example, we can assess people's empirical character by their patterns of behavior and speech and by what we infer to be their thoughts and feelings, but a person's *free will*, as it is in itself, is ultimately inscrutable. We have *Ideas* of God, freedom, and even immortality that can inform our thoughts and hopes, but we can never perceive, intuit, or comprehend the objects of these thoughts. Famously, Kant says that he has given a critique of reason in order to make room for faith, but the *Critique of Pure Reason* does not provide his argument for faith. The *Groundwork*, then, must work from the assumption that ethics cannot be derived from religion, even though Kant later argues that elements of religious faith can be supported by moral arguments.[1]

These methodological and epistemological points are the important background for the *Groundwork for the Metaphysics of Morals* (Kant 2002 [1785]), but Kant's explicit argument in the *Groundwork* starts and proceeds from more familiar ideas about what is most worthy of choice. The main themes are presented and defended in a preface and three sections, some highlights of which are sketched in the following sections.

2.   Preface: Aims and Methods

Here Kant relates ethics as a rational discipline to other branches of knowledge, explaining that although its prescriptions are substantive, ethics must be based on principles of pure reason. Empirical studies of matters related to ethics, labeled *practical anthropology*, are distinguished from *moral philosophy proper*, which is concerned with *a priori* principles of a pure rational will. Kant's focus, *a pure rational will*, is contrasted with Christian Wolff's focus on *the will in general* (which includes non-rational and conditionally rational choices). The aim of the *Groundwork*, Kant explains, is to seek out and establish the supreme principle of morality. Seeking out the supreme principle, which is the task of the first two sections of the *Groundwork*, requires not only finding apt expressions of it but also showing that the principle expressed is the *only* principle that could satisfy the presupposition of common morality that moral duties are based on such a Categorical Imperative. The task of *establishing* the supreme moral principle requires defense of the claim that moral duties are, as common morality presupposes, in fact based on a Categorical Imperative, that is, they are unconditional requirements of reason even for imperfectly rational beings, like us, who can follow rational principles but can also fail to do so. In the *Groundwork* (1785) Kant aims to lay out only foundations for a whole system of moral principles based on reason, but he also planned to return to develop such a moral system, or *metaphysics of morals*, in a later work, *The Metaphysics of Morals* (1797–8). This subsequent work, he anticipates, would show the adequacy of his first principles in application, thereby clarifying and confirming those principles though not by itself securely proving them.

3.   Section One: The Principle of a Good Will

Here Kant famously claims that only a good will is good without qualification, that only acts from duty have moral worth, and that such acts are morally worthy because of their underlying principle rather than what they achieve or aim to achieve. The principle of a good will, expressed in morally worthy acts, is to respect and conform to universal law, and this, Kant argues, implies acting only on maxims that one can will as universal law. The primary aim of this first section is to identify features of our common rational cognition of morality and show, by an analytical method, that these entail a commitment to the supreme moral principle and that this principle enables us to identify maxims on which it is wrong or morally unworthy to act. Kant explains that, even if they do not always use it well, ordinary people have the rational capacity to determine whether or not what they propose to do is morally permissible. Nevertheless moral philosophy is still needed to combat sophistry and confusion, and to provide a deeper understanding of our moral thought and practice.

To expand on these basic points briefly, the first section opens with the ringing declaration that only a good will is good without qualification (*GMS* 4: 393). This proposition is not just about what is worth having when considered apart from further effects. Innocent pleasures and deserved happiness are good in that way. A person's happiness if consistent with moral principles is both good to the agent and among the things that others have some reason to promote. The point of saying that a good will is *good without qualification* is not simply to say that it is non-instrumentally good but to affirm that when our various desires and values conflict, nothing should take precedence over what one does or would will as a person who has a *good will* committed to following the moral law. Other things that we may value – such as talent, power, wealth, and even happiness – are good to have and pursue only so long as they can be pursued and enjoyed without violating the principle(s) of a good will.

Kant does not mean here to endorse the self-righteous attitude that all that matters is "keeping one's own hands clean" regardless of what others do or suffer as a result. Rather, to give priority to our good will in deliberation is simply to treat duty as trumping any other things that we may desire. This does not yet *specify* what our *duty* is. A good will is "good without qualification" and so we must never abandon our good will in any context regardless of what others are doing and even if harmful consequences will predictably follow. That is, we must regard our best informed judgment that, all things considered, it is our duty to do something as decisive in our deliberations. This is not to deny, however, that what others may do or suffer as a result of our decisions is generally relevant, though not always decisive, when we try to determine what it is our duty to do in a given situation.

A second major idea that Kant finds in common rational knowledge of morality is that only acts from duty have moral worth (*GMS* 4: 397–9). Here Kant sets aside cases where a person acts contrary to duty. Many people think that a person could be morally commendable even when act-ing contrary to duty if the person was conscientiously trying to do right and acted wrongly solely because of a mistaken belief about what is morally required. Kant, however, does not focus on such cases here, presumably because these cases are not necessary to consider for the project at hand, which is to identify and analyze the basic principle on which a person with a good will acts. For this Kant focuses on the paradigm case in which one acts *from duty* by doing what is in fact morally required because it is morally required.

According to Kant, one cannot tell for certain whether anyone, including oneself, has ever acted solely from duty as opposed to acting to impress others, to avoid censure, to express personal prefer-ences, and so on. Nevertheless, the ideal of doing what is right because it is right can inspire us as we deliberate about what to do. In Kant's view, acting this way would have a special *moral worth* as manifesting a moral commitment that everyone should have. Moral worth, however, is not like a gold star, a reward for virtue, or an earned right to be praised by others. There is no way to measure or even identify it with certainty, and although we should strive for the strength of will (or *virtue*) always to conform to duty and do so *from duty* (at least when inclinations tempt us to do otherwise), this does not mean that we have a duty to accumulate a record of as many exemplary acts of moral worth as possible. One person of good will may face extraordinary moral challenges and temptations and so act with explicit thoughts of duty more often than another, but the first is not necessarily a better person than the second because, assuming that the second also has a good will, presumably she too would act similarly if facing the same challenges and temptations. The moral goodness of a person is not measured by the number of a person's morally worthy deeds but by the quality of that person's will. Kant's point, seen in context, is that only acts from duty would fully express a person's morally *good will* in action. This proposition is not offered as a comprehensive theory of comparative praiseworthiness but rather as a step in Kant's project in the first section of the *Groundwork*, which is to "seek out" the fundamental principle of an unqualifiedly good will.

The search continues as Kant asks what gives acts from duty their moral worth? (*GMS* 4: 399). In other words, what about such acts identifies them as acts of good will? It is not that they have desirable consequences, for even with the best possible will a person may be unsuccessful in achiev-ing his or her ends and by chance even a bad will can bring about desirable outcomes. Furthermore, the identifying mark of a good will is not even *the intention* to produce certain results, for a person of good will is not concerned only with consequences. Of course, people of good will include the happiness of others, self-improvement, and so on, among their ends, but always with constraints on the means that they will use to promote the ends. We cannot identify any type of end (such as happiness) such that aiming to promote it shows that a person is acting from a good will. Instead the essential mark of an act of good will is the underlying principle on which the act is based independently of the agent's personal wishes and desires. Kant proceeds to identify the principle as *respect for law* or *to conform to universal law as such* (GMS 4: 400–1). *Laws* in this context are by definition necessary and universal rational principles, and so we can infer at least that a good will respects and conforms to universal law by obeying necessary and universal rational principles, whatever these may be (which is not yet specified).

Kant next describes the principle of a good will as "I ought never to act in such a way *that I could not also will that my maxim should become a universal law*" (GMS 4: 402). This is essentially the same principle that Kant later declares to be the only possible Categorical Imperative and a way of testing whether or not one's maxims are permissible to act on. Kant does not fill in the argument to show how this action-guiding principle expresses or follows from the preceding "Conform to universal law as such." Instead he proceeds to illustrates how the principle, or a variant of it,[2] can show that it is morally wrong, even if prudentially expedient, to make a lying promise to extricate oneself from a distressful predicament. He expresses confidence that ordinary reason is sufficient to know the difference between right and wrong, but explains that philosophy may be needed to combat the confusions and self-serving quibbling that otherwise might lead us astray.

4. Section Two: Duty Presupposes the Categorical Imperative and Autonomy of the Will

In the next section Kant makes a partly new attempt to seek out the supreme principle of morality, now starting from the idea of duty rather than from the idea of a good will. He first repeatedly insists that all moral philosophy must be based on a priori principles (GMS 4: 406–13). Contrasting his view with popular philosophy, which mixes conceptual and empirical claims, he argues that only one principle could be a purely rational moral principle (GMS 4: 413–21). That principle, which he calls the Categorical Imperative, ultimately turns out to be more or less equivalent to the claim that we ought always to act as free and rational beings with the capacity and disposition to govern ourselves by rational principles independently of our sensuous impulses and inclinations (GMS 4: 421–40).

The starting point of this section is the common distinction between what we must do to promote our own desire-based interests and what we are morally required to do whether or not it serves those interests (GMS 4: 413–7). Rational requirements to promote desire-based interests are what Kant calls *hypothetical imperatives* whereas moral requirements are (or are based on) *categorical imperatives*. All imperatives are principles that a fully rational person would follow in the relevant context and which therefore imperfectly rational beings *ought* to follow (GMS 4: 413). Hypothetical imperatives, however, are rational requirements that are doubly conditional: they are binding only if they do not violate categorical (moral) requirements and only insofar as they promote our personal ends or (more generally) the end of attaining happiness that we have by natural necessity. Categorical imperatives are principles that any fully rational person would follow regardless of whether doing so promotes the person's personal ends or happiness.

Famously Kant formulates several versions of the supreme moral principle (*the* Categorical Imperative), arguing that these are at bottom the same and suggesting that they progressively reveal various aspects of the fundamental requirements of morality (GMS 4: 421–40).[3] In brief, the main formulations are (1) act only on maxims that you can will as universal laws; (2) act so that you always treat humanity, in your own person or in the person of any other, never simply as a means but always at the same time as an end in itself; and (3) always act as if you were an autonomous lawmaker in a possible kingdom of ends in which the rational members make the laws to which they are subject while abstracting from personal differences (*GMS* 4: 421–40). Kant illustrates the application of the first two of these principles by describing four cases. In each situation a person considers doing something that Kant regards as wrong: making a lying promise to get a loan, committing suicide to escape discomfort and troubles, neglecting to cultivate one's talents simply because one prefers a life of ease, and refusing to give aid to the needy when one easily could (*GMS* 4: 421–3, 429–30). There is a vast literature concerning the interpretation of these formulations and the relations among them, but I respectfully pass over these controversies here in order to focus on the outlines of the main argument of the *Groundwork*.[4] Even the number of formulations remains controversial, but from the preceding list drawn from Kant's review (*GMS* 4: 346), clearly (1) attempts to re-articulate formally the basic idea of the Golden Rule, and (2) affirms human dignity as a barrier to unrestrained consequentialist thinking, and (3) sketches abstractly the ideal of a community in which all moral agents are authors of the moral laws to which they are subject.

Kant argues progressively from formula to formula, ending with the striking conclusion that autonomy of the will is the supreme principle of morality (*GMS* 4: 440). In effect, he argues, to act morally is to follow the Categorical Imperative, which amounts to acting as a fully rational and free person. Freedom here is not license to do as one pleases but autonomy of the will, which (as indicated at the beginning of the next section) entails both *freedom negatively conceived*, a rational capacity and disposition to act independently of determination by alien causes, and *freedom positively conceived*, a rational capacity and disposition to govern oneself in accordance with rational principles that (in a sense) one gives to oneself (*GMS* 4: 446–7). All previous moral theories, Kant argues, have failed to appreciate the central role of this autonomy of the will. In various ways, insofar as they are substantive, the previous theories – ethical egoism, moral sense theories, divine command theories, and rationalist perfection theories – give us only reasons to act based on hypothetical imperatives, which, as Kant has argued, cannot support the unconditional demands of morality (*GMS* 4: 441–4).

Kant ends section two with a surprising concession that for all he has shown there may be no genuine categorical imperative and so morality may be an illusion (*GMS* 4: 445). His argument so far proceeded analytically from the common idea of moral duty. It attempted to show that, assuming we are subject to moral duty, we must follow its supreme principle, the Categorical Imperative, and that this is true if and only if as rational agents we have autonomy of the will. The argument is conditional, leaving open the possibility that we are mistaken in assuming that we have duties. Assuming, then, that we are imperfect rational agents and, as Kant has argued, imperfect rational agents have moral duties as specified by the Categorical Imperative *if* (but only if) they have autonomy of the will, it remains for the third section to show that we imperfectly rational agents have autonomy of the will or, what is supposed to be the same from a practical standpoint, we must necessarily conceive of ourselves as having autonomy of the will. This would "establish" the supreme moral principle as a rational principle of choice.

5. Section Three: Practical Reason Presupposes Autonomy of the Will

In the third section of the *Groundwork* Kant responds to the lingering worry left in the preceding section that morality might be a mere phantom of the brain. This may seem surprising because it is not a primary aim of Kant's moral theory to respond to those who doubt the judgments of ordinary morality, and indeed he has already expressed in section 1 his confidence that common reason is capable of discerning right from wrong. So what *is* his aim? What would it mean for morality to be a mere illusion? Recall that Kant has in effect analyzed the moral judgment that we have a duty as a prescription or prohibition that is categorically imperative, implying that we have compelling and overriding reasons to follow it. A moral duty is supposed to be an unconditional rational requirement, which any fully rational person would follow (in the specified conditions) and that imperfect rational beings ought to follow if they can. That we have rational capacities of some kind but are not fully rational is not in question here. What the preceding discussion has not yet shown is that the moral requirements that we believe in are really, as they purport to be, rational imperatives for us that we "ought" and even "must" follow. If we were fully rational without inclinations, Kant argues, we would necessarily conform to the moral requirements. And he argues that if we were entirely natural beings whose behavior is determined by inclinations, then we would be incapable of governing ourselves by rational moral principles. But as human beings we are in between: we are neither purely rational nor completely governed by inclinations (*GMS* 4: 453–4). What Kant needs to show is that we have the capacity or freedom to follow rational requirements even when they conflict with our inclinations. In section 2 Kant purports to have shown that any *fully* rational person, acting rationally, would follow the principles expressed in the formulations of the Categorical Imperative, and so any imperfectly rational person who can follow them has a moral obligation to do so. What he has argued, then, is that *if free*, that is, capable of governing ourselves by moral principles, we imperfectly rational beings are under moral obligation to follow them.

Another way of expressing the doubt that remains at the end of the preceding section is to say that we do not yet know whether or not the principle of a good will, which Kant has argued is the only principle that could be a Categorical Imperative, is really a Categorical Imperative (*GMS* 4: 445). That may seem puzzling because he has apparently articulated several formulations of what he repeatedly *calls* "the Categorical Imperative," arguing that *only* this principle (or these formulations) could be a Categorical Imperative in the strictest sense – a requirement that is unconditionally rational for anyone to follow. What Kant has shown in the previous discussion is only that certain shared ideas in ordinary morality presuppose that there is such a rational principle and that it serves as the basis of common moral judgments about what duties we have. So there would really be a Categorical Imperative, as morality presupposes as its basis, if imperfectly rational beings such as us have the freedom to act as we would if we were fully rational, even though we often we fail to do so.

Kant's argument in response to these concerns is notoriously difficult to follow, and interpretations remain controversial. Here I only sketch the main steps as I understand them. Kant begins with the idea of a *will*, characterizing it as an ability of living rational beings to cause events in accord with the idea of a law (*GMS* 4: 446). Then he defines *a free will in a negative sense* as a will that can work independently of determination by alien causes. So a free will can make things happen in the world without being deterministically caused or motivated by sensuous inclinations and desires. Then Kant argues that *a will that is free in a negative sense must also be free in a positive sense* (autonomy). The key idea here is that a free will cannot be lawless, and so rational beings with free wills must be subject to *laws*, that is, universal rational principles that they necessarily acknowledge as their own or "give to themselves." Next Kant re-affirms (from section 2) that *if a will is free in the positive sense (autonomy), then it is subject to the moral law* as expressed by the Categorical Imperative. Any rational being, then, is subject to the moral law *if that person has a will that is free in the negative sense*.

The next subsection (*GMS* 4: 447–8) attempts to remove the conditional clause. That is, Kant argues that all rational beings necessarily have wills that are free in the negative sense, or at least we must presume this from the standpoint of practice (choice and action), which means it is a valid principle for determining what we ought to do. The main argument is this: (1) we cannot act except under the idea of freedom, taking ourselves to have free wills when we choose and act, (2) anyone who cannot act except under the idea of freedom, is free from a practical standpoint (i.e. the practical laws are binding for such a person just as they would be if the person were free), (3) therefore, we are free from a practical standpoint.

This basic argument is followed by a lengthy response to the imagined objection that his reasoning is circular (*GMS* 4: 449–50). Kant's answer is No, because we can and must see ourselves as members of not only a "sensible world" in which all phenomenal events are caused but also an "intelligible world" in which we can think and make choices free from determination by such causes. As moral agents and even in theoretical thinking, we cannot help but regard ourselves (with others) as having the capacity to reason without being determined by sensuous causes and so as negatively and positively free. Such freedom is an idea we must use from a practical standpoint but it cannot be comprehended in empirical terms.

6. Questions of Interpretation

Serious scholars often disagree, and here are some of the persistent controversies. For example, contemporary writers disagree about whether Kant is committed to a strong version of the *guise of the good* thesis. Did Kant believe that when we choose to act we necessarily see our act as objectively and completely good?[5] Kant no doubt thought that when one *wills* to do something then one regards acting in that way to be good *in some sense* (*KpV* 5: 63–4). But good in what sense? When we choose to do something then we generally regard it as good to do at least in a subjective sense, for example, that doing it pleases us or is likely to get us something that we want. Also Kant held that when one *wills fully in accord with reason* then one wills only what is objectively and completely good to do – that is, either unconditionally good or good subject to some condition that is in fact satisfied. More controversial is whether in willing to do something one necessarily takes it to be good (or at least permissible) for anyone to do. The relevant texts are complicated. Kant at times seems to identify *the will* with practical reason (*GMS* 4: 413), and practical reason determines both what is instrumentally good and what is good in itself. And yet Kant seems to imply that we often do will to act contrary to reason (*GMS* 4: 413, 454–5). In later works Kant distinguishes between two senses of *will* – practical reason (*Wille*) and choice (*Willkür*), but it is uncertain to what extent the distinction is implicit in the *Groundwork*.[6]

Why does this controversy matter? The strongest versions of the guise of the good thesis seem to have troubling implications. For example, if I always take what I will to be objectively, universally and unconditionally good, then I cannot knowingly will to do something that I believe to be bad or wrong. All wrongdoing would be due to moral errors or perhaps self-deception. Weakness of will and willful wrongdoing, as commonly understood, would be impossible. It is also not clear how Kant interprets weakness of will (Hill 2012c). In his view, the will is not a physical power that could be literally strong or weak like a muscle, but instead in all voluntary actions, including weak-willed wrongdoing, what we will are maxims that "incorporate" our incentives (Allison 2011; Reath 2015). Would, then, a person doing wrong from weakness of will have simultaneously two conflicting maxims, an ineffective good moral maxim as well as the bad maxim on which he actually acts?[7]

Another controversy that persists concerns how to interpret the several formulations of the Categorical Imperative and the relations among them. The extent to which Kant meant for formulations of the Categorical Imperative to serve as practical guides to moral decision making remains controversial despite passages that strongly suggest that at least some of them can serve this role. Scholars also differ about which formulation, if any, is the most comprehensive and illuminating of the basic requirements of morality. Onora O'Neill (1989), Oliver Sensen (2011), Barbara Herman (1993), and Jens Timmermann (2011), for example, give priority to the formulas of universal law, treating the later formulations as more or less the same or derivatives. Allen Wood (1999) treats the later formulations as more illuminating and grounded in moral realist metaphysics. John Rawls (1999), by contrast, develops a constructivist reading of the formulations that retains the priority of the (appropriately reconstructed) universal formula. My own work has emphasized the kingdom of ends formula as combining aspects of the supreme principle expressed in the earlier formulations.[8] These controversies matter not only because they are about how to understand Kant's supreme moral principle and its role in moral judgment but also because they concern crucial steps in Kant's overall argument that all previous moral theories are mistaken and morality is not based on an illusion.

Questions also remain unsettled about the content of the formulations as well as their relative priority.[9] For example, how specific are *maxims* meant to be? Are they a person's broad generic life-governing principles, or more specific expressions of one's intentions in particular contexts?[10] Is the formula of universal law that Kant introduces distinct from the often conflated formula of autonomy?[11] We are to treat humanity in each person as an end in itself, but what is *humanity*? For example, is it the same as *a good will*[12] or the capacity for having a good will, all aspects of our rational nature, or simply the capacity to set ends for oneself?[13] How are we to understand *legislation* in the kingdom of ends? Are we to think of ideal rational lawmakers *jointly* legislating moral principles by which they will be governed (by analogy to state legislation) or are we to imagine *individuals* willing that their personal maxims be adopted by (or permissible for) everyone?[14]

Here, briefly, are three further questions that concern particular texts.

First, to what degree does the moral law leave room for the pursuit of our personal projects? Kant says that to harmonize positively with humanity as an end in itself everyone must endeavor "*as far as he can* to promote the ends of others" and that "for this idea is to have its full effect in me" the ends of any person who is an end in himself must "be also, so far as possible, my ends" (*GMS* 4: 430). Does this mean that we must always promote the happiness of others instead of our own at every opportunity unless we are trying to fulfill some other competing duty? Commentators disagree about this and whether Kant acknowledges any sense in which an act can be morally good to do but not required.[15]

Second, does Kant's argument in the second paragraph of *Groundwork* III (*GMS* 4: 446–7) imply that we act freely only when we act on the moral law? It may seem so because Kant argues that negative freedom of will is also positive freedom (autonomy), and the principle expressive of autonomy ("being a law to itself") is "acting on no other maxim than one that can also have being itself a universal law for its object" (*GMS* 4: 447). If this is a version of the Categorical Imperative, the apparent implication is that only acts based on the moral law are free and therefore all wrong acts are unfree and so we are not responsible for them. Most scholars reject this interpretation, but the texts suggesting it require explanation.

Third, what exactly was the circular reasoning that in *Groundwork* III Kant dramatically pretends that he has fallen into? (*GMS* 4: 448–50). How did he think that in the end he could avoid the charge? In both the *Groundwork* and the *Critique of Practical Reason* Kant defends what has been called the reciprocity thesis: one is subject to the moral law *if and only if* one is free. Kant apparently thought that he might be read as arguing both (1) we know that we are subject to the moral law *because* we know that we are free and (2) we know we are free *because* we know that we are subject to the moral law (*KpV* 5: 5n). This, of course, would be circular reasoning. In the *Critique of Practical Reason* Kant clearly adopts the second line of argument,[16] but was this a reversal of the argument in *Groundwork* III? It seems so because in the first two paragraphs of *Groundwork* III Kant argues explicitly that if negatively free a will must be free positively and so must be subject to the moral law (even if not always following it). And in the fourth paragraph he argues that every rational agent, from a practical standpoint, is negatively free. Thus so far, in the early paragraphs, the argument is (1), that is, because we know (or have warranted belief) that we are free, we know that are subject to the moral law. Why then did he raise the suspicion that he also argued for (2), inferring freedom from morality? Did he worry that his claim that we cannot act except under the idea of freedom was based on our sense that we can always resist sensuous desires to do our duty? In any case, he seems to respond by offering a non-moral argument that we must think of ourselves as free. That is, even in theoretical thinking one must take oneself to belong to the intelligible world, which is not governed by empirical causal laws, and to do so is to think of oneself as free. There are other ways to interpret the apparent circularity and the intended escape, and we may wonder whether Kant's ideas of freedom and the intelligible world are sufficient for his purpose if these are, as he says, ultimately inexplicable.

Notes

1 *KpV*, esp. 5: 122–148. See also *RGV*.
2 "Act as though the maxim of your action were to become by your will a universal law of nature" (*GMS* 4: 421).
3 (*GMS* 4: 436). In order to distinguish Kant's comprehensive moral principle from more specific moral principles that he sometimes calls categorical imperatives, I capitalize the term when it refers to versions of his comprehensive moral principle.
4 See, for example, Allison (2011), Baron (1995), Cummiskey (1996), Dean (2006), Guyer (2007), Korsgaard (1996), Herman (1993), O'Neill (1989), Rawls (1999), Reath (2015), Sedgwick (2008), Sensen (2011), Timmermann (2011), Wood (1999, 2008).
5 For some discussion of this issue, see Hill (2002c, 2008, 2012b); Reath (2015); Engstrom (2009).
6 For example, *MS* (6: 213–14) and *RGV* (6: 25–6).
7 See Hill (2012c), 107–128.
8 See, for example, Hill (2012d).
9 For a review of various interpretations, see Hill (2012a).
10 See O'Neill (1989: 83–88).
11 See Wood (1999: 156–90).
12 See Dean (2006: 1–106).
13 See Korsgaard (1996: 106–32).
14 See Hill (2002a).
15 See Baron and Seymour Falmy (2009) and Hill, Jr. (1992, 2002b).
16 *KpV* (5: 5n).

References

Allison, H. (2011) *Kant's Groundwork for the Metaphysics of Morals*, Oxford: Oxford University Press.
Baron, M. (1995) *Kantian Ethics Almost Without Apology*, Ithaca: Cornell University Press.
Baron, M. and Seymour-Falmy, M. (2009) "Beneficence and Other Duties of Love in the *Metaphysics of Morals*," in T.E. Hill, Jr. (ed.), *The Blackwell Guide to Kant's Ethics*, Malden, MA: Wiley-Blackwell, pp. 211–28.
Cummiskey, D. (1996) *Kantian Consequentialism*, New York: Oxford University Press.
Dean, R. (2006) *The Value of Humanity in Kant's Moral Theory*, Oxford: Oxford University Press.
Engstrom, S. (2009) *The Form of Practical Knowledge*, Cambridge, MA: Harvard University Press.
Guyer, P. (2007) *Kant's Groundwork for the Metaphysics of Morals*, London and New York: Continuum.
Herman, B. (1993) *The Practice of Moral Judgment*, Cambridge, MA: Harvard University Press.
Hill, Jr. T.E. (1992) "Kant on Imperfect Duty and Supererogation," in *Dignity and Practical Reason in Kant's Moral Theory*, Ithaca: Cornell University Press, pp. 147–75.
Hill, Jr. T.E. (2002a) "Hypothetical Consent in Kantian Constructivism," in *Human Welfare and Moral Worth*, Oxford: Oxford University Press, pp. 61–96.
Hill, Jr. T.E. (2002b) "Meeting Needs and Doing Favors," in *Human Welfare and Moral Worth: Kantian Perspectives*, Oxford: Oxford University Press, pp. 201–43.
Hill, Jr. T.E. (2002c) "Personal Values and Setting Oneself Ends," in *Human Welfare and Moral Worth*, Oxford: Oxford University Press, pp. 244–74.
Hill, Jr. T.E. (2008) "Legislating the Moral Law and Taking One's Choices to Be Good," *Philosophical Books* 49(2): 97–106.

Hill, Jr. T.E. (2012a) "Kantian Normative Ethics," in *Virtue, Rules, and Justice: Kantian Aspirations*, Oxford: Oxford University Press, pp. 35–70.

Hill, Jr. T.E. (2012b) "Practical Reason, the Moral Law, and Choice: Comments on Stephen Engstrom's *The Form of Practical Knowledge*," *Analytic Philosophy* 53(1): 71–7.

Hill, Jr. T.E. (2012c) "Kant on Weakness of Will," in *Virtue, Rules, and Justice: Kantian Aspirations*, Oxford: Oxford University Press, pp. 107–28.

Hill, Jr. T.E. (2012d) "The Dignity of Persons: Kant, Problems, and a Proposal," in *Virtue, Rules, and Justice: Kantian Aspirations*, Oxford: Oxford University Press, pp. 185–202.

Kant, I. (1965 [1781/1787]) *Critique of Pure Reason*, N.-K. Smith (trans.), New York: St. Martin's Press.

Kant, I. (2002 [1785]) *Groundwork for the Metaphysics of Morals*, T.E. Hill, Jr. (ed.) and A. Zweig (trans.), Oxford: Oxford University Press.

Korsgaard, C. (1996) *Creating the Kingdom of Ends*, Cambridge: Cambridge University Press.

O'Neill, O. (1989) *Constructions of Reason*, Cambridge: Cambridge University Press.

Rawls, J. (1999) "Kantian Constructivism in Moral Theory," in S. Freeman (ed.), *Collected Papers*, Cambridge, MA: Harvard University Press, pp. 303–58.

Reath, A. (2015) "Did Kant Hold That Rational Volition Is *Sub Ratione Boni*?" in M. Timmons and R. Johnson (eds.), *Reason, Value, and Respect*, Oxford: Oxford University Press, pp. 232–55.

Sedgwick, S. (2008) *Kant's Groundwork of the Metaphysics of Morals: An Introduction*, Cambridge: Cambridge University Press.

Sensen, O. (2011) *Kant on Human Dignity*, Berlin and Boston: Walter de Gruyter.

Timmermann, J. (2011) *Kant's Groundwork of the Metaphysics of Morals: A Critical Guide*, Cambridge: Cambridge University Press.

Wood, A. (1999) *Kant's Ethical Thought*, Cambridge: Cambridge University Press.

Wood, A. (2008) *Kantian Ethics*, Cambridge: Cambridge University Press.

Further Reading

P. Guyer, *Groundwork of the Metaphysics of Morals: Critical Essays*, 2nd ed. (Lantham, MD and Oxford: Roman & Littlefield Publishers, 1998) is a critical commentary from twelve Kant scholars. P. Guyer, *Kant* (Abingdon: Routledge, 2004) is general introduction to Kant's philosophy by a distinguished Kant scholar. T.E. Hill, Jr. (ed.), *Blackwell Guide to Kant's Ethics* (Malden, MA: Wiley-Blackwell Publishers, 2009) contains accessible essays introducing a wide range of topics in Kant's ethics. J. Rawls, *Lectures on the History of Moral Philosophy*, B. Herman (ed.) (Cambridge, MA: Harvard University Press, 2000), pp. 143–325, is a commentary by a deservedly influential moral and political philosopher.

13

THE SECOND *CRITIQUE*

Preface and Introduction

Valentin Mureşan

★★★

1. Preliminary Overview

The *Critique of Practical Reason* (*KpV* – 2002b [1788]) was published only three years after the *Groundwork of the Metaphysics of Morals* and twelve years before the *Metaphysics of Morals*. Originally conceived as a part of the second edition of the *Critique of Pure Reason* (1998 [1787]) (with the provisional title *Critique of Pure Practical Reason*), the *KpV* became finally a self-contained work, having a precise function in Kant's practical philosophy: to lay the foundation for the system of the metaphysics of morals. In 1797, Kant published *The Metaphysics of Morals* launching a new discipline which contained the "*system* of pure practical reason" "developed from" the second *Critique* (*KpV* 5: 8), that is, the whole system of a priori duties of human beings *as such*, derived from a priori grounds (Beck 1963: 16).[1] The distinct disciplinary levels of the system of practical philosophy – starting from "anthropology" and going towards the "metaphysics of morals" through the "critique of practical reason" – bring into prominence "the theoretical form of the entire system of Kant's practical philosophy" created in order to provide a "transcendental-metaphysical foundation of ethics" (Pârvu 2013: 5).

KpV plays the role of a canon of practical reason, that is, it provides the sum total of the principles of practical reason's correct use (A796/B824). It is an instrument for grounding the metaphysics of morals by a preliminary conceptual clarification, which consists in a critical examination of all a priori and pure concepts, which are needed to explain rational action conceived of as universal moral duty. The *KpV* has a decisive contribution to removing and forestalling the confusions and misunderstandings which can impede the moral law's acceptance and diminish its efficacy (Engstrom 2002: xxviii). Metaphorically speaking, it is "a complete dissection of reason's practical use" (*KpV* 5: 5). Kant considered that "only a comprehensive *Critique of Practical Reason* can remove all this misinterpretation [of Kant's Critical philosophy] and put the consistent way of thinking, which indeed amounts to its greatest merit, in a clear light" (*KpV* 5: 6–7).

As usual, the Preface anticipates and the Introduction briefly presents most of the issues that will be addressed in the main text, but they also contain replies to some ingenious reviewers of the *KrV* and *GMS*. By analogy with the *KrV*, the second *Critique* has two parts: the Doctrine of Elements

DOI: 10.4324/9781003406617-18

and the Doctrine of Method. As if Kant intended to outline his main project, that is, defending the possibility a non-empiricist moral theory, the first part of the Doctrine of Elements, the Analytic, begins with the question "Is pure reason practical?" or, in other words, "Can reason by itself determine the will?" Then, the clarification of an impressive list of controversial problems is attempted by critical analysis. For instance, Kant sets himself the task of elucidating the concept of a causality suitable to rational beings, raising, among others, the following questions: How can we derive the idea of absolute freedom from that of morality? What kinds of imperatives are there and what is the nature of practical necessity? Can we justify the supreme principle of morality otherwise than by a "transcendental deduction"? What is a "fact of reason"? What is the nature of a "suprasensible" being and what is the significance of our twofold nature? How could freedom be a causality of pure reason? What role does the supreme good play and how to defend the strategy of beginning in ethics with the concept of law, rather than that of good? How is moral evaluation possible and what is the meaning of a "typic"? How can the principle of morality function as a motive?

The second section of Part I, the Dialectic, includes "critiques" of the antinomy of practical reason, reflections on the "postulates" of pure practical reason and a discussion of the relation between the highest good and the supreme principle of morality. The book ends with a short chapter dedicated to the Doctrine of Method. As already mentioned, after the second *Critique*, *The Metaphysics of Morals* restricts the focus of discussion to the derivation of the system of a priori duties of "human beings as such" from the supreme principle of morality and proposes some incomplete exercises of applying the a priori duties to cases in experience.

The Kantian sui generis "critique" does not refer to a psychological process, as Kant's language suggests, but to an intersubjective activity of building a "systematic practical philosophy, seen as a *science*" (*KpV* 5: 12).[2] This is a new kind of scientific theory inspired by the structure of the Newtonian theory of mathematical physics[3] interpreted in a non-empiricist way. The second *Critique* is designed to contribute to the accomplishment of the "metaphysical revolution" promised by Kant in the *KrV*, being an introduction to the "system of practical reason" and leading us towards a "methodic science of pure reason". In what follows, the focus will be on the aim of the Second *Critique* (Section 2), its methodology and a suggested new interpretative line on Kant's project of a scientific practical philosophy (Sections 3 and 4), followed by a brief conclusion (Section 5).

2. The Main Aim of the Second *Critique*

Without any doubt, there are several aims this work tries to achieve. Generally speaking, it was written to discover the conditions of possibility, the scope, and the limits, of practical reason. These aims, in their turn, also presuppose the need for a clarification of the "principle of all duty", its "formula" and its justification. But the *main* aim of the *KpV* is related to Kant's great project of setting up a non-empiricist theory of morals under the form of a unified theory of speculative and practical reason. The first step in exploring this project – as the beginning of the Preface shows – is the elucidation of the determining (motivational) mechanism of ethical actions, starting from the old and solid "belief-desire" theory which dominated the history of empiricism in ethics.[4] The main aim of the book is summarised by the seemingly odd question from the beginning of the Preface, namely, whether "*there is pure practical reason*" (*KpV* 5: 3) or, in other words, whether there are actions performed from the motive of duty alone. This is a question about ethical motivation. It uncovers Kant's belief that the empiricist tradition in ethics, beginning with Aristotle's "belief-desire" theory of motivation, may and should be replaced by a rationalist theory, a theory grounded a priori. We may call this theory "cognitivist internalism" ("cognitivist" because the principles of reason alone motivate the actions without any help from additional ends and empirical incentives, and "internalism" because the reasons for moral action are internal, that is, exclusively principles of practical reason). Instead of looking for a theory based on perception and empirical judgments, we look for a theory in which emotion and inclination towards empirical ends are excluded from the process of moral assessment and motivation. Empiricism in ethics, based on an outmoded "mixed moral philosophy" of motivation,[5] is unsatisfactory because it implies moral relativism (which is arguably ethically contradictory) and is capable of leading us only accidentally to the good, while, on the contrary, the motivation theory based on "the pure presentation of duty" has "an influence on the human heart so much more powerful than all other incentives" (*GMS* 4: 410–1).

Kant's ethical theory is usually regarded as a theory of duty. A duty is an *action* (or an action-type) to which someone is bound by a categorical imperative. An action is something more than unintentional behaviour, it is always a "rational" correlation between means and ends, in the sense of being guided by *principles* – subjective ("maxims") or objective ("laws"). Could we have purely rational laws of the will? More exactly, Kant's question in the Introduction is "whether pure reason is sufficient by itself alone to determine the will or whether reason can be a determining basis of the will only if it is empirically conditioned", as the "belief-desire" theory together with a "universal empiricism" doctrine would claim? (*KpV* 5: 15).

The will of the human agent has always two determining sources: rational (practical laws) and empirical (inclinations). If we imagine an *ideal* model of an agent, from which the empirical ingredients are totally excluded and only pure reason remains, we could prove and make intelligible that "pure practical reason is *possible*" inside this ideal framework (*KpV* 5: 12n). This presupposes a "new language" and a *new theoretical structure* – a theory based on a new concept of causality, the atemporal "causality through freedom" which governs the laws of practical reason in a hypothetical world of freedom, a world of absolutely free rational beings, the opposite of the world of necessity, the future Laplacean world. Therefore, we have to present clearly "the practical capacity of reason", more exactly to explain its concepts and "universal determinative rules", going then back to the point where the concrete duties of human being's experience are derived from these non-empirical principles. The main task of the *Critique* is to contribute to the setting up of a frame-theory which discovers the general epistemological conditions in which the supreme principle of morality is possible as a universal rule which determines the will.

Being a kind of causality (of rational beings), the will involves the concept of "law". The ideal world of freedom is not lawless. But it is not governed by natural causal laws (as the world of necessity is); on the contrary, it is completely independent of any determination by external causes and by the causal laws of the deterministic physical world. Therefore, the will may be thought in only one way: as governed by *its own* "practical" laws, a property called "freedom" in the positive sense or "autonomy"; the concept of freedom in the sense of autonomy is the "keystone of the whole edifice of a system of pure reason" (*KpV* 5: 4). Freedom is the condition of the moral law (which requires just this autonomy) and "its reality is proved by an apodictic law of practical reason" (*KpV* 5: 4). If autonomy exists, then pure reason exists as practical reason, since it includes its own determining ground. Kant abandoned in the *KpV* the project of the third part of *GMS*, that is, to "deduce" a priori the moral law (*KpV* 5: 31); he proposes now a very controversial solution – that developed around the concept of the "fact of reason" (*KpV* 5: 31).

In brief, if we want to represent the human agent as acting under the moral law, we have to think him as absolutely independent of the external factors governed by deterministic natural laws (and, hence, he should be thought of as "free in the negative sense"). This ideal world of freedom, populated only by free wills (regarded as instances of a sui generis kind of causality), is governed by a self-imposed system of *practical* laws, that is, is a world of freedom in the positive sense ("autonomy").

Autonomy is the condition of the moral law (*KpV* 5: 3). If we want to think a human being under the moral law, we have to think human beings as absolutely free. Hence, Kant concludes, "[w]ith this pure practical power of reason, transcendental freedom is now also established" (*KpV* 5: 3). Difficulties will certainly arise from the details of the arguments, but for the purpose of this chapter, the important aspect is Kant's emphasis on a sui generis, lawful and at the same time free causality. The focus on the laws and rules of this causality governing our moral world leads Kant, by analogy with theoretical philosophy, to the idea of a practical philosophy with scientific character. In the next two sections we will examine this methodological aspect of Kant's Critical philosophy.

3. Critical Methodology

The use by Kant of a strange language is not the result of an excess of imagination, but a symptom of his efforts to get most of the disciplines, including metaphysics, to face a radical reform, a reform which consists essentially in checking whether the human mind is able to achieve objective knowledge and rational morality. For instance, to reach these aims, he enjoins metaphysics "to follow the secure path of science"; this means to look for a *new style of theorising in science and philosophy* in general, following the example of physicists and geometers, who work in the most advanced natural sciences. Concerning metaphysics Kant claims that "fate thus far has not favoured it to the point of enabling it to enter upon the secure path of a science" (Bxiv). Logic, the old method of dogmatic metaphysics, "has been so successful in following the secure path of a science" due to its "limitations"; because logic is required to abstract from all objects of cognition and their differences, in this discipline "the understanding deals with nothing more than itself and its form" (Bix). By contrast, it is more difficult for a discipline to acquire a scientific character when reason deals not only with itself, but also with objects. In the absence of an alternative method, as indicated by metaphysics' and other disciplines' "mere groping about" (Bvii), we have to find a new method of thought. What is this new method? What is this methodological tool of the science of universal practical reason?

Kant began to approach this subject-matter several years earlier in a period in which his independent thinking started to gradually manifest itself, even if his original philosophy was not yet articulated. The excerpt that follows, taken from a paper written for a competition organised by the Academy of Berlin (1763), is a convincing anticipation of the new method:

> The true method of metaphysics is basically the same as that introduced by *Newton* into natural science and which has been of such benefit to it. *Newton's* method maintains that one ought, on the basis of certain experience and, if need be, with the help of geometry, to seek out the rules in accordance with which certain phenomena of nature occur. Even if one does not discover the fundamental principle of these occurrences in the bodies themselves, it is nonetheless certain that they operate in accordance with this law. Complex natural events are explained once it has been clearly shown how they are governed by these well-established rules.
>
> (*UD* 2: 286)

Here Kant presents Newton's method as taking experience and, in fact, a certain experience, as the starting point. With the help of mathematics, geometry in particular, the kinds of phenomena illustrated by the specific experience under consideration are presented as occurring in accordance with certain rules. The fundamental principle given by the set of these rules will govern the occurrence of similar phenomena, although this principle is already identified, and it is not observed in the objects constituting these phenomena.

Kant thinks that the same method will work in metaphysics – the experience will be given by "an immediate and self-evident inner consciousness", to the rules there correspond "characteristic marks" of a certain thing, and the explanatory work will be given by these marks as "found in the concept of any general property" (*UD*: 2: 286).

Later, in 1787, in the second edition of the *KrV*, Kant wrote that old-fashioned metaphysics is obsolete, whereas its classical method, logic, is insufficient. To keep metaphysics alive we must move it on the sure path of the great science, "properly and objectively called so"; sciences, such as physics and geometry, by a "sudden revolution", became the model of all knowledge; by "imitating" them, we express our need for a "new method of thought" (Bix–Bxx):

> [T]his critique of pure speculative reason consists in that attempt to transform the accepted procedure of metaphysics, undertaking an entire revolution according to the example of geometers and natural scientists. It is a treatise on the method, not a system of the science itself.
>
> (Bxxii)

One of the most suggestive presentations of this new "rational method", can be found at the end of the *KpV*, in a chapter dedicated to the applications of this theory, having the title the Doctrine of Method. This procedure is later called the method of "rational generalization" (or "transcendental" for a priori grounding the theories) in contrast to the method of "inductive generalization" (A764–5/B792–3):

> The fall of a stone, the motion of a sling, resolved into their elements and into the forces manifesting themselves in these [actions] and treated mathematically, ultimately produced that clear insight – unchangeable throughout the future – into the world structure which, as observation proceeds, can hope to keep always expanding but need never fear having to regress.
>
> Now, this example can counsel us to enter upon this same path in dealing with moral predispositions of our nature and can give us hope of a similar good result. We do, after all, have at hand the examples of the morally judging reason. If we now dissect these examples but, lacking *mathematics*, take up in repeated experiments on common human understanding a procedure – similar to *chemistry* – of *separation* of the empirical from the rational that may be found in them, this can allow us to cognise both of them *pure* and, with certainty, what each can accomplish by itself.
>
> (*KpV* 5: 163)

We see here again Kant's commitment to the broadly Newtonian methodology from the natural sciences (Brading 2013). There is, first, the experience of a phenomenon to be explained; there is, secondly, the mathematical approach, which is meant to lead to the formulation of the rules in accordance with which the phenomenon occurs; finally, such rules are regarded as laws governing the world and regulating the occurrence of similar phenomena.

Interestingly, however, the quotation also introduces some qualifications concerning the appropriate methodology for practical philosophy. As Kant notes, mathematics is lacking in the case of moral theory and we need to replace it with chemistry. Accordingly, the procedure is not one of rule-formulation and prediction, but of analysis and separation. In moral philosophy, we begin with examples of moral judgments and proceed to the identification and separation of the empirical and rational aspects. The standards on the basis of which moral judgments are passed are non-empirical, a priori, and they are also supposed to provide the motivation for the performance of morally right actions. It should be remembered, however, that the purpose of this discussion of methodology is given by the purpose of the Doctrine of Method in the Second *Critique*, and this is primarily pedagogical. Nevertheless, although the discussion here has a specific purpose, we will see that, in fact, Kant's general view of the methodology of practical philosophy is that it does not include mathematics.

A significant feature of Kant's second *Critique* is that it is not a "doctrine". Following the terminology of the *Metaphysical First Grounds of Natural Science* (*MAN*), we define a "doctrine" as the sum of the laws of a given domain. A "theory" is such a set of (even practical) laws, which have a certain degree of universality and do not depend on particular circumstances. A doctrine becomes a "science proper" when it is a system of laws or duties which form a totality and are ordered following some principles; the science proper is based on rational, a priori, principles, not on empirical ones. Characteristic of science is its apodictic certainty assured by its a priori status.

A proper science of nature presupposes a "pure part", a *metaphysics of nature*, and an "applied part," which is based on empirical principles (*MAN* 4: 467, 469; Bxxiv, 2002a). The same is supposed to be the case for the science of freedom. It has a set of a priori (but impure) laws (duties) for human beings as such derived from the completely a priori (pure) supreme principle of morality. Hence, Kant's ethical theory has two parts, one pure, the other, empirical. The first includes the supreme principle of morality, the principles of derivation and the complete system of 14 a priori human duties. The second part includes the applications of the 14 "metaphysical first principles of ethics" to cases of experience. Kant adds a decisive condition, not for science in general, but for the science of natural bodies: in every special doctrine of nature there is only "as much *proper* science as there is *mathematics* therein" (*MAN* 4: 470). For this reason chemistry or psychology are not considered sciences proper.

Has the doctrine of freedom the same fate? No, because Kant claims that mathematics should be used only for phenomena that are fit to being treated mathematically. Psychology and ethics are not among them; these sciences "are possible without mathematics".[6] Therefore, we may have a *science of ethics* without mathematics, but one which is similar in structure and methods to the science of nature in general. The Preface and Introduction to the *KpV* announce also the objective of the *Metaphysics of Morals*: to find the a priori principles – particularly their condition, extent and boundaries – as a firm basis for "a *scientific* system of [practical] philosophy" (*KpV* 5: 12).

The emphasis on the methodological continuity between theoretical and practical philosophy is an important aspect of the second *Critique*'s Preface and Introduction, but commentators usually discuss it within the broader frame of Kant's *systematic* philosophy and focus on the transcendental and Critical aspects of the common method. Nevertheless, the scientific character of Kant's methodology in both his theoretical and practical philosophy is neither a new topic of interest nor one completely overlooked today.[7]

The secondary literature on the scientific character of Kant's methodology in moral philosophy is still scant. It is very likely this will be a topic that will attract more interest, especially in the context of the current need for directions with guiding force in practical philosophy. One argumentative path which the discussion can follow starts from debates in contemporary epistemology, particularly in the philosophy of science, on the nature of scientific theories. In particular, the distinction between statement and semantic views of scientific theories may inspire debates on the features that a science of the moral world and moral objectivity would appropriately have and may even contribute to progress on debates concerning the justification of particular principles on the basis of the Categorical Imperative. Moreover, this direction of further research is particularly promising given that there are several kinds of semantic reconstructive accounts, and some may be more appropriate for a Kantian science of the moral world than others.[8]

Before concluding, I would like to focus on a specific interpretative issue, which can illustrate the potential benefit of an approach to Kant's practical philosophy from the perspective of an emphasis on the scientific character of his methodology. Given the purpose of this chapter, the comments in the following section will have a strictly tentative and suggestive nature. More work would be needed to substantiate the suggested position and to show that the adumbrated alternative can bring some plausible results; I expect still more work will be needed to show that this would be the argumentative line which would better fit Kant's methodological commitments.

4. The "Formula"

One of the merits of the Preface and Introduction to the *KpV* is that of warning us that the concept of "formula" – in this context, at least – has also a *mathematical* origin, and not only a logical-linguistic one. Many commentators adopt what we can call *the formulation view*: they accept the translation of "Formel" with "(linguistic) formulation" or, in the best case, they use "formula" and "formulation" alternatively and seemingly interchangeably. This can be seen as a consequence of a still dominant linguistic approach in philosophy. As mentioned, Kant thinks that the kind of scientific approach we can take in ethics would not be as informed by mathematics as other natural sciences. Nevertheless, given the importance of mathematics for what he regards as a genuinely scientific discipline, it is not surprising to see him continuing to develop the analogy with mathematics with regard to some aspects of his ethical theory.

One potentially fruitful result of examining this analogy can be noticed by looking at debates on the relation between specific moral principles and duties, and Kant's Categorical Imperative with its various forms. Attempts to justify specific principles and duties through a 'derivation' from one of the forms of Categorical Imperative usually give rise to counterexamples and debates which are mostly inconclusive. In some instances, interpreters simply conclude that Kant never intended to author an ethical theory which would derive specific principles or duties, and that Kant's examples are merely illustrative and without normative intention. Other readers note that some of the forms of the Categorical Imperative are not supposed or fit to play the role of a second-order criterion which can justify specific standards of action, and some regard such forms as serving only "a rhetorical function" (Timmermann 2007: 106).[9]

Let us see what Kant says in the Preface to the *KpV*:

> [A reviewer objected that] no new principle of morality has been put forth in it [the *Groundwork*] but only a *new formula*. [. . .] But whoever knows what a *formula* means to a mathematician, a formula that determines quite precisely and keeps one from missing what is to be done in order to comply with an assignment, will not consider a formula that does this with regard to all duty as such to be something insignificant and dispensable.
>
> (*KpV* 5: 8n)

Following this analogy between a mathematical formula and an ethical principle may be fruitful beyond Kant's intention to formulate a reply to one of his critics. As he presents it, a formula states the problem to be solved, for example "what is the cube volume?" or "what is the model of all duty in general?", and gives us the method to solve it – an algorithm to calculate the cube volume or a procedure to derive a priori the duties of human beings without missing the target.[10] There are several contexts where Kant uses the term "Formula [*Formel*]" in the sense presented here: as a proposition which stipulates the conditions of possibility of a class of things through their "formula", which is their *general model*. One possible illustration – although a mere analogy – is the following reflection:

> The principle [*Principium*] or the norm [*Norm*] of all analytic propositions is the principle [*Satz*] of contradiction and of identity. This [principle – *Satz*] is (if I consider both [the law of contradiction and of identity] together) no *axiom* but only a formula, i.e., a general *model* [*ein allgemein Modell*] of analytic propositions; for it contains no *medium terminum*.
>
> (*Refl.* 4634)[11]

This fragment is about the *formula of analytic propositions*. This consists of the laws of contradiction and identity taken together, and offers a general model of analytic propositions. There is no middle term through which analytic propositions are derived. Consider now the analogy with the moral case (assuming, that is, that such an analogy were intended); we could consider the various particular duties to correspond to the analytic propositions in Kant's discussion. These particular duties would then have as a model two (or more) laws taken together – this would be the formula of duties. As a general model of duties, the formula would not be an axiom,[12] stipulating the essential conditions an action-type must satisfy to be "subsumed" to this model.

Let us pursue the analogy and consider the moral law or the supreme principle of morality to play the role of the general model of particular duties. Corresponding to the laws of contradiction and identity constituting the formula of duty, we can consider the three forms of Categorical Imperative Kant discusses in the second part of the *GMS*, and in particular at 4: 436–7 – of Universal Law, Humanity, and Kingdom of Ends. Together, perhaps as a kind of synthesis, these constitute the formula of duty or the moral law.

It is worth mentioning, first, that Kant presents the relation between these three forms of the Categorical Imperative as similar to the "progression" of the categories of quantity: the third principle is the union through synthesis of the other two[13] (*GMS* 4: 436). This establishes a systematic link to Kant's comments on the table of categories in the Analytic of Concepts: "[I]n each case the third category of the class arises from the combination of the second category with the first one of the same class" (B110). Yet, this prompts questions about the strength of the analogy, since the supreme principle of morality in our case is supposed to be a combination of all three forms of the Categorical Imperative. While we seem to reach the limit of the analogy, there is an answer to this possible objection too. Thus, in the *GMS* Kant talks about "*access* for the moral law" or the supreme principle of morality, which is obtained by a combination of the three forms; more exactly, "it is very useful to bring one and the same action under the three concepts mentioned above [the three forms of the Categorical Imperative] and thereby, as far as possible, bring it closer to intuition" (*GMS* 4: 437). This suggests that what Kant has in mind here (assuming again the analogy with the formula of analytic propositions holds) is not simply a formula of duties which justifies particular duties, but a general model through the application of which these particular duties move asymptotically closer to intuition.

We can speculate further and consider the form (formula) of autonomy as the model of all duties in the sense that in a moral world unified by the moral law, this moral law is a formal principle, that is, it only tells us what an obligation is. It is the origin of the practical laws which guide each rational being's actions. This guidance is done by duties, which are action-types absolutely and objectively prescribed by reason (how we *ought* to act) (*MS* 6: 226).

Therefore, when Kant uses the phrase "the formula of [. . .] all duty" or "the principle of all duty" (*GMS* 4: 425) – that is, the supreme principle of morality from which all duties are "derivable" – he very probably has in view the *general model* of all duty (plus the procedure to "derive" them). This interpretative suggestion seems also confirmed when Kant talks about a "model" in reference to the "moral world" of holy wills and of holy laws in relation to the world of finite rational beings and their maxims that approximate the first to the limit (*KpV* 5: 33). Finally, in speaking about "derivation", Kant does not have in mind some kind of simple logical deduction, but a special kind of reasoning,[14] guided by some derivation formulas (FUL, FH, FKE), the outcome of which is not simply the justification of particular duties, but what Kant regards as the process of bringing them closer to intuition.

When he developed the empirical part of his theory, Kant also spoke of the "subsumption" of the material maxim under the aforementioned principles and, reciprocally, of the principles of duty's "application" to the maxims in phenomena; this can be seen as further textual support for an interpretation, where the relation is that of satisfying a model.[15] This is specific to a type of theory inspired from the (mathematical) natural sciences. Yet, as already mentioned, these are meant as tentative suggestions as starting points for further research.

5. Conclusion

At the beginning of the Preface to the *KpV*, Kant warns the reader that the first question and the main concern of the *KpV* is whether pure reason can be practical, that is, as stated in the Introduction, whether "pure reason is sufficient by itself alone to determine the will, or whether reason can be a determining basis of the will only as empirically conditioned" (*KpV* 5: 15). This means to ask if pure reason could be an a priori basis for "a scientific system of [practical] philosophy" (*KpV* 5: 12). This is because such a determining basis of the will would be regarded by Kant as a type of causality and he regards causality as necessarily law-governed. Hence, a scientific system of practical philosophy distinct from the system of natural laws and providing an account of our moral world relies on a positive answer given in the *Analytic*, thus opening the way for a critical debate on the conditions of possibility of a *metaphysics of morals*. This "critique" is done as part of a special discipline called the "critique of practical reason," which can clarify the system of a priori duties in the metaphysics of morals, using the supreme principle of morality already identified in the *GMS* (although justified in a different way here). Another general conclusion is that only objective validity – therefore only an a priori approach – can assure the foundation of a universal and necessary agreement in the process of building a scientific theory proper, including an ethical one, based on moral laws. For, avoiding the attractions of a plausible "universal empiricism", the second *Critique* offers the instruments to justify a priori moral principles under which the "counsels" or "orders" of experience are "subsumed". The Critique in general is the core part of the "transcendental"[16] program. The *Critique of Practical Reason* is situated at the core of Kant's original program of reinventing moral philosophy.

Notes

1 Talking about the transition from *KrV* to *KpV*, Kant says that reason and its concepts are "in a *transition* to a use of them [here, in *KpV*] that is entirely different from the use that it made of them *there* [in *KrV*]" (*KpV* 5:7).

2 In Kant's vocabulary, a "science" is a body or a system of knowledge ordered according to *principles*. Depending on the nature of the principles, the science may be "a science properly so-called when the principles are a priori and a science improperly so-called" when the principles are empirical ("laws of experience").

3 A. M. Friedman remarks that the explanation of the process of scientific knowledge was done in Kant's time by using the language of our faculties of knowledge. This explains why, although Kant takes as a model

a non-psychological view of scientific knowledge, he frames his approach in the ambiguous terms of the psychological faculties of knowledge (Friedman 2010: 65, 67).

4 According to this model, we are motivated to act by desires and our actions are guided by our beliefs about the world and about how to satisfy those desires.

5 "It is surprising how otherwise acute men can believe that they find a distinction between the *lower* and the *higher power of desire* according to whether the **presentations** linked with the feeling of pleasure have their origin *in the senses* or in *understanding*" (*KpV* 5:22–3 – e. in original). This is the empiricist mixed moral philosophy Kant criticizes, because it ultimately leads to, as Kant puts it, the euthanasia of pure reason.

6 "A pure philosophy of nature in general, that is, that which investigates only what constitutes the concept of a nature in general, may indeed be possible even without mathematics" (*MAN* 4: 470). But "a pure doctrine of nature concerning determinate natural things (doctrine of body or doctrine of soul) is only possible by means of mathematics" (*MAN* 4: 471).

7 In her PhD thesis, Nataliya Palatnik focuses precisely on Kant's method, its Newtonian character and his science of the moral world within the framework of the Newtonian methodology. She traces back the interest in this approach to the middle of the 19th century, but also refers to more recent discussion (Palatnik 2015: 2, 10). For instance, Hermann von Helmholtz (1995 [1862]) contrasts the speculative philosophy of some of the representatives of German Idealism with Kant's adherence to the fundamental principles of natural scientists. More recently, Friedman (2012) talks about Kant's methodological combination of mathematical sciences and practical reason in his account of our specifically human perspective. For some more speculative, but reconstructive discussions of Kant's practical philosophy within the framework of a methodological emphasis on the scientific character of Kant's approach, see Pârvu (2013) and Mureşan (2013).

8 For instance, on some accounts, the set-theoretic kind (e.g., Stegmüller 1976 develops this meta-theory using examples of physical theories) seems the most appropriate reconstructive frame of Kant's theory of pure practical reason. Such reconstructive attempts would make more evident the Kantian project of placing practical philosophy on the secure path of science and showing the "scientific form of practical philosophy" (Pârvu 2013: 11).

9 For instance, for Hannah Arendt, "the judgement of the particular – [. . .] this is right, this is wrong – has no place in Kant's moral philosophy" (1992: 15). Timmermann refers to one of the Autonomy-based forms of the Categorical Imperative. By contrast, Houston Smit and Mark Timmons (2013) argue that most of the duties Kant presents in the Doctrine of Virtue can be derived from a specific form of the Categorical Imperative, namely, the Formula of Humanity.

10 A similar way of describing mathematical problems can be found in Kant's lectures on the metaphysics of morals; there Kant regards mathematical problems as problematic imperatives: "[In . . .] mathematical problems, [. . .] the laws for solving the problem constitute the imperative, in that they prescribe what has to be done should one wish to solve it, e.g., divide a straight line into two equal parts" (*V-MS/Vigil* 27: 486).

11 "Das Principium oder die norm aller analytischen Sätze ist der Satz des Wiederspruchs und der identitaet. Er ist (wennich sie beyde zusammen nehme) kein *axioma,* sondern eine Formel, d. i. ein allgemein Modell analytischer sätze; denn er enthält keinen *medium terminum*."

12 An axiom is a synthetic a priori *proposition* evident by itself, from which one could *logically* deduce the moral duties as theorems. There are no logical deductions of this type, nor any instance of the term "syllogism" in the contexts where the "applications" were discussed.

13 "A progression takes place here, as through the categories of the *unity* of the form of the will (its universality), the *plurality* of the matter (of objects, i.e., of ends) aand the *allness* or totality of the system of these" (*GMS* 4: 436).

14 Through this reasoning process, the *empty* formal duty expressed by the FUL is filled with some factual-nomic content by applying it to maxims of human nature, without losing its a priori character.

15 The pure moral law (the "holy" one) is an idea of reason "which necessarily serves as a *model* to which all finite rational beings can only approximate without end"; "the progress of one's maxims toward this model is unended" (*KpV* 5: 33).

16 Transcendental philosophy is the exposition of the rules of "*pure* thinking through which objects can be cognized fully a priori" (*GMS* 4: 390); the status of a transcendental *practical* philosophy is controversial, although one can say that it is the attempt to show that the will and the moral action may be determined only by pure practical reason. This is the central topic of the *KpV*.

References

Arendt, H. (1992) *Lectures on Kant's Political Philosophy*, Chicago: The University of Chicago Press.

Beck, L.W. (1963) *A Commentary to Kant's Critique of Practical Reason*, Chicago: The University of Chicago Press.

Brading, K. (2013) "Newton's Law-Constitutive Approach to Bodies: A Response to Descartes," in R. Schliesser and A. Janick (eds.), *Interpreting Newton*, Cambridge: Cambridge University Press.

Engstrom, S. (2002) "Introduction," in I. Kant (ed.) and W.S. Pluhar (trans.), *Critique of Practical Reason*, Cambridge, MA: Hackett.

Friedman, A.M. (2010) "Einstein, Kant, and the A Priori," in M. Suarez *et al.* (eds.), *EPSA Philosophical Issues in the Sciences*, ch. 7, Berlin: Springer.

Friedman, A.M. (2012) "Reconsidering the Dynamics of Reason: Response to Ferrari, Mormann, Nordmann, and Uebel," *Studies in History and Philosophy of Science* 43(1): 47–53.

Kant, I. (1992) "Inquiry Concerning the Distinctness of the Principles of Natural Theology and Morality," in D. Walford and R. Meerbote (eds.), *Theoretical Philosophy (1755–1770)*, Cambridge: Cambridge University Press.

Kant, I. (1998 [1781/1787]) *Critique of Pure Reason*, P. Guyer and A. Wood (trans.), Cambridge: Cambridge University Press.

Kant, I. (2002a) "Metaphysical First Grounds of Natural Science," in H. Allison and P. Heath (eds.), *Theoretical Philosophy after 1781*, M. Friedman (trans.), Cambridge: Cambridge University Press.

Kant, I. (2002b [1788]) *Critique of Practical Reason*, W.S. Pluhar (trans.), Cambridge, MA: Hackett.

Mureşan, V. (2013) "How Many Formulas? An Alternative Reading," in V. Mureşan and S. Majima (eds.), *Applied Ethics*, Sapporo: Hokkaido University.

Palatnik, N. (2015) *Kant's Science of the Moral World and Moral Objectivity*, doctoral dissertation, Cambridge: Harvard University.

Pârvu, I. (2013) "What Does 'Metaphysics' Mean in Kant's *Groundwork of the Metaphysics of Morals*," in V. Mureşan and S. Majima (eds.), *Applied Ethics*, Sapporo: Hokkaido University Press.

Smit, H. and Timmons, M. (2013) "Kant's Grounding Project in *The Doctrine of Virtue*," in M. Timmons and S. Baiasu (eds.), *Kant on Practical Justification: Interpretive Essays*, New York: Oxford University Press.

Stegmüller, W. (1976) *The Structure and Dynamics of Theories*, Berlin: Springer.

Timmermann, J. (2007) *Kant's Groundwork of the Metaphysics of Morals: A Commentary*, Cambridge: Cambridge University Press.

von Helmholtz, H. (1995 [1862]) *Science and Culture: Popular and Philosophical Essays*, D. Cahan (ed.), Chicago: University of Chicago Press.

Further Reading

A. Reath and J. Timmermann, *Kant's Critique of Practical Reason: A Critical Guide* (Cambridge: Cambridge University Press, 2010) is a collection of essays on the main sections of the *Critique* including an extensive bibliography. L.W. Beck, *A Commentary on Kant's Critique of Practical Reason* (Chicago: University of Chicago Press, 1960), and G. Sala, *Kants "Kritik der praktischen Vernunft". Ein Kommentar* (Darmstadt: Wissenschaftliche Buchgesellschaft, 2004) include discussions of the Preface and Introduction. Otfried Höffe, "Einführung in die *Kritik der praktischen Vernunft*" and A. Wood, "Preface and Introduction (3–16)," in O. Höffe (ed.), *Immanuel Kant: Kritik der praktischen Vernunft* (Berlin: Akademie Verlag, 2002) are two essays exactly on the topics of this chapter. Other essays in this cooperative commentary are also relevant for the issues discussed in this chapter, in particular the essays by Onora O'Neill, "Autonomy and the Fact of Reason in the *Kritik der praktischen Vernunft* (§§7–8, 30–41)" and Karl Ameriks, "Pure Reason of Itself Alone Suffices to Determine the Will (42–57)".

14

THE ANALYTIC OF PURE PRACTICAL REASON

Andrews Reath

***

1. The Aims of the *Critique* and Its Place in Kant's System

The *Critique of Practical Reason* has two principal aims. One is to "show *that there is pure practical reason*, and for this purpose it criticizes reason's entire *practical faculty*" (*KpV* 5: 3). That is, it shows that reason issues a priori practical principles that apply to us simply as rational agents independently of subjective interests. In a word, if pure reason is practical, then reason alone, independently of desire, can direct us how to act. The second aim is to establish the reality of transcendental freedom – a capacity to initiate action independently of temporally prior causes, including empirically given interests (*KpV* 5: 3). Both aims are achieved by the argument of Chapter I of the Analytic, in which Kant uses an analysis of the faculty of pure practical reason to derive a statement of its "fundamental law" and then appeals to features of ordinary moral consciousness to establish its authority (*KpV* 5: 30–2).

The rest of this section locates the *Critique* in Kant's moral conception and in his philosophical system. Section 2 gives an overview of the main argument in Chapter I of the Analytic, and Section 3 discusses the significance of the "fact of reason." Section 4 comments briefly on Chapters II and III and the Critical Elucidation.

The *Groundwork of the Metaphysics of Morals* and the second *Critique* are both parts of Kant's foundational project in moral theory, whose aim is to articulate the fundamental principle of morality and show that it has a basis in reason a priori. Both works take on the question whether pure reason is practical, though Kant refers to this issue explicitly only in the *Critique*.

Whether pure reason is practical – whether reason generates a priori principles of conduct and can move the will – is a fundamental question in moral theory, the answer to which shapes one's understanding of morality at the most basic level. Kant thinks that it is part of the common idea of duty that moral requirements apply with unconditional necessity (*GMS* 4: 389). Ordinary moral thought understands moral requirements as "categorical imperatives" that apply independently of and take priority over inclination-based interests. But the authority that we assign to such principles is genuine only if they are based in reason a priori. In understanding moral requirements as categorical imperatives, ordinary moral thought thus assumes that pure reason is practical. But is it?

DOI: 10.4324/9781003406617-19

The empiricist tradition denies that reason by itself is practical and thus rejects Kant's understanding of morality. Empiricists explain the normative force of morality by appeal to empirically given features of our psychology, such as a capacity to sympathize with the pleasures and pains of others, sensitivity to the approval of others, and so on. The rationalist tradition prior to Kant agrees that morality is a set of rational principles, but, according to Kant, falls short in showing how such principles are possible because it does not take on the question of what it would be for pure reason to be practical. Though Leibniz and Wolff held that the content of morality is grasped through reason, they explain its authority and motivating power through a disposition to take pleasure in the thought of perfection, which they think is a basic feature of our psychology. Thus both traditions take moral requirements to be hypothetical imperatives whose normative force is conditional on having certain empirically given interests. By contrast, Kant's project is to establish the possibility of genuine categorical imperatives, thereby vindicating ordinary moral thought, by showing that the basic principle of morality is a principle of pure practical reason.

The *Groundwork* carries this project out in two clearly demarcated stages. *Groundwork* I and II formulate the basic principle presupposed by ordinary moral thought by analyzing various concepts. *Groundwork* I derives a statement of the Categorical Imperative (CI) from analyses of the common idea of duty and that of a good will, while *Groundwork* II derives several related formulations of the CI from analysis of pure practical reason. But mere analysis of a set of concepts cannot establish their objective validity and our title to employ them. It may be that our ordinary conception of moral requirement presupposes that pure reason is practical, but that does not show that we human beings have the requisite rational capacities for such principles to apply to us. The analytical stages of the *Groundwork* leave open the possibility that the authority of morality is illusory.

That component of the project occupies *Groundwork* III, which is synthetic in that it appeals to certain features of human agency given to us through our practical self-consciousness. Kant refers to this stage of the argument as a "deduction" of the CI (*GMS* 4: 447, 454). The third section opens with further analytical arguments showing that a rational being with a will necessarily acts under the idea of freedom and that any such agent is committed to the morality (*GMS* 4: 446–8). Kant now needs to show that we are rational agents of the kind presupposed by this argument. The details are obscure, but very generally Kant argues that warrant for ascribing ourselves free agency is found in our capacity for theoretical reason. Our awareness of the spontaneity of theoretical reason – as a capacity for "pure self-activity" (*GMS* 4: 452) – gives us membership in an intelligible world, and thereby confirms the presumption that our faculty of desire is a rational will. But then we human beings necessarily act under the idea of freedom, and since we identify with our free agency as our "proper self" (*GMS* 4: 457–8, 461), our self-conception as free agents commits us to the authority morality. What is important for our purposes is that this "deduction" appeals to the spontaneity of *theoretical* reason to warrant the ascription of (transcendental) freedom to our wills; once our free agency is established, the authority of morality follows.

Chapter I of the Analytic of the *Critique* develops an argument with the same structure. The analytic stage (*KpV* 5: 19–30, §§1–6) is a compressed version of arguments found in parts of *Groundwork* II and of the opening of *Groundwork* III. By analyzing what is presupposed if pure reason is practical, Kant derives a statement of the fundamental principle of pure practical reason, which turns out to be the moral law – more precisely, the Universal Law formulation of the CI. However the synthetic stage of the argument is importantly different. Kant claims that the moral law neither allows nor needs a "deduction" in his technical sense (*KpV* 5: 46–7) and that its authority is established as a "fact of reason" (*KpV* 5: 31ff., 47). Since the "fact of reason" is one of the important notions in the second *Critique*, we discuss it in Section 3. The point for now is that the authority of morality is established through features of ordinary moral consciousness – that in ordinary practical reasoning we recognize the authority of morality as a source of unconditional requirements, that we can act on such requirements simply because we ought to, and that we identify with our moral capacities as core features of our self-conception.

One apparent difference between the two works is that where the "deduction" in *Groundwork* III first needs to establish our free agency on grounds that are independent of morality, in the *Critique* Kant does not appeal to anything outside of moral consciousness to establish the authority of morality. The moral law "is firmly established of itself" and "has no need of justifying grounds" (*KpV* 5: 47). A second difference is that in the *Critique* our recognition of the authority of morality establishes our freedom. "It is . . . the moral law . . . that first offers itself to us . . . [and] leads directly to the concept of freedom" (*KpV* 5: 29). Ordinary moral consciousness discloses important features about the kinds of agents that we are (e.g., that are transcendentally free, etc.). In this respect, the fact of reason contains synthetic a priori claims about human agency that take the place of the claims about our membership in an intelligible world that *Groundwork* III uses to ascribe freedom to our will.

The "fact of reason" is important to Kant's moral theory, but the *Critique*, as one of the three *Critiques*, is also important for Kant's critical system. A "Critique" is a critical examination of the powers and limits of a domain of rational cognition that is called for where we purport to have a body of synthetic a priori cognition, to show how it is possible (*KpV* 5: 8). A Critique is appropriate in the moral domain because common sense morality presents us with synthetic a priori practical principles – substantive practical principles that are necessary and a priori, and not based on empirically given interests. How could there be practical requirements like that, one might ask? Only if pure reason is practical – but is it? Since both the *Groundwork* and the second *Critique* take on this question, they fit squarely into Kant's critical project as applied to moral cognition.

The *Critique* contributes to Kant's system in another way by resolving, from a practical point of view, a set of metaphysical questions that reason in its theoretical use leaves unanswered – in the Analytic the question of free will, and later in the Dialectic the questions of God and immortality. In the *Critique of Pure Reason*, Kant shows that theoretical reason forms the idea of transcendentally free causality because of its demand for completeness in explanation, and the Resolution of the Third Antinomy, appealing to the distinction between phenomena and noumena, shows that transcendentally free agency is not ruled out by causal determinism in nature. But since theoretical reason cannot establish the reality of transcendental freedom, it remains agnostic about it. The second *Critique*, however, provides positive grounds for asserting that moral agents are transcendentally free. In revealing that we can act from moral requirements simply because we ought to, the fact of reason shows that we can act from requirements that originate in pure practical reason independently of empirically given interests. It thus reveals that our rational agency is a form of causality that satisfies the definition of transcendental freedom, and furthermore, supplies a statement of the principle that governs this causal power – the moral law (*KpV* 5: 47–50). Kant makes it clear that the reality of transcendental freedom is "objective [. . .] though only practical" (*KpV* 5: 49). Since it is established through features of moral consciousness, not through any sensible intuition, it is not an item of theoretical knowledge that can enter into the explanation of events. The argument is thus not an illicit extension of theoretical knowledge beyond the limits of possible experience.

2.   The Argument of Chapter I of the Analytic

Chapter I is structured as a deductive argument that begins with a Definition of "practical law" (§1), proceeding from there through a series of Theorems and Corollaries to a statement of the "Fundamental Principle of Pure Practical Reason" (§7). This structure reflects the fact that Kant is using an analysis of pure practical reason to arrive at a statement of its fundamental principle (just as in *Groundwork* II, he extracts the first formulation of the CI from "the mere concept of a categorical imperative" – *GMS* 4: 420). The question of the *Critique* is whether "pure reason of itself alone suffices to determine the will" (*KpV* 5: 15). But if "*pure* reason can contain within itself a practical ground, that is, one sufficient to determine the will, then there are practical laws" (*KpV* 5: 19). If pure reason is practical, then it issues some practical laws. The "Definition" [*Erklärung*] of practical law is a practical principle that is objective and "[holds] for the will of every rational being" (*KpV* 5: 19) – or as Kant makes clear in the subsequent Remark, "determines the will simply as will", independently of an agent's contingently given interests. A practical law – if there are such principles – applies with necessity to the will of any rational agent (*KpV* 5: 20–1). With this concept in hand, Kant asks what conditions a principle must satisfy to hold as a practical law.

Theorem I (§2) tells us that no "material practical principle" can hold as a practical law. Such principles "presuppose an *object* (matter) of the faculty of desire as the determining ground of the will" (*KpV* 5: 21). Here Kant does not mean to claim that no principle that directs one to an end can be a practical law. He thinks that any practical principle must contain some end in order to determine the will (*GMS* 4: 427, *KpV* 5: 34, *MS* 6: 385), and he recognizes moral requirements to adopt ends – for example, the duties of virtue (*MS* 6: 386–95). Rather, a material practical principle is one whose normative force depends on a contingent interest in some end that one has as a matter of psychological fact. Kant tells us that all such principles determine choice "through the representation of an object and that relation of the representation to the subject . . . called pleasure in the reality of the object" (*KpV* 5: 21). In other words, material practical principles provide a ground of choice through the fact that an agent takes satisfaction in or has an empirically given desire for the relevant end. Roughly, taking satisfaction in or having an inclination-based interest in the end is a condition of seeing reason to adopt the end or act on the principle. Since a practical law applies necessarily to any agent, its normative force cannot depend on empirically given interests – or as Kant says, "on the subjective condition of receptivity to pleasure or displeasure" (*KpV* 5: 21). Therefore no "material practical principle" can serve as a practical law.

Theorem II (§3) generalizes this point, holding that all material practical principles "come under the general principle of self-love or one's own happiness" (*KpV* 5: 22). This claim is puzzling, since as defined, material practical principles can incorporate other-regarding desires. Agents acting from natural sympathy or affection for loved ones could be acting for the well-being of another, but their principles of action could be "material" in Kant's sense. Similarly, Hutcheson or Hume's moral sense theories and Wolff's perfectionism count as "material principles of morality" (*KpV* 5: 39). But it is unclear why such principles fall under the principle of self-love or one's own happiness. The best way to make sense of Theorem II is to see it as articulating a shared structural feature of any practical principle whose normative force depends on an empirically given interest in some end that is rationally optional. The argumentation for Theorem II is dense, but the basic idea is that a material practical principle provides a ground of choice "through the feeling of agreeableness that the subject expects" from the realization of the end, which is a function of the "receptivity of the subject". Since "happiness" is "consciousness of the agreeableness of life uninterruptedly accompanying [one's] whole existence", when one bases one's choice on the fact that one expects to take satisfaction in, or (what is the same thing) has an empirically given desire for some end, one acts from the principle of happiness in a broad sense (*KpV* 5: 22). Note that if we understand the principle of happiness in this way, Kant is not claiming that action on a material practical principle is always *for the sake of* one's own happiness. Given differences in the receptivity of human agents, he can allow that individuals take satisfaction in and act for the sake of many different kinds of ends, including those that are not self-regarding in the ordinary sense. However Kant is claiming that despite the differences among human ends, all action on "material practical principles" shares a common structural feature ("are wholly of the same kind") – namely that the ground of choice is the satisfaction expected from some end or an agent's empirically given desires. The principle of happiness thus represents one form of human choice.[1]

Continuing the argument, Theorem III (§4) asserts that a principle can serve as a practical law only if it provides a ground of choice through its form rather than its matter. A practical law will have some matter; in order to determine choice, it must direct an agent to some specific end or action (Cf *KpV* 5: 34). But the ground of choice – the source of its normative authority – cannot be an empirically given interest in the end or action that is the matter. If it were, it would be a material principle and Kant has shown that no such principle can serve as a practical law. But what is the alternative? We know from the definition of a practical law that any such principles apply necessarily to any rational agent as such (have the formal features of necessity and universality). Theorem III concludes that a practical law provides a ground of choice through its having "the *form* of giving universal law" (*KpV* 5: 27) – that is, the source of its authority is simply that it is suited to make a demand on any rational agent.

Now in fact the Theorem is slightly more complex. It claims that "if a rational being is to think of his maxims as practical universal laws", he can do so only through their form. The context then is that of a deliberating agent concerned with the demands of pure practical reason. One conforms to pure practical reason by acting from maxims with the form of universal law-giving simply because or on condition that they have the form of law-giving. The subsequent Remark indicates that one determines whether a maxim has that form by asking whether the maxim can at the same time be willed as universal law without inconsistency (*KpV* 5: 27–8) – as a principle that all agents can agree that any agent may accept and act from (cf. Engstrom 2009: 115–17). Theorem III thus points toward the "fundamental law" that determines what it is to exercise pure practical reason (stated later in §7): one conforms to pure practical reason by acting from maxims that have or are consistent with the form of universal law-giving simply because they have that form. Furthermore, since this principle is recognizable as the moral law, this analysis connects morality to reason; the "fundamental law of pure practical reason" turns out to be the principle underlying ordinary moral reasoning.

In Theorem III, Kant is drawing a connection between form and normative necessity.[2] Indeed he appears to claim that the only possible source of the normative authority of a practical law lies in its having the form of universal law-giving. But why think that? Why can't some substantive value or end provide a necessary ground of choice for any rational agent in itself through its intrinsic features, without the mediation of an empirically given interest – that is, why couldn't such a value be the basis of a practical law? Kant answers the second question in Chapter II of the Analytic (discussed in Section 4). To address the first briefly, Kant's view is that the form of universal law-giving is the normative ground of choice that is internal to pure practical reason, and as such the only ground that can govern choice necessarily. As a product of pure practical reason, a practical law provides a ground of choice through the form of law-giving because one exercises pure practical reason just by acting on principles with the form of universal law-giving because they have that form. Simplifying, pure practical reason issues practical laws that are necessary and universal; to act from such principles simply because they are necessary is what it is to conform to pure practical reason. That means that the associated "fundamental law" is the formal principle internal to pure practical reasoning – the principle through which one exercises the capacity for pure practical reasoning, to which any agent is committed simply as such a reasoner.

Kant now makes a final analytical move that Henry Allison has termed the "Reciprocity Thesis" (Allison 1990: Ch. 11), arguing that "freedom and unconditional practical law reciprocally imply each other." In Problem I (§5), Kant argues that a will determinable by the law-giving form of its maxims is a free will, while in Problem II (§6) he argues that if a will is free, its basic principle is to act on maxims that have the form of law. The argument for the first prong depends on the claim that the law-giving form of a maxim is a rational ground that is not an object of appearances. If so, a will determined by the law-giving form of its maxims operates independently of sensible determining grounds and of natural causal laws, and thus satisfies the definition of transcendental freedom. The argument for the converse (a reprise of an argument given in *Groundwork* III at *G* 4: 446–7) holds that a free will operates independently of empirical conditions, but nonetheless acts on some principle. This independence condition implies that the ground of choice is not an empirically given interest in the matter of its principles. Theorem III has shown that the alternative is to act only on maxims that have the form of law-giving (simply because they have that form . . .). Thus, its basic principle is the fundamental law of pure practical reason. Space does not permit adequate treatment of these compressed arguments here. However what Kant appears to be getting at is that a pure will determinable by the law-giving form of its maxims operates according to the formal principle of pure practical reason – a law that arises from the nature of pure practical reason. Because it operates according to its own internal principle, independently of externally given factors, a pure will has the marks of a self-determining causality (cf. Allison 1990: Ch. 11; Korsgaard 1996: Ch. 6; Reath 2010: 51–4).

To this point, Kant's analysis has shown that a practical law provides a ground of choice through its having the form of universal law-giving (§4) and points to the fundamental law of pure practical reason recognizable as the Universal Law version of the CI. Further, he has argued that an agent with the capacity to act from this principle is transcendentally free, and conversely that this law is the fundamental principle of free agency. These analytical claims, however, do not show that pure practical reason applies to or is active in human beings. But at *KpV* 5: 30, a shift takes place. Kant develops the famous "gallows example", in which one's prince threatens one with death unless one give false testimony against an innocent person whom the prince wishes to destroy. Could one resist the prince's clearly unjust demand? Kant writes that one might not assert that one would resist the prince,

> but he must admit without hesitation that it would be possible for him. He judges therefore, that he can do something because he is aware that he ought to do it and cognizes freedom within him, which, without the moral law would have remained unknown to him.
>
> (*KpV* 5: 30)

This example provides a thought experiment to show that we recognize the authority of morality and have the ability to comply with moral requirements even at great cost to ourselves. The thought experiment illustrates two aspects of the fact of reason – our acknowledgment of the deliberative priority of moral principle, which carries with it awareness of our ability to act from duty that reveals our free agency.

When Kant states the "Fundamental Law" in §7, he presents it as an imperative that is indeed authoritative for us, claiming that it is established as a "fact of reason."

> Consciousness of this fundamental law may be called a fact of reason . . . because it forces itself upon us as of itself as a synthetic a priori proposition . . . [it is] the sole fact of pure reason which, by it [this law] announces itself as originally law-giving.
>
> (*KpV* 5: 31)

The two principal aims of the Critique have now been accomplished in outline. First, the fact of reason establishes a fundamental practical law – the moral law – thereby showing that pure reason is practical. And Kant's analysis confirms that the principle underlying common moral thought is based in pure practical reason. Second, the fact of reason includes our awareness of our capacity to set aside sensibly given interests and conform to practical law simply because we ought to. Combined with the solution to Problem I, it therefore establishes our transcendental freedom. "[F]reedom is real, for this idea reveals itself through the moral law" (*KpV* 5: 4).

Theorem IV (§8) may seem like an afterthought, but by reflecting on what has just been established Kant introduces the crucial idea of autonomy, claiming that "autonomy of the will is the sole principle of all moral laws" and that "heteronomy of choice [. . .] does not ground any obligation at all" (*KpV* 5: 33). By autonomy of the will, Kant means that the nature of pure practical reason (the pure will) is the source of its own fundamental principle (Reath 2013). Since the argument of §§1–7 has based the moral law in the very nature of pure practical reason, it has shown that the will has autonomy in this sense and that the moral law is the principle that the will or practical reason gives to itself. Otherwise put, it has established that the principle of determining choice through the law-giving form of one's maxims, independently of any empirically given interest in their matter, is the formal principle that expresses the nature of pure practical reason. Furthermore, moral obligation is genuinely categorical only if based in the autonomy of the will, since only a principle that is internal to pure practical reason in this way can govern choice unconditionally. As Kant makes clear toward the end of the section, foundational theories that ground the authority of morality in some object that is given to the will, such as moral sense theories, perfectionist theories, or divine command theories do not yield practical laws. They are at best principles whose normative force is conditional on an agent having an interest in that object as a matter of psychological fact (*KpV* 5: 39–41). Kant concludes: "the formal practical principle of pure reason [. . .] is the sole principle that can be fit for categorical imperatives, that is, practical laws" (*KpV* 5: 41).

3.   The Fact of Reason [*Faktum der Vernunft*]

The idea that the "fundamental law of pure practical reason", or moral law, is given as a "fact of reason" is a central but puzzling feature of the *Critique*. Scholars disagree about how the fact of reason is to be interpreted and whether, by appealing to this idea, the *Critique* completely abandons the strategy of justification employed in the *Groundwork*. Assuming that the two works do take different approaches to the authority of morality, there is also disagreement about the philosophical merits of appeal to the fact of reason. Some commentators regard it as an unfortunate reversion to a form of rational intuitionism or dogmatism, while others view it as an important advance, both in Kant's thinking and in moral theory.[3] We cannot resolve these issues here, but will present the fact of reason as an importantly different approach to foundational questions that is worth taking seriously as a position in moral theory.

Kant refers to the fact of reason both as consciousness of the law of pure practical reason (*KpV* 5: 31) and as consciousness of freedom (*KpV* 5: 42). Both are aspects of the fact of reason, but the first is clearly fundamental (Rawls 2000: 258–61). The first explicit mention of the fact of reason is in the Remark to §7, where Kant presents the law of pure practical reason as an authoritative imperative. He is very clear that what reveals our freedom is our awareness that we can act from this principle (*KpV* 5: 4, 29–30, 47–8). (Kant can say that "consciousness of freedom of the will" is "inseparably connected with, indeed identical" with the fact of reason (*KpV* 5: 42) because our recognition of the authority of the moral law includes awareness of our ability to act from its demands.)

One important interpretation of the fact of reason has been developed by Rawls. He argues that when Kant refers to our "consciousness" of the moral law, he means that we are conscious of its *authority* in "everyday moral thought, feeling and judgment" (Rawls 2000: 255, 260; see also

268–71). Our acceptance of the authority of morality and the deliberative priority of moral considerations in practical reasoning is seen in the standards to which we hold ourselves and various judgments that we make about right action (*KpV* 5: 30, 32, 91–2), in the operation of conscience, and in various moral emotions including the feeling of respect (*KpV* 5: 72ff). Moreover our acceptance of the authority of morality is stable on reflection. We identify with our moral capacities and it is a deep feature of our self-conception as persons that we stand in moral relations to others. The significance of the fact of reason on this reading is that the authority of morality is in some sense self-standing, and not based on anything outside of on-going, critical moral reflection. For example, there is no need to base it on theoretical reason or a conception of free agency established independently of morality, as Kant appears to do in *Groundwork* III. ("Consciousness of this fundamental law may be called a fact of reason because one cannot reason it out from antecedent data of reason, for example, from consciousness of freedom" – *KpV* 5: 31.)

Another interpretive approach begins from the etymology of "*Faktum*." The German "*Faktum*" derives from the Latin "*factum*", meaning or "deed" or "action" ("what is done"), and in at least one passage Kant uses the Latin "*factum*" as a gloss for the German "*Tat*" (deed) (*MdS* 6: 227. Cf. Engstrom 2002: xli–ii; Willaschek 1991; Kleingeld 2010: 61–2). This etymology suggests that Kant's "*Faktum der Vernunft*" may be understood as the deed of reason, or what reason does in us – a meaning a step removed from the modern usage of "fact" (cf. Ware 2014). On this reading, the idea behind the fact of reason is that the reality of pure practical reason is established by a deed of reason, and what reason does is to present us with a law whose authority is exhibited in a pattern of ordinary practical judgments in which we acknowledge the priority of moral considerations.

These two approaches are easily combined. The second focuses on the fact that the concern of the *Critique* is to establish the reality of pure practical reason (pure practical reason establishes its reality through what it does), while the first focuses on the fact that the reality of pure practical reason is displayed in ordinary moral consciousness (what pure practical reason does is present us with moral requirements whose authority we acknowledge in ordinary practical reasoning).

Kant's emphasis on the "common practical use of reason" (*KpV* 5: 91) in discussing the fact of reason indicates that it is not a reversion to intuitionism and suggests a response to the dogmatism objection. Kant is not claiming that the authority of the moral law is a self-evident truth, and the fact of reason is not a static recognition of the authority of morality. The authority of morality is confirmed by a pattern of practical judgments that we make in ordinary contexts.

> But that pure reason . . . is practical of itself alone: this one had to be able to show from the most common practical use of reason, by confirming the supreme practical principle as one that every natural human reason cognizes . . . as the supreme law of its will.
>
> (*KpV* 5: 91)

Indeed the moral theorist can "at any time set up an experiment with every practical human reason in order to distinguish the moral (pure) determining ground from the empirical" (*KpV* 5: 92; cf. 5: 32). The theorist can construct examples and set up thought experiments to show that we do recognize the priority of the moral (as Kant does in the "gallows example" at *KpV* 5: 30). For example, Kant suggests that any decent person who considers lying for one's own advantage will distinguish the reasons based on one's own happiness from moral considerations and will judge that one ought to give priority to the latter ("his practical reason . . . unites with what maintains in him respect for his own person (truthfulness)" – *KpV* 5: 93) That we can set up such thought experiments "at any time" indicates that such judgments about the authority of morality are stable on reflection and that they are deeply rooted in our self-conception as persons.

4. The Balance of the Analytic

Chapters II, III and the Critical Elucidation appear to address a series of separate problems. Chapter II takes up the good as "the object of practical reason" – by which Kant means an object that one is led to adopt through sound practical reasoning – and responds to an objection that had been raised to his moral conception. Kant first tries to establish a fundamental moral law; but one might think that a moral conception must begin from some conception of what is good, then derive principles of conduct from what will promote or realize that good. Chapter III is a description of "respect" for morality as the basic moral motive or incentive [*Triebfeder*] that elaborates a footnote found in *Groundwork* I (*GMS* 4: 401n). The Critical Elucidation, in addition to reflecting on the overall structure of the Analytic, covers ground similar to the Resolution of the Third Antinomy (A532–8/B560–86), to show that Kant's robust conception of transcendental freedom is consistent with causal determinism in nature. But Kant gives a rationale for this order of topics based on the distinctive features of practical reason. Since theoretical reason aims at knowledge of objects given in sensible intuition, the Analytic of the first *Critique* first takes up the a priori forms of sensibility and proceeds from there to the pure concepts of the understanding and then to the a priori principles of understanding. But since practical reason is concerned with the realization of objects that it represents as good, its Analytic proceeds in reverse order. It begins from the a priori principles by which reason determines the will and then considers the objects that it adopts under the direction of these principles, and finally the motivational effect of the moral law on our sensibility (*KpV* 5: 89–90). Furthermore, each chapter adds important elements to the moral conception developed in Chapter I. Our discussion will comment briefly on Chapters II and III.

The main aim of Chapter II is to respond to what Kant acknowledges is "the paradox of method" in his moral conception: "that the concepts of good and evil must not be determined before the moral law [. . .] but only [. . .] after it and by means of it" (*KpV* 5: 63). Almost all moral theories in the tradition prior to Kant are based on a conception of what is good that is uncritically assumed, either because it is a value thought to be self-evident or one which human beings are presumed to care about. Examples of the good that Kant has in mind include happiness, perfection, conformity with the moral sense, and the divine will, and the traditional theories in different ways base principles of conduct on the relevant conception of value (*KpV* 5: 40, 64). Kant classifies all such principles as "material principles of morality" (*KpV* 5: 39) because they make their fundamental principle a "material" principle in the sense of Theorems I and II – a principle whose normative force depends on an antecedent interest in some end. Kant argues that all such theories fail because they cannot show that moral principles are genuine practical laws. In attempting to ground morality on some externally given object or value without first showing that it is rationally necessary to take interest in it, such theories employ the method of heteronomy. Thus, they can show at best that moral principles are hypothetical imperatives. The problem is that since these theories *begin* from some conception of the good, they have no rational standard by which to assess and to establish the rational necessity of the proposed value. As Kant says:

> suppose that we wanted to begin with the concept of the good in order to derive from it laws of the will . . . since this concept had no practical a priori law for its standard, the criterion of good and evil could be placed in nothing other than the agreement of the object with our feeling of pleasure.
>
> (*KpV* 5: 63)

The resulting principle would have normative force only for agents with an antecedent interest in that conception of good. The only way to establish genuine unconditional requirements is through a critical examination of the necessary commitments of rational agency that uncovers the formal principle of pure practical reason – a principle to which any rational agent is committed qua rational. That is, one must first establish a practical law. This is Kant's method of autonomy (*KpV* 5: 63–5; see Reath 2010: 50–1).

It is central to Kant's moral conception that morally good conduct is motivated by the immediate recognition of the authority of morality – that is, by respect for morality. But in order to function as an "incentive" or effective motivating ground, a human being's recognition of the authority of morality must counteract certain tendencies to regard inclinations as good reasons for action and to make claims on their behalf – volitional propensities that Kant terms "self-love" and "self-conceit". Thus Kant also regards respect as the feeling that follows when our recognition of the authority of morality limits these sensible tendencies. Chapter III gives an account of how recognition of the authority of morality functions as an incentive in human beings by describing the effects of that recognition on our faculty of desire. Respect as moral feeling has a negative dimension insofar as it results from checking self-love and "striking down" self-conceit; but insofar as it results from our own rational activity, it has a positive and elevating dimension as well. Throughout this discussion, while Kant describes "respect" as moral feeling, he stresses that it is not an "antecedent feeling" in the subject – a sensible disposition that aligns with moral demands. Respect "is not the incentive to morality; instead it is morality itself subjectively considered as an incentive" (*KpV* 5: 76). As we have seen, the aim of the *Critique* is to show that pure reason is practical through the fact of reason. By describing the way in which we experience the authority of morality, this chapter confirms the fact of reason and the general claim that the capacity for pure practical reason is active in us.

Notes

1 Cf. Reath (2006: Ch. 2) and Reath (2015: xx–xi).
2 For further discussion, including of the idea of a "formal principle", see Reath (2010).
3 While Henrich (1960) and Beck (1960) look for continuity between the *Groundwork* and the *Critique*, Ameriks (1982) argues that the fact of reason is a reversal of the strategy of the *Groundwork*. For recent discussion see Timmermann (2010). Ameriks (1982: 218–19, 2003: 254), Guyer (2007: 462), and Wood (2008: 134–5) are critical of the fact of reason, while Rawls (2000: 264–8) regards it as an important turn in moral theory. Another recent defense of the idea is Ware (2014). Kleingeld (2010) is a good discussion that provides an overview of different approaches.

References

Allison, H. (1990) *Kant's Theory of Freedom*, Cambridge: Cambridge University Press.
Ameriks, K. (1982) *Kant's Theory of Mind*, Oxford and New York: Oxford University Press.
Ameriks, K. (2003) *Interpreting Kant's Critiques*, Oxford and New York: Oxford University Press.
Beck, L.W. (1960) *A Commentary on Kant's Critique of Practical Reason*, Chicago: University of Chicago Press.
Engstrom, S. (2002) "Introduction," in I. Kant (ed.), W.S. Pluhar (trans.), *Critique of Practical Reason*, Indianapolis/Cambridge, MA: Hackett Publishing.
Engstrom, S. (2009) *The Form of Practical Knowledge*, Cambridge, MA: Harvard University Press.
Guyer, P. (2007) "Naturalistic and Transcendental Moments in Kant's Moral Philosophy," *Inquiry* 50: 444–64.
Henrich, D. (1960) "Der Begriff der sittlichen Einsicht und Kants Lehre vom Faktum der Vernunft," in D. Henrich (ed.), *Die Gegenwart der Griechen in neuern Denken* (Tübingen: J.C. Mohr); translated (1994) as "The Concept of Moral Insight and Kant's Doctrine of the Fact of Reason," in D. Henrich (ed.) and R. Velkley (trans.), *The Unity of Reason*, Cambridge, MA: Harvard University Press.
Kleingeld, P. (2010) "Moral Consciousness and the 'Fact of Reason'," in A. Reath and J. Timmermann (eds.), *Kant's Critique of Practical Reason: A Critical Guide*, Cambridge: Cambridge University Press.
Korsgaard, C. (1996) *Creating the Kingdom of Ends*, Cambridge: Cambridge University Press.
Rawls, J. (2000) *Lectures on the History of Moral Philosophy*, Cambridge: Harvard University Press.

Reath, A. (2006) *Agency and Autonomy in Kant's Moral Theory*, Oxford and New York: Oxford University Press.

Reath, A. (2010) "Formal Principles and the Form of a Law," in A. Reath and J. Timmermann (eds.), *Kant's Critique of Practical Reason: A Critical Guide*, Cambridge: Cambridge University Press.

Reath, A. (2013) "Kant's Conception of Autonomy," in O. Sensen (ed.), *Kant on Moral Autonomy*, Cambridge: Cambridge University Press.

Reath, A. (2015) "Introduction to the Critique of Practical Reason," in I. Kant (ed.), M.J. Gregor (trans.), *Critique of Practical Reason*, 2nd ed., Cambridge University Press (with revised introduction).

Timmermann, J. (2010) "Reversal or Retreat? Kant's Deductions of Freedom and Morality," in A. Reath and J. Timmermann (eds.), *Kant's Critique of Practical Reason: A Critical Guide*, Cambridge: Cambridge University Press.

Ware, O. (2014) "Rethinking Kant's Fact of Reason," *Philosopher's Imprint* 14: 32.

Willaschek, M. (1991) "Die Tat der Vernunft: Zur Bedeutung der Kantischen These vom 'Factum der Vernunft'," in G. Funke (ed.), *Akten des Siebenten Internationalen Kant-Kongress*, Bonn: Bouvier.

Wood, A. (2008) *Kantian Ethics*, Cambridge: Cambridge University Press.

Further Reading

L.W. Beck's *A Commentary on Kant's Critique of Practical Reason* (Chicago: University of Chicago Press, 1960) is an older but still useful commentary on the entire work. Stephen Engstrom, "Introduction," in W. Pluhar (trans.), *Kant, Critique of Practical Reason* (Indianapolis: Hackett Publishing, 1996); A. Reath, "Introduction," in *Kant, Critique of Practical Reason*, M.J. Gregor (trans.), revised ed. (Cambridge: Cambridge University Press, 2015) provide overviews of the main themes and arguments of the *Critique* (and the latter contains a bibliographical essay on secondary work through to 2014). A. Reath and J. Timmermann, *Kant's Critique of Practical Reason: A Critical Guide* (Cambridge: Cambridge University Press, 2010) is a collection of essays on the main sections of the *Critique* with an extensive bibliography (through to 2010). For discussions of the "fact of reason", see the references in note 3. Discussions of "respect" as the moral incentive include Chapter 1 of A. Reath, *Agency and Autonomy in Kant's Moral Theory* (Oxford and New York: Oxford University Press, 2006); S. Engstrom, "The *Triebfeder* of Pure Practical Reason," in A. Reath and J. Timmermann (eds.), *Kant's Critique of Practical Reason: A Critical Guide* (Cambridge: Cambridge University Press, 2010); M. Zinkin, "Respect for the Law and the Use of Dynamical Terms," *Archiv für Geschichte Philosophie* 88 (2006): 31–53; R. McCarty, *Kant's Theory of Action* (Oxford and New York: Oxford University Press, 2009), J. DeWitt, "Respect for the Moral Law: The Emotional Side of Reason," *Philosophy* 89 (2014): 31–62; O. Ware, "Kant on Moral Sensibility and Moral Motivation," *Journal of the History of Philosophy* 52 (2014): 727–46.

15

DIALECTIC OF PURE PRACTICAL REASON

Oliver Sensen

★★★

1. Introduction

Imagine a situation in which behaving morally will cause you unhappiness. For instance, you have been told that you are the most qualified applicant for a particular job. But you also realize that others are lying on their CVs which make them look more qualified than you. Let us assume that you have no way of proving that they are lying, and that if you do not get the job, you would have to leave the profession you love, causing you great unhappiness. It is unthinkable to you that you could lie on your CV, but you realize that you will not get the job without it. In behaving morally, do you not have to hope that you will also become happy? What is the relation between morally good behavior and happiness, and what is the result if you have no indication that moral behavior will lead to happiness in this life?

It is questions like these that form the systematic background of the 'Dialectic' of the *Critique of Practical Reason* (1788). The second *Critique*, like the first, is divided into a 'Doctrine of Elements' (*KpV* 5: 19–148), and a 'Doctrine of Method' (*KpV* 5: 151–63), and the 'Doctrine of Elements' consists of an 'Analytic' (*KpV* 5: 19–106), as well as a 'Dialectic.' The 'Dialectic' itself is divided into two chapters. The first brief chapter is a general introduction to the idea of a dialectic of practical reason (*KpV* 5: 107–10), and it is followed by the main chapter: "On the dialectic of pure reason in determining the concept of the highest good" (*KpV* 5: 111). The main chapter is again divided into nine sections. Introductory remarks on the highest good are followed by the antinomy of practical reason (Sections I and II), the immortality of the soul as well as the existence of God (Sections IV and V). These sections are supported by general reflections on the insight one can get from practical reason, and the demand for the highest good (Sections VI to IX).

The central part of the 'Dialectic' is therefore the antinomy of how morality and happiness are related. There are a few issues that make the passage difficult to understand. One issue is that Kant does not fully spell out his reasoning, and the passage can be read very differently. A second issue is that Kant presents different accounts in other writings on this subject (cf. Pasternack 2014: 31–60), and it is not clear whether the views of the second *Critique* are his final, well-considered opinion. But the main systematic issue is that Kant himself has made the task of solving the relationship

DOI: 10.4324/9781003406617-20

between morality and happiness harder to solve because he had argued in the 'Analytic' that morality and happiness have no necessary connection, and that one even has to abstract from all considerations of happiness in acting morally (cf. *KpV* 5: 19–28). This leads to the charge that Kant might be inconsistent in bringing back happiness in the 'Dialectic.'

In shedding light on the issues of the 'Dialectic,' I shall first explain the questions more fully than Kant states them and elucidate why it is part of a dialectic (section 2). I shall then present his solution and analyze his argument for a justified belief in immortality, and a rewarding God (section 3). Finally, I shall address the issue whether Kant is inconsistent in trying to combine morality and happiness (section 4). If morality requires that one abstract from all considerations of happiness, how is it possible to still hope for happiness, and to pursue it?

2.   The 'Dialectic' and Its Problem

The problem of morality and happiness is created by reason itself: "Pure reason always has its dialectic" (*KpV* 5: 107). By this Kant means that even in practical matters reason creates a conflict when applying one of its basic principles. The basic principle is that reason presupposes "the unconditioned for everything conditioned" (*KpV* 5: 107; cf. A409/B436). Imagine – to give an example from theoretical reason – that you seek an explanation for a given event, for instance the fact that the water in this pond froze. The event of the water freezing is conditioned. It depends on the temperature, atmospheric pressure, purity of the water and so on. But each of these conditions is itself conditioned by something earlier in time. To explain the event fully, one would not only have to cite the totality of all the conditions, but also something that is the unconditioned condition of the subsequent conditions. For otherwise there is "never a first beginning, and thus no completeness of the series on the side of the causes descending one from another" (A445f/B474f). The explanation is only complete if it comes to an end in something – such as the Big Bang or an act of God – that caused the chain of events without itself being caused by a prior event. However, such a first beginning is contrary to the idea of a causally ordered (sensible) nature, according to which everything has a cause in a previous time. In other words, if one believes that the Big Bang caused the water to freeze, one's own reason will ask further: What caused the Big Bang?

In its theoretical use, reason seeks sufficient answers, but it creates a conflict within itself if it seeks the unconditioned complete answer for a given conditioned. There must be a first cause, and there cannot be a first cause. A similar conflict arises in reason's practical use, according to Kant: "But reason in its practical use is no better off. As pure practical reason it likewise seeks the unconditioned for the practical conditioned (which rests on inclinations and natural needs)" (*KpV* 5: 108) (For further similarities and differences between the two antinomies see Sala 2004: 234–43; Watkins 2010).

Kant's claim is that in its practical use reason "seeks the unconditioned totality of the object of pure practical reason, under the name of the *highest good*" (*KpV* 5: 108). In this section, I will unfold the meaning of this claim by asking three questions: (1) What is the highest good? (2) Why should one seek it? (3) What exactly does one have to do to promote it?

(1) What does Kant mean by the "highest good"? When reason seeks the unconditioned, this can be of two kinds. In our previous example of the water freezing, the unconditioned could refer to the first cause that was not itself caused, for example, the Big Bang, or it could refer to the complete explanation of the event, that is, the whole series of conditions, including all the intermediate steps (cf. A417/B445). Likewise, in the practical sphere the highest good could refer to the unconditioned condition of all goodness, or to the whole and complete good. Kant here puts the first one aside: "That *virtue* (as worthiness to be happy) is [. . .] the *supreme* good has been proved in the

Analytic" (*KpV* 5: 110). Instead, Kant focuses on "the whole and complete good as the object of the faculty of desire of rational finite beings" and "for this, *happiness* is also required" (*KpV* 5: 110).

Kant defines happiness as: "the state of a rational being in the world in the whole of whose existence *everything goes according to his wish and will*" (*KpV* 5: 124), and it includes the satisfaction of the sensible side of our nature (cf. Bader 2015: 185; but see Fugate 2014). Kant argues that in the highest good virtue and happiness stand in exact proportion to each other. The reason for this claim seems to be that earlier in the second *Critique* Kant had argued that it is the moral law that determines the value of something: the "*good* [. . .] *must not be determined before the moral law* [. . .] *but only* [. . .] *after it and by means of it*" (*KpV* 5: 62f; cf. *GMS* 4: 436). The moral law or Categorical Imperative commands the will to be "*giving universal law through all its maxims*" (*GMS* 4: 432, cf. 421). This leads to the idea that happiness is only good insofar as it is in accordance with morality (cf. Engstrom 1992: 751–8), and introduces the idea of proportionality. The highest good as complete good is therefore "happiness distributed in exact proportion to morality" (*KpV* 5: 110).

This general characterization covers several dimensions of the highest good. For instance, it is, on the one hand, a *description* of what is good for a person, but then it is also something one *ought* to bring about, on the other (cf. Reath 1988: 595). Second, Kant speaks in the same paragraph of "the highest good in a *person*" and "of a possible world" (*KpV* 5: 110f). These are two different things. Is reason concerned with *my own* complete good, or with the good of the whole world (cf. Bader 2015: 202)? A third distinction concerns the degree of the highest good. Is only that a complete good that has the *maximum* of virtue and happiness, or is a lower degree also an instance of the highest good, as long as virtue and happiness stand in the right proportion (cf. Engstrom 1992: 768)? There are further distinctions one can draw within the highest good, for instance, whether one regards happiness as the sum of all inclinations or as beatitude and complete independence of inclinations (cf. *KpV* 5: 119). Kant uses all of these and does not always distinguish clearly between them.

(2) Why *should* one bring about the highest good? The highest good is not merely a description of what is unconditionally good for a human being, but also something that is commanded to bring about. But if this is so, is it part of what the moral law commands directly, or is it somehow an additional prescription?

On the one hand, Kant says that bringing about the highest good "belongs to duty" (*KpV* 5: 126), and that the highest good is something "the moral law makes it our duty to take as the object of our endeavors" (*KpV* 5: 129; cf. *RGV* 6: 5). One could argue that the duty to bring about the highest good is already contained in the duty to promote the happiness of others, as Kant argues, for instance, in the fourth example of the *Groundwork* (cf. *GMS* 4: 423, 431; Engstrom 1992: 772). Kant even seems to say about both that one should promote them "as much as possible" (*GMS* 4: 430; cf. *KpV* 5: 119). But there also seem to be differences between the duty to promote the happiness of others, and the duty to promote the highest good. One difference is that the duty to promote the highest good includes the condition of proportionality (see page 180 above), which the duty to promote happiness does not. This could be explained away, however, in that the proportionality condition only applies to an omniscient and all-powerful being, and that since human beings lack these properties, we only have the duty to promote the happiness of others (cf. Engstrom 1992: 772).

But there are further differences. In the case of the duty to promote the happiness of others, the only thing that is commanded is to adopt a maxim, not to bring about a particular outcome, such as the highest good (cf. Bader 2015: 206). Furthermore, in the context of the promotion of happiness, Kant never mentions the need to postulate the existence of God, which is an essential part of the duty to promote the highest good (see pages 182–6). The duty to promote the happiness of others in the *Groundwork* does not seem to be the same as the duty to promote the highest good.

Accordingly, in several passages in the 'Dialectic' Kant uses a weaker language, saying that the highest good is "attached inseparably to an a priori unconditionally valid *practical* law" (*KpV* 5: 122) or "necessarily connected with the moral lawgiving of pure reason" (*KpV* 5: 124). This leaves open the possibility that it needs an additional step to get from the supreme moral law to the duty to bring about the highest good. In the *Religion* Kant is more explicit when he states that the highest good "exceeds the concept of duty that morality contains (and which does not presuppose any matter [. . .], but only [. . .] formal laws)" (*RGV* 6: 6n). The command to adopt the highest good as an end is therefore "introduced by the moral law itself, and yet through it practical reason reaches beyond the law" (*RGV* 6: 6n). What is added to the moral law, and why is it added by reason?

Kant specifies the addition to the moral law as "an a priori necessary object of our will [. . .] inseparably bound up with the moral law" (*KpV* 5: 114), or as something "reason points out to all rational beings as the goal of all their moral wishes" (*KpV* 5: 115), or as "a *purpose* given a priori, that is, an end as object (of the will)" (*KpV* 5: 134). So what is added is a goal or purpose, in other words: that when we think about the *consequences* of moral actions: "it is one of the inescapable limitations of human beings [. . .] to be concerned in every action with its result, seeking something in it [. . .] that they can *love*" (*RGV* 6: 7n). This is not something that is commanded by the supreme moral law itself, and Kant – famously – claims that we should disregard the consequences and follow the moral law for its own sake (*GMS* 4: 393, *RGV* 6: 7n). But this does not mean that we are not also *interested* in the consequences.

How can one understand this? One possibility is that the highest good is the sum of all of one's duties, and gives a complete picture of the "totality" (*KpV* 5: 108) of what one should do (cf. Kleingeld 2016: 45–7). However, there is reason to believe that this is not all that Kant has in mind. The complete set of duties does not involve consequences, but maxims, and one still would not be allowed to be guided by the consequences of one's actions. Rather, it seems to me that Kant has a special perspective in mind. In the heat of the moment, the agent should follow the moral law for its own sake (cf. *KpV* 5: 109f). But the same agent can also ask in a special reflection what kind of world she would create with her moral actions. This is a different outlook, which one can compare to Butler's "cool hour" (2006, Sermon XI: 117) of reflection.

The consequences of one's actions one can hope for under this special perspective can be of two sorts: (a) for oneself: "If I do what I should, what may I then hope?" (A805/B833) In the normal saying that it is commanded to bring about the highest good, what is commanded is merely the first part, virtue or the worthiness to be happy. The second part, happiness itself, is nothing that is commanded, but merely hoped for. The first is "*immediately* within our power," the second "is not in our power" (*KpV* 5: 119) and can therefore not be commanded. The second part is merely about the "expectation of a happiness proportionate" (*KpV* 5: 119) to morality, or in short: "an object of hope" (*KpV* 5: 128).

Looked at from a different perspective, (b), one can think about the consequences of one's actions from "the perfect volition of a rational being that would at the same time have all power, even if we think of such a being only for the sake of the experiment" (*KpV* 5: 110). From this God's-eye-perspective, in which we have all the power and knowledge, we can envision a world in accordance with the highest moral law or a moral world (cf. A808/B836). It is a perspective of reason in the sense that we are impartial and not governed by our own concerns: "He would thus feel himself compelled by reason to acknowledge this judgment with complete impartiality, as if rendered by somebody else yet at the same time his own, and in this way the human being evinces the need, effected in him by morality, of adding to the thought of his duties a final end as well, as their consequence" (*RGV* 6: 6). But what is important to note is that this is not our normal perspective. We do not have all the power, omniscience, and perfect impartiality, even if we can take this perspective.

There are, therefore, two ways in which the realization of the highest good is commanded. Everything that is commanded rests on the Categorical Imperative. It is the "categorical imperative, which as such only affirms what obligation is" (*MS* 6: 225). Whatever is commanded about the highest good, rests on the imperative. However, it only becomes a command *about* the highest good, if (1) one adds to what is commanded the *hope* to become happy, or (2) if one looks at the results of morality from an impartial, ideal perspective.

(3) The previous discussion of why one should bring about the highest good already indicated what more specifically one has to do to bring it about. The main requirement is to pursue one's own virtue, "that is, a disposition conformed with law *from respect* for law" (*KpV* 5: 128). There is no duty to make others virtuous. Kant holds that one cannot force another to adopt a particular disposition (cf. *MS* 6: 386). There is also no duty to bring about the exact proportion of virtue and happiness in oneself or others. This is because one does not even know in one's own case how virtuous one is (Cf. *GMS* 4: 406–8). As mentioned before, the duty to pursue one's own virtue does not introduce any new duties. It does not "increase the number of morality's duties" (*RGV* 6: 5). A right moral disposition adds to doing what the moral law says is the right thing to do that one does it simply because it is right: "it must also be done *for the sake of the law*" (*GMS* 4: 390).

The Kant literature debates whether Kant shifts the emphasis from thinking about one's own highest good to a duty of bringing about the highest good for the world at large (cf. Reath 1988; Guyer 2005: 289; Pasternack 2014: 31–6). In the *Critique of Practical Reason* Kant seems to talk about both aspects. He does believe that the highest good is not just about one's own happiness, but that there is also a duty "to bring about the highest good in the world" (*KpV* 5: 126). However, both seem to be included in what we have said before. If one follows the moral directives, one can think what the consequences of one's actions will be, and in particular ask whether one will also become happy. But one can also think more ideally about what world would come about *if* all others would be virtuous as well (cf. *GMS* 4: 438). In this sense, the question of the highest good is at the same time about one's own happiness, as well as about creating a moral community (cf. *RGV* 6: 97f).

3. The Antinomy and Its Solution

For Kant the command to pursue the highest good leads to an antinomy. In the theoretical sphere, I have argued earlier in section 2, reason gets into contradictions when it seeks the unconditioned condition for explaining physical phenomena. In order to give a fully sufficient explanation of an event, for instance, reason can argue that there must be a first cause and that there cannot be one. The problem arises if we look at past conditions, the "*antecendentia*" (A411/B438). In the practical sphere, by contrast, we look at the future consequences of a morally good action, the *consequentia*.

But why does this lead to a contradiction? An antinomy arises because, on the one hand, we ought to pursue the highest good, and it seems that an 'ought' implies a 'can': "we *ought* to strive to promote the highest good (which must therefore be possible)" (*KpV* 5: 125), but, on the other hand, it does not seem possible that we can bring about the highest good. Kant holds this thesis because he had argued earlier in the *Critique of Practical Reason* that morality and happiness are not – other than the views he ascribes to the Ancient Stoics and Epicureans – analytically connected but are "quite *different elements*" (*KpV* 5: 112), and he further argued one does not causally lead to the other. The motive for happiness does not lead to a moral disposition, and – as far as we can tell – a morally good disposition does not necessarily lead to happiness in this world (cf. *KpV* 5: 113).

Kant resolves the antinomy in that the highest good is possible if the soul is immortal, and if there is a God who can bring about happiness in proportion to virtue. Kant puts forth the postulate of immortality in order to explain how it is possible for an individual to become worthy of happiness, and God to bring about happiness (cf. *KpV* 5: 124). On the surface, the argument seems pretty straightforward: "It is a duty to realize the highest good [. . .]; therefore, it must be possible; hence it is also unavoidable [. . .] to assume what is necessary for its objective possibility" (*KpV* 5: 144n). Since he identifies the immortality of the soul, as well as God's existence, as necessary conditions of the possibility of the highest good, the argument can be summarized as follows:

(1) One ought to bring about the highest good.
(2) Ought implies can.
(3) One can only bring about the highest good if the soul is immortal and God exists.
(4) Therefore one needs to postulate the immortality of the soul and God's existence.

The solution to the antinomy can therefore be read as an argument for the existence of God, and the immortality of the soul. As such both arguments have been heavily criticized. The secondary literature mostly agrees that the argument for the existence of God does not establish theoretical knowledge. However, scholars point out that Kant intends the proof merely as a practical proof, that is, as providing moral faith for our practice (Wood 1970: 145–52); it is further said to be a proof that only grows out of a subjective necessity of our pure reason (Sala 2004: 292), and is solely regulative for our practice (DiCenso 2011: 216). Others believe that even that fails, and that the proof merely satisfies a need of an "all-too-human reason" (Beck 1960: 254), or that the ideal of the highest good does not need the existence of God in order to function as an ideal (see Sussman 2015: 220). Likewise, the argument for the immortality of the soul is subject to criticism (cf. Beck 1960: 268; Allison 1990: 172f). A close look at the arguments, however, will show that Kant himself qualifies his claims in important respects.

(1) As I have argued in the first section, Kant already qualifies the first premise. It is not strictly speaking commanded to bring about the highest good. For finite human beings, it is commanded to form a good will and develop virtue, the first part of the highest good. Only if one reflects upon the consequences of one's action from an ideal perspective, that is, a perspective under which one is omniscient and all powerful, would one have a duty to bring about happiness in exact proportion of virtue as well. There will therefore be two arguments. The first goes from the command to become a virtuous person to the immortality of the soul, and runs:

I ought to acquire virtue.
Ought implies can.
I can only acquire virtue if my soul is immortal.
Therefore I must postulate the immortality of the soul.

The second argument takes the ideal perspective into account, but since it is not our actual situation, it needs to postulate the existence of God:

I ought (under an ideal perspective) to bring about happiness in proportion to virtue.
Ought implies can.
(Since the ideal perspective is not my actual situation) happiness can only be brought about if there is a God.
Therefore I must postulate the existence of God.

Both arguments share the second premise that ought implies can. Is that premise sound?

(2) The second premise, ought implies can, is a plausible thought that appears throughout Kant's writings. But is this a valid inference, and if so, why is it valid? For instance, Kant cannot merely have a psychological claim in mind, for he himself acknowledges that there could be the phenomenon of a conscience that is too strong (cf. *V-Mo/Collins* 27: 356). We might feel that we ought to do something, for example, to help others in need, although in fact this goes beyond our powers, or

beyond what is commanded. We might *feel* an Ought although we cannot accomplish it. So, what exactly is Kant's claim?

It seems to me that Kant uses at least two different versions of 'ought implies can.' In one version he uses it as a *Modus Tollens*, and as such it mainly forms a limit on what moral theories can demand: "People are always preaching about what ought to be done, and nobody thinks about whether it can be done [. . .]. Consideration of rules is useless if one cannot make man ready to follow them" (*V-Mo/Collins* 27: 244). If someone (physically) cannot do something, it cannot be commanded of him that he do so: "thus a man, for example, has no obligation to stop hiccupping, for it is not in his power" (*V-Mo/Collins* 27: 261).

In this version, one can simplify Kant's argument as a *Modus Tollens*:

If I ought, then I can.

I cannot.

Therefore, I am not obligated to do it.

This argument seems very plausible. However, at first glance, it does not seem to be what Kant has in mind in the 'Dialectic' of the *Critique of Practical Reason*. The main reason is that the direction of the 'Dialectic' argument is not to prove that we are not obligated to do something, but that we can do something. He does not seem to use a *Modus Tollens*, but a *Modus Ponens*.

Kant uses a *Modus Ponens* argument in the gallows example of the second *Critique*. There he uses the moral 'ought' to conclude that we are justified in assuming freedom. Imagine a situation in which no desire speaks for performing the morally good action. If one is nonetheless aware that one ought to do the moral action, this ought gives one a sense that one could determine oneself independently of desires and therefore act freely: "He judges, therefore, that he can do something because he is aware that he ought to do it and cognizes freedom within him, which, without the moral law, would have remained unknown to him" (*KpV* 5: 30). In this second sense the argument has the following simplified form:

If I ought, then I can

I ought

Therefore, (I am justified in assuming) that I can

This argument, too, seems plausible. This is especially so since Kant is not claiming that one positively knows that one is free. For one does not know whether one will act in accordance with the Ought (cf. *V-MS/Vigil* 27: 507), and even after the action one cannot be sure why exactly one acted (cf. *GMS* 4: 406–8). But it is plausible that one has a psychological sense of being able to act independently of one's desires, and this is all Kant needs for practical purposes, that is, in order to act morally (cf. *KpV* 5: 108, 135; *KU* 5: 470). This, however, would not be enough to establish that one really can bring about the highest good. So, how does Kant use 'ought implies can' in the 'Dialectic'?

The result of the discussion so far suggests that 'ought implies can' is not an axiom, or a fundamental law that is valid a priori in its own right (cf. also Rödl 2013). Rather the principle gets its plausibility from other considerations: It is pragmatically pointless to demand something that cannot be fulfilled, and the experience of an ought gives one a sense that one could do the required action. However, 'ought implies can' is the result of these pragmatic and empirical considerations, not its foundation. Might Kant have something stronger in mind? In theoretical philosophy, it seems that necessity involves possibility. If something has to happen, and it cannot be otherwise, then it is also possible. But does the same principle apply in the practical sphere?

There is an important difference. In Kant's theoretical sphere, the necessary elements of the mind, such as space, time, and causality create how the world appears (cf. Bxvi). A necessity in thought creates a necessity in how the world appears. But in the practical sphere, there is no connection between the moral law and the laws of nature (cf. *KpV* 5: 113). A moral necessity does not by itself guarantee that it is possible in nature. One could argue that God might have established a harmony between these two spheres, but this is exactly what the argument aims to establish, not something that can be presupposed at the outset.

So, how does 'ought implies can' function in the resolution of the antinomy? It seems that Kant uses the *Modus Tollens* version of the argument after all. From the 'Analytic' in the *Critique of Practical Reason* he takes the existence of the moral ought: "Pure reason [. . .] gives (to the human being) a universal law, which we call the *moral law*" (*KpV* 5: 31). This law, if one thinks about the consequences, is tied to the highest good. Were the highest good impossible, then the moral law that commands it would also be pointless: "If, therefore, the highest good is impossible in accordance with practical rules, then the moral law, which commands us to promote it, must be fantastic [. . .] and must therefore in itself be false" (*KpV* 5: 114). This is the *Modus Tollens* version of 'ought implies can,' and has the same plausibility as it has in other cases. The second premise, 'ought implies can,' is therefore the conclusion of the longer *Modus Tollens* argument. However, since Kant acknowledges a gap between moral necessity and laws of nature, is the argument strong enough to give theoretical knowledge of God and immortality? I shall start with the immortality argument.

(3) The first argument applies to the postulate of the immortality of the soul. One ought to bring about one's own virtue, and this Ought would be pointless if one could not do it. In the third premise, Kant asserts that one can acquire virtue only if the soul is immortal. However, the third premise is not fully spelled out, and if one thinks about it, it is not clear what the exact point is supposed to be. A straightforward reading is that in this life, because of the claims of our inclinations, we are never fully capable of having a full strength of virtue (cf. *KpV* 5: 123; Engstrom 1992: 762). However, this does not seem to explain the temporal aspect of immortality. Presumably, if the soul continues to exist after death, there would be no inclinations that could weaken the strength of will, and so the full strength of virtue would be instantly given. Why would it need a continued existence after death?

One explanation is that Kant is not concerned with a one-time strength of will, but with an extensive magnitude of good acts. Virtue is then acquired the more virtuous deeds one performs, and in its sum an immortal soul would approximate perfection (cf. Bader 2015: 192). However, if there is no sensibility after death, would this not also eliminate time as well as succession, and how would an immortal soul act after death at all? Kant's argument is therefore not fully spelled out, and open to interpretation. This is not helped by the fact that in the first *Critique*, he seems to invoke the immortality of the soul to explain the possibility of happiness, not of virtue (cf. A809f/B837f).

But it is not only the content of the argument that is unclear, but also its status. Again, a straightforward reading of the argument would hold that we gain theoretical knowledge that the soul is immortal. But in fact, Kant's claim is considerably weaker. He defines a postulate not as theoretical knowledge, but as "a *theoretical* proposition, though one not demonstrable as such, insofar as it is attached inseparably to an a priori unconditionally valid *practical* law" (*KpV* 5: 122). The claim is not that we know that the soul is immortal, but that we are entitled to assume it "only for practical use" (*KpV* 5: 135), that is, for acting morally. Accordingly, when Kant considers the issue more fully in the *Religion*, he puts forth a much weaker premise. He does not use 'ought implies can,' but "ought implies *hope* that can" (*RGV* 6: 51). The moral Ought justifies not knowledge, but that "he may hope" (*KpV* 5: 123) to acquire virtue (on Kant's notion of hope see Willaschek 2010: 180f; Chignell 2014).

(4) Kant also qualifies the second argument that he uses to support the postulate of God's existence. In the argument, Kant says that from an ideal perspective one should bring about happiness

in exact proportion to virtue. Since ought implies can, but the ideal perspective is not our actual perspective, we have to assume the existence of God in order for happiness to come about. On an ambitious reading of the argument, one would conclude from the existence of the moral law to the existence of God. As such, the argument has been heavily criticized in the literature (see page 183). However, it is important to see that Kant himself qualifies the argument in at least three important respects.

(a) As I have noted before, bringing about happiness in proportion to virtue "is not in our power" (*KpV* 5: 119), and it therefore cannot be commanded. We can put ourselves into this perspective and think about the consequences that would come about if we were a "wise and all-powerful distributor" (*KpV* 5: 128), but we do not have these powers. Bringing about this aspect of the highest good is, accordingly, not commanded, and achieving happiness – for oneself or others – "is therefore made solely an object of hope" (*KpV* 5: 129). Inasmuch as God is necessary for achieving happiness, God's existence too is not an object of knowledge, but merely of hope.

(b) However, Kant does not even argue that we *have to* assume the existence of God in order to hope for happiness. Kant says that regarding "*the way*" in which happiness results from moral behavior "we have a *choice*" (*KpV* 5: 144f; cf. Willaschek 2010: 191f). Kant thinks that it could be the case that natural laws are such that they will bring about happiness in proportion to virtue, he just thinks that "our reason finds it *impossible* [. . .] to conceive," and that a "moral interest [. . .] turns the scale" (*KpV* 5: 145). The argument therefore does not claim that one has to assume the existence of God in order that one can hope for happiness.

(c) Finally, in virtue of being a postulate, the argument is meant "only for practical use" (*KpV* 5: 135), that is, to "determine [. . .] the maxims of our rational conduct" (*KpV* 5: 108), or in short: to act. Practical knowledge is therefore not theoretical knowledge of the existence of God, which was gained from the moral law a practical premise (similarly Ameriks 2012: 257). Rather the argument justifies that we assume the "possibility of *making real* [. . .] the highest good" (*KpV* 5: 135). If we would know that the highest good is impossible, the command to bring it about would be pointless. With the argument, however, we now have a way to think that it is possible that the highest good could come about. Therefore, we are justified in acting accordingly, but it serves only for performing the action, "not for any speculative purpose" (*KpV* 5: 138).

4. Consistency

Even if Kant's claims about the highest good and the postulates are more modest than they might seem at first glance, there remains the question whether Kant is inconsistent in bringing back considerations of happiness and God. In his main discussions about moral philosophy, he says that we should "put aside entirely" (*GMS* 4: 400) considerations of happiness when we determine the moral course of action, and also that we should not base it on a belief in a rewarding God (cf. *KpV* 5: 41). Is Kant's discussion of the highest good an attempt to bring in through the backdoor happiness and God, and is he not inconsistent in doing this? A version of these issues has become to be known as the Beck-Silber debate (cf. Beck 1960: 242–5; Silber 1963; Baiasu 2018). I shall point out three reasons why Kant does not seem to be inconsistent after all.

(1) Kant emphasizes right in the first chapter that "the highest good [. . .] is not [. . .] to be taken as [. . .] *determining ground*" of moral actions (*KpV* 5: 109). In other words: The hope for one's own happiness is not what one should have in mind during the action. One can again distinguish between two perspectives: In the heat of action, the only right moral motive is duty and respect for the moral law. But in a cool hour of reflection, when one thinks of the consequences of one's actions, it is natural for us to hope for one's own happiness as well. In addition, Kant confirms that

the 'Dialectic' does not change his views on the role of God: "it is not [. . .] necessary to assume the existence of God *as a ground of all obligation in general* (for this rests [. . .] solely on the *autonomy of reason itself*)" (*KpV* 5: 125f).

(2) Kant is also not inconsistent because he does not argue that we can have theoretical knowledge of God and his rewards. It is therefore not something certain on which one can base one's actions. The postulates give "comforting hope, though not certitude" (*KpV* 5: 123n). Kant even argues that any prior knowledge of God and his rewards would undermine the right moral motive (cf. *KpV* 5: 147; and Timmermann 2015).

(3) Furthermore, the comforting hope one can entertain in a cool hour of reflection that moral behavior might be rewarded "cannot be called happiness" (*KpV* 5: 119), because it is "only a negative satisfaction" (*KpV* 5: 117), not a positive feeling of happiness. If one realizes that behaving morally will cause one unhappiness in this world, the thought that one might be rewarded in an afterlife is at this point – partly because of its uncertainty – merely consolation: "This consolation is not happiness" (*KpV* 5: 88), however.

5. Conclusion

In the 'Dialectic' of the *Critique of Practical Reason*, Kant addresses a further dimension of our moral thought, that is, that we think about the consequences of our actions, including our own happiness. This need is not just a sensible desire, but "a need *of pure practical reason*" (*KpV* 5: 142). Kant's determination of the highest good is in accordance with the moral law, and his discussion of happiness and God is not inconsistent with the tenets of his moral philosophy, and "everything stands together in the most perfect harmony" (Cf. KpV 5: 110).

References

Allison, H. (1990) *Kant's Theory of Freedom*, Cambridge: Cambridge University Press.

Ameriks, K. (2012) *Kant's Elliptical Path*, Oxford: Oxford University Press.

Bader, R. (2015) "Kant's Theory of the Highest Good," in J. Aufderheide and R. Bader (eds.), *The Highest Good in Aristotle and Kant*, Oxford: Oxford University Press, pp. 183–213.

Baiasu, S. (2018) "Nature and Freedom: The Highest Good and the Beck/Silber Debate Today," in V. Waibel, M. Ruffing and D. Wagner (eds.), *Natur und Freiheit*, Berlin: Walter de Gruyter, pp. 1715–20.

Beck, L.W. (1960) *A Commentary on Kant's Critique of Practical Reason*, Chicago: University of Chicago Press.

Butler, J. (2006) "Sermon XI," in D. White (ed.), *The Works of Bishop Butler*, Rochester: University of Rochester Press, pp. 110–18.

Chignell, A. (2014) "Rational Hope, Possibility, and Divine Action," in G. Michaelson (ed.), *Religion Within the Bounds of Mere Reason: A Critical Guide*, Cambridge: Cambridge University Press, pp. 98–117.

DiCenso, J. (2011) *Kant, Religion, and Politics*, Cambridge: Cambridge University Press.

Engstrom, S. (1992) "The Concept of the Highest Good in Kant's Moral Theory," *Philosophy and Phenomenological Research* 52: 747–80.

Fugate, C. (2014) "The Highest Good and Kant's Proof(s) of God's Existence," *History of Philosophical Quarterly* 31: 137–58.

Guyer, P. (2005) *Kant's System of Nature and Freedom*, Cambridge: Cambridge University Press.

Kleingeld, P. (2016) "Kant on 'Good', the Good, and the Duty to Promote the Highest Good," in T. Höwing (ed.), *The Highest Good in Kant's Philosophy*, Berlin: Walter de Gruyter, pp. 33–50.

Pasternack, L. (2014) *Kant on Religion Within the Boundaries of Mere Reason*, London: Routledge.

Reath, A. (1988) "Two Conceptions of the Highest Good," *Journal of the History of Philosophy* 26: 593–619.

Rödl, S. (2013) "Why Ought Implies Can," in M. Timmons and S. Baiasu (eds.), *Kant on Practical Justification*, Oxford: Oxford University Press, pp. 42–56.

Sala, G. (2004) *Kants "Kritik der praktischen Vernunft. Ein Kommentar,"* Darmstadt: Wissenschaftliche Buchgesellschaft.

Silber, J. (1963) "The Importance of the Highest Good in Kant's Ethics," *Ethics* 73: 179–97.

Sussman, D. (2015) "The Highest Good: Who Needs It?" in J. Aufderheide and R. Bader (eds.), *The Highest Good in Aristotle and Kant*, Oxford: Oxford University Press, pp. 214–28.

Timmermann, J. (2015) "Why Some Things Must Remain Unknown: Kant on Faith, Moral Motivation, and the Highest Good," in J. Aufderheide and R. Bader (eds.), *The Highest Good in Aristotle and Kant*, Oxford: Oxford University Press, pp. 229–42.

Watkins, E. (2010) "The Antinomy of Practical Reason: Reason, the Unconditioned and the Highest Good," in A. Reath and J. Timmermann (eds.), *Kant's Critique of Practical Reason: A Critical Guide*, Cambridge: Cambridge University Press, pp. 145–67.

Willaschek, M. (2010) "The Primacy of Practical Reason and the Idea of a Practical Postulate," in A. Reath and J. Timmermann (eds.), *Kant's Critique of Practical Reason: A Critical Guide*, Cambridge: Cambridge University Press, pp. 168–96.

Wood, A. (1970) *Kant's Moral Religion*, Ithaca: Cornell University Press.

Further Reading

L. Pasternack, *Kant on Religion Within the Boundaries of Mere Reason* (London: Routledge, 2014) gives an excellent introduction to the topics of the "Dialectic" and compares it to Kant's treatment in other works, while A. Wood, *Kant's Moral Religion* (Ithaca: Cornell University Press, 1970) provides a thorough discussion. L.W. Beck, *A Commentary on Kant's Critique of Practical Reason* (Chicago: University of Chicago Press, 1960); G. Sala, *Kants "Kritik der praktischen Vernunft": Ein Kommentar* (Darmstadt: Wissenschaftliche Buchgesellschaft, 2004) provide a detailed commentary of the "Dialectic" itself. Three collections of essays, J. Aufderheide and R. Bader (eds.), *The Highest Good in Aristotle and Kant* (Oxford: Oxford University Press, 2015); T. Höwing (ed.), *The Highest Good in Kant's Philosophy* (Berlin: Walter de Gruyter, 2016); A. Reath and J. Timmermann (eds.), *Kant's Critique of Practical Reason: A Critical Guide* (Cambridge: Cambridge University Press, 2010) bring together leading scholars who discuss the highest good and the "Dialectic" respectively.

16

METHOD OF PURE PRACTICAL REASON[1]

Robert Johnson

★★★

Two things fill the mind with ever new and increasing wonder and awe, the oftener and more steadily we reflect on them: the starry heavens above me and the moral law within me.

(*KpV* 5: 161)[2]

1. Introduction

In the *Critique of Practical* Reason, The *Method* is the entirety of the second part of the *Critique of Practical Reason*. Its aim is to provide an idea of "the way in which we can secure to the laws of pure practical reason access to the human mind and an influence on its maxims" (*KpV* 5: 151).

Kant took himself to have established that morality is composed of "laws of pure practical reason" and that a Good Will wills on the basis of maxims that could serve as such laws. It is a fair question how that could be possible. How might laws, rules or principles that do not appeal to any natural human interest "secure access to the human mind", especially if this is what is required for our actions to have genuine moral worth and for our wills to be good? How, in concrete terms, could an autonomous principle motivate? The *Method* addresses this question.

Unsurprisingly, the *Method*'s answer relies on Kant's views in the first part of the second *Critique*. He thinks not only *can* an autonomous law motivate, but, because cognition of one's own freedom follows upon the cognition of such a law, it is "the strongest incentive to the good". Kant explicitly ties this strongest of incentives not only to cognition of one's freedom, but to the sense of self-worth that is to arise during the course of this method. And that he does so might suggest a certain picture of how the laws of pure practical reason gain "access" to the mind: Those insufficiently motivated by Moral Law need only be led to behold the unqualified value of their own rational agency. That inspiring vision will summon sufficient will to conform even to morality's most challenging requirements. However, in my view Kant's appeals to this sense of self-worth, important as they are, do not imply that moral persuasion is supposed to unveil the value of one's own rational agency. The order in which Kant presents our cognitions of the moral law and of freedom, and as well as the proper progression of moral persuasion, although not incompatible with such an aim, do not require it. Thus, although the *Method* reveals the depth of Kant's faith in the Enlightenment ideals he

 DOI: 10.4324/9781003406617-21

eloquently expresses in his concluding remarks about "the moral law within" us, it does not reveal a foundational value at work in his conception of practical reason.[3]

2. Moral Persuasion

I will mainly use the phrase "moral persuasion", even if much of Kant's own discussion is couched in terms of "moral education". I mean to be talking about a fairly common activity encompassing not only teaching the young (Kant's example is a 10-year-old) but also advice to wayward adults in need of edification, and persuasion is good general term for the activity Kant envisages in these pages. This is especially so because there is no moral information a minimally rational person lacks and could be provided as a part of such an education.

The audience of moral persuasion is not supposed to be cynics, but those who for some reason are not, or not yet, wholeheartedly receptive to morality. Although the *Method* relies heavily on anecdotes from ordinary experience of moralizing, it is not really an argument based on observations to be used as evidence for a theoretical position that an autonomous law can motivate us. It advocates a certain manner of going about moral education that, he asserts, has "never yet been widely used" (*KpV* 5: 153).

Kant begins with an admission about the audience of moral persuasion that we should handle carefully:

> Certainly it cannot be denied that in order to bring either an as yet uneducated or a degraded mind into the path of the morally good, some preparatory guidance is needed to attract it by a view to its own advantage or to frighten it by fear of harm.
>
> (*KpV* 5: 152)

This may sound harsh, but I believe the basic point is not. Persuasion aimed at the morally "uneducated or degraded mind" has to begin, perhaps obviously, by appealing to *non-moral* interests. Kant may have assumed that non-moral interests always resolve into self-interest. This assumption, together with his position about morally "uneducated or degraded" minds, would imply that invariably the beginning of moral persuasion is self-interest. But the *Method* does not require that controversial assumption. We could just as easily assume, for instance, that human beings also possess intrinsic interests in the well-being of others. Then a "preparatory" starting point could easily be non-moral intrinsic interest in the well-being of some other person or persons.

Kant is describing the starting point of persuasion someone who is not yet particularly moved by moral considerations. This can in some respects be thought of like conceiving of a moral "state of nature". Imagining such a state allows us to clearly address questions about the origin of political interest, such as, How might people come to possess a sense of justice? The issue here is about morality in general, How might people come to possess a sufficiently effective interest in morality (construed as the Categorical Imperative)? Part of the answer one might have thought depends on what interests one thinks human psychology comes naturally equipped with. But, importantly, Kant does not assume the target of moral persuasion *lacks moral interest*. His method does not suppose, for instance, that the aim is to instill something that is missing. Rather, an interest in morality, supposing it exists in some degree, in the object of moral persuasion is assumed by Kant to be in some sense so weak that appealing immediately to it would not provide "access to the mind" for genuinely moral maxims.

A philosopher who assumes that all human interests somehow originate in self-interest would of course have to explain how human beings can nevertheless pursue charity or justice when it isn't in their own interest. Kant rejects such assumptions because they are incompatible with the idea that morality is composed of autonomous laws. Any such assumptions about human nature cannot characterize the psychological starting place of moral persuasion.[4] So it is important that we not think that he wants to explain moral interest in terms of non-moral interest, and obviously not in terms of self-interest. Moral persuasion does *begin* with non-moral interest but it doesn't follow that this is in any way an *origin* of moral interest, whatever non-moral interests might turn out to be. It begins with the presumption of the absence of an immediate and sufficient respect for the moral law that characterizes the end-point of moral edification.

But some moral interest, it seems, is not far away. As soon as "these leading strings have had some effect", the appeal to non-moral interests, though presumably necessary, should end. Immediately,

> the pure moral motive must be brought to mind [. . .] because, in teaching a man to feel his own worth, it gives his mind a power, *unexpected even by himself*, to pull himself loose from all sensuous attachments (so far as they would dominate him) and, in the independence of his intelligible nature and in the greatness of soul to which he sees himself called, to find himself richly compensated for the sacrifice he makes.
>
> (*KpV* 5: 152, my emphasis)

What "gives his mind a power" is not the feeling of self-worth but "the pure moral motive" when it is "brought to mind." Cognition of the moral law in its "purity" brings another cognition, the cognition of one's freedom, which is a source of the feeling of self-worth. More on this later. For now, note that it is the cognition of one's freedom that is the source of the motivational "power" that the audience of moral persuasion then acquires. Kant presents this sort of moral persuasion in such a way that it produces a kind of self-respect, a "feeling one's own worth". He thinks of this as initially a moment of moral enlightenment, something "unexpected". Promptly abandoning an initial appeal to the "leading strings" of non-moral interests is thus necessary to avoid, not only the effect of what Kant regards as the only sufficiently reliable motive to act morally, but the recognition of one's *independence* of those non-moral interests. It is necessary to achieve a kind of self-respect.

Although it will be obvious to those familiar with Kant's overall views, while he speaks of recognizing one's own "greatness of soul" as a "compensation for the sacrifice" morality can demand, he is not suggesting that moral persuasion appeals to one's enlightened self-interest. Though there is apparently a kind of satisfaction that comes from recognizing one's freedom, Kant is not claiming that this satisfaction is itself supposed to be the motivation to comply with the Moral Law. He is not, that is, suggesting that when we drop the "leading strings" of non-moral interest we then pick up the more noble strings of a "satisfaction" arising from a view of our "greatness of soul". Respect for the moral law alone is, of course, the sole sufficient interest.

More importantly, there is a theoretical picture Kant's presentation of his *Method* might suggest, but is in fact not required. Kant describes the proper method of moral edification as drawing a person's attention to their "intelligible nature". And he refers to this intelligible nature alongside remarks about the importance of our sense of self-worth. I would describe the tempting, though controversial picture this might encourage in this way:

> Human beings possess something of unique value, free rational agency, that stands apart from, even outside of, nature. It is important for each to get a clear and direct view of this uniquely valuable item existing within themselves because it is only a clear view of this value that can produce a reliable inspiration and motivation to conform to the demands of the moral law.

On this reading, moral persuasion is primarily a matter of guiding someone to an unimpeded vision of the intrinsic value of their own rational agency. Once this special fact about the value of their agency, their own "greatness of soul" is clearly in view, motivation to conform to the Moral Law even in the most difficult of circumstances will then follow.

While Kant's florid prose, here and elsewhere, may suggest this picture to some, the view is unnecessary. The interpretation supposes that Kantian moral theory relies on controversial metaphysical claims about our "intelligible natures". It also relies on a controversial claim about the foundation of morality. That claim is that it is in becoming aware of the intrinsic value of one's own humanity that moral progress begins, and one is thereafter more motivated to conform to moral requirements. I think that while the method Kant describes and argues for is not inconsistent with this reading of Kant's ethical theory, it does not require it.

Moral persuasion, as depicted in the *Method* does not *seem* to aim at producing a clear view, un-occluded by natural interests, of a unique value in its audience so that this vision of "the good" can produce a powerful motivation to act morally. It aims at drawing attention to the Moral Law, what morality requires, with the resulting further cognition of their own capacity to conform to that law. The recognition of one's capacity to act then gives rise to a sense of one's supreme value. The progression is thus from the cognition of being bound by the moral law, to the cognition of having the capacity to act as that law requires, ending with 'feeling' of one's own worth. The progression is not that one first cognizes the supreme value of one's humanity, and then acquires a powerful motivation leading one to conform to what the moral law requires.

That Kant's *Method* does not propose as a method the unveiling of the value of one's own agency can also be seen by considering the structure of his example of moral persuasion earlier in the *Critique* in which he is discussing what Henry Allison dubbed the "Reciprocity Thesis" (1986). It will be worthwhile to consider carefully the structure of that example:

> Suppose that someone says his lust is irresistible when the desired object and opportunity are present. Ask him whether he would not control his passion if, in front of the house where he has this opportunity, a gallows were erected on which he would be hanged immediately after gratifying his lust. We do not have to guess very long what his answer would be. But ask him whether he thinks it would be possible for him to overcome his love of life, however great it may be, if his sovereign threatened him with the same sudden death unless he made a false deposition against an honorable man whom the ruler wished to destroy under a plausible pretext. Whether he would or not he perhaps will not venture to say; but that it would be possible for him he would certainly admit without hesitation.
>
> (*KpV* 5: 30)

Call this example, GALLOWS. GALLOWS presents the reader with a thought experiment that has three parts or stages, concluding of course, with the person's thought that it is possible for them to refrain from something morality forbids.

We begin with a supposed "irresistible lust". People often use the phrase (or its cognates), "I couldn't help myself (or wouldn't be able to . . .)". One might hear this about anything desirable, but the example assumes an interest in sex is particularly powerful, and surely this is why Kant uses it. It is important that in this succession of cognitions, the succession begins in such a way that it will make sense that the person will come to cognize something about the Moral Law and the capacity of the will. The epistemic condition of genuinely thinking about pursuing some desire is that "I have no choice" or "I can't help myself" is not merely a condition of being unaware that one does have a choice or that one can help oneself. It is, if the progression of cognitions Kant here discusses is accurate, a condition in which the *unconditional authority* of the Moral Law is not fully cognized. I say "not fully cognized" because any normal adult is in Kant's view cognizant of the Moral Law and its authority. Knowing what one ought to do in any circumstance is not supposed to be an achievement. So the fact that Kant in his discussion of the Reciprocity Thesis, and especially in his example, alludes to a kind of *lack* of cognition, means that that lack must be consistent with possessing sufficient knowledge of the Moral Law and its bindingness to qualify as a rational agent. Cognition of the moral law, in the relevant sense, is cognition of a sort that leads to a further distinct cognition of one's freedom. But it has to be a kind of "full appreciation" of the authority of that law that a person might lack, yet at the same time cognize that law as binding in some lesser sense (sufficient for moral agency).

What a person cognizes is something about their own *agency*. They aren't cognizing something about what thoughts they are capable of, what they can see or hear, nothing about themselves as *knowers*. They cognize something about themselves inasmuch as they are *agents*. Moreover, it is a *practical cognition* about what they must do, and, as a result, can do, that "I am unconditionally bound" and "I am free", or more colloquially that "I *can* help myself".

This, then, is the first stage of the example, the stage of someone's saying or thinking "I can't help it" with regard to some passion. The second stage puts the lie to that thought. We are to imagine telling this wanton that certainly they *could* help it if their death were the certain consequence of satisfying that passion. One might think Kant has gone too far with this consequence. Wouldn't some lesser consequence show the same point, say, "Suppose you would lose an arm, or everything you own, or . . ."? Evidently Kant wants to us to think in "all in" terms when speaking of our natural motivations so that he can swiftly make his point about the recognition of our freedom. He wants to mark a kind of progression of cognitions that ends with what he himself thinks of as a cognition of our *independence* of the order of nature, as beings inhabiting an intelligible realm. And that cognition requires that there be some recognition that one can choose against *all* of one's interests that have an origin in our *sensible* natures.

Kant is *not* claiming that the mere *risk* of death is enough to get the person to come to realize that they *can* after all help it, though that might be enough for most people. The reason I say this is that obviously some are willing to *risk* their own death to satisfy some desires. The point of having the noose erected outside of the house is to *remove* the ordinary possibility that one might avoid the consequence. We are to conclude that the person, whether he goes through with it or not, at that point knows they *can* help it. In *some* sense they understand, or come to know, that they are free not to gratify that particular desire.

The subtext of this second stage of the example may well be that there is a hierarchy among desires – and by 'desires' I mean what Kant would call 'sensuous' desires, not 'higher desires' he discusses elsewhere in the *Critique* – at the top of which is the desire to survive. In some sense or other the desire for survival carries more weight than other desires, such as sexual desire. And although little hangs on it, I think the pragmatic implication of Kant's use of sexual desire here is that he thought that *ceteris paribus* among all of the other desires, sexual desire is probably next most weighty. But although the desire for survival may carry more weight than other desires, the example is clearly not meant to portray persuasion as asking a person to join you in predicting that the desire for survival will "overwhelm" everything else in some sort of Hobbesian bear pit of desire in their psychology. Persuasion here is asking the person to consider whether he would *control* his passion, and, without getting into the details of what that might mean within Kantian moral psychology, what it at the least implies is that there is *willing* here, that it is possible to freely decide not to do something that sexual passion has led one to say "I just can't help" doing. Such a decision would be on the basis of considering forfeiting one's own life over against fulfilling one's sexual desire.

The second stage of the example involves one's coming to know about oneself that, no matter how much one might want something, one *can* decide not to pursue it because one might want something else *even more*. But although Kant is confident that most would opt for survival given this choice, *this* choice is obviously not one that the person being persuaded faces. The method of persuasion in this case uses a counterfactual. The option of fulfilling a sexual desire is actual while the hangman's noose is not. What is supposed to be shown to the person being persuaded is thus not that they will die if they fulfill their passion, and not even that they *might* die. It is that even if no such threat exists, they are facing a choice, not simply giving in to the inevitable, when they face a powerful desire. And this is an aspect of their freedom.

One should ask, then, Why not stop here? Kant has asked us to imagine leading a person to the realization that, contrary to what they had proclaimed or thought, they *can* help pursuing the object of a passion, indeed a very powerful one. We can now generalize: for any other desire that seems so urgent as to be irresistable, the gallows will show them otherwise. Perhaps, if the fear of death isn't universally more powerful than any other desire, one might even say that, for *any* desire that seems so urgent as to be irresistible, there at least *could be* some other desire that is more powerful, even if not a desire for survival. Isn't this sufficient to deliver the desired cognition of their freedom?

It is not. Yes, the person *could* help pursuing the object of their passion, but its still open to us to think this is only because they *couldn't* help doing something else, namely, saving their own life. In a battle of the *I-couldn't-help-it* the desire for survival might be reasonably expected to win. So one could, for each individual passion, pair it with GALLOWS (or some other stronger urge) and normally expect that a person *can* help pursuing that passion. But it seems necessary, within the example and what it is supposed to illustrate, first to introduce the possibility of choice – that is, the existence of freedom – *within* the realm of desire, without making this freedom a choice for the Moral Law. So at this stage of the example, what the person comes to cognize is that, yes, they *can* help it, but this falls short of cognizing their autonomy.[5]

In cognizing that, in fact, they *could* help indulging a given passion by way of recognizing that they would forgo it on the pain of a threat of death, they cognize their *freedom* from that passion. The advantage I believe Kant wants to gain by using the threat of death is that it trumps almost *any* passion, and so the cognition we're supposed to imagine this person coming to is not simply their freedom from sexual desire, but their freedom from *any* desire save the desire for survival. So this second stage of the example does suffice for an awareness of a kind of freedom. However, it is not cognition of a freedom from *all* sensuous desires, much less cognition of something ennobling about oneself.

However, this raises the possibility that, in this second stage of the example, the strength of the desire that is supposed to be the competing option is a disposable aspect of that option. I don't think one can draw many conclusions about the fact that Kant does not here consider whether one might face the gallows for something else one desires, but perhaps there are such examples, or at least possible examples (say, experiencing an infinitely meaningful and intense pleasure). The point is supposed to be that, for any given desire, we can decide not to pursue it in favor of pursuing some other desire. If one thinks "I can't help it", one can see, not only that the possible threat of death shows that you could help it, but also that one *might* choose to fulfill a desire that is not as strong as either of these options.

The third stage of the example, then, is the stage in which the person is supposed to fully cognize their freedom. We are to imagine asking whether the person could face the hangman's noose – the same gallows that revealed that they could help satisfying even the most urgent of desires – rather than tell a lie that will have serious consequences for some innocent other. The supposition is that the latter contains a demand of an *unconditional practical law*. That is, it is not supposed to be open for further deliberation whether all things considered the agent *might* be morally permitted to lie (or not be blameworthy for doing so) because the stakes are so high. And Kant states confidently that he believes anyone would acknowledge that of course they *could* face the gallows instead of lying in the circumstance, even if they would not go so far as to say they *would* do so. Our wanton would acknowledge that they are capable of facing death rather than lying, and there is no reason to doubt it. Kant then draws the conclusion that the wanton acknowledges *because* he ought not lie he *can* resist lying, even if it means death, and that the acknowledgement that he *can* is an acknowledgment of his free agency. He can because he ought.

But we might well wonder about this further implication, that it is only when faced with the unqualified demand contained in the Moral Law that we do (can? would?) acknowledge this. Recall in the second stage of the example, there seems to be left open the possibility that *not only* might we resist an urgent passion in the name of saving our life, but in the name of simply *some more urgent* – indeed perhaps not even stronger – conflicting passion. It is debatable whether human nature is uniform when it comes to which desires are strongest. Sexual passion is high on the list for most, and the desire for survival seems about as close to a universal human desire. But the "I can't help it" thought can attach to lesser desires, and even when it attaches to these, there is no reason to think that we might not resist them in the name of just a further desire (again, think of an infinitely meaningful experience). Why is our freedom not revealed simply in the thought that, for any desire, we could resist it in the name of some further desire that is more urgent? Indeed, is there an upper limit on urgency?

The Moral Law, in making a categorical, unqualified demand, is supposed to be making a demand that contravenes *any other demand* from our 'natural' interests. And it is in our recognition of our capacity to conform to such a demand that we recognize that our wills belong to a *non-natural* order. That recognition is supposed, in turn, to give us a picture of ourselves as having a sort of incomparable dignity. Saying that our dignity is related to our membership in a non-natural, rational order of things is at best an ornate way of referring to a way of understanding practical principles as the outcomes of a sort of joint legislation by us as rational agents. And, importantly, this sense of our own worth *follows upon* the recognition of our freedom to conform with the Moral Law. It is, importantly, not that we come to recognize the value of our rational agency which in turn motivates us to act.

The order of cognitions represented in GALLOWS reflects the path of moral development in the *Method*. That path has at its core self-respect, "teaching a man to feel his own worth" by leading him from cognition of the Moral Law to an "unexpected" power found in his membership of an intelligible world existing independently of the order of natural causes. Kant clearly relies on the order of practical knowledge his earlier discussion presented. First, one encounters the subordination of one's will to an unqualified command in the Moral Law, and through that presentation of the law, one recognizes the freedom of one's will to conform itself to that.

When Kant refers to "leading strings" one needs to make use of in cultivating the uncultivated mind, he is not merely talking about children, as in, say, advising one to offer a child a reward if they share a toy, or punish them for not sharing. He apparently has in mind some venue for moral instruction in general, such as mentorship, advising, 'Sunday School' or perhaps even a kind of ethical civics class. The aim of moral persuasion is not to guarantee that a person acts morally but to help to put that person into position to do so.

But even if his topic is not the moral instruction of children, it frames the core of his discussion (*KpV* 5: 154–9). Everyday gossip about seemingly noble acts reveals a "propensity of reason" [*Hange der Vernunft*] to look for even the distant possibility of a non-moral ground. Educators, he claims, should make use of this propensity. He predicts that even children who aren't ready for intellectual subtlety would quickly become astute and interested because they'd feel their judgment strengthening. Teachers could be confident that their knowing and approving of pure conduct, and noting with sorrow or contempt the least deviation from it, would leave a lasting impression of esteem for one and disgust for the other.

Kant asks us to imagine a 10-year-old being presented with an example reminiscent of GALLOWS (at *KpV* 5: 156; call this GALLOWS II). The differences in the two examples are instructive. GALLOWS has a three part structure, beginning with an agent's ignorance of their own practical freedom; next, a recognition that for any given situation in which that agent might think they have no choices there are in fact alternatives; and finally ending with a recognition that no interest from the "order of nature" in oneself closes off the possibility of obeying the demands of morality. GALLOWS II ends likewise in the Moral Law being a bridge of sorts to beholding one's own freedom. However, in this case the example considers a child who is yet unaware of their own freedom being told about the example of a Good Will. Suppose, Kant says, we were to describe to such a child a situation in which someone tries to get an honest man to join others in falsely accusing an innocent powerless person (Kant is evidently thinking of Anne Boleyn). First offered gifts, he rejects them. Of course, Kant notes, the child would at this point applaud the merit, but these are merely *gains foregone*. What about threats of *loss*? Suppose his best friends renounce him, his family disinherits him, and powerful people persecute and harass him. Indeed, again as in GALLOWS, Kant presents us with the figure of an errant 'prince' who threatens him with prison or death. Even his own family pleads with him to give in for their sakes. Yet he does not waver in his resolve to be honest. Step by step, Kant claims, the youth will be moved from approval to admiration, from admiration to marvel, from marvel to veneration and "a lively wish that he himself could be such man".

There is again a clear progression in GALLOW II. In it, we begin, not as in GALLOWS, with someone in the grip of a non-moral passion, but a Good Will presented with a moral demand not to bear false witness in a life and death circumstance. This Good Will is then tempted with advantages, but presumably does not even consider them. One can speculate at this first stage how various moral characters might respond to bigger, more impressive rewards, ending at the extreme with a figure much like Jesus in the desert being offered "all the kingdoms of the world". It is interesting that Kant is not particularly impressed with this stage of "meritorious" action, and he does not expect the 10-year-old to express more than "approval." By contrast, the Good Will deserves "admiration" for enduring the loss of inheritance and friendship, and marvel and veneration for facing the loss of freedom and life, and losses to his family.

The example illustrates an increasingly narrow basis of motivation culminating with solely the Moral Law itself. Once other interests are subtracted from it, the thought of duty alone is supposed to be the most powerful motivation. First, remove any advantages of acting dutifully. Next, add disadvantages of increasing importance to the agent, ending in loss of life and the anguish of loved ones. The direction is meant to *isolate* duty so that a law of pure practical reason is the only thing that counts in favor of refusing to bear false witness. We are meant to conclude that this can trump all other "incentives which derive from one's own happiness", no matter how dear, and no matter how high they are piled up against it. The idea, again, is that it is at this moment that the hypothetical agent finds, and the 10-year-old audience member is supposed to acknowledge in that agent, that his will inhabits a non-natural realm, and this enhances his sense of self-worth. But, again, the judgment of the value of one's rational agency follows upon the recognition of one's already present capacity to conform to moral requirements no matter how difficult. Oversimplifying, it is not the judgment of one's own value as a free rational agent that makes one able to overcome any obstacle in doing one's duty; it is the latter judgment that generates the former.

In GALLOWS as well as GALLOWS II, Kant argues that moral education, done properly, gives rise to a sense of self-worth. However, the point is to focus the mind of the subject on the moral law itself:[6]

> I assert further that, if in the admired action the motive from which it was done was esteem for duty, this respect for the law, and not any pretension to inner greatness of mind or noble and meritorious sentiment, is that which has the most power over the mind of the spectator. Consequently, duty, not merit, has not only the most definite influence but, when seen in the true light of its inviolability, also the most penetrating influence on the mind.
>
> (*KpV* 5: 156–7)

Here Kant locates the source of our freedom to overcome all natural interests in the moral law itself. In so doing he distinguishes between two sorts of evaluations. The first is merit [*Verdienst*], and about this sort of evaluation he is quite guarded. In several spots, in the *Methodology* as well as elsewhere, Kant counsels against being overly dazzled by "so-called noble (super-meritorious) actions, which so fill our sentimental writings" (*KpV* 5: 155). I think the best term for what Kant is thinking of as 'merit' is *moral praiseworthiness*. I think it would be wrong to think he does not regard it as a positive moral evaluation; clearly he thinks that it is. Instead, he's thinking of *merit* as reflecting a kind of *achievement* and in the case of *moral merit* it is a *moral achievement*. However, the sense of self-worth that arises in moral education is another kind of evaluation, *moral worth*, and this does not necessarily reflect any *achievement*. In GALLOWS and GALLOWS II, the subject of moral persuasion is not supposed to discover something *praiseworthy* in themselves when they come to be aware of something they were unaware of before, the power to overcome any natural inclination. What they cognize is something that is present in *any rational will*.

GALLOWS II exhibits the point from the *Analytic* that we come to know of the freedom of our own wills through cognition of the Moral Law. That point is that "reason exhibits" the Moral Law as a command that applies to our wills independently of any "sensuous condition". It is by stripping away every sensuous condition counting in favor of the Moral Law that one gains a clear cognition of it. In having that unsullied cognition presented as an unqualified demand, cognition of one's freedom follows.

3. Conclusion

Kant's discussion of the subtlety of practical reasoning in, for instance, gossip, as well as the impact of properly presented examples of Good Will, are in service of Kant's primary point: To gain access to the mind, the Moral Law needs to be displayed in its purest form. So presented it will give rise to consciousness of our freedom. Kant then sums this up by laying out its 'course' of his method. It has two steps or exercises. The first is making it "as if by habit" that we judge conformity with moral laws of our own and others' actions. The second is calling attention to motivation solely by duty "by a vivid exhibition of the moral disposition in examples" (*KpV* 5: 159–60).

I want to end by noting a central feature of Kant's moral philosophy that emerges out of his discussion in the *Method*. Kant is insistent that the error of other moral views is that they are *heteronomous*, while he takes himself to have attempted to give an account of morality as fully *autonomous*.

The importance to Kant of his doing so is squarely in view in the *Method*. Again and again he comes back to what he regards as the central fact about morality:

> Duty, not merit, has not only the most definite influence [over the mind of the spectator to the Good Will] but, when seen in the true light of its inviolability, also the most penetrating influence on the mind.

(*KpV* 5: 157)

Autonomous principles are principles that contain no non-moral incentives. It is only when they are in this way cognized – as autonomous – that we become conscious of our freedom. And consciousness of our freedom "is the best, indeed the only, guard that can keep ignoble and corrupting influences from bursting in upon the mind" (*KpV* 5: 161).

Notes

1 Thanks to Adam Cureton, Markus Kohl, and Matt McGrath for discussion of these topics.
2 I use Lewis White Beck's translation of the *Critique of Practical Reason* (1985).
3 Among the best and most thorough defenses of the reading of Kant's ethics that I oppose, the reading in which there is a fundamental value that grounds morality, is Paul Guyer's work, for instance, in *Virtues of Freedom* (2016).
4 E.g., *GMS* 4: 441–5.
5 For something like this alternative picture, see, e.g., Markus Kohl (2015).
6 See my "Kant's conception of Merit" (1996).

References

Allison, H.E. (1986) "Morality and Freedom: Kant's Reciprocity Thesis," *The Philosophical Review* 95: 393–425.
Guyer, P. (2016) *Virtues of Freedom*, Oxford: Oxford University Press.
Johnson, R. (1996) "Kant's Conception of Merit," *Pacific Philosophical Quarterly* 77: 313–37.
Kant, I. (1985) *Critique of Practical Reason*, L.W. Beck (ed. and trans.), New York: Palgrave Macmillan.
Kohl, M. (2015) "Kant on Determinism and the Categorical Imperative," *Ethics* 125: 331–56.

Further Reading

I think it's fair to say that the *Methodology* part of the 2nd *Critique* has been widely ignored. As such, there is not the same wealth of commentary on it as there is on almost every other part of Kant's ethics. For a comprehensive picture of his views on moral education, one should also read part II of the *Tugendlehre*, the *Doctrine of the Methods of Ethics* (*MS* 6: 477–486). Stefano Bacin gives a thorough and accurate overview of the *Methodology* in "The Meaning of the *Critique of Practical Reason* for Moral Beings: The Doctrine of Method of Pure Practical Reason," in A. Reath and J. Timmermann (eds.), *Cambridge Critical Guide to the Critique of Practical Reason* (Cambridge: Cambridge University Press, 2010); K. Roth and C. Surprenant (eds.), *Kant and Education: Interpretations and Commentary* (London: Routledge, 2012), contains 16 essays on Kant's views on moral education. Felicitas Munzel, in both her *Kant's Conception of Moral Character* (1999), and in her contribution on moral education in this volume, contains valuable perspectives on these and related topics.

III. TELEOLOGICAL PHILOSOPHY

17

THE THIRD *CRITIQUE*

Preface and Introductions

Gabriele Tomasi

★★★

In late December 1787, Kant wrote to the Jena professor Carl Leonhard Reinhold, author of the *Letters on the Kantian Philosophy* (1790–92), disclosing that he was at work on the critique of taste and had discovered "a new sort of a priori principles, different from those heretofore observed." "There are three faculties of the mind," he writes in the letter: the faculty of cognition, the faculty of pleasure and displeasure, and the faculty of desire. As he reminds Reinhold, a priori principles for the first of these had been uncovered in the *Critique of Pure Reason*, and those governing the third faculty had been treated in the *Critique of Practical Reason* (*Br* 10: 514).[1] What Kant here reveals is his discovery of a priori principles for the second faculty, to be discussed in a manuscript entitled the *Critique of Taste*, which he hoped would be "completed although not in print by Easter" (*Br* 10: 515). In fact, it would take Kant another two years to complete the work that would be published as the *Critique of the Power of Judgment* (1790),[2] bringing to conclusion what he came to see as a necessary trilogy.[3]

Kant did not initially conceive of the critical project in this way; in the letter to Reinhold, however, he seems to acknowledge the necessity of his findings. He writes that "the analysis" of the three faculties allowed him "to discover something systematic" in the human mind, putting him "on the path [. . .] to recognize three parts of philosophy, each of which has its a priori principles [. . .] – theoretical philosophy, teleology, and practical philosophy" (*Br* 10: 514–5). Kant had long thought it impossible to find a priori principles for the power of judgment (cf. *KrV* B 35), but he now saw that each faculty of the mental triad had its own principles. Although he speaks in the plural in the letter, we will see that there is really only one principle of the power of judgment, that is, that of the purposiveness of nature. Thanks to this principle, the power of judgment is not reducible to one of the other faculties and has its own critique.[4] Furthermore, Kant goes as far as to attribute to the "second faculty," or to its critique, the task of being "an intermediary between understanding and reason" (*KU* 5: 168), or between the two distinct conceptual domains of these faculties, that is, nature and freedom. Kant deals with each of these complex topics in his Introduction to the work, touching on themes including the division of philosophy, the nature and role of the power of judgment, and the nature and application of its principle. In what follows, I will offer a sketch of his arguments.[5]

DOI: 10.4324/9781003406617-23

1. On the Division of Philosophy as a Distinction Between Conceptual Domains

The Introduction to the third *Critique* opens with a critical reflection on the customary division of philosophy into the theoretical and the practical. Kant tries to put this division on a stronger footing. Interestingly, there is no trace here of the tripartite division of philosophy hinted at in the letter to Reinhold. As we will see, what was anticipated in the letter as a third part, namely teleology, is here conceived of as "a means for combining the two parts of philosophy into one whole" (*KU* 5: 176), according to Kant's understanding of the concept of purposiveness as a mediating concept.

Kant moves from a conception of philosophy as a kind of rational cognition of things by means of concepts to arguing that a division of philosophy into different parts is justified only if it is based on a specific distinction or opposition between the principles belonging to the different parts. On his view, the only distinction of this sort in philosophy is that between the (pure) concepts of the understanding, which he here calls "the *concepts of nature*," and "the *concept of freedom*." The former are constitutive with regard to theoretical knowledge: they make objective discrimination in experience possible and offer grounds for synthetic a priori knowledge. The latter includes "a negative principle (of mere opposition)" with regard to theoretical knowledge and is constitutive of practical knowledge; that is, it sets up "principles for the determination of the will." Since this categorical distinction is complete – there are "only two sorts of concepts that allow an equal number of distinct principles of the possibility of their objects" – philosophy is "justifiably" divided into the theoretical and the practical (*KU* 5: 171).

The crucial aspect of Kant's proposal is his identification of practical philosophy with "the practical legislation of reason in accordance with the concept of freedom" (*KU* 5: 171). It is based on an analysis of what a practical principle is and argues against the misuse of the term "practical" to describe what is only "technically practical" (as with, for example, the rules "of art and skill in general, as well as those of prudence" (*KU* 5: 172–3)).[6] On Kant's view, the mere embodiment of theoretical knowledge about causal relations in rules that presuppose a determination of a will to some end must surely take the form of practical propositions, because they represent something as possible through a will. However, they do not belong *ipso facto* to practical philosophy; they could well be "mere corollaries" of theoretical philosophy. By contrast, the special practical propositions that require a second part of philosophy for themselves alone "under the name of practical philosophy" are *morally* practical precepts, namely practical propositions "which are grounded entirely on the concept of freedom" and exclude the determination of the will "from nature" (*KU* 5: 173).

This conception of the division of philosophy into the theoretical and the practical, however interesting (and disputable) on its own, is crucial here because it allows Kant to set the scene for the mediating role of the critique of the power of judgment, or for the place of this critique in the system of philosophy. In fact, once he has justified the division, the question of the relation between the two parts of philosophy arises. To prepare his answer, Kant puts forward, in the second section of the Introduction, some reflections "on the domain of philosophy in general" (*KU* 5: 174).

Using a political metaphor, he claims that our cognitive faculty has two domains: that of the concepts of nature and that of the concept of freedom (a domain (*ditio*) being the part of a "territory (*territorium*)" in which a type of concept is a priori legislative). The intriguing point is that the two distinct types of concept on which he grounds the division of philosophy, while having different domains, share the same territory of possible experience. This implies that the faculties through which the legislation of these concepts takes place – understanding and reason – are also normative "on one and the same territory of experience": the laws of nature describe how the world *is*, the moral law dictates how it *should* be. How this sharing of territory is to be interpreted is hard to say. Kant does not merely affirm the coexistence of these two modes of legislation (that is, ultimately, of determinism and libertarianism). Rather, his position is complex, and the text reflects this, expressing both his incompatibilism and his compatibilism.

Kant can affirm the coexistence of determinism and libertarianism because he had already proved, in his resolution of the third antinomy in the *Critique of Pure Reason*, the possibility of "at least conceiving" of it "without contradiction" (*KU* 5: 174–5). This compatibilism comes to light here in the claim that the supersensible "should have an influence" on the sensible; "namely the concept of freedom *should* make the end that is imposed by its laws real in the sensible world" (*KU* 5: 176). On the other hand, Kant's incompatibilism is expressed by the idea that the "two different domains" of the concepts of nature and the concept of freedom "do not constitute *one* domain," because the concept of freedom involves reference to the supersensible or to an atemporal reality beyond or underlying the sensible world. Kant speaks of "an incalculable gulf fixed between the domain of the concept of nature, [. . .] and the domain of the concept of freedom," as if there were two different worlds (*KU* 5: 175–6). Actually, Kant's belief that determinism is incompatible with libertarianism allows for what Adrian Moore calls a "relativistic compatibilism,"[7] the core of which is a distinction between two ways of viewing our own actions (cf. *GMS* 4: 450–52). This compatibilism is welcome to the extent that it does not admit of a reduction of one domain to the other, but it is unclear whether it offers a solution to the challenging problem of the compatibility of the effects of the two kinds of legislation.[8]

The actions we perform in order to fulfill the duties the moral law imposes on us are phenomena of the sensible world: a world that Kant sees as governed by causal laws such that every event in it is completely determined by antecedent physical causes. He assumes that it must be possible to conceive of nature "in such a way that the lawfulness of its form is at least in agreement with the possibility of the ends that are to be realized in it in accordance with the laws of freedom" (*KU* 5: 176), but by claiming this he is apparently asking us to think something unthinkable: an amalgam of the determination of the will in accordance with the concept of freedom and the concept of a physical event. If, as stated in a passage from the second *Critique*, the moral law is to furnish the sensible world "with the form of a world of the understanding" (*KpV* 5: 43), the form of nature, its causal fabric, should make room for the effects of acts the cause of which is not in the causal series.

Kant attempts to resolve the problem by moving to the supersensible: there must be "a ground of the *unity* of the supersensible that grounds nature with that which the concept of freedom contains practically" (*KU* 5: 176). Interestingly, he does not phrase the question in the metaphysical terms of a transition from freedom to nature; instead, he formulates it as a transition from a "manner of thinking" in accordance with the concept of freedom to one in accordance with the concepts of nature, suggesting that what is crucial is the possibility, for a moral agent, of conceiving of nature as amenable to the realization of moral ends. In turning to the concept of a supersensible ground, Kant points out that his move cannot have a cognitive character: that concept "does not suffice for cognition of it either theoretically or practically, and thus has no proper domain of its own" (*KU* 5: 176). This characterization is interesting; it parallels that of the principle of the power of judgment, of which Kant says that it "may not constitute a special part of a system of pure philosophy, between the theoretical and the practical part" (*KU* 5: 168). It is precisely the critique of that power that Kant presents, in the third section of the Introduction, as a "means for combining the two parts of philosophy into one whole" (*KU* 5: 176).

2. The Intermediary, or a Power With No Domain

Kant does not offer a direct argument for the unifying role of the *Critique of the Power of Judgment*. Rather, he tries to make this plausible on the basis of two analogies. The first aims to attribute to the power of judgment, if not a legislation of its own (for it does not have a "field of objects as its domain" (*KU* 5: 177) and therefore does not constitute a special part of a system of pure philosophy), then at least a proper a priori principle of its own "for seeking laws" (*KU* 5: 177) since, like understanding and reason, it belongs to "the family of the higher faculties of cognition."[9] The second, more complex and challenging analogy capitalizes on the "something systematic" in the human mind hinted at in the letter to Reinhold. Very roughly, the idea is that each faculty of cognition is legislative for a faculty of the soul. According to Kant's conception of the soul, "between the faculty of cognition and that of desire there is the feeling of pleasure, just as the power of judgment is contained between the understanding and reason." This conception grounds the hypothesis that the power of judgment is legislative for the feeling of pleasure and displeasure, much as the understanding is legislative for the faculty of cognition (insofar as "it is related as a faculty of a *theoretical cognition* to nature") and reason (in which alone the concept of freedom has its place) is legislative a priori for the faculty of desire "as a higher faculty" (*KU* 5: 177–8).[10]

Kant considers this second analogy "of still greater importance" than the one based on the kinship of the power of judgment "with the family of faculties of cognition" (*KU* 5: 177), presumably because it offers the ground for building an answer to the problem of unifying the two parts of philosophy. Kant's conjecture exploits the necessary combination of pleasure or displeasure with the faculty of desire. He argues that, "just as in its logical use it makes possible the transition from understanding to reason," connecting concepts into judgments that might be used as premises in syllogisms, the power of judgment can effect "a transition from the pure faculty of cognition, i.e., from the domain of the concepts of nature, to the domain of the concept of freedom" (*KU* 5: 178–9). This is nothing more than a suggestion. Kant has not yet proved the connection between the power of judgment and the feeling of pleasure and displeasure. Nor, given that feeling has a connection with the faculty of desire, has he shown how the power of judgment can connect the faculties of cognition and desire.

The first of these desiderata will be satisfied later in the Introduction. Assuming as a sort of principle that "the attainment of every aim is combined with the feeling of pleasure," Kant will point out that a feeling of pleasure might be determined merely through the relation of the object to the faculty of cognition. The paradigmatic case he has in mind is the discovery of the possibility of unifying "two or more empirically heterogeneous laws of nature under a principle that comprehends them both" (*KU* 5: 187). As Jochen Bojanowski suggests, a preliminary consideration regarding the second desideratum is that through the feeling of pleasure – for which the power of judgment is legislative – we can act as causes of the reality of objects we desire and have represented through our understanding.[11] Be that as it may, Kant has given some reason to suppose that the power of judgment has a proper a priori principle and therefore has its own critique, as part of a critique of pure reason. Furthermore, in offering a provisional determination of the systematic place of the critique of the power of judgment, he has suggested that it can connect the two parts of philosophy. All this should now be proved.

3.   On the Principle of the Reflecting Power of Judgment

That the power of judgment has an a priori principle for itself and is therefore an a priori legislative faculty is what Kant shows in Section IV of the Introduction. Beginning with the definition of the power of judgment "in general" as "the faculty for thinking of the particular as contained under the universal," he then draws a distinction between two contrasting ways in which this operation may occur: if the universal (be it a concept, a principle, or a law) is given, "then the power of judgment, which subsumes the particular under it [. . .] is *determining*"; if, however, only the particular is given, for which the universal is to be found, "then the power of judgment is merely *reflecting*" (*KU* 5: 179).

Roughly, the subsumption of the given particular amounts either to its conceptual determination as a thing of such-and-such a type or to the related operation of thinking a particular concept or law under a higher-level concept or law. Commenting on the determining power of judgment, Kant refers particularly to the "universal transcendental laws, *a priori* given by the understanding" (*KU* 5: 179). On his view, these a priori laws "pertain only to the possibility of a nature (as object of the senses) in general" (*KU* 5: 179). However, he acknowledges that, alongside this nomological level and grounded in it, there is a second nomological level, namely that of empirical laws. These laws pertain to the "manifold of forms in nature" and are left "undetermined" by transcendental laws (*KU* 5: 179–80).

The *status* of these laws is rather problematic.[12] Laws are objective rules that have an a priori origin in our understanding (or reason). This is apparently not the case for empirical laws. Not being a priori, they lack real universality and necessity. Kant notes that, for "the insight of *our* understanding" (*KU* 5: 180), they appear contingent: it may appear that nature could have been organized differently (cf. *KU* §61, 5: 360). Following Kant, let us take the law of causality as an example: while phenomena necessarily have a causal order, their having the order they actually do may seem contingent to us.[13] This state of affairs raises a hard question for Kant, since he assumes that the concept of law implies the idea of necessity. Consequently, either he must somehow redeem this idea or he cannot consider the empirical rules connecting natural objects or events as laws.

Kant cuts through the dilemma, suggesting that in order to call the empirical rules "laws," "as is also required by the concept of a nature," we have to consider them from the point of view of their integration in a comprehensive systematic unity of nature: they must be regarded as necessary "on a principle of the unity of the manifold, even if that principle is unknown to us" (*KU* 5: 180). Kant's reasoning is that, just as we can comprehend the necessity of the transcendental laws by seeing them as products of the spontaneity of our understanding, we can likewise conceive of the necessity of the particular laws of nature by considering their systematic connection as a product of an understanding, albeit one more wide-ranging than our own. This is how the reflecting power of judgment must consider them, since its task is to ascend "from the particular in nature to the universal," which might mean either finding empirical concepts for the given particulars or finding systemically organized empirical laws that explain their behavior – a task it can carry out only if it assumes that nature has a sort of unity with regard to its empirical laws.

With these considerations, the principle of the reflecting power of judgment is finally introduced, and its correspondence to treating nature as if "an understanding" (even though "not ours") "contained the ground of the unity of the manifold of its empirical laws" (*KU* 5: 180) is established. According to Kant, just as the universal laws of nature "have their ground in our understanding" (*KU* 5: 180), so must the reflecting power of judgment conceive of nature as if an (infinite) understanding had given its particular laws "for the sake of our faculty of cognition, in order to make possible a system of experience" in accordance with them.[14] Kant notes that the correspondence of something with that constitution of things that is possible only in accordance with ends "is called the purposiveness of its form"; therefore, he maintains that "the principle of the power of judgment in regard to the form of things in nature under empirical laws in general is the *purposiveness of nature in its multiplicity*" (*KU* 5: 180).

Three things are worth noting at this point. First, since the principle of the purposiveness of nature should ground "the possibility of the systematic subordination of empirical principles under one another," it cannot be borrowed from experience; it is an a priori principle that the reflecting power of judgment gives to itself, not to nature, as a law.[15] Second, the fact that it is stated as an "as if" (*als ob*) clause qualifies it as a mere regulative principle, or a "subjective principle (maxim) of the power of judgment" (*KU* 5: 184). As such, it says nothing about the fabric of the world and is only a rule for reflecting on it with regard to "the connection of appearances in nature that are given in accordance with empirical laws" (*KU* 5: 181). Nevertheless, and third, since it makes possible "a system of experience in accordance with particular laws of nature" (it makes nature cognizable by us), the principle of the reflecting power of judgment also counts as "a transcendental principle" (*KU* 5: 180): a principle that contains the a priori condition "under which alone things can become objects of our cognition." Kant does not consider it a metaphysical principle because, although it applies to empirical objects, its application does not rest on any empirical feature of these objects (cf. *KU* 5: 181–2).

Having introduced and qualified the a priori principle of the reflecting power of judgment, Kant now has to justify or deduce it. This is the task of Section V, which, containing the deduction (the *quid juris*) of the principle of the formal purposiveness of nature as a transcendental principle of the power of judgment, is at the same time the formal and the theoretical center of the Introduction. As pointed out by Reinhard Brandt, according to the pattern I–IV/V/VI–IX, Sections I–IV have set the stage for the introduction of the principle of the power of judgment, namely the principle of the formal purposiveness of nature; Section V presents and deduces it as a transcendental principle; and Sections VI–IX illustrate the outcome of this deduction.[16]

4. The Deduction of the Principle of the Purposiveness of Nature

In Section V, Kant's first concern is to show that "the concept of a purposiveness of nature belongs among the transcendental principles." He claims that this "can readily be seen" (*KU* 5: 182) from the maxims that the power of judgment follows in the investigation of nature. Rules such as the *lex parsimoniae* and the *lex continui in natura* pertain to the possibility of the cognition of nature as determined by a manifold of particular laws and presuppose that nature is organized so as to be cognizable by our understanding. More importantly, they are not psychological rules: they "do not say what happens, i.e., in accordance with which rule our powers of cognition actually perform their role." Rather, they say how things "ought to be judged"; they are normative principles, and as such they cannot be "merely empirical" (*KU* 5: 182). From this, Kant concludes that the purposiveness of nature for our cognitive faculties, which is "obvious" in these principles, is a transcendental principle of judgment – namely, a principle that represents an a priori condition of our knowledge of nature – and therefore requires a transcendental deduction (*KU* 5: 182).

In a second step, Kant recalls that, although the transcendental laws without which nature "could not be conceived" are the necessary ground of the possibility of experience, they do not completely determine the objects of empirical cognition. To cite again the example of causality: it is a universal law of nature that "all alteration has its cause," but distinct kinds of objects, "besides what they have in common as belonging to nature in general, can still be causes in infinitely many ways," and each of these ways must have its rule (*KU* 5: 183). This observation offers the basis for the deductive argument, which resumes the necessity question. Kant notes that the rules that pertain to the particular, empirical causal relations are laws, and hence they bring "necessity" with them; however, "as far as our insight goes" they are contingent: we cannot know them a priori, and experience does not teach any necessity. The consequence is that we must also judge the unity of nature as a system of empirical laws as contingent. However, since such a unity is a necessary condition for the possibility of a "thoroughgoing interconnection of empirical cognitions into a whole of experience," the power of judgment must assume as an a priori principle for its own use that "what is contingent for human insight in the particular (empirical) laws of nature nevertheless contains a lawful unity, not fathomable by us but still thinkable, in the combination of its manifold into one experience possible in itself" (*KU* 5: 183–4). On Kant's view, this assumption has normative force: in investigating nature, we *ought* to consider it as if it were purposive, because this is just what knowing it involves.

From Kant's deduction, the principle of the purposiveness of nature emerges once again as subjective, regulative, and nevertheless transcendental: the deduction establishes as subjectively necessary a view of nature that the understanding recognizes "objectively as contingent." The heart of the deduction is the thought that if an agreement of nature with our faculty of cognition were not presupposed a priori by the power of judgment, we would have "no guideline" for an experience of nature in all the multiplicity of its empirical laws and for research into them (*KU* 5: 185). In fact, nature, while compliant with the universal laws of the understanding, could nevertheless display a specific diversity of empirical laws so great that it would be impossible for our understanding to discover an order in them. In the face of this possibility, which Henry Allison describes as "the spectre of empirical chaos,"[17] the deduction articulates Kant's belief that, without the presupposition of the purposiveness of nature for our understanding "in its necessary business of finding the universal for the particular," we could not "make progress in experience" and acquire cognition (*KU* 5: 186). Knowledge of the empirical laws *as laws* would simply be impossible (cf. *KU* 5: 184–5).

5. Pleasure and Purposiveness

Having justified the principle of the purposiveness of nature, Kant now explicitly faces an issue he had previously only hinted at (cf. *KU* 5: 184) – namely, as the title of Section VI announces, the combination of the feeling of pleasure with the concept of the purposiveness of nature. What the title announces is slightly puzzling, however. Arguing at a general level, Kant is going to discuss a pleasure that is connected to the achievement of a cognitive goal. Afterwards, distinguishing an aesthetic from a logical representation of the purposiveness of nature, he will deal in Section VII with a kind of pleasure – the satisfaction connected with the beautiful – that is not combined with the attainment of a particular cognitive aim but which rests on the relation of the form of the object "to the cognitive faculties of the subject in the apprehension of it."[18] In Section VIII, he will deal with the representation of a kind of purposiveness in which the form of the object is related "to a determinate cognition of the object under a given concept and has nothing to do with a feeling of pleasure in things but rather with the understanding in judging them" (*KU* 5: 192).[19]

Put briefly, Kant speaks of an "aesthetic representation of the purposiveness" of an object (as distinct from a logical or conceptual representation) when, instead of being used in a cognition, the representation of the object is "immediately connected with the feeling of pleasure," and this because of the suitability of the form of the object "to the cognitive faculties that are in play in the reflecting power of judgment" – namely imagination and understanding (*KU* 5: 189–90). Therefore, he will regard natural beauty "as the *presentation* of the concept of formal (merely subjective) purposiveness" (*KU* 5: 193). As for what the title of Section VIII announces as the "logical representation of the purposiveness of nature," this will turn out to be what the term "teleology" expresses: a consideration of a real (objective) purposiveness "through understanding and reason (logically, in accordance with concepts)" (*KU* 5: 193).

This articulation of the representation of the purposiveness of nature grounds the division of the third *Critique* into two parts (cf. *KU* 5: 193);[20] with that said, it is unclear how it relates to what is at issue in Section VI. On the one hand, the satisfaction associated with the beautiful is not combined with the attainment of particular cognitive aims; on the other, Kant will make no reference to the feeling of pleasure in relation to teleology.[21] What is the point, then, of Section VI? Is Kant simply preparing the ground for his account of how pleasure is likewise connected to a representation of purposiveness that "precedes the cognition of an object"? (*KU* 5: 189).[22]

While all this is unclear, how Kant proves the combination of the feeling of pleasure with the concept of the purposiveness of nature is more perspicuous. He builds a syllogism, the main premise of which is the sentence "the attainment of every aim is combined with the feeling of pleasure." Its second premise is the assumption that discovering an order of nature is a task for the understanding, since it is a necessary end for it "to introduce" into the cognition of nature "unity of principles" (*KU* 5: 187). The conclusion drawn is that we are delighted "when we encounter such a systematic unity among merely empirical laws" (*KU* 5: 184).[23] Presumably, Kant can see this as evidence for the combination of the feeling of pleasure with the concept of the purposiveness of nature because he assumes that this principle, namely the perspective of a unity of nature in the multiplicity of its empirical laws – a principle that the power of judgment attributes to nature – is the condition of the attainment of the end of the understanding.

An observation by Kant in this context calls for comment. He claims that, since the principle of the reflecting power of judgment is an a priori representation,

> the feeling of pleasure is also determined through a ground that is *a priori* and valid for every-one; and indeed merely through the relation of the object to the faculty of cognition, without the concept of purposiveness in this case having the least regard to the faculty of desire.
>
> (*KU* 5: 187)

It may appear that Kant is anticipating a point that will be crucial to the justification of the claim to universal validity that "so essentially belongs" to judgments of taste (*KU* 5: 214).[24] As we have seen, the problem is that the pleasure he speaks of in Section VI cannot be the pleasure associated with the beautiful since any relation to an end is emphatically ruled out by Kant in the aesthetic domain. What he says in this section can be preliminary at most and simply reveals his orientation toward an understanding of the pleasure connected to the principle of the power of judgment as a pleasure that results from the relation of its object to the faculty of cognition. Indeed, Kant will claim in Section VII that the ground of the pleasure that determines the judgment of taste

> is to be found in the universal though subjective condition of reflecting judgments, namely the purposive correspondence of an object (be it a product of nature or of art) with the rela-tionship of the cognitive faculties among themselves (of the imagination and the understand-ing) that is required for every empirical cognition.
>
> (*KU* 5: 191)

6. Concluding Remarks

I have offered an outline of the main themes dealt with in the Introduction to the third *Critique*. As we have seen, two issues come to the fore. On the one hand, the work should bridge the gulf between the domain of the concept of nature and the domain of the concept of freedom (cf. *KU* 5: 175–6). On the other hand, it should deal with the pressing issue of the possibility of a system of nature or the unity of nature as a system of experience (cf. *Br* 11: 49). These two issues inter-sect. In fact, the idea of a system of nature that Kant develops in teleological terms in the second part of the work ultimately leads to the question of the final end.[25] On Kant's view, this end is the highest good,[26] which he sees as being connected to the fundamental issue of the (moral) vocation of human beings (cf. *KU* §§83–7). From this point of view, the first part of the work dealing with the aesthetic power of judgment, although "essential" since it shows that the power of judgment contains "a principle" that it lays "at the basis of its reflection on nature entirely *a priori*" – namely that of a formal purposiveness of nature (*KU* 5: 193) – is a sort of prelude or preparation that should lead, in the second part, from nature to freedom.

Such a perspective on the whole of the third *Critique* is suggested by Kant himself in the concluding section of the Introduction. Under the title "On the connection of the legislations of understanding and reason through the power of judgment," he situates the work in the context of the (what are now) three critiques and again takes up the topic of Sections I–II.[27] Kant here envisages a determination of the sensible by the "supersensible in the subject," or an effect of a "causality through freedom" that takes place in the world "in accordance" with the "formal laws" of such causality (*KU* 5: 195). The effect in question is "the final end," namely the highest good that "should exist" but "can become actual only in nature and in accord with its laws" (*KU* 5: 196). With respect to this, Kant suggests that, "in the concept of a purposiveness of nature," the power of judgment provides the mediating concept between nature and freedom that makes room for the possibility of the final end (*KU* 5: 196).[28]

What these considerations show is that Kant's interest in discussing the power of judgment in relation to both aesthetics and teleology is ultimately practical, as this is the interest that underlies the whole of his philosophy. He believes that the purposiveness of nature for our faculty of cognition hints at its agreement with the pure moral concept of the highest good as an "effect" of freedom in the world. Revealingly, the Introduction closes by pointing out that "the spontaneity in the play of the faculties of cognition," the agreement of which contains the ground of our satisfaction in the beautiful, makes the concept of a purposiveness of nature "suitable for mediating the connection of the domain of the concept of nature with the concept of freedom in its consequences" (*KU* 5: 197).

Notes

1 The translations used are from Kant 1999 and Kant 2000 (Cambridge Edition of the Works of Immanuel Kant).

2 On *Entstehungsgeschichte* and the publication of the work, see Zammito 1992; Giordanetti 1999; Klemme 2006: XVII–XXXV. Kant speaks of a critique of the power of judgment, of which the critique of taste is only a part, at the close of a letter to Reinhold of 12.5.1789 (cf. *Br* 11:39).

3 That the discovery of a further a priori principle implies a reconception of the critical project seems to be suggested in the Preface, where Kant describes the first *Critique* as pertaining only to the understanding (cf. *KU* 5: 167) and claims that a "critique of pure reason" would be incomplete if the power of judgment "were not dealt with as a special part of it" (*KU* 5: 168). The expression "critique of pure reason" seems to evoke an inclusive whole that is articulated in three parts, namely the three critiques (cf. Brandt 2007: 521–31), as if Kant were now looking, to use Alfredo Ferrarin's words, to "*reason as a whole*," to which the three cognitive faculties of the mind belong as "the different modalities of a unitary power" (Ferrarin 2015: 24).

4 For a clear statement of the task of the *Critique of the Power of Judgment*, cf. the Preface to the work (*KU* 5: 168).

5 As is well known, the text Kant had printed as the introduction to the *Critique of the Power of Judgment* – to which I will exclusively refer – is actually the "second" introduction to the work. The original introduction, or *Erste Einleitung* (cf. *EEKU* 20: 193–251), was twice as long, and Kant replaced it at the very last stage of manuscript preparation, presumably not only because of its length. The second introduction has the characteristics of a new text rather than an abridgment of the first. On the formation, publication and content of the first introduction, cf. Frank and Zanetti (1996: 1160–204), Klemme (2006: 473–83), and Sánchez Madrid (2011).

6 Cf. Bojanowski 2008: 26–30.

7 Moore 2003: 100. For a discussion of the question, see Moore 2003: 90–112; Wolff 2013.

8 The gulf question also has an apparently less metaphysical and more anthropological side, concerning, as Michael Rohlf claims, the gulf that separates our sensible interest in our desires and inclinations from

the moral disposition and how someone can move from the former realm to the latter. Cf. Rohlf 2008. Kant gives some prominence to this side of the gulf question when he reformulates it in Section IX of the Introduction.

9 If the power of judgment were legislative and had a domain, it would also ground a "doctrine," but in this case its function as a *Verbindungsmittel* between theoretical and practical philosophy would imply, as Jochen Bojanowski observes, a reduction of the two parts of philosophy to the same principle, and the division of philosophy would have no justification. Cf. Bojanowski 2008: 31.

10 What Kant claims "provisionally" (*KU* 5: 178) here is restated in a more assertive way in the last section of the Introduction (cf. *KU* 5: 196–97), after he has justified the a priori principle of the power of judgment.

11 Cf. Bojanowski 2008: 32.

12 On Kant on laws of nature, cf. Watkins 2014a; Friedman 2014. On his conception of empirical laws in particular, see Guyer 2005: 38–55.

13 Cf. Brandt 2008: 45–7.

14 For a discussion of Kant's argument, cf. Guyer 2005: 60–8, 346–52.

15 Kant uses the term "heautonomy" (*KU* 5: 186) to describe the act of self-legislation by the reflecting power of judgment. It is a term he coins to emphasize that the power of judgment is "both source and referent of its own normativity" (Allison 2001: 41).

16 Cf. Brandt 2007: 400–1.

17 Cf. Allison 2001: 38–9.

18 It is worth mentioning that Kant only seems to be interested in the positive side of the story. Section VI announces a combination "of the feeling of pleasure with the concept of the purposiveness of nature"; likewise, Section VII discusses pleasure as a representation of purposiveness. The non-suitability or non-purposiveness of nature to our cognitive faculties and the related displeasure remain in the background (cf. *KU* 5: 188).

19 On why, according to Kant, we must regard organisms as purposes, cf. Ginsborg 2001.

20 How the two parts connect is problematic. The rational necessity of a formal purposiveness of nature is the element common to both. Purposiveness, the key principle of the power of judgment, might be represented as either subjective or objective, and just as beauty might be regarded as a symbol of the concept of formal (merely subjective) purposiveness, "natural ends" (namely organized living beings) can be considered "as the presentation of the concept of a real (objective) purposiveness" (*KU* 5: 193). However, this is far from saying that what fastens the two parts of the *Critique of the Power of Judgment* together is more substantial than the mere unity of the power of judgment (cf. Brandt 2007: 457–9).

21 In the Preface, he had already claimed that, "in the case of the logical judging of nature," the principle of the power of judgment "has no immediate relation to the feeling of pleasure and displeasure" (*KU* 5:169; cf. also 5:192).

22 For a discussion of the point, cf. Allison 2001: 55–9.

23 Cf. Guyer 2005: 68–73 for interpretation.

24 Cf. Brandt 2008: 45.

25 On nature as a system of ends, cf. Watkins 2014b.

26 "The moral law, as the formal rational condition of the use of our freedom [. . .] determines for us, and indeed does so *a priori*, a final end, to strive after which it makes obligatory for us, and this is the highest good in the world possible through freedom" (*KU* 5:450).

27 For a comment, cf. Allison 2001: 206–18.

28 In contrast to what happens in the Methodology of the Teleological Power of Judgment, where Kant deals extensively with the final end, he mentions here neither God nor the immortality of the soul as conditions for its attainment. On Kant's argument in that context, cf. Guyer 2005: 293–303, 314–42.

References

Allison, H.E. (2001) *Kant's Theory of Taste: A Reading of the Critique of Aesthetic Judgment*, Cambridge and New York: Cambridge University Press.

Bojanowski, J. (2008) "Kant über das Prinzip der Einheit von theoretischer und praktischer Philosophie (Einleitung I–V)," in O. Höffe (ed.), *Immanuel Kant: Kritik der Urteilskraft*, Berlin: Akademie Verlag, pp. 23–39.

Brandt, R. (2007) *Die Bestimmung des Menschen bei Kant*, Hamburg: Meiner.

Brandt, R. (2008) "Von der ästhetischen und logischen Vorstellung der Zweckmäßigkeit der Natur (Einleitung VI–IX)," in O. Höffe (ed.), *Immanuel Kant: Kritik der Urteilskraft*, Berlin: Akademie Verlag, pp. 41–58.

Ferrarin, A. (2015) *The Powers of Pure Reason: Kant and the Idea of Cosmic Philosophy*, Chicago: The University of Chicago Press.

Frank, M. and Zanetti, V. (1996) "Kommentar," in M. Frank und V. Zanetti (eds.), *Immanuel Kant: Schriften zur Ästhetik und Naturphilosophie*, Frankfurt am Main: Deutscher Klassiker Verlag.

Friedman, M. (2014) "Laws of Nature and Causal Necessity," *Kant-Studien* 105: 531–53.

Ginsborg, H. (2001) "Kant on Understanding Organisms as Natural Purposes," in E. Watkins (ed.), *Kant and the Sciences*, New York: Oxford University Press, pp. 231–58.

Giordanetti, P. (1999) "Kants Entdeckung der Apriorität des Geschmacksurteil: Zur Genese der *Kritik der Urteilskraft*," in H.F. Klemme, B. Ludwig, M. Pauen and W. Stark (eds.), *Aufklärung und Interpretation: Studien zu Kants Philosophie und ihren Umkreis*, Würzburg: Königshausen & Neumann, pp. 171–96.

Guyer, P. (2005) *Kant's System of Nature and Freedom: Selected Essays*, Oxford: Clarendon Press.

Kant, I. (1999) *Correspondence*, A. Zweig (ed.), Cambridge and New York: Cambridge University Press.

Kant, I. (2000) *Critique of the Power of Judgment*, P. Guyer (trans.), E. Matthews and P. Guyer (eds.), Cambridge and New York: Cambridge University Press.

Klemme, H. (2006) "Einleitung," in I. Kant, *Kritik der Urteilskraft*, Hamburg: Meiner.

Moore, A.W. (2003) *Noble in Reason, Infinite in Faculty: Themes and Variations in Kant's Moral and Religious Philosophy*, London and New York: Routledge.

Rohlf, M. (2008) "The Transition from Nature to Freedom in Kant's Third *Critique*," *Kant-Studien* 99: 339–60.

Sánchez Madrid, N. (2011) "Introducción," in I. Kant, N. Sánchez (ed. and trans.), *Primera Introducción de la Crítica del Juicio*, bilingual ed., Madrid: Escolar y Mayo.

Watkins, E. (2014a) "What Is, for Kant, a Law of Nature?" *Kant-Studien* 105: 471–90.

Watkins, E. (2014b) "Nature in General as a System of Ends," in I. Goy and E. Watkins (eds.), *Kant's Theory of Biology*, Berlin and Boston: Walter de Gruyter, pp. 117–30.

Wolff, M. (2013) "Kant über Freiheit und Determinismus," in W. Euler and B. Tuschling (eds.), *Kants Metaphysik der Sitten in der Diskussion: Ein Arbeitsgespräch an der Herzog August Bibliothek Wolfenbüttel 2009*, Berlin: Duncker & Humblot, pp. 27–42.

Zammito, J.H. (1992) *The Genesis of Kant's Critique of Judgment*, Chicago and London: The University of Chicago Press.

Further Reading

W. Euler, *Natur und Freiheit: Kommentar zu den Einleitungen in Kants "Kritik der Urteilskraft"* (Hamburg: Meiner, 2018) is a clear and very detailed commentary on both introductions to the third *Critique*. A. Falduto, *The Faculties of the Human Mind and the Case of Moral Feeling in Kant's Philosophy* (Berlin and Boston: Walter de Gruyter, 2014), ch. 4, contains a clear and well-informed account of Kant's systematic classification of the faculties of the mind. R. Hanna and A.W. Moore, "Reason, Freedom and Kant: An Exchange," *Kantian Review* 12 (2007): 113–33 is a thought-provoking paper on what, in the Introduction to the *Critique of the Power of Judgment*, emerges as "the gulf problem." A. Nuzzo, "Reflective Judgment, Determinative Judgment, and the Problem of Particularity," *Washington University Jurisprudence Review* 6 (2013): 7–25 provides an informative account of this crucial distinction from the third *Critique*. C. Pollock, *Kant's Theory of Normativity. Exploring the Space of Reason* (Cambridge: Cambridge University Press, 2017) deals with the foundational issues touched on in the Introduction. R. Zuckert, *Kant on Beauty and Biology: An Interpretation of the Critique of Judgment* (New York: Cambridge University Press, 2007) offers very useful reflections on many of the themes only hinted at in the Introduction. The volume of essays M. Massimi and A. Breitenbach (eds.), *Kant and the Laws of Nature* (Cambridge: Cambridge University Press, 2017) offers a systematic exploration of Kant's view on the laws of physics and biology.

18

ANALYTIC OF THE BEAUTIFUL

Fiona Hughes

★★★

The "Analytic of the Beautiful" offers an analysis of the principal features of aesthetic judgments of taste. These are disinterested as to quality, subjectively universal as to quantity, display purposiveness without purpose as their characteristic relation, while their modality is to stand in necessary connection with pleasure. Interpretations differ as to the distinctness of, and relations between, these 'Moments' of beauty, as well as the relation in which the universality and necessity claims stand to the later "Deduction" of taste.[1]

The major critical debates – which by no means exhaust the philosophical interest of the Analytic – concern the following questions.

(i) Are there distinct judgmental and affective components in a judgment of taste and, if so, in what relation do they stand to one another?[2]
(ii) How exactly are judgments of taste linked to cognition?[3]
(iii) What does it mean to say that judgments of beauty are subjective and what implications does this have for the relation in which they stand to objects?

In this chapter I address the latter question, which lies behind central elements of the Analytic such as the claim that aesthetic judgments are not concerned with the existence of objects, as well as having implications for the significance of Kant's aesthetic formalism. In particular, I will examine whether the object plays a legitimate role in the determination of taste.

When the object has not been excluded in interpretations of Kant's judgments of taste, it has been seen as a problem or, at best, marginalised.[4] The motivation for concluding that the object is excluded in Kant's analysis of aesthetic judgment can be traced back to his declaration that taste is subjective and not concerned with the object's existence[5] (*KU* 5: 203–4). However, it would be too quick to conclude that for Kant taste stands in no relation to an object. Indeed Kant draws a distinction between simply liking an object and also liking its existence (*KU* 5: 209). Moreover, the "Analytic of Beauty" begins thus: "If we wish to decide whether something [*etwas*] is beautiful or not [. . .]"[6] (*KU* 5: 203). For Kant the "something" that is beautiful is an object. Guyer argues,

DOI: 10.4324/9781003406617-24

however, that Kant's introduction of the object into his account of taste leads him astray (1979: 209). Allison agrees with Guyer that Kant made a mistake in treating aesthetic and perceptual form as equivalent, but argues that he need not have so restricted the qualifying features for beautiful objects (2001: 135–6). Allison, however, goes on to marginalise the object in insisting – along with Guyer and Ginsborg – that the determining factor for judgments of taste lies not at all in the object and only in the mental state (Ginsborg 1998: 449; Guyer 1979: 253; Allison 2001: 128–9).[7] As these commentators rightly point out, it cannot be the case that for Kant beauty is grounded in the object as opposed to a mental state – as this would be contrary to the Copernican Revolution. Moreover, Kant sets up an alternative between the subjective universality of taste being grounded in the judgment or in our pleasure in the object and rules out the latter on the grounds that this would destroy the very universality aimed at by resulting only in agreeableness (*KU* 5: 217). Nonetheless, I will show how the object has a necessary role to play in the determination of a judgment of taste. I will also offer a partial defence of the link Kant makes between aesthetic and spatio-temporal form.

Kant says very little about what it is that an object must be like if it is to count as beautiful. While he tells us in some detail about the relation between the mental powers necessary for taste, the only feature of the beautiful object he mentions overtly is its form (*KU* 5: 217–18, 224–5). Two principal objections ensue. Firstly, if beauty is equivalent to spatio-temporal form, then Kant's theory would seem to entail that all objects are beautiful.[8] Secondly, Kant is criticised for excluding all features other than formal ones.[9] Thus, the verdict is that Kant's account of aesthetic form is too unrestricted in referring to any spatio-temporal form whatsoever and too restricted in referring only to spatio-temporal form. Allison answers both these objections by prising apart aesthetic and spatio-temporal form (2001: 184–92).

The notion of design is central for Kant's discussion of the role played by the object's form in judgments of taste. I argue that design is not any spatio-temporal form whatsoever and that only free design worthy of our gaze and looking *as if* – but not – motivated by a purpose qualifies as the object of a pure judgment of taste. Design, I argue, is not something in the object rather than in the mind and, rather, exhibits the relation between mind and object necessary for any experience of an object. Design arises only when form is free from the constraints of cognition and thus does not arise in respect of all objects. To be free from the constraints of cognition is not, however, to have a form other than cognitive form – as Allison would have it – because taste must display 'cognition in general' or the general form of a cognitive judgment in the cooperation of imagination and understanding.

I start by analysing Kant's discussions of design in the "Analytic of Beauty" and argue that this concept has implications for all beautiful objects – despite its apparent restriction to the visual arts. I go on to augment the rather brief account of design in the "Analytic" by linking it to the discussion of "monogram" in the "Schematism" chapter of the *Critique of Pure Reason*. Both monogram and design qualify as drawing or outline. I will show how the account of the monogram explains the link between mental activity and form that is necessary if design is to be understood as displaying the necessary structural relation between mind and object.

I conclude that design's essential role for taste is as an outline that holds up the object for our attention. The beautiful object – and not just an image of it – comes to the fore through design. I suggest that the connection Hogarth makes between line and volume shows that design need not be merely a tracing of the outer edge of the object. Admittedly, Kant's accounts of features such as color and tone are unsatisfactory. However, this is not to say that he was wrong to claim that design is essential for aesthetic judgment.

1.   Design as "Outline" in the *Critique of Judgment*

For Kant, sensible form [*Gestalt*] exhibited as the design [*Zeichnung*] of the beautiful object is the *sine qua non* of the visual arts:

> In painting, in sculpture, indeed in all the visual arts, including architecture and horticulture insofar as they are fine arts, what is essential is design, the suitability of which for taste is grounded not in what gratifies us in sensation, but merely in what we like because of its form [*Form*].
>
> (*KU* 5: 225)[10]

Design, which is necessary for pure judgments of beauty about fine artworks, concerns their form and does not arise from sensations. Design is the drawing of a line or "outline" [*Abriß*] (*KU* 5: 225). Colors, by contrast, arise from sensation and cannot make the object [*den Gegenstand an sich*] "beautiful and worthy of being intuited [*anschauungswürdig*]"[11] (*KU* 5: 225). The negative implication is clear: design makes the beautiful object worthy of being looked at in its own right, rather than as the content of cognitive or moral judgments. Speaking in the same tenor of the universal validity of *all* beautiful objects, Kant in an earlier section remarks: "We want to submit the object [*Objekt*] to our own eyes"[12] (*KU* 5: 216). Colors merely make the object more vivid or charming, whereas when something is beautiful in respect of its form, its design draws our eyes to it.

The contrast between design and color in the fine arts is consistent with the overall argument of Section 14 where form is the defining characteristic of a beautiful sensory object – whether natural or artistic. Beauty, Kant says, is something "we attribute to an object on account of its form [*Form*]" (*KU* 5: 225). It is only approximately half way through Section 14 that he turns to the relation between art and design. The freedom with which he moves between discussions of natural and artistic beauty throughout the Analytic is reinforced by his next remarking that *all* objects of sense have a form qualifying as either shape [*Gestalt*] or play [*Spiel*] (*KU* 5: 225). Although this comment may not even be restricted to aesthetic objects, while the minimal examples he supplies are from art alone, the conclusion he draws surely refers to aesthetic objects in general for he remarks, without restriction, that design and composition – the play between several shapes or forms – jointly "constitute the proper object [*den eigentlichen Gegenstand*] of a pure judgment of taste"[13] (*KU* 5: 225). While we might think that composition arises only in respect of artworks, it is arguable that a landscape can be seen as a composition insofar as it is a dynamic organisation of forms seen by a spectator from a certain perspective.

Thus I am arguing that even though Kant most explicitly associates design with beautiful artistic form in Section 14, the idea of drawing or tracing out a form is, at the very least, illuminating for beautiful forms in nature. And what distinguishes beautiful from ordinary perceptual form is its quality of attracting – and holding – our gaze through a presentation of design. When we see something beautiful we experience a self-reproducing pleasure that arises as a lingering contemplation of this object (*KU* 5: 222).

Kant previously qualified design as a free drawing or outline:

> Flowers, free designs [*freie Zeichnungen*], lines aimlessly intertwined and called foliage: these have no significance, depend on no determinate concept, and yet we like them.
>
> (*KU* 5: 207)

We can now see that the way in which design holds our gaze depends on the freedom of its outline. It is as though it had been sketched "free hand". He does not develop the idea of free design, but the freedom of beauty is central for his account.[14] We must conclude that in Section 14 he carries forward this sense of design as distinctively free sensible form.

Admittedly, the phrase "free designs" could be read here as the second in a list of discrete items and referring exclusively to artworks. However, it is plausible that the phrase also refers to apparently free patterns found in nature. Read in this way, "free designs" contributes to a developing idea of aesthetic form. The beautiful flower displays a free pattern in the configuration of, for instance, its petals as does the beautiful painting of that flower. Foliage is a natural phenomenon, but also an artistic decoration inspired by nature – for instance, a style of wallpaper fashionable in the late eighteenth century (*KU* 5: 229). In both cases there is an easy transition from the patterns displayed by natural phenomena to artworks. Thus patterns displayed by natural objects can be considered as designs simply because they look as if they were freely sketched.

So far we have seen that design as form or outline makes the object worth looking at and that it is free. Next we discover that design displays another characteristic of beauty, namely, of looking *as if* it were determined by some – but not by any specific – purpose. The beautiful form of an object is explicitly linked with design in the sense of intention or purpose in the "General Comment" at the end of the Analytic:

> [I]n apprehending a given object of sense [. . .] the object may offer just the sort of form [*Form*] in the combination of its manifold as the imagination, if it were left freely to its own devices, would design [*entwerfen würde*] in harmony with the understanding's lawfulness in general.
>
> (*KU* 5: 241)[15]

Admittedly, Kant does not use *Zeichnung* or its verbal form *zeichnen* in this passage. However, *entwerfen* means to design, to sketch, to draw or to outline and thus the sense of design as drawing is maintained when the link between pattern and purpose is explicitly brought out. The shift is from 'design' as a product of imagination to the related activity of the imagination producing beautiful forms.

An object we empirically apprehend – Kant makes no distinction between natural beauty and artworks – looks as if it were freely designed by imagination and yet at the same time we are bound to what is actual, that is, to something given to our senses as a 'definite' [*bestimmte*] form. [*ibid.*] Kant uses the subjunctive mood to express the ambiguous freedom of imagination, which appears free to design what is already in existence and yet is in harmony with the laws of understanding. The outline of the beautiful object gives the dual impression of being determined by an intention, while at the same time free. The subjective side of the same relational story is that in aesthetically appreciating a beautiful object we view it *as if* it arose from a purpose, although we view it as free from determination *by* a purpose. Even beautiful artistic objects look as if they arose without intention – although we know this not to be the case. Later Kant says that beauty in nature must look as if it were art, while beautiful art must look as if it were nature (*KU* 5: 306). In neither case – whether its form is in fact the result of an intention or not – do we view the object as arising from a purpose when we respond to it aesthetically. What matters in an aesthetic judgment is how the object appears to the eye or its "mode of presentation [*Vorstellungsart*]" (*KU* 5: 221). When we see the formal patterning of an object as free we call that object beautiful, regardless of its purpose within the order of nature [*Naturzweck*] (*KU* 5: 229). This is the sense in which in finding something beautiful we are, according to Kant, disinterested with regard to the existence of the object (*KU* 5: 204).

Kant calls this curious conjunction of implying a purpose, while at the same time denying any such, "purposiveness without purpose" [*Zweckmäßigkeit ohne Zweck*]. This is a purposiveness arising only formally in the subjunctive mood, that is, *as if* it were the result of an intention. The purposiveness of form of the object – its design – is determined neither by the object's mere existence nor by the intention of a subject – human or divine – and lies only in our way of presenting, that is, the way in which the object's free outline makes us want to linger in our apprehension of it (*KU* 5: 221).

I have uncovered three interconnected characteristics of design, which coincide with central features of Kant's analysis of judgments of taste. The beautiful object intrinsically attracts our gaze, displays a free outline and implies purposiveness while excluding any determining purpose.[16] Kant's introduction of design in Section 14 is not a *faux pas* and, rather, accounts for the role of the object in respect of the main elements of the Analytic of the Beautiful.

2. Monogram as Delineation of the Sensible Concept in the 'Schematism' Chapter

We have seen that the beautiful object's purposiveness without purpose arises from the activity of imagination. However, Kant does not give a systematic account of the connection between design and imagination in the third *Critique*. In order to make good this missing link, I now turn to the connection between sensible form and imagination in the "Schematism" chapter of the *Critique of Pure Reason*. This will prepare the way for establishing something further about design, namely that it arises as a peculiarly harmonious relation between the activity of judging and an object. Indeed, this is the condition of the possibility of the three features I have already brought to light.

Kant's schema mediates between concept and intuition. Experience of an object requires the combination of these two components, thus a schema is a condition of the possibility of the experience of objects. In the first instance, Kant presents the schema as mediating between category and appearance, thus making possible a cognitive judgment as the determination of a particular sensory given under a universal concept. The schema as "a transcendental determination of time" is homogeneous with both the category – the ground of determination or unity – and with time – the *a priori* form of sensible objects[17] (A138–9/B177–8). Kant goes on to distinguish two sorts of schema. The schema of a sensible concept – a monogram – makes images possible, while the schema of the pure concepts of the understanding (the categories) "can never be brought into any image whatsoever" (A141–2/B180–1). In this discussion I focus on the monogram as sensible schema.

The sensible schema is first presented as "a rule of synthesis of the imagination, in respect to pure figures in space" (A141/B180). In other words, the schema is the principle in accordance with which the pure sensible concept of a triangle, for instance, takes sensible form. The sensible schema as rule is a "representation of a universal procedure of imagination in providing an image for a concept" (A140/B179–80). The schema can only be thought, as it is not yet determined as any particular size or type – equilateral, isosceles or scalene – as would be required for an image (A140–1/B179–80). But as the thinking of the schema is carried out by the imagination, the capacity for synthesis, we must conclude that "thinking" – as "representation" – in this case refers not to a proposition or formula, but to the very carrying out of a rule.[18]

What does Kant mean by calling the sensible schema a monogram? A monogram is commonly a species of signature made up of the interlinked initial letters of a name.[19] However, Paton proposes that Kant uses the term with the more general sense of a sketch or outline (2013: 36). I will establish that the monogram is a signature of imagination in sketching the outline – or form – of objects through a process of synthesis.

The monogram has been taken to apply only to pure figures in space, that is, geometric forms.[20] However, Kant says that the monogram pertains to "figures in space," now omitting the earlier restriction to pure figures (A141–2/B181). Kant gives the example of the empirical sensible concept "dog", acting as a rule "according to which my imagination can delineate [*verzeichnen*] the figure of a four-footed animal in a general manner" without restricting the construction of imagination to the image of any particular dog (A141/B180). *Verzeichnen* has the root *zeichnen*, that is, to draw, outline or sketch.[21] Such delineation is the necessary *a priori* condition of any image of a dog as representative of a particular breed or of an individual dog. The monogram delineates by synthesising a form or shape for this empirical and general – not in this case pure – sensible concept. Thus when Kant refers to "the schema of sensible concepts, such as of figures in space" as a monogram of pure *a priori* imagination, he does not drop the word "pure" with regard to "sensible concepts" through inattention or abbreviation (A141–2/B181). He means that the *a priori* synthesising activity of imagination is required for both pure and empirical sensible concepts. A monogram delineates a figure – be it a triangle or a dog – in space.

The figure is the sensible form of the object. The link between sensible schema and form is explicit in one of the most famous statements from the first *Critique*:

> This schematism of our understanding, in its application to appearances and their mere form, is an art concealed in the depths of the human soul, whose real modes of activity nature is hardly likely ever to allow us to discover, and to have open to our gaze.
>
> (A141/B180–1)

The synthesis of imagination delineates a figure, that is, the form of an object. This is a form or figure *in* space and time, rather than the forms of space and time that are the general background conditions of all experience.

A monogram traces the outline or form of the object, which even though it is a necessary condition for an image is distinct from the latter. The image is a reproduction arising from the reproductive use of imagination, whereas the monogram is a product of pure a priori imagination, which delineates or sketches the shape of the object in space and time prior to any determination under a concept (A141–2/B181). HENCE "pure a priori imagination" in the "Schematism" is nothing other than what is called "productive imagination" in both editions of the Transcendental Deduction (A123/B152).

3.   What the Monogram as Sensible Schema Tells Us About Design

The further aspect of design I am in the process of uncovering is that it is not found privatively in either an object or a mental state and arises, rather, as a relation between mind and object. The account of the monogram is instructive for this by:

(i)   providing a more elaborated account of the productive role of imagination than does the Analytic of Beauty;

(ii) explaining, in particular, the link between form and productive imagination that is presupposed rather than analysed in the third *Critique*;

(iii) establishing the distinction between pure and empirical sensible forms with respect to the a priori synthesis of imagination.

(i) The systematic connection between design and monogram as sensible schema is grounded in their source in the same mental power. Aesthetic judgments arise from the free lawfulness of the imagination, which is both productive and spontaneous [*produktiv und selbsttätig*] (*KU* 5: 240). The pure a priori or productive imagination is also the source of the monogram as sensible schema (A141–2/B181). Productive imagination in general is the power of synthesis, which delineates or produces figures in space (A141/B180).

(ii) In the "Analytic of Beauty" productive imagination is "the originator of chosen [*willkürlich*] forms of possible intuitions"[22] (*KU* 5: 240). The "Schematism" chapter explains how productive imagination delineates the general form of objects. In an epistemic judgment synthesis giving rise to form is preparatory for unification under a concept in the determination of an object. In an aesthetic judgment such resolution of the process of synthesis does not arise because imagination stays focussed on the form of the object. Only in the case where the object in respect of its form is worthy of being looked at in its own right does the perceptual form qualify as design and we call the object beautiful.

(iii) Aesthetic judgments are directed to empirical sensible figures, not pure or geometric sensible forms. Geometric forms are not free designs: they cannot qualify as beautiful as they are regular or determined (*KU* 5: 204). A geometric figure displays not purposiveness without purpose, but, rather, objective purposiveness "useful for solving many problems" (*KU* 5: 362). While beauty displays the conditions for cognition in general – the relation between understanding's concepts and the sensible forms or figures produced by imagination – and thus contributes indirectly to cognition, geometric form is directly productive for cognition.

Developing further the last of these points, an aesthetic judgment – although empirical – does not lay claim to objective necessity (*KU* 5: 191). Nonetheless, aesthetic judgments are subject to a transcendental exposition, that is, they have an a priori ground (*KU* 5: 277). This conjunction can now be explained. As the outline or form – that is, design – of the beautiful object is sensible but cannot be geometric, it must be the transcendental form of an empirical sensible object. Whereas in epistemic empirical judgments the transcendental condition – the monogram – is merely presupposed as a background condition, in an aesthetic empirical judgment this condition is displayed as design. The sensible monogram is a delineation of the synthesising activity of the pure productive imagination as a condition for the possibility of experience. Free design displaying purposiveness without purpose shows the transcendental form necessary for all appearances, although only in respect of a singular object worthy of our gaze.

That an object has a spatio-temporal form is a necessary condition of experience; *how* form is delineated or sketched out in any particular case depends on the object in question. Even pure objects of intuition vary in their form and can be triangular, circular or square, and so on. Empirical forms vary considerably more. Only some of these empirical forms fulfil the further condition of being worthy of our looking at them.

Design is a monogram of the pure productive imagination, although not all monograms are beautiful. Design exhibits in an exemplary fashion – as a characteristic signature – the sensory form or monogram presupposed in any appearance, while Kant's account of the monogram explains what it is that design exhibits.

4. Design: Too Unrestricted and Too Restricted?

Having established a number of features of design characteristic of a beautiful object, I will now address two objections mentioned at the outset of this chapter. Firstly, does the link Kant makes between aesthetic judgment and spatio-temporal form entail that all objects are beautiful? If the distinguishing characteristic of beauty – namely sensible form – is shared by all objects then, so the objection goes, we must conclude that all objects are beautiful and this, it is argued, is implausible. Leaving aside any attempt to defend independently the position that all objects are beautiful, my contention is that this cannot be Kant's position for it leaves out a very important element of his argument, namely, the contingency of judgments of beauty.

In the "Introduction" to the *Critique of Judgment* Kant claims that taste is characterised by intrinsic contingency [*inneren Zufälligkeit*] (*KU* 5: 191). The conjunction of contingency with *a priori* structure is characteristic of any empirical singular judgment. Not all of these, however, refer the presentation to a pleasure and arise from a "mere reflection on the form of an object" (*KU* 5: 191). My proposal is that this characteristic renders apparent the contingency shared by all empirical judgments and explains why aesthetic judgments are *intrinsically* contingent. Kant makes abundantly clear that it is not possible to know in advance whether the form of the given object will prompt a harmony of the faculties.[23] "We cannot determine a priori what object will or will not conform to taste; we must try it out" (*KU* 5: 191). Experiencing the object as worthy of our apprehension and taking pleasure in it *is* to see its form as free design. This, like the epistemic monogram, operates as a principle within the activity of judging and is not established propositionally in advance of the experience to which it applies.

Kant reiterates the claim that pleasure arises only contingently in the Analytic: "We cannot possibly tell a priori that some presentation or other (sensation or concept) is connected, as cause, with the feeling of a pleasure or displeasure, as its effect" (*KU* 5: 221). Yet despite its contingency, the judgment of taste nevertheless claims subjective universal validity and necessity (*KU* 5: 236). But there is no conflict between these claims. *When* we find something beautiful, we necessarily find it pleasurable and call on others to share this pleasure. But we cannot tell in advance or a priori *that* something will strike us as beautiful. Thus it cannot be the case that all objects are beautiful, otherwise aesthetic judgments would not be contingent and the pleasure we take in beautiful objects would be a priori and would not require awaiting an empirical presentation. Only when, contingently, a free design holds our gaze do we deem something beautiful.[24]

Having answered the objection that Kant's account of taste in the "Analytic" is not restrictive enough, we now need to address the charge that it is too restrictive. Why, in short, should it be only spatio-temporal form that gives rise to taste? There can be no doubt of the inadequacy of Kant's at best ambivalent account of the contribution of color and tone to beauty.[25] Even when he concedes these features can qualify as beautiful, he does so – following Euler – by granting them temporal status, not by revising his account of beauty's restriction to spatio-temporal form.

Kant's unsatisfactory account of color and tone has led Allison to argue for an understanding of aesthetic as distinct from spatio-temporal form. The harmony of the faculties characteristic of taste requires "an organized manifold of some sort," which need not be limited to – although "*may*" include – "spatio-temporal configuration" and amounts to "merely some kind of diversity for the imagination to unify in its apprehension and present for reflection."[26] Allison provides only one example in support of his alternative strategy. Following Guyer, he refers to a series of paintings by Albers, which Allison says give rise to aesthetic appreciation due to "their confluence of colors rather than their rigid geometrical form."[27] Whatever the virtues of the example – it is not at all evident that Albers' forms are rigid – Allison's point is that color can qualify as beautiful.

What exactly could comprise Allison's preferred version of aesthetic form as "some kind of diversity" giving rise to unification? Certainly, the use of color in a painting can be experienced as "diverse". For instance, Rothko paints with a variety of modulations of color crucial for the expressive effect of his works. And I agree with Allison that Kant requires something like a unification of a manifold that falls short of determinate unity. As Allison argues, the harmony of the faculties cannot just be a response to an isolated sensation and requires some "arranging or ordering of sensible content" (2001: 136). But it is difficult to see what unification of a sensible manifold would involve if it were not unification *in* space. Surely to speak of unification of colors implies a spatial environment where they are laid out and arranged? If this is right, then Allison's Kant requires spatio-temporal form.

While both Guyer and Allison are right in criticising Kant for failing to do justice to the roles played by color and tonality, they have given insufficient reasons for rejecting his claim that spatio-temporal form is essential for taste. Paying more attention to the distinctiveness of design as *free* spatio-temporal form allows us to defend Kant's position.[28] Instead of insisting on the exclusive grounding of taste in the harmony of the faculties – as Guyer does[29] – or offering an alternative way of thinking about the aesthetic form of the object – as Allison does – we can conclude that design is a necessary condition of aesthetic appreciation, even though it is not in every case sufficient. Even the most expressive use of color – as in Albers and Rothko – has to be presented in *some* spatial configuration or, in Kant's terms, as a unified manifold.[30]

Allison anticipates this objection by stating that the spatio-temporal features may not be the features that are reflected on in taste (2001: 369 n48). However, if the outline is not aesthetically pleasing then the beauty of accompanying features will suffer. If the colors are beautiful and yet the distribution of colors on the canvas is not, would we find the painting worthy of **comparable** aesthetic appreciation? This is something that Klee and Matisse – both masters of color – recognised. For them, line and color operate in necessary conjunction with one another (see Merleau-Ponty 1964). And in Albers' *Study for Homage to the Square: Beaming* (1963) the form within which color is presented does not, on close visual examination, look rigid and, I would argue, although comparatively regular, qualifies as a sketchy outline or design. Such a sketchy line is characterised by miniscule gaps and barely discernible deviations.[31] Kant's mistake was in saying that design is *the* (rather than *an*) essential aspect – *das Wesentliche* – in respect of which objects are beautiful: but he was not wrong in claiming that design is essential for taste.[32]

5. Conclusions

I have established a number of interconnected features qualifying an object as beautiful in respect of its form. Design is not characteristic of any spatio-temporal form whatsoever: only those objects that draw our gaze towards them insofar as they display free outlines and prompt a harmony of the faculties qualify as beautiful. Design is thus founded on a relation between mind and object that arises contingently.

From this we can conclude that the beautiful object plays a necessary role within the determination of taste insofar as it prompts a playful mental state. An object worthy of our apprehension on account of its free design stands in a necessary relation to the harmony of the faculties, for the mental state is a response to the beautiful object. Certainly, the determination of the judgment of taste does not arise from the object as prior to the mental state and only insofar as it is an object for reflection. Moreover, this is only the beginning of an account of the precise role the object plays in the determination of taste.

A further provisional conclusion I draw from the account of monogram as sensible schema, is that design is not an image. Aesthetic judgments rely on productive imagination, which delineates or configures objects. While delineation is a necessary condition of the determination of images, design operates indeterminately and freely.[33] If beauty were an image, the object would already be determined, whereas design sketches the object without a determinate conclusion. While it may seem intuitive to think of natural beautiful objects as distinct from images, what would it mean to say the same of visual artworks? An image – in Kant's terms – is a picture [*Bild*], which is a reproduction of something else.[34] In insisting that beauty arises from productive not reproductive imagination, Kant implies that artworks engage us in an original manner rather than as copies of something else.[35] Artworks – like beautiful natural objects – engage us directly through their free design.[36]

But how exactly does design as outline engage us with the object? The prospect I want to open up here draws on Michael Podro's insight into how for Hogarth – Kant's eighteenth-century predecessor – the drawing of a line makes possible the imagining of the volume of the object (Podro 1998: 111; Hogarth 1753). The line is not just a line, as it gives form to the object by tracing out its spatial structure (Podro 1998: 111). The line is thus not so much a restriction, as an enabling condition in the portrayal of objects. Taking up this idea with regard to Kant, I propose that drawing is an imaginative encounter with an object, bringing together its variety (for Hogarth) or its manifold (for Kant).[37] The line is exploratory of what is given in experience as "waving and winding", intertwined and free.[38] The line is not a defining limit, but an outline that holds up the object for our gaze. It is in the play between the possibility of the determination of the object and the latter's resistance to being pinned down that design emerges as a signature of the activity of imagination.

Notes

1 See, for instance, Guyer (1979) and Allison (2001).
2 See, for instance, Guyer (1979), Ginsborg (1991).
3 See, for instance, Guyer (1979), Allison (2001), Hughes (2007).
4 For a marked exception, see Zuckert (2002, 2006, 2007). Unlike Zuckert I argue that for Kant aesthetic form is necessarily spatio-temporal, even though I agree with her that it is not exclusively so (Zuckert 2006: 599).
5 Ginsborg (1991: 309) argues that the judgment of taste is self-referring and "is essentially devoid of content."
6 Pluhar's translation is used throughout unless otherwise signaled.
7 For objectivist readings of Kant's aesthetics, see Ameriks (1983), Kulenkampff (1990). My reading in contrast to both subjectivist and objectivist poles is relational.
8 See Guyer (1979: 297), Meerboote (1982: 81), Fricke (1990: 167).
9 See Guyer (1979: 211–37), Allison (2001: 131–2, 367).
10 Amended translation.
11 Kant's assessment of color is ambivalent as he concedes – although does not sustain – the possibility that color may give rise to pure aesthetic judgments. See his discussion of Euler (*KU* 5: 224).
12 Kant uses *Objekt* and *Gegenstand* interchangeably in this passage. It is clear from the context that both terms refer to sensory objects. See also *KU* (5: 290).
13 He gives no example of the mere play of sensations in temporal composition. However, he is surely thinking of music and "the art of color," both of which he later includes in "the art of the beautiful play of sensations" (*KU* 5: 324).
14 See, for instance, his distinction between free and merely accessory beauty (*KU* 5: 229).
15 Amended translation.
16 Design only arises in conjunction with reflection. I leave this dimension of taste for another discussion.
17 Kemp Smith's translation is used throughout unless otherwise signaled.
18 In other words, the rule is determined in its use. Compare Wittgenstein 1978.
19 Albrecht Dürer used this device to sign his works.
20 See Makkreel (1990: 31), Paton (2013: 35–6 n6).
21 Guyer and Wood translate *verzeichnen* as "to specify." While this is not incorrect, the link with *zeichnen* is lost. Melnick (2008: 82) uses the expression "drawing in thought."
22 Pluhar translates *willkürlich* as "chosen," while Guyer selects "voluntary." The term could also be translated as "arbitrary."
23 This is what I call a 'dual harmony' in Hughes 2010.
24 Zuckert (2006: 611) remarks on the contingency of aesthetic pleasure and insists on its *haeccitas* or individual form (2006: 615).

25 Within Section 14 Kant excludes color and tone from judgments of beauty, only to reverse his view and then return to his initial position. See Hughes (2007) for a proposal for extending Kant's formalism.

26 Allison (2001: 136). Also 368–9 for Allison's criticism of Rogerson 1986 who argues that aesthetic form is exclusive of spatio-temporal form. Zuckert (2006: 610) extends Allison's insight with her idea of an organic or purposive unity of diversity.

27 Allison (2001: 136) referring to Guyer (1979: 231). Guyer refers to Kramer (1973: 364) for a discussion of Albers' series "Homage to the Square" 1950–1976.

28 Guyer (1979: 220–3) for an extended discussion of design exclusively in terms of finality.

29 Guyer (1979: 209) argues that Kant's account of supposed constraints on objects that count as beautiful is "not implied by the idea of the harmony of the faculties itself."

30 The varied colors of Pollock's "Mural" (1943) display sufficient spatial unification for the purposes of Kant's claim, despite his technique of "throwing" color at the canvas.

31 Such deviations in line can also be discerned in works by Mondrian such as "Broadway Boogie Woogie" (1942–3).

32 Moreover, if he did not make this claim the link between cognitive and aesthetic judgments, claimed throughout the Analytic would amount to an idle wheel. See, in particular, *KU* (5:217–8, 238–9, 240–1).

33 See A141–2/B181, where the monogram is the condition of the possibility of the image.

34 See Bergson (2004: 1–85; 1993: 11–80) for a quite different account of images.

35 Kant's insists that fine art does not depend on imitation (*KU* 5:318).

36 I do not wish to exclude reproductive imagination and images from the scope of aesthetic judgments and insist only that design as constitutive of pure judgments of beauty is not an image.

37 Hogarth (1753: 37). See also Podro (1998: 118–19) on how through the variation of the line "we have a sense of participation in the form of the object."

38 Compare Hogarth (1753: 38) with Kant's idea of free design.

References

Albers, J. (1963) *Study for Homage to the Square: Beaming*, London: Tate Modern.

Allison, H. (2001) *Kant's Theory of Taste*, Cambridge: Cambridge University Press.

Ameriks, K. (1983) "Kant and the Objectivity of Taste," *British Journal of Aesthetics* 23: 295–302.

Bergson, H. (1993/1896) *Matière et mémoire*, Quadrige: Presses Universitaires de France, pp. 11–80.

Bergson, H. (2004) *Matter and Memory*, N.M. Paul and W. Scott Palmer (trans.), Mineola, NY: Dover, pp. 1–85.

Fricke, C. (1990) *Kants Theorie des reinen Geschmacksurteils*, Berlin and New York: Walter de Gruyter.

Ginsborg, H. (1991) "On the Key to Kant's Critique of Taste," *Pacific Philosophical Quarterly* 72: 290–313.

Ginsborg, H. (1998) "Kant on the Subjectivity of Taste," in H. Parret (ed.), *Kants Ästhetik, Kant's Aesthetics, L'esthétique de Kant*, Berlin and New York: Walter de Gruyter, pp. 448–65.

Guyer, P. (1979) *Kant and the Claims of Taste*, Cambridge, MA: Harvard University Press.

Hogarth, W. (1753) *The Analysis of Beauty*, http://archiv.ub.uni-heidelberg.de/artdok/1217/1/Davis_Fontes52.pdf

Hughes, F. (2007) *Kant's Aesthetic Epistemology: Form and World*, Edinburgh: Edinburgh University Press.

Hughes, F. (2010) *Reader's Guide to Kant's Critique of Aesthetic Judgement*, London and New York: Continuum.

Kramer, H. (2009/1973) *The Age of the Avant-Garde 1956–1972*, New Brunseick and London: Transaction Publishers.

Kulenkampff, J. (1990) "The Objectivity of Taste: Hume and Kant," *Nous* 24: 93–110.

Makkreel, R. (1990) *Imagination and Interpretation in Kant*, Chicago: University of Chicago Press.

Meerboote, R. (1982) "Reflection on Beauty," in T. Cohen and P. Guyer (eds.), *Essays in Kant's Aesthetics*, Chicago: University of Chicago Press.

Melnick, A. (2008) *Kant's Theory of the Self*, London: Taylor and Francis.

Merleau-Ponty, M. (1964) "Eye and Mind," in J.E. Edie (ed.), *The Primacy of Perception*, Evanston, IL: Northwestern University Press.

Paton, H.J. (2013/1936) *Kant's Metaphysic of Experience*, vol. 2, Abingdon and New York: Routledge.

Podro, M. (1998) *Depiction*, New Haven and London: Yale University Press.

Rogerson, K.R. (1986) *Kant's Aesthetics: The Roles of Form and Expression*, Lanham, MD, New York and London: University Press of America.

Wittgenstein, L. (1978/1953) *Philosophical Investigations*, Oxford: Blackwell.

Zuckert, R. (2002) "A New Look at Kant's Theory of Pleasure," *The Journal of Aesthetics and Art Criticism* 60(3): 239–52.

Zuckert, R. (2006) "The Purposiveness of Form: A Reading of Kant's Aesthetic Formalism," *Journal of the History of Philosophy* 44(4): 599–622.

Zuckert, R. (2007) *Kant on Beauty and Biology: An Interpretation of the Critique of Judgment*, Cambridge: Cambridge University Press.

Further reading

Classical anglophone accounts of Kant's aesthetics: H. Allison, *Kant's Theory of Taste* (Cambridge: Cambridge University Press, 2001); P. Guyer, *Kant and the Claims of Taste* (Cambridge, MA: Harvard University Press, 1979). For readings of the systematic relationship between the first and third critiques: S. Gibbons, *Kant's Theory of Imagination* (Oxford: Clarendon Press, 1994); F. Hughes, *Kant's Aesthetic Epistemology: Form and World* (Edinburgh: Edinburgh University Press, 2007); R. Kukla (ed.), *Aesthetics and Cognition in Kant's Critical Philosophy* (Cambridge: Cambridge University Press, 2007). On the question of the role of the object in Kant's aesthetics: K. Ameriks, "Kant and the Objectivity of Taste," *British Journal of Aesthetics* 23 (1983): 295–302; J. Kulenkampff, "The Objectivity of Taste: Hume and Kant," *Noûs* 24 (1993): 93–110; H. Ginsborg, "On the Key to Kant's Critique of Taste," *Pacific Philosophical Quarterly* 72 (1991): 290–313 (on taste as self-referring); P. Guyer, "Formalism and the Theory of Expression in Kant's Aesthetics," *Kant-Studien* 68 (1977): 46–70 (on a supposed problem in Kant's introduction of the form of the object).

19

ANALYTIC OF THE SUBLIME

Alexander Rueger

★★★

The feeling of the sublime, according to Kant, shares important features with the feeling of beauty.[1] When we call an object 'sublime' we judge it with a kind of pleasure in a disinterested way, claiming universality and necessity for our judgment. But Kant ascribes a structure to the feeling that distinguishes it from the pleasure in beauty, in fact, it distinguishes it so radically that the judgment of the sublime is not a judgment of taste at all. Here, Kant stands apart from much of the tradition in which the sublime was often taken to be the highest degree of beauty.[2]

The broad outline of Kant's view is relatively clear and uncontroversial. When we encounter certain objects in nature that are characterized by their immensity – either in terms of their spatial magnitude or in terms of their power or force – we find our faculty of intuition, the imagination, overwhelmed. The object seems to put up resistance to our comprehension in a way that makes the object appear 'contrapurposive' to us. A feeling of displeasure results that, upon reflection, however, turns out to be a way (perhaps the only way) of accessing aesthetically, through feeling, the superior powers of our mind, that is, our faculty of reason. What was felt as a painful resistance, as a failure of the faculty of intuition, is now experienced as an aesthetic awareness of our intelligible being and its superiority over any merely natural resistance. This awareness is 'purposive' for the ultimate vocation of our mind and is registered in a feeling of pleasure.

Kant's description of the feeling of the sublime follows the tradition that finds a mixture of displeasure and pleasure (or a transformation of one into the other) in the experience. Burke's attempt to explain how "pain" from terror can be the cause of "delight" is mentioned by Kant (5: 277)[3] and he was most likely also familiar with Mendelssohn's theory of "mixed sentiments". Kant refers to these as "Rührung",[4] a feeling "in which agreeableness is produced only by means of a momentary inhibition followed by a stronger outpouring of the vital force" (5: 226; 245).[5] In contrast, however, to Burke's theory, which he subsumes under "empirical psychology", Kant's own ambition is a *transcendental* analysis or exposition of the sublime. It is the "presumed" universality and necessity of judgments of the sublime that point to "an a priori principle in them and elevates them out of empirical psychology [. . .], in order to [. . .] transpose them into transcendental philosophy" (5: 266; cf. 277). In the following I will first clarify Kant's transcendental ambition (Section 1) before I discuss the two modes of the sublime (Sections 2 and 3).

DOI: 10.4324/9781003406617-25

1. Purposiveness and Pleasure in the Sublime

Using the framework established in the Introduction and the Analytic of the Beautiful, Kant analyzes the displeasure involved in the sublime as based on the fact that an object's representation or form is "contrapurposive for our power of judgment, unsuitable for our faculty of presentation, and as it were doing violence to our imagination." The pleasure of taste, by contrast, arises from the "purposiveness in its [the object's] form, through which the object seems as it were to be predetermined for our power of judgment" (5: 245). In general, a "purposiveness judged merely subjectively [. . .] is the relation to the feeling of pleasure and displeasure" (20: 248); that is, a representation that is purposive or suitable for our faculties will be received with satisfaction.

By contrast, that an object is "unsuitable for our faculty of presentation", or even does "violence to our imagination" (5: 245) presumably means that the representation of the object does not agree with the conditions under which the imagination is supposed to operate. Faced with such an object, the faculty of presentation does not achieve what might be considered its aim or interest and this failure is registered with displeasure.[6] We are thus led to the notion of faculty interests that Kant had introduced in the *KpV* (but had used quite extensively much earlier in his lectures[7]): "To every faculty of the mind one can attribute an *interest*, that is, a principle that contains the condition under which alone its exercise is promoted" (5: 119).

If contrapurposiveness of an object is detected through displeasure in the object and if, conversely, purposiveness of an object results in pleasure in it, it would seem that Kant is using the principle, briefly mentioned in the Introduction, that "the attainment of every aim is combined with the feeling of pleasure" (5: 187), where 'aim' is to be taken as referring to a faculty's interest. Given the claim about displeasure, the principle would seem to provide a necessary condition for pleasure, not merely a sufficient one. Let's call this the *achievement principle*.[8]

Several qualifications apply to this principle. First, the condition of logical consistency – that a faculty does not attempt to accomplish an objectively impossible task – is not part of a faculty's interest but rather is "the condition of having reason at all" (5: 120). Second, only contingent satisfaction of an interest results in pleasure: "since this agreement of the object with the faculties of the subject [in the case of beauty] is contingent, it produces the representation of a purposiveness of the object with regard to the cognitive faculties of the subject" (5: 190). This is opposed to the agreement of appearances with the pure concepts of the understanding which is inevitable and is not registered with any feeling (5: 187).

Since the experience of the sublime consists in a combination of displeasure and a feeling of satisfaction, the achievement principle requires that Kant introduce a second-level purposiveness which can coexist with the first-level contrapurposiveness and accounts for the pleasure of the sublime. This "higher purposiveness" (5: 246; cf. 20: 249f.) concerns precisely the (first-level) inadequacy of the imagination: this failure, indicated or "sensibly presented" in the feeling of displeasure, can serve to "provoke and call to mind" – in ways to be discussed – ideas of reason which themselves do not admit of sensible presentation but which are the proper referent of judgments of the sublime (5: 245). Thus it is an interest of reason that is satisfied at the second level and for which the failure of the imagination at the first level is judged to be purposive. It follows from this two-level structure that the natural object that we initially judge to be sublime cannot properly be the referent of the sublime: since judging that X is sublime attributes a positive feature to X, X cannot be the natural object that has been found to be contrapurposive. So the object itself merely "serves for the presentation of a sublimity that can be found [only] in the mind" (5: 245; see Section 3).

The use of the achievement principle in Kant's account of beauty and the sublime raises the question whether this principle is indeed a legitimate ingredient in a *transcendental* analysis. Guyer, who has emphasized the central role of the principle, thinks that it is imported from empirical psychology and thus refutes Kant's transcendental ambition.[9] I suggest, however, that the principle can actually be derived from the "transcendental definition" of pleasure that Kant presents in §10 (cf. also *EEKU* 20: 230f.). Even though 'pleasure' is an empirical concept, Kant asserts, we can give an explanation or definition of it "through pure categories" (5: 177n), in this case, the category of causality: "The consciousness of the causality of a representation with respect to the state of the subject, for maintaining it in that state" is what we call pleasure. Conversely, if a representation is associated with displeasure, it contains grounds for our mind's attempt to get rid of it (5: 220). If we presuppose that a faculty F has an interest in having representations that conform with the conditions "under which alone its exercise is promoted", then (i) having a pleasurable representation R, according to the definition, means that R has a tendency to cause its own maintenance in the mind; and (ii) this R must agree with the operating conditions (the interest) of F, for if R did violate these conditions (i.e., obstruct the operation of F), R could not have the tendency to maintain itself in the mind. In this case, R would contain, as Kant says, the ground for "hindering" its maintenance or for "getting rid of" it (5: 220). Overall, if R is pleasurable according to the transcendental definition, it "attains the aim" of F. Kant may, after all, be justified in using the achievement principle without collapsing the analysis into empirical psychology.

The inadequacy of the imagination can be sensibly presented in the feeling of displeasure. There is, however, no (positive) feeling for the ideas of reason relevant in the sublime. This is the basis for the often noted structural similarity between the way the feeling of the sublime arises and the way Kant analyzes the arising of the feeling of respect for the moral law in the incentives chapter of the *KpV*.[10] The moral law can effect this feeling only indirectly, through the pain it induces when it is "thwarting all our inclinations" (5:73). The violation of the interest of the senses – here, inclinations – results in displeasure or pain. Kant adds the apparently analytic principle that the removal of an obstacle automatically promotes the interest of reason (the determination of the will): "there is indeed no feeling for this law, but inasmuch as it moves resistance out of the way, in the judgment of reason this removal of a hindrance is esteemed equivalent to a positive furthering of its causality" (5:75; cf. 79). Analogously, the immense object in nature offers resistance to being grasped by the senses – it is judged to be contrapurposive and occasions a feeling of displeasure. But this resistance is at the same time the measure of our positive aesthetic response, our becoming aware of the superior faculty of reason. The superiority of reason is felt through the amount of resistance that has to be overcome; there is no *direct* feeling for the superiority:[11] "In aesthetic judging (without a concept) the superiority over obstacles can only be judged in accordance with the magnitude of the resistance" (5: 260). The failure of the imagination (and the associated displeasure) is therefore a "merely negative presentation" of the infinite – but it is the only presentation possible (5: 274).[12]

All of these considerations are summed up in one of the final characterizations Kant gives of the sublime: "That is sublime which pleases immediately through its resistance to the interest of the senses" (5: 267).

2. The Mathematical Sublime

Under the heading "On the mathematical sublime" (§25) Kant gives a "nominal definition" that covers, at least approximately, *both* kinds of the sublime, the mathematical and the dynamical: "We call sublime that which is absolutely great" (5: 248). Even though Kant emphasizes that to be great and to be a magnitude are "quite different concepts," the division of the Analytic of the Sublime is based on the distinction between extensive and intensive magnitudes.[13] In the *Metaphysik Dohna* lectures (from 1792–3) Kant gives a relevant characterization of the distinction:

"The magnitude of a quantum considered as an aggregate is extensive. The magnitude of a quantum *considered as a ground* is intensive" (*V-Met/Dohna* 28: 637). The latter magnitude is a degree, measuring the strength or power of the ground. Accordingly, in the experience of the mathematical sublime we consider the size of an object as an aggregate of units and estimate its greatness; in the dynamical sublime we experience an object as a "ground" or power that has (potentially) immense effects on us.

If we apply the framework of faculty interests to the two modes of the sublime, we have to identify in each case the conditions under which the imagination fails to achieve its aims and the higher interest that is served by this failure.

Kant starts from the traditional characterization of the sublime in terms of greatness. What can be great? Spatial magnitudes, of course, but – surprisingly – also virtue, public freedom and justice, or the accuracy of a measurement (5: 249). This is the first indication that Kant understands 'great' and 'greatness' in a wide sense – as is common at the time.[14] Although the main discussion of the mathematical sublime is in terms of the estimation of spatial magnitudes, the wider usage of 'great' becomes important when Kant switches from the sensible sense of greatness to an "intelligible" sense, that is, when he applies "great" to noumena (e.g., 5: 255; see 2.(iii)).

Estimation of magnitude comes in two modes: *mathematical* estimation involves the determining power of judgment, while *aesthetic* estimation results in a judgment of the reflecting power. Since the judgment of the sublime is supposed to be a reflecting judgment, it is the aesthetic mode that will be relevant for it. Mathematical estimation assigns definite (numerical) quantities to the size of objects and thus answers the question 'how large?', while aesthetic estimation only answers 'is it large (or great)?' Each mode, of course, requires a standard or unit and thus the estimation is relative to the choice of standard. In the aesthetic case, the standard is "subjective" but nevertheless valid for everyone; the judgments then take the form, for example, 'This person is great (tall)', where the comparison standard is a normal-sized human being. Such (reflecting) judgments, says Kant, express estimation of what is "simply great".[15] Judgments of the sublime, however, concern what is "absolutely great" or "great beyond all comparison" (5: 248). How do we arrive at aesthetic estimations of the latter sort?

Each mode of estimation contains two operations: (i) the *apprehension* of the sensible manifold and (ii) the *comprehension* of the manifold. The latter can be either logical/mathematical (in the concept of numbers) or aesthetic (comprehension in one intuition). If I have chosen a unit, say, a meter, I can "run through" (apprehend) the manifold of a given object and mathematically comprehend it as a numerical multiple of the unit ('14 meters'). The chosen unit *itself* can be mathematically comprehended with respect to a different unit (1 m = 100 cm). Kant argues that, on pain of an infinite regress, this process of mathematical comprehension ultimately has to start from a basic measure which itself is comprehended aesthetically, "grasp[ed] [. . .] in one intuition" (5: 251). Although mathematical estimation, with its arbitrary choice of units, has no limits in its application, its fundamental dependence on aesthetic comprehension proves to be important for the judgment of the sublime.

In contrast to the limitlessness of mathematical comprehension, Kant claims that in aesthetic comprehension of units, a limit or maximum, "the aesthetically greatest basic measure", can be reached (5: 252).[16] Reaching this limit – call it M – is the mechanism by which the experience of the sublime is triggered. When the imagination "runs through" a given manifold and tries to aesthetically comprehend it in one intuition, this procedure succeeds only up to "a greatest point beyond which it cannot go" for what is apprehended first "already begin[s] to fade in the imagination" while it goes on to apprehend further parts of the manifold (5: 252). Thus, aesthetic comprehension cannot go beyond M.

This limit for the imagination when dealing with *finite* magnitudes does not seem to have anything to do with an unsuccessful attempt to comprehend something "absolutely great" or infinite.[17] This is how it should be since there are no infinite objects in nature, and the imagination does not engage in trying to estimate infinity. Kant clearly emphasizes this: "Nature is thus sublime in those of its appearances the intuition of which brings with them the idea of infinity." In the imagination's attempt to go beyond M this "idea of infinity" is induced in the mind. This happens when – and only when – the imagination is felt to be inadequate even in its "greatest effort [. . .] in the estimation of the magnitude of an object." In the *aesthetic* estimation, of course; in mathematical estimation, with the help of number concepts, we "can make any measure adequate for any given magnitude" (5: 255).

In what way is this idea of infinity induced? Kant explains this in terms of the *analogy* between M and the notion of infinity.[18] Only in aesthetic comprehension there is "a greatest; and about this I say that if it is judged as an absolute measure, beyond which no greater is subjectively (for the judging subject) possible, it brings with it the idea of the sublime," that is, the idea of infinity (5: 251). When the imagination reaches M, it cannot aesthetically form a unit so that what was large with respect to M becomes small with respect to a larger unit. Since the infinite is that against which everything else is small (5: 250), M thus is a "subjective" representative of infinity. M is a subjectively *absolute* limit and, compared with it, every other unit is small. But apprehension goes further with the given magnitude if it exceeds M; in fact, Kant points out, the structure of the world shows us that there are always larger units that are beyond the grasp of imagination (5: 256f.). What is largest for the imagination is actually small. Hence, although the effort to go beyond M triggers the idea of infinity, M is a hopelessly inadequate presentation of the idea of infinity.

The maximal effort of the imagination to aesthetically comprehend, says Kant, "is a *relation* to something absolutely great" (5: 258; my emphasis). This "relation" is one of analogy with, or symbolization of, reason's idea of infinity. At the same time, the failure of the imagination to go beyond M reveals that no sensible (finite) standard can be adequate for what reason can think in this idea.[19] This failure induces the feeling of reason's "preeminence", a superiority that "cannot be made intuitable through anything except the inadequacy" of the imagination (5: 258). Its futile effort therefore is "also a relation to the law of reason", a symbolic correspondence with reason's law.

It remains to be discussed (i) why the imagination engages in the futile effort to go beyond M at all, (ii) which faculty interests are being frustrated (and why), and (iii) what notion of infinity Kant is employing.

(i) Why should the imagination be driven to provide larger and larger (aesthetically comprehended) units, even though these are obviously not needed for mathematical estimation? Kant's answer seems to be that it is the "law of reason" or the "voice of reason, which requires totality for all given magnitudes", where 'totality' means comprehension in one intuition (5: 254).[20] He illustrates the process at the end of §26. We choose a mountain to "serve as unit for the number that expresses the diameter of the earth, in order to make the latter *intuitable*" (5: 256; my emphasis). What is made to be intuitable is the large magnitude, the diameter of the earth; for this we need a suitably large unit, hence a relatively small number that multiplies it. So the move to larger units ("for shortening the numerical series") is driven not so much by the demand of convenience for the understanding but by the desire to make large magnitudes intuitable. The imagination here does not try to comprehend the large magnitude itself but provides larger and larger units, which inevitably leads to the maximum and the failure of the imagination to go beyond it. Kant's example of the interior of St. Peter's in Rome (5: 252) seems to be intended to illustrate this at a sub-astronomical scale.[21]

(ii) Is it really the imagination's *own* interest, as I claimed, that is not satisfied in this process rather than an interest of reason? The imagination's task is to comprehend (aesthetically); not being able to go beyond M is a failure with respect to this aim, even though the understanding doesn't require it for logical estimation. This finite failure (i) evokes the ideas of infinity and (ii) motivates the comparison with reason's capacity. The voice of reason is what drives the imagination to expand but the blockage of the expansion is a frustration of the imagination's own interest. If we were dealing with a failure with respect to an interest of reason, then the displeasure would not be analogous to the moral case. The painful aspect of the moral feeling is due not to the fact that sensibility/inclinations cannot reach an aim set by reason but that their own interests are frustrated.

Why does the failure of mathematical estimation – which involves understanding and imagination – to grasp infinity not call up the idea of reason's superiority? Because, says Kant, it has been shown to be objectively impossible to attain "to absolute totality through the progression of the measurement of things." This is "an impossibility of thinking the infinite as ever given" and thus not merely a subjective impossibility, an "incapacity for grasping it; for there nothing at all turns on the degree of comprehension in one intuition as a measure" (5: 259).

Why is then reason's demand for the imagination to comprehend even infinity not also incoherent and thus of no effect on feeling? The relevant difference here is that in aesthetic comprehension – comprehension "in the unity not of thought but of intuition" – the imagination "suspends" the progression of time, or "cancels the time condition",[22] and therefore, what is impossible *in time* might seem attainable for the imagination when it suspends time:

> the comprehension in one moment of that which is successively apprehended, is a regression, which in turn cancels the time condition in the progression of the imagination and makes simultaneity intuitable (5: 258f.).

The aesthetic maximum of comprehension, of course, shows that the imagination cannot live up to this seeming possibility. Only this "subjective" failure or shortcoming results in displeasure (because the object is seen as subjectively contrapurposive); the objective impossibility does not result in painful feeling – presumably for the same reason that agreement of appearances with the categories is not registered with pleasure (see Section 1). And because mathematical comprehension does not reach a limit, there is no felt blockage that would initiate the thought of reason's superiority. Only in the aesthetic failure do we find this idea arising.

(iii) Which notion of infinity is at work in the discussion of the mathematical sublime? Not the mathematical concept where comprehension into a totality is "objectively impossible". "In the case of nature as appearance, [. . .] infinity comprehended [. . .] is a self-contradictory concept (on account of the impossibility of the absolute totality of an endless progression)" (5: 255; cf. 259). Hence, whatever concept reason forms of infinity, it must be a different one. Indeed, the notion Kant invokes applies to reason's "idea of a noumenon" by which "the infinite of the sensible world is completely comprehended in the pure intellectual estimation of magnitude under a concept" (5: 255). But with this concept of infinity it makes no literal sense to say that the supersensible is "greater than" any sensible magnitude (even though Kant engages in this talk).[23]

The *prima facie* strange comparison of the greatness of ideas with the smallness of sensible things presumably rests on the view, presented, for example, in *GMS*, that the "world of understanding", the supersensible, contains the "ground" of the phenomenal world and that "what belongs to mere appearance is necessarily subordinated by reason to the nature of the thing in itself" (4: 453, 461).

(The ground, traditionally, is always "greater" than the consequence.) This points, even in the mathematical sublime, to practical reason (cf. 5: 256).[24]

In sum: At the *first level*, the failure of the imagination with respect to its own interest (of aesthetic comprehension beyond the maximum) results in displeasure, according to the achievement principle. Reflection on this, the work of the (aesthetic) power of judgment, leads to the *second level*, at which the failure of the imagination is judged to be purposive with respect to the aim of reason and is registered with pleasure.[25] But it is, I have suggested, important that the imagination fail at a *finite* task because only this ('subjective') failure results in displeasure.

3. The Dynamical Sublime and the Relation to Morality

In the dynamical sublime a natural object is experienced, on the *first level*, as "fearful" (5: 260), as being capable of destroying our physical being through its enormous power. The "irresistibility of its power [. . .] makes us, considered as natural beings, recognize our physical powerlessness" (5: 261). At this level, the imagination is presenting the object as a threat to our happiness, to "those things about which we are concerned (goods, health, and life)" (5: 262; cf. 269).[26] The aesthetic judging of the object "stretches imagination to its limit", not, as in the mathematical case, to the limit of its "enlargement", but to the limit of "its power over the mind" (5: 268). That is, the imagination, in the face of the object's apparent power, cannot uphold a representation of our wellbeing or physical survival. If we imagine, counterfactually, that we wanted to resist the power, we realize that "all resistance would be completely futile" (5: 260). As in the mathematical case, we aesthetically judge this through displeasure.

In reflection, however, at the *second level*, the first-level failure of the imagination arouses "our power (which is not part of nature) to regard those things [our wellbeing] [. . .] as trivial"; we become aware of our superiority over nature, as intelligible beings, whose "highest principles" (our moral principles) cannot be affected by any natural force (5: 261f.). We find in us "a power to assert our independence" from the influences of nature and, in analogy to the mathematical case, the capacity "to diminish the value of what is great" according to the standard of nature "and so to place what is absolutely great only in its (the subject's) own vocation" (5: 269). Again, we experience, at this second level, "a pleasure that is possible only by means of a displeasure" (5: 260).

Usually – and in line with some passages in Kant (in particular, 5: 247) – we think of the mathematical sublime as related to theoretical reason while it is the dynamical mode that is related to practical reason. But it is clear from the text that Kant intended practical reason or "moral ideas" to be what both kinds of the sublime are directed at.[27] In both versions of the sublime experience Kant finds a symbolic presentation of the relation in which reason and sensibility stand in morality – a relation of dominance or violence "since human nature does not agree with that [morally] good of its own accord, but only through the dominion [*Gewalt*] that reason exercises over sensibility" (5: 271). In the *aesthetic* judgment on the sublime, this "dominion" is "represented as being exercised by the imagination itself, as an instrument of reason" (5: 269).[28] This apparently refers to the mechanism of aesthetic comprehension through which the imagination does violence to sensibility in the attempt to comprehend in one moment what, for inner sense, requires progression in time (5: 259). This is one of the senses in which the mathematical sublime functions as a symbol of morality.[29]

The mediating role of the imagination is required in order to preserve the *aesthetic* character of the judgment of the sublime and to distinguish it from moral judgments (where reason's influence is direct, as it is in the feeling of respect). Since the imagination operates with intuitions of objects in nature, we naturally take, in such an aesthetic judgment, the object, given in intuition, to be the ground or carrier of the sublime quality. This is the basis for the "subreption" that we are subject to when we call natural objects sublime. And as much as the notion of subreption seems to indicate a mistake or an illusion, it turns out to be required to ensure the aesthetic nature of our judgment: it is precisely the subreption, Kant says, that makes "as it were intuitable the superiority of the rational vocation of our cognitive faculty over the greatest faculty of sensibility" (5: 257). In order to have "as it were" an intuition of what is properly not intuitable, the subreption is required.[30]

The nature of this subreption has been the matter of some debate. If we look for a precedent, however, it is not likely the famous transcendental subreption from *KrV*.[31] More plausibly, it is similar to the kind of "optical illusion" Kant diagnoses in *KpV* as a *vitium subreptionis*. The moral law determines the will to do some action X which results in our taking pleasure in X (as morally good). This, Kant points out, is often taken by us in reverse order: it seems to us that our pleasure in X leads to the determination of our will, since the "inward effect", the impulse to act, is the same in both cases. The subreption here consists in our taking "what we ourselves do as something that we merely passively feel" (5: 116f.). This is analogous, in the sublime experience, to our confusing the feeling of respect for the idea of humanity in us with respect for an object of nature because we take what we accomplish ourselves (reason) to be a feature of an object that we passively receive.[32]

Interestingly, with respect to the *KpV* subreption, Kant says that "even the illusion that takes the subjective side of this intellectual determinability of the will as something aesthetic" is "sublime" (5: 117). The *vitium* itself is admirable! I suggest that, as in the case of the sublime, the subreption in *KpV* provides an indirect sensible presentation of what cannot be sensibly represented at all, viz., the act of the rational determination of our will. If an *aesthetic* presentation is to be given, it *has* to take the form of the optical illusion. But since it is the indirect presentation of the moral determination of our will, it deserves appreciation – it is sublime. As long as the judgment of the sublime is an aesthetic judgment, the subreption takes place; an explicit awareness of our moral vocation on this occasion would be the result of further reflection.[33]

Even though the subreption is necessary to secure the aesthetic character of judgments of the sublime, it is only when we recognize the 'mistake' that we are able to give their deduction, that is, the justification of their claim to universal and necessary validity. Kant points out in §30 that, in contrast to the case of judgments of taste, a deduction of judgments of the sublime is already contained in the exposition of these judgments. A separate argument is not needed here because we properly judge as sublime not an object in nature but a feature of our mind, the supersensible vocation of our faculties. The representation of the object is merely "*used* in a subjectively purposive way" (5: 280), namely, to arouse a feeling in us for a "purposiveness lying in the subject a priori," that is, the fact that even the disharmonious relation of the imagination and reason (in the experience of the sublime) is suitable for making us aware of our vocation (20: 249f.; cf. 5: 192). Since the representation of the object – or, rather, its contrapurposiveness and the attending displeasure – is merely used for the aim of arousing a feeling of our supersensible vocation, all that is required for a justification of the universality claim of the feeling is a demonstration that this aim has universal validity. But this has been done in moral philosophy (cf. 5: 292) and can be presupposed here since it is not the aim of the (reflecting) power of judgment.[34] [35]

Notes

1   My comments will not address some topics already discussed in more recent literature: I leave out the question of the possibility and status of the sublime in art; the varieties of the sublime beyond the ones explicitly mentioned in the Analytic (e.g., the so-called moral sublime); and a more detailed discussion of the ways in which the sublime contributes to morality. All of these topics have been treated ably and at length in Clewis' recent study (2009). For views that disagree with Clewis on some issues, see, e.g., Abaci (2008) (on art), McBay (2012) (on the moral sublime) and Doran (2015).

2 This holds for Baumgarten – for whom "aesthetic magnitude" is an ingredient in beauty – and his disciple Meier who characterizes the sublime as "maximal beauty" (*allergrösste Schönheit*; [1748: 169]), but also for many British authors before Burke.

3 Cf. Burke (1759, sections I.iv and IV.vi). All references to Kant's AA5 are to *KU*.

4 Often translated as 'emotion' but 'stirring' would be better.

5 See Mendelssohn (1771b: 142–7); Beiser (2009: 213f., 217–24); Guyer (2014: 347–51).

6 This contrapurposiveness can have to do with the object's 'formlessness' (e.g., 5:244; 247; 280) but as we will see (section 2), lack of form – whatever this may mean – is not a necessary condition (cf. also Clewis [2009: 69–72]).

7 See, e.g., *V-Met L1/Pölitz* from the mid-1770s (28:245–53).

8 Guyer has long been suggesting that this is Kant's general theory of pleasure (1997: 70ff.). For a rejection of this claim see Allison (2001: 56). For Guyer's discussion of the sublime under this point of view see (1993: 205–28).

9 Guyer (1997: 72).

10 See e.g., Guyer (1993: 359); Allison (2001: 326f.); Doran (2015: 189–95). For a dissenting view cf. Park (2009: 188).

11 Hence Kant's term "negative pleasure" (5: 245).

12 This is why the Jewish ban on images of anything divine is for Kant a most sublime passage: it presents negatively what can otherwise not be presented (5:274).

13 Following perhaps Mendelssohn who distinguished the "Sinnlichunermessliche" and the "Unermessliche der Stärke" (1771a: 217–19). Cf. Guyer (2014: 361f.).

14 Cf. Baumgarten's concept of "aesthetic magnitude" which means the "weight and significance" of objects (1750: §177ff.) and Sulzer, s.v. 'Gross. Grösse' (1771: 490–9).

15 In the estimation of an object as "simply great", says Kant, "we always combine a kind of respect with the representation" (5:249) but it is not clear that the feeling in this case has the structure of what he calls "Rührung". Cf. Allison (2001: 312f.).

16 Even though the transcendental nature of Kant's discussion can perhaps be defended to some extent (as I have tried in section 1), the claim about the aesthetic maximum is clearly empirical.

17 This is in contrast to readings that understand the imagination "attempt[ing] to estimate aesthetically [. . .] an infinite magnitude, a task that requires an impossible aesthetic unit of measure" (Budd [2002: 76]) or arriving "at infinity itself as the only appropriate measure. But by this time the imagination is simply overwhelmed" (Crowther [1989: 97]). What is important is that the imagination is overwhelmed already at a finite task, not only when it tries to accomplish something impossible.

18 Crowther (1989: 105) hints at this but believes that it actually plays no role in the production of the experience of the sublime. Cf. also Lyotard (1994: 101).

19 See below, section 2 (iii), for discussion of this idea of infinity.

20 It is not altogether clear how this claim is to be understood (though most commentators accept it at face value). It would seem that reason cannot simply operate on the imagination if the judgment of sublimity is supposed to be an aesthetic judgment. Cf. Park (2009: 152).

21 The other example in this context, the pyramids, is more difficult to interpret. See Allison (2001: 317f.) for a plausible reading.

22 The imagination does "violence to inner sense" and frustrates sensibility's interest (5:259). See below, 3. Cf. also Makkreel 1984.

23 Budd notices this (2002: 77n8). Cf. the lectures *V-Met/Mron* (1782–3), *V-Met L2/Pölitz* (1790) (29: 834–9; 28: 568f.) and *V-Phil-Th/Pölitz* from 1783–4 (28:1017f). Here Kant makes a tentative distinction between the mathematical infinite (applicable to phenomena but not to noumena) and the "metaphysical" infinite (the unlimited, which applies to noumena). At (28:568f.) Kant seems to reject the otherwise intriguing proposal by Moore (1988) that the metaphysical infinite manifests itself to finite minds as the mathematical infinite.

24 As noticed, e.g., by Crowther (1989: 100) and Matthews (1996: 171f.).

25 In the terminology of the *EEKU*: we detect, at the first level, "internal" contrapurposiveness; at the second, we find "relative" purposiveness (20: 249f.). Although the frustration of the imagination's interest is clearly the main issue on the first level of the analysis, there are remarks in Kant's text (emphasized, e.g., by Lyotard [1994: 150–3; 187–90]) that point to a pleasure of the imagination when it "feels itself to be unbounded precisely because of this elimination of the limits of sensibility", which "expands the soul" (5: 274; cf. 5: 269). Admittedly, such remarks do not sit easily with the interpretation I suggested. Clewis (2007: 83)

argues that this pleasure in the 'expansion of the soul' can arise only on the basis of the humiliation of the imagination by reason; for Lyotard it is the pleasure of "sacrifice" (1994: 188). I should note, though, that as far as I can see, Kant never actually talks about pleasure in these remarks.

26 Happiness, according to *GMS*, is an "ideal of the imagination" (4: 418).

27 E.g., Crowther, Matthews, and Allison have emphasized this (see fn. 24).

28 Insofar as the imagination is an "instrument of reason" in the experience of the sublime, it can be said to "acquire an enlargement and power which is greater than that which it sacrifices" and be itself "superior to nature" (5: 269).

29 Since the imagination is engaged in this violence with every 'normal' act of comprehension, we have to assume that the resultant displeasure becomes noticeable only when the comprehended manifold reaches the aesthetic maximum. Cf. also Guyer's reading of the sublime as a symbol of negative freedom (2005: 227–30).

30 Cassirer noted this: "Our view remains aesthetic only if it does not recognize the vocation of our mind's powers in and of itself but, as it were, through the medium of an intuition of nature" (1921: 353).

31 See Clewis' discussion (2009: 72–9).

32 Doran (2015: 201) briefly notes this analogy but otherwise it does not seem to have been discussed.

33 Cf. Guyer (2005: 160). Here I disagree with Myskja (2002: 158) and Clewis (2009: 78, 219f.).

34 See Allison (2001: 332).

35 Thanks to Susan Hahn for many helpful suggestions.

References

Abaci, U. (2008) "Kant's Justified Dismissal of Artistic Sublimity," *Journal of Aesthetics and Art Criticism* 66: 237–51.

Allison, H. (2001) *Kant's Theory of Taste*, Cambridge: Cambridge University Press.

Baumgarten, A. (1750/1961) *Aesthetica*, part I, reprint, Hildesheim: Olms.

Beiser, F. (2009) *Diotima's Children*, Oxford: Oxford University Press.

Budd, M. (2002) *The Aesthetic Appreciation of Nature*, Oxford: Oxford University Press.

Burke, E. (1759/1998) *A Philosophical Enquiry into the Origin of Our Ideas of the Sublime and Beautiful*, 2nd ed., Oxford: Oxford University Press.

Cassirer, E. (1921) *Kants Leben und Lehre*, 2nd ed., Berlin: B. Cassirer.

Clewis, R. (2009) *The Kantian Sublime and the Revelation of Freedom*, Cambridge: Cambridge University Press.

Crowther, P. (1989) *The Kantian Sublime*, Oxford: Oxford University Press.

Doran, R. (2015) *The Theory of the Sublime from Longinus to Kant*, Cambridge: Cambridge University Press.

Guyer, P. (1993) *Kant and the Experience of Freedom*, Cambridge: Cambridge University Press.

Guyer, P. (1997) *Kant and the Claims of Taste*, 2nd ed., Cambridge: Cambridge University Press.

Guyer, P. (2005) *The Values of Beauty*, Cambridge: Cambridge University Press.

Guyer, P. (2014) *A History of Modern Aesthetics*, vol. I, Cambridge: Cambridge University Press.

Lyotard, J.-F. (1994) *Lessons on the Analytic of the Sublime*, Stanford: Stanford University Press.

Makkreel, R. (1984) "Imagination and Temporality in Kant's Theory of the Sublime," *Journal of Aesthetics and Art Criticism* 42: 303–15.

Matthews, P. (1996) "Kant's Sublime: A Form of Pure Aesthetic Reflective Judgment," *Journal of Aesthetics and Art Criticism* 54: 165–80.

McBay, M. (2012) "The Moral Source of the Kantian Sublime," in T. Costelloe (ed.), *The Sublime: From Antiquity to the Present*, Cambridge: Cambridge University Press, pp. 37–49.

Meier, G.F. (1748) *Anfangsgründe aller schönen Wissenschaften*, vol. I, Halle: Hemmerde.

Mendelssohn, M. (1771a/2006) "Über das Erhabene und Naïve in den schönen Wissenschaften," in A. Pollock (ed.), *Ästhetische Schriften*, Hamburg: Meiner, pp. 216–59.

Mendelssohn, M. (1771b/2006) "Rhapsodie," in A. Pollock (ed.), *Ästhetische Schriften*, Hamburg: Meiner, pp. 142–87.

Moore, A.W. (1988) "Aspects of the Infinite in Kant," *Mind* 97: 205–23.

Myskja, B. (2002) *The Sublime in Kant and Beckett*, Berlin: Walter de Gruyter.

Park, K.H. (2009) *Kant über das Erhabene*, Würzburg: Königshausen & Neumann.

Sulzer, J.G. (1771) *Allgemeine Theorie der schönen Künste*, vol. I, Leipzig: Weidmann.

Further Reading

H. Allison, *Kant's Theory of Taste* (Cambridge: Cambridge University Press, 2001), ch. 13: Very clear discussion which, inter alia, reconstructs Kant's claim that the sublime has less significance within the third Critique than the beautiful. R. Clewis, *The Kantian Sublime and the Revelation of Freedom* (Cambridge: Cambridge University Press, 2009): Detailed discussion of earlier literature with an emphasis on the role of the sublime in promoting morality. P. Guyer, *Kant and the Experience of Freedom* (Cambridge: Cambridge University Press, 1993), ch. 6: Corrects in interesting ways Guyer's earlier neglect of the sublime in Kant's aesthetic theory. M. McBay, *The Sublime* (Cambridge: Cambridge University Press, 2018): The most recent monograph on the topic with an extended exploration of connections with ancient philosophy. R. Zuckert, "Kant's Account of the Sublime as Critique," *Kant-Yearbook* 11 (2019): 101–19: Focuses on the mathematical sublime and argues that Kant's analysis of the sublime does not overstep the limits of the critical framework.

20

DIALECTIC OF THE AESTHETIC POWER OF JUDGMENT

Tanehisa Otabe

★★★

The Critique of the Aesthetic Power of Judgment is divided into the Analytic and the Dialectic according to Kant's conception of transcendental logic in the first Critique. While in the Analytic Kant's goal is to "resolve the faculty of taste into its elements and to unite them ultimately in the idea of a common sense" (*KU* 5: 240),[1] in the Dialectic he considers a conflict that inevitably arises from the Analytic that makes his analysis of the judgment of taste doubtful. This is a conflict between two propositions concerning the principles of taste: the thesis "The judgment of taste is not based on concepts," and the antithesis "The judgment of taste is based on concepts" (*KU* 5: 338). What is at issue is, therefore, not a conflict between first-order aesthetic judgments, for example, "this rose is beautiful" and "this rose is not beautiful," but rather a conflict between the second-order principles underlying first-order judgments of taste.[2] Kant resolves the conflict by showing that the concept to which the object is supposedly related in the judgment of taste is understood differently in the two propositions and that no real contradiction exists. He thereby introduces the distinction between a determinate concept and an indeterminate concept, identifying an indeterminate concept with reason's concept of a supersensible substrate. This solution to the conflict leads to the final section of the Dialectic entitled "On beauty as a symbol of morality," in which Kant addresses the transition from the sensible to the supersensible.

In the following I first make clear how Kant establishes the antinomy of taste (§56). Second, I consider his (rather formal) solution of the antinomy based on the distinction between a determinate and an indeterminate concept (§57). I next examine what he means by the supersensible substrate, referring to his conception of the philosophical system in Section IX of the Second Introduction. The following section then addresses his theory of beauty as a symbol of morality (§59), answering the question of whether or not his move to the supersensible in the Dialectic is compatible with the central doctrine of the autonomy of the beautiful in the Analytic. Finally, I briefly address the historical influences of the Dialectic with special regard to Friedrich Schiller's 1795 work "On the Aesthetic Education of Human Beings in a Series of Letters."

DOI: 10.4324/9781003406617-26

1. Presentation of the Antinomy of Taste

Kant examines two commonplaces of taste in section 56: "Everyone has his own taste," and "There is no disputing about taste" (*KU* 5: 338).

The first commonplace holds that the determining ground of a judgment of taste is "merely subjective (gratification or pain)," and one therefore neither can nor actually does demand "the necessary assent of others" (*KU* 5: 338). This maxim serves even to justify a lack of taste.

The second commonplace seems similar to the first. However, this negative implies a positive proposition: one can argue about a judgment of taste, even though the judgment cannot be disputed. This is tantamount to saying that the determining ground of a judgment of taste "may even be objective," even though one cannot bring it to determinate concepts as grounds of proofs. We argue to have our judgments of taste confirmed by others and "come to mutual agreement" (*KU* 5: 338). In this sense, a proposition that derives from the second commonplace can be opposed to the first commonplace.

Kant formulates the antinomy of taste as follows (*KU* 5: 338):

Thesis. "The judgment of taste is not based on concepts."
Antithesis. "The judgment of taste is based on concepts."

The thesis is true. It would otherwise be possible to "decide by means of proofs," which contradicts his analysis of the judgment of taste in the Analytic, especially in the first moment (sections 1–5). The antithesis is also true. It would otherwise not even be possible to "lay claim to the necessary assent of others to this judgment," which also contradicts his analysis of the judgment of taste in the Analytic, especially in the fourth moment (sections 18–22) (*KU* 5: 338–9). This opposition is based on the subjectivism and objectivism of taste.

These two propositions or principles are, as Kant notes at the beginning of section 57, "nothing other than the two peculiarities of the judgment of taste represented above in the Analytic" (5: 339), namely in sections 33 and 32, respectively:

The judgment of taste is not determinable by grounds of proof at all, just as if it were merely subjective.

(*KU* 5: 284)

The judgment of taste determines its object with regard to satisfaction (as beauty) with a claim to the assent of everyone, as if it were objective.

(*KU* 5: 281)

The thesis and antithesis in the Dialectic appear to correspond to the two peculiarities that were discussed in the Analytic. If so, the question is why the need for the Dialectic. To answer, we have to first make clear how Kant addressed these two peculiarities in the Analytic.

The issue is the determinations: "as if it were merely subjective" and "as if it were objective." The first determination means that "I must be sensitive to the pleasure immediately in the representation of an object, and I cannot be talked into it by means of any proofs" (*KU* 5: 285). In this respect the judgment of taste has "merely subjective validity" (*KU* 5: 285). The second determination, by contrast, means that a judgment of taste is not only valid for the person who makes it, but "universally valid," as if the predicate "beautiful" designated an objective property. It follows that Kant understands by these two peculiarities the "subjective universality" that a judgment of taste demands (*KU* 5: 280).

Kant explains the subjective universality of a judgment of taste as follows: an objective cognitive judgment requires as a "subjective condition" the "agreement" of "the imagination (for the intuition and the composition of the manifold of intuitions), and the understanding (for the concept as representation of the unity of this composition)" (*KU* 5: 287). This subjective condition must be "the same" in all human beings. Otherwise we could not communicate our cognitions to one another (*KU* 5: 290n.). Now, the judgment of taste is "grounded only on the subjective formal condition of a judgment in general" (*KU* 5: 287). That is, a judgment of taste, "S is beautiful," is neither determined by a certain sensitive intuition offered by the object S (in which case S is to be called agreeable), nor a certain concept that determines the object S (in which case S is to be called good). The judgment is based solely on the "agreement of the imagination and the understanding" as the "subjective formal condition" that each judgment has to satisfy. That is, the judgment of taste contains "a principle of subsumption, not of intuition under concepts," as is the case with an objective cognitive judgment that pertains to a certain content, but "of the faculty of intuition [. . .] (i.e., of the imagination) under the faculty of concepts (i.e., the understanding)" (*KU* 5: 287). This principle of a subsumption which is subjective and formal enables the subjective universality of a judgment of taste.

This argument in the Analytic, which elucidates the possibility of a judgment of taste according to its two peculiarities, suits the task of the Analytic to resolve the faculty of taste into its elements.

As compared to the argument in the Analytic, the thesis and the antithesis in the Dialectic do not refer to moments or aspects of a judgment of taste, but to its general principle.[3] The two peculiarities and the thesis/antithesis differ, therefore, in the roles they perform, or purposes they serve, in the respective context of the Analytic and the Dialectic. I next discuss Kant's solution of the antinomy of taste.

2. Solution of the Antinomy of Taste

The antinomy may be understood as follows:

Thesis. The judgment of taste is not based on concepts of the understanding, but on sensation; that is, "agreeableness" is the "determining ground of taste."

(*KU* 5: 341)

Antithesis. The judgment of taste is based on concepts of the understanding, namely "the principle of perfection" is the determining ground of taste.

(*KU* 5: 341)

We are faced here with the opposition between empiricism and rationalism. According to the Analytic, however, both the agreeableness and the perfection of an object are essentially different from the beautiful (*KU* 5: 221). If the antinomy were to be understood in this way, then, we could only resolve it "by showing that both of the opposed [. . .] propositions are false" (*KU* 5: 341), which is not what Kant means by the antinomy of taste.

In order that the antinomy can be resolved, the thesis and antithesis made compatible, we have to show that the same term "concept" is "not taken in the same sense in the two maxims" (*KU* 5: 339). Kant adds that "this twofold sense or point of view in judging is necessary in our transcendental power of judgment," and that "the semblance involved in the confusion of the one with the other is, as a natural illusion, unavoidable" (*KU* 5: 339). The preceding empiricist and rationalist propositions understand by "concepts" the concepts of the understanding. To regard all concepts as concepts of the understanding is certainly natural. The concepts are, however, not confined to those of the understanding. As Kant points out:

> A concept can be either determinable or else in itself indeterminate and also indeterminable. The concept of the understanding, which is determinable by means of predicates of the sensible intuition that can correspond to it, is of the first sort; of the second sort, however, is the transcendental concept of reason of the supersensible, which is the basis of all that intuition, and which thus cannot be further determined theoretically.
>
> (*KU* 5: 339)

Kant understands concepts in either-or terms; that is, concepts are either determinable or indeterminate and indeterminable. Given this distinction, we can resolve the antinomy by saying:

> The judgment of taste is "not based on determinate concepts" of the understanding.
> The judgment of taste is "based on some, although indeterminate concept" of reason.
>
> (*KU* 5: 340)

The questions here become what Kant means by "determination," and if these either-or terms are valid. For the answer to the first question, Kant does not use the term "determine" in the following way: "the understanding determines the sensibility" (B161n.) or "how a product of the imagination should be, [. . .] is determined through concepts" (*KU* 5: 241). Here, what is to be – or cannot be – determined is a concept, and to determine a concept is to confirm it by a corresponding sensible intuition. A determinable concept is, therefore, a concept of the understanding to which a sensible intuition can correspond, while an indeterminate and indeterminable concept is a concept of reason to which no sensible intuition can be adequate. Viewed from this perspective, the thesis and the antithesis are compatible because concepts of understanding and of reason do not exclude each other. That is, no contradiction exists in saying that the judgment of taste is not based on concepts of the understanding, but is based on concepts of reason.

We move to the second question: whether or not the either-or scheme of concepts is justifiable. Here we have to consider Kant's definition of the beautiful in the Analytic. Kant argues in the Analytic that what is beautiful does "not depend on any determinate concept and yet pleases," and that "the satisfaction in the beautiful must depend upon reflection on an object that leads to some sort of concept (it is indeterminate which)" (*KU* 5: 207). However, this indeterminate concept that pertains to the judgment of taste is not a concept of reason, but rather an "indeterminate concept of the understanding" (*KU* 5: 244). That is, a concept of reason and a concept of the understanding can both be indeterminate. Kant further says that "the beautiful" is the "presentation of an indeterminate concept of the understanding," while the "sublime" is "that of a similar [i.e. indeterminate] concept of reason" (*KU* 5: 244). He also calls concepts of reason "determinate (practical) ideas" (*KU* 5: 256). This means that concepts of the understanding and those of reason can be determinate. The question is whether there is any contradiction in his view of concepts between the Analytic and the Dialectic.

Kant's argument is consistent because in the Analytic he uses the words "determinate/indeterminate" in terms of concepts in another way than in the Dialectic. Here a concept is determinate if it has a conceptually determined and defined content. When Kant mentions an indeterminate concept in the Analytic, it is not something on which the judgment of taste "is based," as is in the antithesis of the antinomy (*KU* 5: 338).[4] It is rather something to which an empirical intuition of the imagination is related, or, using Kant's wording, under which it is subsumed, that is, presented in intuition by the imagination. In the judgment of taste the concept of the understanding is indeterminate because, as we have seen, the principle of subsumption is not that "of intuitions under concepts," as is the case with the objective cognitive judgment, but solely that "of the imagination under the understanding" (*KU* 5: 287). That is, the judgment of taste "without a concept of the object" (*KU* 5: 217) is "grounded only on the subjective formal condition of a judgment in general" (*KU* 5: 287). The "powers of cognition" are thus "in a free play, since no determinate concept restricts them to a particular rule of cognition" (*KU* 5: 217). The indeterminableness of the concepts is also a prerequisite for art to be beautiful because the artist adds "to a concept [of the understanding]" (i.e., a determinate concept of the object to be represented) "a representation of the imagination that belongs to its presentation, but which by itself stimulates so much thinking that it can never be grasped in a determinate concept, hence which aesthetically enlarges the concept itself in an unbounded way" (*KU* 5: 314–15). A concept of the understanding becomes indeterminate when it is enlarged not by "logical attributes" (*KU* 5: 315) that represent what lies in the concept, but by a "multitude of sensations and supplementary representations" (*KU* 5: 316).

In the Analytic of the Sublime, Kant similarly states that, "in judging a thing to be sublime," the imagination is "related to reason, in order to correspond subjectively with its ideas (though which is undetermined)" (*KU* 5: 256). The ideas of reason partake in the judgment on the sublime in that its foundation is "in the predisposition to the feeling for (practical) ideas, i.e., to the moral feeling" (*KU* 5: 266), thereby leaving the ideas undetermined, since only practical reason can determine them (cf. *KU* 5: 256).

It follows that in the Analytic Kant addresses an indeterminate concept in terms of the relationship between the imagination and the understanding or reason. When Kant refers to an indeterminate concept in the Dialectic, however, he understands something completely different. This difference will also serve to elucidate the relationship between the Analytic and the Dialectic.

3. Purposiveness of the Nature

The thesis of the antinomy that "the judgment of taste is not based on concepts" (*KU* 5: 338) derives immediately from the Analytic, because it means that the judgment of taste is "not based on determinate concepts" of the understanding (*KU* 5: 340) and needs no further explanation. The main issue in resolving the antinomy is, therefore, the meaning of concepts in the antithesis: "The judgment of taste is based on concepts" (*KU* 5: 339). The concept on which the judgment of taste is grounded is an "indeterminate concept" of reason. Kant explains as follows:

> I say that the judgment of taste is based on a concept (of a general ground for the subjective purposiveness of nature for the power of judgment), from which, however, nothing can be cognized and proved with regard to the object, because it is in itself indeterminable and unfit for cognition; yet at the same time by means of this very concept it acquires validity for everyone [. . .], because its determining ground may lie in the concept of that which can be regarded as the supersensible substratum of humanity.
>
> (*KU* 5: 340)

While in the Analytic Kant remarks that the judgment of taste is "not grounded on concepts" (*KU* 5: 209) because it is not a cognitive judgment, he still argues in the Dialectic that the judgment of taste is "based on a concept" (*KU* 5: 340). Yet there is no contradiction between the Analytic and the Dialectic because the concept is not taken in the same sense in the two propositions. That is, the concept on which the judgment of taste is based is not a concept of the understanding but of reason.

Here, the intertwined questions become, first, what a "concept (of a general ground for the subjective purposiveness of nature for the power of judgment)" means, second, why it is an indeterminate concept of reason, and, finally, how it serves to ground the judgment of taste. By "resolving the faculty of taste into its elements" (*KU* 5: 240), the Analytic explicated that the judgment of taste is "grounded only on the subjective formal condition of a judgment in general" (*KU* 5: 287), that is, on the "harmony of the faculties of cognition" (*KU* 5: 218). This explication in the Analytic is justifiable because it is based on the analysis of the faculty of taste. What is at issue in the Dialectic is, however, if and, if so, how this "subjective formal condition" of the power of judgment conforms to nature. This conformity, the "purposiveness of nature for the power of judgment" (*KU* 5: 340), is not justifiable by the analysis of the power of judgment itself. It is rather a subjective principle for the power of judgment to reflect upon nature. That is why the "purposiveness of nature for the power of judgment" is characterized as "subjective," and the "concept (of a general ground for the subjective purposiveness of nature for the power of judgment)" is designated as an indeterminate concept of reason. This concept is undoubtedly unfit for objective cognition and thus provides "no proof for the judgment of taste" (*KU* 5: 340), but it still concerns a "determining ground" (*KU* 5: 340) of the judgment of taste in that, without this concept, that is, unless nature (outside us) conformed to the power of judgment (inside us), a judgment of taste would not be possible because the subjective condition of the power of judgment is fulfilled only when nature conforms to the power of judgment. In this sense, Kant designates this indeterminate concept of the "purposiveness of nature for the power of judgment" as an "idea" of the "intelligible substratum of nature outside us and within us" (*KU* 5: 345, 344).[5]

At this point we should look briefly at the Second Introduction. In section V, Kant introduces the concept of the "purposiveness [of nature] for our faculty of cognition" as a specific principle of the power of judgment to reflect on nature (and not to determine it), remarking that it is "neither a concept of nature, nor a concept of freedom" (*KU* 5: 185). Kant thus principally distinguishes the power of judgment from the understanding and reason. The principle of the power of judgment, however, serves to mediate between nature and freedom, or between the understanding and reason. In section IX he outlines this mediation:

> The understanding gives [. . .] an indication of the supersensible substratum of nature; but it leaves this entirely undetermined. The power of judgment, through its a priori principle for judging nature [. . .], provides for its supersensible substratum (in us as well as outside us) determinability through the intellectual faculty. But reason provides determination for the same substratum through its practical law a priori; and thus the power of judgment makes possible the transition from the domain of the concept of nature to that of the concept of freedom.
>
> (*KU* 5: 196)

In view of Kant's argument in section 57, I here address only the relationship between the understanding and the power of judgment. I will return to the relationship between the power of judgment and reason in the next section. The purposiveness of nature means that nature, as appearance that works mechanically, is able to accept purposes posed by reason. Purposive nature is, therefore, something other than the nature cognized by the understanding as appearance, and can thus be called its supersensible substratum. The understanding, the task of which lies in cognition of nature, indicates its supersensible substratum (or noumena) without any further determination than "something = x" (A250), because it is beyond the scope of the understanding (A255–6/B 311). By contrast, the power of judgment, the task of which is not to determine but to reflect on nature, views the same supersensible substratum as nature capable of accepting purposes. Kant thus claims that the supersensible substratum is undetermined by the understanding, while the power of judgment provides it with determinability.[6]

Now the relationship between the Dialectic and the Analytic is clarified. In the Analytic Kant asserts that "the principle of taste is the subjective principle of the power of judgment in general" (*KU* 5: 286); that is, the judgment of taste is "grounded only on the subjective formal condition of a judgment in general" (*KU* 5: 287). In the Dialectic, by contrast, Kant reconsiders the subjective principle of taste in relation to "the concept of a purposiveness of nature" (*KU* 5: 182) introduced in the Introduction, indicating its systematic role of mediating between nature and freedom, or between the understanding and reason. In the final paragraph of Remark II of section 57, Kant explicitly considers the relationship of the three Critiques, characterizing the three ideas as follows:

> [F]irst, that of supersensible in general, without further determination, as the substratum of nature; second, the very same thing, as the principle of the subjective purposiveness of nature for our faculty of cognition; third, the very same thing, as the principle of the ends of freedom and principle of the correspondence of these ends with nature in the moral sphere.
>
> (*KU* 5: 346 – slightly modified[7])

This passage from section 57 precisely corresponds to the earlier citation from section IX of the Second Introduction (*KU* 5: 196), which evidences Kant's primary concern in the Dialectic to integrate his theory concerning the judgment of taste in the Analytic into his systematic discourse in the Second Introduction.

4.   Beauty and Morality

Section 59 is entitled: "On beauty as a symbol of morality." We here have to answer two questions: What is a symbol and why is beauty a symbol of morality?

We begin with the first question. Kant is conscious of his unique usage of the word "symbol." As he points out, the "use of the word symbolic in contrast to the intuitive kind of representation" has been "accepted by recent logicians" (*KU* 5: 351). For example, Baumgarten insists in his *Metaphysics* as follows:

> If the sign is joined together in perception with the signified, and the perception of the sign is greater than the perception of the signified, this COGNITION is called SYMBOLIC. If the perception of the signified is greater than the perception of the sign, the COGNITION will be INTUITIVE (intuition).[8]

A cognition is intuitive when we perceive objects by means of signs that make us aware of the objects the signs refer to, rather than of the signs themselves, that is, when the signs become quasi-transparent and the signified is perceived as if immediately. Based on this distinction between symbolic and intuitive cognition, Lessing outlines the following theory of artistic illusion in his 1766 essay *Laocoon*:

> The poet wants to make the ideas he awakens in us so vivid that, from the rapidity with which they arise, we believe that we perceive the real and sensible impressions of the objects they

refer to. In this moment of illusion, we should cease to be conscious of the means which the poet uses for this purpose, that is, his words.[9]

The distinction between symbolic and intuitive cognition thus plays a decisive role in eighteenth-century aesthetic theory.[10]

Opposing this usage of the word "symbolic," Kant asserts that "the symbolic kind of representation is merely a species of the intuitive" (*KU* 5: 351), and that "the intuitive in cognition is either schematic, by means of demonstration, or symbolic, as a representation based on mere analogy" (*KU* 5: 351 n.). That is, both schemata and symbols belong to the intuitive presentation of concepts. They are distinguished in two respects: first, which concepts they intuitively present, and, second, how they present them.

Kant already dealt thoroughly with schemata in the first *Critique*. Given the concept of a triangle, we can draw a triangle and make concrete the concept of a triangle by creating an image of it. This operation attributed to the imagination is called schematism. A drawn image of a triangle – an "example" (*KU* 5: 351) of a triangle – is, however, equilateral, isosceles, or scalene, and can never be "adequate to the concept of triangle." A scheme of the triangular is, therefore, not a drawn triangle, but rather "a rule" for drawing it and "can never exist anywhere except in thought" (A141/B180).

Symbols, by contrast, are an intuitive presentation of the concepts of reason. However, "no intuition adequate to the concepts of reason can be given at all." There can be, therefore, no schemata for them. The question is how they are presented intuitively.

The symbols do this presentation of the concept by means of an analogy (for which empirical intuitions are also employed), in which the power of judgment performs a double task: first applying the concept to the object of a sensible intuition, and then, second, applying the mere rule of reflection on that intuition to an entirely different object (i.e. an idea of reason), of which the first is only the symbol (*KU* 5: 352).

An analogical relationship A: B = C: D illustrates Kant's theory of symbols. Given a concept of the understanding B and a concept of reason (i.e. an idea) D, the empirical intuition A corresponds to a concept B, but there can be no empirical intuition C adequate to a concept D. A symbolic presentation makes the idea D sensible by using the intuition A instead of a nonexistent intuition C. The power of judgment performs two tasks. First, it relates a concept B to the object of a sensible intuition A, and, second, it ascribes a reflection (or the rule of reflection) on the object of a sensible intuition A to an idea D.

Kant's example of a symbol of a despotic state is a handmill (*KU* 5: 352). When we reflect on a sensible intuition A presenting the concept of handmill, we notice a relationship of dominance between the mill and the grain, whose relationship is also found in a despotic state D. A handmill thus serves as a symbol of a despotic state when we ascribe our reflection on a handmill to a despotic state. In an analogy, therefore, the similarity lies merely in "the form of the reflection" and "not the content" (*KU* 5: 351).

A symbolic presentation can thus be characterised as follows: First, based on an analogy, it is only an indirect presentation, in contrast to a schema which directly presents a concept of the understanding. Second, an empirical intuition A is a symbol in terms of a concept D, but an example in terms of a concept B. The difference between an example and a symbol is not decided by the properties of an intuition A, but by the procedure of the power of judgment. An intuition A is an example if the power of judgment subsumes an intuition A under a concept B, while it is a symbol if the power of judgment ascribes a reflection on an intuition A to an idea D. Third, there is no necessary relationship between an intuition A and an idea D. In concrete terms, a symbol of a despotic state is not necessarily a handmill, and a handmill can symbolise another idea. What an intuition A symbolises depends on which characteristics of the intuition A the power of judgment remarks. Fourth, the power of judgment makes sensible an idea D by means of an intuition A, providing thereby no cognition of an idea D, because only a reflection on an intuition A determined by a concept B is ascribed to an idea D, and a concept B that determines an intuition A cannot be a predicate of an idea D.

We now move to the second question: why beauty is a symbol of morality. That beauty is a symbol of morality does not mean, by the definition of a symbol, that there is any similarity between them, but rather that reflection on a beautiful object can be ascribed to morality:

> [In the judgment of taste] the mind is at the same time aware of a certain ennoblement and elevation above the mere receptivity for a pleasure from sensible impressions. [. . .] In this faculty [of taste] the power of judgment does not see itself, as is otherwise the case in empirical judging, as subjected to a heteronomy of the laws of experience; in regard to the objects of such a pure satisfaction it gives the law to itself, just as reason does with regard to the faculty of desire.
>
> (*KU* 5: 353)

Here Kant contrasts the aesthetic judgment on the beautiful with that on the agreeable, stating that the aesthetic judgment on the beautiful is certainly triggered by an empirical intuition, but is not at all "passive" (*KU* 5: 222), as is the case with the aesthetic judgment on the agreeable, but is "free and grounded in autonomy" (*KU* 5: 350). It is so in that the aesthetic judgment on the beautiful has its principle in the "correspondence of the faculties of cognition with each other (of imagination and of understanding)" (*KU* 5: 342). The reason the beautiful is regarded as a symbol of morality is that the judgment of taste on a beautiful object is grounded in autonomy, which is also the case with the moral judgment.

Recalling the preceding property of a symbol – that there is no necessary relationship between an intuition that serves as a symbol and an idea presented by it – we can say that there is no necessary relationship between beauty and morality. Both beauty and morality are autonomous; that is, beauty neither grounds morality, nor is it grounded on morality. It does not follow, however, that the relationship between beauty and morality is merely arbitrary. In the case of symbolising a despotic state by means of a handmill, the power of judgment is not necessarily restricted to the intuition of a handmill. Other intuitions are also available for the purpose. In this sense, the power of judgment looks at the intuition of a handmill from an outsider's perspective. In the case of a symbolic representation of morality by means of beauty, however, the power of judgment does not find the similarity between beauty and morality from an outsider's perspective, but by reflecting on its own activity. The relationship between beauty and morality, which is based on a self-reflecting activity of the power of judgment, is not arbitrary. The judgment of taste is intrinsically directed to the moral judgment, as Kant points out: "that is the intelligible, upon which [. . .] taste looks out" (*KU* 5: 353 – slightly modified). Beauty is a symbol of morality not despite, but because of its autonomy. Kant concludes section 59 as follows:

> Taste as it were makes possible the transition from sensible charm to the habitual moral interest without too violent a leap by representing the imagination even in its freedom as purposively determinable for the understanding and teaching us to find a free satisfaction in the objects of the senses even without any sensible charm.
>
> (*KU* 5: 354)

The beautiful (that pertains to an empirical intuition and is nevertheless autonomous) acts as a bridge between the (solely heteronomous) agreeable and the (purely autonomous) good, thereby negating not the difference between the three. There is, therefore, no contradiction between the central doctrine of the autonomy of the beautiful in the Analytic and the remark on beauty as a symbol of morality in the Dialectic.[11]

5.   Historical Influences

It should be concluded, from what has been said so far, that the primary task of the Dialectic is to incorporate the theory of the judgment of taste in the Analytic into the systematic discourse in the Introduction. The task is accomplished by the concept of the purposiveness of nature as a principle of the power of judgment, prescribing to the beautiful a transitive or intermediate role between receptivity and activity. The following is a brief sketch of the historical influence of the Dialectic with special regard to Friedrich Schiller's 1795 work "On the Aesthetic Education of Human Beings in a Series of Letters."

Concerning the question how "a transition from feeling to thinking," or from "passivity" to "activity" is possible (Schiller 1982: 131), Schiller states that,

in order to exchange passivity for autonomy, a passive determination for an active one, one must [. . .] be momentarily free from all determination whatsoever, and pass through a state of pure determinability,

(141 – italics in the original)

designating this intermediate state as "aesthetic." Schiller thus far follows Kant's perspective on the systematic role of the power of judgment.

Schiller goes further, however, to argue that even though we are "nothing in the aesthetic state" because of the "absence of any specific determination" (145), we are, for that very reason, in a state of "unlimited determinability" (141). This testifies that "thereby something infinite is achieved," that is, "humanity" – that inheres in our nature "as potentia," but is lost to us "in practice" with every determinate condition that we enter – is "restored" (147). Schiller's originality lies in considering the aesthetic state that is characterised by unlimited determinability not only as an intermediate step, but also as the state exemplifying the idea of humanity. He assigns to the aesthetic the role of providing us with the freedom that the determinations of sensibility and understanding deprive us of, and thereby integrating our life anew, offering us "the possibility of becoming human beings" (149). Mediated by Schiller, Kant's Dialectics of the third *Critique* continues to echo in Western aesthetics.[12]

Notes

1   Unless noted otherwise, translations are from the Cambridge Edition of the Works of Immanuel Kant, series editors Paul Guyer and Allen W. Wood (New York: Cambridge University Press, 1992). All italics are in original.
2   See Allison 2001: 237.
3   See Allison 2001: 242.
4   In section 5 Kant explicitly declares that the judgment of taste is "neither *grounded* on concepts nor *aimed* at them" (*KU* 5: 209).
5   See further: "the mere pure rational concept of the supersensible, which grounds the object (and also the judging subject) as an object of sense, consequently as an appearance" (5: 340).

6　It is important not to confuse the present discussion with the account of determinate and indeterminate concepts in section 57. There it was a matter of presenting a concept in a sensible intuition and not of making an idea conceptually determinable. See Allison 2001: 247.

7　The German original is: "*drittens* eben desselben, als Prinzips der Zwecke der Freiheit und Prinzips der Übereinstimmung derselben mit jener im Sittlichen." What is at issue is which nouns are the antecedents for the two pronouns, "derselben" and "jener." Guyer's and Matthews' translation – "*third*, the very same thing, as the principle of the ends of freedom and principle of the correspondence of freedom with those ends in the moral sphere" (Kant 2000: 221) – is grammatically incorrect. Meredith (Kant 1957: 215), Philonenko (Kant 1989: 169) and Gargiulo (Kant 2008: 1100) relate them to "Zwecke" and "Freiheit," which is grammatically correct. Pluhar's interpretation is more convincing: "*third*, the idea of the same supersensible as the principle of the purposes of freedom and of the harmony of these purposes with nature in the moral sphere" (Kant 1987: 220). See Banham (2000: 119); Allison (2001: 384).

8　Baumgarten 2013: 227 <§620> (slightly modified – emphasis in the original). Kant possessed the fourth (1757) edition of Baumgarten's *Metaphysics*. Section 620 is the same in the four editions (1739, 1743, 1750 and 1757).

9　Lessing 1962: 85 (slightly modified).

10　See Wellbery (1984) and Otabe (1995).

11　For a contrasting view, see Shaper (1992: 379). Guyer has a similar perspective, commenting that the "metaphysics of the Dialectic make no real contribution to Kant's theory of the universal voice [in the Analytic]" (Guyer 1997: 311).

12　More than two hundred years later, Jacques Rancière advocates the "aesthetic regime of the arts" (Rancière 2013: 18) because of its "indetermination between activity and passivity" (2009: 107), stating that "Schiller's aesthetic state" is "a pure instance of suspension" and "the moment of formation and education of a specific type of humanity" (2013: 23f.). However, Rancière pays no attention to the affirmative implications Schiller (and also Kant) gave to the concept of determinability, and negatively uses the adjective "determinable" (2010: 137, 141).

References

Allison, H.E. (2001) *Kant's Theory of Taste: A Reading of the Critique of Aesthetic Judgment*, Cambridge: Cambridge University Press.

Banham, G. (2000) *Kant and the Ends of Aesthetics*, London: Palgrave Macmillan.

Baumgarten, A. (2013 [1739]) *Metaphysics: A Critical Translation with Kant's Elucidations, Selected Notes, and Related Materials*, C.D. Fugate and J. Hymers (trans.), London and New York: Bloomsbury.

Guyer, P. (1997) *Kant and the Claim of Taste*, 2nd ed., Cambridge: Cambridge University Press.

Kant, I. (1957) *Critique of Judgment*, J.C. Meredith (trans.), Oxford: Clarendon Press.

Kant, I. (1987) *Critique of Judgment*, W.S. Pluhar (trans.), Indianapolis: Hackett Publishing Company, Inc.

Kant, I. (1989) *Critique de la faculté de juger*, A. Philonenko (trans.), Paris: Librairie philosophique J. Vrin.

Kant, I. (2000) *Critique of the Power of Judgment*, P. Guyer and E. Matthews (trans.), Cambridge: Cambridge University Press.

Kant, I. (2008) "Critica del Giudizio," in A. Gargiulo (trans.), *Le Tre Critiche*, Milano: Mondadori.

Lessing, E. (1962 [1766]) *Laocoön: An Essay on the Limits of Painting and Poetry*, E.A. McCormick (trans.), Indianapolis and New York: The Bobbs-Merrill Company, Inc.

Otabe, T. (1995) "From 'Clothing' to 'Organ of Reason': An Essay on the Theories of Metaphor in German Philosophy in the Age of Enlightenment," in Z. Radman (ed.), *From a Metaphorical Point of View: A Multidisciplinary Approach to the Cognitive Content of Metaphor*, Berlin and New York: Walter de Gruyter, pp. 7–25.

Rancière, J. (2009) *The Emancipated Spectator*, G. Elliott (trans.), London and New York: Verso.

Rancière, J. (2010) *Dissensus: On Politics and Aesthetics*, S. Corcoran (trans.), London and New York: Continuum International Publishing Group.

Rancière, J. (2013) *The Politics of Aesthetics: The Distribution of the Sensible*, G. Rockhill (trans.), London: Bloomsbury.

Schiller, F. (1982 [1795]) *On the Aesthetic Education of Man in a Series of Letters*, E. M. Willkinson and L. A. Willoughby (trans.), Oxford: Clarendon Press.

Shaper, E. (1992) "Taste, Sublimity, and Genius: The Aesthetics of Nature and Art," in P. Guyer (ed.), *Cambridge Companion to Kant*, Cambridge: Cambridge University Press, pp. 367–93.

Wellbery, D. (1984) *Lessing's Laocoon: Semiotics and Aesthetic in the Age of Reason*, New York: Cambridge University Press.

Further Reading

W. Bartuschat, *Zum systematischen Ort von Kants Kritik der Urteilskraft* (Frankfurt am Main: Vittorio Klostermann, 1972): A reconstruction of the third Critique as a whole including a minute explanation of the concept of the supersensible substratum from the systematic point of view. R. Brand, "Analytic/Dialectic," in E. Shaper and W. Vossenkuhl (eds.), *Reading Kant: New Perspectives on Transcendental Arguments and Critical Philosophy* (Oxford: Basil Blackwell Ltd., 1989), pp. 179–95: A detailed account of the concepts of Analytic and Dialectic in all three Critiques. P. Giordanetti, "Kant: Die moralische Grundlegung der Ästhetik," in H.-G. Sandkühler (ed.), *Handbuch Deutscher Idealismus* (Stuttgart: Metzler, 2005), pp. 297–304: A concise account of the relationship between beauty and morality in Kant's aesthetic theory. C.H. Wenzel, *An Introduction to Kant's Aesthetics: Core Concepts and Problems* (Malden, MA: Blackwell, 2005, esp. Ch. 6), pp. 106–27: Ch. 6 includes an introductory and instructive treatment of the Dialectic of the third *Critique*.

21

ANALYTIC OF TELEOLOGICAL JUDGEMENT

Christian Onof and Dennis Schulting

***

In this chapter, we examine eight sections of Kant's *Critique of Judgement* (CJ), which cover an introduction and the Analytic of Teleological Judgement. They are rich in content insofar as they (i) introduce a set of distinctions between types of purposiveness, (ii) refer to a number of issues discussed previously (e.g. in the *Critique of Pure Reason*, hereafter CPR), such as geometric cognition and the relation between sensibility and the understanding, (iii) raise issues of compatibility with the conditions of objective knowledge identified in CPR, and (iv) present the principles governing teleological judgements of nature. We discuss these issues and briefly address two concerns the Analytic gives rise to, namely its compatibility with Kant's earlier claims of causal determinism and with contemporary biology.

1. Subjective and Objective Purposiveness

Section 61 (§61) of CJ constitutes the articulation between the two parts of CJ. It introduces Part II, that is, the Critique of Teleological Judgement (hereafter CTJ). It functions both as a linking section and justification for including the objective purposiveness of nature in CJ: unlike aesthetic judgements, judgements of objective purposiveness of nature, the topic of CTJ, were not a recognised domain of philosophy. Additionally, Kant's examination of our theoretical cognition of nature was arguably completed in CPR, so his revisiting it calls for some justification.

As far as the first task is concerned, Kant could have contented himself with the observation that, since Part I has shown that aesthetic judgements are found to be judgements of purposiveness (without a purpose, *KU* 5: 236), they may justifiably share the platform with CTJ. That would, however, be a *post facto* justification, and hardly adequate to the systematicity of Kant's critical investigation. Moreover, it would leave it unclear why subjectively purposive aesthetic judgements (*KU* 5: 203) should be examined in the same work as objectively purposive ones. Kant addresses this concern in the very first paragraph of §61. He reminds us that what has been discussed under the heading of an examination of aesthetic judgement, in Part I, is relevant to our investigation of nature. That is, there are transcendental principles that "provide us with a good basis for assuming that nature in its particular laws is *subjectively* purposive" for our cognition, so that natural products will contain forms that are "*beautiful*" (*KU* 5: 359).[1] They are beautiful insofar as their "variety and unity" (*KU*

 DOI: 10.4324/9781003406617-27

5: 359) lead to the kind of "attunement of the cognitive powers" (*KU* 5: 238) that provides the pleasure upon which a judgement of beauty is based. In the Critique of Aesthetic Judgement, Kant had already indicated that this attunement is the "subjective condition of [the process of] cognition" (*KU* 5: 238). Now, in §61 he explains that there are transcendental principles providing us with a basis for judging the particular laws of nature to be purposive for our investigation of it, so that we should expect to find the products of such laws to be conducive to the attunement of our cognitive faculties required for cognition, and to be judged as beautiful.

Kant is not saying that, whenever we make a cognitive judgement, we experience a pleasure providing the basis for a judgement of beauty. Rather, when, in cognising certain products of nature, we turn our attention to the "variety and unity" (*KU* 5: 359) of the laws producing them, without seeking to cognise them, we thereby attend to what brings about the attunement of our mental powers. In thus attending to nature's purposiveness for our cognition, the conditions are met for an experience of beauty grounded in our pleasure in this attunement. The words "variety and unity" refer to transcendental principles (*KU* 5: 359), but which ones?

In line with the "articulation" function of this section, Kant is directly referring to the substantial introduction to CJ which presents the systematic organisation of the work. There, he explains that "the concept of a purposiveness of nature belongs among the transcendental principles" (*KU* 5: 182) of our cognition. This principle is expressed in terms of maxims guiding the pursuit of knowledge, which take nature as displaying *a unity in the diversity of its empirical laws* which is purposive for our cognition (*KU* 5: 185). This principle[2] is subjective, unlike CPR's regulative principles (Onof 2020),[3] but nonetheless transcendental *qua a priori* condition of cognition.

Kant has thus established the connection between the two parts of CJ by showing how the transcendental principle of the subjective purposiveness of nature points to the possibility of an experience of beauty induced by the pleasure experienced in contemplating the unity nature presents us with in the diversity of its particular laws, as manifested in certain natural products. Kant's next task is to introduce the move from such subjective purposiveness to an objective purposiveness of nature, thus addressing what the title of §61 announces, and what is the central topic of the Analytic of Teleological Judgement.

Kant makes two negative points about such objective purposiveness. First, we have no basis for judging that there is a distinct purposive "lawfulness of nature" (*KU* 5: 359): such a judging would require our being able to know purposes that are not ours, and not nature's either (since nature is not an intelligent being), but which are manifested in a type of lawfulness distinct from that of the Second Analogy of CPR. Second, the idea of objective purposiveness is, on the contrary, what we use to point to the contingency of certain natural forms, for instance the bone structure of birds which we judge as "utterly contingent" in terms of efficient causality (*KU* 5: 360).

That last point, however, also has a positive connotation: it is clear that we could not hope to investigate such natural products without appealing to an *"analogy in terms of purposes"* through which we make "reflective" judgements (*KU* 5: 360). The analogy is with a causality that would reside in the *concept* of an object and through which the object is produced. Such judgements cannot be determinative because that would amount to importing a new causality into natural science, for which we only have evidence in ourselves (*KU* 5: 361), that is, in our practical freedom (A803/B831).

2. Formal and Material Objective Purposiveness

The Analytic of Teleological Judgement, like the Analytics of CPR and the *Critique of Practical Reason* (hereafter CPrR), establishes important distinctions. Since the overall topic is objective purposiveness, Kant starts by distinguishing *formal* from *real (material)* purposiveness (*KU* 5: 364). The presentation of the first is the occasion for Kant to return to his analysis of judgements of geometry from CPR (e.g. A714–19/B742–7), now adding formal purposive judgements to them. To understand how the latter are related to the former, it is important to have a clear conception of Kant's account of how geometric construction yields synthetic a priori truths.[4] Kant takes the example of what we now call the theorem of angles subtended by the same arc at the circumference (Shawyer 2010: 7). This states that, if we consider a triangle specified by its base and "vertical angle" (AB and *γ* respectively in Figure 21.1; *KU* 5: 362), we find that the locus of third points of such triangles, that is, the points at the vertical angle (point C in Figure 21.1), is in a circle including A and B (let O be its centre). In referring to this theorem, Kant starts with a circle and "the unity of many rules resulting from the construction of that concept" (*KU* 5: 364). What does that mean?

Let us assume that we first construct a circle going through A and B. The aforementioned theorem results from observing that the rule by which we construct the circle *is also the rule* by which we construct all points C which define identical angles.[5] In a geometric proof, in producing an intuition through the figurative synthesis involving the schemata of a set of geometric concepts, I grasp (find "spontaneously" – *KU* 5: 362) that this is *the same construction* as would have been carried out under a different rule (schema of a second set of concepts). So, the synthetic *a priori* judgement obtained through geometric construction is that of the *unity of two* (non-analytically related) *rules of construction*.[6]

We can now understand how Kant defines formal purposive judgements in terms of "the unity of many rules resulting from the construction of that concept" (*KU* 5: 364). The idea is that in constructing the circle, other rules can be considered – Kant gives the example of four points on the circle whose intersecting lines define two rectangles with identical areas (*KU* 5: 362).[7] So the construction of the circle is purposive in that it provides the basis for "infinitely many splendid properties of this figure" (*KU* 5: 362), that is, many rules can thus be unified. Such purposiveness is objective but merely formal and thus does not refer to a purpose (*KU* 5: 364).

Kant distinguishes this *formal objective purposiveness* from the *formal subjective purposiveness* of aesthetic judgements, and from the *real (material) objective purposiveness* that will concern him in the following sections. First, such geometric findings are conducive to "admiration" (*KU* 5: 364), which Kant distinguishes from amazement in that the first is just an effect of purposiveness, while amazement occurs when we cannot reconcile a presentation with the principles of cognition (*KU* 5: 365). Although such admiration is commonly described as of the "beauty" of geometric figures, the judgement of purposiveness which gives rise to it is not aesthetic, insofar as it is not "judging

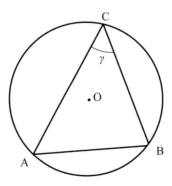

Figure 21.1   Circle of Centre O and Angle *γ* Subtended by Arc (AB)

without a concept" based upon the pleasure felt in the "free play of our cognitive faculties" (*KU* 5: 366). Second, such formal objective purposiveness is to be distinguished from the purposiveness we judge as residing in certain arrangements of "*things* outside of me" (*KU* 5: 364), for example, the ordering of paths in a garden. Here, the judgement which is no longer *a priori* relies upon the concept of a purpose: it is a judgement of real objective purposiveness.

Before moving on, we should note Kant's dwelling extensively on the purposiveness of geometric constructions, even showing leniency towards the enthusiasm (*Begeisterung*) of the Platonists for mathematics (*KU* 5: 363).[8] Kant makes a point of singling out what his critical theory identifies as the ultimate object of our admiration of geometric figures: the *unexplained* purposive "compatibility [*Vereinbarung*] of that form of sensible intuition (which is called space) with the faculty of concepts (the understanding)" (*KU* 5: 365), an agreement which "enlarges the mind" (*KU* 5: 365) insofar as it leads us to thinking of the ultimate basis of this harmony. In so doing, Kant is echoing his comment about schematism as a "hidden art in the depths of the human soul" (B180/A141) but also thereby clarifying two issues: (i) that it may have a supersensible basis; (ii) that it is manifested in the harmony between the understanding and space.[9] This latter point places constraints on acceptable interpretations of space as form of intuition. If this form is interpreted as essentially a pre-conceptual notion, while space itself is produced by the understanding through the figurative synthesis (e.g. Longuenesse 2005: 67–77; Friedman 2012), then there would no longer appear to be any unexplained harmony between space and the understanding (see Onof and Schulting 2015).

3.   Extrinsic and Intrinsic Material Objective Purposiveness

Kant's example of a garden, which is of a "product of art" (*KU* 5: 366), was one of *intrinsic (material objective) purposiveness* insofar as the arrangement of its parts has some purpose. In §63, Kant distinguishes this from making a claim about *extrinsic (material objective) purposiveness*, for example, that through an "ancient deposit of sandy strata" nature pursues the purpose of enabling extensive "pine forests" to establish themselves (*KU* 5: 367). This is not intrinsic because it identifies a purpose that is only relative insofar as it is a means for another purpose (*KU* 5: 367). But establishing the truth of this judgement would require that I first identify some *natural product* that is a *purpose of nature*. Kant pours cold water over the idea of determining extrinsic purposes of nature because of the problem of determining anything as a purpose of nature. Thus, commenting upon how the environment in cold climates is purposive for its inhabitants, he points out that "it is not clear why people should have to live in those regions at all" (*KU* 5: 369; see also *KU* 5: 378).

Intrinsic purposiveness has, so far, only been characterised for products of art. But if Kant thinks the idea of objective purposiveness of nature is worth investigating, it is because, while we are not able to *determine* natural products as objective purposes of nature, objective purposiveness may be useful to *reflect* upon nature and natural products. This is the topic he starts tackling in §64.

4.   Intrinsic Material Objective Purposiveness in Natural Products

To judge that something is possible merely as a purpose is to judge that this thing's[10] form[11] could not have arisen from the mere efficient causality of what Kant now calls "the mechanism of nature" (*KU* 5: 369). So the form of the thing is *contingent* as far as empirical laws are concerned (*KU* 5: 370). Now Kant adds that reason, in seeking to understand the conditions of production of a natural product, must always "cognize not only the product's form, but the form's necessity as well" (*KU* 5: 370). Here, Kant is referring to the demand of reason for a totality of conditions for the existence of the thing, not applied to a series (Fourth Antinomy), but to all the grounds for the production of the thing in question. Since this thing's existence (or production) is a contingent fact, even when all empirical laws are taken into account, the question is, where can reason find the complement of sufficiency?

Contingency versus necessity: Before addressing this question, an immediate concern looms here, when confronting this claim of contingency of the natural product's form with the Second Analogy, according to which "there must [. . .] lie in that which in general precedes an occurrence the condition for a rule, in accordance with which this occurrence always and necessarily follows" (A193/B238–9). This would seem to contradict the "contingency of [a natural product's] form with respect to all empirical laws of nature in relation to reason" (*KU* 5: 370) since this is precisely the possibility that some determination of the thing's current state does not follow from a rule/law.[12] While that raises issues that will be dealt with in the Antinomy of Judgement (*KU* 5: 387),[13] we must first dispel this appearance of contradiction arising from the Analytic.

To do so, we note that Kant mostly refers to a *thing* in these sections. Things are posited (as existing) when cognising an object.[14] We experience certain things, for example, natural products, by synthesis of the manifold in intuition of their spatio-temporal manifestations under the categories (by means of schemata in the figurative synthesis, B151–2). However, when thereby bringing, in virtue of intellectual synthesis, this unified intuition under a concept in terms of causality in particular, we find a lack of determinacy.[15] Unlike the case of CPR's objects, this is not the cue for seeking further determinations under the categories according to regulative principles of pure reason (A671/B699) since all natural/physical laws have already been taken into account. The complement of sufficiency must be sought elsewhere.[16] This contingency however holds "as far as reason is concerned" (A671/B699): it is logically possible that a higher cognition should be able to explain these things mechanistically (see *KU* 5: 406).

Contingency and purposiveness: To return to the question of where reason can find the complement of sufficiency required to make sense of what is a contingent product of nature with respect to all physical laws, Kant's answer is a crucial claim for CTJ since it accounts for the central role of the notion of objective purposiveness in our cognition of nature and its products. Kant says that "the very contingency of the thing's form is a basis for regarding the product as if it had come about through a causality that only reason can have" (*KU* 5: 370). That is, the thing's contingency with respect to all physical laws entails that reason can only resort to a concept as providing the ground for the necessity of the thing insofar as a will (practical reason) could act on this concept as its purpose, thereby producing the thing.

What justifies this answer? One response is that it is a simple claim Kant makes further (*KU* 5: 372–3) referring back to CPR: "[O]ne can think of causality in only two ways: either according to nature or from freedom" (A532/B560). In CJ, Kant claims that the understanding can conceive of the (mechanical) causality of "efficient causes (*nexus effectivus*)" and reason "that of final causes (*nexus finalis*)" (*KU* 5: 372), and we cannot conceive of "more than these two kinds of causality" (*KU* 5: 373). The claims in the two *Critiques* are distinct insofar as a *final* cause need not be a *first* cause (transcendental freedom). The connection, however, is the concept of *practical freedom*. This concept is grounded on that of transcendental freedom (A533/B561) and we represent the latter in terms of the former (A547/B575). The representation of a causality other than the efficient causality of nature is therefore in terms of "a faculty of determining oneself from oneself, independently of necessitation by sensible impulses" (A534/B562). This is exactly a representation in terms of a will with its own purposes (*KU* 5: 370) which justifies the claim that we conceive of causality either as efficient or final (*KU* 5: 372).[17] It follows that what is contingent in terms of all physical laws can be thought only in terms of an agent's purposes, a point well illustrated by Kant's example of a "regular hexagon drawn in the sand" in an "apparently uninhabited land" (*KU* 5: 370).

Since this introduction of final causes also characterises the thought of a product of *art*,[18] more is needed if the thing in question is a product of *nature*. That is, we need to characterise its being intrinsically purposive, rather than merely relatively purposive for an external designer (see Kreines 2005: 278–80).[19] This defines a second requirement provisionally described as a thing's being "*cause and effect of itself*" (*KU* 5: 370). Kant illustrates this by considering how the tree, *qua* species, or *qua* individual, or *part* of the tree, can be said to produce itself, that is, "both generating itself and being generated by itself ceaselessly" (*KU* 5: 371).

In §65, Kant further clarifies this by indicating that, rather than a concept causing the organisation of the parts within the unity of the whole, as in the case of a product of art, a purpose of nature is characterised by the parts being organised in a way *we can think of* as causing them. That is, the causal role of the concept in the case of the product of art is here taken over by the role played by the formal organisation of the parts as basis for a purposive judgement.[20] Insofar as these are judged as intrinsic and not relative purposes, this second requirement for considering products of nature reflectively as objective purposes, is their being "*self-organizing*" beings (*KU* 5: 374).[21] With this, Kant has introduced a "regulative concept for the reflecting power of judgment" (*KU* 5: 375) when applied to what he calls "organized beings" which are characterised by the fact that they have a "*formative* power" reducible to any "*motive* power" (*KU* 5: 374).

Kant now adds that, insofar as a thing is judged as a purpose of nature, so are its parts: not only does each part "exist [. . .] *for the sake of the others* and on account of the whole" (*KU* 5: 373), as in a product of art, but "each [part] produces the others reciprocally" (*KU* 5: 374). Kant thereby clarifies that the causal connection referred to in the provisional characterisation of a natural purpose (*KU* 5: 370) is judged to be a final cause.[22] To justify this, note that, while each part may, trivially, be viewed as efficient cause of the whole, the latter can be judged only as final cause of the parts required for its existence. The causal link from part to part, which transitively combines these two, is therefore one of final causality. That is, the concept of any thing that is a part of an organised being can be judged as final cause of any other part that is required for its existence, since without this other part, the first one would not be a part of this organised being. Note however that for Kant the condition "required for its existence" is not spelt out, and yet it is necessary for the claim to hold (see final section of this chapter).

With this answer to the question of what provides a further account (beyond mechanism) of the existence of a thing and its necessity, Kant has shown how teleology enables us to judge certain products of nature problematically *as objects*, but as objects constrained by empirical (mechanical) laws under the aegis of final causes: "Organized beings [. . .] thus first provide objective reality to the concept of [. . .] an end of *nature*" (*KU* 5: 376).

5.   The Principles for Judging Intrinsic Purposiveness

Having characterised natural intrinsic (material objective) purposiveness and thereby extended (problematically) the domain of objectivity, Kant needs to clarify the principle guiding judgements of intrinsic purposiveness for the products of nature, that is, the new type of object, analogously to the principles of the pure understanding for the type of object examined in CPR.

In §66, the *principle for purposive judgements of organised beings* is presented: "Nothing in it is in vain" insofar as, in it, "*everything is an end and reciprocally a means*" (*KU* 5: 376). Kant is referring to his earlier claim that reason seeks to cognise not only the product of nature's form, but also the form's necessity (*KU* 5: 370). This principle complements that of "the general doctrine of nature that *nothing* happens by *chance*" (*KU* 5: 376); the latter is a short version of the Second Analogy stating that every event is a rule-governed occurrence.

In §67, Kant shows that, once teleology is invoked for products of nature, it "necessarily leads to the idea of the whole of nature as a system in accordance with the rule of ends," that is, a *principle of the purposiveness of nature*, "to which idea all of the mechanism of nature in accordance with principles of reason must now be subordinated" (*KU* 5: 378–9). The first part of this claim follows from the fact that if a product of nature is judged as purposive, then so must nature which produces it. In this way, hypothetical judgements of extrinsic purposiveness[23] now find a place in relation to what has been judged as a natural purpose (*KU* 5: 378–9). As far as the second part of the claim is concerned, Kant has just reminded us of the universality of the Second Analogy, so the claim of subordination cannot be understood as restricting this universality in any way. Rather, it is a principle that deals with the systematic organisation of nature, and this lies beyond the scope of the Second Analogy (see *KU* 5: 183). The latter principle is therefore subordinated to the systematic organisation defined by the former. Additionally, Kant indicates that the systematicity of nature should be taken as guiding principle of reason independently of our judgements about natural purposes (*KU* 5: 380–1): this is a reminder of the "principles of systematic unity" of nature of CPR which, similarly, rest upon "the purposive unity of things" (A686/B714).

The *principle of purposiveness of nature* is a regulative principle of reflective judgement, designed to enable us to "extend natural science" (*KU* 5: 379, 383). As explained earlier, it enables the consideration of new objects. It judges nature "as if" it were intentionally produced, rather than judging it to be purposively designed by God (*KU* 5: 381).[24] This "principle of teleology" is (i) unlike the principle of the formal purposiveness of nature (*KU* 5: 181–4), that is, of its *subjective* purposiveness for our cognition (Onof 2020: 36), insofar as the former deals with *objective* purposiveness and thereby is "an internal principle of natural science" (*KU* 5: 381); and it is (ii) unlike the regulative principle of the purposive unity of things which has an objective status (A648–50/B676–8) since this deals with the unity of knowledge of what is already an object, while the principle of teleology applies to things that are objectively underdetermined: it enables *reflecting upon them as objects*. It is therefore a subjective principle playing an objective role in natural science,[25] namely that of guiding investigation into products of nature (*KU* 5: 383).[26] Kant does not claim that the introduction of teleology "explains" natural products: it is only insofar as "we could produce" something, that is, in terms of a parts–whole account characteristic of "mechanism,"[27] that we can have complete insight into that thing (*KU* 5: 384). Nevertheless, it enables us to "solve problems" (*KU* 5: 382) by introducing "another method for our use of reason in our investigation" (*KU* 5: 383) and providing insights into nature's "organisation" and systematicity (*KU* 5: 384).[28]

Kant adds that "to avoid even the least suspicion" of introducing any "supernatural cause" into "physics," the intentions referred to in judgements of purposiveness are "ascribe[d] [. . .] to nature, that is, to matter" (*KU* 5: 383). Is this compatible with Kant's also claiming that judging things as natural purposes involves referring them "to a supersensible determining ground" (*KU* 5: 377)? It is on a *dual-aspect* view of the relation between appearances and reality in-itself. While natural science focuses upon appearances, things identified through objective determinations have an intelligible aspect (supersensible basis).

In the following sections, we address two sets of concerns raised by the claims made in CJ's Analytic.

6. Teleology and Determinism

In the Resolution of the Third Antinomy (RTA), Kant claims that

> all the actions of the human being in appearance are determined in accord with the order of nature [. . .]; and if we could investigate all the appearances of his power of choice down to their basis, then there would be no human action that we could not predict with certainty.
>
> (A549–50/B577–8)

The necessity which is claimed here does not seem compatible with the contingency claimed for organised beings and, by implication, human organisms; moreover, the account we provided earlier of the compatibility of the Second Analogy with this contingency does not suffice here because the claim of determinism in the RTA leaves no room for any contingency over and above what empirical laws determine.

To address this issue, first, note that the claim of strong determinism of the RTA (which is not obviously derivable from the Second Analogy) refers to *psychological* determinism (Allison 1990: 31) as the reference to "the appearances of his power of choice" (A549/B577) indicates. This means that when Kant says that this agent's actions are determined, he is referring to the psychological dimension of the action, which we can, for simplicity, think of as the formation of an intention to act involving a representation of the action's purpose. What Kant does not address in the RTA is the further question of the implementation of this intention *in outer sense*.[29] This implementation is the unfolding of an action whose final cause is the agent's purpose. In terms of the causality of *outer sense*, this amounts to a further determination of the behaviour of this agent, *qua organism*, over and above what physical laws of outer sense determine. So it is perfectly compatible with the contingency that Kant identifies in the form of natural products such as organisms. Further, it actually fills in Kant's account of mind-body interaction in terms of a mind-body account (see Ameriks 2000: 89–91).

7. Kant's Analysis of Teleological Judgements and Contemporary Science

There are two important reasons for which some of Kant's claims may appear unsustainable today. First, consider his claim that all the parts of a thing that is a natural purpose have to be purposive. This would seem to be false on two grounds (see Guyer 2005b).

(i) It is well known that organisms may carry inherited features which no longer play any role in sustaining the organism's functions (Muller 2002), such as the appendix in the case of humans (Breitenbach 2009: 35). A teleological account of such features would therefore seem out of place. However, the organism is to be judged not only as organism *qua* individual, but also as organism *qua* member of a species (*KU* 5: 371). In the latter sense, insofar as such features were useful in the survival of an ancestor of an individual organism, they are therefore purposive *for the existence* (as noted earlier) of the species it belongs to. (ii) Relatedly, more and more of the processes (e.g. reproduction, growth) characterising organisms are now being explained causally. A teleological account of such processes would thus seem to be surplus to requirement. However, it is one thing to describe the process of growth of an organism in terms of the role of enzymes, and another to account for this process as a *function* necessary to the organism's and/or species's existence: the latter requires teleological judgements.[30] Kant makes the point forcefully for the simple processes involved in the constitution of structural features of an organism:

> [I]n, e.g., an animal body, many parts could be conceived as consequences of merely mechanical laws [. . .]. Yet the cause that provides the *appropriate* material, modifies it, forms it, and deposits it in its *appropriate* place must always be judged teleologically.
>
> (*KU* 5: 377, our emphasis)[31]

The importance of this passage should not be underestimated as it shows that, however much the processes that support life have been, and will be, given mechanistic explanations, there would be a loss of content in replacing the teleological claim by such mechanistic accounts of supporting processes.[32]

The second issue is the theory of evolution. It has been argued (e.g. Mayr 1974) that the advent of this theory (together with modern genetics) implies that an *a posteriori* explanation can be given which dispenses with any reference to teleology (Breitenbach 2009: 47–8). That is: (i) the purposive arrangement of the parts of the organism is explained as a result of adaptation through variation and natural selection; and (ii) the role of the interaction of parts in the organism's development and survival is explained in terms of processes governed by its genetic code, that is, efficient causality. We have already addressed the second issue. As to the first, variation occurs as a result of random mutations.[33] An appeal to randomness, on its own, disqualifies the account as one in terms of efficient causes. The problem is that what supplements it, that is, accounts of the "errors" in the molecular processes responsible for the replication of DNA for instance, does not explain why rates of mutation result which allow biological species, that is, the objects of biology, to establish themselves (by propagation).[34] In Kant's vocabulary, biology thereby arguably lacks in systematicity (*KU* 5: 381). This causal explanatory gap implies that teleological judgements about the possibility of suitable rates of mutation for the existence of the theory's objects is unavoidable.[35]

While this cannot be discussed further here, we should note the existence of attempts to model optimal rates of mutation by drawing upon the concept of top-down (i.e. whole-part) causality, that is, effects upon parts of a system not fully analysable by considering the parts as "bottom-up" causes (efficient causality as we know it), but requires the system itself to be a top-down cause (Ellis 2012; see also Roth 2014). So, as with Kant's motivation for introducing purposiveness, that is, "contingency in terms of all empirical laws" (*KU* 5: 370) of bottom-up causality, top-down causality would provide the further determination of an account of how "a thing is possible" (*KU* 5: 369). It is fruitful as a mathematical model of how, on certain fitness criteria, optimal rates can be obtained (Ellis 2012: 130).[36] This is a controversial notion which we perhaps cannot understand (see Kim 2006), but as such, it is congenial to Kant's noting that a higher understanding might be able to account in terms of efficient (no longer part-whole) causes for what we can judge only teleologically (*KU* 5: 406ff).

To conclude, the Analytic of Teleological Judgement has shown how reflectively judging nature and some natural products as objective real intrinsic purposes of nature defines regulative principles guiding our investigation of nature. We have dispelled worries about potential conflicts with the Second Analogy and Kant's claims of causal determinism in CPR. That there remain concerns about the compatibility of the use of both teleological and mechanical explanations in natural science is a topic Kant addresses in the Antinomy of Judgement.

Notes

1 We made use of both the Cambridge Edition and Pluhar translations for Kant's *Critique of Judgement* (see respectively Kant 2001, 1987), without explicitly mentioning this wherever this work is quoted. The same holds for the *Critique of Pure Reason*, for which we used the Cambridge edition (Kant 1998), without explicitly mentioning this wherever this work is quoted.

2 One could also use the plural, i.e. refer to *principles*, if we consider the maxims in question as so many principles, hence the plural at *KU* 5: 359.

3 The importance of this essential difference is overlooked by many commentators who thereby take the principle of purposiveness to supersede that of the systematic unity of nature of CPR (e.g. Guyer 2005a) and even contradict it (Horstmann 1989).

4 This is not spelt out in detail in the literature (e.g. Schabel 2006). Callanan (2016: 73–6) correctly indicates that Kant's example of a proof (A716–17/B745) is not a reading-off of a truth from a figure.

5 To be precise, to describe the whole circle, i.e. the two arcs linking A to B, two supplementary angles are required..

6 We agree with Friedman's (2012: 237–8) identification of the role of schemata but, as Carson (1997), not with his equating the function of "iterative [. . .] constructive operations" with that of "quantificational statements."

7 This is the Intersecting Chords Theorem (Shawyer 2010: 14).

8 Cf. the note on Plato in *On a Recently Prominent Tone of Superiority in Philosophy* (*VT* 8: 391).

9 See Breitenbach (2015: 964) for an illuminating account of this as explaining how a geometric "demonstration" can be judged as "beautiful" (*KU* 5: 366).

10 It is noteworthy that Kant uses "thing" rather than "object" here. Indeed, what is at stake is not the further determination of an object, but the thing that the objective determinations identify.

11 This concerns form, but it is not formal purposiveness because it is the form of a real thing, i.e. a matter of real (material) purposiveness.

12 We take it that the Second Analogy affirms that "every occurrence must fall under a causal law" (Allison 2004: 259), but such laws could in principle exhibit orderless diversity (*KU* 5:185).

13 This antinomy deals explicitly with the compatibility of mechanistic and teleological judgements and solves it by clarifying their merely reflective nature, but here, only the tension between contingency and necessity is at stake.

14 This existence is also that of the thing *qua* thing-in-itself on a metaphysical dual-aspect theory (Allais 2015; Onof 2019; Schulting 2021).

15 Further on this topic, see Onof (2022) and Schulting (2018: 299–309).

16 On mechanical inexplicability, see McLaughlin (1990: 152–6) and Ginsborg (2004).

17 We may of course represent as final causality that which is actually natural causality (A803/B931).

18 That the parts are there *only* for the whole also follows from the analysis of relative purposiveness (Kreines 2005: 278–9).

19 This is evident from what we have just indicated, i.e. the fact that what is not mechanical causality for us must be understood as causality from freedom (A532/B560). That is why it is not the purposiveness of the production of artefacts that is used in teleological accounts of natural purposes, but our own purposive activity (see Breitenbach 2009: 43).

20 This is the role the concept of *information* plays in genetics: the spatial arrangement of bases A, C, G and T on the DNA molecule defines a code for the synthesis of proteins; we judge it purposively by saying it codes for these tasks.

21 Our contemporary concept of *self-organised criticality* is different: features of a whole emerge from the mere (mechanical) causal interactions of parts, e.g. in natural swarm behaviour (Johnson and Lam 2010) or social cognition (Marsh and Onof 2008).

22 Angela Breitenbach (2009: 34–5) shows the limitations of Wright's (1973) causal account of biological functions (see below).

23 Categorical judgements of extrinsic purposiveness would require that a natural purpose be determined, that is, a final purpose of nature (*KU* 5: 378; cf. *KU* 5: 434–6).

24 In the light of the principle of teleology, the aesthetic free play of our faculties contemplating nature is now judged as *objectively* purposive (*KU* 5: 380).

25 The mere regulative status of the principle of teleology is consistent with biology's not being a "proper science" for Kant (*MAN* 4: 470; see Illetterati 2014: 96), and its not being dignified with a name separate from physics (*KU* 5: 382).

26 It is not however a pragmatic principle connected with *empirical* limitations of our cognition (Dennett 1993; see Cohen 2007: 118–19), but with *essential* limitations of our *type* of cognition.

27 This conception of mechanism is in line with McLaughlin's (1990: 154ff.) reading of *KU* 5: 408 rather than Teufel's (2011: 223–6). McLaughlin (2014:158–64) finds the relation understanding–space as the most promising key to justifying this conception. We would argue that the issue is: how is the pure category of causality applied to space? While any part is grounded on the whole of space (Onof and Schulting 2015:44), the (figurative) synthesis of such a part is dependent upon a manifold of similarly grounded constituent parts. The supersensible grounds for this are not epistemically accessible (*KU* 5:365).

28 See Kreines (2005: 273).

29 For Kant, "laws of corporeal appearances" must be treated separately from "what belongs merely to inner sense" (A683/B711).

30 Kant thus disagrees that teleological statements can be translated into teleology-free statements, a widespread view in contemporary philosophy of biology (e.g. Wright 1976; see Breitenbach 2009: 37). Geiger (2009: 540–2) shows that Kant's claim that judging a thing as purposive/self-organised is judging something about it we cannot grasp with mere mechanical causality (*KU* 5: 409), namely "how it produces itself," is analytical.

31 "[A]ppropriate" refers to norms. Quarfood (2004: 139–42) shows the problems encountered by purely naturalistic theories (etiological or causal) in accounting for "biological normality."

32 Thus "by reference to mechanical laws we simply cannot make sense of the particular organic dependency relation" (Breitenbach 2009: 42ff). The importance of this dependency explains the development of the concept of a sense of mechanism in contemporary philosophy of biology (Garson 2013).

33 On the theory, these rates themselves are determined through natural selection (Sniegowski *et al.* 2000).

34 One cause of mutation is in the process of DNA replication which involves deletion/replication of nucleotides (building blocks of DNA). A source of "error" is the slippage that occurs in areas of the genome with repetitive nucleotides. Researchers are gaining more understanding of these processes (Ganai and Johansson 2016), but this does not provide a mechanistic explanation of why these occur with frequencies appropriate for the propagation of a species.

35 This is because efficient causality does not provide an account of how such a species can "produce itself"; see footnotes 30–2.

36 The introduction of fitness criteria would imply that the rates of mutation are not merely naturally selected for (see footnote 34). In this respect, note the directed mutation controversy (e.g. Stumpf *et al.* 2007).

References

Allais, L. (2015) *Manifest Reality: Kant's Idealism and his Realism*, Oxford: Oxford University Press.

Allison, H. (1990) *Kant's Theory of Freedom*, Cambridge: Cambridge University Press.

Allison, H. (2004) *Kant's Transcendental Idealism: An Interpretation and Defense*, New Haven and London: Yale University Press.

Ameriks, K. (2000) *Kant's Theory of Mind: An Analysis of the Paralogisms of Pure Reason*, Oxford: Clarendon Press.

Breitenbach, A. (2009) "Teleology in Biology: A Kantian Perspective," *Kant Yearbook* 1: 31–56.

Breitenbach, A. (2015) "Beauty in Proofs: Kant on Aesthetics in Mathematics," *European Journal of Philosophy* 23: 955–77.

Callanan, J. (2016) "Kant on the Acquisition of Geometrical Concepts," in E. Carson and L. Schabel (eds.), *Kant: Studies on Mathematics in the Critical Philosophy*, London: Routledge, pp. 580–604.

Carson, E. (1997) "Kant on Intuition in Geometry," *Canadian Journal of Philosophy* 27(4): 489–512.

Cohen, A.A. (2007) "A Kantian Stance on Teleology and Biology," *South African Journal of Philosophy* 26(2): 109–21.

Dennett, D. (1993) "Evolution, Teleology, Intentionality," *Behavioral and Brain Sciences* 16(2): 389–91.

Ellis, G.F.R. (2012) "Top-Down Causation and Emergence: Some Comments on Mechanisms," *Royal Society: Interface Focus* 2(1): 126–40.

Friedman, M. (2012) "Kant on Geometry and Spatial Intuition," *Synthese* 186: 231–55.

Ganai, R.A. and Johansson, E. (2016) "DNA Replication – A Matter of Fidelity," *Molecular Cell Review* 62: 745–55.

Garson, J. (2013) "The Functional Sense of Mechanism," *Philosophy of Science* 80(3): 317–33.

Geiger, I. (2009) "Is Teleological Judgement (Still) Necessary? Kant's Arguments in the Analytic and in the Dialectic of Teleological Judgement," *British Journal for the History of Philosophy* 17(3): 533–66.

Ginsborg, H. (2004) "Two Kinds of Mechanical Inexplicability in Kant and Aristotle," *Journal of the History of Philosophy* 42(1): 33–65.

Guyer, P. (2005a) *Kant's System of Nature and Freedom: Selected Essays*, Oxford: Oxford University Press.

Guyer, P. (2005b) "Purpose in Nature: What Is Living and What Is Dead in Kant's Teleology?" in *Kant's System of Nature and Freedom: Selected Essays*, Oxford: Blackwell, pp. 343–72.

Horstmann, R.-P. (1989) "Why Must There Be a Transcendental Deduction in Kant's *Critique of Judgment*?" in E. Förster (ed.), *Kant's Transcendental Deductions*, Stanford: Stanford University Press, pp. 157–76.

Illetterati, L. (2014) "Teleological Judgments: Between Technique and Nature," in I. Goy and E. Watkins (eds.), *Kant's Theory of Biology*, Berlin: Walter de Gruyter, pp. 81–98.

Johnson, B.R. and Lam, S.K. (2010) "Self-Organization, Natural Selection and Evolution: Cellular Hardware and Genetic Software," *BioScience* 60(11): 879–85.

Kant, I. (1987) *Critique of Judgment*, W. Pluhar (ed. and trans.), Indianapolis: Hackett.

Kant, I. (1998) *Critique of Pure Reason*, P. Guyer and A.W. Wood (eds. and trans.), Cambridge: Cambridge University Press.

Kant, I. (2001) *Critique of the Power of Judgment*, P. Guyer and E. Matthews (ed. and trans.), Cambridge: Cambridge University Press.

Kim, J. (2006) "On Being Realistic About Emergence," in C.P. Davies (ed.), *The Re-Emergence of Emergence*, Oxford: Oxford University Press, pp. 189–202.

Kreines, J. (2005) "The Inexplicability of Kant's *Naturzweck*: Kant on Teleology, Explanation and Biology," *Archiv für Geschichte der Philosophie* 87: 270–311.

Longuenesse, B. (2005) *Kant and the Human Standpoint*, Cambridge: Cambridge University Press.

Marsh, L. and Onof, C. (2008) "Stigmergic Epistemology, Stigmergic Cognition," *Cognitive Systems Research* 9(1–2): 136–49.

Mayr, C. (1974) "Teleological and Teleonomic. A New Analysis," in R.S. Cohen and M.W. Wartofsky (eds.), *Methodological and Historical Essays in Natural and Social Sciences*, Dordrecht: D. Reidel, pp. 91–117.

McLaughlin, P. (1990) *Kant's Critique of Teleology in Biological Explanation*, Lewiston, NY: Edwin Mellen Press.

McLaughlin, P. (2014) "Mechanical Explanations in the 'Critique of the Teleological Power of Judgement'," in I. Goy and E. Watkins (eds.), *Kant's Theory of Biology*, Berlin: Walter de Gruyter, pp. 149–65.

Muller, G.B. (2002) "Vestigial Organs and Structures," in M. Pagel (ed.), *Encyclopedia of Evolution*, Oxford: Oxford University Press, pp. 1131–3.

Onof, C. (2019) "Reality in-Itself and the Ground of Causality," *Kantian Review* 24(2): 197–222.

Onof, C. (2020) "The Role of Regulative Principles and Their Relation to Reflective Judgement," in S. Baiasu and A. Vanzo (eds.), *Kant and the Continental Tradition: Sensibility, Nature, and Religion*, London: Routledge, pp. 101–30.

Onof, C. (2022) "The Transcendental Synthesis of the Imagination and the Structure of the B Deduction," in G. Motta, D. Schulting and U. Thiel (eds.), *Kant's Transcendental Deduction and the Theory of Apperception: New Interpretations*, Berlin and Boston: Walter de Gruyter, pp. 437–59.

Onof, C. and Schulting, D. (2015) "Space as Form of Intuition and as Formal Intuition: on the Note to B160 in Kant's *Critique of Pure Reason*," *Philosophical Review* 124(1): 1–58.

Quarfood, M. (2004) *Transcendental Idealism and the Organism: Essays on Kant*, Stockholm: Almqvist & Wiksell.

Roth, S. (2014) "Kant, Polanyi, and Molecular Biology," in I. Goy and E. Watkins (eds.), *Kant's Theory of Biology*, Berlin: Walter de Gruyter, pp. 275–92.

Schabel, L. (2006) "Kant's Philosophy of Mathematics," in P. Guyer (ed.), *The Cambridge Companion to Kant and Modern Philosophy*, Cambridge: Cambridge University Press, pp. 94–128.

Schulting, D. (2018) *Kant's Deduction From Apperception: An Essay on the Transcendental Deduction of the Categories*, Berlin and Boston: Walter de Gruyter.

Schulting, D. (2021) *The Bounds of Transcendental Logic*, London/New York: Palgrave.

Shawyer, B. (2010) *Explorations in Geometry*, London: World Scientific.

Sniegowski, P.D., Gerrish, P.J., Johnson, T. and Shaver, A. (2000) "The Evolution of Mutation Rates: Separating Causes from Consequences," *Bioessays* 22(12): 1057–66.

Stumpf, J.D., Poteete, A.R. and Foster, P.L. (2007) "Amplification of Lac Cannot Account for Adaptive Mutation to Lac+ in Escherichia Coli," *Journal of Bacteriology* 189(6): 2291–9.

Teufel, T. (2011) "What is the Problem of Teleology in Kant's Critique of the Teleological Power of Judgment?" *SATS: Nordic Journal of Philosophy* 12: 198–236.

Wright, L. (1973) "Functions," *Philosophical Review* 82: 139–68.

Wright, L. (1976) *Teleological Explanations: An Etiological Analysis of Goals and Functions*, Berkeley: University of California Press.

Further Reading

John D. McFarland's, *Kant's Concept of Teleology* (Edinburgh University Press, 1970), is a classical study of the concept of 'teleology' in Kant's first *Critique*, some of the minor works and in the third *Critique*.

Kant's views on biological teleology are placed in the larger context of transcendental idealism by Marcel Quarfood in his *Transcendental Idealism and the Organism. Essays on Kant* (Stockholm: Almqvist & Wiksell, 2004).

Luca Illetterati, "Teleological Judgments: Between Technique and Nature," in I. Goy and E. Watkins (eds.), *Kant's Theory of Biology* (Berlin: Walter de Gruyter, 2014), pp. 81–98, shows the philosophical interest and contemporary relevance of Kant's discussion of the methodology of biology.

In her paper "Teleology in Biology: A Kantian Perspective" (*Kant Yearbook* (2009) 1: 31–56), Angela Breitenbach addresses the contemporary discussion of the concept of function in the philosophy of biology and shows that by not interpreting teleology naturalistically, Kant's approach can make a positive contribution to it.

22

TELEOLOGICAL POWER OF JUDGMENT – DIALECTIC

Thomas Teufel

★★★

1. Introduction

The "Dialectic of the Teleological Power of Judgment" (*KU* 5: 385, §§69–78) is the second of three main parts of the "Critique of the Teleological Power of Judgment,"[1] which itself is the second of two parts – Aesthetics and Teleology – of the *Critique of the Power of Judgment*. Following the model of the *Critique of Pure Reason* and the *Critique of Practical Reason*, the teleological Dialectic is positioned between an Analytic[2] and a Method.[3] A Transcendental Analytic is concerned with a phenomenological and conceptual analysis of the type of cognition under investigation in the respective *Critique*[4] – in the present case, teleological judging. A Transcendental Method is concerned with principles of the proper use of that type of cognition.[5] The principal task of a Transcendental Dialectic, in this scheme, is to address certain "sophistical" (A339/B397) forms of reasoning associated with that type of cognition that must be disarmed before principles of its proper use can be canvassed.[6] Central among those sophistical forms of reasoning are antithetical conflicts Kant calls antinomies. In the case of the teleological Dialectic, Kant identifies one such antithetical conflict. The central task of the teleological Dialectic is the presentation and resolution of this teleological[7] antinomy.

Formally speaking, all Kantian antinomies consist in the confrontation of a thesis with a contradictorily opposed antithesis – together with the observation that our human intellects are unavoidably committed to the truth of both. The task of a Transcendental Dialectic is, then, to show that what at first appears to be a potentially crippling epistemic predicament can nevertheless be resolved with the help of transcendental philosophy. Even then, the opposing positions unavoidably continue to *appear* to be in conflict because we naturally continue to take each at face value. Transcendental philosophy serves as the reminder that face-value (in Kant's terms, 'dogmatic') interpretations of the antithetical positions are not, in fact, reflective of any deeper epistemic truth. However unavoidable they may be, such interpretations are in fact a mistake (not unlike the mistaken perceptual judgments involved in, say, the Müller-Lyer or the moon illusion).[8] An antinomical conflict, in short, is the "natural and unavoidable" (*KU* 5: 340) appearance of a nevertheless transcendental-philosophically resolvable contradiction. Since it is thus concerned with rationally

DOI: 10.4324/9781003406617-28

dispelling misleading appearances, Kant also calls the dialectical portion of a transcendental Critique a "logic of illusion" (A61/B86; A293/B249).

But there is an important difference between the illusions Kant dispels in the first two *Critiques* and the antinomy Kant seeks to resolve in the Teleology of the third *Critique*; giving the latter resolution special urgency. The conflicts at the heart of Kant's previous antinomies are symptoms of deeply entrenched dogmatisms that transcendental philosophy has come on the scene to expose. While the contradictorily opposed positions are generated by the nature of reason itself, their opposition proves pernicious only because of the dogmatic rationalist or dogmatic empiricist interpretations we naturally give to them. Transcendental critique, as the critique of these interpretations, is, then, the critique of dogmatism. By contrast, the antinomy at the heart of the teleological Dialectic is the natural and unavoidable appearance of a contradiction that arises on the grounds of critical philosophy *itself*. Neither of the contradictorily opposed positions is generated by reason and its outsize ambitions, both are instead fully supported by due principles of transcendental philosophy.

This has two important consequences. First, the stakes of the teleological Dialectic in the third *Critique* are different than those in the Dialectics of the first and second *Critique*. Had transcendental philosophy proved unable to resolve dogmatic conflicts in the first and second *Critique*, it would have proved to be an ineffective philosophical tool for ridding *reason* of contradiction. By contrast, were transcendental philosophy to prove unable to resolve the contradiction at the heart of the teleological Dialectic, it would prove to be an ineffective philosophical tool for ridding *itself* of contradiction. It would, in consequence (absent other, non-transcendental resolutions), prove to be a self-contradictory philosophical tool. Second, and related, since both thesis and antithesis are duly critical positions, the resolution of the antinomy in the teleological Dialectic cannot consist in showing that dogmatic interpretations of these positions are a mistake.[9] The resolution does not lie in a critical re-interpretation of competing dogmatic positions but in a transcendental-logical re-interpretation of (the scope of) competing critical positions.

Moving from these broadly formal considerations to matters of content, we must ask what the teleological antinomy is about. The deepest source of the antinomy in the teleological Dialectic is Kant's introduction of a new fundamental principle into critical philosophy – the transcendental "principle of the purposiveness of nature" (*KU* 5: 181), governing the newly introduced "reflecting power of judgment" (*KU* 5: 180). This principle is predicated on a non-mechanistic form of causality, namely, purposiveness, or "the causality of a concept with respect to its object" (*KU* 5: 210).[10] The principle's attribution of this non-mechanistic form of causality to nature makes the reflecting power of judgment sit *prima facie* uneasy vis-à-vis transcendental philosophy's foundational commitment to the principle of nature's universal mechanism.

That the teleological antinomy traces, respectively, to the reflecting power of judgment (specifically, to the transcendental principle of nature's purposiveness) and to the understanding (specifically, to the transcendental causal principle in the guise of the principle of universal mechanism)[11] – and, so, is at bottom a conflict *between* those cognitive faculties – is reflected in the antinomy's title. Kant does not call it an 'Antinomy of Teleology,' as parallelism with the "Antinomy of Taste" (*KU* 5: 338) in the Critique of the Aesthetic Power of Judgment would suggest. Instead, Kant reserves the honorific "antinomy of the reflecting power of judgment" (*KU* 5: 387) for this latest conflict, tying it to the cognitive faculty itself, rather than merely to one of its applications. The titular suggestion is that the antinomy in the teleological Dialectic has deeper roots than the antinomy in the aesthetic Dialectic, namely, that it is *the* antinomy in the *Critique of the* (Reflecting) *Power of Judgment*:[12] the place where reflecting cognition is finally shown in its dialectical complications.

Tension between transcendental philosophy's mechanistic and teleological commitments had, to be sure, been palpable throughout the third *Critique*. It finally bursts into the open in the Teleology as a question about the scope and limits of judging natural structures and processes according to mechanistic principles alone. The immediate catalyst for this question is the apparent necessity of appealing to non-mechanistic (specifically, teleological) principles when investigating organisms in nature. Kant introduces the prospect of such a necessity in the Analytic of the Teleological Power of Judgment.[13] We consider organic structures and processes in functional (i.e., non-mechanistic, teleological) terms with a seemingly inevitable literalism that does not extend to our study of *non*-organic natural structures and processes. We consider biological organisms – but not mountain ranges, weather systems or planetary orbits – "natural purposes" (*KU* 5: 369).

But while Kant's introduction, in the Analytic of the Teleological Power of Judgment, of the *prospect* of the necessity of non-mechanistic judgments of organic structures and processes in nature suffices to identify the structure of a *potentially* antinomical conflict between principles of mechanistic and non-mechanistic judging, it does not yet suffice to show that we are dealing with a genuine antinomy. This is because Kant does not *justify* the purported necessity of non-mechanistic judging in the Analytic of the Teleological Power of Judgment.[14]

Moreover, while the warrant for the necessity of non-mechanistic judging can, in the framework of the third *Critique*, only come from the transcendental principle of nature's purposiveness, the nature of the link between particular teleological judgments and the transcendental principle of nature's purposiveness remains, up to this point in the third *Critique*, fully mysterious. Before Kant can show that the *prima facie* conflict between mechanistic and non-mechanistic judging of organic processes raises a genuine question about the mutual consistency of the transcendental causal principle and the transcendental principle of purposiveness, he must show that appealing to non-mechanistic principles in judging organic processes is necessary and rooted in the transcendental principle of purposiveness.

These desiderata determine the structure of the teleological Dialectic as well as of the remainder of this chapter. After an initial presentation of the teleological antinomy in §§69–71 (see section 2, next), Kant first considers transcendental-logically *un*-justified teleological judgments in §§72–74 (see section 3), followed by an account of transcendental-logically *justified* teleological judgments in §§75–77 (see section 4); this, finally, puts him in a position to resolve the antinomy in §78 (see section 5).

2. The Teleological Antinomy (§§69–71)

The alleged necessity of judging particular organic processes in nature teleologically conjures a patent but initially unspecific threat of a conflict with universal mechanism. Kant's first task in the teleological Dialectic is to present this conflict with formal precision as one fit for treatment in the dialectical portion of a transcendental critique – namely, as the natural and unavoidable appearance of a logical contradiction that is (nevertheless) open to transcendental-philosophical resolution.

Kant's strategy for accomplishing this has, however, traditionally left his commentators at a loss. That is because Kant formulates the conflict between competing interpretations of nature's mechanism in terms of merely "regulative principles" (*KU* 5: 387) or subjective "maxims" (*KU* 5: 387) of the reflecting power of judgment:

> *The first maxim* is the *thesis*: All generation of material things and their forms must be judged possible in accordance with merely mechanistic laws.
>
> *The second maxim* is the *antithesis*: Some products of material nature cannot be judged as possible according to merely mechanistic laws (judging them requires an entirely different law of causality, namely that of final causes).
>
> (*KU* 5: 387)

Before considering the claims of these maxims more closely, we must address three preliminaries concerning (*a*) their normative force, (*b*) the nature of their opposition, and (*c*) the conception of mechanism espoused in them.

First, it is clear that the two regulative maxims would be fully compatible (indeed, complementary) if they were merely heuristic principles; that is to say, if they were merely subjectively necessary methodological recommendations, and not rationally binding in any stronger sense than that. Since many treat a principle's regulativity as tantamount to such mere heuristicity, one of the perennial difficulties commentators confront in Kant's teleological antinomy is to show how patently compatible principles can possibly give rise to an unavoidable appearance of a contradiction. The literature is replete with imaginative solutions to this problem.[15]

But the problem is manifestly not Kant's. For Kant, a principle's regulativity indicates its domain. Regulative principles govern a *subjective* domain: acts of (reflecting or determining) judgment. *Qua* judgment-determining principles, they are *practical* principles (as opposed to object-determining, theoretical principles); specifically, they are technical-practical principles of cognitive conduct: they instruct cognitive agents how to judge in given circumstances and under the presupposition of given ends of judging.

It is evident even from a cursory look at Kant's presentation in the third *Critique* that being subjective in this sense does not restrict a principle's normative force to a merely subjective form of necessity. Exhibit A in this regard is the principle of nature's purposiveness itself. *Qua* principle of the reflecting power of judgment governing exercises of judgment, it is a *regulative* principle, or a merely "subjective principle (maxim)" (*KU* 5: 184). *Qua* supreme principle of the reflecting power of judgment it is, however, *a priori* and fully transcendentally necessary; or so Kant hopes to show in his "deduction" (*KU* 5: 184) of it.[16] A principle's subjective domain does not entail a merely subjective form of necessity; nor does its transcendental necessity entail constitutivity.[17] While all heuristic (i.e., subjectively necessary) principles are *eo ipso* regulative (i.e., judgment-determining) principles, not all regulative principles are *eo ipso* heuristic. *A fortiori*, the regulativity of the maxims in the antinomy of the reflecting power of judgment does not, by itself, entail that they are merely methodological recommendations either. As we will see, their bindingness is, instead, a form of technical-practical necessity; and this fully suffices to make them contradictory opposites.

Turning to the nature of that opposition, it is clear, second, that the antinomy does not arise from the confrontation of two different maxims – one mechanistic, one teleological – but from different interpretations of the same, mechanistic maxim. For convenience, I will call this underlying maxim the Maxim of Mechanistic Judging.[18] It takes the form of a hypothetical imperative of cognitive conduct. As both the thesis and the antithesis suggest, this imperative is binding for investigators of nature concerned with an explanation of "the generation of material things and their forms" or of "products of material nature" (*KU* 5: 387). Investigators who seek to understand the generation or production of material things are engaged in a science of origins Kant calls "natural history" (*KU* 5: 428). The demand of the Maxim of Mechanistic Judging can be formulated as the instrumental imperative: "if you seek to judge causal origins in nature, then you must judge them in accordance with mechanistic laws."

The antinomical conflict in the teleological Dialectic arises because the consequent of this instrumental imperative can be given an unlimited (thesis) interpretation or a limited (antithesis) interpretation. According to the thesis interpretation, "*All* [causal origins in nature] must be judged [. . .] in accordance with merely mechanistic laws" (*KU* 5: 387; my emphasis). According to the antithesis interpretation, "*Some* [causal origins in nature] cannot be judged [. . .] according to merely mechanistic laws" (*KU* 5: 387; my emphasis).

The teleological alternative, which Kant adds parenthetically to the antinomy's antithesis position, presents the reason why one might think to limit the sway of the Maxim of Mechanistic Judging. It thus points forward to the resolution of the antinomical conflict. But it is important to note that it does not contribute to the logical presentation of the antinomy itself. Formally speaking, then, since the antinomy in the teleological Dialectic arises from unlimited and limited interpretations of an underlying Maxim of Mechanistic Judging, it is, in all strictness, an antinomy of mechanism.

Third, the conception of mechanism at issue in the teleological antinomy is best understood in light of Kant's discussion of causal principles in the introduction to the third *Critique*. Kant there distinguishes a "transcendental" (*KU* 5: 181) from a "metaphysical" version of the causal principle governing "bodies as substances" (*KU* 5: 181). According to the transcendental version, "their alteration must have a cause" (*KU* 5: 181). According to the metaphysical version, "their alteration must have an *external* cause" (*KU* 5: 181; my emphasis). The difference between the two principles is that the metaphysical causal principle substitutes "the empirical concept of a body (as a moveable thing in space)" for the merely "ontological predicate" (*KU* 5: 181) of a substance. This transforms the relevant conception of cause into that of an inert, transeunt, material cause, thus issuing in a formulation of causal mechanism already familiar from Kant's Second Law of Mechanics: "Every change of matter has an external cause" (*MAN* 4: 543).[19]

Let us now turn to the claims of the contradictorily opposed maxims themselves in order to see just which position concerning mechanistic judging each advocates. For the thesis, this task is relatively straightforward. Its claim is nothing but the first *Critique's* commitment to universal causal mechanism turned into a research-guiding imperative. This imperative demands, with technical-practical bindingness (i.e., on pain of practical irrationality, or of willing the end without willing the universally necessary means to that end),[20] that anyone engaged in the project of natural history or of investigating the causal ancestry of natural objects must in *all* explanations of that ancestry appeal *only* to mechanistic causal laws. The justification for that demand stems from the category of causality subject to the specifications of the metaphysical causal principle, according to which natural causes are *all and only* mechanistic. Not only are mechanistic explanations thus universally necessary for a natural account of the phenomena in question, they are, moreover, universally sufficient: no non-mechanistic causes (whether dynamical, psychological, teleological, or supernatural) are to be permitted in our explanation of causal ancestries in nature.

The contours of the antinomy of the teleological Dialectic become clearer when we consider just which part of the thesis the antithesis opposes. Here the textual facts are perhaps surprising, given how widely Kant is believed to be advocating a form of "Mechanical Inexplicability" (Ginsborg 2015: 281) of organic processes in nature and a corresponding form of neo-Aristotelian realism about teleological causes.[21] As it turns out, the antithesis does *not* call into question (instead, it fully concedes) the universal necessity of mechanistic judging *even* of organic processes in nature.

In his explication of the antithesis, following his presentation of the antinomy, Kant insists that recognizing the occasional necessity of non-mechanistic judging does *not* mean that "those forms [of organic nature] would not be possible in accordance with the mechanism of nature" (*KU* 5: 388), nor that "reflection in accordance with the first maxim is thereby suspended" (*KU* 5: 388). But reflection in accordance with the first maxim would be suspended whenever non-mechanistic judging of causal origins in nature proves necessary, if the point of the antithesis were to say that such cases limit the universal *necessity* of the maxim of mechanistic judging. By insisting that reflection in accordance with the first maxim is *not* "thereby" (*KU* 5: 388) suspended, Kant emphasizes that the antithesis only disputes the universal *sufficiency* of the maxim of mechanistic judging. The antithesis thus invokes the possibility of phenomena with respect to which an alternative form of judging is occasionally *co*-necessary. Nor should this be surprising. After all, the antithesis denies the possibility of judging organic processes "according to *merely* mechanistic laws" (*KU* 5: 387; my emphasis) – it does not deny the possibility (nor, for that matter, the necessity) of judging them according to mechanistic laws altogether.

To sum up, the thesis *proclaims*, while the antithesis *denies*, that mechanistic judging of the generation of material things in nature is both universally necessary *and* universally sufficient. Kant's task for the remainder of the teleological Dialectic is, then, twofold. First, Kant needs to show that the appearance of this conflict is indeed unavoidable. That is to say, Kant needs to show that mechanistic and *non*-mechanistic (specifically teleological) forms of judging the generation of material things in nature are indeed occasionally *co*-necessary. Failing that, the thesis would be vindicated, as it would always prove to be both necessary *and* sufficient to judge causal ancestries in nature mechanistically. The apparent necessity of appealing to non-mechanistic patterns of explanation when addressing organic processes in nature would then turn out to be just that: a perhaps alluring or expedient but ultimately ungrounded and misleading fiction. No genuinely antinomical conflict would consequently arise in the teleological Dialectic. Any deeper role for the principle of nature's purposiveness in biological explanation and for teleology at large would turn out to be imaginary.

Second, Kant needs to show that this conflict is transcendental-philosophically resolvable. That is to say, he needs to show how the occasional necessity of *non*-mechanistic judging (if any) *can* coexist with the unceasing necessity of *mechanistic* judging to which both thesis and antithesis are committed. The problem addressed in Kant's teleological Dialectic is, accordingly, how students of natural history can possibly be required to judge organic processes in nature both mechanistically *and* non-mechanistically *at the same time*.

3.   Dogmatism – Transcendental-logically *Un*-Justified Forms of Teleological Judging (§§72–74)

Kant seeks to establish the necessity of non-mechanistic (specifically, teleological) forms of judging by following a two-pronged strategy. In the present section, I discuss the first, negative part of this strategy, pursued in §§72–4. Starting with the phenomenological fact (analyzed but not justified in the transcendental Analytic) of the "similarity to purposes that we find in [nature's] products" (*KU* 5: 390), Kant now surveys a range of *illegitimate* ways in which one might seek to justify that similarity. Kant's account of these illegitimate ways of justifying the purpose-likeness of nature – or of nature's "technique" (*KU* 5: 390), as Kant now calls it – is itself divided into two parts. While Kant considers all illegitimate attempts to ground teleological judging under the heading of dogmatism, he splits them into a set of four traditional metaphysical dogmatisms (§§72–3) and into a form of dogmatism that (perhaps surprisingly) arises within critical philosophy itself. This 'critical dogmatism' consists, roughly, in teleology considered under first-*Critique* strictures but as yet in the absence of its proper third-*Critique* justification (§74).

It is hard to suppress the suspicion that Kant embarks on his discussion of the four non-critical, metaphysical dogmatisms primarily out of a desire to give his account a veneer of historical completeness. Kant is fully explicit about the fact that none of these traditional views could conceivably qualify as an interpretation of either the antinomy's thesis or antithesis position. After all, both thesis and antithesis derive from the duly critical metaphysical causal principle, which itself derives from the transcendental causal principle (see section 2 earlier in the chapter). Moreover, both thesis and antithesis are subjective, regulative principles. *Ex hypothesi*, principles of traditional metaphysical dogmatism do not satisfy either of these criteria. Accordingly, even by the lights of Kant's *via negativa* in §§72–4, his demonstration that dogmatic metaphysical interpretations of teleology must be considered illegitimate at best illuminates the overall lay of the philosophical land, but it does not advance Kant's own argument by much.

The first two of the four metaphysical dogmatisms Kant discusses in §§72–3 are what, today, we would consider reductivist or deflationist positions. The two views consider teleological properties in nature as *not* metaphysically real and, so, as merely apparent or ideal. The consequent "idealism of purposiveness" (*KU*: 5: 391) holds that teleological judging is not grounded in any kind of genuine purposive causality. Instead, the "similarity to purposes that we find in [nature's] products" (*KU* 5: 390) either has a purely accidental, natural ground or, conversely, a non-accidental, non-natural ("hyper-physical," *KU* 5: 392) ground. Kant calls the first of these idealisms "casuality" (*KU* 5: 391) and identifies it with the views of Epicurus and Democritus; he calls the second "fatality" (*KU* 5: 391) and identifies it with Spinoza.

Since purposiveness, for Kant, names a type of causality that *concepts* can exhibit with respect to their objects, any non-critical, dogmatic explanation of nature's apparent purposiveness must appeal to an actual intellect as the locus of the causally efficacious concepts so posited. By that measure, however, casuality fails entirely since it seeks to ground the purpose-like character of organic beings in "blind chance" (*KU* 5: 393); consequently, "nothing is explained" (*KU* 5: 393). Fatality fares marginally better, since it locates the source of everything in nature in the unity of the divine intellect. Unfortunately, Spinoza's divine intellect is itself governed by "blind necessity" (*KU* 5: 394) which (much like casuality's blind chance) is inconsistent with the volitional contingency inherent in a form of causality whose efficaciousness is determined by antecedent representations of its effects.

The remaining two metaphysical dogmatisms treat teleological properties in nature as real. The consequent "realism of purposiveness" (*KU* 5: 391) then either finds a genuine "analogue of a faculty acting in accordance with an intention" (*KU* 5: 392) in natural beings themselves, or else posits "an intentionally productive (originally living) intelligent being" (*KU* 5: 392) outside of nature. Kant calls the former position, which considers matter itself to be alive, "hylozoism" (*KU* 5: 392), and identifies the latter as "theism" (*KU* 5: 392). According to Kant, hylozoism is self-contradictory, since the idea of "a living matter" (*KU* 5: 394) contradicts matter's essential inertia. Of all the non-critical dogmatisms Kant discusses, only theism is considered at least minimally intellectually respectable. While theism's dogmatic conception of a creator-God is open to neither empirical confirmation nor logical proof – and, so, fails as a proper theoretical grounding of teleology – it is at least not self-contradictory.

Kant's discussion of *critical* dogmatism in §74 is more informative. The notion of 'critical dogmatism' is, of course, perplexing. In order to allow for it, Kant now considers "dogmatic" the use of any concept that is "lawful for the determining [. . .] power of judgment" (*KU* 5: 395). This significantly broadens Kant's first-*Critique* conception of dogmatism. Kant in effect now claims that *all* determining judgments – whether metaphysical in the sense discredited by the *Critique of Pure Reason* or *a priori* and constitutive in the sense championed there – are *dogmatic* judgments. Framing dogmatism in this way has two advantages. First, it brings the rather unusual teleological Dialectic (which arises on the grounds of critical philosophy itself), in line with Dialectics of yore by casting its resolution as an instance of vanquishing dogmatism. While this may seem disingenuous, it has the important second advantage of suggesting that what ailed earlier attempts at grounding teleology was not so much the nature of the ground sought (whether unduly metaphysical or duly critical) but failure to understand the nature of the judgments to be so grounded.

For, the flip side of Kant's broadened definition of dogmatism is a tightened conception of criticism. Kant now says that the critical treatment of a concept is "that which is lawful merely for the reflecting power of judgment" (*KU* 5: 396). The momentous nature of this definition for Kant's critical philosophy can hardly be overstated. Since Kant evidently does not seek to withdraw the title of 'Critique' from his earlier towering achievements (by now exposing critical philosophy before 1790 as so many iterations of illicit dogmatisms), Kant's point can only be that what made those earlier *Critiques* 'critical' is subject to reevaluation in light of the discovery of the new reflecting power of judgment. Specifically, Kant now recognizes the regulativity (i.e., the judgment-determining nature) of *all* ostensibly theoretical transcendental principles canvassed in critical philosophy – including the regulativity of constitutive transcendental principles (i.e., of the categories). While this may sound like a contradiction in terms (indeed, like heresy!) by the standards of the Appendix to the Transcendental Dialectic of the *Critique of Pure Reason*, the central takeaway from Kant's *Critique of the Power of Judgment* – Kant's *mature* exploration of the topic of regulativity – is that 'constitutive' and 'regulative' are not *co*-ordinate but *sub*-ordinate concepts. Constitutive principles are not *opposed to* – they are a *kind of* – regulative principle (namely, the kind that determines determining judgments).

Concerning the matter at hand, Kant's new account of the critical use of concepts means that teleological judgments cannot be given "objective reality" (*KU* 5: 396), because the concept of a natural purpose cannot be abstracted from experience.[22] The concept of a natural purpose must, instead, be considered "in relation to our cognitive faculties, hence in relation to the subjective conditions for thinking it" (*KU* 5: 395). *Qua* critical concept, the concept of a natural purpose must, more specifically, be considered in relation to the reflecting power of judgment. But if teleological judgments are thus not exercises of the determining power of judgment and instead stand under principles of, or are "lawful merely for" (*KU* 5: 396), the reflecting power of judgment, then their legitimacy (if any) can only derive from the legitimacy (if any) of that reflecting power. Exploring the link between teleology and the reflecting power of judgment and its principle is, accordingly, the line of thought Kant must pursue in the second, positive part of his attempt to establish the necessity of non-mechanistic, specifically teleological forms of judging.

4. Criticism – Transcendental-logically *Justified* Forms of Teleological Judging (§§75–77)

Sections 75–7 contain some of the richest and most deeply suggestive, but also some of the densest and least perspicuous passages in all of Kant's critical oeuvre. The ostensible reason for this is that Kant here must not only ground the necessity of particular teleological judgments of biological nature in the necessity of the transcendental principle of nature's purposiveness, but that this requires him to justify the transcendental necessity of the principle of nature's purposiveness itself – a task he did not manage to complete in the principle's official transcendental deduction in §V of the Introduction to the *Critique of the Power of Judgment*.[23] His success on both of these scores can charitably be described as mixed. In the end, the Dialectic contains at best an intriguing hint at Kant's envisioned strategy for a transcendental deduction of the principle of nature's purposiveness and even less of a hint at how singular reflecting teleological judgments may be related to that transcendental principle.

Kant revisits the matter of the transcendental necessity of the principle of nature's purposiveness in §§76–7 by discussing the "special character" (*KU* 5: 405), "peculiarity" (*KU* 5: 407), and "constitution" (*KU* 5: 399, 407) of our human understanding. In simplest terms, the character of our human understanding is discursive. This means that the understanding subsumes (representations of) particular, spatio-temporally located or locatable individuals under pure and empirical concepts in determining judgments. While the act of integrating sensible and conceptual representations (intuitions and concepts) into judgments is combinatorial – hence, synthetic – the fact that we do not ourselves generate the intuitive content for our cognitive judgments and instead are fundamentally receptive with respect to that content means that the basic direction of our combinatorial activity goes *from* concepts *to* objects: we bring our conceptualizations *to* the world of sense. In that regard, our understanding is analytic, "it must go from the analytical universal (from concepts) to the particular" (*KU* 5: 404, see *KU* 5: 408).

But if our intellects thus determine an infinitely rich sensible manifold by means of merely finitely complex concepts, then much in that manifold must *ex hypothesi* remain conceptually *un*-determined, while our concepts (and theories), conversely, remain intuitively *under*-determined.[24] Kant puts the point this way: "the particular as such contains something contingent with regard to the universal" (*KU* 5: 404). This contingency of the particular suggests an arbitrariness in the organization of conceptual schemes that, perhaps most worryingly, threatens to undermine the claim to necessity inherent in our empirical causal laws. Addressing this threat, Kant notes at the end of §76 that such arbitrariness must be counteracted by a non-arbitrariness assumption concerning the "unity, hence lawfulness, in the connection of particular laws of nature (which lawfulness of the contingent is called purposiveness)" (*KU* 5: 404). Unfortunately, just as in Kant's "deduction" of the "transcendental concept of a purposiveness of nature" (*KU* 5: 184) in the Introduction, this line of thought at best presents a cognitive desideratum, it does not by itself constitute a cogent transcendental deduction[25] – and Kant knows it.

In focusing on the peculiarity of our human understanding, a thought that had been in the background in the Introduction now comes to the fore – and Kant pursues it single-mindedly in his justly famous §77. For, in considering the contingency of "the particular" (*das Besondere*), Kant no longer simply means the particularity of individual laws of nature or of individual spatio-temporal objects – particulars which involve already more or less extensive conceptualization. Instead, Kant now considers the universal and the particular as "two entirely heterogeneous elements . . . required for the exercise of [our cognitive] faculties" (*KU* 5: 402). That is to say, he now explores the point of contact between conceptual universality and sensible particularity "as such" (*KU* 5: 404). And to do *that* is to treat sensible particularity – or what he now calls "the manifoldness of . . . the particular (of the given empirical intuition)" (*KU* 5: 407) – as utterly un-synthesized sensible content.[26]

Kant's surprising claim about sensible particularity at this foundational level is that "through the universal of our (human) understanding the particular is *not determined*" (*KU* 5: 406, my emphasis), or, again, that our discursive understanding "*determines nothing* with respect to the manifoldness of [the particular of the given empirical intuition]" (*KU* 5: 407, my emphasis). Kant's claim here is not simply that the particular at this foundational level can be determined in a variety of incommensurate or even inconsistent ways. Kant's claim is that it would not be possible to determine the particular in this sense *at all* – the particular in this sense would remain strictly *un*-determinable – were it not for the intervention of a transcendental principle of nature's purposiveness.

The thought is surprising, because, according to Kant's official account in the *Critique of Pure Reason*, the understanding begins its determining business precisely when its spontaneous syntheses "run through and then . . . take together" (A99) an as yet un-synthesized sensible manifold. The spontaneity of these syntheses means that no further transcendental-logical justification or governing principle is necessary – nor, on pain of regress, possible – in order to account for the understanding's cognitive syntheses.

What, then, might the transcendental-philosophical problem lurking in the particular "as such" that Kant's transcendental principle of nature's purposiveness is supposed to address be? Unfortunately, Kant does not say. But if one considers Kant's remarks on sensible particularity over the course of the third *Critique* in their totality, one can glean the following. There is a transcendentally necessary assumption present in all our cognitive syntheses that is neither a conceptual determination (because all conceptual determination instead presupposes it), nor a sensible intuition (because, *qua* assumption, it is an exercise of our higher cognitive powers). The assumption is that intuitive manifolds – or the 'manifoldness of the particular of the given empirical intuition' – in fact *are* manifolds; which is to say: that they exhibit at least minimal apprehensible structure.

Kant's negative insight in the third *Critique* is that, by the principles of his earlier theoretical philosophy, we are not entitled to this assumption on either intuitive or demonstrative grounds. Kant's positive insight is that it is an assumption of nature's *purposiveness*, because the only way we can think of anything as exhibiting any structure at all – even minimal apprehensible structure – is to consider it as the effect or product of an associated structuring concept. And Kant's technical term for that type of causality is purposiveness.[27] It is thus an assumption that governs *any* determining synthesis, without itself being a determining synthesis. It is, in short, not an object-determining or constitutive principle of the understanding, but a judgment-determining or regulative assumption of the reflecting power of judgment – albeit a transcendentally necessary regulative assumption, since, without it, there could be no determining syntheses and, hence, no cognition at all (empirical or otherwise).

Now, assuming that something like this were to explain the claim and transcendental status of the principle of nature's purposiveness, it still leaves the question of the necessity of singular teleological judgments unanswered. We know that this necessity cannot be grounded in any empirically discernible features of biological phenomena. To be sure, even Kant had initially suggested such features, pointing to organisms' peculiar form of reciprocal causality in §65 of the Analytic. But it is sometimes overlooked that this is part of a *reductio* that leads the whole notion of empirical markers of purposiveness *ad absurdum* by the end of that same section. While Kant notes that judging "some forms of nature" (*KU* 5: 387) in accordance with teleological principles is necessary "upon occasional prompting" (*KU* 5: 387), his fundamental tenet concerning nature's purposiveness is not only that purposiveness is not a 'dogmatic' concept for the determining power of judgment – but that "such a thing cannot be perceived" (*KU* 5: 189). Neither subject to the understanding's determining syntheses nor perceptible, the 'occasional prompting' which necessitates teleological judging is, accordingly, not the sort that could possibly be part of self-conscious human experience if all our intellects had to go by were the spatio-temporal and categorial cognitive framework presented in the *Critique of Pure Reason*. Kant's suggestion (borne out in his resolution to the Antinomy in §78) is that the necessity of particular teleological judgments of biological phenomena is instead the consequence of a human cognitive apparatus equipped with a transcendental principle of nature's purposiveness, which, so equipped, now resonates with aspects of "the supersensible" (*KU* 5: 412) that would otherwise remain beyond the reach of self-conscious human awareness.

Unfortunately, just what the nature of that resonance may be is not addressed in the Dialectic of the Teleological Power of Judgment. Instead, Kant treats the necessity of teleological judgments that register it as if it were a straightforward consequence of his account and not in need of further explanation. Much the same holds for the *apriority* of reflecting aesthetic judgments of natural and artistic beauty in the Critique of the Aesthetic Power of Judgment. This suggests that both forms of *a priori* reflecting judgment in the third *Critique* – *a priori* reflecting (aesthetic) judgments of a purposiveness *without* purpose, and *a priori* reflecting (teleological) judgments of a purposiveness *with* purpose – are consequences of an interaction between the transcendental principle of nature's purposiveness and supersensible reality whose character can only be determined by a holistic interpretation of the third *Critique*; an interpretation that exceeds the scope of what can be attempted here.

5. Resolution of the Antinomy (§78)

Kant's appeal to the supersensible does, however, provide the clue to his straightforward resolution of the antinomy of the reflecting power of judgment. According to the thesis position, abiding by the maxim of mechanistic judging is both universally necessary and universally sufficient for judging the generation of material entities in nature. The antithesis concedes this, noting only that certain dimensions of our cognitive engagement with biological phenomena are rooted in supersensible reality – compelling appeal to teleological concepts. This leaves the maxim of mechanistic judging fully *necessary* for any comprehensive *natural* explanation of biological phenomena. But it does suggest that mechanistic judging, while moreover fully *sufficient* for any comprehensive *natural* explanation of biological phenomena, is not sufficient for an explanation of *all* dimensions of our cognitive engagement with those phenomena. Furthermore, since our supersensibly grounded teleological judging of biological phenomena occurs in response to what are in all other respects empirically given objects, it inevitably *appears* to have the sort of objective empirical import that our transcendental analysis revealed a critical concept merely for the reflecting power of judgment cannot have. Accordingly, even as the conflict between an (empirically) unlimited but (supersensibly) limited scope of the maxim of mechanistic judging is (thus) transcendental-philosophically resolvable, both positions naturally and unavoidably continue to appear to contradict each other.

Notes

1 I say 'three main parts' because an introductory section (§61) is not assigned to either Analytic, Dialectic or Method.
2 "Analytic of the Teleological Power of Judgment" (*KU* 5: 362, §§62–68).
3 "Appendix: Methodology of the Teleological Power of Judgment" (*KU* 5: 416, §§79–91).
4 See Chapters 7, 8, 14, and 21 in this volume.
5 See Chapters 11, 16, and 23 in this volume.
6 See Chapters 10 and 15 in this volume.
7 But see section 2 in this chapter.
8 See A297/B354.
9 For Kant's views on dogmatism and criticism in §74, see section 3 in this chapter.
10 See Teufel 2011a.
11 See section 2 in this chapter.
12 See Teufel 2012.
13 See Chapter 21 in this volume.
14 This is one of the significant differences between the teleological Analytic in the *Critique of the Power of Judgment* and the Analytic of Concepts of the *Critique of Pure Reason*. While the Analytic of Concepts contains a fully formed transcendental-philosophical justification of the type of cognition under investigation (namely, the transcendental deduction of the categories), the teleological Analytic contains nothing of the sort.
15 See, e.g., McLaughlin (1990: 154ff.), Allison (2003: 224ff.), Quarfood (2004: 167f., 190ff.), Ginsborg (2015: Ch. 12), Watkins (2009: 197–221).
16 "The Principle of the Formal Purposiveness of Nature is a Transcendental Principle" (*KU* 5:181).
17 See Teufel (2017).
18 See Teufel (2011b).
19 See Teufel (2012).
20 See *GMS*, 4: 417.
21 See McLaughlin (1990).
22 See also *KU* 5: 189, 399.
23 See Teufel (2017).
24 See also *EEKU* 20: 215.
25 Teufel (2017: 114f.).
26 Allison (2001: 39), Teufel (2012).
27 "[T]he causality of a concept with respect to its object is purposiveness" (*KU* 5: 220).

References

Allison, H.E. (2001) *Kant's Theory of Taste*, Cambridge: Cambridge University Press.

Allison, H.E. (2003) "Kant's Antinomy of Teleological Judgment," in P. Guyer (ed.), *Kant's Critique of the Power of Judgment: Critical Essays*, Lanham, MD: Rowman & Littlefield, pp. 219–36.

Ginsborg, H. (2015) *The Normativity of Nature: Essays on Kant's Critique of Judgment*, Oxford: Oxford University Press.

McLaughlin, P. (1990) *Kant's Critique of Teleology in Biological Explanation: Antinomy and Teleology*, Lewiston: Edwin Mellon Press.

Quarfood, M. (2004) *Transcendental Idealism and the Organism*, Stockholm Studies in Philosophy 26, Stockholm: Almqvist & Wiksell.

Teufel, T. (2011a) "Kant's Non-Teleological Conception of Purposiveness," *Kant-Studien* 102(2): 232–52.

Teufel, T. (2011b) "What Is the Problem of Teleology in Kant's 'Critique of the Teleological Power of Judgment'," *SATS* 12: 198–236.

Teufel, T. (2012) "What Does Kant Mean by 'Power of Judgment' in His *Critique of the Power of Judgment?*" *Kantian Review* 17(2): 297–326.

Teufel, T. (2017) "Kant's Transcendental Principle of Purposiveness and the Maxim of the Lawfulness of Empirical Laws," in M. Massimi and A. Breitenbach (eds.), *Kant and the Laws of Nature*, Cambridge: Cambridge University Press, pp. 108–27.

Watkins, E. (2009) "The Antinomy of Teleological Judgment," *Kant Yearbook* 1: 197–221.

Further Reading

I. Goy, *Kants Theorie der Biologie* (Berlin: Walter de Gruyter, 2017) contains a section-by-section commentary on the Critique of the Teleological Power of Judgment, an original interpretation of Kant's critical *teleology* (connecting it with Kant's critical *theology*), and an excellent discussion of 17th- and 18th-century life sciences. P. Guyer, *Kant's System of Nature and Freedom* (Oxford: Oxford University Press, 2005) is a collection of essays from the early 1990s to the early 2000s, organized around the idea that Kant's teleological thought and views on nature's systematicity are of a piece with his concerns with our rationality and freedom. H. Van den Berg, *Kant on Proper Science* (Dordrecht: Springer, 2014) explains Kant's philosophy of biology in the *Critique of the Power of Judgment* (as well as in the *Opus Postumum*) as an integral part of – rather than orthogonal to – Kant's philosophy of science. R. Zuckert, *Kant on Beauty and Biology* (Cambridge: Cambridge University Press, 2007) makes the rare attempt to interpret the *Critique of the Power of Judgment* as a unified whole, integrating the book's aesthetic and teleological doctrines in an overarching theory of reflecting judgment.

23

METHOD OF THE TELEOLOGICAL POWER OF JUDGMENT[1]

Ido Geiger

★★★

1. Introduction

The long last part of the third *Critique* contends with two topics. The first shorter part explains how the principle of teleology is to be employed in empirical research of organic nature; it also offers a fascinating speculation suggesting how it might be used to view organic nature as a single whole that evolved step-by-step from matter (§§80–1). The second presents a partly new argument for the assumption of the highest good and the government of a benevolent God, but also repeats and gives pride of place to the familiar argument to these conclusions (§§82–91). This second part can be divided into three: 1) an argument from organized nature to the assumption of the highest good and a moral creator (§§82–4); 2) a presentation and comparison of the physicoteleological argument for the assumption of God as world-architect and the ethicotheological argument for the assumption of the highest good and a benevolent world-author (§§85–9 and the concluding General Remark on the Teleology); and 3) an epistemological reflection on the status of the latter argument and the important notion of practical affirmation or moral faith (§§90–1).

The division of the Methodology into two parts is suggested by its introductory section (§79). Kant asks what place teleology has within theoretical philosophy (cf., *KU* 5: 194): Does it belong to the doctrine of nature or to theology as concerned with the "original ground of the world as the sum total of all objects of experience" (*KU* 5: 416)? His answer is that teleology belongs to neither doctrine but rather to the critique of reflective judgment. Nevertheless, the "most important use of it can be made within theology" (*KU* 5: 416). Furthermore, "it can and must provide the method for how nature must be judged in accordance with the principle of final causes" (*KU* 5: 417).

2. The Methodology of Biology (§§80–81)

The principal task of the Analytic of Teleological Judgment (§§61–8) is analyzing what it means to speak of a natural object, as we do, as if it were self-organizing. Kant states that such claims cannot be factual ones. The concept of self-organization

DOI: 10.4324/9781003406617-29

cannot rest merely on grounds in experience, but must have as its ground some sort of *a priori*
principle, even if it is merely regulative and even if that end lies only in the idea of the one
who judges and never in any efficient cause.

(*KU* 5: 376)

The forces of nature do not operate with a view to ends they aim to construct. As Kant often
remarks, the forces of nature are blind (see, e.g.: *KU* 5: 376, 377, 381; see also: *KU* 5: 379, 387,
390, *EEKU* 20: 235). To attribute self-organization to an object is not to assert that it is self-
organizing and that its organization is the effect of purposive efficient causation. In other words, it
is neither a commitment to theism (creationism) nor to hylozoism (vitalism).[2] Rather, it is to think
of it as though it were self-organizing, to be guided in empirical research by the idea that it is self-
organizing, This is what Kant means by calling the idea a regulative principle, "a *maxim* for the
judging of the inner purposiveness of organized beings" (*KU* 5: 376).

In the first part of the Methodology (§§80–1), Kant specifies the implications of this view for the
empirical investigation of organic phenomena. He elaborates what shape explanations of organic
processes take and what role mechanistic causality plays in them. Kant takes for granted that we all
characterize certain wholes as self-organizing:

No one has doubted the correctness of the fundamental principle that certain things in nature
(organized beings) and their possibility must be judged in accordance with the concept of
final causes.

(KU 5: 389)

But to gain insight into these organized wholes we must identify the causal mechanisms that serve
them. The causal explanation of organized beings is strictly mechanistic, which means the explanation of a whole as a function of the properties and blind causal powers of its parts. Kant draws a
sharp distinction between describing something as self-organizing and in this employing teleological
language, on the one hand, and, on the other, explanations of it as the effect of blind mechanistic
causality. Indeed, it is only by identifying such mechanisms that researchers gain insight into nature.
Explanations in biology begin by characterizing an organized whole and proceed by detecting a
mechanism through which a further organized state or structure appears. The processes given as
principal examples are growth, reproduction, interdependence of organs and systems, including
regeneration and compensation for malformed organs (*KU* 5: 371–2).

If, therefore, the investigator of nature is not to work entirely in vain, he must, in the judging
of things whose concept as natural ends is indubitably established (organized beings), always
base them on some original organization, which uses that mechanism itself in order to produce other organized forms or to develop its own into new configurations.

(*KU* 5: 418)

Thus, organization is an assumption attributed to natural objects and their states; forces – and thus
explanations – are exclusively mechanistic. Explanations of organic processes begin and end with
descriptions of organized wholes or states; but the forces active in these processes are mechanistic.

It is for these insights that Kant praises Blumenbach (*KU* 5: 423–4; see also, *Br* 11: 184–5), who
"begins all physical explanation of these formations with organized matter" (*KU* 5: 424; see also,
ÜGTP 8: 180n). At the same time, "he leaves natural mechanism an indeterminable but at the

273

same time also unmistakable role under this inscrutable *principle* of an original *organization*" (*KU* 5: 424). It cannot be stressed enough that despite its name Kant sees Blumenbach's formative drive (*Bildungstrieb*) not as a teleological force or agency, but as an original organization; it is, furthermore, mechanistic forces that are sought to explain further organization "standing, as it were, under the guidance and direction of the former principle" (*KU* 5: 424).[3] It is this very methodology that Kant employs in his papers on the biological concept of human races, alluded to in §80 (*KU* 5: 420).

These two points of emphasis are also central to the long speculative passage, characterized as "a daring adventure of reason" (*KU* 5: 419n).

> The agreement of so many genera of animals in a certain common schema, which seems to lie at the basis not only of their skeletal structure but also of the arrangement of their other parts, and by which a remarkable simplicity of basic design has been able to produce such a great variety of species by the shortening of one part and the elongation of another, by the involution of this part and the evolution of another, allows the mind at least a weak ray of hope that something may be accomplished here with the principle of the mechanism of nature, without which there can be no natural science at all. This analogy of forms [. . .] strengthens the suspicion of a real kinship among them in their generation from a common proto-mother, through the gradual approach of one animal genus to the other, from that in which the principle of ends seems best confirmed, namely human beings, down to polyps, and from this even further to mosses and lichens, and finally to the lowest level of nature that we can observe, that of raw matter: from which, and from its forces governed by mechanical laws [. . .] the entire technique of nature, which is so incomprehensible to us in organized beings that we believe ourselves compelled to conceive of another principle for them, seems to derive.
>
> (*KU* 5: 418–19)[4]

Kant boldly speculates that we may yet discover that the entire range of organic species evolved from one another and have their origin in matter and that this gradual process of generation is governed by mechanistic causality. This might seem to be a denial of the claim that biological explanations necessarily begin with an organized whole. But Kant is quick to emphasize that the daring speculation accords with the methodology he champions.

> And yet ultimately he [the **archaeologist** of nature] must attribute to this universal mother an organization purposively aimed at all these creatures, for otherwise the possibility of the purposive form of the products of the animal and vegetable kingdom cannot be conceived at all. In that case, however, he has merely put off the explanation, and cannot presume to have made the generation of those two kingdoms independent from the condition of final causes.
>
> (*KU* 5: 419–20)

From a modern perspective, Kant is certainly far from understanding the evolution of life. However, Darwinian evolutionary theory and its synthesis with genetic theory apparently employ the methodology he recommends. The theories begin with the attribution of organization to matter and explain further organization by identifying the blind mechanistic processes that bring it about. Comparison with the bold speculation reveals that Darwin's achievement lies not only in the discovery of the mechanistic principles of random variation and natural selection. It also lies in showing that better adapted and more complex organization arises from what is less or less well organized.[5] But these epochal insights are not the end of teleological judgments of organic phenomena.[6]

In §81, Kant offers a principled methodological assessment of the competing contemporary theories of generation.[7] First, according to occasionalism, God "would immediately provide the organic formation to the matter commingling in every impregnation" (*KU* 5: 422). This approach Kant calls hyperphysics, because it attributes no effective causality to nature: "no one who cares anything for philosophy will assume this system" (*KU* 5: 422).

Kant then distinguishes two types of preformation theories. The theory of individual preformation hold that all individuals that will ever exist are pre-formed and contained one within either the sperm (spermism/animalculism) or ovum (ovism) of another. It too holds that the form of every individual comes "immediately from the hand of the creator" (*KU* 5: 423). But it makes a great difference whether these forms "arise supernaturally, at the origin or during the course of the world" (*KU* 5: 423). For the former possibility "left something to nature" (*KU* 5: 423). But the theory suffers from decisive weaknesses: It too is not a wholly naturalistic theory, because the preservation of embryos requires positing a "multitude of supernatural arrangements" (*KU* 5: 423), and because it explains miscarriages as designed to astonish future anatomists; it is not parsimonious, because many more prefigured beings must exist than are ever developed; finally, the "the generation of half-breeds" (*KU* 5: 423) constitutes powerful empirical counter-evidence to it.

For theories of epigenesis or generic preformation, "the productive capacity of the progenitor is still preformed in accordance with internally purposive dispositions that were imparted to its stock" (*KU* 5: 423). The theory is naturalistic, considering nature "as itself producing rather than merely developing" (*KU* 5: 424). It can also explain the crucial fact of the existence of half-breeds. Kant does not explain what precisely he means by saying that there was a need to limit "an excessively presumptuous use of it" (*KU* 5: 424). But it is here that Kant credits Blumenbach for his great contribution to the theory. The problem must be the attribution of the capacity for organization to the forces acting in these processes.[8] For its solution is precisely the distinction between original organization and blind mechanistic forces. It is true that the theory assumes a great deal of organization as its point of departure. But this is the "least possible appeal to the supernatural" (*KU* 5: 424); furthermore, the issue of first beginnings is one "on which physics always founders, no matter what chain of causes it tries" (*KU* 5: 424).

Finally, another theme of these sections invites scrutiny. In the *Metaphysical Foundations of Natural Science*, Kant distinguishes the description of nature from rational science. The former consists of

> *natural description*, as a system of classification for natural things in accordance with their similarities, and *natural history*, as a systematic presentation of natural things at various times and places.
>
> (MAN 4: 468)

The latter systematically presents "an interconnection of grounds and consequences" (*MAN* 4: 468), which contains the natural causal laws of merely observational sciences and sciences properly so-called that have constructed the *a priori* principles of a special metaphysics. The Methodology is of great importance for understanding this distinction and the relations between its terms. It reveals that the teleological description of organisms and their different states goes hand-in-hand with seeking causal explanations of the mechanisms governing organic processes. Kant's daring speculation reveals, furthermore, that the value of the archaeology of nature, and of natural history generally (see, *KU* 5: 428n), is to prepare the ground for causally informative rational science.[9]

3.   The Ultimate End of Nature and the Final End of Creation (§§82–84)

The argument for the assumption of a benevolent God and the highest good presented in §§82–84 is not well-organized. The first two sections are long and rambling and do not contain all the elements the argument requires; specifically, Kant states but does not explain until the last section why the final end of creation must be sought beyond nature (cf., *KU* 5: 378). The third section is shorter, clearer and seems to present a more compact version of the argument, consequently presenting the discussion of the ultimate end of nature in the longer argument as something of a digression. As we shall see, the partly new argument presented here merely sets the stage for the more important but familiar ethicotheological argument for the highest good and a benevolent creator in §87. Here is one way of outlining a longer version of the preparatory argument:

1) The internal purposiveness attributed to organized beings necessarily leads us to think of nature as a single teleological system connected by relations of external purposiveness.
2) The idea of nature as such a purposive whole inevitably raises the question of the ultimate end of nature [*letzter Zweck der Natur*]. The only candidate is the human being as a practically rational being, "who by means of his reason can make a system of ends out of an aggregate of purposively formed things" (*KU* 5: 427).
3) But the idea of happiness as the overarching end of human beings as rational and natural beings cannot serve to constitute a system of ends. It can "assume no determinate universal and fixed law at all" (*KU* 5: 430). Furthermore, we necessarily seek the final end of creation [*Endzweck der Schöpfung*]; but the ultimate end of nature cannot be the final end of creation, because everything in or related to nature is conditioned; but the final end of creation must be unconditioned. If we assume

> an **intentionally acting** cause, then we cannot stop at the question why things in the world (organized beings) have this or that form, or are placed by nature in relation to this or that other thing [. . .] we must also raise the question of the objective ground that could have determined this productive understanding to an effect of this sort, which is then the final end for which such things exist.
>
> (*KU* 5: 434–5)

4) Only the human being, as moral, contains within himself an unconditioned or absolute end. It alone qualifies as the final end of creation, viz., "the highest good in the world".

> (*KU* 5: 435)

> Now of the human being (and thus of every rational being in the world), as a moral being, it cannot be further asked why (*quem in finem* [to what end]) it exists. His existence contains the highest end itself, to which, as far as he is able, he can subject the whole of nature.
>
> (*KU* 5: 435)

Several points require comment. First, it is not clear that Kant is entitled to claim that the attribution of internal purposiveness leads *necessarily* to the idea of nature as single teleological system constituted by relations of external purposiveness.[10] Nor is it clear that we *inevitably* ask after the final end of nature so conceived. After all, we are considering nature *as though* it were a purposive whole and this distinct manner of thought might not contain all aspects of our ordinary thinking about intentional agency. Indeed, there is good reason to think that the final end of a transcendent being is inscrutable.

Second, the conclusion of the second step is justified in a particularly confusing passage. Kant describes a familiar enough picture of the great chain of being, according to which the plant kingdom is a means to the subsistence of the herbivorous animals, and these means for the car-nivores, and all these exist for man, who is the ultimate end of nature, because "he is the only being on earth who forms concepts of ends for himself and who by means of his reason can make a system of ends out of an aggregate of purposively formed things" (*KU* 5: 426–7). This appears to be the conclusion Kant wants to reach. But he then proceeds to offer a competing picture, suggested by Linnaeus, in which man "has only the rank of a means" (*KU* 5: 427). The real point of these and the following paragraphs is to offer an argument rather than rely on more or less familiar ideas. Kant reminds us that the notion of the purposiveness of nature, according to which we judge organisms, is not objective, but a subjective principle of reflective judgment: "given the nature of our understanding and our reason we cannot conceive of them except in accordance with final causes" (*KU* 5: 429). It is precisely because the purposiveness of nature is an idea according to which we reflect upon nature that it is only for us rational beings that nature can form a purposive whole: only the human being "by means of his reason can make a system of ends."[11]

Third, the third and fourth steps of the argument deploy claims Kant makes in earlier writ-ings, highlighting what importance the notion of natural purposiveness has for his thinking even before it is made a principal concern of the third *Critique*. Kant claims in the *Groundwork* that happiness cannot be the end of the human being as "an organized being, that is, one pur-posively constituted for life" (*GMS* 4: 395; see also, *KpV* 5: 28). He also discusses in §83, in some detail, the central line of thought of his "Idea for a Universal History with a Cosmopoli-tan Aim" that does offer a teleological account of the end for which human nature is designed. Kant claims there that 'unsociable sociability' or competitive human antagonism is the natural mechanism through which human beings develop their capacity to attain ends they set them-selves and that it gradually and unwittingly drives humankind towards the *"achievement of a civil society universally administering right"* (*IaG* 8: 22). This attainment of a perpetual cosmopolitan peace is the halfway mark to the attainment of a cosmopolitan moral community. In the words of the Methodology, it is

> a deeply hidden but perhaps intentional effort of supreme reason if not to establish then at least to prepare the way for the lawfulness together with the freedom of the states and by means of that the unity of a morally grounded system of them.
>
> (*KU* 5: 433)

It is interesting to recall the very first proposition of the essay: "*All natural predispositions of a creature are determined sometime to develop themselves completely and purposively*" (*IaG* 8: 18). The third *Critique* thus justifies the framing methodological assumption of the earlier essay as well as enlists its central argument for service within the critical framework.[12]

Fourth, the last point could perhaps be worked into the outline of the argument, for it is Kant's claim that the attainment of a cosmopolitan state of right is the ultimate end of nature. It is impor-tant to see clearly though that we are declared to be the titular lords of nature, because of our rational capacity to set ourselves ends and this leads to examining our two overarching ends, viz., happiness and morality. But when we come to understand what the ultimate end of nature is, we learn that "the development of the natural predispositions in the human race, and the end of nature itself [. . .] is not our end" (*KU* 5: 432). The ultimate end of nature is not an end we set, but one towards which we are unwittingly driven; it is one we "ascribe to nature in regard to the human species" (*KU* 5: 431).

It is particularly important to see that the argument takes a practical turn in its very first step. This step might initially appear to repeat a very important transition in the Analytic of Teleological Judgment. There Kant claims that the concept of a natural end

> necessarily leads to the idea of a whole of nature as a system in accordance with the rule of ends, to which idea all the mechanism of nature in accordance with principles of reason must now be subordinated (at least in order to test natural appearance by this idea).
>
> (*KU* 5: 379)

However, the purposive system of which Kant is speaking is a system of empirical laws; the assumption is a guideline "for extending natural science in accordance with another principle, namely that of final causes, yet without harm to the mechanism of nature" (*KU* 5: 379).[13] But in the argument we are examining, this sense of nature as a purposive theoretical whole is nowhere in sight. The second step asks what the ultimate end of nature is. But the answer that it is designed to be known, that it is a system purposive for our cognitive theoretical capacities, is apparently not an option. The reason that "can make a system of ends out of an aggregate of purposively formed things" (*KU* 5: 427) is clearly practical reason. And this explains, in turn, why, in the third and fourth steps, the options considered as ways of bringing systematic unity to this aggregate are happiness and morality – our two overarching practical ends.

4. Physicotheology or Ethicotheology? (§§85–89; General Remark on the Teleology)

That the moral-teleological argument takes a practical turn in its very first step is confirmed and the significance of this fact expounded in §§85–86. Their aim, succinctly, is to emphasize that physicoteleology, that is, theoretical reflection on the purposiveness of organized beings and of nature as a whole, can only lead to the assumption of "an intelligent world-cause (as the highest artist)" (*KU* 5: 438; see also *KU* 5: 480). In contrast, ethicotheology or moral theology leads to the fully determinate idea of God (see, KU 5: 196; cf., EEKU 20: 246–7).

> In relation to the **highest good** possible under his rule alone, namely the existence of rational beings under moral laws, we will conceive of this original being as **omniscient**, so that even what is inmost in their dispositions (which is what constitutes the real moral value of the actions of rational beings in the world) is not hidden from him; as **omnipotent**, so that he can make the whole of nature suitable for this highest end; as **omnibenevolent** and at the same time **just**, because these two properties (united as **wisdom**) constitute the conditions of the causality of a supreme cause of the world as a highest good under moral laws; and likewise all of the remaining transcendental properties, such as **eternity**, **omnipresence**, etc.
>
> (*KU* 5: 444)

As Kant stresses, physicotheology, the attempt to argue from the purposiveness of nature for our theoretical capacities to the existence of a God possessing all transcendental properties, is no more than a "misunderstood physical teleology" (*KU* 5: 442); and physical teleology, properly construed, is merely a preparation or propaedeutic for ethicotheology (*KU* 5: 442).[14] Indeed, the latter argument does not build upon the former. As the ground for ethicotheology, our moral vocation is adequate

by itself, and urges attention to the ends of nature and research into the inconceivably great art that lies hidden behind its forms in order to provide incidental confirmation from natural ends for the ideas created by pure practical reason.

(KU 5: 444–5; see also KU 5: 478–9)

Thus, the section titled On the Moral Proof of the Existence of God (§87) presents the familiar argument for the highest good and a benevolent God that takes our moral vocation as its starting point. Significantly, Kant poses again the problem set as a task in the Introduction to the book, that is, bridging the "incalculable gulf [*unübersehbare Kluft*]" (*KU* 5: 175) separating the practical worldview of moral agency and the theoretical worldview of nature.[15]

> Now from this moral teleology, which concerns the relation of our own causality to ends and even to a final end that must be aimed at by us in the world, and thus the reciprocal relation of the world to that moral end and the external possibility of its accomplishment (to which no physical teleology can guide us), there arises the necessary question of whether it compels our rational judging to go beyond the world and to seek an intelligent supreme principle for that relation of nature to what is moral in us, in order to represent nature as purposive even in relation to the morally internal legislation and its possible execution.
>
> (KU 5: 447–8)

The general line of argument he goes on to draw is familiar.[16]

1) The subjective condition under which we act, as finite rational agents, is the pursuit of happiness. But as rational moral agents, we are bound by the objective moral law. Thus, our final end is "**happiness** – under the objective condition of the concordance of humans with the law of **morality**, as the worthiness to be happy" (*KU* 5: 450).
2) But we cannot conceive of these two requirements being "both **connected** by merely natural causes" (*KU* 5: 450).
3) Consequently,

> we must assume a moral cause of the world (an author of the world) in order to set before ourselves a final end, in accordance with the moral law; and insofar as that final end is necessary, to that extent (i.e., in the same degree and for the same reason) is it also necessary to assume the former, namely, that there is a God.
>
> (KU 5: 450)

Kant goes on to emphasize several points. First, our moral obligations are in no way dependent upon coming to believe in the highest good and a benevolent God (*KU* 5: 450–3). Second, the "reality of a highest morally legislative author is thus adequately established merely **for the practical use** of our reason, without determining anything in regard to its existence theoretically" (*KU* 5: 456). Third, the argument is not at all new but has been familiar to common human reason ever since "human beings began to reflect on right and wrong" (*KU* 5: 458; see also *KU* 5: 476–8). Finally, the practically rational idea of God as the moral author of the world is the right sort of religious disposition and has the advantage of protecting us from delusional religious enthusiasm as well as from anthropomorphic idolatry (*KU* 5: 459; cf., *KU* 5: 481–2).

That the line of thought the argument presents is familiar might be quite disappointing. For it might be thought that Kant raised the problem of the chasm between nature and freedom in the third *Critique* – even though he had argued for the highest good and a benevolent God in earlier texts – because he came to think that the practical argument demands further support.[17] The practical argument shows that as finite moral agents we necessarily set the highest good as our final end and that setting this end is tantamount to belief in a benevolent God. This might nevertheless raise for us the question of whether there are any theoretical grounds for affirming what the practical standpoint entails. It might be thought that answering this question in the negative means failing to bridge the chasm between nature and freedom, precisely because what as moral agents we inevitably believe is something which we have no theoretical grounds to affirm or uphold.[18]

If this were the problem posed, it would demand a unique philosophical argument to solve it. It would demand reaching the one idea from both the practical standpoint of moral agency and the theoretical standpoint of reflection upon nature. Metaphorically, the bridge with which Kant connects the castle of freedom to the domain of nature is a drawbridge lowered from the practical side. It fits snugly and enables easy crossing, for physical teleology serves as a stepping-stone onto the bridge – although, Kant emphasizes, it can bear no weight. The problem he does not pose calls, however, for a bridge that finds secure support in the two domains it spans.

Are there Kantian resources for constructing such a bridge? I think there are. Kant claims that theoretical reflection on nature does lead necessarily to the assumption of a God who designed a world purposive for theoretical cognition. He insists that it can take us no further. But the idea of a nature purposive for theoretical cognition can be viewed as inflecting our moral duty in a distinct way: To the extent possible, it is our duty to bring the order of nature into systematic accord with what our moral duties demand – thus removing obstacles to moral success and enhancing the effectiveness of the pursuit of moral ends. We can perhaps do little to alter the physical world. But good knowledge of it is a condition of effective moral agency. Furthermore, we might distinguish here the immutable laws of physical nature from alterable laws governing human societies and individual psychology. Shaping human nature and the human world in ways that make moral agency effective can be viewed as our moral duty. The task of bringing the natural world into greater systematic accord with the system of moral laws makes sense, precisely because we assume that the laws of nature constitute an ordered system.

Kant does not take this route in the third *Critique*. But he concludes his "Idea for a Universal History" by claiming that it can serve not merely for the explanation of human history but also for presenting humankind as progressing towards the attainment of its vocation.

> Such a *justification* [*Rechtfertigung*] of nature – or better, of *providence* [*Vorsehung*] – is no unimportant motive for choosing a particular viewpoint for considering the world. For what does it help to praise the splendor and wisdom of creation in the nonrational realm of nature, and to recommend it to our consideration, if that part of the great showplace of the highest wisdom that contains the end of all this – the history of humankind – is to remain a ceaseless objection against it, the prospect of which necessitates our turning our eyes away from it in disgust and, in despair of ever encountering a completed rational aim in it, to hope for the latter only in another world?
>
> (*IaG* 8: 30)

The end of Kant's philosophy of history is defending the claim that human prudence and the desire for happiness unwittingly lead to a cosmopolitan state of right, which in its external form is in accord with the demands of morality.[19] The representation of human history as progressing towards the attainment of its moral vocation is precisely a theoretical perspective that entails a moral duty in this world. This justification of nature calls upon us to work with providence.

It bears stressing that belief in the realizability of the highest good is "a *theoretical* presupposition [. . .] attached inseparably to an a priori unconditionally valid *practical* law" (*KpV* 5: 122; see also, *KrV*

A805–6/B833–4, A809/B837). The concept sets no new moral duty. The promotion of the highest good "is commanded by the moral law, let the outcome of this effort be whatever it will" (*KU* 5: 451). On the other hand, theoretical reflection upon the purposiveness of nature sets the highest good as a practical end. What practical reflection reveals we can rationally take to be true is a task we can rationally work towards according to theoretical reflection. Thus the bridge spanning the domains of nature and freedom is, on the one side, grounded in a theoretical postulate and, on the other side, affirmed – in the sense of being made firm or securing rather than stating as fact – by giving more concrete form to our moral duty. The argument thus remains true to Kant's denial of the possibility of physicotheology.[20]

It is further worth noting that both in the Introduction and in the Methodology Kant poses the problem of the gap between freedom and nature in very general terms as a problem of the fate of moral agency in the natural world. But his solution to the problem focuses on only one part of the natural world, that is, on human nature and more specifically on happiness as the natural end of finite rational agents. The argument just sketched enables us to view the bridging problem as the broader metaphysical question Kant himself formulates.

A final important question. In the Methodology, Kant employs physical teleology as a propaedeutic for ethicotheology. But he praises and gives pride of place to the latter familiar argument. Why is it important to present again an argument that is in essence already well-known to readers of the first and second *Critiques*?

In these earlier texts, I suggest, the argument to the highest good is presented as the solution to the problem of finite practical agency: we desire happiness but are bound by moral laws. In the third *Critique*, Kant relocates the problem. He lays great emphasis on the exhaustive division of philosophy into theoretical and practical philosophy and accordingly on the distinction between concepts of nature and the concept of freedom. The pursuit of happiness, he surprisingly declares, properly belongs to theoretical rather than practical philosophy:

> For if the concept determining the causality is a concept of nature, then the principles are **technically practical**, but if it is a concept of freedom, then these are **morally practical**; and since in the division of a rational science what is at issue is entirely this sort of difference of objects, the cognition of which requires distinct principles, the former will belong to theoretical philosophy (as a doctrine of nature), while the latter will entirely by itself constitute the second part, namely practical philosophy (as a doctrine of morals).
>
> (*KU* 5: 172)

Accordingly, the task of the Methodology is to bridge the gap between nature and freedom and between theoretical and practical philosophy. This explains Kant's otherwise perplexing claim that the power of judgment is "an intermediary [*Mittelglied*] between the understanding and reason" (*KU* 5: 177; see also *KU* 5: 168). Kant appears to be saying that the argument to the highest good has its proper place in the third *Critique* and in this way contributes to bringing the "entire critical enterprise to an end" (*KU* 5: 170).

5. Moral Faith or Practically Grounded Affirmation [*Fürwahrhalten*] (§§90–91)

The last two sections of the Methodology (§§90–91) are devoted to an epistemological reflection on the main claims of the preceding sections. The failure of physicotheology is first explained by reason's native pursuit of unity: It attributes all natural organization to a single intelligent author; and attributes to this author all transcendental properties. Kant does not object to the former attribution and recognizes the popular usefulness of the latter. However, the precise delineation of physical from moral teleology serves to reveal "where the real nerve of the proof lies" and "to separate what belongs merely to persuasion [*Überredung*] from that which leads to conviction [*Überzeugung*] (two types of approval [*Beifall*] that differ not merely in degree but in kind)" (*KU* 5: 462).

How does the ethicotheological proof lead to conviction? No theoretical proof of the existence of God as the moral author of the world is possible. Such arguments attempt to determine what an object is but "we have no material at all for the determination of the idea of the supersensible, since we would have to derive any such material from things in the sensible world" (*KU* 5: 466). This might be read as denying the possibility of any theoretical argument regarding the supersensible. But Kant is apparently only denying again the possibility of constructing a theoretical proof of God as moral author of the world. Indeed, as an example of a valid theoretical argument by analogy Kant gives the analogy between artworks and human agency, on the one hand, and, on the other, natural ends and a divine intelligence (*KU* 5: 465). But whether the intelligent author of the world had a final end in creation "can never be revealed to us by theoretical research into nature" (*KU* 5: 441).

But there are also proofs that focus on how we human beings judge and are thus grounded on "sufficient principles for the reflecting power of judgment" (*KU* 5: 463). Such a proof

> if it is based on a practical principle of reason (which is thus universally and necessarily valid), then it can make a sufficient claim of conviction from a purely practical point of view, i.e., moral conviction.
>
> (*KU* 5: 463)

Remarkably, Kant says, there is among the ideas of reason a single fact, viz., "the idea of **freedom**, the reality of which, as a particular kind of causality [. . .] can be established through practical laws of pure reason" (*KU* 5: 468). But if

> the supreme principle of all moral laws is a postulate, then the possibility of its highest object and thus also of the condition under which alone we can conceive of this possibility is thereby also postulated along with it.
>
> (*KU* 5: 470)

Our affirmation of the existence of God and the highest good is though "an affirmation in a purely practical respect, that is, a moral faith" (*KU* 5: 470).[21]

6. Conclusion

Despite its thought-provoking evolutionary speculation and its obvious contribution to the task Kant describes as bridging the gap between nature and freedom, the Methodology of Teleological Judgment is still a relatively neglected part of Kant's critical philosophy. It invites further scrutiny from those interested in Kant's conception of teleology and biology, in particular, and those working on Kant's multifaceted idea of God.

Notes

1 This research was supported by the Israel Science Foundation (grant No. 659/19).
2 See: *KU* 5:374, 392, 394–395; see also: *TG* 2:330; *MAN* 4:544. See: Zumbach 1984: 79–86. Cf., Lenoir 1989: 29.

3 See, McLaughlin 1982. See also: Lenoir 1980, 1989: 17–35; Richards 2000.
4 See also, ÜGTP 8: 179–180. Cf., RezHerder 8: 54.
5 See, Roth 2008: 280. Cf., Guyer 2005: 323–4n16.
6 See, Ginsborg 2004: 62–5. Cf., Lovejoy 1968.
7 See: Roe 1981: 1–20; McLaughlin 1990: 7–24; Roth 2008; Richards: 13–16.
8 See, Roth 2008: 283.
9 See also: *VvRM* 2: 435n; 443; *BBM* 8: 100n, 102; *ÜGTP* 8: 161–162.
10 See, Guyer 2005: 326–7.
11 Cf., Freudiger 1996: 430.
12 See, Kleingeld 1998: 327–9.
13 See: Guyer 2005: 325–8; Breitenbach 2009: 143–7.
14 For other discussions of physicotheology see: *BDG* 2:116–126; *KrV* A620–630/B648–658; *V-Phil-Th/ Pölitz* 28: 1007–1010.
15 Freudiger (1996), Gfeller (1998), Guyer (2005), Nuzzo (2005: 360–7) and Cunico (2008) concur that Kant attempts to solve the bridging problem in the Methodology. But the relation between the domains is a recurring theme. Important discussions include the experience of the sublimity of nature, interest in the beauty of nature (§42) and beauty as a symbol of morality (§59). Schrader (1953: 205–6), White (1979), Dahlstrom (2008: 10–15) and Friedlander (2015) find the bridge in these and other discussions.
16 See: *KrV* A804–819/B832–847; *KpV* 5: 124–132; *V-Phil-Th/Pölitz* 28: 1071–6; *RGV* 6: 6–8.
17 See, Guyer 2005: 317.
18 See, Dahlstrom 2008: 9–10. Cf., Freudiger 1996: 432–5.
19 See, Geiger 2013.
20 Cf., Sellars 1963: 40.
21 See: *KrV* A828–831/B856–959; *KpV* 5: 142–146; *V-Phil-Th/Pölitz* 28: 1010–12, 1082–4.

References

Breitenbach, A. (2009) *Die Analogie von Vernunft und Natur: Eine Umweltphilosophie nach Kant*, Berlin: Walter de Gruyter.
Cunico, G. (2008) "Erklärungen für das Übersinnliche: physikotheologischer und moralischer Gottesbeweis (§§85–9)," in O. Höffe (ed.), *Immanuel Kant: Kritik der Urteilskraft*, Berlin: Akademie Verlag, pp. 309–29.
Dahlstrom, D. (2008) "The Unity of Kant's Critical Philosophy," in *Philosophical Legacies: Essays on the Thought of Kant, Hegel, and Their Contemporaries*, Washington, DC: The Catholic University of America Press, pp. 1–16.
Freudiger, J. (1996) "Kants Schlußstein: Wie die Teleologie die Einheit der Vernunft stiftet," *Kant-Studien* 87: 423–35.
Friedlander, E. (2015) *Expressions of Judgment: An Essay on Kant's Aesthetics*, Cambridge, MA: Harvard University Press.
Geiger, I. (2013) "Can Universal History Underwrite Kant's Substantive Conception of Moral Value?" in S. Bacin, A. Ferrarin, C. La Rocca and M. Ruffing (eds.), *Kant und die Philosophie in weltbürgerlicher Absicht: Akten des XI. Internationalen Kant Kongresses*, Berlin: Walter de Gruyter, pp. 247–57.
Gfeller, T. (1998) "Wie tragfähig ist der teleologische Brückenschlag? Zu Kants *Kritik der teleologischen Urteilskraft*," *Zeitschrift für Philosophische Forschung* 52: 215–36.
Ginsborg, H. (2004) "Two Kinds of Mechanical Inexplicability in Kant and Aristotle," *Journal of the History of Philosophy* 42: 33–65.
Guyer, P. (2005) "From Nature to Morality: Kant's New Argument in the 'Critique of Teleological Judgment'," in *Kant's System of Nature and Freedom: Selected Essays*, Oxford: Clarendon Press, pp. 314–42.
Kleingeld, P. (1998) "Kant on the Unity of Theoretical and Practical Reason," *Review of Metaphysics* 52: 311–39.
Lenoir, T. (1980) "Kant, Blumenbach and Vital Materialism in German Biology," *Isis* 71: 77–108.
Lenoir, T. (1989) *The Strategy of Life: Teleology and Mechanics in Nineteenth Century German Biology*, Chicago: University of Chicago Press.
Lovejoy, A.O. (1968) "Kant and Evolution," in B. Glass, O. Temkin and W.L. Strauss Jr. (eds.), *Forerunners of Darwin 1745–1859*, Baltimore: Johns Hopkins University Press, pp. 173–206.
McLaughlin, P. (1982) "Blumenbach und der Bildungstrieb: Zum Verhältnis von epigenetischer Embryologie und typologischem Artbegriff," *Medizinhistorisches Journal* 17: 357–72.

McLaughlin, P. (1990) *Kant's Critique of Teleology in Biological Explanation: Antinomy and Teleology*, Lewiston: Edwin Mellon Press.

Nuzzo, A. (2005) *Kant and the Unity of Reason*, West Lafayette: Purdue University Press.

Richards, R. (2000) "Kant and Blumenbach on the *Bildungstrieb*: A Historical Misunderstanding," *Studies in History and Philosophy of Science Part C: Studies in History and Philosophy of Biological and Biomedical Sciences* 31: 11–32.

Roe, S.A. (1981) *Matter, Life, and Generation: Eighteenth-Century Embryology and the Haller-Wolff Debate*, Cambridge: Cambridge University Press.

Roth, S. (2008) "Kant und die Biologie seiner Zeit (§§79–81)," in O. Höffe (ed.), *Immanuel Kant: Kritik der Urteilskraft*, Berlin: Akademie Verlag, pp. 275–87.

Schrader, G. (1953) "The Status of Teleological Judgment in the Critical Philosophy," *Kant-Studien* 45: 204–35.

Sellars, W. (1963) "Philosophy and the Scientific Image of Man," in *Science, Perception and Reality*, Atascadero: Ridgeview Publishing.

White, D.A. (1979) "On Bridging the Gulf between Nature and Morality in the *Critique of Judgment*," *Journal of Aesthetics and Art Criticism* 38: 179–88.

Zumbach, C. (1984) *The Transcendent Science: Kant's Conception of Biological Methodology*, The Hague: Martinus Nijhoff.

Further Reading

K. Ameriks, "Status des Glaubens (§§90–1) und Allgemeine Anmerkung über Teleologie," in O. Höffe (ed.), *Immanuel Kant: Kritik der Urteilskraft* (Berlin: Akademie Verlag, 2008), pp. 331–49: The first two sections offer a detailed and illuminating analysis of §§90–1 and relate them to the pertinent discussions of the first *Critique* and *Logic*. A. Chignell, "Belief in Kant," in *Philosophical Review* 116 (2007): 323–60: An indispensable paper for the broader context and implications of Kant's notion of pure practical affirmation or holding to be true. G. Cunico, "Erklärungen für das Übersinnliche: Physikotheologischer und moralischer Gottesbeweis (§§85–9)," in O. Höffe (ed.), *Immanuel Kant: Kritik der Urteilskraft* (Berlin: Akademie Verlag, 2008), pp. 309–29: A perspicuous and detailed presentation of the argument of §§85–9. J. Freudiger, "Kants Schlußstein. Wie die Teleologie die Einheit der Vernunft stiftet," *Kant-Studien* 87 (1996): 423–35: A lucid critical examination of the Methodology and its answer to the problem of bridging the chasm between nature and freedom. P. Guyer, "From Nature to Morality: Kant's New Argument in the 'Critique of Teleological Judgment'," in *Kant's System of Nature and Freedom: Selected Essays* (Oxford: Clarendon Press, 2005), pp. 314–42: A detailed reconstruction of the argument of the Critique of Teleological Judgment and defense of the claim that it offers a new theoretical grounding of the highest good and a benevolent God. A.W. Wood *Kant's Moral Religion* (Ithaca: Cornell University Press, 1970): The classic reconstruction of Kant's defense of moral faith.

B. Doctrinal Part

I. METAPHYSICS OF MORALS

24

KANT'S "INTRODUCTION" TO THE *METAPHYSICS OF MORALS*

Otfried Höffe

★★★

The *Metaphysics of Morals* of 1797 is a book which Kant had worked on for many years. Already, in a letter from December 31, 1765 (more than three decades before the final publication and still prior to the so-called silent decade), Kant wrote to the philosopher and mathematician Johann Heinrich Lambert concerning a "*metaphys.: origin of practical worldly wisdom*". Twenty years later, in the pro-grammatic, preliminary engagement of a metaphysics of morals, the *Groundwork of the Metaphysics of Morals*, that intention resounds in the title.

Although Kant had in mind the project of a metaphysics of morals for many years, he wrote it in his own typical manner, taking time to allow for the development and maturing of his thought: that is, only *after* he had completed his Critical work. Just as with the text as a whole, the "Preface" and above all the "Introduction" are densely written, reminiscent almost of encyclopedia articles. Schopenhauer views this choice uncharitably, describing Kant's *Doctrine of Right* simply as the prod-uct of the author's own senility (cf. *The World as Will and Representation*, vol. 1, Book 4, § 62). Schopenhauer accuses Kant of producing an "odd mixture of irreconcilable errors" (i.e., weaknesses in fundamental ideas and arguments).

This accusation, however, can be rejected for the most part (as an initial attempt, see Höffe 2014: Ch. IX). On the contrary, one finds no sign of senility, or, plumbing the depths of polemical condescension, unnecessary loquaciousness. Kant writes with great density because he has often and thoroughly thought through the themes of his metaphysics, articulating them backwards and forwards so that he now can present and ground them succinctly, without detours and with limited meanderings.[1]

1. Section I: Idea of and Necessity for a Metaphysics of Morals

Decisive – and in comparison to earlier writings, relatively new – is the differential analysis between the idea (and necessity) of a metaphysics and the duty to have a metaphysics of morals. Natural science's concern for objects of external sense allows us to "accept many principles as universal on the evidence of experience" without an *a priori* deduction (*RL* 6: 215). Chemists even depend "entirely on experience" and, nonetheless, assume necessity and universality (*RL* 6: 215). Such

DOI: 10.4324/9781003406617-31

approaches are fundamentally and completely denied to moral laws. Indeed, moral laws are different even in kind to the prudential demands made by a doctrine of happiness which needs to appeal fundamentally and completely to experience. Happiness has to do so, because only experience "can teach what brings us joy" (*RL* 6: 215); purportedly rational reflections on the basis of experience are dismissed by Kant as an "apparently a priori reasoning" (*RL* 6: 215). These are nothing other than experiences raised by induction to generality. More importantly, they belong to a "tenuous" generality because "everyone must be allowed countless exceptions" (*RL* 6: 216).

From the perspective of that empiricism which dominates our sense of ethics today, these theses sound irreconcilably provocative. Yet, for Kant, they are self-evident theses. In Kant's oeuvre, this had been so since the *Groundwork* or even earlier. The *Critique of Pure Reason* (A823/B851) argues that morality is concerned with "absolutely necessary" ends while the metaphysics of morals is concerned with *a priori* principles (B869/A841). According to Kant's thesis, which is convincing up to this day, this is because, when talking about morality, one is not concerned with what the German word "Sitten" means, namely, "manners and customs" (*RL* 6: 216). It is astonishing, though, that Kant makes this clear only in *The Metaphysics of Morals* and not earlier – in the "Preface" to the *Groundwork*, at least. In the *Groundwork*, however, Kant is already clear enough. What is at stake is a "pure will" completely determined "from a priori principles" (*GMS* 4: 390). Now, in *The Metaphysics of Morals*, Kant states it even more explicitly, that, because of the categorical "ought", everything depends upon an absolute (not comparatively generalizable) and upon a universal (not generalized) legal legislation (*RL*, 6: 216).

No less consistent and convincing is what at first appears to be an astonishing thesis: that it is a duty to have a metaphysics of morals. The thesis is astonishing only as long as one takes metaphysics to be a merely cognitive endeavor, which, of course, applies to the metaphysics of natural science but not to that of morality.[2]

In order to understand Kant's thesis, we must distinguish between two concepts, more precisely, between two aspects, and, in addition, between two levels, of a metaphysics of morals. The text named the *Metaphysics of Morals*, to be sure, has a cognitive character, because it illuminates what the normal person has, "only in an obscure way," but nonetheless "within himself" (*RL* 6: 216). Thus, it enlightens man about himself, so that there are two levels: the level of obscure knowledge and the level of bright and enlightened knowledge.

How, then, can there be a duty? The duty in question is not a cognitive duty to bring something vaguely known into the bright light of knowledge, but a moral duty to have a clear apprehension of that which is only vaguely known. Kant gives no argument for this claim. A creative interpretation is required here that adheres closely to Kant's convictions.

What follows seems to fit with those convictions. What is required morally is not knowledge, but a moral *attitude* as the readiness to lead one's life from a moral point of view. In some respects, it is a second-order duty, that, when applied systematically, becomes a pre-duty or pre-command: it is the duty to subjugate oneself to duty. Morality is similar to Kant's notion of the fact of reason. This attitude has an "autopoietical character" that calls forth one to moral judgment (Höffe 2012: 154). Reason, too, asks that one should create or constitute oneself as a free being with practical reason. This task is, for Kant, a moral duty, and corresponds to an antecedent 'ought', to a proto-categorical imperative.

As is well-known, Kant's philosophical ethics of autonomy systematically diverges fundamentally from Aristotle's ethics of *eudaimonia*. Nonetheless, here it shows itself to be in conformity with Aristotle's notion of a three-dimensionally practical philosophy: (moral) action is not merely the subject-matter. This action (gr. *praxis*), which is concerned with the overcoming of the "grossest" (including cognitive) and "most pernicious errors" (i.e., what is morally harmful in the highest sense, *RL* 6: 215), is also aimed at. Finally, morality is already present, not so much as an 'is', but most of all as a duty.

2. Section II: A Rich Tableau of Concepts

In answer to the question of how human mental capacities are related to moral laws, Kant develops[3] rich and complicated range of concepts. He goes on to expand these concepts further in the section on the "Division" (Sect. IV (III)) and the section on the "preliminary concepts" (Sect. III (IV)). The nuances attending this terminology satisfies the aspiration to "scholastic precision" (*RL* 6: 206) mentioned in the Preface. Every theory of action, moral psychology, and meta-ethics would do well to take it as a conceptual model.

According to the title of the section, one might expect at first an exhaustive tableau of human mental capacities that, then, would serve as the background for profiling moral laws. This expectation is dashed in two respects. Kant does not present every mental capacity as he does in the Introduction to the *Critique of the Power of Judgment* where he discusses three: the faculty of cognition, the feeling of pleasure and displeasure, and the faculty of desire (*KU* 5: 177). In this text Kant is concerned immediately with the capacity relevant for praxis, the faculty of desire. The counterpart for the theoretical realm, the faculty of cognition, is not mentioned, whereas the feeling of pleasure and displeasure is mentioned because it is in part connected to the faculty of desire.

When it comes to the faculty of desire, Kant begins with something that is easily overlooked, a capacity that is not specifically human. This is the capacity of a being "to act in accordance with its representations" that he calls life (*RL* 6: 211). Kant does not say to whom or what he attributes this capacity. Unquestionably, it is not possessed by every living being, plants for obvious example. When it comes to higher, more developed, animals, one can hardly deny its presence. The *Critique of the Power of Judgment* attributes to "the animals" the capacity to act according to representations, which is why, "they are still of the same genus as human beings (as living beings)" (*KU* 5: 464). To be sure, one would hardly attribute this capacity to all animals (e.g., cockroaches and ants) so that Kant would have been more precise if he had spoken just of "animals" and not "the animals." We can also not draw from this passage – a passage which is concerned not with a theory of animals, but is part of the doctrine of method of the teleological judgment – that Kant would consider beings who lack this capacity (e.g., plants) not as living beings at all. Thankfully, since the respective questions are of an empirical nature, they are not relevant for the central aim of Section II (I). This is because only beings with practical reason engage in the relationship to the moral law referred to in the title of the section – the beings in question are, if we put aside angels and God, human beings.

With remarkable consistency and trenchant succinctness, Kant proceeds by means of three steps, which he never expressly distinguishes. First, he develops the concepts of pleasure and displeasure which are contrary to the moral law because they are "merely subjective" (*RL* 6: 211). Kant elaborates on these concepts by connecting them with two modes of action of the faculty of desire: desire and aversion. Next, Kant introduces the concepts of feeling and practical pleasure (in contrast to mere contemplative pleasure), and, in a further step, he presents the concepts of desire, inclination, interest, and concupiscence (*RL* 6: 213). The concept of interest constitutes a shift from subjective concepts to concepts which are explicitly morally relevant. However, because interest judges according to "a general rule" (*RL* 6: 212), it admits of, as a special case, universal rules or "pure rational principles" (*RL* 6: 212) by which it becomes a "pure interest of reason" (*RL* 6: 213), and a "sense-free inclination" emerges (*RL* 6: 213).

In the second step, Kant turns to concepts that lead to morality but are not yet specifically moral concepts: choice, wish and will. The third step eventually leads to the genuinely moral concepts of freedom of choice (as opposed to animal choice) and to the positive and negative concept of freedom. Subsequently, the concepts of moral, juridical and ethical laws follow, as well as the concepts of legality and morality.

This tableau of concepts is already so rich that one is astonished to encounter their further development in the later Section III (IV). In any event, one must relativize the later section's title of "preliminary concept." As we can see, concepts that are "common to both parts of *The Metaphysics of Morals*" (*RL* 6: 222) are already developed in Section II (I), which is devoted to mental capacities. What follows is a closer discussion of some of those concepts.

Decisive to Kant's understanding of metaphysics is a pair of concepts that are not found before, appearing in neither the *Groundwork* nor in the *Critique of Practical Reason*. The two related, but distinct, concepts of choice ("Willkür") and will ("Wille") appear for the first time in Section II (I) of the Introduction to *The Metaphysics of Morals*. Both are found under "the faculty of desire in accordance with concepts" (*RL* 6: 213) and consist of a "faculty to do or to refrain from doing as one pleases" (*RL* 6: 213). Their difference lies in the following: When it comes to choice, the faculty of desire is directed towards "one's action" (*RL* 6: 213), whereas with will the concern is with "the ground determining choice to action" (*RL* 6: 213). In this latter case, one no longer is determined by something external, which, then, is tantamount to practical reason itself (*RL* 6: 213; cf. also *GMS* 4: 413).

Kant, here, speaks simply of practical reason, without giving any further qualification. He admits all three possible forms of reason: that of technically practical, pragmatically practical, and morally practical. These forms increase in their demands, but no demands are made explicit in this particular passage. The least demanding form is what we are left with. When the notion of practical reason is left unqualified, we are dealing with technically practical reason, that is, reason in its hypothetical and technical interpretation with its respective principles. The same threefold distinction – albeit not mentioned explicitly by Kant – holds for the the concept of the will. The will can take on a technical, pragmatic, and moral form. Since, again, we do not get any further qualification, Kant seems to mean the most basic form of the will, that is, the technically rational will.

Höwing (2013: 37–42) goes to great lengths to determine what Kant might understand by a "faculty to do or to refrain from doing as one pleases" (*RL* 6: 213). Höwing's conclusion is convincing inasmuch as the relevant principles are not yet moral-practical principles. We can arrive at this conclusion more quickly when we take a closer look at the text itself and distinguish, as I have done here, the three steps in Kant's presentation of his conceptual tableau. Such a reading interprets the passage on the "faculty of desire in accordance with concepts" (*RL* 6: 213) as leading towards morality, but not yet employing moral concepts. Three observations support this interpretation. First, one encounters the notion of "pure," hence, moral, practical reason for the first time only in the next paragraph (*RL* 6: 213). Second, the final concept of the paragraph leading to morality – practical reason – is not qualified in any further sense; hence, it is not yet morally qualified. Third, even "to do or refrain from doing as one pleases" lacks any moral qualification.

One encounters "free choice" where a determination occurs independently of merely sensible impulses, by means of pure reason, unlike in mere animals. In accordance with the negative concept of freedom, the will here is a pure will because it is independent of sensible impulses. Positive freedom consists in "the ability of pure reason to be of itself practical" (*RL* 6: 214). In contrast to an occasional misunderstanding, pure practical reason does not consist in a (theoretical) ability to *perceive* the demands of morality but, rather, in the capacity to *act* morally on the basis of maxims.

The condition for an appropriate maxim consists in its "qualifying as universal law" (*RL* 6: 214). Even if Kant speaks here of an "imperative" (*RL* 6: 214) without the supplement "categorical," it is the categorical imperative he is talking about, in its basic form, found in Section III (IV) (cf. *RL* 6:

224). The three forms of the categorical imperative which Kant distinguishes in the *Groundwork* (the formulas of natural law, human end, and kingdom of ends) are found neither in Section III (IV), nor here in Section II (I). Kant's explanation for the imperative (*RL* 6: 214), however, is already known from the *Groundwork* and the *Critique of Practical Reason* (cf. *KpV* §7). Because pure reason as a faculty of principles "does not have within it the matter of the law (. . .), there is nothing it can make the supreme law and determining ground of choice except the form" (*RL* 6: 214).

In his famous essay, "Two Concepts of Liberty," Isaiah Berlin accuses Kant of only knowing the positive and not the more important concept of negative freedom. This accusation is astonishing because it contradicts Kant's understanding of (negative) freedom as independence from sensible impulses (*RL* 6: 213) that one finds already in his earliest writings and is here simply repeated.

Just as there are two forms of metaphysics – that of natural science and of morality – so, too, there are two kind of laws, natural laws and the laws of freedom. The latter are also called "moral" laws (*RL* 6: 214). These laws of freedom occur in two forms. These two forms should not be equated with the distinction between the Doctrine of Right and the Doctrine of Virtue. Laws of freedom are "juridical" inasmuch as they direct the conformity to laws, of external actions (*RL* 6: 214). If the laws of freedom *themselves* also serve as determining grounds for action, they are to be considered "ethical" (*RL* 6: 214).

At this point, Kant delivers a further alternative. He then expands this alternative in the following section (one cannot summarize more simply the complex phenomenon of morality). Kant argues that freedom can be taken in an external and also in an internal sense with regard to choice. Externally freedom is concerned with legality. Internally freedom is concerned with morality. Although there are two forms of laws of freedom – juridical and ethical – we do have an analogous situation to theoretical philosophy's concept of two forms of intuition: space (with respect to outer sense) and time (with respect to inner sense). The juridical laws of freedom correspond to space; ethical laws of freedom correspond to time. Just as in the case of theoretical reason where time is concerned with both outer and inner objects, so here morality is concerned not only with the external but also the internal use of freedom, "although they should not [in the sense of: need not] always be considered in this respect" (*RL* 6: 214).

3. Section IV (III): On the Division of a Metaphysics of Morals

In light of the disputed sequence of the sections, one might be advised to link Section IV (III) to Section II (I) due to its similar treatment of faculties. On the one hand, Section IV (III) provides a more precise discussion of Section II's (I's) not yet developed concepts of the juridical (i.e., *Jus*) and the ethical. Justice and ethics, as well as concepts like "legality-morality" and "external-internal legislation", are paired in each section. In other words, they are part of that dichotomous character that, according to Kant's *Lecture on Logic* (cf. *Log* 9: Note 1 to §113), constitutes the sole *a priori* division of principles. On the other hand and in support of maintaining the traditional sequence of the sections, Kant employs concepts here such as duty and obligation that are *not* introduced until Section III's (IV's) treatment of preliminary concepts. Moreover, the footnote given to the title of Section IV (III) provides grounds for placing Section III (IV) (on preliminary concepts) prior to Section IV (III) (concerned with the organizational structure of a metaphysics of morals). Reflections on "the division of a system" fit better at the end of an introduction. In light of the disagreement over the sequencing, I especially hold to the traditional sequencing because the sequence does not affect an objective discussion of the themes. At best, one can say that Kant did not reach final clarity with the composition of the introduction. This lack of clarity is hastened by the conceptual pairing of the "juridical-ethical" as well as that of "legality-morality." While this pairing is treated twice, it is absent in the list of shared preliminary concepts. Furthermore, the concept of maxims plays a role already in Section II (I) (*RL* 6: 214) but is not actually discussed until Section III (IV) (*RL* 6: 225). Not least, what is given in the footnote as the "highest divided concept" of "right or wrong" as "*aut fas aut nefas*" [i.e."proper or improper"] (*RL* 6: 218) is not found in the preliminary concepts of Section III (IV). There, one finds "*right* or *wrong*" paired with another Latin concept, that of "*rectum aut minus rectum*" (*RL* 6: 223), contrasted to just ("justum") and unjust ("injustum") (cf. *RL* 6: 224). Final clarity here is difficult to determine.

Section IV (III) begins with a concept of lawgiving whose qualification by the term "all" (*RL* 6: 218) appears to be plainly general. In fact, we are here concerned with actions and thus practical legislation solely. Since Kant mentions two options: not only "reason alone," hence morality as prescriptive, but also "the choice of another" (ibid.), he could be speaking of the lawgiving of plain, and not yet moral, practical reason. The "two elements" of practical lawgiving – a law as the objective, normative element and an incentive as a subjective, motivational element (cf. *RL* 6: 218) – support such a reading. These two elements apply as well to sub-moral, hypothetical-practical laws that, to be sure, have as imperatives of prudence only the rank of empirical counsels (cf. *GMS* 4: 418). However, a more careful reading discovers that the "two elements" are genuinely moral.

With regard to the law, the respective action is represented as a duty (*RL* 6: 218). Furthermore, what is referred to as the incentive is explained by the concept of obligation, which unequivocally has a moral nature according to the preliminary concepts as "the necessity of a free action under a categorical imperative of reason" (*RL* 6: 222). In this respect, the brackets after "all lawgiving," with its two possibilities of an "internal or external action," together with "by reason alone or by the choice of another" (*RL* 6: 218) anticipate the alternative between ethical or juridical laws, introduced in the next paragraph. For, this alternative concerns two different incentives: either one makes the "duty the incentive" (i.e., ethical lawgiving); or "an incentive other than the idea of duty" is permitted (i.e., juridical lawgiving; *RL* 6: 219). A few lines later Kant speaks of rightful and ethical legislation; and even later of doctrine of rights (or *ius*) and ethics. The three conceptual pairings of ethical-juridical lawgiving, rightful-ethical legislation, and the doctrine of right's *ius*-ethics turn out to be equivalent.

Subsequently to this discussion, we get a lucid definition of legality (lawfulness) as the (non-) conformity of an action with law with the supplement: "irrespective of the incentive to it" (*RL* 6: 219). When it comes to morality, by contrast, the idea of duty "is also the incentive to the action" (*RL* 6: 219).

Consequently, Kant explains that ethical lawgiving (therefore ethics generally) applies the notion of duty to both internal and external actions, because it applies to "everything that is a duty in general" (*RL* 6: 219). When it comes to Kant's precise formulation, though, one encounters a small discrepancy. On the one hand, not only ethics but also "ethical lawgiving" covers all duties; on the other hand, a part of lawgiving is not included in ethics, but rather in *ius* (cf. *RL* 6: 219). Kant employs the example of the precept "*pacta sunt servanda*", which he – inconsistently – translates as "contract" (*RL* 6: 219); elsewhere as "promises agreed to must be kept" (*RL* 6: 220); and even as "keeping with promises made in a contract" (*RL* 6: 220).

Leaving these small linguistic discrepancies aside, Kant's conceptual tableau proves to be highly complex, yet, nonetheless, congruent with our fundamental moral intentions. In this respect, it appears to be superior to the simplified concepts employed by many moral and legal philosophers today; it is highly suitable for the problem area of law and morality (see Höffe 2008: Part II, esp. Ch. 5). One such question of this problem area is whether duties apply to external or to internal actions. The answer frames the discussion of legal or ethical lawgiving – duties of right or duties of virtue. It is an altogether different question whether one only fulfils duties simply because they are duties, regardless of what the actions are to which they are applied. Since acting from duty alone, that is, morality, includes all duties, ethics needs to be examined from two perspectives. On the one hand, there are duties specific to ethics that go beyond what is demanded by legal morality; and, on the other hand, all duties belong to ethics, not only those that are its specific duties.

Kant does not elaborate his concept of internal action, that is, that which is distinctive of ethical lawgiving. If one invokes the Introduction to the Doctrine of Virtue, we could think of the notion of "self-constraint" (*TL* 6: 379). It makes sense that Kant, in this respect, speaks, of "internal lawgiving" (*RL* 6: 220 and 221).

In the last two paragraphs devoted to the further examination of *ius* and ethics, one encounters examples of different forms of lawgiving. It is part of juridical lawgiving – duties of right of which one can be coerced (*RL* 6: 220) and duties "of narrow obligation" (*TL* 6: 390) – to fulfil one's promise. Alternatively, it is a virtue to fulfil it without being externally coerced (*TL* 6: 390). Ethical lawgiving is by contrast exclusively (!) internal with its "directly-ethical duties" (*RL* 6: 221) of "wide obligation" (*TL* 6: 390) and demands "actions of benevolence" (*RL*, 6: 220). To internal lawgiving, finally, belong all duties – the directly ethical, that is, genuinely ethical duties as well as the indirectly ethical duties, that is, the duties of right.

4. Section III (IV): Preliminary Concepts

The longest section of the "Introduction," which consists of eight pages and is almost as long as the other three sections together, alludes to the tradition of scholastic philosophy. It does so by virtue of the subtitle that is placed in brackets, "*Philosophia practica universalis*." It is especially referring to Christian Wolff's text from 1738–39 with the same title. In the Preface to the *Groundwork*, Kant distanced himself sharply from the "celebrated Wolff" (*GMS* 4: 390). Despite his invocation of Wolff's text in the subtitle here, Kant by no means retracts his criticism of him (i.e., the absence of a pure *a priori* principle). In stark contrast, Kant begins with a pure *a priori* concept – that of freedom defined as a pure rational concept (*RL* 6: 221).

Kant neither explains his criterion for selecting and organising the concepts to follow, nor is such a criterion easy to detect from the text. The majority of the concepts and their sequencing can be explained by the vital task Kant sets for *The Metaphysics of Morals*. That task is to develop not only a legal- but also virtue-relevant theory of action. He means to do this in conjunction with the initial and guiding concept of freedom that is characteristic not of pure (i.e., "holy": *RL* 6: 222) but, rather, of free creatures which are sensuously stimulated. With the allusion of his subtitle, Kant means to show that in his *Metaphysics of Morals* he wishes to treat that same broad and comprehensive topic area of the doctrine of right and virtue as Wolff had done. In fact (and in contrast to Wolff), Kant develops a genuine and rigorous theory of freedom.

Section III (IV) develops, thus, concepts which are common to both parts of *The Metaphysics of Morals* (*RL* 6: 222). More precisely, they are *preliminary* concepts and, as such, concepts which are not specific to one of the two parts. Above all, these are concepts that are not discussed in either part because of their generality. This procedure has the astonishing consequence that a conceptual pairing that is so central for law as "person" and "thing" (*RL* 6: 223) appears only in the passage on preliminary concepts and not – not even additionally – in the *Doctrine of Right* proper.

When it comes to Kant's concept of the person in the *Metaphysics of Morals* we must consider an important passage in the *Doctrine of Virtue*. Its content should have appeared already among the preliminary concepts because of its meaning and validity for both parts of the *Metaphysics of Morals*. Within the passage "On Servility" in § 11 of the *Doctrine of Virtue*, one reads that a human being "regarded as a person, that is, as the subject of a morally practical reason" is "exalted above any price" (*TL* 6: 434). Persons possess a dignity, described as an "absolute inner worth," because they can demand respect "from all other rational beings in the world" and "which he must also not forfeit" (*TL* 6: 435).

When in §B of the Introduction to the *Doctrine of Right* Kant speaks of a "universal law of freedom" (*RL* 6: 230), one is meant to recall the preliminary concepts for adequate understanding. Where it comes to differentiations, they break down again dichotomously: theoretical-practical philosophy, negative-positive freedom, technical-categorical imperative, permitted-unpermitted, person–thing, right–wrong, and so on.

Kant begins with the concept of freedom, declares it to be a pure rational concept, which makes it regulative, rather than constitutive, for theoretical philosophy. When it comes to its practical application, however, freedom demonstrates its reality by practical principles (*RL* 6: 221) – here Kant alludes to his theory as being the "fact of reason".

"Unconditional practical laws," or "moral" laws (*RL* 6: 221), are based on this concept of freedom. When it comes to the qualification of laws, "moral" is here employed as a pure rational discipline (see *GMS* 4: 388) with its specific form of obligation. Morals are not used in the sense of their belonging to natural inclination.

These practical laws take on the character of imperatives when applied to sensible, free, beings, that is, rational natural beings. Given their unconditionality, they take on the character of categorical imperatives. Two things are striking here. First, there is more than one, single, unconditional practical law (on this plurality, see *RL* 6: 227). The singular categorical imperative, more familiar to the Kant reader, appears only later in the text (*RL* 6: 225). Second, Kant does not contrast the categorical imperatives to the hypothetical imperatives as he does in the *Groundwork*. Hypothetical imperatives don't appear in the Introduction at all, even if the criterion "command only conditionally" (*RL* 6: 221) notionally corresponds to that of a hypothetical imperative. In the *Groundwork*, Kant introduces a subset of hypothetical technical imperatives. However, the Introduction treats them as a whole ("All other imperatives are technical" – *RL* 6: 222). Pragmatic imperatives are not discussed. This is explained by a remark in the *Groundwork* concerning the (pragmatic) imperatives of prudence. They "agree entirely with those of skill", that is, with (technical) imperatives of skill, if there is "a determined concept of happiness" (*GMS* 4: 417). This demand is not fulfilled, according to Kant, in the Introduction's discussion of preliminary concepts.

Presumably, this is because Kant is primarily concerned with sensible rational beings. He is, therefore, not consistent in maintaining the distinction between imperatively indifferent practical laws and the (categorical) imperative. On the one hand, already in §7 of the *Critique of Practical Reason*, he does not introduce this imperatively indifferent law but the categorical imperative under the title "Fundamental Law of Pure Practical Reason." Similarly in the *Metaphysics of Morals*, a bit later, he will speak of the categorical imperative in the singular as "the supreme principle of the doctrine of morals" (*RL* 6: 226), and, again later, the (moral practical) law is qualified twice in a manner not applied to all rational beings (i.e., not to pure, holy beings) but merely to sensible rational beings. On the other hand, Kant calls the law a "proposition that contains a categorical imperative (a command)" (*RL* 6: 227).

When Kant turns to the concepts of morally possible or impossible actions, he is interested exclusively in morally necessary actions. In doing so, he implicitly criticizes the British *moral sense* philosophers. While adherence to what is morally necessary is connected "with a pleasure [. . .] of a distinctive kind", it is a moral feeling which, for two reasons, we take no account of "in practical laws of reason" (*RL* 6: 221). First, this feeling has nothing to do with "the basis of practical laws but only with the subjective effect in the mind" (*RL* 6: 221). Second, this feeling does not add anything "objectively, i.e., in the judgment of reason" (*RL* 6: 221). The Preface to the *Doctrine of Virtue* underscores this. Moral feeling is subjectively, and not objectively, practical. Here one is to think of that – intellectually effected – feeling of respect for the moral law (cf. *KpV* 5: 75, see also *KU* §12). Consequently, a feeling always belongs to "the order of nature" (*TL* 6: 376).

From the many additional preliminary concepts that are introduced, let us take a closer look at the following: According to the concept which Kant has introduced as a silent attack on Wolff, obligation is "the necessity of a free action under a categorical imperative," not restricted to, but strengthened by, the addition "of reason" (*RL* 6: 222). The bond of obligation to the categorical imperative is so tight that Kant can reverse its terms in his imagination while retaining their logical cohesion. A few paragraphs later he writes: "The categorical imperative [. . .] as such only affirms what obligation is" (*RL* 6: 2: 225). This is followed by the familiar basic formula of the categorical imperative, which in the whole *Metaphysics of Morals* appears only here, in the Introduction: "act upon a maxim that can also hold as a universal law" (*RL* 6: 225; see also 226). The justification why the categorical imperative can serve for universal lawgiving and the importance of the concept of maxims follow immediately.

Let us return to Kant's concept of obligation. It is a strictly normative and purely moral concept. The legal notion of obligation in civic law, usually occurring in the plural as liabilities, plays no role here when it comes to the task of a metaphysics of morals. What is to be recognized is that in this context obligation is, according to the criterion of necessity, a singular thing. (This is why Kant in the *Doctrine of Virtue* speaks of "only *one* obligation of virtue, whereas there are *many* duties of virtue" – *TL* 6: 410.) Later, Kant speaks of obligation also in the plural, but then in a different sense that is closer to the concept of duties (cf. *RL* 6: 224).

Kant explains that "the ground of the possibility of categorical imperatives" lies in its exclusive connection to the freedom of choice (*RL* 6: 222). The additional concepts are related to freedom, or the obligation resulting from freedom, as well. Duty is labelled as the "matter of obligation" (*RL* 6: 2: 222). An action is a deed insofar as it is viewed "under obligatory laws" that are imputable to the agent as author. A person is a subject capable of this kind of imputation, where everything else is a thing. A deed that conforms to duty is "right"; whereas deeds contrary to duty are "wrong."

Kant introduces next a set of paired concepts ("just and unjust") that he rarely employs. In the context of the paired concepts of "right and wrong," "just and unjust" are concerned with a subset of external laws. They are equated with the Latin notions of *iustum* and *iniustum*, which appear in §B of the "Introduction" to the *Doctrine of Right* in German as *Recht* and *Unrecht*. Assuming that there is a consistency to the concepts, what appears in the Introduction as "*recht-unrecht*" ["right-wrong"] is concerned with the whole, whereas "*Recht-Unrecht*" ["just-unjust"] is concerned with that subset that is treated in the Introduction as related to external laws and, there, can be translated as "just-unjust."

The next paragraph is probably the most frequently discussed piece of the entire Introduction: It consists of four (in part lengthy) sentences amounting to eighteen lines concerned with the topic of "conflict of duties." Without providing any example, the first sentence defines the theme: a conflict of duties occurs where a duty "wholly or in part" cancels another duty (*RL* 6: 224). The second sentence explains that duties that are opposed to one another are "inconceivable." Kant gives a cogent, two-part argument: For one thing, because of the concepts of duty and obligation, particular actions have an objective practical necessity, for another thing, "two rules opposed to each other" cannot "be necessary at the same time" (*RL* 6: 224). The third sentence states it is only possible that there are two grounds of obligation, one of which "is not a duty." If, then, two such grounds of obligation conflict, Kant, in the fourth sentence, claims that practical philosophy (which, according to *RL* 6: 216 has as its object "freedom of choice") announces that the duty lies not to the stronger obligation, but to the stronger *ground* of obligation. The stronger ground should have priority.

I would like to offer a tentative interpretation of this topic, which in fact is a complex field of themes. My interpretation asks, initially, what examples apply to the sentences 2 and 3. The popular example for sentence 2, concerned with the conflict of duties, is one that Kant himself gives in his treatise "On a Supposed Right to Lie from Philanthropy": the conflict between the prohibition of lying and the requirement to offer aid. According to his critics, Kant here demonstrates himself to be an inhuman rigorist. However, his arguments are not so easily dismissible. First, as an absolute duty with narrow obligation (cf. *TL* 6: 390), the prohibition of lying admits of no exception, whereas the requirement to offer aid – as a duty of virtue and as an imperfect duty with wider obligation (cf. *TL* 6: 390) – prescribes no concrete, particular action. Second, a lie, defined as "an intentionally untrue declaration to another (. . .) always harms another, even if not another individual, nevertheless humanity generally, inasmuch as it makes the source of right unusable" (*VRML* 8: 426). Put into a nutshell, if we have a conflict between a duty of right and a duty of virtue, a duty of virtue which would infringe the duty of right, would indeed be contrary to duty. Furthermore, Kant knows of no conflict between two genuine (i.e. moral, not positivistic) duties of right – and there are good reasons to presume that such a conflict is difficult to imagine.

The criterion of "stronger obligation" mentioned in sentence 4, but rejected by Kant, cannot hold because the necessity involved in the definition of obligation allows for no "more or less" but only for "either necessary or not necessary." Kant does not present this argument himself. What example can one give of two actions that obligate from grounds which vary in their strength? The ground for obligation, in Kant's context, seems to be weaker than obligation itself; therefore, it involves less than necessity. If we imagine two non-necessary demands (e.g., in the Kantian spirit, two prudential imperatives aiming at one's personal well-being), it seems to be clear that in the case that two such imperatives conflict, one follows that counsel that, with greater probability or to a greater degree, serves one's own welfare.

Therefore, despite the common charge that Kant is an inhuman rigorist, Kant's thesis that there can be no conflict between duties is by no means odd; it may be, even, correct.

Notes

1 Kant, a careful and thoughtful author, could hardly have allowed for the sequence that are the divisions of the "Introduction to the Metaphysics of Morals" as we have it, in the Akademie Ausgabe. These motivated a number of changes by Bernd Ludwig, in his 1988 edition (see "Translator's note on the text of *The metaphysics of morals*", in Kant (1996: 356–7). The Cambridge Edition adopts two of these changes and, significantly, the change of the sections of "Introduction to the Metaphysics of Morals", which are reordered: II, I, IV, III. Here only sections I and II are reordered, whereas III and IV are kept as in the Akademie Ausgabe. For the sake of clarity, I will, in what follows, additionally give the original sequence, as printed in the *Akademie Ausgabe*, in brackets.
2 See Chapter 13, in this volume, on how the metaphysics of morals is both a cognitive and practical endeavor.
3 In what was earlier labeled Section I, now Section II – see note 1. For a detailed discussion, see also section 3 of this chapter.

References

Höffe, O. (2008) *Praktische Philosophie: Das Modell des Aristoteles*, 4th ed., Berlin: Akademie Verlag.
Höffe, O. (2012) *Kants Kritik der praktischen Vernunft. Eine Philosophie der Freiheit*, München: Beck.
Höffe, O. (2014) *Immanuel Kant*, New York: SUNY.
Höwing, T. (2013) "Das Verhältnis der Vermögen des menschlichen Gemüts zu den Sittengesetzen," in A. Trampota, O. Sensen and J. Timmermann (eds.), *Kants "Tugendlehre": A Comprehensive Commentary*, Berlin and Boston: Walter de Gruyter, pp. 25–58.
Kant, I. (1996) *Practical Philosophy*, M.J. Gregor (ed. and trans.), Cambridge: Cambridge University Press.

Further Reading

For other discussions of the text in Kant, which is the focus of this chapter, see M. Baum, "Prior Concepts of the Metaphysics of Morals," in A Trampota, O. Sensen and J. Timmermann (eds.), *Kants "Tugendlehre": A Comprehensive Commentary* (Berlin and Boston: Walter de Gruyter, 2013), pp. 113–38; A. Wood, "Kant's Doctrine of Right: Introduction," in O. Höffe (ed.), *Immanuel Kant: Metaphysische Anfangsgründe der Rechtslehre* (Berlin: Akademie Verlag, 1999), pp. 19–49; G. Zöller, "Idee und Notwendigkeit einer Metaphysik der Sitten," in A. Trampota, O. Sensen and J. Timmermann (eds.), *Kants "Tugendlehre": A Comprehensive Commentary* (Berlin and Boston: Walter de Gruyter, 2013), pp. 11–24; and, with attention also drawn to the Doctrine of virtue, B. Ludwig, "Die Einteilung der Metaphysik im Allgemeinen und die der Tugenlehre im Besonderen," in A. Trampota, O. Sensen and J. Timmermann (eds.), *Kants "Tugendlehre": A Comprehensive Commentary* (Berlin and Boston: Walter de Gruyter, 2013), pp. 59–84; O. Höffe, *Kants Kritik der reinen Vernunft: Die Grundlegung der modernen Philosophie* (Beck: München, 2004) offers a good presentation of the theoretical background of Kant's practical philosophy. For the distinction between ethics and legal philosophy in Kant, see S. Schadow, "Recht und Ethik in Kants Metaphysik der Sitten," in A. Trampota, O. Sensen and J. Timmermann (eds.), *Kants "Tugendlehre": A Comprehensive Commentary* (Berlin and Boston: Walter de Gruyter, 2013), pp. 85–112.

25

DOCTRINE OF RIGHT

Howard Williams

★★★

1. Introduction

There are two major influences that help shape Kant's doctrine of right. They are both historical and philosophical, but in different degrees. The first of these influences is the natural law tradition in political theory, which forms the historical context within which Kant spells out his doctrine. Particularly important in establishing this tradition in so far as it influences Kant are: Jean-Jacques Rousseau, who had a major impact on Kant's practical philosophy in general; Thomas Hobbes and John Locke, in their writings on the state of nature and the foundation of property rights; Grotius and Vattel, in determining Kant's views on international law. Kant becomes closely acquainted with this tradition through his reading of Gottfried Achenwall, whose text *Ius Naturae* (1763) provided the foundation for Kant's courses on Natural Law which he taught over many years (Byrd and Hruschka 2010: 15–19).

The second main influence (and here the weight is on the philosophical side) on Kant's treatment of right is his own critical system. In rereading the natural law tradition Kant shapes it to his own philosophical ends in the light of the main conclusions of his critical philosophy. All three *Critiques* have a significant impact on his theory of right: the first through its limitations on our empirical knowledge; the second through its prioritizing of practical reason where theoretical reason is inconclusive; the third for its legitimation of the use of teleology in a practical, political and historical context. It is axiomatic for Kant that "for the doctrine of right, the first part of the doctrine of morals, there is required a system derived from reason which could be called the *metaphysics of right*" (*MS* 6: 205). Right falls within his critical system of philosophy spelled out in the three volumes beginning with the *Critique of Pure Reason*. Kant has a holistic view of right or law. The basic principles of right are deduced a priori for the individual, however, the deduction does not end at the individual. Right and the positive law that embody it are connected from the individual level through to the national, international and cosmopolitan level. So just as there can be no theory of right that applies exclusively to the individual – we have to look to the institutions within a state that realize right – so also in outlining the sphere of law that is safeguarded by the state we need also to look to the international legal structure that will take us beyond individual and state right.

DOI: 10.4324/9781003406617-32

2. Natural Right

Kant has an ambivalent attitude to the idea of natural right. On the one hand, he is prepared to conduct his enquiries into the theory of law and politics under the framework of natural law (which had been the prevailing tradition in German-speaking countries up to his time) and he is prepared occasionally to invoke natural right in a rhetorical way to support demands in the improvement of human society in his times; yet on the other hand he hardly takes over any of the framework of natural right thinking in its original form. In effect it is possible to argue that in his legal and political theory he replaces the older natural right with his own a priori theory of right. Concepts, such as the "state of nature," the "social contract," "innate freedom" are now seen in this context. As an example of Kant's rhetorical use of the term natural right, we can look to the third Definitive Article of *Toward Perpetual Peace*, where he speaks of

> the inhospitableness of the inhabitants of the sea coasts (for example, the Barbary Coast) in robbing ships in adjacent seas or enslaving stranded seafarers, or that of the inhabitants of deserts (the Arabian Bedouins) in regarding approach to nomadic tribes as a right to plunder them [as being contrary] to natural right.
>
> (*EF* 8: 358)

He deploys the term to condemn what he regards as hostile and lawless behavior which arises in parts of the world to which civil society has not extended. In using the term here Kant wants to tap into a widely felt sense of injustice amongst all people when they witness extreme unfairness and disregard for morality of this kind. He is happy to take advantage of the general connotations of the term in his day, which derive from the natural law tradition in philosophy and jurisprudence. Yet, on the other side, Kant's more specific, technical use of the term in his Doctrine of Right tends towards a disregarding of the conventional uses of the term and an absorption of it within the framework of his own critical philosophy. He takes no precursor in political philosophy as a full authority in the field, relying on his own judgement in taking his own philosophy beyond the previously received wisdom.

As a systematic dimension of Kant's critical philosophy, natural right is dealt with in the Doctrine of Right of the first part of the *Metaphysics of Morals* (first published in 1797). Right requires external coercive laws and they may be of two kinds: natural laws and positive laws. Kant describes natural laws as the type of external laws "that can be recognized as obligatory a priori by reason even without external law giving" (*MS* 6: 224). Thus even in the absence of legislation from a state, natural laws should be obeyed without question by human individuals. There can be neither legal nor moral grounds for disregarding them even where there is no state to apply coercion. By contrast, those laws that "do not bind without actual external lawgiving (and so without it would not be laws) are called *positive* laws" (*MS* 6: 224). For Kant, it is possible to conceive of a system of external laws that contains only positive laws, but "then a natural law would still have to precede it, which would establish the authority of the lawgiver" (*MS* 6: 224). So, as Kant sees it, any actual legal order must have at its foundation natural right even though it may proceed on the basis solely of statutory right. All external legislation must concur with natural right. Thus natural right is not only at the systematic heart of Kant's practical philosophy but also at the center of his understanding of politics and law. However, this is a natural right with unique Kantian features. It is natural right based on the a priori principles of Kant's critical philosophy. We need now to look more closely at those principles.

3. Right Based on A Priori Principles

A key issue for us as we look into Kant's legal philosophy is the nature of the relationship between Kant's pure moral theory – outlined most strikingly in the *Groundwork to the Metaphysics of Morals* (1785) – and the theory of right on which his legal and political philosophy is based. There is no doubting that this is a complex relationship and it is not always clearly expressed by Kant himself (Baiasu 2016: 2–9). Indeed it is possible to argue that there are different accounts of the relationship that Kant gives which do not wholly coincide with each other. What I shall argue for here is a view that I take to predominate in Kant's writings on politics and law and the account I believe to be the most coherent. For Kant neither fully separates morality and right (as does Fichte) nor does he subordinate morality to right (as with Hegel). Right is seen as a separate and distinct part of morality, playing an equal part with virtue in realizing our freedom. The Doctrine of Right precedes the Doctrine of Virtue in Kant's *Metaphysics of Morals*.

We have always to begin with the pure moral theory. This is spelled out in the *Groundwork* and the *Critique of Practical Reason*. Systematicity for Kant within philosophy has to be gained by adopting a metaphysical approach that abstracts from all direct experience. Legal and political philosophy has to depart from a priori ideas (*MS* 6: 215). The pure moral philosophy offers a very clear starting point in that it sets out the principles we should adopt if we are to conduct ourselves decently in our relationships with others and in regard to ourselves. This implies that the Categorical Imperative has to play a foundational role in the philosophy of right. In politics and legal affairs we cannot simply abandon our moral selves. The requirements of the Categorical Imperative, particularly as exemplified by the formulas of the universal law and humanity, should provide a framework for our reasoning about law and politics. But how is this delicate relationship between morality and law to be spelled out? It is not possible that rules that are deemed appropriate for our individual conduct (ethics) can be carried over wholly unaffected into rules that are necessary to our social and collective conduct (right). Indeed the principles that govern pure moral deliberation have to do with our motivation or disposition in acting, and in the sphere of legal and political deliberation we have need of rules that will regulate our actual actions and their effects. The rules of the *Groundwork* are wholly metaphysical: they are concerned with our motivations as rational intellectual beings. The rules of the Doctrine of Right have to do with the external, phenomenal world even though they take their origins in our intellectual existence. The rules of right have to be conditioned by the a priori reflections of pure moral philosophy but they have also to take into account matters encountered in experience. There is an impure element to moral theory as it is deployed in right and politics.[1]

One striking way of putting this is to say that the moral theory of the *Groundwork* has to do with the conditions of human freedom in general, whereas the Doctrine of Right has to do with the conditions of our external freedom, as beings of sense and intellect in a phenomenal world amongst other similar beings. The *Groundwork* outlines the moral law which provides the metaphysical basis for our freedom in general. The moral law assumes the possibility that each rational human individual has the power to determine their maxims in acting. Moral laws are ones that are appropriate for beings that have this power of choice. But moral laws (which are the laws of freedom) can be of two kinds:

> As directed merely to external actions and their conformity to law they are called *juridical* laws; but if they also require that they (the laws) themselves be the determining grounds of actions, they are *ethical* laws, and then one says that conformity with juridical laws is the *legality* of an action and conformity with ethical laws is its *morality*.
>
> (*MS* 6: 214)

There is a symbiotic relation between the moral and the legal in Kant's philosophy. Within the pure moral framework of the categorical imperative we see that the human individual is the kind of being that belongs both to the sphere of the intelligent and the natural world. The human being is capable of acting according to the moral law, however, in belonging also to the natural world, we are drawn by our senses and inclinations, and ultimately our own poor deliberations, to aims and actions that run contrary to moral law. Thus, when it comes to external actions, the incentive to comply with law, which is provided by our freedom, has to be supplemented by a natural (physical) incentive. Kant puts it in this way:

> All lawgiving can therefore be distinguished with respect to the incentives [. . .]. That lawgiving which makes an action a duty and also makes this duty the incentive is *ethical*. But that lawgiving which does not include the incentive of duty in the law and so admits an incentive other than the idea of duty itself is *juridical*.
>
> (*MS* 6: 218–19)

With juridical law, the incentive that is not drawn from duty has to be

> drawn from *pathological* determining grounds of choice, inclinations and aversions, and among these from aversions; for it is a lawgiving which constrains, not an allurement, which invites.
>
> (*MS* 6: 219)

Although external law making introduces this pathological incentive to do our duty, it is not as a result removed from the sphere of moral theory. For as Kant makes evident, we retain the ethical duty to obey the law for its own sake – even with coercive external law – but should we not find that constraint sufficient we assent to the additional incentive of the possibility of pathological coercion. The possibility of the application of coercion to ensure that we obey juridical laws has for Kant to be seen as an integral part of a metaphysics of morals and not an additional condition that is derived from a standpoint wholly external to the teaching of the categorical imperative. The ethical and the legal spheres are indeed distinct but they are not wholly separate from each other. The doctrine of the Categorical Imperative, and the condition it implies, never to attempt to use other individuals solely as means but always also as ends, applies also to external lawgiving or right.

4. Property and Contract

The right to property is, in keeping with practical reason, justified neither solely historically nor empirically. Although the concepts of the state of nature and the social contract appear in Kant's political theory in helping derive our rights to things, they are not dealt with in the same manner as in the political theory of his precursors, such as Hobbes, Locke and Rousseau. They are not external or historical conditions that we are to imagine as a presupposition of a story that leads to the establishment of property ownership, rather they are concepts that are necessarily required to embrace if we are to act as property owners. Just as the categories of the transcendental logic are required so that we can constitute an objective world for our understanding, so we have to presuppose the concept of property ownership (of a 'mine and thine'), deriving from a hypothetical state of nature and social contract, if we are to inhabit a settled social world. We are able to exchange property and enjoy property rights because there are fellow human beings that grasp the idea of property ownership and are prepared to conduct themselves in relation to others in a manner that realizes it.

Social and political freedom are only possible through the acceptance of a "universal principle of right":

> Any action is right if it can coexist with everyone's freedom in accordance with a universal law, or if on its maxim the freedom of choice of each can coexist with everyone's freedom in accordance with a universal law.
>
> (*MS* 6: 230)

Such external freedom is thoroughly reciprocal. We cannot grant to ourselves more freedom than we are prepared to grant others. It presupposes our equality. We do not have the right to subject others to any coercive restraints on their actions which we will not accept ourselves. This freedom presupposes the legislative standpoint in which each has the right to participate in making the laws to which we are all subject. In practice Kant accepts it is impossible for each person to act as a co-legislator, but those who legislate must be seen and see themselves as representatives of each and every person. Kant's republicanism requires that we have, as citizens, to see ourselves as co-participants in making the laws to which we are subject. This is implied by our innate freedom which we share with all rational beings who are also natural beings. We recognise that we have to subject ourselves to the possibility of coercion if we are live in a society with other beings like ourselves.

> Freedom (independence from being constrained by another's choice), insofar as it can coexist with the freedom of every other in accordance with a universal law, is the only original right belonging to every man by virtue of his humanity.
>
> (*MS* 6: 237)

The principal concepts, which Kant uses in his theory of right, such as the state of nature, the original contract, the original common ownership of the earth's surface, are all a priori concepts. He regards them as concepts we have to share in order for us live to in a civil society. They are metaphysical propositions that have to be generally accepted if we are to be part of a rightful society with others. For Kant "all propositions about right are a priori propositions, since they are laws of reason (*dictamina rationis*)" (*MS* 6: 250). Kant thinks that the need for us to use a priori teachings comes particularly to the fore in the deduction of our right to own property. We cannot, he thinks, argue that we have a right to a thing merely upon the basis of our happening to have it in our physical possession at the time. Mere empirical possession does not imply that an object is necessarily ours. Rather we require that others recognize that entitlement to ownership and so we can maintain a thing is ours even if we are not at the time physically holding it. Kant calls possession which is merely the holding of a thing "empirical possession." And it is then "only possession in appearance" (*MS* 6: 249). What is needed to form an effective society with others is a rational possession. At the heart of rational possession or ownership is the

> proposition about the possibility of possessing a thing external to myself, which puts aside any conditions of empirical possession in space and time (and hence presupposes the possibility of *possession noumenon*), goes beyond those limiting conditions; and since it affirms possession of something even without holding it, as necessary for the concept of something external that is mine or yours, it is synthetic.
>
> (*MS* 6: 250)

The ownership of property is never merely an empirical fact that we can establish through mere observation. Property ownership is not a proposition of theoretical philosophy about a condition in the world. It is rather a condition which requires for its affirmation a grasp of practical philosophy. In this respect, practical philosophy can offer us a great deal more than theoretical philosophy.

> No one need be surprised that *theoretical* principles about external objects that are mine or yours get lost in the intelligible and represent no extension of cognition, since no theoretical deduction can be given for the possibility of the concept of freedom on which they are based. It can only be inferred from the practical laws of reason (the categorical imperative), as a fact of reason.
>
> (*MS* 6: 252)

We can easily discover for ourselves that we cannot know from observation who owns what. Neither does possession on its own nor use confer right. Only from the perspective of practical philosophy can ownership potentially be established through the deduction and recognition of the a priori possibility of an ownership which persists even in the absence of our presence to hold it. As Kant puts it,

> the concept of merely rightful possession is not an empirical concept (dependent on conditions of space and time) and yet it has practical reality, that is, it must be applicable to objects of experience, cognition of which is dependent upon those conditions. [. . .] Since the concept of a right is simply a rational concept, it cannot be applied *directly* to objects of experience and to the concepts of empirical *possession*, but first must be applied to the understanding's pure concept of *possession* in general. So the concept to which the concept of right is directly applied is not that of *holding* (*detention*), which is an empirical way of thinking possession, but first must be applied to the understanding's pure concept of possession in general.
>
> (*MS* 6: 253)

The general recognition of this aspect of the doctrine of right is a vital step in making possible a settled human society.

Kant accepts that the presence in our minds of the idea of property – a personal ownership that can be asserted in the absence of our being there to assert it – is not enough to bring property into being in the world. Historically the first property rights were established by force and had to be maintained primarily by force.[2] However, what makes property possible in a more secure and persistent way is the existence of the kind of society where the mutual recognition of property rights is an established rule in the minds and actions of individuals. Given that we are both rational and natural beings the actual maintenance of property rights in a society requires the combination of the rational acceptance of the normative standing of property rights and an external coercive power to enforce those rights where they are (for whatever reason) violated. Thus "something can be acquired conclusively only in a civil constitution; in a state of nature it can also be acquired, but only provisionally" (*MS* 6: 264). A civil condition comes into existence with the coincidence of the existence of a general coercive authority and the recognition by all of the a priori conditions of right. The general coercive authority has to be bound by the conditions of right if it is legitimately to enjoy full effectiveness. It may then legitimately punish those who fail to abide by the conditions of right. All this has to be present if we are to enjoy property rights.

> When you cannot avoid living side by side with all others, you ought to leave the state of nature and proceed with them into a rightful condition, that is, a condition of distributive justice.
>
> (*MS* 6: 307)

In a condition of distributive justice, the law says what objects "are capable of being covered externally by law, in terms of their matter, that is, what way of being in possession is rightful" (*MS* 6: 306).

But even then, the property we own within a particular national civil society is only provisionally so. In a world that is divided up into independent sovereign states that do not fully recognize each other's authority to make and administer laws there is an "indeterminacy, with respect to quantity as well as quality, of the external object that can be acquired (of the sole, original external acquisition)" (*MS* 6: 266) which is extraordinarily difficult to resolve. No matter how we suppose it might be resolved for one people by referring to a social contract they may presume to have agreed to, this still leaves the matter unfinished. For "even if it is resolved through the original contract, such acquisition will always remain only provisional unless this contract extends to the entire human race" (*MS* 6: 266). There is a telling criticism of competitive capitalism inherent in Kant's theory of property. The ownership of individuals at a personal and state level is made possible only by the use of the idea of original common ownership. We all get to own what we possess by recognizing the interdependence of all property claims. All laws of property ownership have to be guided by our original right of common ownership. Within right itself there is "this rational idea of a peaceful, even if not friendly, thoroughgoing community of all nations on the earth that come into relations affecting one another" (*MS* 6: 352).

5. The Social or the Original Contract

Kant gives his own twist to Rousseau's famous doctrine announced in *The Social Contract* (1762) which provides a defence of popular sovereignty.[3] Rousseau was deploying a term that had wide currency in political philosophy. Kant deploys the idea in his own distinct sense to convey an understanding of the idea of an original contract which is somewhat mid-way between the uses of Locke and Rousseau, on the one hand, and Hobbes, on the other. With Kant, the concept of an original contract provides, as with his predecessors Locke and Rousseau, the basis for the criticism of unjust governments, but not, by contrast, for their overthrow. The right of criticism, based upon the ideas of innate right and embodied in the concept of a social contract, does not translate into a right to act as subjects directly to overthrow offending circumstances and officials. In the manner of Hobbes, Kant argues that the power of the sovereign should not be resisted, and so even when the sovereign acts badly it should be obeyed. The original contract provides a popular foundation to sovereignty, but it is not an idea that subjects can themselves apply directly to politics. The reforms that might be required if a society is measured by the ideal of a social contract have to be carried out by the already existing sovereign. Reform has to be from the top down and not from the bottom up. Another way of putting it is to say that the original contract is a model that all genuine civil societies have to follow and one we have to assume, as rulers and subjects, if we are to act lawfully. It is indeed a rule for those in government to follow, but since their task is partly also to enforce (with coercion if necessary) the laws of the society they cannot be coerced into acting according to the ideal of the social contract.

The idea of the original contract falls in with the a priori standards of reasoning Kant has already applied to the emergence of property as an institution. Just as with property, where we have to suppose there is a synthetic a priori proposition, which permits individuals to regard things as their own, even when they are not physically holding them, so for a rightful society to come about we have to assume that the terms of the original contract have been accepted by all sides. This should not be seen as occurring in an actual event, but rather it has to be morally assumed on all sides (*TP* 8: 297). This is:

> *only an idea* of reason, which, however, has its undoubted practical reality, namely to bind every legislator to give his laws in such a way that they *could* have arisen from the united will of a whole people, and to regard each subject, insofar as he wants to be a citizen, as if he has joined in voting for such a will. For this is the touchstone of any public law's conformity with right. In other words, if a public law is so constituted that a whole people *could not possibly* give its consent to it (as, e.g., that a certain class of *subjects* should have hereditary privilege or *ruling rank*), it is unjust.
>
> (*TP* 8: 297)

The original contract represents from a Kantian perspective a normative standard by which to measure, accept or criticize the laws of a state and the policies of its rulers. That the normative standard is not wholly met does not of itself serve to undermine the authority of the laws or rulers. Rather it can provide an opportunity for laws to be improved and rulers to increase the effectiveness of their administration. Government and rulers have to submit themselves to the authority of reason in public debate, but in permitting and heeding that public debate they reinforce, rather than undermine their authority. For Kant "the people too has its inalienable rights against the state, although these cannot be coercive rights" (*TP* 8: 304). Subjects must be allowed to speak up in the hearing of their ruler:

> A citizen must have, with the approval of the ruler himself, the authorization to make known publicly his opinions about what it is in the ruler's arrangements that seems to him to be a wrong against the commonwealth.
>
> (*TP* 8: 304)

Kant presents rulers as the servants of the public. He thinks there are limits to the case that rulers might make for advancing a new rule. For instance, Kant does not think a ruler can institute a law that would permit the creation of a caste of people that would enjoy a privileged inherited status (*TP* 8: 297). Kant does not allow rulers to regard their role simply as prudential guardians of the status quo. They have always to pay heed to the "public well-being (*Heil des Staates*)" and what first must be "taken into account is precisely that lawful constitution which secures everyone his freedom by laws" (*TP* 8: 298). Where such a constitution is lacking the ruler must seek to bring it about and where it is under threat steps should be taken to safeguard it.

Thus, Kant's social contract favors popular sovereignty, but in a highly cautious way. The people should never interpret the original contract in a manner such that threatens the irresistible power of the executive in carrying out the laws. Change should be effected by alterations in the law which authorize the executive to act in a different manner. And "if the existing constitution cannot be well reconciled with the idea of the original contract," the sovereign should be allowed to change it "so as to allow to continue in existence that form which is essentially required for a people to constitute a state" (*MS* 6: 340). Effective law making and the proper execution of laws have to be permitted to continue uninterrupted within a state, even as it may change its own constitution. In championing change to bring an existing society more in to line with the idea of the original contract, Kant much prefers the model of metamorphosis to the model of revolution. The latter metaphor implies the very dangerous possibility of the death of the state at the same time as it is supposed to transform itself radically.[4]

6. Republicanism and Cosmopolitanism

Kant has a very wide-ranging understanding of the role of the social contract as a normative standard by which to measure the performance of a state. Adhering to the original contract requires a good deal more than simply adhering to the principle of popular sovereignty. Popular sovereignty has to comply with the innate freedom that each individual should enjoy. Kant defines our innate freedom as "independence from being constrained by another" individual's arbitrary will (*MS* 6: 237). Kant puts this definition in a more striking and radical form later when he says that this independence also implies

> a human being's quality of being *his own master* (*sui iuris*), as well as being a human being *beyond reproach* (*iusti*), since before he performs any act affecting rights he has done no wrong to anyone.
>
> (*MS* 6: 238)

What is most remarkable in this statement of the implications of our innate right is its universality. In principle, Kant's critical philosophy of right makes no distinctions of race, gender and nationality. Of course, Kant does not always follow through this universalist dimension in his own more empirical discussions of European and world politics, but it is there always in the background as a measure of legal and political advance.

It is implicit in the idea of right itself that we should obey only those laws to which we could give our consent. Only this form of legislation conforms to the idea of freedom which requires that one should be free from the arbitrary constraining will of any other. Now, the "only constitution that accords with right" is "a pure republic"; this is "the kind of government suited to the idea of the original contract" (*MS* 6: 340). A republic is the only form of government

> which makes freedom the principle and indeed the condition for any exercise of coercion, as is required by a rightful constitution of a state in the strict sense of the word.
>
> (*MS* 6: 340)

The gradual metamorphosis that brings this about is essential. "Only it will finally lead to what is literally a state"; it is "the constitution in which law itself rules and depends on no particular person" (*MS* 6: 340). The republic, as the embodiment of the idea of the state, is highlighted in the first definitive article *Toward Perpetual Peace* as one of the principal means of establishing world peace. Kant argues that all constitutions should gradually transform into republican ones. In such republican states the laws will be made by the people's representatives, carried out by their representatives in the executive and implemented by independent judges in the courts. Neither of these three powers should interfere with the power of their partners. Kant believes that states with republican constitutions will be predisposed towards peace since the people who carry the main burden (both financially and in combat) of prosecuting a war will themselves be asked to give their verdict on the possible declaring of war.

Since these republics will be founded upon right they will see the need to join up with other republics to create a federation of peace. Thus the second definitive article of Perpetual Peace requires all states to enter such a federation, even if they are not already republics (*ZeF* 8: 356). As themselves agents of law, states should not require coercion. Certainly sovereign states cannot be coerced to act as good international citizens; they must learn to do so guided by the principles of morality and law informed by reason.

What sets the seal, however, for the realization of the practical goals of Kant's critical system in politics and right is the emergence of a third layer of law which Kant calls cosmopolitan right. Cosmopolitan right is law for the world-citizens who must inevitably emerge through the growth of republican rule and the dissemination of the rule of law. Kant defines cosmopolitan right in a very simple way by saying such a right "shall be limited to conditions of universal hospitality" (*ZeF* 8: 357). By hospitality, Kant means that we should not turn down the request of visitors for entry if it would lead to their destruction. Kant anticipated the contemporary right to refugee status that exists since the founding of the United Nations, its Charter and its various declarations. Kant also found it compatible with cosmopolitan right the manner in which China and Japan had restricted the incursions of European people in his day, confining their entry and allowing them (in China's case) to settle only in enclaves on their coast (*ZeF* 8: 359). In contrast, he regarded as a horrifying breach of the rule of hospitality the way in which "civilized, especially commercial, states in our part of the world" treat the territories they visit (*ZeF* 8: 358). The right of hospitality demonstrates the thoroughgoing nature of Kant's grasp of law: as an interrelated, interdependent system from the ground up. The innate right of freedom which all human individuals enjoy under practical reason translates itself inexorably into a cosmopolitan right to be treated with the dignity befalling a human being on all parts of the globe.

> Since the (narrower or wider) community of the nations of the earth has now gone so far that a violation of right on one place of the earth is felt in all, the idea of cosmopolitan right is no fantastic and exaggerated way of representing right; it is, instead a supplement to the unwritten code of the right of a state and the right of nations necessary for the sake of any public rights of human beings.
>
> (*TP* 8: 360)

Here the radical dimension of Kant's idea of our innate right comes to the fore.

Kant's doctrine of right provides a radical, critical vision that challenges contemporary theories of property, economic justice and international relations. This challenge can be seen in just war theory,[5] and its attendant debates.[6] The a priori principles of right and property ownership run counter to the assertive forms of nationalism and exploitative forms of acquisition that still disfigure world society today.

Notes

1 See Robert Louden (2002).
2 See Allen Wood (2014: 712–13).
3 Cf. Susan Shell (1996: 4–5, 81–2).
4 See Williams (2003: 160–74).
5 Cf. Susan Shell (2005) and Orend (2000).
6 See Williams (2012).

References

Achenwall, G. (1763) *Ius Naturae*, 5th ed., Göttingen: Bossiegel.

Baiasu, S. (2016) "Right's Complex Relation to Ethics in Kant: The Limits of Independentism," *Kant-Studien* 107(1): 2–33.

Byrd, B. and Hruschka, J. (2010) *Kant's Doctrine of Right: A Commentary*, Cambridge: Cambridge University Press.

Louden, R. (2002) *Kant's Impure Ethics*, Oxford: Oxford University Press.

Orend, B. (2000) *War and International Justice: A Kantian Perspective*, Waterloo: Wilfrid Laurier University Press.

Rousseau, J.-J. (1995 [1762]) "The Social Contract," in V. Gourevitch (ed. and trans.), *The Social Contract and Other Later Political Writings*, Cambridge: Cambridge University Press.

Shell, S. (1996) *The Embodiment of Reason*, Chicago: University of Chicago Press.

Shell, S. (2005) "Kant on Unjust War and 'Unjust Enemies': Reflections on a Pleonasm," *Kantian Review* 10: 82–111.

Williams, H. (2003) *Kant's Critique of Hobbes*, Cardiff: University of Wales Press.

Williams, H. (2012) *Kant and the End of War*, Basingstoke: Palgrave Macmillan.

Wood, A. (2014) 'Kant's Political Philosophy', in M. Altman (ed.), *The Palgrave Handbook of German Idealism*, New York: Palgrave Macmillan.

Further Reading

K. Flikschuh, *Kant and Modern Political Philosophy* (New York: Cambridge University Press, 2000) – a detailed discussion of Kant's political philosophy with particular emphasis on the role of metaphysics. For a reconstruction of Kant's political project with the aim of presenting a contemporary convincing picture, see A. Ripstein, *Force and Freedom: Kant's Legal and Political Philosophy* (Cambridge, MA: Harvard University Press, 2009). For an account of Kant's concept of law, see R. Alexy, "Kant's Non-Positivistic Concept of Law," *Kantian Review* 24(4) (2019): 497–512; for a focus on the link between ethical and juridical philosophy and defending the independence of juridical philosophy from ethics in Kant, see M. Willaschek, "Why the Doctrine of Right Does not Belong in the Metaphysics of Morals: On Some Basic Distinctions in Kant's Moral Philosophy," *Jahrbuch für Recht und Ethik/Annual Review of Law and Ethics* 5 (1997): 205–27. Good discussions of Kant's account of international relations can be found in: G. Cavallar, *Kant and the Theory and Practice of International Right*, 2nd rev. ed. (Cardiff: University of Wales Press, 2020); L. Caranti, *Kant's Political Legacy: Human Rights, Peace, Progress* (Cardiff: University of Wales Press, 2017). For excellent accounts of Kant's cosmopolitanism, the following are recommended: O. Höffe, *Kant's Cosmopolitan Theory of Law and Peace* (New York: Cambridge University Press, 2006); P. Kleingeld, *Kant and Cosmopolitanism: The Philosophical Ideal of World Citizenship* (Cambridge: Cambridge University Press, 2012).

26

THE DOCTRINE OF VIRTUE

Mark Timmons

★★★

The Doctrine of Virtue, Part II of the two-part 1797 *Metaphysics of Morals*, represents Kant's effort to set forth the metaphysical first principles of ethics, from which a fairly comprehensive system of ethical duties can be derived, thus completing Kant's systematic treatment of moral philosophy. It begins with a short preface emphasizing that a doctrine of virtue (and duty in general) is not properly grounded in either feeling or happiness, but rather requires grounding in metaphysical first principles. The preface is followed by a substantive introduction, organized into eighteen sub-sections, which collectively cover a broad range of topics that Kant considered preparatory to the rest of the book, which itself has two main divisions: the Doctrine of the Elements of Ethics and the Doctrine of the Methods of Ethics. The first division is concerned with setting forth and justify-ing a system of mid-level duties, while the second is concerned with moral pedagogy. The book's conclusion comments on the reason for not bringing religion (as a doctrine of duties to God) into the system of philosophical ethics.

What mainly serves to distinguish *The Doctrine of Virtue* (*TL*, henceforth) from the earlier *Groundwork of the Metaphysics of Morals* (1785) and *Critique of Practical Reason* (1788) is (1) Kant's presentation of ethics as fundamentally a doctrine of ends, (2) the development of his conception of virtue, and (3) his presentation and defense of a fairly comprehensive system of ethical duties that occupies the main part of the work. Accordingly, in what follows I will concentrate on these three topics, taking them up in order. I conclude by mentioning some of the important topics in *TL* not covered in this chapter.

1. Ethics as a Doctrine of Ends

Kant explains at the beginning of the introduction to *TL*, that "ethics" had been used in ancient times to refer to the entire doctrine of duties. Later, it was reserved exclusively for the part that concerns duties of virtue (the subject matter of *TL*), which is to be distinguished from duties of right, the subject matter of the Part I of *The Metaphysics of Morals*, *The Doctrine of Right*. In *TL*'s introduction, Kant draws a number of distinctions between these two types of duty, including (1) a "formal" difference that pertains to the kind of rational constraint associated with each type, and (2)

 DOI: 10.4324/9781003406617-33

a "material" difference in the kinds of duty they involve. Let us take these up in order in explaining how ethics (so understood) is essentially a doctrine of ends.

According to Kant, the notion of duty, because it only applies to non-holy rational agents whose choice and action may not accord with requirements of the moral law, includes the notion of a rational constraint on choice and action. Both duties of right and duties of virtue are subject to moral *self*-constraint ("inner constraint") which is exercised when, in opposition to those inclinations based in self-love that motivate one to act against duty, one acts solely from the thought that some action is one's duty. However, only duties of right also admit of "external constraint" in the form of coercion by others (including the state). Thus, one formal distinguishing difference is that duties of right do, but duties of virtue do not, admit of external constraint (*TL* 6: 410).[1] A reason for this concerns the material difference between the two doctrines of morals.

Regarding the material difference, a doctrine of virtue unlike a doctrine of right considers ends of action. Kant characterizes an end as "an object of the choice (of a rational being), through the representation of which choice is determined to an action to bring this object about" (*TL* 6: 381). The ends of one's actions are thus the purposes for which one acts; they provide one with reasons for engaging in (and refraining from) activities that contribute to one's ends. Ends of action are, in Kant's terminology, the "matter" of choice. And insofar as an action is something one does on purpose, "every action," according to Kant, "has its end" (*TL* 6: 385). To explain in what sense a doctrine of virtue is a doctrine of ends, and why the material difference between the two doctrines explains that lately noted formal difference, we must clarify some of the distinctions Kant draws regarding ends.

First, Kant distinguishes between subjective and objective ends. Subjective ends are those adopted based on inclination, which are "discretionary" in the sense that one is not morally required to pursue them. (Kant also refers to such ends as "relative" and "arbitrary.") For example, in choosing to become a lawyer, one adopts an end (or, more precisely, a set of ends) that provide one with reasons to engage in those activities essential to becoming a practicing lawyer. Presumably, one adopts such an end because one believes that successfully pursing this career will contribute to one's happiness. By contrast, objective, non-discretionary ends are ones that all non-holy rational beings have an obligation to adopt.

Second, within the category of objective ends, Kant distinguishes between ends-in-themselves and ends as states of affairs one might intend to bring about or promote. Kant's conception of an end-in-itself is that of a *status* that all rational beings have by nature. This notion of an end, central to Kant's moral philosophy, figures in the humanity formulation of the Categorical Imperative (CI): "So act that you use humanity, whether in your own person or in the person of any other, always at the same time as an end, never merely as a means" (*GMS* 4: 429). In so acting, one respects humanity. Kant claims that this status "must in every maxim serve as a limiting condition of all merely relative and arbitrary ends" (*GMS* 4: 436), that is, as a limit on the means through which one pursues such ends, as well as limiting the ends one may adopt on the basis of inclination. So, for example, making a lying promise for the purpose of financial gain constitutes treating another person merely as a means and thus a failure to respect humanity as an end-in-itself.

But in addition to this negative limiting role, Kant claims that respect for humanity also requires that one "further" humanity by adopting ends of action, understood as possible states of affairs that one might hope to bring about or at least promote. That there are such ends that one has a duty to adopt – "obligatory ends" – constitutes the distinctive material difference between the doctrine of right and the doctrine of virtue. One way Kant has of drawing this material distinction is to claim that while the doctrine of right only sets forth laws for actions pursuant to discretionary ends based on self-love, the doctrine of virtue sets forth laws that constrain one to have an end. The two most fundamental obligatory ends are those of self-perfection and the happiness of others which, as we shall see in section 3, structures Kant's normative ethical theory. That the doctrine of virtue is fundamentally a doctrine of obligatory ends explains why the duties featured in this part of a doctrine of morals can only be subject to internal constraint. Kant explains: "I can indeed be constrained by others to perform *actions* that are directed as means to an end, but I can never be constrained by others *to have an end*: only I myself can make something my end" (*TL* 6: 381).

However, one may ask why a doctrine of morals includes a doctrine of obligatory ends? Kant himself raises the question in relation to promoting the happiness of others when he writes: "Would it not be better for the well-being of the world generally if human morality were limited to duties of right, fulfilled with the utmost conscientiousness, and benevolence were considered morally indifferent?" (*TL* 6: 358). Kant answers that there *must* be obligatory ends, because "were there no such ends, then all ends would hold for practical reason only as a means to other ends; and since there can be no action without an end, a *categorical* imperative would be impossible" (*TL* 6: 385). Kant's reasoning here is faulty, or at least incomplete, because arguably without obligatory ends there could still be categorical imperatives that impose constraints on the pursuit of ends that we adopt based on self-love. That is, humanity as an end in itself could serve this constraining role without there being ends grounding positivist duties. Granted, the import of such imperatives would be entirely negative – ruling out ends and actions that conflict with duty. There not being obligatory ends, then, is seemingly compatible with there being categorical imperatives. Commentators who have noticed this fault in the argument have attempted to build on Kant's reasoning to show how, with additional premises, the argument can be improved to secure the claim that there must be such obligatory ends. I will not pause to discuss these charitable interpretations. However, even if the argument in question cannot be made to work, it is open to Kant to argue directly that adopting the ends of self-perfection and the happiness of others is obligatory.[2] (See, for example, *TL* 6: 392–4.)

2. Virtue

Kant distinguishes virtue or a virtuous disposition, something singular, from the many individual virtues featured in his system. The duty to strive toward having a virtuous disposition is one component of the obligatory end of self-perfection and for Kant it is "the highest unconditional end of pure practical reason (which is still a duty)" (*TL* 6: 396). This section summarizes some key ideas regarding the presuppositions, conception, and acquisition of virtue in Kant's work.

Kant's conception of virtue presupposes his rich and subtle account of moral agency – a topic too complex to delve into here. It will suffice for present purposes to make note of a few of its central elements. *First*, human beings exercise their freedom of choice by adopting and acting on maxims (more or less general intentions) for reasons – considerations that one takes to favor a chosen course of action. *Second*, Kant is a motivational dualist in the sense that there are two ultimate sources of reason for action that can motivate one to act. (1) One source is one's sensible nature involving natural likes and dislikes that give rise to desires and aversions (inclinations) on the basis of which one comes to have interests in the obtaining or not obtaining of certain possible states of affairs. In taking such an interest, one construes the object of the interest as in some sense good which provides one with a reason to pursue the object in question and consequently leads one to adopt and act on maxims that one believes will serve such interests. All such motivation based on "interests of inclination," according to Kant, is a matter of pursuing one's self-love. (2) The other source is the moral law which, operating as a source of reasons for action, grounds duties the apprehension of which in particular instances results in the thought of some action being one's duty, which is capable of being a sufficient motivating reason to act accordingly. *Third*, in human beings, these two sources of motivation can come into conflict – a conflict Kant often refers to as conflict between inclination and duty. *Fourth*, Kant views human beings as a species as having an innate propensity to allow, if not take, considerations of self-love to outweigh in normative significance considerations of duty and morality generally. This is Kant's notion of "radical evil" that he discusses at length in Book I of his 1793 *Religion within the Boundaries of Mere Reason*. *Fifth*, and finally, Kant nevertheless holds that human beings, by nature, have a predisposition to good and in particular a "predisposition to personality," understood as one's "susceptibility to respect for the moral law *as of itself a sufficient incentive to the power of choice*" (*RGV* 6: 27).[3] One's highest vocation in life, then, is to overcome radical evil by striving to realize as fully as humanly possible one's predisposition to good.

Regarding virtue, Kant distinguishes the "formal" nature of virtue from its "material nature," the latter having to do with specific ends and virtues taken up in the following section. A concise description of Kant's formal conception is found in the first paragraph of section IX in *TL*'s introduction. With brackets inserted, the paragraph begins:

> [1] *Virtue* is the strength of a human being's maxims in fulfilling his duty. – Strength of any kind can be cognized only by the obstacles it can overcome, and [2] in the case of virtue these obstacles are natural inclinations [3] which can come into conflict with the human being's moral resolution.
>
> (*TL* 6: 394)

The first bracketed remark may be read as an extremely compressed definition of virtue, followed by an unpacking of it (suggested by the dash). Regarding the reference to human beings in 1, in a later passage (at *TL* 6: 405), Kant notes that the concept of virtue only applies to non-holy rational beings (including human beings). A holy being is one whose nature is such that it always and necessarily conforms to the moral law; a being whose will is not susceptible to the kinds of obstacles mentioned in 2. Remark 2, then, draws out something implicit in 1, against the background of Kant's conception of human agency including the thesis of motivational dualism. The moral resolution mentioned in 3 refers to one's commitment to act on maxims of duty. Thus, Kant is thinking of agents who intend to do what they take to be their duty (they have adopted a maxim of duty) but, in addition, the "resolve" of such agents to act accordingly (the strength of their maxims in fulfilling duty) is strong enough to overcome contrary-to-duty inclinations. Furthermore, the sort of resolve in question is a *moral* resolve involving the capacity for self-constraint, and so

> [4] virtue is not merely a self-constraint (for then one natural inclination could strive to overcome another), but [5] also a self-constraint in accordance with a principle of inner freedom, and so [6] through the mere representation of one's duty in accordance with its formal law.
>
> (*TL* 6: 394)

Comment 4 rules out cases in which an agent has inclinations that favor doing incompatible things on some occasion (to play, to study) and where one of them proves motivationally strongest. But more generally, though Kant does not make this explicit here, this comment rules out prudential self-constraint as equivalent to virtue.[4] The constraint essential to virtue is *moral* self-constraint of the sort indicated in 5 and 6.

Inner freedom, for Kant, is to be contrasted with outer freedom. The latter refers to an ability to act without external hindrance from others. Inner freedom as the *capacity* for moral self-constraint is autonomy of the will (*TL* 6: 396); fully realized, it is what Kant refers to as "autocracy" of the will (*MS* 6: 383). The "principle of inner freedom" Kant is referring to in 5 is indicated in 6: the principle of fulfilling one's duties from the sole incentive (motive) of duty or, as Kant says, "through the mere representation of one's duty." Kant has various ways of referring to this incentive, including: *the thought of duty, representation of the law,* and *respect for the moral law.* It is this third way of referring to it that (at least intuitively) fits best with the idea of virtue as involving motivational strength. Successfully striving to become virtuous (a matter of degree) involves strengthening one's respect for the moral law.

So, the task set by the duty to strive to become virtuous is to realize one's capacity for inner freedom by strengthening one's feeling of respect for the law so that one is able to fulfill one's duties from the sole incentive of duty. In doing so, one exercises one's inner freedom by realizing one's predisposition to good. But then how does one go about this task of virtue acquisition? Here is Kant's short answer: "the way to acquire it is to enhance the moral incentive [. . .] both by contemplating the dignity of the pure rational law in us (*contemplatione*) and by practicing virtue (*exercitio*)" (*TL* 6: 397). It is the longer answer that will occupy us in the remainder of this section, which outlines Kant's conception of virtue acquisition and explains the roles of contemplation and practice in its acquisition.

The two most fundamental elements involved in becoming virtuous are: (1) having a proper normative orientation of the will and (2) strengthening one's moral resolve. Let us consider these in order.

The normative orientation in question requires that one come to have a good disposition (*Gesinnung*) by subordinating non-moral incentives to moral incentives. Such subordination may be understood as having both a cognitive and conative component. The cognitive component involves taking moral reasons that impose strict requirements on one's behavior to be normatively superior to both reasons of self-love and to moral reasons that merely favor without strictly requiring action. It also involves taking moral reasons for action that favor without requiring (associated with wide duties such as beneficence) to provide one with sufficient (though not necessarily overriding) reasons for action in cases where such action would not violate a strict moral obligation or involve excessive self-sacrifice. The conative component, then, involves adopting as one's fundamental maxim – a maxim of virtue governing all other maxims that reflects the cognitive component. Roughly, this involves adopting with firm resolve the maxim of always acting in accord with and solely from moral reasons that impose strict requirements and being strongly disposed to act in accord with and solely from moral reasons that merely favor without requiring. To have this sort of orientation is to recognize moral reasons and the moral law that grounds them as being normatively authoritative, and therefore marks one's exit from a state of moral "depravity" characterized negatively as having an evil disposition.

Kant writes that the decision to adopt this maxim of virtue must be done all at once, that it requires a "revolution in the disposition of the human being" (*RGV* 6: 47, see also *Anth* 7: 294), since committing oneself to "break away from [vice] gradually, would itself be impure and often vicious" (*MS* 6: 477). Kant admits that we lack insight into how this revolution is possible (*RGV* 6: 50). But something in one's moral education or perhaps just one's reflection must help trigger it. Presumably, contemplation of the dignity of the moral law – of its authoritativeness – plays a role in coming to embrace this normative orientation of the will. In various places Kant describes the phenomenology of such contemplation as something more than merely apprehending that in fact moral reasons have the kind of authority just mentioned. Fully appreciating the law's authority includes experiences of the law "checking self-love" and "striking down self-conceit" – experiences that have both a negative effect on feeling, but also "awakens *respect* [for the law] insofar as it is a determining ground" (*KpV* 5: 74). Such experiences are presumably part of what leads one to have a proper normative orientation.

But of course having this sort orientation is compatible with being subject to bouts of akrasia and motivational impurity (i.e. instances where incentives of self-love must cooperate with the incentive of respect for the moral law in order for one to be sufficiently motivated to comply with duty). Kant writes that "it is only the strength of one's resolution . . . that is properly called *virtue*" (*MS* 6: 390). One's task, then, is to strengthen one's respect for the authority of the law so that considerations of strict moral requirement become motivationally dominant in a way that excludes cooperating incentives of self-love. Doing so, as noted earlier, is a matter of realizing one's inner freedom which involves both a negative and a positive task. The negative task is to prevent "sensuous impulses" (feelings and inclinations) from interfering with one's moral resolution. The positive task involves the cultivation and thus strengthening of one's respect for the law – the positive component of the practice of virtue, achieved through contemplation and practice. In the Doctrine of Method, Kant emphasizes the importance of recognizing both the dignity of virtue as being exalted over all other ends and one's capacity to act from respect for the law and contrary to all competing inclinations. Contemplation of this dignity (mentioned earlier in connection with having a proper normative orientation) and awareness of one's power "must produce an exaltation in his soul which only inspires it the more to hold duty sacred, the more it is assailed" (*TL* 6: 483). Further, the practice of virtue at a more concrete level involves the cultivation of the virtues, which not only requires avoiding vice, but engaging in activities that positively contribute to the cultivation of such virtues as sympathetic participation in the lives of others. The hoped-for effect of contemplation and practice is a strengthening of one's moral resolve, inspiring a positive interest in morality. Finally, the practice of virtue aims for a frame of mind that is not only "a tranquil mind with a considered and firm resolution to put the law of virtue into practice," but because of the feeling of elevation that accompanies self-mastery, this naturally leads to a "*valiant* and *cheerful* mind in fulfilling its duties" (*TL* 6: 484).

Because, for Kant, virtue as strength is something one must acquire, his view allows for gradations in degree of virtue. Although Kant does not explicitly distinguish being in a state of mere continence from being in a virtuous state of mind characterized by tranquility and cheer, his view allows for such a distinction. A virtuous person of mere continence is one who has a good disposition, having undergone a revolution of the will, but must struggle to overcome contrary-to-duty inclinations, perhaps succumbing to occasional bouts of weakness. A more fully virtuous person is one who has been able to strengthen her moral resolve and thus her respect for the law by acquiring a range of particular virtues that help inoculate her against succumbing to and even being seriously tempted by any contrary-to-duty inclinations she may have. Yet, the "propensity to evil," that is, the susceptibility to the influence of contrary to duty inclinations, is something that is inextirpable (*RGV* 6: 43). Thus, it is not possible for human beings to reach a state in which the susceptibility (however remote for a fully virtuous human being) is eliminated. Rather, as Kant puts it, "Virtue is always in progress . . . it is an ideal which is unobtainable" (*MS* 6: 409, see also *KpV* 5: 32–3, 83–4). The ideal in question is holiness which, strictly, transcends virtue as strength in combatting a propensity to evil, since a holy will lacks this propensity.

3. The Duties of Virtue

In the general introduction to MS, Kant explains that the categorical imperative "affirms what obligation is" and shortly thereafter remarks that the "simplicity of this law in comparison with the great and various consequences that can be drawn from it must seem astonishing at first" (*MS* 6: 225). Kant attempts to draw out some of the various consequences in *TL* by setting forth a system of mid-level moral duties and associated virtues – duties to oneself and duties to others – that constitute the fundamentals of Kant's normative ethical theory. For many of these duties, Kant's reasoning for why they are duties (and not, for instance, mere counsels of prudence) is that they are ultimately grounded in the formula of humanity (FH).[5] In the remainder of this section, I will provide an overview of Kant's system of duties of virtue.

The main division in the Elements is between duties to oneself (Part I) and duties to others (Part II), corresponding respectively to the chief obligatory ends of self-perfection and promoting the happiness of others.[6] For each of these duties, Kant includes a short section in which he briefly discusses the duty and (typically) offers dignity-based reasons intended to justify and explain why they are duties (and not just counsels of prudence). There are ten such sections in Part I, and six in Part II. Kant concludes many of the sections with "casuistical questions" about difficult cases and other matters of fine detail calling for careful moral judgment that he leaves for his readers to ponder.

Part I begins with negative duties to oneself, all of which have to do with "preservation" of one's nature, divided into those pertaining to oneself as an animal being and those pertaining to oneself merely as a moral being – a being endowed with inner freedom and thus a being with dignity. Together, these negative duties comprise the set of perfect duties to oneself. Associated with each of them are specific virtues and vices. Below is a summary table, accompanied by some brief comments. I have taken liberties in labeling some of these; the ones Kant explicitly refers to in *MS* are indicated by an asterisk.

The duties qua animal concern "nature's ends" (*TL* 6: 420) of self-preservation, preservation of the species, and preservation of one's capacity to enjoy life. However, Kant does not argue that suicide, non-procreative sex, and overindulgence in food and drink are wrong simply because they violate or are contrary to these ends. To do so would represent an appeal to a teleology of ends, which in effect would require that conformity to such ends requires that one have a desire or inclination to so conform, resulting in a heteronomy rather than autonomy of choice. Rather, he argues that each type of action in its own way involves treating one's animal nature merely as a means in the sense that one in effect allows sensuous inclinations to rule one's will, thus inverting the proper order of non-moral and moral incentives. Regarding negative duties to oneself as a moral being only, Kant remarks that to engage in lying, avarice, or servility is to "adopt principles that are directly contrary to his character as a moral being (in terms of its very form), that is, to inner freedom, the innate dignity of a human being" (*TL* 6: 420). Kant's derivations of these duties, then, are best interpreted as involving a failure to respect one's humanity and thus their wrongness

Table 26.1 Self-regarding duties with corresponding virtues and vices

Negative Duties to Oneself	Corresponding Virtue/Vice
Qua Animal Being	
Suicide and Self-Mutilation	[Nameless]
Masturbation	Chastity★/Lewdness★
Drunkenness and Gluttony	Temperance/Intemperance
Qua Moral Being	
Lying	Honesty/Dishonesty
Avarice	Frugality/Miserliness★
Servility	True Humility★/Servility★
Positive Duties to Oneself	
Cultivation of Conscience	Conscientiousness★/Unconscientiousness
Moral Self-Scrutiny	Scrupulousness/Unscrupulousness
Natural Self-Perfection	Industriousness/Sloth
Moral Self-Perfection	Virtuous Disposition★/Viciousness

is explained by the humanity formulation. These duties are "narrow" in the sense that they are relatively specific in what they require, so one has less latitude in complying with them compared to "wide" positive duties featured in *TL*.

The positive duties to oneself require one to go beyond mere preservation of one's animal and moral nature – to not only "live in accordance with nature," but to ' "*make yourself more perfect* than nature has made you' " (*TL* 6: 419). In connection with the duty of natural perfection, Kant mentions the natural powers of "spirit (at the disposal of one's reason), mind (at the disposal of one's understanding), and body" (*TL* 6: 444–5). Since one's end-setting capacity is central to Kant's conception of humanity, fully realizing such a capacity is an aspect of respecting one's dignity. As a wide duty, "[w]hich of these natural perfections should take *precedence*" (*TL* 6: 443) as well as how to go about cultivating one's natural perfections is left to the individual. The positive duty of moral self-perfection includes the duty to know what one's duties are, expressed in the command, "Be perfect," and to make respect for the moral law the sole and sufficient motive in fulfilling one's duties "Be holy." This is the duty to strive to acquire a virtuous disposition discussed in the previous section.

The positive duties of conscientiousness (the duty to be one's own innate judge) and self-scrutiny are best viewed as aspects of the duty of moral self-perfection. The first of these involves cultivating one's conscience – an innate capacity to judge whether one's actions comply with the moral law. This duty does not require that one acquire a conscience; having one is one of the presuppositions on the part of one's sensible nature that enables one to be aware of duty. "The duty here is only to cultivate one's conscience, to sharpen one's attentiveness to the voice of the inner judge, and to use every means to obtain a hearing for it" (*TL* 6: 401). While the duty of conscientiousness involves comparing one's actions and omissions against the moral law, the duty self-scrutiny involves focusing attention on one's character to determine whether it is "good or evil, whether the source of your actions is pure or impure, and what can be imputed to you [. . .] as belonging to your moral *condition*" (*TL* 6: 441). Kant refers to it as the "first command" of all duties to oneself. Presumably, this duty is "first," since a first step in striving toward and then maintaining a virtuous disposition requires knowledge of one's own character; complying with this duty "counteracts that *egotistical* self-esteem which takes mere wishes . . . as proof of a good heart" (Ibid.). It is thus an aspect of the practice of virtue (mentioned in the previous section) and requires "impartiality in judging oneself in comparison with the law, and sincerity in acknowledging to oneself one's inner moral worth or lack of worth" (Ibid.). Only by such an honest assessment is one able to comply with the duty of moral self-perfection and in this way is an aspect of that duty.

Part II of the Elements concerns the obligatory end of promoting the happiness of others, as well as avoiding the vices of disrespect, which Kant respectively divides into duties of love and duties of respect. The distinction between them, as Kant explains, has to do with whether performing one of these duties results in putting others under obligation. Those that do are duties of love, those that do not are duties of respect. See the next page for a summary chart.

A few comments are in order, beginning with the duties of love. *First*, the duty of beneficence requires that one adopt the maxim of making "others' *ends* my own (provided only that there are not immoral)" (*TL* 6: 450, see also *TL* 6: 452). Kant refers to this duty as one of "active, practical benevolence" that goes beyond mere well-wishing and includes the willingness to "sacrifice a part of my welfare to others without the hope of return" (*TL* 6: 393). However, because it is "impossible to assign determinate limits to the extent of this sacrifice" (Ibid.), it is a wide duty – one that "has in it a latitude for doing more or less" (Ibid.). *Second*, the duty of sympathetic participation is to cultivate one's natural feelings of sympathetic joy and sadness at another's state of joy or pain in order to "use this as a means for promoting the sort of active rational benevolence" (*TL* 6: 456) that constitutes duty of beneficence. For this reason, Kant refers to this duty as only a "conditional" duty, but no

Table 26.2 Other-regarding duties and corresponding virtues and vices

Positive Duties of Love	Corresponding Virtues/Vices
Beneficence	Beneficence/Envy
Gratitude	Gratitude/Ingratitude
Sympathetic Feeling	Sympathy/Malice, *Schadenfreude*[7]
Negative Duties of Respect	Modesty/Immodesty
Arrogance	Modesty/Arrogance
Defamation	[Nameless]
Ridicule	[Nameless]

less important since developing one's sympathetic feelings can motivate one to do "what the representation of duty alone might not accomplish" (*TL* 6: 457). But, apart from its role in motivation, cultivating such feelings for others presumably enables one to acquire a sensitivity to the particular needs of others and knowledge of how best to respond to those needs, and so cultivating such a sensitivity would seem to be the emotional core of the virtue of beneficence fully developed. *Third,* Kant describes gratitude as "*honoring* a person because of a benefit he has rendered us" (*TL* 6: 454). However, gratitude as a virtue includes having a genuinely grateful disposition – appreciativeness – as its emotional core. For the person with this virtue, expressions of gratitude serve to combine a "*cordiality* of a benevolent disposition with *sensitivity* to benevolence . . . and so to cultivate one's love of human beings" (*TL* 6: 456).

Kant devotes a section to what he refers to as the vices of hatred that are contrary to the duties of love. They include envy, ingratitude, and malice (including *Schadenfreude*) which, for reasons of space, I will skip over.[8]

Regarding the duties of respect, Kant remarks that under this heading "virtues were not so much commanded as rather vices opposed to them censured" (*TL* 6: 467). However, Kant begins his discussion of these duties by mentioning "modesty" (*Bescheidenheit*) as "a willing restriction of one's self-love in view of the self-love of others" (*TL* 6: 462). The lack of modesty in one's claim to be loved by others is egotism, while lack of modesty in one's demands to be respected by others is self-conceit or arrogance. Defamation and ridicule as vices would seem to be forms arrogance, and so modesty might be thought of as the single, most generic virtue regarding duties of respect, and arrogance as the generic vice. Avoiding these vices (and perhaps related others) is tantamount to being a modest person; of having the virtue of modesty.

Finally, it is worth noting the following three aspects of Kant's doctrine of virtue. *First,* as mentioned at the outset, Kant's aim in the Elements is to derive a set of mid-level duties at a general level of description. But, as Kant points out, his grounding project "cannot dispense with principles of application, and we shall often have to take as our object the particular *nature* of man, which is known only by experience, in order to show in it what can be inferred from universal moral principles. But this will in no way detract from the purity of these principles or cast doubt on their a priori source" (*MS* 6: 216). The relevance of facts about human nature is made clear in Chapter II of the Elements, "On ethical duties of human beings toward one another with regard to their condition." In this chapter (all of one paragraph long) Kant makes a set of remarks stating that in order to reach moral verdicts about particular cases by applying the rules associated with the various duties, one must take into account morally relevant facts about one's circumstances, including facts about the individuals with whom one interacts. Kant mentions rank, sex, age, health, prosperity, or poverty as among the relevant facts about others that can affect one's duties. As Kant explains, the duties one has that take into consideration one's circumstances cannot be included within the major divisions of a metaphysics of morals, since metaphysics only concerns those elements that are knowable a priori.

Second, it is unclear whether Kant considered the various negative duties to oneself and others as absolute prohibitions. Kant held that "perfect" (narrow) duties outweigh imperfect (wide) duties, in cases where there are grounds (reasons) for complying with duties of both sort. But the questions raised in the sections on casuistry appended to the perfect duties suggest that Kant could allow for exceptions to such if one has a strong enough *moral* reason to act otherwise. On this point, see especially Kant's casuistical remarks appended to the perfect duty to refrain from suicide.

Third, I would argue that merely complying with (acting in conformity with) the various duties of virtue (its "legality") does not require that one's motive be the sole motive of duty, thus preserving the legality/morality distinction in Kant's ethics (see Timmons 2002/2017). However, an "ethical action," as Kant understands this notion, is one whose sole motive is respect for the moral law (*MS* 6: 394) – also referred to as a "virtuous action."

4. Conclusion

I will conclude by just mentioning other important topics Kant treats in *TL*. (1) In the brief introduction to the Elements, Kant discusses an apparent contradiction in the very idea of a duty to oneself, which he resolves by distinguishing human being as a "sensible" being and as an "intelligible" being. (2) At the end of his discussion of the negative duties to oneself, Kant includes an "episodic section" in which he explains why human beings only have duties to humans (including oneself); that with respect to animals, we only have duties *with regard to* them, and not to them. In this same section, Kant also explains why we only have a duty *with regard to* "what lies entirely beyond the limits of our experience" (*TL* 6: 443), including God. (3) The conclusion of the Elements discusses moral friendship as an appropriate combination love and respect between friends, and ends with an appendix "On the virtues of social intercourse," that concerns "externals" such as affability, sociability, courtesy, hospitality, and gentleness which are useful in promoting a virtuous disposition "by at least making virtue fashionable" (*TL* 6: 474). (4) The Doctrine of the Methods, as mentioned in the introduction (and touched on briefly in section 2), concerns moral education and the practice of ethics, and should be read in conjunction with part II of *KpV*, "The Doctrine of Method of Pure Practical Reason," *Lectures on Pedagogy* and the *Anthropology*.

Notes

1 References to Kant in English translation are from the following: *Practical Philosophy* which includes *Critique of Practical Reason,* and the *Metaphysics of Morals*, M.J. Gregor (trans.) (Cambridge: Cambridge University Press, 1996); *Religion Within the Boundaries of Mere Reason*, G. di Giovanni (trans.), revised ed. (Cambridge: Cambridge University Press, 2018); *Anthropology from a Pragmatic Point of View*, R.B. Louden (trans.) (Cambridge: Cambridge University Press, 2006).

2 While Kant argues for the duty to promote the happiness of others, he does not provide an argument for the duty of self-perfection.

3 The predisposition to good also includes predispositions to animality and humanity. See *RGV* 6: 26–7.

4 Nor is virtue a matter of having a firm resolution to comply with duty out of self-love. In the *Religion*, Kant refers to this as virtue "in a legal sense," which he explicitly distinguishes from genuine moral virtue. See *RGV* 6: 47.

5 For an analysis of Kant's arguments for the duties of virtue, see Timmons 2021: Chs. 10–14.

6 Kant argues that because duty involves self-constraint and that one's own happiness is something one is naturally inclined to pursue, there is no duty to promote one's own happiness (unless doing so is necessary

to comply with duty). And although a component of one's duty to promote the happiness of others includes their moral well-being, Kant claims that this duty is only negative (*TL* 6: 394). Kant denies that making the end of others' perfection is a positive duty we have toward others; for the perfection of others is something only they can accomplish, and "it is self-contradictory to require that I do . . . something that only the other himself can do" (*TL* 6: 386).

7 What Kant calls "malice proper" (*TL* 6: 460) is the realization in action of malevolent joy (*Schadenfreude*) taken immediately in the misfortune of others

8 For discussion of these vices and their psychological source, see Smit and Timmons 2015. Reprinted in Timmons 2017.

References

Smit, H. and Timmons, M. (2015) "Love, Emulation, and the Psychology of the Devilish Vices," in L. Denis and O. Sensen (eds.), *Kant's Lectures on Ethics: A Critical Guide*, ch. 15, Cambridge: Cambridge University Press, pp. 256–76.

Timmons, M. (2002) "Motive and Rightness in Kant's Ethics," in M. Timmons (ed.), *Kant's Metaphysics of Morals: Interpretative Essays*, Oxford and New York: Oxford University Press. Reprinted in Timmons, 2017, ch. 5, pp. 139–74.

Timmons, M. (2017) *Significance and System: Essays on Kant's Ethics*, Oxford and New York: Oxford University Press.

Timmons, M. (2021) *Kant's Doctrine of Virtue: A Guide*, Oxford and New York: Oxford University Press.

Further Reading

M. Gregor, *Laws of Freedom* (New York: Barnes & Noble, Inc., 1963) is the first book-length treatment in English of MS with eight of the twelve chapters devoted to *TL*. M. Timmons, *Kant's Doctrine of Virtue: A Guide* is a commentary on *TL* along with coverage of the General Introduction to *The Metaphysics of Morals* (New York and Oxford: Oxford University Press, 2021); A.M. Baxley, *Kant's Theory of Virtue* (Cambridge: Cambridge University Press, 2010) contains a full treatment of Kant's conception of virtue and related topics. Part II of Melissa Merritt's *Kant on Reflection and Virtue* (Cambridge: Cambridge University Press, 2020) develops an interpretation of Kantian virtue as a skill. M. Timmons (ed.), *Kant's Metaphysics of Morals: Interpretative Essays* (Oxford: Oxford University Press, 2002) features seventeen chapters by scholars, eight of them on various topics in *TL*, and includes an extensive bibliography of articles and books on the entire MS up to 2002. The following three collections contain highly recommended essays by leading scholars: M. Betzler (ed.), *Kant's Ethics of Virtue* (New York: Walter de Gruyter, 2008); L. Denis (ed.), *Kant's Metaphysics of Morals: A Critical Guide* (Cambridge: Cambridge University Press, 2015); A. Trampota, O. Sensen and J. Timmermann (eds.), *Kant's Tugendlehre: A Comprehensive Commentary* (Berlin and Boston: Walter de Gruyter, 2013).

II. RELIGION

27

RELIGION

Stephen R. Palmquist

***

1. Religion in Perspective

The nature and operation of the Kantian mind is nowhere more subtly illustrated and applied than in Kant's theory of religion. Among his writings that deal with this unique feature of human life and thought – arguably the feature most central to our experience and understanding of life's *meaning* – the definitive expression of his position is his 1793/1794 book, *Religion within the Bounds of Bare Reason*. Despite being the only book other than the *Critique of Pure Reason* for which Kant prepared a significantly revised second edition,[1] *Religion* has begun to receive the attention it deserves from English Kant-scholarship only relatively recently: ever-increasing interest since 1990, featuring the publication of at least 45 monographs and anthologies that focus on Kant's theology and/or theory of religion,[2] reached a crescendo in the mid-2010s, with four commentaries on *Religion* appearing over a five-year period: DiCenso (2012) offers a largely political and pedagogical reading of Kant's theories, sticking closely to the text; Pasternack (2014) does the best job of setting *Religion* within the context of Kant's three *Critiques* and exploring its relevance to Kant's core doctrine of the highest good; Miller (2015) is the briefest and most introductory, lacking depth in its coverage of many salient issues; and Palmquist (2016), the longest and most comprehensive, presents a revised and thoroughly annotated edition of Pluhar's entire 2008 translation, with short snippets interspersed by a paragraph or two of comment on each portion of text.[3] Nevertheless, the riches of Kant's *Religion* have only just begun to be tapped.

Of the 38 monographs on Kant's theology and philosophy of religion that have appeared in English since 1990, seven others (in addition to the four commentaries just mentioned) have a major emphasis on interpreting *Religion*. (Those dealing with more generally *theological* themes are more relevant to the next chapter in this volume.) Michalson (1990), lamenting that Kant's conflicting commitments caused him to "wobble" between incompatible positions, aptly illustrates the traditional "reductionist" interpretation of *Religion*. Axinn (1994) provides an analytically informed reading of the entire text of *Religion*, urging readers to take Kant's apparent inconsistencies as accurate expressions of the ambivalence of the human situation. Part I of Hare (1996) interprets *Religion* as Kant's attempt to translate basic Christian doctrines (e.g., original sin and salvation by grace) into

 DOI: 10.4324/9781003406617-35

the philosophical language of Kantian ethics, but argues that his attempt fails because of its inability to explain *how* we overcome "the moral gap" between God's requirements and our ability to fulfill them. Palmquist (2000) devotes Part Three to a step-by-step account of the arguments proposed in *Religion*, based on Kant's distinction between two "experiments" (more on this follows in §2), the other three parts setting this interpretation in the broader context of Kant's Critical theological and personal vision of a new (quasi-mystical) way of life. Part 1 of Firestone and Jacobs (2008) offers a helpful overview of the two main trends in reading *Religion* (i.e., the so-called traditional, reductionist interpretation and the new "affirmative" interpretation); Part 2 then provides a highly innovative (but in places, rather strained) reading of selected portions of Kant's text. Muchnik (2010) thoroughly analyzes Kant's theory of evil, putting Kant's perplexing arguments into the context of his theory of history.[4] And Wood (2020) revises and updates his earlier interpretations of Kant's theory of religion in light of these recent trends.

This chapter sketches key controversies that have arisen in the recent literature on *Religion*. This first section examines several general issues salient to the overall interpretation of *Religion*. The next two sections then focus, respectively, on issues arising primarily out of the first half of *Religion*, composed of what Kant calls the First Piece and Second Piece,[5] and on the second half of the book, composed of the Third Piece and Fourth Piece. As with all of Kant's writings, most interpreters ignore the question of what he intended the architectonic relationship between these four main parts to be. There are, however, some notable exceptions. Pasternack (2014: 9, 216), for example, identifies a "chiastic" ("ABBA") structure, whereby the parts move from "corruption" (A) through two stages of "moral redemption" (B) and back to corruption. Others have emphasized that the first half focuses more on issues relating to individual salvation, while the second concerns salvation via community-building.[6] While I argue that individual and social elements are mixed together in each piece (Palmquist 2000, 2016), I disagree with Pasternack's take on the Fourth Piece, which I see as emphasizing the *proper response* to the corrupting influence of our evil nature, in communities of religious believers (i.e., on evil as *rehabilitated* through genuine service to God in a church). Kant discusses pseudo-service in Part Four only to contrast it with genuine service of God.

In §VII.1 of Palmquist (2000) I argued that *Religion*'s fourfold division corresponds directly to the four epistemological "perspectives" that govern the architectonic structure of the argument in the first *Critique*: adopting the perspective of the Transcendental Aesthetic, the First Piece sets out the *transcendental* conditions for being religious (we must recognize an innate corruption that infects a human nature that is essentially good); the Second Piece then sets out, in the manner of the Analytic of Concepts, *logical* conditions for salvation (inscrutable assistance through conceptualizing a divine Word of grace must empower individual believers to be virtuous in situations where virtue had previously seemed impossible); likewise, the Third Piece adopts the perspective of the *Critique*'s Analytic of Principles by defending the *empirical* conditions for salvation (reformed individuals must cooperate, forming an ethical community united under the concept of an inwardly/morally legislating God – i.e., a *church*); finally, adopting the Dialectic's perspective, the Fourth Piece develops the *hypothetical* conditions whereby communities of believers can hope to satisfy God's demand for holiness (religious believers must employ symbols and rituals that bridge the gap between our moral failings and what we are capable of doing in our own power).[7] Firestone (2012) claimed that the main purpose of Palmquist (2000) was to provide a further verification of the hermeneutic strategy adopted by Palmquist (1993) (i.e., the claim that interpreters must consider the architectonic structure of Kant's system before interpreting any of its specific arguments); he thus assumed none of the arguments or interpretations in Palmquist 2000 could stand on their own, alleging that any interpreter who rejects or lacks interest in the architectonic hermeneutic may safely ignore the interpretations elucidated therein. I responded in Palmquist (2016) by demonstrating that the claims defended in Palmquist (2000) are grounded in a plain reading of Kant's text – regardless of whether or not one accepts the architectonic superstructure that (I claim) informs Kant's religious system.

A more basic debate in the literature concerns what Firestone and Palmquist (2006) called the "traditional" and the "affirmative" interpretations of *Religion*: although uncertainties later arose as to what these terms might denote (cf. Jacobs [2012] and Palmquist [2012]), the distinction was initially meant to differentiate between those who see *Religion* as an exercise in moral reductionism (whereby Kant is allegedly reducing anything genuinely religious to mere morality) and those who see Kantian religion as an attempt to *raise* morality to something essentially different from "bare" (*bloßen*) morality – an option first defended (with explicit reference to Kant's use of the "bare" vs "clothed" metaphor) in Palmquist (1992), then adopted by Hare (1996) and others. Although more and more (especially younger) scholars now defend a non-reductionist reading of Kantian religion (e.g., a conference focused on the affirmative reading of Kant's theory of religion, held at the University of Notre Dame in the Spring of 2023, had over 20 presenters), this debate is anything but settled: the recent commentaries by DiCenso and Miller confirm that the traditional view of *Religion*, as a morally reductionist appendix to Kant's ethics, still has supporters.

Each Preface to *Religion* raises an issue that has generated controversy. The first edition defends the right of "philosophical theologians" to examine established religious traditions and employ passages from their scriptures as aids to reasoning without being subject to the government censorship that Kant thinks is rightly required for publications by biblical theologians. Kant's justification is that biblical theologians (when they become pastors, or when their writings are read by working pastors) have a direct influence on the general public (whose welfare the government has a responsibility to protect), whereas philosophers who deal with religious topics aim only to influence biblical theologians, as part of debates internal to academia. Kant's self-defense appears to have worked for a short time; but shortly after the *second* edition appeared, Wöllner (the king's censor) wrote Kant a stern letter of reproach, accusing him of distorting and disparaging the teachings of Scripture and Christianity.[8] As Kant famously claimed in his response to Wöllner (see note 8), his procedure in *Religion* made "no *appraisal* of Christianity" (7: 8), so it "cannot be guilty of *disparaging* it." Pasternack (2014) boldly and repeatedly claims (as argued more fully in Pasternack [2015]) that Kant was "prevaricating" when he made this claim: *Religion* obviously *does* appraise Christian doctrines and scriptural passages in many ways. I respond to this accusation in Palmquist (2016), suggesting that in Kant's mind both of his two "experiments" remain well within the bounds of rational religion, so that any assessments of doctrines or interpretations of scriptures that take place in *Religion* are meant not as mandates for ordinary church-goers, but as grist for the mill of scholarly debate between academic philosophers and theologians.[9] Exactly what is the relationship between a Kantian (philosophical) view of religion and a standard ("biblical") theological view? The jury on this issue has yet to consider all the evidence, to say nothing of having reached a widely accepted verdict, though a key consideration surely is that a philosophical theory of religion must engage in "conflict" (i.e., rational debate) with biblical theologians *without* claiming to speak with anything other than the authority of reason (see Palmquist [2006]).

Closely related to this first controversy is an insight conveyed by DiCenso (2012), who claims that Kant's central purpose in *Religion* is *pedagogical*. I pick up this suggestion and develop it further in Palmquist (2016), demonstrating that, indeed, Kant filled *Religion* with specific and sometimes pointed recommendations to theology students who might someday become pastors. (Contrary to what Wood [2020] implies [see note 9], many of Kant's recommendations seem to advise clerics who seek to implement rational religion that they will need to interpret Christianity's beliefs, symbols, and rituals in ways that differ from the ways many clerics actually teach their congregations – these being the very recommendations Pasternack reads as "appraisals.") At 6:10 Kant explicitly states that he hopes *Religion* will become a *textbook* for a new course in the philosophical study of religion; Palmquist (2015b) demonstrates that what Kant had in mind here was something very different from the Lectures on Philosophical Theology that he had previously taught (the latter relating more to the topic of Hare's chapter in this volume). One reason this pedagogical emphasis was previously overlooked is that the attention scholars pay to each piece tends to decrease as the book progresses: the First Piece is twice as likely to be discussed as the Second Piece, and the Third Piece half as likely as the Second, while the Fourth Piece has been virtually ignored by most interpreters until recently. *Religion's* pedagogical emphasis follows the opposite trend, so those who carefully scrutinize the conclusions Kant draws and the examples he gives in the Fourth Piece are far more likely to recognize this theme; those who focus only on the First Piece are likely to remain incredulous. Perhaps Kant hoped the biblical theologians reading *Religion* would use it to appraise Christian tradition *on their own*, without Kant himself having to do so explicitly.

The controversy generated by the second edition Preface concerns the nature and function of the two "experiments" (*Versuchen*) that Kant introduces at 6:10 and 6:12, respectively. Early interpretations such as Hare (1996) adopt what Firestone and Jacobs (2008) call "the translation thesis," which identifies Kant's so-called first experiment as the moral philosophy of the second *Critique* and *Groundwork*, the "second experiment" being the entire project of *Religion*. By contrast, I argued at length (in Part Three of Palmquist [2000]) that both experiments are intertwined within *Religion*: the first experiment normally occupies Kant's attention in the earlier portions of each piece, while the later portions implement the second. This pattern is most obvious in the Second and Third Pieces: in each case, the two main divisions obviously correspond to Kant's effort first to identify what the elements of a rational religion actually *are*, and second to examine passages of Scripture and/or traditional doctrines to see whether these are compatible (or can be made compatible) with rational religion. Firestone and Jacobs, taking the translation thesis as their only substantive interlocutor on this issue and remaining silent about the alternative proposal offered in Palmquist (2000), make the intriguing claim that the first experiment is Kant's *sole* concern in the first three Pieces, while the Fourth Piece puts aside the first experiment and conducts only the second. Palmquist (2012) offers a detailed critique of their novel claim; Pasternack (2014) then adds further criticisms, favoring the option I had defended in Palmquist (2000). However, Pasternack (2017) makes an *about face*: after offering a masterful summary of the debate up to that point, he declares that the entire issue is based on nothing other than a mistranslation of "*Versuch*" at 6:12, which he suggests probably refers merely to the fact that the second *edition* is Kant's second "attempt" to defend the arguments in *Religion*.

Pasternack (2017) insists that the whole debate regarding the nature and location of the two "experiments" in *Religion* must now cease, as Kant scholars should acknowledge that it is merely a sad series of missteps that hurts the discipline. Fortunately, his attempt to conduct what might be called a "hermenectomy" on the discipline is bound to fail, because the claim he takes to be bogus (as first put forward in Palmquist [1992]) is not dependent on how one translates Kant's use of *Versuch* in the second Preface; rather, the claim that Kant's two *Versuche* provide the interpretive key to unlocking the mysteries of Kant's *Religion* is grounded on the fact that Kant explicitly links his usage to his *concentric circle* analogy, presented in the same passage (and onto which Kant's reference to two *Versuche* can be directly mapped). Wood (2020, 11–14) adopts essentially the same strategy I have employed, arguing that Pasternack's attempt to "dismantle the conundrum" is far from putting an end to this debate over the nature and placement of Kant's two experiments in *Religion*.

A promising new fourth alternative has yet to be explored fully in the published literature: accurately identifying and locating the two experiments might depend on what Kant means by "natural religion". In the introduction to Part One of the Fourth Piece (and less explicitly in various other passages) Kant first discusses the *source* of a religion, distinguishing a natural/rational from a historical/revealed source, then discusses the *mode of spreading* a religion, identifying religion in this sense as either natural or *scholarly*. When Firestone and Jacobs (2008) claim that Kant focuses solely on the first experiment throughout the text of *Religion* until he finally turns to the second experiment in the Fourth Piece, interpreters may be tempted (as I initially was) merely to pass this off as a poorly reasoned anomaly in the literature, hardly worth the effort of giving reasons for rejecting it (see e.g., Wood [2020, 17n]). But their claim may retain a significant measure of validity if Firestone and Jacobs are interpreting Kant's experimental method in *Religion* as two ways of examining the *spread* of religion, whereas other interpreters have typically assumed that it refers to the *source* of religion. This is not the place to defend such an interpretation in detail,[10] but for those unconvinced by Pasternack (2017), it may provide a way to reconcile the conflicting voices: insofar as Kant is concerned with *spreading* religion, Firestone and Jacobs are correct to see a radical shift of emphasis in the Fourth Piece, even though all four Pieces deal with *both* experiments (as Palmquist [2000] and Pasternack [2014] claim), insofar as this metaphor refers to the *source* of religion. This is a good example of a perspectival resolution to an otherwise seemingly intractable hermeneutic dispute.

A final general issue relates to terminology: English-speaking Kant scholars typically give too little attention to the problem of accurately translating Kant's key terms. A major accomplishment over the past two decades has been the publication of Kant's writings in a single, mostly consistent English series; yet the Cambridge Edition only intensifies the need for Kantians in coming decades not to take the status quo for granted, but to think carefully about how best to *translate* the complex terminology Kant employs to describe features of the mind.[11] This is particularly important for understanding Kant's theory of religion, where the religious implications of his terms can easily be eclipsed by translations that do not sufficiently consider the historical/theological context. In Palmquist (2016), I suggest new translations for many of Kant's key religious terms: *bloß* can be translated "merely" when it functions as an adverb, but as an adjective Kant often uses it (e.g., in the title of *Religion*) as a metaphor that is best rendered "bare"; *Gesinnung* refers not so much to a "disposition," connoting a metaphysical constituent of human nature, as to a form of principled commitment that religious people typically call their "conviction";[12] *Lebenswandel* refers not to a vague "way of life" but to a person's concrete, day-to-day "lifestyle"; because *Willkür* is not etymologically related to any of Kant's five words for *power*, its standard rendering as "power of choice" is inaccurate, whereas the same meaning can be expressed as "volition," without such misleading connotations; *Schwärmerei* refers to a disturbed *state of mind*, not to any "ism," so the standard options ("fanaticism" or "enthusiasm") are both misleading, whereas "delirium" aptly conveys the disease-like mental state that tends to accompany some religious ways of thinking; Kant applies the term *Wohlgefallen* exclusively to the *correct* way human beings relate to God's moral nature, but "well-pleasing" mistakenly suggests that God has sensual desires that we can somehow "please" (the way human beings often pander after the will and whim of human authorities), whereas "satisfaction" accurately reflects Kant's view that human beings *can* satisfy God's will through morally good behavior.[13] As relevant, I shall use these new translations in the discussion that follows.

2. The Goodness of Human Nature and Its Struggle With Innate Evil

A defining feature of the Kantian mind is the role *sensibility* plays in all human knowing. This feature drives the key arguments in *Religion* just as in the first *Critique*. The difference is that, as in the third *Critique*, Kant's aim in *Religion* is to bridge "nature" (as represented by the first *Critique*) and "freedom" (as represented by the second *Critique*).[14] To those who neglect this bridging function of *Religion* in Kant's system, the ubiquity of sensibility on its pages might appear to confirm the impression that Kant is merely supplementing his ethics: those who claim that the body and its mental correlate (i.e., sensibility) are the source of evil for Kant have not read the text with sufficient care. For although Kant does have his eye on freedom and the moral law in *Religion*, every bit as much as in the second *Critique*, there is a crucial difference here: sensibility is no longer merely an *obstacle* that threatens to eclipse human goodness; rather, Kant depicts it (using the term "animality") as the first and foremost aspect of our predisposition to *good*. A religious tradition that properly recognizes this feature of human nature will employ the products of sensibility as *symbols* to do what moral philosophy on its own cannot do: if we can avoid the temptation to take religious symbols literally (i.e., to let sensibility lead the way in moral choice), then they can effectively bridge nature and freedom. While more and more commentators are coming to appreciate the crucial role of symbols in Kantian religion (see e.g., Chignell 2010; Wood 2020), there is still much work to be done in this area.

The single most hotly debated controversy in *Religion* up to now has been the problem of how to understand Kant's arguments for the universal and necessary presence of evil in human nature. The two main options are to assume that Kant wanted to provide an a priori proof of evil but failed to do so (and therefore to attempt to construct one on his behalf, as Henry Allison, Seiriol Morgan, and Pablo Muchnik have done) or to argue that evil for Kant has *no* a priori source but has entirely empirical roots in human society (as Allen Wood has claimed). In Palmquist (2008) I review these options in detail, arguing that the text of the First Piece conveys something *like* a transcendental argument for evil; but because resolving this issue has few (if any) significant implications for understanding Kant's theory of *religion* (as opposed to his ethics), I shall comment no further on it here. The more future scholars of *Religion* get over the tendency to be bogged down with a problem that Kant regarded as essentially inscrutable and therefore unresolvable, the better. For Kant, Christian symbolism of the serpent and its role in the story of the Fall into evil is appropriate precisely because it conveys the message that we actually have no idea where evil "comes from"; all we know is that *if* we judge anyone's volition to be condemnable, then we must *presuppose* – in a manner that I call "*quasi*-transcendental" – that evil infects humanity's essentially good nature at the outset, just as biblical imagery suggests.

Kant's theory of evil would be significantly easier to understand if the problem of finding appropriate translations for his key terms were given more attention (as the essays in Schlüter 2020 do, more generally). A brief example will suffice to make this point. Kant argues in the First Piece that evil originates in the human *Gesinnung*; as long as we stick with the 150-year-old convention of using "disposition," employed in Abbott's 1873 translation, interpreters will tend to interpret this as a *metaphysical* claim. Yet, I argue in Palmquist (2015a), its status as a claim about human *volition* is more obvious if we translate the word as "conviction." Kant's point is that human volition (*Willkür*) operates at two levels: our day-to-day choices are grounded in deep convictions that (whether or not we consciously formulate them as such) are necessarily *either* good *or* evil. We human beings have no "thing" or *part* (alongside or within our body or our mind) that Kant would call our "disposition." Rather, *Gesinnung* is a *principle of mental orientation*; a study of Kant's use of various modifiers turns up the interesting fact that he usually refers to *moral* convictions throughout the first three Pieces of *Religion*, but then focuses in on a special kind of "*religious* conviction" (first mentioned as the last two words of the Third Piece) only in the Fourth Piece. As such, it turns out that *Gesinnung* plays a previously unnoticed role in Kant's theory of propositional attitudes, as one of the two forms of *convincing* or (as I sometimes call it) "convincement" (*Überzeugung*): just as cognition (*Erkenntis*) is an objective process of logical convincing that leads to knowledge (*Wissen*), so conviction (*Gesinnung*) is a subjective process of moral convincing that, if good, leads to faith (*Glaube*).[15]

A properly religious understanding of Kantian *Gesinnung* clarifies not only Kant's doctrine of radical evil, but also a controversial problem that has plagued readers of the Second Piece. Many have lamented that Kant has no discernable role for grace even though (given his defense of human-ity's radically evil nature) his religious system sorely needs one. The problem results from the fact that many readers look for something that (on Kant's view) only biblical theologians could rightly provide: definite confirmation of the *historical* conditions for God to grant assistance to human beings. Kant's first-experiment concern, by contrast, is to understand the *logic* of salvation in such a way that anyone who chooses to believe in a given historical claim that God has provided a means of assistance can do so without crippling their moral nature. Thus he explicitly states that his arguments regarding the idea of justification by grace in Section One constitute a *deduction* (*RGV* 6: 76) – a term Kant associates with the logical perspective in his systematic works. His second-experiment focus (in Section 2) then considers whether (and if so, to what extent) Christian Scrip-ture contains this rationally deduced theory of salvation. In a nutshell, he claims that we must have experienced a genuine change of heart, such that our volition is grounded in *moral convictions* rather than in convictions determined by animal self-love, in order to have good reason to hope that God will forgive our shortcomings. Moreover, because we cannot directly *intuit* our own convictions, our only way of collecting evidence regarding their moral status is to examine our lifestyle: good deeds, as such, cannot save us; but they can provide much-needed assurance that our conviction is good. In other words, Kant constructs an *ethics* of grace, not a theological appraisal of whether or not any particular account of salvation is historically true.[16]

No part of Kant's project in *Religion* involves endorsing (or denying) the Christian account of salvation; rather, his point is to explain to all religious believers *how* to believe in divine grace: their belief must empower them to adopt a lifestyle that, rationally speaking, could be lived only by a person with good convictions. Far from not having any theory on divine grace, Kant regards belief in divine grace as *necessary* for a rational conception of the possibility of human virtue in the face of evil (and so, for religion); but to avoid the danger of religious belief becoming an excuse for wallow-ing in evil, we must interpret this (and all such Christian) doctrine(s) as referring to what *we ourselves* must do to have any rational hope of being saved.

3. Instantiating the Ethical Community Through the Church

Religion's Third and Fourth Pieces argue that, because even good-hearted people tend to corrupt each other when they are together, humanity's salvation ultimately rests on people intentionally forming what Kant famously calls an "ethical community." While interpreters such as DiCenso see Kant as pursuing a primarily political goal at this point (see also Rossi 2005, 2020), religion serving as but one of several means to that end (the other means being secular forms of social organization), Kant explicitly argues in Sections 1–4 of Division One of the Third Piece that an ethical commu-nity *cannot* be political/secular but is viable only if it takes the religious form of a *church*. (Political structures do play a crucial role in shaping human destiny for Kant, but as I argued in Palmquist [1994], Kant explicitly limits their role to that of creating the *external* conditions for the *possibil-ity* of peace; politics is powerless to bring about the *inward* revolution of the ethical community whereby peace is actually realized.) The crucial step in his argument here in Division One comes in Sections 2 and 3, which constitute what I call a special "religious argument for God's existence" (Palmquist 2010a). While Byrne (2007) sees Kant's argument in these sections as just another (failed) attempt to base God's existence on the highest good, I have maintained that Kant sidesteps any dependence on the highest good in this passage.

That even Kant's view of the church is dependent on his prior account of the mind's structure becomes clear when he introduces the four basic requirements for an authentic expression of the "invisible" core that characterizes any true church: harking back to the first *Critique*, he aligns these requirements with his table of categories: the church's *quantity* must be *universal*; its *quality*, that of *integrity (Lauterkeit)*; its *relation, freedom* (both internal, between members, and external, vis-à-vis the political regime); and its *modality, unchangeable* in its adherence to these requirements (whereas all other formative aspects of the church must be subject to revision). Considering that Kant explicitly appeals to the church as the key to the "victory" humanity may hope to have over evil, it is quite surprising how little work has been done to develop and apply a Kantian ecclesiology. Accordingly, in several previous articles (e.g., Palmquist [2013], [2017], and [2020]) and in Parts Three and Four of Palmquist (2016), I show that, after Kant introduces this crucial distinction, his arguments throughout the remainder of the book revolve around one or another of these four categorial requirements.

The Kantian "invisible church" consists of all "well-meaning" [*wohldenkende*] or "goodly minded [*Wohlgesinnte*] persons" – that is, those who seek to implement the four requirements. This provides the basis for an approach to religious pluralism that has only briefly been touched upon in the literature. Section 5 (*RGV* 6: 102–9) sets out a much-neglected view of historical faiths as playing an essential (though only prudential) role in the historical development of religion. In particular, the Third Piece portrays the Kantian mind as recognizing its own private nature and its resulting tendency to *stray* from what is rational, yet as willingly engaging in *public* interactions in hopes of refining humanity's rational nature. This commitment to engage in public life gives the Kantian mind a necessarily dual emphasis. On the one hand, we must use political structures (historical faiths as well as secular governments) to protect human freedom from those who would usurp freedom from the many for the sake of the interests of a few, but on the other, we must recognize that political structures can only take us so far (see Palmquist 1994): without being religious, we can never fully realize the potential of our nature. This is why Kant (again, highly controversially) insists in Section 6 that interpretations of Scripture in a church setting must be *moral*, even if this requires going against the original author's likely intent (*RGV* 6: 109–14).

Probably the most widely discussed controversy sparked by the Third Piece was initiated by Quinn (1990), who negatively assesses Kant's claim that "a remarkable antinomy" arises when reason attempts to understand "sanctifying faith" (*RGV* 6: 116–21). Here again we see *Religion* aptly illustrating Kant's view of the mind's operations: reason necessarily contradicts itself *whenever* it answers questions about metaphysical issues that transcend experience. This antinomy is remarkable because each side presupposes the necessary *priority* of the other. If faith in God's grace precedes our ability to do good, we must presuppose that the believer did *something* good to merit receiving grace; yet if doing good comes first, we must presuppose God's grace, since no human deed could suffice to merit God's assistance. While many have struggled to understand how Kant sought to resolve the antinomy, often assuming he was defending the second option, Palmquist (2016) focuses on Kant's claim to "cut the knot (by means of a practical maxim)" (*RGV* 6: 119): both sides end up defending the same claim, *if* we give priority to practical reason, for both faith in God's grace and the duty to be good are grounded in the "archetype" [*Urbild*] of perfection, discussed in the Second Piece.

A potentially disturbing feature of the Kantian mind comes to the fore in Division Two of the Third Piece, where Kant insists that, because Judaism does not exhibit true (rational) religion, it cannot be regarded as a genuine precursor of Christianity. Those who accuse Kant of anti-Semitism misunderstand a basic feature of Kant's theory of meaning: while *concepts* properly express essential properties of things, the objects that fall under such concepts *never* fully satisfy the ideal type (Godlove 2014). For Kant, "Christianity" and "Judaism" refer primarily not to historical traditions, but to ideal embodiments of two concepts: "pure rational faith" and "statutory faith", respectively. Thinking clearly *requires* making such distinctions but does not justify adopting a judgmental attitude against individuals who belong to those traditions. Otherwise, Kant could not so readily admit that *historical* Christianity has been just as statute-oriented, just as neglectful of the inward core of true religion, as early Judaism was (6: 130–1).

The often-neglected Fourth Piece actually presents some of Kant's most important claims – for anyone who takes organized religion seriously. Here Kant distinguishes "natural" from "revealed" religion, and (to the dismay of his anti-religious readers) refuses to deny the possibility of revelation. Rather, he argues in Part One, Section One that the Gospels contain such a complete expression of rational religion, and appeared so suddenly, that they can safely be treated as revealed. While Section Two expresses some harsh words about the tendency of unenlightened religious people to depend on biblical scholars for instruction in religion, his basic message is that properly trained biblical scholars can play a crucial role in *spreading* pure rational faith. Part Two sets out several help-ful principles designed to assist church-goers (and their leaders) in properly prioritizing the moral and non-moral aspects of their traditions. While many readers assume he is flatly rejecting religious rituals as "pseudo-service," Kant's actual pedagogical advice boils down to the claim that morally good actions serve God *directly*, while non-moral rituals can serve God *in*directly by empowering us to do our duty more consistently. While the main emphasis of the Fourth Piece is often regarded as negative (e.g., Pasternack 2014) – Kant rails against the abuse of power in the name of God that is all-too-common among church leaders – its systematic function is positive: to affirm the role of *conscience* as the ultimate guide in matters of faith. Indeed, Kantian religion is so thoroughly *inward* that its many resonances with Kierkegaard's philosophy cry out for further exploration.

4. Concluding Reflections: Prospects for Future Research

In addition to the various points already mentioned regarding prospects for future research on *Religion*, a number of potentially fruitful themes permeate the book. Taking hints from themes raised in the recent commentaries and anthologies, we can ask: Just how far could one go in using *Religion* as a textbook for training clerics in the art of moral pedagogy? Does Kant's approach have practical (ecclesiastical) applications that could extend beyond the university and into actual church congregations? And does the highest good play a crucial role in *Religion*? If so, does this mean that the Kantian highest good *must* be a religious (rather than a secular) ideal? Indeed, if one grants that radical evil blocks us from being virtuous, then Kantian religion saves us from this fate through a special form of *mental* empowerment: by holding up the idea of *holiness* (i.e., the archetype) as a hypothesis, the Kantian mind motivates us to *become* virtuous where previously the moral gap caused by our radical evil seemed too great to overcome. Those whose lifestyle provides evidence that their *convictions* are holy have a reasonable hope to receive divine assistance; by *believing* one's convictions are good, a religious person gains new hope of being virtuous in this life.

Finally, an intriguing new question raised by recent research on *Religion* is: Why did Kant write a second edition of *Religion*, especially so soon after publishing the first edition? The second edition not only has a new Preface, a renamed section, and a lengthy new paragraph added to the main text, but also nearly 30 new footnotes, some of them quite long, and hundreds of minor changes. I have argued in Palmquist (2016) that many of these additions and changes function as responses to a 1793 book written (in Latin) by the highly influential Tübingen theologian, Gottlob Christian Storr, which offers a rather harsh (though constructive) critique of *Religion*'s first edition. Prior to 1793, Storr had taught Kant's philosophy of religion – Schelling, Hegel, and Hölderlin being among his students – and his book argues that Critical philosophy is even more resoundingly Christian than Kant affirms in *Religion*. In the second Preface (6: 13) Kant expresses apparently heartfelt thanks to Storr, promising to write a thorough reply at a later date – a promise whose fulfilment may have been *Conflict of the Faculties* (1797).

All of this suggests that Kant was more concerned to have *Religion* understood by Christian theologians than by Fichte, whose 1792 *Attempt at a Critique of All Revelation* appears to have had comparatively little direct influence on *Religion* (aside from perhaps prompting Kant to write *Religion* in the first place, to show what he *really* thought about religion – given that Fichte's book was initially published anonymously and many guessed Kant was its author). If *Religion*'s second edition was largely a response to Storr – arguably the eighteenth century's greatest German biblical theologian – then Kant's attempt to persuade Storr seems to have failed, for Kant was censored only *after* publishing the second edition. (Indeed, Storr was so influential that he may well have had something to do with the timing of Wöllner's letter of censure: some of Kant's new footnotes probably offended Storr, making him even more disillusioned with his beloved Kant than he had been after reading the first edition.) Historically, *Religion* has been interpreted primarily through the eyes of the German idealists named earlier; yet if Kant himself showed more interest in responding to Storr than to Fichte, then perhaps a whole new way of reading *Religion* is called for. This in turn may suggest that the Kantian mind is better suited to the task of reforming historical religious traditions such as Christianity than to the task the German idealists attempted, that of creating new metaphysical systems.

Notes

1 At the publisher's request Kant prepared a second edition of *Critique of Judgment*, but made only minor changes and wrote no new preface.
2 The next paragraph briefly summarizes seven key works published in English since 1990. By contrast, a total of only 11 monographs (and no anthologies) on Kant's overall philosophy of religion appeared in the 1970s and 1980s. As my focus here is on recent studies, I shall not discuss this older work. The second half of the Editors' Introduction to Firestone and Palmquist (2006) provides a more detailed overview of key works published from 1970 to 2004.
3 All quotations from *Religion* in this chapter are from Kant's text as presented in Palmquist (2016), which starts from Kant (2008).
4 Of the seven English anthologies on Kant's theology and philosophy of religion since 1990, Anderson-Gold and Muchnik (2009) and Michalson (2014) most consistently focus on essays interpreting *Religion*; Rossi and Wreen (1991) and Firestone and Palmquist (2006) cast a broader look at Kant's *corpus*, the latter emphasizing various ways of reading Kant's view of religion more affirmatively than the former. See also two recent German anthologies: Fischer and Forschner (2010) and Hiltscher and Klingner (2012).
5 Kant's use of *Stück* ("piece") alludes to the fact that the book's four essays were originally submitted as separate "pieces" – that is, as a series of four articles – for publication in *Berlin Monthly*; when the second essay failed to pass the censor's scrutiny, Kant compiled all four pieces as *Religion*.
6 E.g., Palmquist (2000: VI.3, VII.1, note VII.15); Firestone and Jacobs (2008: 25, 184); and Muchnik (2010: xvi, xxviii).
7 Palmquist (1993: Chs. VII–VIII) shows how these same four perspectives form the architectonic structure of the arguments of the first and second *Critiques*. Chapter IX then offers two ways of reading the third *Critique* as following the same fourfold pattern.
8 Kant quotes Wöllner's letter along with his own response in the Preface to *The Conflict of the Faculties* (1797). Significantly, Kant himself stated explicitly in *Religion* (6:175n) that he had no wish "to disparage one [sect] [. . .] by comparison with another." For when historical faiths get religion *right*, "they all deserve equal respect," just as they deserve "equal rebuke" if they pervert true religion.
9 Wood (2020: 22–6) responds to Pasternack's accusation in a similar manner, appealing to Kant's focus on the university as the proper context for philosophical debate that does not appraise in the sense that a pastor must do when speaking from the pulpit. In Palmquist (2006), written before Pasternack's intriguing accusation appeared, I argue that Kant erred by limiting the philosopher's role to the ivory tower: church leaders would do well to immerse themselves in the Kantian mind prior to entering the ministry. If there was any prevarication on Kant's part, it was in harboring the inward hope that *Religion* would have an impact on what pastors preach, while implying in the first Preface that he intended to have no such influence.

10 My thanks to Brandon Love for bringing this interpretive strategy to my attention in his unpublished paper, "Kant's Experimental Method of Reduction as the Key to Understanding Kant's Two Experiments in *Religion*." In 2016, his paper received a "revise and resubmit" from a prominent Kant journal, with one reviewer offering 12 pages of harsh criticism that read in some places like an early draft of Pasternack (2017). By this time, Love had shifted his research focus away from the role of the two experiments in *Religion* and towards a deeper understanding of Kant's overall strategy of applying an "experimental method" to transcendental philosophy in order to revolutionize metaphysics in general. As such, Love (2018) thoroughly (though only implicitly) refutes Pasternack's assumption that Kant's apparent reference to two "experiments" is merely an anomaly created by poor translation. Love effectively demonstrates that Kant's main argumentative method, from the first *Critique* onward, was an intentional application of the Baconian experimental method, one good example of which occurs in the prefaces of *Religion*.

11 See Schlüter [2020] for a collection of essays that goes a long way towards addressing this concern for more scholarly attention to be given to the issue of accurate translation.

12 See Palmquist (2015a) for a full defense of this translation.

13 For a detailed defense of these and other new conventions, see Part 2 of the Glossary in Palmquist (2016).

14 See Palmquist (1993: Ch. 3).

15 For a further defense of this claim, see Palmquist (2015a: §4, especially Figure 1).

16 Palmquist (2010b) presents a detailed defense of this account of Kantian grace. See also Palmquist (2007).

References

Anderson-Gold, S. and Muchnik, P. (eds.) (2009) *Kant's Anatomy of Evil*, Cambridge: Cambridge University Press.

Axinn, S. (1994) *The Logic of Hope: Extensions of Kant's View of Religion*, Amsterdam and Atlanta: Rodopi.

Byrne, P. (2007) *Kant on God*, Aldershot: Ashgate.

Chignell, A. (2010) "The Devil, the Virgin, and the Envoy: Symbols of Moral Struggle in *Religion* II.2," in O. Höffe (ed.), *Klassiker Auslegen: Religion innerhalb der Grenzen der blossen Vernunft*, Berlin: Akademie Verlag, pp. 111–30.

DiCenso, J. (2012) *Kant's Religion Within the Boundaries of Mere Reason: A Commentary*, Cambridge: Cambridge University Press.

Firestone, C.L. (2012) "A Response to Critics of *In Defense of Kant's Religion*," *Faith and Philosophy* 29(2): 193–209.

Firestone, C.L. and Jacobs, N. (2008) *In Defense of Kant's Religion*, Bloomington: Indiana University Press.

Firestone, C.L. and Palmquist, S.R. (eds.) (2006) *Kant and the New Philosophy of Religion*, Bloomington: Indiana University Press.

Fischer, N. and Forschner, M. (eds.) (2010) *Die Gottesfrage in der Philosophie Immanuel Kants*, Freiburg im Breisgau: Verlag Herder.

Godlove, T.F. (2014) *Kant and the Meaning of Religion*, New York: Columbia University Press.

Hare, J.E. (1996) *The Moral Gap: Kantian Ethics, Human Limits, and God's Assistance*, Oxford: Clarendon.

Hiltscher, R. and Klingner, S. (eds.) (2012) *Kant und die Religion – Die Religionen und Kant*, Hildesheim: Georg Olms Verlag.

Jacobs, N. (2012) "A Reply to Critics of *In Defense of Kant's Religion*," *Faith and Philosophy* 29(2): 210–28.

Kant, I. (2008) *Religion Within the Bounds of Bare Reason*, W.S. Pluhar (trans.), Indianapolis: Hackett.

Love, B. (2018) *Kant's Baconian Method as a Transformation of Aristotelian Transcendental Philosophy – A Propaedeutic*, PhD dissertation, Hong Kong: Baptist University.

Michalson, G.E. (ed.) (1990) *Fallen Freedom: Kant on Radical Evil and Moral Regeneration*, Cambridge: Cambridge University Press.

Michalson, G.E. (ed.) (2014) *Kant's Religion within the Boundaries of Mere Reason: A Critical Guide*, Cambridge: Cambridge University Press.

Miller, E.N. (2015) *Kant's 'Religion within the Boundaries of Mere Reason': A Reader's Guide*, London: Bloomsbury Academic.

Muchnik, P. (2010) *Kant's Theory of Evil: An Essay on the Dangers of Self-love and the Apriority of History*, Lanham, MD: Lexington Books.

Palmquist, S.R. (1992) "Does Kant Reduce Religion to Morality?" *Kant-Studien* 83(2): 129–48.

Palmquist, S.R. (1993) *Kant's System of Perspectives: An Architectonic Interpretation of Kant's Critical Philosophy*, Lanham: University Press of America.

Palmquist, S.R. (1994) "'The Kingdom of God Is at Hand!' (Did *Kant* Really Say *That?*)," *History of Philosophy Quarterly* 11(4): 421–37.

Palmquist, S.R. (2000) *Kant's Critical Religion: Volume Two of Kant's System of Perspectives*, Aldershot: Ashgate.

Palmquist, S.R. (2006) "Philosophers in the Public Square: A Religious Resolution of Kant's *Conflict of the Faculties*," in C.L. Firestone and S.R. Palmquist (eds.), *Kant and the New Philosophy of Religion*, Bloomington: Indiana University Press, pp. 230–54.

Palmquist, S.R. (2007) "Kantian Redemption: A Critical Challenge to Christian Views of Faith and Works," *Philosophia Christi* 9(1): 29–38.

Palmquist, S.R. (2008) "Kant's Quasi-Transcendental Argument for a Necessary and Universal Evil Propensity in Human Nature," *The Southern Journal of Philosophy* 46(2): 261–97.

Palmquist, S.R. (2010a) "Kant's Religious Argument for the Existence of God – The Ultimate Dependence of Human Destiny on Divine Assistance," *Faith and Philosophy* 26(1): 3–22.

Palmquist, S.R. (2010b) "Kant's Ethics of Grace: Perspectival Solutions to the Moral Difficulties with Divine Assistance," *The Journal of Religion* 90(4): 530–53.

Palmquist, S.R. (2012) "To Tell the Truth on Kant and Christianity: Will the Real Affirmative Interpreter *Please* Stand Up?" *Faith and Philosophy* 29(3): 340–6.

Palmquist, S.R. (2013) "A Daoist Model for a Kantian Church," *Comparative Philosophy* 4(1): 67–89.

Palmquist, S.R. (2015a) "What Is Kantian *Gesinnung*? On the Priority of Volition Over Metaphysics and Psychology in Kant's *Religion*," *Kantian Review* 20(2): 235–64.

Palmquist, S.R. (2015b) "Kant's Lectures as a Training-Ground for the Moral Pedagogy of *Religion*," in R. Clewis (ed.), *Reading Kant's Lectures*, New York and Berlin: Walter de Gruyter, pp. 367–92.

Palmquist, S.R. (2016) *Comprehensive Commentary on Kant's Religion Within the Bounds of Bare Reason*, Chichester: Wiley-Blackwell.

Palmquist, S.R. (2017) "Kant's Model for Building the True Church: Transcending 'Might Makes Right' and 'Should Makes Good' Through the Idea of a Non-Coercive Theocracy," *Diametros* 14(54): 76–94.

Palmquist, S.R. (2020) "How Political Is the Kantian Church?" *Diametros* 17(65): 95–113.

Pasternack, L.R. (2014) *Routledge Philosophy Guidebook to Immanuel Kant's Religion Within the Boundaries of Mere Reason: An Interpretation and Defense*, London: Routledge.

Pasternack, L.R. (2015) "Kant's 'Appraisal' of Christianity: Biblical Interpretation and the Pure Rational System of Religion," *Journal of the History of Philosophy* 53(3): 485–506.

Pasternack, L.R. (2017) "The 'Two Experiments' in Kant's *Religion*: Dismantling the Conundrum," *Kantian Review* 22: 107–31.

Quinn, P. (1990) "Saving Faith from Kant's Remarkable Antinomy," *Faith and Philosophy* 7(4): 418–33.

Rossi, P. (2005) *The Social Authority of Reason: Kant's Critique, Radical Evil, and the Destiny of Humankind*, New York: SUNY Press.

Rossi, P. (2020) *The Ethical Commonwealth in History: Peace-Making as the Moral Vocation of Humanity*, Cambridge: Cambridge University Press.

Rossi, P. and Wreen, M. (1991) *Kant's Philosophy of Religion Reconsidered*, Bloomington: Indiana University Press.

Schlüter, G. (ed.) (2020) *Kants Schriften in Übersetzungen*, Hamburg: Felix Meiner Verlag.

Storr, G.C. (1793) *Annotationes quaedam theologicae ad philosophicam Kantii de religion doctrinam [Various Theological Notes on Kant's Philosophical Doctrine of Religion]*, Tübingen: Bornium.

Wood, A. (2020) *Kant and Religion*, Cambridge: Cambridge University Press.

Further Reading

Seminal works that still influence contemporary interpreters of Kant's *Religion* are A. Wood, *Kant's Moral Religion* (Ithaca: Cornell University Press, 1970/2009) and M. Despland, *Kant on History and Religion* (Montreal: McGill-Queen's University Press, 1973). S. Palmquist, *Kant's Critical Religion: Volume Two of Kant's System of Perspectives* (Aldershot: Ashgate, 2000; London: Routledge, 2019), interprets *Religion* as a system whose coherence rests on its argument's perspectival structure; C.L. Firestone and N. Jacobs, *In Defense of Kant's Religion* (Bloomington: Indiana University Press, 2008), likewise respond to various conundrums that challenge the cogency of Kant's argument, but without interpreting Kant perspectivally. The most notable of the various recent commentaries are L. Pasternack, *Routledge Philosophy Guidebook to Immanuel Kant's Religion Within the Boundaries of Mere Reason: An Interpretation and Defense* (London: Routledge, 2014), who argues that the highest good is operative throughout *Religion*, and S. Palmquist, *Comprehensive Commentary on Kant's Religion Within the Bounds of Bare Reason* (Chichester: Wiley-Blackwell, 2016), who recommends various novel translations of Kant's terminology while commenting on every sentence in *Religion*. A. Wood's recent sequel, *Kant and Religion* (Cambridge: Cambridge University Press, 2020), portrays Kant's *Religion* as an attempt to reform Christianity through symbolic interpretations of doctrines and rituals. Two important collections of essays are C.L. Firestone and S.R. Palmquist (eds.), *Kant and the New Philosophy of Religion* (Bloomington: Indiana University Press, 2006), and G.E. Michaelson (ed.), *Kant's Religion Within the Boundaries of Mere Reason: A Critical Guide* (Cambridge: Cambridge University Press, 2014).

28

KANT ON RELIGION AND THEOLOGY

John E. Hare

★★★

To cover Kant's views on religion and theology as a whole is too large a topic for the assigned word limit, and this chapter focuses on Kant's *moral* theology since that is the center of his theological interest. There is a brief discussion of what he thinks we can say about religion and theology within the *theoretical* use of reason, but only by way of context for his views about the practical use. For the same reason of space there is little discussion of the pre-critical work and the *Opus Postumum*.

1. The Head of the Kingdom of Ends

A good place to start the discussion of Kant's critical period is his familiar notion of the kingdom of ends. He introduces this idea in the *Groundwork of the Metaphysics of Morals* in elaborating his final formulation or formula of the Categorical Imperative, the supreme principle of morality. He says (*GMS* 4: 434) that morality consists in the reference of all actions to the lawgiving by which alone a kingdom of ends is possible.[1] A kingdom is a systematic union of various rational beings through common laws, and since we are all ends in ourselves (in accordance with the formula of humanity), the kingdom we compose by our systematic union is a kingdom of ends. But why is this a *kingdom*? Christine Korsgaard glosses the idea as "a republic of all rational beings" (1996: 99, 127). R.M. Hare says, "[t]he kingdom of ends is not really a kingdom, but a democracy with equality before the law" (1997: 26). J. L. Mackie is more accurate here. He says, "[b]ut for the need to give God a special place in it [the kingdom of ends] would have been better called a commonwealth of ends" (1977: 45). Kant talks about a kingdom because he wants a systematic union with a head, or king, or sovereign, who is different from the other members of the kingdom. We find this distinction in the same place in *Groundwork*. Kant says of the sovereign that he

> cannot hold the position of sovereign merely by the maxims of his will but only in case he is a completely independent being, without needs and with unlimited resources adequate to his will.

> (*GMS* 4: 434)

DOI: 10.4324/9781003406617-36

Only God can meet this condition, because only God has no needs and unlimited resources adequate to his will. This role of God is the second of the three roles Kant distinguishes, by analogy with the roles of human sovereigns, of legislating, running the kingdom in accordance with the law, and judging our conformity in heart and in behavior to the promulgated law. His brief work *On the Miscarriage of all Philosophical Trials in Theodicy* is a particularly clear discussion of these three divine roles (*MpVT*).[2] God is not legislator of the moral law in the sense that he creates the law. The law is necessary, in the same way that it is necessary that a triangle has three angles, and no one creates it.[3] But God is the "author of the obligation in accordance with the law" (*MS* 6: 227).[4] God also judges our compliance, and can look at our hearts in a way that we ourselves cannot. The notion of God as judge figures largely in Kant's account of conscience, and we return to this later. But for present purposes the most important role is the second, God's executive role in running the kingdom in accordance with the law. This is important because it lies at the basis of Kant's moral argument for the existence of God. This argument comes towards the end of all three *Critiques*, but also in a succinct form at the beginning of the first preface of *Religion within the Boundaries of Mere Reason* (henceforth, *Religion*).

2. The Argument for the Existence of God

Religion was first published in 1793, with a second edition in 1794. The first sentence of the preface to the first edition (*RGV* 6: 3) is a useful text for displaying two fundamentally different interpretations of the work as a whole. Kant writes:

> So far as morality is based on the conception of the human being as one who is free but who also, just because of that, binds himself through his reason to unconditional laws, it is in need neither of the idea of another being above him in order that he recognize his duty, nor, that he observe it, of an incentive other than the law itself.

There are two contrasting interpretations of what Kant means by this, one that I will call a 'reductive' interpretation and one a 'theist' interpretation. The reductive interpretation argues as follows: Kant is saying that if we are free and bind ourselves to universal laws, then we do not need the idea of a transcendent being either to recognize or to do our duty; but we are free and we do bind ourselves to universal laws, and therefore we do not need the idea of a transcendent God. Thus A. C. Grayling argues on the basis of this sentence, "Immanuel Kant was an atheist."[5] I call this interpretation 'reductive' because it ends up *reducing* religion to morality. The theist interpretation, by contrast, emphasizes the first three words of the sentence, "*So far as* we are free and bind ourselves." On this interpretation, Kant is referring to the fact that we are not only free and moral agents, but we are also creatures of sense and creatures of need. If we were only free and morally good, we would not need the idea of God, but that is because we would in effect *be* God. Only God has this kind of non-composite holy nature. We humans are composite, and because we are composite we *do* need the idea of a transcendent God, and indeed the work of such a God, if we are to lead morally good lives in a rationally stable way. This is why, as Kant goes on to say in the third paragraph of this very same preface, "Morality inevitably leads to religion" (*RGV* 6: 6).

The argument needs spelling out. We need the distinction between my ends that are also my duties and my ends that are not also my duties, as this is laid out in the *Metaphysics of Morals* (*MS* 6: 386–8). The ends that are also my duties are my own perfection and the happiness of others. A person's own happiness is an end that every human being has by virtue of the impulses of human nature, but it is not a duty. There is nothing wrong with pursuing my own happiness, and indeed "to be happy is necessarily the demand of every rational but finite being and therefore an unavoidable determining ground of its faculty of desire" (*KpV* 5: 25). But moral permission is only granted to a pursuit of happiness that is consistent with duty. The perfection of others is also their own duty, but not mine. When we combine in a morally permissible way an agent's own happiness, her perfection, the happiness of others, and their perfection, we get an end that morality itself gives to us creatures of sense and creatures of need, and that Kant calls "the highest good": the happiness of all proportioned to the virtue of all (or, put differently, proportioned to their worthiness to be happy).

Now we can go back to the argument in the preface to the first edition of *Religion* that morality inevitably leads to religion. An end can only be pursued in a rationally stable way if the agent believes that the end is really possible.[6] Real possibility is more than merely logical possibility, because it has to be grounded in what is actual. But we do not see within our own agency, or within the world as far as we experience it with the senses, a ground of the required kind, that is, an existent power that can bring about this proportioning of happiness and virtue. This means that in order to make the pursuit of the highest good rationally stable, we have to believe in the existence of a "supersensible author of nature" who has the power and the will to do this because, in the words of the *Groundwork* already quoted, he like us wills the common laws of the kingdom, but he is also unlike us a "completely independent being, without needs and with unlimited resources adequate to his will."[7] Note that the mere possibility of the existence of God would not be enough for this purpose.

3.   The Priority of Practical Reason

We need to understand here the difference between regulative and constitutive principles. A regulative principle is one that we allow to govern our thought in order to make certain rational objectives possible, but it does not carry an existence claim. A constitutive principle carries an existence claim. Within the *theoretical* or speculative use of reason, God functions by and large as a regulative principle and not as a constitutive principle.[8] In the same way purposiveness within nature can function as a regulative principle for science; Kant proposes that we have to think this way in order to make progress in understanding how things work in nature. But within the practical use of reason God functions as a constitutive principle, "since [the highest good] is possible only under the condition of the *existence* of God" (*KpV* 5: 125, emphasis added). Kant then argues for the *primacy* of practical reason. By 'primacy' among two or more things connected by reason he means "the prerogative of one to be the first determining ground of the connection with all the rest" (*KpV* 5: 119). What we have here is a connecting-up operation. An existence claim, by its content, belongs with the theoretical or speculative use of reason rather than the practical, which is concerned with what we should *do*. But if we gave priority to the speculative, that would mean that practical reason would not be allowed to "assume and think as given anything further than what *speculative* reason of itself could offer it from its insight" (*KpV* 5: 120). But speculative reason has no such insight, and practical reason would be confined to the domain in which "manifest examples [can] be shown in experience" (*KpV* 5: 120). God is not in this domain, since God is not accessible to experience. Kant proposes, instead, that speculative reason has to defer in cases where two conditions are met. First, practical reason needs a belief in the existence of something. Second, no disproof of its existence is available within the theoretical use of reason. In such a case, speculative reason "must accept these propositions and, although they are transcendent for it, try to unite them, as a foreign possession handed over to it, with its own concepts" (*KpV* 5: 120). These propositions (like the assertion of the existence of God and of immortality, but also, with a different status, of God's assistance in the revolution of the will) are speculative extensions or "increments" (*KpV* 5: 134) required by practical reason, that is, required for anyone who wants to believe in a rationally stable way that we are under the moral law. Consciousness of our being under this law is what he calls "the fact of reason" (*KpV* 5: 31).

4. Our Duties as God's Commands

This distinction between regulative principles and constitutive principles clarifies to what extent it is right to see Kant as proposing a kind of divine command theory of ethics. He says, throughout the corpus, that we have to recognize our duties as God's commands. But what does he mean by this? One representative passage is from the fourth part of *Religion* (6: 154): "Religion is (subjectively considered) the recognition of all our duties as divine commands." We should tie this thought to the same divine executive power as was central in the argument in *Religion* that morality inevitably leads to religion. Kant is not a divine command theorist in the sense that he thinks divine command is what makes something right or wrong. As stated earlier, he thinks the moral law is necessary. But he also thinks that we have to believe the promulgated law is administered in the world by an omnipotent being for whom it is a principle (though not an obligation, in the absence of contrary inclinations to be restrained), if our pursuit of the highest good is to be rationally stable. This explains the phrase "subjectively considered" in the passage just quoted; the recognition is required by a rational need of ours. The footnote to this passage says that we do not need and cannot have assertoric *knowledge* in religion, even of the existence of God (since we do not have insight into supersensible objects); but we do need an assertoric practical *faith* that the highest good can be realized, and this requires the idea of God, even though, again, we must not pretend to be able to secure objective reality for God through theoretical cognition. Kant does not use the term "regulative" here, but we can connect a passage from the third *Critique* (5: 445), where Kant asks us to imagine a person who

> finds himself under the pressure of many duties that he is willing to perform and can perform only through voluntary sacrifice: he will feel within him a need that in performing them he will also have carried out something commanded, and have obeyed some sovereign.

But even though this need does not itself prove the existence of such a commander, it can be connected up ("because of pure reason's maxim to strive to unify principles as much as we can," as Kant goes on to say at *KU* 5: 456) with the postulation of the existence of such a being required by practical reason.

Kant's account of conscience should be treated similarly to his account of divine command. The same passage of the third *Critique* is helpful. Kant goes on:

> Again, suppose that perhaps he has unthinkingly violated his duty, yet without having made himself answerable to other people: still, within him he will sternly reprimand himself in words that sound as if they were spoken by a judge to whom he had to account for his action.
>
> (*KU* 5: 445–6)

A passage on conscience in the *Metaphysics of Morals* (6: 438–40) makes much the same point.[9] The judge has to be pictured as not merely human, since the job requires seeing into hearts, which humans cannot do. But Kant is careful to say that this idea of a judge does not entitle us to an existence claim.

> This other may be an actual person or a merely ideal person that reason creates for itself. [. . .]
> [An agent may not] *assume* that such a supreme being *actually exists* outside himself.
>
> (*MS* 6: 438–9)

Kant is also careful to note that this other person must also have all power in order to give effect to his laws, and "our reason cannot pursue further his power (as ruler of the world) in this function" (*MS* 6: 438n). That is to say, we can suppose our own reason gives us the law, and condemns our failure, but we cannot suppose our own reason rules the world. The divine power, the executive function, or what we might call "providence," cannot be merely ideal if the law is to have its proper effect.

If we think of our duties as God's command, does this make morality heteronomous? There is a passage in the *Groundwork* (4: 442–3) that is often taken this way.[10] Kant distinguishes between autonomy, where we both will and are subject to the law, and heteronomy, where something else (in Greek, *heteros*) is the source. Under heteronomy he distinguishes empirical and rational principles, and gives two of each. It is heteronomous to make our happiness or some moral feeling the source of the law (the two empirical principles), and it is heteronomous to make perfection (unless we mean moral perfection, which is circular) or "a divine, all-perfect will" the source (the two rational principles). If we do not derive the perfection of the divine will from our own moral concepts, Kant says,

> the concept of his will still left to us, made up of the attributes of desire for glory and dominion combined with dreadful representations of power and vengefulness, would have to be the foundation for a system of morals that would be directly opposed to morality.
>
> (*GMS* 4: 443)

One target of Kant's attack here is Christian August Crusius, whom Kant elsewhere mentions explicitly in connection with the view that locates the determining ground of morality externally in the will of God (*KpV* 5: 40, *V-Mo/Collins* 27: 262–3). The problem with Crusius is that he added to the two practical drives Kant accepts (the drive to increase our own perfection and the disinterested drive for perfection) a third drive, "a natural drive to recognize a divine moral law" and to be drawn towards it out of a sense of dependence on the God who prescribes the command to us and will punish us if we disobey (Crusius 1990: 132). Kant's concern is with the conception of God's will that we will be left with if we subtract from it our moral concepts; we will be left with God's desire for glory and vengeance. But this concern should not prevent us believing that our duties are God's commands. Autonomy does not mean that we create the law, but that we will it as a law for us. There is nothing heteronomous about thinking that this law is in God's will prior to being in ours.

5. The Revolution of the Will

Two more specific things are attributed to divine action by a speculative extension or increment from practical reason. The first is the accomplishment in us of what Kant calls "a revolution of the will." The problem here is that we are born with both a predisposition to the good, which is essential to human beings, and a propensity to evil, which is not. The predisposition is responsive to the moral law, and this law makes duty a precondition of the pursuit of happiness. The propensity reverses these two incentives, making happiness the precondition of doing our duty. Kant holds that we are born with radical evil, under the evil maxim that subordinates duty to happiness, and we are therefore unable to reverse the order of incentives by our own powers (which would require a maxim already good).

> This evil is *radical*, since it corrupts the ground of all maxims; as natural propensity, it is also not to be *extirpated* through human forces, for this could only happen through good maxims – something that cannot take place if the subjective supreme ground of all maxims is presupposed to be corrupted.
>
> (*RGV* 6: 37)

Kant recognizes a problem here, that a revolution of the will must be possible because the moral life is obligatory. He recognizes that Spener, the famous pietist, already saw the problem (*SF* 7: 54). The solution is an Augustinian or Lutheran one. While 'ought' implies 'can', it does not imply 'can by our own devices'. The revolution can be accomplished, but only by divine assistance. It is true that Kant says in the first General Remark in *Religion* (6: 44) "[t]he human being must make or have made *himself* into whatever he is or should become in a moral sense, good or evil."[11] But Kant does not say here that all improvement is our own work, but all *moral* improvement. This is his standard usage. Thus in the same work at 6: 21 he says that choosing the good can only "be called 'moral'" if it is a deed of freedom. In the first General Remark he goes on, three sentences later: "Granted that some supernatural cooperation is also needed to his becoming good or better" (*RGV* 6: 44). This divine assistance is what Kant calls "an effect of grace." He says that "we can admit an effect of grace as something incomprehensible but cannot incorporate it into our maxims for either theoretical or practical use" (*RGV* 6: 53). Theoretical use is ruled out because the assistance is not, even in principle, sensible. Practical use is ruled out because the assistance is not something *we* do, but something God does. Kant has a term for where such beliefs belong: they belong in the "*parerga* to religion within the boundaries of pure reason; they do not belong within it yet border on it" (*RGV* 6: 52).

To explain this, we need to return to the preface to the second edition of *Religion*. A boundary, unlike a limit, presupposes something on both sides of it. The title "Religion within the Boundaries of Mere Reason" suggests there is a religion outside those boundaries. In the second preface, Kant suggests we see revelation as two concentric circles, or as a wider sphere of faith including a narrower one within itself. Historical revelation to particular people at particular times and places is the wider sphere, and the revelation to reason, which abstracts from all experience, is the narrower one (*RGV* 6: 12–13). His own practice is within the narrower circle. In the first preface he distinguishes biblical theology and philosophical theology (*RGV* 6: 9). The biblical theologian studies the Bible, either for the care of souls as a divine, or as a scholar. Philosophical theology is

> a property held in trust by another faculty. This theology must have complete freedom to expand as far as its science reaches, provided that it stays within the boundaries of mere reason and makes indeed use of history, languages, the books of all peoples, even the Bible, in order to confirm and explain its propositions, but only for itself, without carrying these propositions over into biblical theology or wishing to modify its public doctrines, which is a privilege of divines.
>
> (*RGV* 6: 9)

By using the same phrase to describe philosophical theology as he uses as the title for his own book, Kant makes the claim to be himself a philosophical theologian. He therefore also claims to leave biblical theology unmodified. But, to return to the language of the second preface, he can try the project of departing from the pure rational religion, starting from some alleged revelation in the wider sphere, comparing it with the moral concepts, and seeing whether it leads back to the same pure rational system of religion from which he departed. If it does, then we will have found not merely compatibility between Scripture and reason, but unity, "so that whoever follows the one (under the guidance of the moral concepts) will not fail to come across the other as well" (*RGV* 6: 13). It is helpful to use the language here of "translation," though Kant does not himself use it. The project is to see whether we can translate doctrines from the wider sphere into the narrower sphere using the moral concepts.

With this picture of the two circles or spheres in mind, we can understand what Kant means by locating belief in effects of grace in the "parerga to religion within the boundaries of pure reason." "Parerga" means, literally, "works beside one's main work." There is an area, Kant is saying, outside the pure religion of reason but immediately adjacent to it, in the sense of being an extension into the territory of the wider sphere that we can allow as required to solve a problem internal to the pure religion, namely the problem of how a revolution of the will can be accomplished. He does not, however, describe belief in effects of grace as a postulate of practical reason; the postulates belong within the pure religion and the parerga do not.

6. Pure Rationalism

In relation to Scripture Kant is, in his own term, a "pure rationalist" (*RGV* 6: 154–5).[12] We would expect this, since he is defending a "pure religion of reason". He distinguishes himself from the *naturalist* who denies the reality of any supernatural divine revelation. Pure rationalism, by contrast, would "allow this revelation, yet claim that to take cognizance of it and accept it as actual is not necessarily required for religion" (*RGV* 6: 154–5). Note the double modality in this statement. Special revelation is not necessarily necessary for religion. Kant means that it may be necessary as a vehicle, because we would not have come up with the doctrines of the pure religion without it. It may still be necessary for people in Kant's own time. But it is not necessarily necessary, because there may come an age, for example in heaven or an eschatological new earth, when we do not need it. This double modality is repeated elsewhere. In the second edition there is a pattern of responding to worries about the first edition by theological conservatives. In the first edition Kant says that the historical faith will cease (*RGV* 6: 135n). In the second edition he adds: "Not that it 'will cease' (for it might always be useful and necessary, perhaps, as a vehicle) but that 'it can cease'; whereby is intended only the intrinsic firmness of pure moral faith" (*RGV* 6: 135n). But if Kant is a pure rationalist, then his project is not reductive; he does not mean to reduce the wider sphere to the narrower one, but to "allow" it.

To say that philosophical theology intends not to modify biblical theology does not mean that Kant always succeeds in this intention. There are several places in *Religion* where he seems to interfere with biblical theology, and I will briefly mention three. First, in dealing with the story of Abraham's willingness to sacrifice his son on Mt. Moriah, Kant says in *Religion* (6: 186–7) that we should not take something to be a command of God if it conflicts with something that is demonstrably certain, namely that an innocent should not be killed. In *Conflict of the Faculties* (7: 63), published in 1798, he goes beyond this in a skeptical direction, saying that we cannot apprehend any command from an infinite being or be acquainted with it as such. In *Religion* his point is that we cannot be sure that the command is God's. In *Conflict* his point is that we can be sure that it is not. This is typical of the difference between the two works. The *Opus Postumum* goes considerably further in a skeptical direction. The more modest position in *Religion* is more consistent with Kant's other commitments about the limits of our proper certainty. Second, Kant dismisses the penal substitution theory of the atonement (*RGV* 6: 72). The debt that we incur by being under the evil maxim is not, he says,

> a *transmissible* liability which can be made over to somebody else, in the manner of a financial debt. [. . .] It is a debt of sins which only the culprit, not the innocent, can bear, however magnanimous the innocent might be in wanting to take the debt upon himself for the other.
>
> (*RGV* 6: 72)

It is true that Kant goes on to give a "translation" of the doctrine of the atonement in terms of the new man paying the penalty on behalf of the old, but this is allowable just because it is in one sense the same person (and in another sense, not). Third, Kant says the doctrine of double election, that some are predestined to eternal happiness and others reprobated to eternal punishment, "is, if taken according to the letter, the *salto mortale* of human reason" (*RGV* 6: 121).

The insistence that we interpret Scripture through the moral concepts is not, however, in itself reductive. It is the general practice from at least the time of Origen to distinguish the four different senses of Scripture, of which one is the tropological or moral. This should not be understood as interpreting Scripture through the lens of something *external* to it, since the moral principles, centrally the command to love the neighbor as the self, are already in Scripture. Kant's favorite passage is Jesus' Sermon on the Mount (*Matthew* 5–7), and he continually returns to it. The Categorical Imperative is best understood as a philosophical clarification of the golden rule.

7. Immortality

I said that there were *two* more specific things attributed to divine action. The first was the divine assistance in producing a revolution of the will. The second is God's action in rewarding a life under the good maxim with eternal happiness. This is, like belief in the existence of God, a postulate of practical reason (*KpV* 5: 122–4). We must believe that the complete conformity of our dispositions with the moral law is really possible (as we must believe this for the highest good, of which our virtue is the condition). Again, there is a problem for practical reason (like Spener's problem treated earlier), that as far as we can tell in this life we do not seem to be capable of that moral perfection which alone could be justly rewarded by eternal happiness. The solution is presented in the following difficult passage:

> For a rational but finite being only endless progress from lower to higher stages of moral perfection is possible. *The eternal being*, to whom the temporal condition is nothing, sees in what is to us an endless series the whole of conformity with the moral law, and the holiness that his command inflexibly requires in order to be commensurable with his justice in the share he determines for each in the highest good is to be found whole in a single intellectual intuition of the existence of rational beings.

The term "intellectual intuition" at the end of this passage refers to the kind of intuition that God has and we do not. Our intuition is receptive; we receive phenomena from outside us. God's intuition is productive; God makes the things in intuiting them. So the passage is distinguishing between how we experience ourselves to be, which is an endless series, and how God produces us to be, which is all at once. There is a similar distinction that Kant draws in *Religion* (6: 47–8) between revolution and reform (or reformation) in *this* life. The revolution of the will that we have been talking about is all at once, and is seen as a completed whole by God, but what we experience is a continuing series of battles in time by which we gradually get better.

There is something God does here and something we do. We should not hope to understand the relation between these, because our understanding is limited to what can in principle be experienced. But we can say this much: if we aim at what is morally good, this is the result in us of the predisposition to good, or the seed (or germ) of goodness, which responds to the moral law. This seed does not issue, absent a revolution of the will, in the fruit of a morally good life, but it is nonetheless active. Perhaps this activity is not separated in time from God's assistance, and together (but inscrutably) these produce the free choice of the good maxim, which is enough for God to see atemporally and reward in sequence the "worthiness to be happy."[13] If so, this doctrine has a strong tendency to universalism about salvation, for all humans have the predisposition to good, and have it essentially.

8. Theology Within the Theoretical Use of Reason

The final topic for this chapter is the theology that is the work of reason in its theoretical employment. Kant says, in the preface to the second edition of the first *Critique* (Bxxx), that we have to "deny knowledge in order to make room for faith." It is important that the first, negative, part of this project is conceived purposively. The pretensions of human knowledge are exposed, including its theological pretensions, but the purpose is to see that our reason in its theoretical employment cannot either prove *or disprove* the propositions that reason in its practical employment requires us to believe. As stated earlier, speculative reason has to defer to practical reason, and accept "as a foreign possession handed over to it" the proposition that something exists, if "no disproof of its existence is available within the theoretical use of reason" (*KpV* 5: 120). Kant conspicuously mounts attacks on the three traditional proofs within theoretical reason for the existence of God. It is not my project to critique these attacks. They focus on the ontological argument, in a form from Christian Wolff (1741: vol. 2, para 21).[14] Kant's overall strategy is to show what is wrong with the ontological argument, namely that existence is not a predicate, and then to show that the cosmological argument and the physico-teleological argument depend upon the ontological argument. For our present purposes, it is worth pointing out two things about this section of the text. The first is that the physico-teleological argument *does* succeed, according to Kant, in showing the existence of an architect of the world (though not a creator of the world) who is wise and free and has unity (A627/B655). The second is that even if the three traditional arguments fail, the basic error is one of trying to apply to the supersensible what belongs only to the sensible, and this error would be made by theoretical disproofs of the existence of God as much as by proofs. "The same grounds for considering human reason incapable of asserting the existence of such a being [. . .] also suffice to prove the unsuitability of all counter-assertions" (A641/B669). When the veto power, so to speak, of theoretical reason is removed, the primacy of practical reason prevails.

To conclude, Kant is interested in the unity of reason. In the third *Critique* (*KU* 5: 456–8) he returns to the topic of physical teleology, and reaffirms that "for theoretically reflective judgment, physical teleology sufficiently proved, from the purposes of nature, [the existence of] an intelligent cause." He then connects this up in a kind of finishing loop with the moral teleology that practical reflective judgment attributes to creation from a practical point of view.

Now the objective reality of the idea of God, as moral author of the world, cannot be established by [appeal to] physical purposes *alone*. Yet if we combine our cognition of physical purposes with that of the moral purpose, then, because of pure reason's maxim to strive to unify principles as much as we can, physical purposes are very important, since they support the practical reality of the idea of God by the reality that from a theoretical point of view it already has for judgment.

Kant's architectonic conception is that when we are concerned with the practical sphere, a *regulative* principle required by a rational need is also *constitutive*, that is, determinative practically (but not theoretically). In all three *Critiques* he says that the aim of his project is to establish belief in freedom, God and immortality (A800/B828, *KpV* 5: 121, *KU* 5: 473).[15] I have sometimes written, as Kant does, about practical reason and theoretical reason, as though these were two different faculties. But in fact there is only one reason, with various employments, and it is this reason that believes in the existence of God. But Kant wants to insist, as he does in the last sentence of *Religion*, that even though there is only one reason, there is directionality to its commitments. We move, he says, "not from grace to virtue, but rather from virtue to grace" (*Religion* 6: 202).

Notes

1 I have used the translation in the *Cambridge Edition of the Works of Immanuel Kant*, except for the third *Critique*, where I have used the translation by Werner Pluhar (Kant 1987).
2 I have given a fuller account in "Kant, Job, and the Problem of Evil" (Hare 2016). See also *RGV* (6: 139).
3 For the analogy, see Kant's lectures on ethics (Collins), *V-Mo/Collins* (27: 283).
4 Patrick Kain shows the development of Kant's expression of this point, in Kain (2004).
5 See A. C. Grayling (2007). For a more developed statement with the same conclusion, see Peter Byrne (2007). The argument is formulated just this way in Merold Westphal (1998). Stephen Palmquist distinguishes the competing schools at the beginning of his *Comprehensive Commentary on Kant's* Religion within the Bound of bare Reason (2015: 1–7).
6 The term "stable" here is drawn from Volckmann's notes on Kant's lectures on the philosophy of religion (*V-Th/Volckmann* 28: 1151).
7 Kant makes the argument in *On the Only Possible Argument* (1763 – *BDG*) that God is the ground of *all* possibility, and for this reason we have to believe in God's existence. But the present point is different, and less ambitious. There is a good discussion in Christopher Insole (2013: 37–47).
8 See A635/B663: "A theoretical cognition is *speculative* if it pertains to an object or concepts of an object to which one cannot attain in any experience."
9 See my Hare (2013: 101–7).
10 See R.M. Hare (1997: 27). See also my (2001: Ch. 3).
11 This is what Nicholas Wolterstorff calls "the Stoic maxim", in "Conundrums in Kant's Rational Religion" (1991: 48) and he thinks Kant incoherent. But he does not see the point about the usage of the word "moral".
12 I am here dissenting from Allen Wood (1991). Chris Firestone and Nathan Jacobs (2008: 211–20) argue that Kant is agnostic as between pure rationalism and supernaturalism, as two different forms of rationalism. But this would be an odd usage.
13 Gordon Michalson in *Fallen Freedom* (1990: 122–42) despairs of salvaging any coherent doctrine of moral regeneration from *Religion*, but inscrutability does not imply incoherence or 'irony'.
14 It is hard to resist the impression that Kant begs the question against the argument, when asserting that there is no contradiction in saying there is no God. See Alvin Plantinga, "Kant's Objection to the Ontological Argument," 1966.
15 I do not have space to discuss what Kant means by "belief" here. See Insole (2013: 152–71).

References

Byrne, P. (2007) *Kant on God*, Aldershot: Ashgate.
Crusius, C.A. (1990) "Guide to Rational Living," in J.B. Schneewind (ed.), *Moral Philosophy from Montaigne to Kant*, vol. 2, Cambridge: Cambridge University Press.

Firestone, C. and Jacobs, N. (2008) *In Defense of Kant's Religion*, Bloomington: Indiana University Press.

Grayling, A.C. (2007) "Reasonable Bounds," *New Humanist*, https://newhumanist.org.uk/articles/996/rea sonable-bounds (last accessed: 3/1/2021).

Hare, J.E. (2001) *God's Call*, Grand Rapids: Eerdmans.

Hare, J.E. (2013) "Conscience and the Moral Epistemology of Divine Command Theory," in M. Bergmann and P. Kain (eds.), *Challenges to Moral and Religious Belief: Disagreement and Evolution*, Oxford: Oxford University Press.

Hare, J.E. (2016) "Kant, Job and the Problem of Evil," in J. Sterba (ed.), *Contemporary Moral Theory and the Problem of Evil*, Bloomington: Indiana University Press.

Hare, R.M. (1997) *Sorting Out Ethics*, Oxford: Clarendon Press.

Insole, C. (2013) *Kant and the Creation of Freedom*, Oxford: Oxford University Press.

Kain, P. (2004) "Self-Legislation in Kant's Moral Philosophy," *Archiv für Geschichte der Philosophie* 86: 257–306.

Kant, I. (1987 [1790]) *Critique of Judgement*, W.S. Pluhar (ed. and trans.), Indianapolis, IN: Hackett.

Korsgaard, C. (1996) *The Sources of Normativity*, Cambridge: Cambridge University Press.

Mackie, J.L. (1977) *Ethics: Inventing Right and Wrong*, Harmondsworth: Penguin.

Michalson, G. (1990) *Fallen Freedom*, Cambridge: Cambridge University Press.

Palmquist, S. (2015) *Comprehensive Commentary on Kant's Religion Within the Bounds of Bare Reason*, Chichester: Wiley-Blackwell.

Plantinga, A. (1966) "Kant's Objection to the Ontological Argument," *Journal of Philosophy* 63: 537–46.

Westphal, M. (1998) "Commanded Love and Moral Autonomy: The Kierkegaard-Habermas Debate," *Kierkegaard Studies* 3: 1–22.

Wolff, C. (1741) *Theologia Naturalis*, vol. 2, Frankfurt and Leipzig.

Wolterstorff, N. (1991) "Conundrums in Kant's Rational Religion," in P.J. Rossi and M. Wreen (eds.), *Kant's Philosophy of Religion Reconsidered*, Bloomington: Indiana University Press, pp. 40–53.

Wood, A. (1991) "Kant's Deism," in P.J. Rossi and M. Wreen (eds.), *Kant's Philosophy of Religion Reconsidered*, Bloomington: Indianan University Press, pp. 1–21.

Further Reading

P. Byrne, *Kant on God* (Aldershot: Ashgate, 2007) – this is an account of Kant's religion that claims it is antithetical to Christianity and much closer to deism. C. Firestone and N. Jacobs, *In Defense of Kant's Religion* (Bloomington, IN: Indiana University Press, 2008): a defense of the religious seriousness and the coherence of Kant's account of religion, and claims that it incorporates Christian essentials within the confines of reason. C. Insole, *Kant and the Creation of Freedom: A Theological Problem* (Oxford: Oxford University Press, 2013) – this is a learned account of how Kant reached his particular account of freedom in the critical period, emphasizing the problem of theological determinism. C. Insole, *The Intolerable God* (Oxford: Oxford University Press, 2019): a more popular account of Kant's theological development than the preceding, but still one that takes seriously the continuities as well as the differences between Kant's earlier work and the critical period. B. Lipscomb and J. Krueger (eds.), *Kant's Moral Metaphysics* (Berlin: Walter de Gruyter, 2010) – this is a collection of excellent articles about moral metaphysics, freedom, the highest good, epistemology and the supersensible, and religious epistemology. G. Michalson, *Fallen Freedom: Kant on Radical Evil and Moral Regeneration* (Cambridge: Cambridge University Press, 1990): a book about the possibility of accomplishing a 'revolution of the will' given radical evil. The book concludes that Kant does not in the end give a coherent account. S. Palmquist, *Comprehensive Commentary on Kant's Religion Within the Bounds of Bare Reason* (Chichester: Wiley-Blackwell, 2015) – this is, as the title implies, a very full treatment of the text of Kant's *Religion*, defending its coherence and its indebtedness in many respects to the Lutheranism of Kant's youth. P. Rossi and M. Wreen (eds.), *Kant's Philosophy of Religion Reconsidered* (Bloomington, IN: Indiana University Press, 1991) – this collection of essays, and the conference that gave rise to it, was a watershed in the rediscovery of the centrality to Kant of his moral theology at the end of the twentieth century.

III. HISTORY AND POLITICS

29

THE EARLY ESSAYS

Kant's Idea of History

Allen W. Wood

***

Kant's writings on human history appear at first glance to constitute only a small part of his literary output and to have only marginal significance for his philosophy. Unlike some other great modern philosophers, such as Leibniz, Hume and Hegel, Kant was not himself a historian; he was not even a very well read historian of philosophy. Further, Kant, along with his entire century, also acquired, during the following one, a reputation for being 'ahistorical'. This last judgment, however, is a basic and enormous error. Correcting it must be our first order of business.

Ernst Cassirer pointed out many years ago that the intellectual tools of nineteenth-century historicism were forged by the philosophy of the Enlightenment (Cassirer 1951). Kant's philosophy, moreover, *is* historical – even in its own self-conception. Both Prefaces to the *Critique of Pure Reason* describe the task of that work in precisely historical terms – the A Preface by an elaborate political analogy with the ongoing modernization of European states, the B Preface by analogy with the history of science (in particular, the sciences of logic, mathematics and physics) (Aviii–xiii/Bvii–xvi). Kant's reflections on both politics and religion rest on a historical conception of the state and the church and are self-consciously designed for his own age, an age of enlightenment. Moreover, Kant's conception of human nature itself – "the character of the human species" – and that means the nature of reason, as the uniquely self-creating and self-developing faculty of the mind – is historical through and through. At the end of *Anthropology from a Pragmatic Point of View*, the character of the human species is presented as

> a character that [the human being] himself creates, insofar as he is capable of perfecting himself according to ends that he himself adopts. By means of this the human being, as an animal endowed with the capacity of reason (*animal rationabilis*) can make out of himself a rational animal (*animal rationale*).
>
> (*Anth* 7: 321)

Human reason for Kant is essentially something historically self-created and self-creating. Reason, he says, is developed only historically, "*only in the species and not in the individual*" (*IaG* 8: 18; cf. *Anth* 7: 329). "The first character of the human being is the capacity as a rational being to obtain a character as such for his own person and for the society in which nature has placed him" (*Anth* 7: 329). The development of the species–character through reason is even the collective historical vocation of humanity. It consists in the open-ended development of its rational species capacities. In short: To anyone properly acquainted with Kant's writings on anthropology and history, the common charge that Kant's philosophy is "ahistorical" is fundamentally, wildly and conspicuously false.

1. Philosophical History and Moral Faith

In Kant's writings about history, it is especially noticeable that his project of understanding human history is bound up with certain rational aims and hopes, which are sometimes related by Kant himself to religious hopes. He describes the hope for perpetual peace by saying that "philosophy too can have its chiliastic beliefs" – its millenarian expectations (*IaG* 8: 27). Thus it is not uncommon for expositions of Kant's philosophy of history to interpret his entire philosophy of history as motivated by practical considerations and consisting in large part of rational hopes analogous to his "practical postulates" of God, freedom and immortality. Kant's theory of history is then seen as basically an expression of moral-religious hope, and not a program for empirical-factual inquiry.

There is this much truth in such a picture: Kant no doubt sometimes looked at history in light of our moral vocation and the moral-religious hopes grounded on it. This approach is particularly prominent in his reply to Moses Mendelssohn's rejection of the idea of moral progress in history, found in the third part of Kant's essay on theory and practice (*TP* 8: 307–13). Yet such a reading of Kant's philosophy of history as a whole, and especially of the *Idea for a Universal History* – is fundamentally mistaken. On the contrary, in this essay Kant is concerned to reconcile and integrate a *purely theoretical* concern with making theoretically intelligible the welter of contingent facts of which human history consists, with our inevitable and proper concern about the course of history as historical beings and moral agents. For human history is a field of empirical inquiry, but also a process in which we as human agents are involved and interested. To ignore this last fact is fundamentally to misunderstand what history is about.

A close look at the text of *Idea for a Universal History* reveals that Kant's starting point for the philosophy of history in general is purely theoretical. He introduces no moral-religious considerations until the Ninth (and last) proposition of that essay. Kant proceeds from considerations of theoretical reason, projecting the "idea" (or *a priori* rational concept) of a purely theoretical program for making comprehensible sense of the accidental facts of human history. And then he attempts to bring history as a theoretical object of study, so conceived, into *convergence* with our practical concerns, finally uniting our theoretical understanding of history with our moral-religious hopes as historical beings. This can be done only by beginning with the studying of history from a purely theoretical standpoint, since otherwise there would be nothing with which to bring our practical hopes into convergence.

In Kant's view, it would be intellectually dishonest to appeal to practical faith to decide dubious matters of empirical fact. The historical ends regarding which we might have practically grounded hope – for instance, the end of perpetual peace between nations differ from the pure ideal of the highest good, in that they are not set solely *a priori* by reason. They are instead formed through the application of *a priori* practical principles to the empirical conditions of human life. The very conception of these ends depends on propositions that must be arrived at through the working out of Kant's *theoretical* philosophy of history. Sometimes students of Kant's philosophy are tempted to treat certain general but empirical conditions of human life, even certain historically evolved conditions of society, as if they were *a priori* conditions of rational nature generally, and therefore to seek *a priori* status for certain features of Kant's philosophy that are empirically and historically conditioned. This has often happened with his doctrine of the radical propensity to evil in human nature expounded in the *Religion* (*RGV*). It also happens with his philosophy of history. Such misunderstandings badly distort the shape of Kant's philosophy.

For example: The mere existence of a plurality of rational beings does not yet make it imperative on Kantian principles to found a civil union among them guaranteeing external freedom according to universal laws. In addition, it must be assumed that they are in some form of interaction with one another, able to violate one another's external freedom and able to be mutually protected from such violation through the application of external constraint. Kant further assumes that people's exercise of their freedom involves their separate use of portions of the external world, especially portions of the earth's surface. Kant's philosophy of history treats these circumstances of human life as the product of a historical evolution, specifically of the emergence of an agricultural mode of life. It is also a historical development (that is even distinctive of Kant's philosophy of history) that political states come into conflict with one another, and that the teleology of nature, as well as the aims of morality, come to require that people create an international federation of states maintaining international peace between them. It would therefore be incoherent, or at least question-begging, to attempt to base the philosophy of history itself solely on beliefs held purely on practical grounds.

2. Natural Teleology and History

For Kant, an *idea* is an *a priori* concept formed by reason to which no empirical object can perfectly correspond, but which is to be used regulatively in the empirical investigation of nature. The "idea" referred to in the title of Kant's essay on history is the a priori concept of a *theoretical* project whose aim is to ground the empirical inquiry into human history in accordance with Kant's theory of natural teleology (of which, however, he did not give a full account until the *Critique of the Power of Judgment* six years later). More specifically, it is a regulative idea devised in accordance with Kant's conception of the natural teleology of human beings regarded as an animal species.

Kant regards living organisms generally as beings whose arrangement and behavior exhibits conceptualizable regularities that cannot be explained by being brought under the kinds of (mechanical) causal laws that make physical phenomena intelligible to us. Instead, they can be brought under the regulative concept of an "organized being" – a being whose internal arrangements and behavior produces its own organic form, and which can therefore be described as "*both cause and effect of itself*" (*KU* 5: 370). No being in nature corresponds perfectly to this concept, but there are beings in nature (living organisms) that approximate to it, and the investigation of their life processes is governed by a set of regulative principles or maxims, amounting to the assumption (which is not to be taken dogmatically, but used only heuristically) that in an organized being "everything is an end and reciprocally a means as well" (*KU* 5: 376) – in other words, that the life processes of the organism *maximize* the teleological intelligibility we are looking for. For Kant, we assume we have everything to gain by assuming maximal teleological interconnection in organized beings, since this will guide us toward discovering whatever teleology is present there; the absence of teleology represents only an empirical limit to the intelligibility of the organism for us. Thus there is never a cognitive gain to us in being satisfied that teleology is absent.

> Since human beings do not, in the pursuit of their endeavors, follow merely their instincts as do animals, and yet also do not, as would rational citizens of the world, proceed in accordance with a previously arranged plan, it does not seem possible to present a systematic history of them (as could be given for bees or beavers, for instance).
>
> (*IaG* 8: 17)

There are, however, observable regularities among the free actions of human beings as regards their effects – those connected to births, marriages and deaths, for example (*IaG* 8: 17). Because human beings do not co-ordinate their actions "as would rational citizens of the world, [. . .] in accordance with a previously arranged plan," this purposiveness must be unconscious, unintended; it must be a *natural* purposiveness, like that found in plants and animals. Kant's idea for a universal history is a regulative idea for the empirical investigation of history, guided by the heuristic assumption that human history is guided by such a natural teleology.

One heuristic assumption we employ in the investigation of organisms has to do with the development of individual specimens to maturity. It involves the conception of a natural "predisposition" – a global tendency of the organism to develop the set of capacities best suited to carrying on its mode of life. The regulative maxim governing the investigation of predispositions is: "*All of a creature's natural predispositions are destined eventually to develop fully and in accordance with their purpose*" (*IaG* 8: 18). That is, we count something as a natural predisposition of a given organism only if, in the normal and unhindered development of that organism, it develops completely and suitably to the life-processes of the species. In investigating the growth processes of an organism, we conceptualize the global tendencies that show themselves in these processes around the full development of such predispositions. A predatory animal, for example, develops predispositions enabling it to stalk and kill its prey, while the herbivorous prey animal develops predispositions enabling it to hide, flee or repel predators, as well as predispositions enabling it to find and eat the kinds of plants on which it lives.

Kant's First Proposition in the *Idea for a Universal History* invokes this teleological maxim. The Second Proposition applies it, in an extended and creative way, to the human species, in light of its distinctive capacities as a species of *rational* beings. Reason is a capacity that frees those beings that have it from the limitation to only one way of life, and enables them to invent, so to speak, their own nature and their role in the natural world (*MAM* 8: 111–12). It gives human beings what Rousseau called "perfectibility" (Rousseau 1992: 26). The predispositions of rational beings are not fixed by instinct, as they are for other animals, but are devised by human beings themselves in the course of a historical process.

3. The Economic Basis of History

From this follows Kant's Third Proposition:

> *Nature has willed that human beings produce everything that extends beyond the mechanical organiza-tion of their animal existence completely on their own, and that they shall not partake in any happiness or perfection other than that which they attain free of instinct and by means of their own reason.*
>
> (*IaG* 8: 19)

This implies that human predispositions are handed down from one generation of human beings to the next, and modified or augmented through the exercise of reason. Consequently, what we count as the predispositions of the human species are continually developing and growing; the heuristic maxim that nature has ordered things in such a way that all of them eventually develop fully amounts to the claim that human history exhibits a tendency, unintended by human beings themselves, toward the accumulation and boundless development of human faculties and diverse ways of life, with those ways of life predominating that enable these faculties to be exercised to the full and to develop further.

In his essay *Conjectural Beginning of Human History*, Kant distinguishes different phases or stages of human history, based on the historically developed way of life that is dominant in them.[1] In the first phase, people lived as hunter-gatherers; in the next, they tamed animals and lived a pastoral life as nomadic herders (*MAM* 8: 118–19). Then came, in Kant's view, the true revolution in human history, when people developed the capacity to plant and grow crops. Agriculture necessitated a settled mode of life, both in order to reap the harvests they sowed and in order to live off the stored-up products. It required that the producers limit themselves to certain parts of the earth's surface, but also that they defend those parts against others, and in particular against the incursions of those who still practiced the more primitive ways of life, such as the herdsmen who wanted to drive their flocks across the cultivated land. Farming was the most productive mode of life devised so far, creating a surplus, teaching people to plan their lives, defer the satisfaction of their needs, and freeing them to diversify their activities. This led to the creation of towns and the development of diverse practical arts, and a division of labor. Part of the productive surplus could be, and had to be, devoted to the creation of the coercive force needed to protect the rights of property, both in land and stored-up goods, that made the agricultural and urban ways of life possible (*MAM* 8: 119–20). The protection of property, for Kant, as for Locke, Rousseau, and many other modern political theorists, represents the fundamental rationale and function of civil society and the foundation of all those legitimate coercive institutions concerned with the protection of rights and justice.

At this point, Kant's philosophy of history also anticipates the Marxian materialist conception of history. Marx too sees history as divided into stages that are distinguished by modes of production fundamentally distinguished by the degree of development of the productive forces of society. Kant too sees political institutions as based on the property relations corresponding to the prevailing mode of production. Kant's theory lacks the Marxian conception of class conflict as the determinant of social dynamics, but Kant does view social change as involving conflict between higher and lower productive modes – such as the conflict between the pastoral and agricultural ways of life.

4. Unsociable Sociability

In another way, however, Kant's philosophy of history also grounds social progress just as deeply on social conflict. For in his Fourth Proposition in the *Idea for a Universal History*, Kant identifies the mechanism through which he thinks human predispositions unfold in history. This mechanism is social antagonism, a propensity in human nature to compete with other human beings, to have his own way against their will and to achieve superior rank or status in the opinion of others. Alluding to a remark by Montaigne (one of Kant's favorite authors), he calls this propensity of human nature "unsociable sociability."[2] This means it is simultaneously a propensity to be dependent on others (for one's hoped for superiority to them) and also a propensity to come into conflict with others (thus behaving unsociably toward them within this relation of interdependency). Through unsociable sociability, we seek honor, power and wealth, that is, superiority to others exercised over them (respectively) through their opinion, their fear, or their interest. These are the three objects of the social passions (*Anth* 7: 271–5), that is, inclinations that are difficult for us to control through reason. In the *Critique of Practical Reason*, unsociable sociability appears as "self-conceit" (*KpV* 5: 72); in *Religion Within the Boundaries of Mere Reason*, it appears as the radical propensity to evil in human nature (*RGV* 6: 18–89).[3]

Unsociable sociability develops along with the same faculty of reason that enables us to know that it is evil; both are products of society. Acting from our propensity to unsociable sociability is something we do freely, and for which we are to blame. But there is natural purposiveness in unsociable sociability – in other words, nature employs this propensity to further the development of the predispositions of the human species. When people seek to gain superiority over others, they make themselves both unhappy and evil. But in the process they develop capacities that are passed along to later generations and enrich both human nature and human history.

5. The Political State

As a mechanism for developing human predispositions, unsociable sociability reaches a limit at the point where human conflict disrupts the stable life of civilization that is needed for the preservation and further development of human faculties. If life and property become insecure, then people have no opportunity to perfect themselves and no incentive to accumulate products of labor, which may be taken from them before they can be enjoyed. At a certain point, therefore, nature's end of endlessly developing the predispositions of the human species requires a stable and ordered society, a condition of peace with justice. When civilization reaches this point, natural purposiveness requires another device alongside unsociable sociability to balance its counter-purposive effects. This device, which Kant introduces in the Fifth and Sixth Propositions of *Idea for a Universal History*, is the establishment of "*a **civil society** which administers right universally*" (IaG 8: 22). This civil society, characterized by a coercive power protecting rights and property, is the political state. It is a voluntary creation of human beings themselves, and is subject to ideal rational principles (of right or justice) that people are capable of recognizing and obeying; but in promoting the full development of our species predispositions, the establishment of a political state also accords with natural teleology.

The creation of a perfect civil constitution for the state presents itself to the human species as a "problem" to be solved by people themselves, because in addition to being an end of nature (needed to facilitate nature's more basic end of developing human faculties), justice among human beings also presents itself to them as a demand of reason, something they unconditionally ought to achieve.

In the Seventh Proposition, Kant argues that this problem cannot be solved as long as states remain in a permanent state of war in relation to one another. Not only are wars themselves destructive of the conditions needed to develop human faculties. Even worse, in Kant's view, is the fact that the continuous need to be prepared for war distorts the state by putting power in the hands of those who would govern in the spirit of military despotism and by diverting human talents and resources to aims irrelevant or hostile to human progress. Kant is not ignorant of the arguments, advanced in his century by Turgot and renewed in the last century by partisans of the Cold War, that military technologies too can serve human progress.[4] Nor is he unsusceptible to the idea, most often associated with Hegel, that the sublimity of war helps to unite the state and raise individuals above the ignoble disposition to complacent self-seeking that characterizes private economic life in peacetime (indeed, Kant expresses this "Hegelian" idea himself, *KU* 5: 263).[5] But he thinks that the stage of history in which armed conflict between states, and the preparations for conflict, are conducive to human progress is past. Further human progress will depend on the creation of an organization of states to preserve peace and justice between them.

Here Kant's works suggest at least two possibilities: a "federation of nations" (*Völkerbund*) or *foedus pacificum* and a "state of nations" (*Völkerstaat*) or *civitas gentium* (ZeF 8: 356–7). The former would be a league or pact between states aiming at maintaining peace and independence among its members, while the latter would be a state whose members are themselves states (not, therefore, a single world-state directly governing human beings – an idea Kant rejects). The suggestion in *Perpetual Peace* is that a federation might evolve toward a "state of nations" (*ZeF* 8: 357).

6. The Theoretical Comprehension of History and Moral Striving

The result is, as Kant puts it in the Eighth Proposition, that both progress toward a perfect state constitution, and the creation of a peaceful international order among states, may be regarded as ends of nature in history.

> *One can regard the history of the human species at large as the realization of a concealed plan of nature, meant to bring into being an internally and **to this end**, externally perfect state constitution, as the only condition in which nature can fully develop all of its predispositions in humankind.*
>
> *(IaG 8: 27)*

It is important to distinguish between two quite different (and largely independent) theses here. The first thesis is a wholly theoretical one: Under the guidance of heuristic or regulative principles of reason, we should attempt to make sense of human history as a process involving an unconscious and unintended teleology of nature, whose ultimate end regarding the human species is the open-ended development of its predispositions, and whose ends, subordinate to this one, also include the creation of a perfectly just civil constitution and a peaceful international order among states. A second thesis, evident at many points in Kant's writings, and extremely important to his philosophy as a whole but of only ancillary significance in the *Idea for a Universal History*, is a practical or moral one: As human beings, we have a *duty* to work together toward devising and realizing the end of a perfect civil constitution administering justice among human beings, and to this end we are also required to seek an order guaranteeing perpetual peace among states.

The first (theoretical) thesis is in no way dependent on the second (practical or moral) thesis. For Kant it is practical reason – not natural purposiveness – that fundamentally sets our moral duties. If something is an end of morality for practical purposes, it does not follow that it should be regarded by theoretical reason as an end of nature. Nor does the fact that something should be treated for heuristic purposes as an end of nature necessarily imply that there is any moral reason to promote it. Kant is quite explicit that natural teleology by itself does not entail any moral duty to co-operate with it:

> When I say that nature *wills* that this or that ought to happen, I do not mean that she imposes a *duty* upon us to act thus (for this can only be done by practical reason acting free of compulsion), but rather that she *does* it herself, regardless of whether we will it so or not (*fata volentem ducunt, nolentem trahunt*).
>
> *(ZeF 8: 365)*[6]

In other words, when we have a duty to do something that accords with nature's ends, natural teleology co-operates with us, but when moral ends oppose natural ends, nature will offer resistance to the good will.

There is one connection between Kant's theoretical theses about history and his practical ones. The former thesis constitutes part of our empirical grounds for the latter. When we look at history as containing a natural purposiveness toward the perfection of civil constitutions, this gives us a moral reason for co-operating with that purposiveness. It is also at most a contingent fact that at the present stage of history the further improvement of civil constitutions must depend on achieving peace between nations. (As we have seen, not everyone – either in Kant's day or our own – even thinks this is a fact at all.) It is therefore only contingent historical facts, along with *a priori* moral principles, that give us any reason to seek perpetual peace as part of the process of striving toward a perfect civil constitution. Only Kant's philosophy of history, regarded as a heuristically motivated project for obtaining and systematizing theoretical knowledge about history, could deliver the kinds of information necessary to warrant our setting perpetual peace between nations and a perfect civil constitution as ends of morality.

It would make no sense to view Kant's philosophy of history itself as motivated entirely by moral faith in, or hope for, the achievement of these historical ends. For the rationale for setting these ends themselves is not wholly *a priori*. It depends on theoretical conclusions of fact that, in the context of Kant's philosophy of history, could be grounded only on the results of his project of theoretical inquiry. To interpret Kant as reasoning in such a manner solely from moral aspirations to historical conclusions is not only to caricature Kantian moral faith as nothing but groundless wishful thinking, but it would also display the moral hopes themselves as grounded on ends that are without adequate rational motivation in the first place. Such an interpretation, therefore, not only fails to correspond to the letter of Kant's texts on the philosophy of history, but it is also an interpretation on which Kant's philosophy of history could make no sense. Kant's philosophy of history makes sense at all only if, in the words of one recent writer on this topic, we see it as satisfying *both* a theoretical and a practical need of reason (Kleingeld 1995: 215). Further, we have to see the mode of satisfaction of the theoretical need as coming prior in the rational order even to the emergence of the practical need, which is partly grounded on it.

Here is a harder question: How far does Kant's philosophy of history give us reason for *expecting* or *predicting* the success of our moral strivings – the actual progress of civil constitutions toward perfection, the actual co-operation of states in a lawful federation maintaining perpetual peace between them? Kant must be seen as thinking that it does provide such reasons, for in *Perpetual Peace* he offers conclusions from the philosophy of history as providing a "guarantee" of the terms of perpetual peace he has outlined (*ZeF* 8: 360–8). Kant realizes that before the skeptical (sometimes cynical, often fearful) heads of state to whom he is addressing his treatise are going to take steps to bring about a peaceful federation, they will need reassurances that the course to which Kant is directing them has some prospect of success in human history. But it is not immediately clear that his philosophy of history can offer them these reassurances while remaining consistent with its own theoretical claims. For Kant, to identify something as an end of nature is to say that we have heuristic or regulative reasons to look at the facts on the assumption that there are natural tendencies at work to actualize it. These heuristic reasons, however, by themselves provide us with no *evidence* that what has been identified as a natural end will actually come about. The heuristic recommendation says only that we maximize intelligibility by *looking for* such evidence; it does *not* say that we are guaranteed to find what we are looking for.

It would not make empirical sense, even for heuristic purposes, to identify something as a *natural* end if we could observe no mechanisms toward achieving it at work in nature. We say that maintaining a constant body temperature is an end of nature in animals because we notice instinctive behaviors and mechanisms that tend toward increasing their body heat when they are too cold and toward losing body heat when they are too warm. Likewise, it is a necessary condition for viewing the achievement of perpetual peace among nations as an end of nature that we should find some mechanisms at work that tend in that direction. Kant cites the fact that nations can be strong militarily only if they are strong economically, and that the more civilized a nation becomes, the more its economic strength depends on peaceful prosperity. Those nations that do not value peaceful relations with their neighbors, therefore, should increasingly be unable to make war successfully on them, and those nations that are in the best position to defend themselves should also be the ones most ready to join in a peaceful federation (see *ZeF* 8: 368, *IaG* 8: 27–8). To be sure, it does this with a certainty that is not sufficient to *foretell* the future of this peace (theoretically), but which is adequate from a practical perspective and makes it a duty to work toward this (not simply chimerical) goal (*ZeF* 8: 368).

7. Critical Assessment of Kant's Philosophy of History

Even when Kant's views are correctly and sympathetically interpreted, how seriously do they deserve to be taken? Kant's philosophy of history depends on postulating, at least for heuristic purposes, a natural teleology in human history, whose goals are both collective and unconscious. This aspect of Kant's theory may make it seem extravagant, speculative, anti-empirical and even obscurantist. His philosophy of history in this respect may seem starkly at odds with his reputation for skeptical modesty and epistemic humility and caution.

Proponents of so-called methodological individualism will say that it makes sense to appeal to historical tendencies or trends only when their existence can be authenticated and explained in terms of the choices and motivations of individuals, by way of providing 'microfoundations' for them. Kant is no methodological individualist, but the unconscious collective ends he posits in human history for regulative purposes are not postulated arbitrarily, and are based in a general way on empirically observable motivations and actions of individuals. The whole aim of the theory itself is to use these unconscious and unintended ends to identify those patterns of conscious and intentional human motivation and action that have historical efficacy, distinguishing these from the accidental factors in human choice whose relation to history is merely accidental and insignificant.

No doubt there is a measure of theoretical adventurousness in Kant's historical teleology that might unnerve a traditional empiricist. But there is often an even greater and less appreciated departure from empiricist caution involved in the abstract idealizations used by methodological individualists in constructing their 'micro-foundations' for the social trends and tendencies they are willing to countenance. In both cases, empiricist reconstructions of theoretical practice tend to underestimate the creative role of theorizing. There are usually macro-level assumptions built into the choices of abstraction and idealization used to construct micro-foundations, and these are all the less subject to empirical constraint and criticism to the extent that they remain unacknowledged. The Kantian choice to begin with the macro-level is admirably forthright in acknowledging the importance of our *a priori* architectonic cognitive ambitions.

A more serious problem for Kant's philosophy of history is that we can no longer believe, for instance, in Kant's heuristically motivated natural teleology as the right way for investigating the structure and behavior of living organisms. Since Darwin, it has been recognized that the unconscious and unintended purposive arrangements in living things have a determinate empirical explanation, based on natural selection. Moreover, this explanation reveals that Kant's heuristic assumption that the teleology in organisms is maximal is empirically and explainably false. When we learn how the organs of a living thing evolved, for instance, we sometimes come to understand why they are not optimally suited for the function they perform. And it might turn out for similar reasons that not everything we rightly conceptualize as one of the "species predispositions" of an organism would have to be fully developed in the normal course of the organism's development. The biological basis of Kant's philosophy of history therefore seems to have been undermined by scientific developments between his time and ours.

Yet it is not so clear that the methodological considerations motivating Kant's philosophy of history are less applicable today than they were in the eighteenth century. Biology may have made advances that undermine the application to it of Kant's heuristically motivated natural teleology, but human history is still an area of inquiry to which no similar empirical theory has been applied with success. It may be that our best chance of making it intelligible is still the regulative-teleological one that Kant adopts. Kant's approach also has the other benefit it had for him, that it enables us to connect an empirical, theoretical study of history to our practical concern with history as historical agents, by identifying historical tendencies (which Kant calls unintended "ends of nature") with which our efforts as moral beings might harmonize. Historical theories since Kant's time (most famously, the historical materialism of Marx) have taken up the idea that historical changes can be understood as functions of the progressive development of collective human capacities, and consequent changes in economic forms over time. Many others besides Marx have used this idea in a wide variety of contexts to deal with social and historical change (for instance, in the wide variety of so-called theories of modernization).

Easier to recognize is the way the practical or moral-religious side of Kant's philosophy of history is still with us. We are also still practically concerned with the direction of economic growth and the relation of it to the prospects for peace between nations. Twentieth-century projects for peace – the League of Nations, the United Nations and the European Union – are all attempts to fulfill hopes that Kant was among the first to articulate. Also still with us is Kant's cosmopolitanism, which is most fundamentally a view about the historicity of human nature. In concluding his attempt to identify the "character of the human species" as a whole, he describes it first in terms of unsociable sociability:

> The character of the species, as evident based on the collected historical experience of all times and among all peoples, is the following: that they, taken collectively (as the human race as a whole), are a mass of persons that exist one next to one another and after one another and who cannot *do without* peaceful coexistence and yet cannot *avoid* constant strife amongst one another.
>
> (*Anth* 7: 331)

Kant asks whether such a species should be considered good or evil. He seems at first to take the misanthropic side – the part of those critics who either censure humanity for its wickedness, or else laugh at it for its folly. These attitudes would be correct, Kant concludes, but for one thing: they themselves reveal in us "a moral predisposition in us, an innate appeal of reason, to work against that tendency [toward evil]" (*Anth* 7: 333). His final conception of human nature, therefore, consists in a *historical* vision of the human species:

> [It] presents the human species not as evil, but rather as a race of rational beings that strive continually to make progress, against obstacles, from evil to the good. Its will would be good in general, but carrying it through is hindered by the fact that reaching the end cannot be expected simply on the basis of a free agreement of *individuals*. Rather reaching that end can only be expected from the progressive organization of the citizens of the earth within and into the species as a system that is cosmopolitically combined.
>
> (A 7: 333)

Notes

1 Kant was influenced here by Adam Ferguson (1995/1767).
2 "Il n'est rien si dissociable et sociable que l'homme: l'un par son vice, l'autre par sa nature" (De Montaigne 1988: 388). "There is nothing so unsociable and sociable as man; the one by his vice, the other by his nature" (De Montaigne 1949: 91).

3 In the *Religion*, Kant's attribution of this propensity to our social condition is explicit (*RGV* 6:27, 93–4). This in no way detracts from the fact that the evil is entirely our responsibility. It means only that, from a regulative-teleological standpoint, we can understand the propensity to evil as the way nature uses evil "as an incentive to culture" (*RGV* 6: 27).

4 See Anne-Robert-Jacques Turgot (1973). For a recent defense of this idea in the Cold War context, see Diane R. Kunz (1997).

5 Compare Hegel (1991: §324).

6 "The fates lead the willing, drive the unwilling" in Seneca (1918), *Moral Epistles*, 18.4.

References

Cassirer, E. (1951) *The Philosophy of the Enlightenment*, F.C.A. Koelln and J.P. Pettegrove (trans.), Princeton: Princeton University Press.

De Montaigne, M.E. (1949) "Of Solitude," in C. Cotton (trans.), W. Hazlitt (rev.), B. Bates (ed.), *Selected Essays*, New York: Random House.

De Montaigne, M.E. (1988) "De la Solitude," in A. Tournon (ed.), *Essais*, vol. I, Paris: Imprimerie nationale Éditions.

Ferguson, A. (1995/1767) *An Essay on the History of Civil Society*, London: Transaction.

Hegel, G.W.F. (1991) *Elements of the Philosophy of Right*, A.W. Wood (ed.), and H.B. Nisbet (trans.), Cambridge: Cambridge University Press.

Kleingeld, P. (1995) *Fortschritt und Vernunft: Zur Geschichtsphilosophie Kants*, Würzburg: Königshausen & Neumann.

Kunz, D.R. (1997) *Guns and Butter: America's Cold War Economic Diplomacy*, New York: The Free Press.

Rousseau, J.-J. (1992) *Discourse on the Origin of Inequality*, D. Cress (trans.), Indianapolis, IN: Hackett.

Seneca (1918) *Epistles*, R.M. Gummere (trans.), Loeb Classical Library 75–7, Cambridge, MA: Harvard University Press.

Turgot, A.-R.-J. (1973) *Turgot on Progress, Sociology and Economics: A Philosophical Review of the Successive Advances of the Human Mind, on Universal History [and] Reflections on the Formation and the Distribution of Wealth*, R.L. Meek (ed. and trans.), Cambridge: Cambridge University Press.

Further reading

A.O. Rorty and J. Schmidt (eds.), *Kant's Idea for a Universal History with a Cosmopolitan Purpose: A Critical Guide* (Cambridge: Cambridge University Press, 2009) includes a series of relevant texts for Kant's idea of history, in particular: H. Allison's "Teleology and History in Kant: The Critical Foundations of Kant's Philosophy of History" focuses on the underlying methodology of Kant's account of history and its connections with the emergent Critical philosophy; J.B. Schneewind's "Good Out of Evil: Kant and the Idea of Unsocial Sociability" examines the notion of unsocial sociability, which plays a crucial role in Kant's philosophy of history, but also more generally in his thought; Eckart Föster's "The hidden plan of nature" discusses another important topic for Kant's account of politics and philosophy by focusing on the 8th Proposition in the *Idea*; three further essays with direct focus on history in this early essay of Kant are also very worth considering: G. Lloyd's "Providence as Progress: Kant's Variations on a Tale of Origins," T. Pinkard's "Norms, Facts, and the Philosophy of History," and R. Bittner's "Philosophy Helps History".

30

THE LATER VIEW

Kant on History and Politics

Susan Shell

★★★

Kant's political thought has recently emerged as a topic of major scholarly concern, after many years of general neglect in the English-speaking world, thanks to the seminal work of scholars such as Patrick Riley (1983), Howard Williams (1983), and – above all – John Rawls (1971), whose pathbreaking writings set in motion a virtual industry of scholarship along "constructivist" lines. More recent work has focused not only the strengths and limitations of this approach (e.g., O'Neill (1989), Flikschuh (2000)) but also on alterative reconstructive readings (e.g., Kersting (1992), Höffe (2006), Ellis (2005), Ripstein (2009)), as well as including philosophically sophisticated textual studies that pay nuanced attention to intellectual and historical context (e.g., Kleingeld (2011), Byrd and Hryschka (2010), Maliks (2015)). Much of the research that has flourished in the most recent years has clustered around particular themes, such as revolution, citizenship, and international law; while other work has addressed with new vigor the place of history and politics within Kant's overall critical scheme (e.g., Wood (1999), Zoeller (2011), Sweet (2013), Huseyinzadegan (2015)).

It is impossible in a brief chapter to do justice to these and other recent contributions to our understanding of Kant's later political and historical thought, and even less to the many controversies this new work has generated. Instead, I will view Kant's late approach to both politics and history through a somewhat narrower, and still largely neglected lens: namely, Kant's own use of the term "politics" both generally and, in later years, as a term of art. Kant's understanding of politics in the latter sense sheds revealing light not only on his late concept of republicanism and accompanying two-tiered strategy for bending the arc of history "toward the better" (*SF* 7: 79) but also on the evolving role of "politics" within Kant's overall critical system.

1. Kant's Pre-revolutionary "Politics"

Prior to the French Revolution, Kant used the term "politics" only rarely and in either a broadly descriptive sense (as in "political geography"), or, even more uncommonly, in the then conventional sense of prudence in affairs of state [*Staatsklugheit*]. Thanks to the pervasive influence of Machiavelli and his followers, the ordinary meaning of "politics" had by the 18th century changed from the high-minded concern of the wise and virtuous statesman (as in Aristotle's *Politics*) to

DOI: 10.4324/9781003406617-39

an explicitly a-moral "reason of state" and, by extension, the self-serving manipulation of others to enhance one's own power, wealth, and glory. That transformation is anticipated in a famous paragraph of Machiavelli's *Prince* (1995), which calls upon rulers to take their bearings from how men live, rather than how they ought to live (Chapter 15). Frederick II's own *Anti-Machiavel* (co-authored with Voltaire, and published in 1740), testifies to the ongoing salience of "politics" in this new, broadly Machiavellian sense both as target for moral and religious opprobrium and as a (secret) model for emulation.

Under the reign of Frederick II (1740–1786), Kant devoted little thematic attention to "politics," a term that is especially uncommon in his writings of the 1780's. At the same time, he also did not hesitate to make use of politics in a roughly Machiavellian sense by appealing to the self-interest of "enlightened" monarchs (such as Frederick II) to promote the enlightenment cause. Rulers could best serve their *own* interests, Kant argued, as well as promote the aim of enlightenment more generally, by permitting the free public use of reason without relinquishing absolute sovereignty. By thus guarding the state against the potentially destabilizing effects of free public discourse, absolutism was more favorable to the transformation of a people's way of thinking – or so Kant urged – than could be assured under a regime in which the people enjoyed greater civil freedom (*WA* 8: 41–2). A perfectly just constitution, as Kant wrote in the same year, is a "society in which *freedom under external laws* can be encountered combined in the greatest possible degree with irresistible power" (*IaG* 8: 22) – a definition perfectly consistent with the principles of Hobbes, so long as lawful freedom replaces mutual survival as the primary goal of civil peace. To be sure, such a society would constitute no more than a "glittering misery" as Kant here puts it, did that civic arrangement not also promise to contribute to a "moralization" of the human race by allowing all the predispositions of humanity to develop freely and without mutual hindrance (*WA* 8: 41). Still, now that the "idea" of universal history from a cosmopolitan standpoint had been announced, at least provisionally, future progress toward that civil and moral end, as here presented, was, if not assured, then at least on track (cf. *Refl* 8019; 19: 583).

It is thus no wonder that Kant devoted little thematic attention during most of the 1780s to politics as such. Frederick's motto "argue as much as you like [. . .] only obey!" was ultimately to be vindicated by and through the critical instruction whose ever wider dissemination Kant had good reason to expect – not least, because it coincided with the self-interest of "enlightened" rulers like Frederick II – rulers wishing to secure not only obedient subjects but also their own future glory (*IaG* 8: 31). Left to their own selfish devices, autocratic monarchs could be counted on to advance the cause of progress more effectively, and with less civil danger, than would otherwise be possible, thanks to nature's "cultivation" thereby of mankind's "propensity [. . .] to *think* freely." The Machiavellian challenge could be met, in other words, by Machiavellian means as reinterpreted by Hobbes and placed in service to a moral aim: namely, a people "capable of *freedom* in acting" (*WA* 8: 41).

2. Kant's Pre-revolutionary Republicanism

Prior to 1789, Kant's "republicanism" can be summarized by a crude but pithy formula: Hobbesian means to Rousseauian ends. As early as the *"Remarks" in Observations on the Beautiful and the Sublime* (1765), Kant had identified two civic ideals: republics, which required civic virtue and simplicity of manners; and monarchies, which were suited to "luxurious" times (like the present). Republics offer "equality (freedom)," whereas monarchies (or what he here calls "the *sovereign* state"), offer "unity but not equality" (*Bem* 20: 166). The "perfect *republic*," according to these same notes, is a "combin[ation]" of equality and unity – a formulation that leaves open the question of whether civic unity can be sustained in modern times without monarchy of some kind.

In subsequent years Kant will combine these ideals in a model of justice in which reciprocal freedom is secured by the irresistible will of an enlightened ruler. Such a ruler can be conceived as effectually sovereign insofar as it "represents" the people in the specific sense of governing in accordance with laws to which people *could* consent without giving up their claim to equal freedom under law. The crucial question is thus not who rules (be it one, few, or many) but whether their "way of ruling" [*Regierungsart*] conforms to what rational people in the preceding sense could will, and accordingly assigns no special value to democracy, or to citizens' active participation in positive lawmaking, over other constitutional forms.[1]

Civic freedom and equality, as Rousseau had seen matters, required the passionate identification of citizens with the wider community; hence his notorious pessimism concerning the possibility of reconciling civic health with progress in the arts and sciences. For all his praise of Rousseau's genius (see, e.g. (*Bem* 20: 43)), Kant never shared in that pessimism. Even in his "Remarks," Kant had sought to reconcile progress in the arts and sciences with civic health by prioritizing the universal, and hence rational, form of the general will, over its particular content (*Bem* 20: 161). The general will on Kant's maturer understanding "gives" the law (by virtue of its form") rather than "making" it (by virtue of its matter). And the existence of a just community no longer depends, as with Rousseau, on passions that are both parochial and difficult to sustain, particularly under conditions of modern enlightenment. Instead, equal freedom under law can be secured, or at least approached, by an appeal to reason – either in a higher, moral sense that takes men as they ought to be, or in a lower, merely prudential sense that takes them as they are. But in neither case, in Kant's writings prior to the French Revolution, need subjects themselves participate in positive law*making* (as with Rousseau). It suffices, from the standpoint of right, that the ruler treat them "in accordance with their dignity" as *potential* lawgiving members of a moral kingdom of ends.

In keeping with this fact, Kant's description of "the perfect republic" (or res publica = public thing) in the *Critique of Pure Reason* makes no provision for popular participation in law making:

> Plato's *Republic* has become proverbial as allegedly a striking example of a dream-built perfection that can reside online in an idle thinker's brain; and *Brucker*[2] finds ridiculous the philosopher's assertion that a prince would never rule well if he did not partake of the ideas. However, we would do better to pursue this thought further. [. . .] Surely a constitution consisting of the *greatest freedom* according to laws through which *the freedom of each can coexist with that of the others* [. . .] is a necessary idea [. . .] that we must lay at the basis not merely in the first drafting of a state constitution but also in all laws.

> (A316/B372–3)

Kant's retort to Brucker, and implicitly, to Machiavelli, advances a republican "idea" that combines a Rousseauian end with Hobbesian means. Rulers treat their subjects "in accordance with their dignity" not by allowing them a share in positive lawmaking but instead through "irresistible" commands as the "hard shell" within which the predisposition "to think freely" can develop to its fullest – and hence the surest way, according to Kant's writings of the period, to promote the moralization of the human race (A316/B372–3, *IaG* 8: 27, *WA* 8: 41–2, *V-NR*/Feyerabend 27: 1383).

3. Kant's Politics After the Death of Fredrick the Great

Two major events whose importance to Kant can hardly be overstated, radically changed his treatment of both "republicanism" and "politics," both broadly speaking and as a term of art: the death of Frederick II in 1786, and the Storming of the Bastille in the summer of 1789. As a result of these events and their aftermath – in one case, the ascendance to the throne of a king distinctly hostile to Kant's larger purposes, on the other, an increasingly radical and violent revolutionary turn in France along with the accompanying domestic reaction, Kant found himself forced to address practical political matters more directly and thematically than previously. In so doing these events also prompted him to revisit his earlier confidence in enlightened monarchy as the surest practical route to human progress.

Accompanying those changes in Kant's external situation was a new understanding on his part of the systematic role and purpose of reflective judgment (first elaborated in the *Critique of Judgment* whose last pages were completed in the final months of 1789). The accompanying a priori principles of teleological judgment not only lent critical grounding and precision to Kant's previously free-standing historical presumption that "All natural predispositions of a creature are determined sometime to develop themselves completely and purposively" (*IaG* 8: 18); they also provided new conceptual tools for his emerging understanding of the state as an "organized" whole.

Two issues loom especially large in this redirection of Kant's focus toward a more direct engagement in political affairs: freedom of religion and the purported right of revolution.

As to the first: under Frederick the Great, Kant had enjoyed wide latitude to publish what he wished – so much so that he dedicated the *Critique of Pure Reason* to Frederick's official censor, who was also a personal friend. His successor, Frederick William II, took a different, and more restrictive view, especially in matters of religious liberty, preferring to confine the officially recognized sects to professing their official doctrines, and restricting others to near silence. Whatever justification such policies might have had from the standpoint of maintaining sectarian peace, they were devastating to Kant's then strategy for the promotion of enlightenment (in his peculiar sense), one that relied, above all else, on freedom to argue publicly, particularly on religious matters (Shell 2009).

The impact of the French Revolution was even more far-reaching. The appearance of a German translation in 1791 of *Burke's Reflections on the Revolution in France*, followed by August Wilhelm Rehburg's endorsement of Burke's work in the same year and the fuller and far more influential translation of Burke's work published by August Gentz in 1793, helped set in motion conservative reaction even prior the execution of Louis XVI and subsequent Terror that seemed to confirm Burke's darkest predictions. That this reaction included sometime followers of Kant such as Gentz and Rehburg was a particular blow, and culminated, in the first instance, to Kant's publication of *On the Common Saying: that may be true in theory, but is of no use in practice* (1793), which can be read as a direct response to Burke's charge, reaffirmed by Gentz and Rehburg, that metaphysics had caused the revolution (*Refl* 23: 127) and which represents Kant's first effort to deal systematically with the question of "application." As Reidar Maliks has recently argued, Kant in this and subsequent political works denies the right of revolution in no uncertain terms, while also insisting on a priori rational principles that, duly carried out, would uphold the civic equality of citizens, including a right, in the case of "active" citizens, to participate in positive lawgiving. In so doing, Kant not only attempts to steer a narrow course between the Revolution's more radical German supporters (such as Forster), and conservative defenders of traditional institutions (such as Rehburg and Genz). Kant thereby marks out, through his own public writings, a course of speech and action that is political in a "true" sense that Kant explicitly describes for the first time.

4. Kant's "True Politics"

Kant's use of the term "politics" increases in the early 1790s, while still keeping its conventional Machiavellian flavor, that is, as a principle of action that is *other* than, if not in outright opposition to, a moral one. This is pointedly the case in Kant's several references, in *Religion within the Boundary of Bare Reason*, to "political interests" (*RGV* 6: 131) and to the "merely political laws" of the Jewish state, whose "political faith" sharply contrasts with "moral faith" and which as such falls entirely outside the boundaries of true religion (*RGV* 6: 125).

It is only with *Perpetual Peace* – the most obviously "political," and politically influential piece, he ever wrote – that "politics" receives more positive coloration, at least potentially, in partial response, perhaps, to Genz's own positive use of the term (Greene 2017). It is also here that Kant for the first time offers an explicit definition of politics, and indeed, not one but two: namely, "as applied doctrine of right [*ausübender Rechtslehre*]" (*ZeF* 8: 370), and "as the art of making use [of nature's mechanism] for governing human beings" (*ZeF* 8: 372).

In what, then, does the "applied doctrine of right" consist, and how, if at all, might it also include "making use of the mechanism of nature to govern human beings"? Kant's subsequent account of what he here calls "the true politics" offers an enticing, if ambiguous, answer:

> The true politics cannot [. . .] take a step [*keinen Schritt thun*] without having already paid homage to morality, and though politics in itself [*für sich selbst*] is a difficult art, its union with morality is no art at all, for as soon as the two enter into conflict, morality cuts the knot that politics cannot untie. The right of human beings must be held sacred, no matter what sacrifice it may cost the dominant authority [*herrschenden Gewalt*]. One cannot here cut things in half and concoct the cross [*Mittelding*] of a pragmatically conditioned right (between right and use); all politics must, rather, bend its knee to right, though it may hope thereby to gradually achieve the level [*Stufe*] where it can shine constantly.
>
> (*ZeF* 8: 380)

Politics pays advance "homage" to morality by "bending the knee" to right, which though it is no "Mittelding," nevertheless combines an act of "using" – a use that it would seem to share with other "arts" devoted to the manipulation of natural objects – with an act of "governing" only possible in the case of objects that are (also) rational beings.

Kant's later comparison, in the *Doctrine of Right*, of the juridical community of persons to the physical community of bodies will shed further light on right's peculiar role in mediating between the laws of nature and those of freedom, and hence in cutting the knot that politics "for itself" cannot unravel. And it may have prompted Kant's attempt, in an early draft of that later work, to distinguish politics as a "science" – that is to say, as a body of knowledge informed by an "idea" – from politics as a branch of prudence:

> Politics as a science is the system of the laws for securing the rights and satisfaction of the people with their internal and external condition.
>
> Just as *prudence* [*Klugheit*] is the skill of using human beings (free beings) as means to one's aims; so *politics* (Staatskunst) is that prudence through which someone understands how to use an entire free people for his aims.
>
> (*VAMS* 23: 346)

Kant's draft adds a further condition with which a true politics must harmonize: namely, that all laws of right be publicizable (*VAMS* 23: 346). And yet the failure of the published version either to call politics a "science" or to provide the extended discussion of the "transcendental principle of public right" Kant had earlier promised (*ZeF* 8: 386), suggests the impossibility, as he may have come to see it, of any strictly "scientific" approach to the task to which politics "properly" addresses itself: namely to make the public "satisfied with its condition" (*ZeF* 8: 386; cf. *VRML* 8: 429; Oki 2018).

Instead, Kant looks to the republican "idea," elaborated along explicitly "organic" lines, and including, for the first time, an insistence that citizens actively participate in lawgiving, to newly facilitate the transition from a politics that "makes use of the mechanism of nature" to govern human beings (*ZeF* 8: 366) to one that treats "the human being, *who is now more than a machine*, in keeping with his dignity" (*WA* 8: 42; cf. *VAMS* 23: 267).

5. Kant's Late Republicanism: From Singular to Systematic Representation

That new emphasis can already be detected in the *Critique of Judgment*, which compares the recent "transformation" of a people into a state to the "organization" of a "direct natural purpose" (or living organism generally):

> The analogy of [a direct natural end [*Naturzweck*]] can shed light on a certain association [*Verbindung*], more encountered in the idea than in reality [*Wirklichkeit*]: thus in speaking of the recent total transformation of a great people into a state the word *organization* was often and very aptly made use of for the establishment [*Einrichtung*] of magistrates, etc., and even for the entire state body. For each member in such a whole should indeed [*freilich*] be not merely a means but also at the same time an end; and each, in cooperating in/co-effecting [*mitwirken*] the possibility the whole, is on the other hand determined in its place and function by the idea of the whole.
>
> (*KU* 5: 375)

The citizen is here for the first time conceived as actively contributing, as "member" of the civic body, to realizing the republican idea. Kant expands upon the nature of this civic body (the "maternal womb," as he will later put it, from which each has arisen and to which each must leave behind a sacred pledge [*TP* 8: 291]), in *Theory and Practice*, which explicitly connects citizenship with the right to vote (*TP* 8: 295). The rightful civil constitution is based, as Kant now puts it, on three "a priori" principles: namely, freedom, equality, and "independence" [*Unabhängigkeit*] as the quality necessary to have a "vote in legislation." Independence, in turn, includes living "by alienating what is one's own," but excludes "serving" others (other than the commonwealth), that is, "giving them permission to make use of one's faculties/means" [*Vermögen*]. And it is thus compatible with the role that Frederick the Great at least *claimed* to occupy: namely of that of "first servant" of the commonwealth (*TP* 8: 295: cf. *ZeF* 8: 352–3).

In keeping with this change, Kant introduces what he calls "the representative system," one roughly based on the one proposed by Abbé Sieyès and subsequently adopted by French lawmakers. Where Kant had earlier left "representation" of the people (in good Hobbesian fashion) to the actual ruler, he now carves out an explicit "representative" role for an elective legislature, albeit one whose relation to positive lawmaking – as distinguished from the fundamental lawgiving by which the constitution is itself established – remains unspecified.

That reticence, in an essay written to defend "metaphysics" against the charge that it had, in Rehberg's words, "caused the revolution," is understandable, and was in any case in keeping with Kant's ongoing claim that even in the absence of such a legislature, rule in accordance with principles of right was sufficient to infuse the "mechanism" of coercive laws with the "spirit of freedom." Such infusion would at least enable citizens "to become rationally convinced that this coercion is in conformity with right," and thus obey without falling "into contradiction with [themselves]" (*TP* 8: 305).

At the same time, the "hard shell" of Kant's pre-revolutionary writings, one that allowed the "predisposition to think freely" to develop to its maximum extent by reducing external friction to a minimum, has been replaced by a "maternal womb" in which moral education can proceed more organically, and through the self-cultivation of a reason freed from the burden of obedience to laws that reason cannot justify.

A similar reticence, and related emphasis on infusing coercive laws with the "spirit" of republicanism, prevails in *Toward Perpetual Peace*, which treats active citizenship and the accompanying right to vote only indirectly, under the rubric of the "representative system," which can be honored in the "*spirit*" by a ruler's "way of governing," as when Frederick II "at least *said* that he was only the highest servant of the state" (*ZeF* 8: 352). Indeed, Kant is here still willing to allow that of all "forms of sovereignty," monarchy, so long as the ruler governs in that spirit, is the state constitution that best accords with the "possibility of republicanism," to which the constitution may hope to be raised by gradual reforms, whereas democracy, or rule by all, can be thus transformed only by "violent revolution" (*ZeF* 8: 353). Republican "hope" thus rests less with aristocracy, and still less, with pure democracy, as Kant now puts it, than with the monarch whose "way of governing" accords with the "spirit of the representative system." At the same time, as Kant here adds, without a representative system every way of governing is "despotic and violent" irrespective of the [official] constitution (*ZeF* 8: 353).

In what, then, does a "representative system" consist? And does its "spirit" suffice indefinitely, or is every way of governing not in accordance with both the spirit and the *letter* of a representative system (ultimately) "despotic and violent," as Kant's last sentence might be taken to imply?

Kant's later *Metaphysics of Morals*, published during the waning days of an increasingly enfeebled monarch, offers the following clarification:

> Every true republic [. . .] is and can be nothing other than a *representative system* of the people, in order to procure its rights in the people's name, through all state citizens united, by means of its delegates [*Abgeordeten*] (deputies).
>
> (*MS* 6: 341)

Whereas he had earlier assigned the representative function to the head of state alone, as "representing" the general will of the people (*TP* 8: 304), the three persons of the general will (legislative, executive, and judicial) (*MS* 6:313) are now said to collectively constitute the relation of general commander [*allgemeinen Oberhaupts*] to those who obey (*MS* 6:316). Headship thus takes a double form: both as the relation of "command" without which a rightful state cannot be thought, and is therefore necessary "in the idea," and as the delegated headship (or executive power) by which actual laws are put into effect. And lawgiving similarly assumes a double form: both as the fundamental civic lawgiving in the "idea" and by virtue of a general will in which all (rational) citizens must share, and as the delegated power of positive lawmaking that applies the fundamental law to actual circumstances, a lawmaking activity in which active citizens are now said to "cooperate" [*mitwirken*]. Accordingly, the "people" of Kant's "true republic," circa 1797, no longer need to be "represented" by a (sole) head of state in order for the concept of right to have effectual existence (as in Kant's earlier writings). Instead, "the united people" are, or can become, the "sovereign itself" (*MS* 6: 341), as in the telling case of Louis XVI, who inadvertently "wasted" his own rulership:

> It was thus a great misstep in judgment on the part of a mighty ruler [*Beherrschers*] of our time when to help himself out of the embarrassment of large state debts he left it to the people to take on this burden and distribute it as it deemed good; for then the

law-giving authority naturally came into the people's hands, not only with regard to the taxation of subjects but also with regard to governing [*Regierung*], namely that it not incur new debts through wastefulness [*Verschwendung*] or war, so that the entire power of ruling [*Herrschergewalt*] of the monarchy entirely vanished [*verschwand*] [. . .] and passed over [*überging*] to the people, to whose lawgiving will the mine and thine of each subject was subjected.

(MS 6: 341–2n)

The rulership of a "wasteful" king could "vanish/be laid waste" without the state thereby descending into lawless anarchy, because the people, as Kant now sees it, can be a "whole" without being "represented" by an independent head of state who wields effectual power, as on his earlier, more strictly Hobbesian model.

Kant's unpublished reflections serve to further illuminate the nature of this sudden constitutional improvement without an accompanying cessation, however temporary, of civic life:

In France the National Assembly was able to alter the constitution even though it was called together, to be sure, only in order to bring order to the credit system [*Creditwesen*] of the nation. For they were representatives of the entire people, whom the king had allowed to decree in accordance with indeterminate plenary power. The king otherwise represented the people; here he was thus negated [*vernichtet*]; because the people themselves were present [*gegenwärtig*] [. . .]. Thus the misfortune of the king comes directly from his own sovereignty, after he had once allowed the people's deputies to assemble, then he was nothing; for his entire lawgiving authority was founded only on his representing the whole people; this also illuminates the injustice of a single person as sovereign. He cannot admit that that which he represents [*repräsentirt*] presents itself [*sich selbst darstelle*]. Because he represents [*vorstellt*] the whole, he becomes nothing when this whole, of which he is not a part but merely the proxy/place holder [*Stellvertreter*], is allowed to present itself [*sich selbst stellen lässt*].

(Refl 8055; 19: 595–6)

Kant's punning plays here on the term "stellen" bring home his current dissatisfaction with his own earlier, more strictly Hobbesian account of representation. The people's representative should not take their place in the manner of a proxy [*Stellvertreter*], but should instead belong to what it represents, as with the people's deputies once summoned by the then ruling sovereign.

An added note suggests, moreover, the importance of active citizenship in giving "substance" to a popular unity that otherwise depends on representation by proxy:

The National Assembly was called in order to save the state by covering with their guarantee [*Guarantie*] (not merely drawing up bills/plans [*Entwürfe*]) all the debts imposed on the state by the extravagance of the government [*Regierung*]. They therefore had to freely [*freiwillig*] guarantee [*verbürgen*] it with their property (they had therefore to put themselves in a condition such that they alone could dispose of their property, hence in a condition of freedom, albeit under laws, but those that they gave themselves, that is, a republican condition or condition of free citizens [*freybürgerlichen*], and the court had itself yielded the right to encumber them. But so that they could achieve this state of citizenry [*Bürgschaft*], they had to establish a constitution that could exercise no authority/force [*Gewaltthätigkeit*] over them.

(Refl 8055; 19: 596; see also 8048; 19: 593)

Kant's verbal play on "Bürger" and "verbürgen" ("citizen" and "to back up" or "guarantee") draws attention to the integrative character of citizenship, and helps explain why, in his final estimation, "self-subsistence" [*Selbständigkeit*] (*MS* 6: 314) replaces "independence" [*Unabhängigkeit*] (*TP* 8: 290) as the essential characteristic of the (active) citizen. For while "independence" is merely the logical negation of "dependence," self-subsistence entails the further, positive quality, on Kant's later account, of being able to manage one's own affairs in reciprocal relation with others. Thus while the savage may be "independent" and in this negative sense "his own master," only one who is capable of sustaining himself collectively without ceasing to be self-directing, counts as "self-subsistent" in a way that makes one capable of voting or "giving voice" [*Stimmgebung*], and thereby "organizing" [*organizeren*] the state in common with others (*MS* 6: 314).

Whereas "active" citizens can be regarded as substances in community with other substances (in accordance with the a priori concept of "relation"), passive citizens "lack civic personhood [*bürgerlichen Persönlichkeit*]" and, as Kant adds, "their existence is, as it were, merely adherence" (*MS* 6: 314). Passive citizens, "exist" in a civic sense, in other words, only insofar as they are maintained by ("inhere in") active citizens (on whom passive citizens depend for their support), just as qualities "exist" only insofar as they "inhere" in substances.

Kant's comparison of the active citizen to substance metaphysically conceived contrasts revealingly with a similar, pre-revolutionary analogy. According to that earlier analogy, *all* citizens exist merely as inherences in the "substance" of state, by which each is maintained, and without which none would have a future he or she could count on (cf. *Refl* #8023; 19: 585; *state* has "*Selbständigkeit*," hence cannot be inherited by another).

> Because an individual human being can suffer [*leiden*] no other security for his future preferences, he is juridically only *accidens*, which can only exist *inhaerendo*. A civil whole is substance.
>
> (*Refl* 8065; 19: 600)

It seems to be the state alone, and not individual citizens, on Kant's pre-revolutionary understanding, that count as self-subsistent, capable of existing in reciprocal community [*commercium*] with others – a commercium here identified not with the individual state, as in his later work, but solely with a "league of nations." Thus, according to the same unpublished reflection:

> The question is whether the end of humanity is the transformation [*Verwandlung*] of substance into accident or whether it is of accident into substance, and the duty of the state toward itself is to preserve itself as a particular state, such that this duty could not be yielded. In the latter case the unity of *commercium* (league of nations [*Völkerbund*]) remains the sole thing that constitutes the end of humanity, not the unity of inherence, not the unity of dependence [dependenz] of a highest referee [*Schiedsrichter*], but the freedom of each individual state under universal laws. Autonomy.
>
> (*Refl* 8065; 19: 600)

The restriction of *Selbstständigkeit* to the state in these comments sheds suggestive light on Kant's changing conception of the *Völkerbund*, between 1784 and 1795, from federation that is both externally coercive and universally inclusive, in the *IaG* (*IaG* 8: 26) in accordance with the principle of "autonomy" as elaborated in the *Groundlaying* (*GMS*), to his later non-coercive and more restrictive conception, in *Toward Perpetual Peace*, of a non-coercive federation of republics (and their like), or to what the *Metaphysics of Morals* calls a "free federation of states." For, states, as organized beings in their own right, have "outgrown" [*entwachsen*], as he tellingly puts it, the constraint of others (*ZeF* 8: 355).

In sum, revolutionary developments in France, including the distinction between active and passive citizenship introduced by the Abbé Sieyès, and deputized rule under a representative National Assembly, seem to have provided Kant convenient conceptual tools for integrating his new understanding of organized being (originally formulated with respect to "natural products") within the framework of his long-standing republican "idea." The "active" citizens of such a state are not just inherent parts (as with citizens as such, in Kant's pre-revolutionary understanding) but substantive members, "organizing [*organiseren*] or cooperating/co-effecting [*mitwirken*] to introduce new laws" (*MS* 6: 315). Autonomy, or subjection to no law that one does not also give, in other words, is no longer limited to the ethical kingdom of ends, or to a republic only in the idea, but has an effectual political reality [*Wirklichkeit*] distinctly its own.

6. Kant's Final Politics: From Mechanism to Organism

In Kant's final productive years, beginning with the *Conflict of the Faculties* (1797) and up through and including the earlier pages of the *Opus Postumum*, Kant's political works aim with increasing directness at facilitating the transition from the mechanical to the organic state[3] – enough, indeed, almost to justify Nietzsche's later (derisive) quip.[4] That transition can also be framed as moving from politics "as the art of making use of the mechanism of nature to govern human beings" to a politics that (also) aims at satisfying public demand for a government in which "the people is co-lawgiving." For "a being endowed with freedom," as he notes in Part Two of the *Conflict of the Faculties*,

> is not satisfied with the pleasure of life's comforts that fall to his portion [*zu Theil werden*] through another ([including] the government); what matters is instead the principle according-ing to which he procures it for himself.
>
> (*SF* 7: 87n)

It follows, Kant continues, that such a being "can and should," according to "the *formal* principle of its will, desire/demand [*verlangen*] no other government for the people to which it belongs than one in which the people is co-lawgiving [*mit gesetetzgebend*]" (*SF* 7: 87n).

To be sure, that demand cannot be translated into active disobedience without itself becoming unjust and hence lapsing into self-contradiction. For "right is still always only an idea" whose "execution" is restricted "to the condition that its means harmonize with morality." To rule autocratically, and yet "in a republican manner" – that is, in accordance with the "spirit of republicanism" and on analogy with it – is thus enough to "make a people satisfied with its constitution" (*SF* 7: 87n). And yet that very spirit, along with the way of ruling that accords with it, lifts the burden of obedience to coercive laws that reason cannot justify and is thereby itself progressively transformative, thus promoting improvement in the constitution without recurrence to a state of nature, improvement that a people "rich in spirit" (*SF* 7: 85) managed all at once, thanks to the singular extravagance of their then reigning monarch.

At the same time, given the *current* state of Europe, as Kant also observes, autocratic rule in a republican spirit may be the better actual constitution, "as the only one by which the people [*Volk*] can maintain itself against mighty neighbors" (*SF* 7: 86n). Kant's final thematic treatment of politics, in an essay published one year later, in in keeping with the latitude of that suggestion. In that in many ways confounding little work, which is otherwise notoriously insistent on the primacy of a priori principles, Kant gives remarkable scope to what he calls "the experiential cognition of human beings." Kant here identifies (for the first time) not just a "task" [*Aufgabe*] of politics (here described as "making a people satisfied with its condition") but also a specific "problem" [Problem], namely:

of how it can be managed [*wie es anzustellen sei*] that in a society however large concord in accordance with principles of freedom and equality is to be maintained (namely, by means of a representative system).

(*VRML* 8: 429)

"This," he continues:

will then be a principle of *politics*, whose arrangement and ordering will contain decrees, drawn from the experiential cognition of human beings, that have in view only the mechanism of legal administration [*Rechtsverwaltung*] and how this can be directed purposively [*zweckmässig*].

(*VRML* 8: 429)

Thanks to that political cognition, as spelled out in Kant's final writings, all peoples can look forward to eventual public "satisfaction," be it actively (as with most all European nations) or passively (as with others that are poorer in "spirit"). More recent self-styled "Kantians" have understandably abandoned the racial anthropology that supports this two-tiered republican model without giving up on its implicit distinction between what the people will and what they ought to will. Indeed, it perhaps one of the lingering ironies of Kant's late works that they may have helped to unleash, through the force and eloquence of their argument, not only the world-wide movements of the last two centuries in support of representative popular government, but also, and in the latter's name, for that rule by an enlightened elite in accordance with what a rational people *should* want – a presumption that may have helped to provoke, however inadvertently, the current populist backlash.

At the same time, anticipations in Kant's earliest moral and political writings of that two-tiered civil model suggests that it is fundamentally rooted neither in his emerging critical system nor in his reaction to external events of the late 1780s and 1790s, but rather in his long-standing effort to address a problem to which he had been initially awakened through his reading of Rousseau: that of reconciling the competing claims of freedom (understood as subjection to no law one does not also give) and modern scientific progress. Whether Kant's late works offer an adequate response to Rousseauian pessimism on this score must here remain an open question.

Notes

1　See, for example, *V-Nr/Feyerabend* (27: 1383).
2　Johann Jakob Brucker, an influential 18th-century German historian. On his role in the dispersal of political "Machiavellianism" (under the rubric of "enlightenment") see Longo (2010).
3　Cf. Huseyinzadegan (2015).
4　See Friedrich Nietzsche (1918), *The Antichrist*, Chapter 11: "Didn't Kant see in the French Revolution the transformation of the state from the inorganic form to the organic?"

References

Byrd, B.S. and Hruschka, J. (2010) *Kant's Doctrine of Right: A Commentary*, New York: Cambridge University Press.

Ellis, E. (2005) *Kant's Politics*, New Haven: Yale University Press.

Flikschuh, K. (2000) *Kant and Modern Political Philosophy*, New York: Cambridge University Press.

Greene, J.A. (2017) *Edmund Burke's German Readers at the End of Enlightenment, 1790–1815*, unpublished dissertation, Cambridge: University of Cambridge.

Höffe, O. (2006) *Kant's Cosmopolitan Theory of Law and Peace*, A. Newton (trans.), New York: Cambridge University Press.

Huseyinzadegan, D. (2015) "Kant's Political *Zweckmässigkeit*," *Kantian Review* 20(3): 421–44.

Kersting, W. (1992) "Politics, Freedom, and Order: Kant's Political Philosophy," in P. Guyer (ed.), *The Cambridge Companion to Kant*, Cambridge: Cambridge University Press, pp. 3–342.

Kleingeld, P. (2011) *Kant and Cosmopolitanism*, New York: Cambridge University Press.

Longo, M. (2010) "A 'Critical' History of Philosophy and the Early Enlightenment: Johann Jacob Brucker," in G. Santinello and G. Piaia (eds.), *Models of the History of Philosophy: International Archives of the History of Ideas/Archives internationales d'histoire des idées*, Dordrecht: Springer.

Machiavelli, N. (1995) *The Prince*, Harvey Mansfield (ed.), Chicago: University of Chicago Press.

Maliks, R. (2015) *Kant's Politics in Context*, New York: Oxford University Press.

Nietzsche, F. (1918) *The Anti-Christ*, H.L. Mencken (trans.), New York: Knopf.

Oki, M. (2018) "The Proper Task of Kantian Politics: The Relation between Politics and Happiness," in L. Krasnoff, N.S. Madrid and P. Satne (eds.), *Kant's Doctrine of Right in the 21st Century*, Cardiff: University of Wales Press.

O'Neill, O. (1989) *Constructions of Reason: Exploration of Kant's Practical Philosophy*, Cambridge: Cambridge University Press.

Rawls, J. (1971) *A Theory of Justice*, Cambridge, MA: Harvard University Press.

Riley, P. (1983) *Kant's Political Philosophy*, Lanham, MD: Rowman & Littlefield.

Ripstein, A. (2009) *Force and Freedom*, Cambridge, MA: Harvard University Press.

Shell, S.M., (2009) *Kant and the Limits of Autonomy*, Cambridge, MA: Harvard University Press.

Sweet, K. (2013) *Kant on Practical Life: From Duty to History*, New York: Cambridge University Press.

Williams, H. (1983) *Kant's Political Philosophy*, New York: St. Martin's Press.

Wood, A.W. (1999) *Kant's Ethical Thought*, New York: Cambridge University Press.

Zoeller, W. (2011) "Kant's Political Anthropology," *Kant Yearbook* 3: 131–61.

Further Reading

L. Caranti, *Kant's Political Legacy* (Cardiff: University of Wales Press, 2019) is a good examination of Kant's political philosophy and its potential impact on our ways of thinking of human rights, peace and history. O. Höffe, *Kant's Cosmopolitan Theory of Law and Peace*, A. Newton (trans.) (New York: Cambridge University Press, 2006) and P. Kleingeld, *Kant and Cosmopolitanism* (New York: Cambridge University Press, 2011) are excellent discussions of Kant's ideal of cosmopolitanism. R. Maliks, *Kant's Politics in Context* (New York: Oxford University Press, 2015) offers a historically informed account of significant aspects of Kant's political philosophy. A. Ripstein, *Force and Freedom* (Cambridge, MA: Harvard University Press, 2009) presents a cogent reconstruction of Kant's political philosophy for the current readers. S.M. Shell, *Kant and the Limits of Autonomy* (Cambridge, MA: Harvard University Press, 2009) offers a focused examination of Kant's idea of autonomy and its relevant for contemporary liberal political theories. H. Williams, *Kant's Political Philosophy* (New York: St. Martin's Press, 1983) is a classic introduction to Kant's political thought.

IV. ANTHROPOLOGY

31

ANTHROPOLOGY

Robert B. Louden

***

In the winter semester of 1772–73, Kant began lecturing on anthropology at the University of Königsberg – a practice he continued annually until he retired from teaching in 1796. In a frequently cited letter to former student Marcus Herz written toward the end of 1773, he describes his new course as follows:

> This winter I am giving, for the second time, a lecture course on anthropology, a subject that I now intend to make into a proper academic discipline. But my plan is quite unique. I intend to use it to disclose the sources of all the [practical] sciences, the science of morality, of skill, of human intercourse, of the way to educate and govern human beings, and thus of everything that pertains to the practical [. . .]. I include so many observations of ordinary life that my auditors have constant occasion to compare their ordinary experience with my remarks and thus, from beginning to end, find my lectures entertaining and never dry. In my spare time, I am trying to prepare a preliminary study for the students out of this very pleasant observation-based doctrine [*Beobachtungslehre*], an analysis of the nature of skill (prudence) and even wisdom that, along with physical geography and distinct from all other learning, can be called knowledge of the world.
>
> (*Br* 10: 145–6)

Anthropology was a new area of academic inquiry at this time – a product of the larger Enlightenment effort to emancipate the empirical study of human nature from theologically based enquiries, best captured by Alexander Pope's famous remark:

> Know then thyself, presume not God to scan:
>   The proper study of Mankind is Man.
>   – *An Essay on Man*, 1773–1734, Epistle II (in Brinton 1956: 57)

DOI: 10.4324/9781003406617-41

Kant was one of the very first to offer an anthropology course within the German university system, and he was also a leader in its development into an academic discipline. But as he notes in his letter to Herz, his own plan was "quite unique." His main goal in teaching the course was to provide students with what he calls "*Weltkenntnis*" or knowledge of the world – a decidedly practical and nonacademic kind of know-how that would "be useful not merely for the *school* but rather for *life* and through which the accomplished apprentice is introduced to the stage of his destiny, namely, the *world*" (VvRM 2: 443; see also V-Anth/Fried 25: 469, V-Anth/Mensch 25: 854). But Kant's intentionally popular manner in conveying this "enlightenment for common life" (V-Anth/Mensch 25: 853) was also quite unique: "our anthropology can be read by everyone, even by women at the dressing-table, because it has much that is entertaining" (V-Anth/Mensch 25: 856–7). For these two reasons as well as others to be elaborated on later, Kant's anthropology writings occupy a virtually unique place within his vast corpus.

1. Origins and Connecting Points

"*Virtually* unique" because his anthropology course did not spring up ex nihilo. Kant also began lecturing on physical geography back in summer semester 1756 when he was an unsalaried *Privatdozent*, and the later anthropology course is to a certain extent an outgrowth of his lectures on physical geography. Indeed, as he also notes in the preceding cited letter to Herz, it is the two disciplines taken together which in his view form a subject "distinct from all other learning," and it is their joint task to provide students with knowledge of the world. In principle, students would acquire a knowledge of nature from the physical geography course, and a knowledge of human beings from the anthropology lectures. As Kant notes in the Preface to Rink's edited version of the *Physical Geography* lectures:

> The experiences of **nature** and the **human being** together constitute **knowledge of the world**. **Anthropology** teaches us **knowledge of the human being**, we owe our **knowledge of nature** to **physical geography**.
>
> (*PG* 9: 157; cf. *V-Anth/Pillau* 25: 733)

But in fact Kant frequently discusses human beings in his geography lectures. For instance, in his 1757 Announcement for the course he states that one of its goals is

> to explain the inclinations of human beings that spring from the zone in which they live, the diversity of their prejudices and way[s] of thinking, insofar as this can serve to acquaint man better with himself.
>
> (*EACG* 2: 9)

And in the 1765 Announcement he notes that the second part of the geography course "considers the *human being*, throughout the world, from the point of view of the variety of his natural properties and the differences in that feature of man which is moral in character" (*NEV* 2: 312). Kant's decision to begin offering a separate course on anthropology in 1772 is motivated in part by his conviction that the human being should be viewed as "a free-acting being" rather than a mere product "belonging to the play of nature" (*Anth* 7: 119, 120; cf. *V-Anth/Pillau* 25: 733). However, in fact it is neither the case that humans are treated exclusively as free-acting beings in the anthropology lectures nor entirely as products of nature in the geography lectures. As a result, there is no bright, clear line to be drawn between Kant's physical geography and anthropology lectures, particularly when we use human beings as the intended line of demarcation. Obviously, the anthropology lectures are much more concerned with human beings than are the geography lectures, but the study of human beings is not the exclusive domain of either discipline.

(Louden 2011: 147)

The first complete English translation of Rink's version of Kant's *Physical Geography* was not published until 2012 (see Kant 2012b: 441–679). In 2009 the *Holstein* (1757–59) transcription of the Lectures on Physical Geography was first published in the German Academy edition (*V-PG* 26.1: 1–320), and Academy volume 26.2 (2020) includes the *Hesse* (1770), *Kaehler* (1774), *Messina* (1778), *Dönhoff* (1782), and *Dohna* (1792) transcriptions of these popular lectures, as well as selections from other transcriptions (*V-PG* 26.2). Multiple volumes of Kant's extensive classroom lectures on ethics, logic, metaphysics, theology, and anthropology have been available for many years, but in comparison with these other areas of Kant's philosophy it is clear that the first half of Kantian *Weltkenntnis* has suffered from neglect by Kant scholars. However, at the same time, the recent appearance of the first complete English translation of Rink's edition of *Physical Geography*, when taken in conjunction with the recent publication of multiple versions of Kant's Lectures on Physical Geography in the German Academy edition, opens up new avenues for research and suggests that this may be "the last frontier" in Kant scholarship (see Louden 2014a).

During the eighteenth century all professors at Prussian universities were expected to lecture from state-approved textbooks. Minister of Education Karl Abraham von Zedlitz (to whom Kant dedicated his first *Critique* – see Aiii/Biii) made a rare exception to this required textbook regulation for Kant's geography course, on the ground that "no 'entirely suitable' textbook was available" (Vorländer 2003: 2: 57). However, for his anthropology lectures Kant used Baumgarten's *Metaphysics* (4th ed., 1757 – first translated into English in Baumgarten 2013) – specifically, the sections on empirical psychology; viz., §§504–739 as his text (see *V-Anth/Mensch* 25: 859, *V-Anth/Mron* 25: 1214). And Kant also used Baumgarten's *Metaphysics* as the text for his lectures on metaphysics – a topic that he first began lecturing on in winter semester 1755–56, one semester before he started lecturing on geography. So his lectures on metaphysics constitute a second background source for the anthropology lectures. Toward the very end of the *Critique of Pure Reason* Kant declares that "empirical psychology must [. . .] be banned entirely from metaphysics," adding that we should grant it only a temporary refuge "until it can establish its own domicile in a complete anthropology (the pendant to the empirical doctrine of nature)" (A848–9/B876–7). This desire to find a proper home for empirical psychology within anthropology is a second motive behind the creation of his new course on anthropology. The influence of Baumgarten's *Metaphysics* is most noticeable in the first part of the anthropology lectures, which makes use of the faculties of the human mind as an organizing principle. Broadly speaking, Kant's discussions here can be seen as adding "empirical meat on the bones" (Jankowiak and Watkins 2014: 58) of his more formal account of the necessary conditions of a priori cognition in the first *Critique*.

A third background source for part of the anthropology lectures – specifically, the discussions of sexes, peoples, and races that occur toward the end of many versions of the lectures – is Sections Three and Four of Kant's 1764 book, *Observations on the Feeling of the Beautiful and Sublime* (*GSE* 2: 228–56). Its title notwithstanding, the *Observations* is not fundamentally a project in aesthetics at all but rather "a work in what Kant would later call 'anthropology from a pragmatic point of view'" (Guyer 2007: 19). Kant's deeply prejudiced views on race, gender, and ethnicity have understandably drawn a great deal of criticism in recent years, in part because they stand in an uneasy relation with the strong universalism of his ethics, which commands us to respect the inherent dignity of every human being (see *GMS* 4: 435) and to recognize that "all human beings are equal to one another" (*V-Mo/Collins* 27: 462). (For further discussion and references, see Helga Varden's contribution to this volume.)

A fourth area that Kant draws on for his anthropology – particularly noticeable in the concluding section of the *Friedländer* transcription entitled "On Education," in which he singles out Basedow's Philanthropinum school in Dessau as "the greatest phenomenon which has appeared in this century for the improvement of the perfection of humanity" (*V-Anth/Fried* 25: 722–3) – is his work on pedagogy. The main texts here are his two short *Essays Regarding the Philanthropinum* (*AP* 2: 445–52) and the *Lectures on Pedagogy*, also edited by Rink (*Päd* 9: 437–99). (For further discussion and references, see Felicitas Munzel's contribution to this volume.)

Finally, the strong teleological assumption evident throughout the anthropology lectures – particularly as regards the destiny or vocation [*Bestimmung*] of the human species – also links them to Kant's later work in the philosophy of history. In *Friedländer* we are informed that "in nature everything is designed to achieve its greatest possible perfection" (*V-Anth/Fried* 25: 694), and this heuristic principle resurfaces later in the First Proposition of the *Idea for a Universal History with a Cosmopolitan Aim* where Kant states: "*All natural predispositions of a creature are determined sometime to develop themselves completely and purposively* [*zweckmässig*]" (*IaG* 8: 18). It is largely for this reason that some commentators have called Kant's philosophy of history work "a component of anthropology" (Brandt and Stark 1997: liii), and it does appear that "the origin of most of Kant's assumptions concerning the historical development of humanity [. . .] lie in his anthropology lectures" (Sturm 2009: 355). (For further discussion and references, see Allen Wood's contribution to this volume.)

However, in the end it may be more fruitful to simply treat all of Kant's writings and lectures on anthropology, history, and education as interconnected "fields of impurity" (Louden 2000: 26–31). Each field makes a key contribution to his extensive attempt to develop an empirical theory of human nature, but they should not be treated in isolation from each other.

2. Texts

Kant's primary anthropology text is *Anthropology from a Pragmatic Point of View* (*Anth* 7: 117–333), first published in 1798, two years after he retired from teaching at the University of Königsberg. In a note at the end of the Preface, he describes this work as "the present manual for my anthropology course" (*Anth* 7: 122n). This book is the closest we have to a verbatim report of what Kant actually said in his anthropology class during his final years of teaching. However, due in part both to the popularity of this particular course and to a long-standing tradition of detailed note-taking in German universities during this time, there also exist numerous transcriptions of Kant's anthropology lectures, the most important of which are now available in book form. Seven sets of student notes from the anthropology course are printed in Academy volume 25: *Collins* (1772–73, *V-Anth/Collins* 25: 7–328), *Parow* (1772–73, *V-Anth/Parow* 25: 243–463), *Friedländer* (1775–6, *V-Anth/Fried* 25: 469–728), *Menschenkunde* (1781–82?, *V-Anth/Mensch* 25: 853–931 – a version of this transcription was first published in 1831: see Kant 1831), *Mrongovius* (1784–85, *V-Anth/Mron* 25: 1209–429), and *Busolt* (1788–9, *V-Anth/Busolt* 25: 1435–531). English translations of the complete texts of *Friedländer* and *Mrongovius* are available in the *Lectures on Anthropology* volume in *The Cambridge Edition of the Works of Immanuel Kant*, along with substantial excerpts from *Menschenkunde* and shorter excerpts from the other four transcriptions (see Kant 2012a). Two additional anthropology transcriptions are also available in Kowalewski (1924) and Tonelli (1976).

Many of these transcriptions are compilations of accounts prepared by different students and auditors of Kant's annual course which were traded and handed down over the years. For these reasons as well as others, caution needs to be exercised in using them: they were not written by Kant, and we cannot always be sure that they accurately represent his views. Kant himself lists several additional reasons for wariness in his letter to Herz of October 20, 1778, when he responds to a request from Zedlitz for a reliable transcription of his lectures:

> Those of my students who are most capable of grasping everything are just the ones who bother least to take explicit and verbatim notes; rather, they write down only the main points, which they can think over afterwards. Those who are most thorough in note-taking are seldom capable of distinguishing the important from the unimportant. They pile a mass of misunderstood stuff under what they may possibly have grasped correctly. Besides, I have almost no private acquaintance with my auditors, and it is difficult for me even to find out which ones might have accomplished something useful [. . .]. [And] since I make improvements or extensions of my lectures from year to year, [. . .] my students cannot very easily help themselves by copying from each other.
>
> (*Br* 10: 242)

In the last sentence of this citation, Kant seems to be implying that a student who obtains a transcription from an earlier version of the course may wind up with an inaccurate account of his current thinking on the subject. But this point also reveals the unique importance of the available lecture transcriptions, the earliest of which date from 1772, when studied in conjunction with Kant's own final version of the lectures from 1798. Taken together, they allow us to track the development of Kant's own conception of the new subject that he was attempting "to make into a proper academic discipline" (*Br* 10: 145). Two recent collections of essays that contain multiple efforts to understand the evolution of Kant's conception of anthropology as well as its relation to other aspects of his philosophy are Jacobs and Kain (2003) and Cohen (2014).

Finally, Kant's own voluminous notes are an additional textual source for his anthropology. Academy volume 15 contains nearly a thousand pages of material relating to the anthropology lectures: "Reflexionen zur Anthropologie" (notes on anthropology) and "Collegentwürfe" (drafts of his anthropology lectures from the 1770s and 1780s). English translations of a small portion of this material (mostly bearing on aesthetics) are available in Kant (2005).

3. What *Is* Kantian Anthropology? A Primer

The popularity and *Weltkenntnis* goals of Kant's anthropology course were discussed earlier, and Kant's earliest biographers testify to his success in achieving both of these aims. Jachmann, for instance, reports that the anthropology lectures were

> an extremely pleasant instruction, which were also attended the most frequently. Here one saw the lofty thinker strolling about in the material world, and the human being and nature illuminated with the torch of original reason. His astute remarks [. . .] were fitted out in lectures filled with wit and genius, which charmed every single listener.
>
> (Jachmann 1804: 31)

Similarly, Rink describes the anthropology lectures as "lively," adding that they were enriched by the "keen observations [. . .] [Kant] mixed in, which he drew either from his own experience or from his reading, such as the best English novelists" (Rink 1805: 46).

But there are several additional interrelated features of Kantian anthropology that serve to further distinguish it from its competitors.

Empirical Science. First, Kant repeatedly describes his anthropology as an empirical science. As we saw earlier, in his 1773 letter to Herz it is tagged as "a very pleasant observation-based doctrine [*Beobachtungslehre*]" (*Br* 10: 146), and in virtually all versions of the anthropology lectures this same emphasis on systematic empirical observation is evident. For instance, in the opening sentence of *Collins* he declares that in the "science of the human being (anthropology) [. . .] the grounds of cognition are drawn from observation and experience" (*V-Anth/Collins* 25: 7). And in the Preface to *Friedländer* he asks: "How does anthropology arise? Through the collection of many observations about human beings by those authors who had acute knowledge of human beings" (*V-Anth/Fried* 25: 472; cf. *V-Anth/Mensch* 25: 856, *V-Anth/Busolt* 25: 1435–6).

However, Kant qualifies his use of the term "empirical" in this context by specifying that the kind of empirical knowledge his anthropology aims at is "general" as opposed to "local" – viz., universal rather than particular. As he notes in *Friedländer*:

> Anthropology is not however a particular, but a general anthropology. In it one comes to know the nature of humanity, not the state of human beings, for the particular properties of human beings always change, but the nature of humanity does not. Anthropology is thus a pragmatic knowledge of what results from our nature.
>
> (*V-Anth/Fried* 25: 471)

The Kantian anthropologist's job is thus to locate core truths about the human species and its destiny, and this quest for universal truths about the human condition does set it at odds with "the relativist bent" (Geertz 2000: 44; cf. 50) that is implicit in much subsequent cultural anthropology. True, in one transcription Kant does claim that the type of "general knowledge of the world" sought by his anthropology "is not empirical but cosmological" (*V-Anth/Pillau* 25: 734), and this is one of several tensions and ambiguities behind his claim that anthropology is empirical. But his language here is unfortunate. The kind of cosmological knowledge he draws attention to in the anthropology texts *is* empirical, but it aims at a very high level of generality, being concerned with knowledge about the human species as a whole rather than limited and partial information about specific groups of people in specific times and places. The latter knowledge lacks practical utility because it "is bound to place and time and provides no rules for acting in common life" (*V-Anth/Pillau* 25: 734; cf. *Anth* 7: 120), whereas what Kantian anthropology seeks is an understanding of the character of the entire human species "as it is known from the experience of all ages and by all peoples" (*Anth* 7: 331).

However, as Hume pointed out earlier ("[m]oral philosophy has, indeed, this peculiar disadvantage, which is not found in natural, that in collecting its experiments, it cannot make them purposely, with premeditation, and after such a manner as to satisfy itself concerning every particular difficulty which may arise" – Hume 1978: xviii–ix), anthropology faces special challenges in its aspiration to become an experimental science, challenges that do not occur in the natural sciences. Human beings' propensity to dissemble, along with their self-consciousness, means that in practice it is very difficult to perform replicable experiments involving their mental states. As Kant remarks in the Preface to his *Anthropology*:

If a human being notices that someone is observing him and trying to study him, he will either appear embarrassed (self-conscious) and *cannot* show himself as he really is; or he dissembles, and does not *want* to be known as he is.

(*Anth* 7: 121; cf. *V-Anth/Mron* 25: 1214, *V-Anth/Busolt* 25: 1437)

Hume responded to this conundrum by arguing that history should form the basis for the new science of man. ("These records of wars, intrigues, factions, and revolutions, are so many collections of experiments, by which the politician or moral philosopher fixes the principles of his science" – Hume 1975: 83.) Kant's response was to cast the net still wider by enlisting the resources of multiple "aids [*Hilfsmittel*]" to anthropology such as "world history, biographies, even plays and novels" (*Anth* 7: 121; cf. *V-Anth/Pillau* 25: 734, *V-Anth/Mensch* 25: 857–8, *V-Anth/Mron* 25: 1213). By incorporating the enduring insights into the human condition uncovered by historians, biographers, playwrights, and novelists in this manner, Kant is thus able to build bridges between the humanities and the human sciences – bridges that were unfortunately destroyed by later social theorists harboring narrower scientistic ambitions.

Pragmatic. But above all, Kantian anthropology is pragmatic – this is by far the most significant marker for his unique conception of anthropology. However, Kant employs the crucial term "pragmatic" in several different ways.

First, a doctrine is pragmatic if it is useful, and Kantian anthropology aims to provide readers with advantageous knowledge that will help them succeed in life and achieve their goals: "One calls all practical knowledge of the human being 'pragmatic' insofar as it serves to fulfill our overall aims" (*V-Anth/Mensch* 25: 855). Second, pragmatic anthropology is prudential: it teaches individuals how to rationally promote their own happiness and welfare. "All pragmatic doctrines are doctrines of prudence" (*V-Anth/Fried* 25: 471), and "the capacity to choose the best means to happiness is prudence" (*V-Anth/Parow* 25: 413). In the *Groundwork*, Kant calls this prudence "in the narrowest sense" (*GMS* 4: 416). Third, pragmatic anthropology, in offering the reader a broad understanding of human nature, also enables him "to use other human beings skillfully for his purposes" (*Anth* 7: 322). Pragmatic anthropology in this third sense is "a knowledge of the art of how one human being has influence on another and can lead him according to his purpose" (*V-Anth/Mensch* 25: 855; cf. *V-Anth/Busolt* 25: 1436). Some readers may sense a slightly sinister air behind this third aspect of pragmatic anthropology, and it does seem to stand in tension with one of the most famous tenets of Kantian ethics; viz., to never treat other human beings merely as a means (see *GMS* 4: 429). Kant probably meant that pragmatic anthropology teaches us how to skillfully use other people to achieve our aims *under moral constraints*, but he does not explicitly say this. And in principle, nothing would seem to prevent someone from using the insights of Kantian anthropology for immoral ends. Unscrupulous advertisers and businesspeople, for instance,

may use their knowledge of human nature to sell people things that they do not need and cannot afford, and shrewd politicians may exploit their knowledge of human nature to advance their own personal agendas for power and control.

(Louden 2006: 354)

Kantian anthropology is an eclectic venture revealing multiple origins, and it can also be applied toward many different purposes.

Pragmatic vs. physiological. Fourth, Kant also uses the term "pragmatic" to mark a contrast between his own conception of anthropology and the "physiological" approach championed by Ernst Platner and other "philosophical physicians" such as la Mettrie. In the Preface to the 1798 *Anthropology* he states:

> A doctrine of the knowledge of the human being, systematically formulated (anthropology), can exist either in a *physiological* or in a *pragmatic* point of view. – Physiological knowledge of the human being concerns the investigation of what *nature* makes of the human being; pragmatic, the investigation of what *he* as a free-acting being makes of himself, or can and should make of himself.
>
> *(Anth* 7: 119; cf. *Br* 10: 145–6)

Kant is not implying here that pragmatic anthropology does not aspire to become an experimental science which seeks to establish causal laws of human behavior. "To observe human beings and their conduct, to bring their phenomena under rules, is the purpose of anthropology" (*V-Anth/Fried* 25: 472; cf. *V-Anth/Busolt* 25: 1435). But he is saying that in pragmatic anthropology any rules of human behavior discovered must be shown to have practical utility. Pragmatic anthropology is not empty theorizing:

> pragmatic anthropology is now our end. It should not be a theoretical anthropology, which merely poses questions and contains in itself only psychological investigations; on the contrary we want to give instruction as to how through observation one might come to be acquainted with the constitution of human beings so as to be able to use them here to our end.
>
> *(V-Anth/Busolt* 25: 1436; cf. *Br* 10: 145–6)

Pragmatic vs. scholastic. This practical, anti-theoretical quality of pragmatic anthropology is also highlighted in Kant's frequent contrasts between pragmatic and "scholastic" anthropologies. "Platner has written a scholastic anthropology," but "one could not obtain any enlightenment for common life from it" (*V-Anth/Mensch* 25: 856, 853). Similarly, the anthropology contained in Baumgarten's empirical psychology "only concerns what is scholastic" (*V-Anth/Mron* 25: 1214). In "*Anthropologia scholastica*" one considers the knowledge of the human being "more as a [kind of] school knowledge," whereas in "*Anthropologia pragmatica*" one "considers the knowledge of the human being as it is useful in society in general" (*V-Anth/Mron* 25: 1210). [In this disparaging use of the term "scholastic," Kant is expressing a typical Enlightenment attitude toward medieval philosophy – see also *GSE* 2: 256. As d'Alembert remarks: "the scholastics emasculated the sciences with their trifling questions" (Kramnick 1995: 9).]

4. Contested Features

However, there remain at least two alleged aspects of Kantian anthropology that have been the source of continual controversy in the growing secondary literature devoted to his theory of human nature. First, to what extent does Kant's pragmatic anthropology also contain a distinctly *moral* anthropology? Although the specific term "moral anthropology" does not occur in any of the extant versions of the lectures on anthropology, in other texts Kant does explicitly refer to a "moral anthropology" that constitutes "the second part" of moral philosophy (*V-Mo/Mron* II 29: 599), "the counterpart of a metaphysics of morals, the other member of the division of practical philosophy as a whole" (*MS* 6: 217; cf. *V-Mo/Collins* 27: 244), as well as to a "practical anthropology" that constitutes "the empirical part of ethics" (*GMS* 4: 388). Some commentators have used this linguistic evidence to conclude that "'pragmatic anthropology' is therefore not the discipline of practical anthropology, variously described by Kant, that was supposed to function as a complement to pure moral philosophy" (Brandt 2003: 92), while others (including the present author) have argued that there are nevertheless multiple moral messages in the lectures on anthropology, messages which when taken together do entitle us to assert "that we do find a distinctively *moral* anthropology within Kant's anthropology lectures" (Louden 2003: 66–7; see also Stark 2003: 20–1). Perhaps the strongest moral message occurs in the final section of most versions of the lectures, where Kant sketches the moral destiny of the human species – a destiny that culminates in the realization of our predisposition toward "cosmopolitical unity" (*Anth* 7: 333; cf. *V-Anth/Fried* 25: 696, *V-Anth/Mron* 25: 1429 – for discussion, see Louden 2014b). A second example of a moral message within the anthropology lectures is connected to Kant's fundamental goal of imparting *Weltkenntnis* to his students. Human beings need accurate empirical knowledge of the world and of human beings in order to correctly and efficaciously apply the a priori or pure principles of morality to the human condition. In the Prolegomena to *Collins* Kant notes explicitly that it is due to the lack of *Weltkenntnis* "that so many practical sciences have remained unfruitful. For example, moral philosophy. [. . .] But most moral philosophers and clergymen lack this knowledge of human nature" (*V-Anth/Collins* 25: 9). Filling this basic gap is one of Kant's primary aims in teaching his anthropology course, because "morals needs anthropology for its *application* to human beings" (*GMS* 4: 412).

A second contested feature centers on the ongoing debate over transcendental anthropology. Kant's repeated descriptions of his own anthropology as an empirical science that "does not at all belong to metaphysics" (*V-Anth/Parow* 25: 244; cf. *V/Anth-Collin* 25: 8) would seem to rule out any connection to a transcendental undertaking that seeks to uncover the a priori requirements for experience, for "[f]rom empirical principles one cannot attain transcendental ones" (*Refl* 4851, 18: 9). But his alluring appeal to the necessity of an "*Anthropologia transcendentalis*" which would provide us with "the self-knowledge of understanding and reason," "without which we have no measure of the dimensions of our knowledge" (*Refl* 903, 15: 395), has understandably captured the attention of many commentators.

While the explicit phrase "*Anthropologia transcendentalis*" occurs only once in Kant's vast corpus (in Latin, in a posthumously published *Reflexion*), it does link up with another famous text that Kant repeats several times. In the *Jäsche Logic* he states:

The field of philosophy in this cosmopolitan sense can be brought down to the following questions:

1. *What can I know?*
2. *What ought I to do?*
3. *What may I hope?*
4. *What is the human being?*

Metaphysics answers the first question, *morals* the second, *religion* the third, and *anthropology* the fourth. Fundamentally, however, one could reckon all of this [*alles dieses*] as anthropology, because the first three questions relate to the last one. (*Log* 9: 25; cf. Kant's letter to Stäudlin of May 4, 1793, *Br* 11: 429, *V-Met-L1/Pölitz* 28: 533–4)

In describing an anthropology that is somehow able to answer all of philosophy's questions, Kant is clearly referring to something that is not merely empirical. And in his conviction that anthropology is the most fundamental and important discipline, he is once again following in Hume's footsteps:

'Tis evident, that all of the sciences have a relation, greater or less, to human nature; and that however wide any of them seem to run from it, they still return back by one passage or another. Even *Mathematics, Natural Philosophy, and Natural Religion,* are in some measure dependent on the science of MAN; since they lie under the cognizance of men, and are judged of by their powers and faculties.

(Hume 1978: xv)

But where in his writings does Kant provide readers with an answer to the crucial question, "What is the human being?" Or rather, where does he address this question in a manner that implies or suggests that he thinks he has also provided an answer to all of philosophy's questions? The anthropology texts do not pretend to operate on this extravagantly high level – for the most part, as we have seen, they offer readers only a "very pleasant observation-based doctrine" (*Br* 10: 146). As Reinhard Brandt notes in his detailed *Kommentar zu Kants Anthropologie*:

> pragmatic anthropology [. . .] does not answer the question, What is the human being? [. . .] Neither the Lectures on Anthropology nor the *Anthropology* of 1798 refers to the question, 'What is the human being?' as its central problem; they do not mention it once.

(Brandt 1999: 16)

However, while most commentators concur that the anthropology lectures themselves do not contain a transcendental anthropology, this still leaves open the possibility that such an anthropology may be found elsewhere in Kant's corpus; for example, within the critical philosophy of the three *Critiques*. Heidegger, Foucault, and many others have pursued one or another version of this thesis over the years, in an attempt to show that "the grounding of metaphysics is a questioning with regard to the human being, i.e., anthropology" (Heidegger 1997: 144 – for discussion and further references, see Louden 2018). But here another problem emerges: does the effort to unite transcendental philosophy with anthropology result in an objectionable epistemological speciesism? Are all philosophical questions simply questions about human beings, or is philosophy bigger than the merely human?

5. "The Eye of True Philosophy"

To the extent that the empirical, pragmatic nature of Kant's anthropology does clearly distinguish it from his better-known transcendental investigations, the traditional picture of Kant as the defender of the necessity of a priori principles in all areas of human thought needs to be bracketed when approaching his extensive work on human nature. And in this respect, Kantian anthropology also seems to prefigure later developments in philosophy such as American pragmatism, naturalism, and the recent experimental turn in ethics, as well as the general attitude of many contemporary thinkers who are "made queasy by the whole idea of the a priori" (Peacocke 2004: 505). However, the unabashedly popular and didactic commitments of Kantian anthropology prevent it from being wholly identified with any of these movements.

But while Kant's anthropology has often been viewed as a merely marginal project by those professional philosophers who are intent on "keeping philosophy pure" (see Rorty 1982), recent scholarship has begun to challenge this received view. For even though Kant's texts do not provide the kind of answer to the question, What is the human being? that can claim to answer all of philosophy's questions, it is clear that he believed that philosophy in the "cosmopolitan sense" (*Log* 9: 25) presupposes anthropology. For this *"worldly concept"* of philosophy "is the science of the final ends of human reason" (*Log* 9: 23), and one needs extensive empirical knowledge of human nature to know what these ends are. Furthermore, "[t]his high concept gives philosophy *dignity,* i.e., an absolute worth" (*Log* 9: 23). And only when the other sciences incorporate this cosmopolitan sense of philosophy into their own missions do they also have dignity, for philosophy in this cosmopolitan sense "is that alone which has *inner* worth, and gives worth to all the other sciences" (*V-Met-L2/ Pölitz* 28: 532; cf. *Log* 9: 24). The "eye of true philosophy" (*Anth* 7: 227; cf. *Log* 9: 45) has both empirical and a priori components, and it is only when both dimensions are granted their rightful place that philosophy in the Kantian sense can fulfill its mission.

References

Baumgarten, A. (2013) *Metaphysics: A Critical Translation with Kant's Elucidations, Selected Notes, and Related Materials*, C.D. Fugate and J. Hymers (ed., trans. and intro.), London: Bloomsbury.

Brandt, R. (1999) *Kommentar zu Kants Anthropologie in pragmatischer Hinsicht*, Hamburg: Felix Meiner.

Brandt, R. (2003) "The Guiding Idea of Kant's Anthropology and the Vocation of the Human Being," in B. Jacobs and P. Kain (eds.), *Essays on Kant's Anthropology*, Cambridge: Cambridge University Press, pp. 85–104.

Brandt, R. and Stark, W. (1997) "Einleitung," in R. Brandt and W. Stark (eds.), *Kant, Immanuel, Vorlesungen über Anthropologie*, Academy vol. 25, Berlin: Walter de Gruyter, pp. VII–CLI.

Brinton, C. (ed.) (1956) *The Portable Age of Reason Reader*, New York: The Viking Press.

Cohen, A. (ed.) (2014) *Kant's Lectures on Anthropology: A Critical Guide*, Cambridge: Cambridge University Press.

Geertz, C. (2000) *Available Light: Anthropological Reflections on Philosophical Topics*, Princeton: Princeton University Press.

Guyer, P. (2007) "Translator's Introduction to *Observations on the Feeling of the Beautiful and Sublime*," in G. Zöller and R.B. Louden (eds.), *Kant, Immanuel, Anthropology, History, and Education*, Cambridge: Cambridge University Press, pp. 18–22.

Hume, D. (1975) *Enquiries Concerning Human Understanding and Concerning the Principles of Morals*, L.A. Selby-Bigge (ed.), 3rd ed., Oxford: Clarendon Press.

Hume, D. (1978) *A Treatise of Human Nature*, L.A. Selby Bigge (ed.), 2nd ed., Oxford: Clarendon Press.

Jachmann, R.B. (1804) *Immanuel Kant geschildert in Briefen an einen Freund*, Königsberg: Friedrich Nicolovius.

Jacobs, B. and Kain, P. (eds.) (2003) *Essays on Kant's Anthropology*, Cambridge: Cambridge University Press.

Jankowiak, T. and Watkins, E. (2014) "Meat on the Bones: Kant's Account of Cognition in the Anthropology Lectures," in A. Cohen (ed.), *Kant's Lectures on Anthropology: A Critical Guide*, Cambridge: Cambridge University Press, pp. 57–75.

Kant, I. (1831) *Immanuel Kant's Menschenkunde oder philosophische Anthropologie*, Nach handschriftlichen Vorlesungen herausgegeben von Fr. Ch. Starke, Leipzig: Die Expedition des europaischen Aufsehers.

Kant, I. (2005) *Notes and Fragments*, C. Bowman, P. Guyer and F. Rauscher (eds.), Cambridge: Cambridge University Press.

Kant, I. (2012a) *Lectures on Anthropology*, A.W. Wood and R.B. Louden (ed.), Cambridge: Cambridge University Press.

Kant, I. (2012b) *Natural Science*, E. Watkins (ed.), Cambridge: Cambridge University Press.

Kowalewski, A. (ed.) (1924) *Die philosophischen Hauptvorlesungen Immanuel Kants. Nach den aufgefundenen Kollegheften des Grafen Heinrich zu Dohn-Wundlacken*, Munich and Leipzig: Rösl and Cie.

Kramnick, I. (ed.) (1995) *The Portable Enlightenment Reader*, New York: Penguin Books.

Louden, R.B. (2000) *Kant's Impure Ethics: From Rational Beings to Human Beings*, New York: Oxford University Press.

Louden, R.B. (2003) "The Second Part of Morals," in B. Jacobs and P. Kain (eds.), *Essays on Kant's Anthropology*, Cambridge: Cambridge University Press, pp. 60–84.

Louden, R.B. (2006) "Applying Kant's Ethics: The Role of Anthropology," in G. Bird (ed.), *A Companion to Kant*, Oxford: Blackwell Publishing, pp. 350–63.

Louden, R.B. (2011) "'The Play of Nature': Human Beings in Kant's Geography," in S. Elden and E. Mendieta (eds.), *Reading Kant's Geography*, Albany: SUNY Press, pp. 139–60.

Louden, R.B. (2014a) "The Last Frontier: The Importance of Kant's *Geography*," *Society and Space* 32: 450–66. Reprinted in R.R. Clewis (ed.) (2015) *Reading Kant's Lectures*, Berlin: Walter de Gruyter, pp. 507–25.

Louden, R.B. (2014b) "Cosmopolitical Unity: The Final Destiny of the Human Species," in A. Cohen (ed.), *Kant's Lectures on Anthropology: A Critical Guide*, Cambridge: Cambridge University Press, pp. 211–29.

Louden, R.B. (2018) "Kant's Anthropology: (Mostly) Empirical Not Transcendental," in F.V. Tommasi (ed.), *Der Zyklop in der Wissenschaft: Kant und die transzendentale Anthropologie*, Hamburg: Felix Meiner, pp. 19–34.

Peacocke, C. (2004) "Moral Rationalism," *Journal of Philosophy* 101: 499–526.

Rink, F.T. (1805) *Ansichten aus Immanuel Kant's Leben*, Königsberg: Göbbels and Unzer.

Rorty, R. (1982) "Keeping Philosophy Pure: An Essay on Wittgenstein," in R. Rorty (ed.), *Consequences of Pragmatism*, Minneapolis: University of Minnesota Press, pp. 19–36.

Stark, W. (2003) "Historical Notes and Interpretive Questions About Kant's Lectures on Anthropology," in B. Jacobs and P. Kain (eds.), *Essays on Kant's Anthropology*, Cambridge: Cambridge University Press, pp. 15–37.

Sturm, T. (2009) *Kant und die Wissenschaften vom Menschen*, Paderborn: Mentis.

Tonelli, G. (ed.) (1976) *Immanuel Kants Menschenkunde: Nach handschriftlichen Vorlesungen herausgegeben von Fr. Ch. Starke. Im Anhang Immanuel Kants Anweisung zur Menschen- und Weltkenntniß. Nach dessen Vorlesungen im Winterhalbjahre 1790–91 herausgegeben von Fr. Ch. Starke*, Hildesheim: Georg Olms.

Vorländer, K. (2003) *Immanuel Kant: Der Mann und das Werk*, 3rd ed., Wiesbaden: Fourier.

Further Reading

A. Cohen, *Kant and the Human Sciences: Biology, Anthropology, and History* (Hampshire: Palgrave Macmillan, 2009) argues that the biological rather than the physical sciences provide Kant's model for the human sciences. M. Foucault, *Introduction to Kant's Anthropology*, R. Nigro (ed.) (Los Angeles: Semiotext(e), 2009) is Foucault's secondary doctoral thesis, defended in 1961, parts of which were later recast as *The Order of Things*. P.R. Frierson, *What is the Human Being?* (London: Routledge, 2013) takes its cue from Kant's famous *Jäsche Logic* remark (see Log 9: 25), and engages Kant's anthropology with a variety of competing post-Kantian theories of human nature. R.B. Louden, *Kant's Human Being: Essays on His Theory of Human Nature* (New York: Oxford University Press, 2011) continues and deepens avenues of exploration initiated in his *Kant's Impure Ethics*. H.L. Wilson, *Kant's Pragmatic Anthropology: Its Origin, Meaning, and Critical Significance* (Albany: SUNY Press, 2006) examines the debate concerning the origin of Kant's anthropology, and also defends its popular orientation. R.B. Louden, *Anthropology from a Kantian Point of View* (Cambridge: Cambridge University Press, 2021), offers a more detailed exploration and defense of the issues discussed in this chapter.

32

KANT ON UNIVERSALITY AND ACCOMMODATING DIFFERENCES (RELIGIOUS, RACIAL, SEXUAL, GENDERED)

Helga Varden

★★★

1. The Puzzle[1]

An enduring source of skepticism towards Kant's practical philosophy is his deep conviction that morality must be understood in terms of universality. Whether we look to Kant's fundamental moral principle (the Categorical Imperative) or to his fundamental principle of right (the Universal Principle of Right), universality lies at the core of the analyses. We see this in his reliance on universalizable maxims and acting from duty when it comes to virtue and on interaction subject only to universal laws in his account of right. A central worry of his critics is that by making universality the bedrock of morality in these ways, Kant fails to appreciate the importance of difference in individual lives, societies, and legal-political institutions when these are realized well. More specifically, Kant's approach seems unable to critique central aspects of normativity, namely the natures and roles of different social identities, including those tied to nations, cultures, sexuality, and gender; those tied to different types of relationships, including differences between intimate and affectionate personal friendships, impersonal relationships involving strangers only, and purely professional relationships; and finally, those tied to different historically situated legal-political systems. Insofar as contemporary Kantian theories maintain this deep commitment to universality, the critics continue, they will inherit the consequences of this serious philosophical mistake.

One of the oldest, most persistent lines of criticism of this kind goes like this: Kant considers the human self a purely rational subject that relates to everything as distinct from itself and that (morally) ought to relate to everything always in a thoroughly moralized, reflective way. Hence, a subject strives to lead a life that is as good and moral as possible (as it should), endeavoring to act only on universalizable maxims (subjective principles of action) from the motivation of duty (a self-reflective mode) with regard to everything and everyone at all times. And since the universalization test for maxims involves checking whether one's actions are consistent with respecting all persons as free and equal, it looks like all good or valuable actions and relations become moralized in a virtuous person's life (since they always involve acting self-reflectively and as motivated by reason, or from duty). In addition, living an emotionally healthy and moral life appears to involve treating

 DOI: 10.4324/9781003406617-42

everyone – strangers and loved ones alike – as if they have an equal normative say and moral importance in our lives. Critics worry that an approach of this kind is unable to capture rich and meaningful human lives with profound, complex, and wonderful loves as well as brutal, devastating, and destabilizing losses. Moreover, it seems to be a morally and emotionally perverted kind of ideal: surely the aim is not to live all aspects of our lives in such thoroughly reflective, moralized ways where everyone is regarded as equally important. Relatedly, such an approach appears incapable of capturing the importance of non-moralized, unreflective emotions and particular persons in emotionally healthy interactions and evaluations. For example, it seems to ignore the central, constructive roles of affectionate love, grief, and forgiveness, as well as the importance of particular histories, cultures, families, and other loved ones in lives lived well.

Variations of this worry regarding the importance of non-moralized, unreflective emotions and particularity in the lives of emotionally healthy human beings have been raised against Kant's philosophy from the start – by philosophers ranging from Fichte, Hegel, and Nietzsche to Beauvoir and Sartre to, more recently, the many related discussions motivating and surrounding the important work in both the "analytic" and "continental" philosophical traditions. For example, over the last few decades, feminists have fruitfully engaged these issues through concepts such as the "relational self" and "care."[2] Other particularly interesting treatments of these topics are found in contemporary work inspired by P. F. Strawson's analysis of reactive attitudes;[3] by Bernard Williams' "one-thought-too-many" objection to universal theories;[4] and, more recently, by Stephen Darwall's concept of the "second personal address" (2006). In addition, some discussions focus on the social nature of gender and sexuality, including its fundamental other-directedness. Perhaps the most influential discussion here is the one initiated by Beauvoir in *The Second Sex* (2011) – one that Judith Butler has continued and enhanced.[5] In addition, there are many accounts of (the importance of) the imperfect and destructive aspects of human nature, such as various issues concerning bad behavior and violence, twisted characters, systemic injustices, and so on. Although we find much extremely interesting work on systemic injustice in all the traditions of analytic philosophy,[6] it seems fair to say that the most interesting discussions to date treating bodily and violent aspects of race, sexuality, and gender have occurred within the postmodern and phenomenological philosophical traditions as well as in the analytic feminist tradition.[7] A particularly influential strand of contemporary thinking concerned with sexuality and gender is found in the related French philosophical tradition[8] and in the works of those inspired by it.[9] Now, importantly and somewhat ironically, scholars working on sexuality, race, and gender often argue that a major problem with Kant's philosophy is not, in a certain sense, its universalism, but its lack thereof. When it comes to issues such as women, non-white people, and non-straight sexual identities and orientations, it appears as if Kant doesn't put that high a price on equality after all. The few times these differences come up in Kant, they are paid attention to in the wrong ways. Instead of standing up to the oppression of social groups, Kant tries to justify it and thereby partakes in the project of rationalizing historically inherited prejudices and injustices in the name of universal moral theory.[10]

Kant's universalism is also often viewed as problematic from the perspective of legal-political philosophy. For example, much legal positivism regards Kant's universalism as impossible to defend since it cannot capture the importance of historical context and diversity of legal-political systems. There are many different legal-political systems, this line of criticism goes, which fail to satisfy Kant's Universal Principle of Right and his theory's liberal system of rights. Nonetheless, they secure a legitimate rule of law for the peoples governed by them. The rule of law does not commit one to principles of freedom, but to recognized laws, rules, or norms only.[11] Common to all these non-Kantian philosophical accounts of legal-political philosophy, ethics, moral psychology, and philosophical anthropology is a shared belief that Kant's universalism is deemed a major theory to refute and overcome.

I argue that Kant's philosophy neither advocates moralized hyper-reflective, alienating ways of being nor seeks to justify Kant's own and others' prejudices in the name of morality's universality. To see this, we need to understand both Kant's account of human nature – of the predisposition to good and the propensity to evil – and how Kant's theory of freedom sets the moral framework within which important non-moralizable concerns of human nature are accommodated. We can then appreciate the ways in which Kant sees both unreflective and reflective normative elements as working together as an integrated whole in emotionally healthy, morally good human beings, historical cultures, and legal-political institutional systems. Contrary to what the skeptics believe, all these concerns lie at the heart of Kant's practical philosophy, and they constitute one main reason why the continuous engagement with and development of Kant's philosophy should not be perceived as perpetuating a serious philosophical mistake, but as utilizing and continuing to develop some of the best, most exciting ideas our philosophical tradition has given us.

2. Kant on Human Nature

This section argues that in his writings on human nature, anthropology, history, and religion, Kant explores the importance of embodiment, of non-moralizable (aspects of) emotions, and of particular others. He also rightly maintains that these normative and partly unreflective (albeit conscious) aspects of ourselves include features that we transform, develop, and integrate by acting on maxims and that we can and sometimes should restrain or correct by reflective means. I furthermore suggest that insofar as we are morally and emotionally healthy mature persons or have succeeded in developing healthy cultures supportive of good legal-political institutional systems, we characteristically move easily between unreflective and reflective ways of being. That is, we move between simply acting in reflexively (unmoralized) self-conscious ways and acting in reflectively (moralized) self-conscious ways. Such ease of transition reveals one way in which importantly non-moralizable and moralizable ways of being – happiness and morality – can come into "close union [. . .] under the limiting conditions of practical reason" (*MS* 6: 426). Once we have clarified these ideas, we can turn, in the third and final section, to Kant's proposal concerning how we make space for the non-moralizable aspects of our human nature within our moral theories of freedom.

A good place to start when exploring Kant's understanding of emotionally healthy, moral being is his account of the predisposition to good in human nature, described in the *Religion*. Here Kant proposes that we see human nature as constituted by a predisposition that is both "original" and "good." It is "original" in that it belongs "with necessity to the possibility of this being," and it is good in that it does "not resist the moral law," but rather "demand[s] compliance with it" (*RGV* 6: 28). The predisposition to good, in other words, enables and is constitutive of emotionally healthy and morally good human being, and it is at the heart of Kant's philosophical account of what a good human life consists in. Kant furthermore argues that this overall predisposition to good can be seen as made up of three distinct predispositions, each distinguished by the complexity of the self-consciousness and reasoning capacities necessarily involved in realizing it.[12] In good human lives and societies (cultures and institutions), these three predispositions are realized in a unified whole. Some more details about each will help to explain.[13]

At the lowest level – in that it both involves the least complex form of self-consciousness and thinking capacities, and is the most basic and emotionally strongest in its capacity to motivate us to action – we find what Kant calls the predisposition to "*animality* [. . .] as a *living being*" (*RGV* 6: 26). It is made up of three conscious drives, namely the drives to self-preservation, to the propagation of the species "through the sexual drive and for the preservation of the offspring thereby begotten through breeding," and, finally, to "community with other human beings through the social drive" (*RGV* 6: 26–7).[14] The predisposition to animality, then, is constitutive of us simply as *living* (conscious) beings, and realizing it (surviving, having sex, and affectionately loving or orienting to others by means of a shared "us") does not require reason as such. Consequently, also non-human animals with less complex forms of consciousness (reflexive self-consciousness in combination with reflection by means of associative thinking) are *alive* in this technical sense of the term; they, too, do the kinds of things this predisposition enables.[15]

Because the predisposition to animality does not necessarily involve reflective self-consciousness (the awareness of myself as an "I") and reasoning powers (using abstract concepts), developing it (as human beings) involves realizing important unreflective or non-moralizable (aspects of) emotions in our basic orientations (to ourselves and others) in the world. We see this in how we develop in terms of survival skills, sexuality and gender (identity and orientation), and affectionate love (being part of a family, among loved ones, in a country, etc.) with the corresponding healthy emotions such as hurt, falling in love, grief, fear of danger, comfort in one's own body and in the world, feeling pleasure after a good and healthy meal, or even a healthy love of country. For Kant, emotionally healthy ways of being are fundamentally tuned in to the kinds of embodied, social beings we are, meaning that when we get these things basically right – when we take pleasure in what is genuinely good for us, as who we are – we realize these aspects of ourselves in ways consistent with our "animalistic" natures, namely as living, embodied, social beings. Exactly because this animalistic predisposition is at its core an unreflective, yet conscious, normative structure of our basic moral psychology, and because it is original and good, realizing ourselves well in these ways is deeply pleasant. Moreover, we will affirm this unreflective way of being as good from the higher self-reflective, moral point of view.

The second predisposition to good in human nature is called the predisposition to "*humanity*," namely "as a living and at the same time *rational* being" (*RGV* 6: 26). This predisposition enables rational end-setting; it is "physical [. . .] and yet *involves comparison* for which reason is required," though it does not require being able to act as motivated by pure practical reason. And, finally, "out of this self-love originates the inclination to *gain worth in the opinion of others*, originally, of course, merely *equal worth*" (*RGV* 6: 27). When the predisposition to humanity is developed well, it centrally involves experiencing a kind of love that is enabled by perceiving and being perceived by another as equally valuable (having "equal worth") as well as taking joy in setting ends of one's own rationally (acting on universalizable maxims). In contrast to other animals – animals that don't have a self-recognitional kind of sociality (e.g., pass the mirror test) and cannot set ends of their own rationally (as they cannot use abstract concepts self-reflectively) – humans learn to exercise freedom by having an awareness of themselves as seen by others (and vice versa) and by becoming able to act on maxims. Indeed, Kant argues in the *Anthropology* that the inability to act when born is the reason why (only) human babies scream when they are born. The scream reveals a frustration at not being able to act, and, so, it reveals the capacity for a representation that other animals don't have – the one that distinguishes them as a *rational* in additional to a *living* being (*Anth* 7: 268).

The preceding, I believe, are central aspects of what Kant means when he says that these two predispositions – to animality and humanity – are "original" and "good" in that they *prepare the way* for morally responsible human being. Developing our animality and humanity together is to, first, attend to what is deeply pleasing for us and to realize ourselves as beings capable of setting ends of our own in a way that is grounded in a trust of ourselves and each other as at home in a shared world. Second, because we can use abstract concepts and engage in reflection, as we mature, we develop, transform, and integrate our animality and humanity in self-reflective ways: we learn to feel, describe, and develop our emotional experiences as well as to rationally choose ends of our own in conjunction with those experiences. Thus, our emotional lives are much more complex than those of other animals (*living beings*), and the world presents itself as distinctly open-ended because we are capable of setting ends of our own (*rationality*) in morally responsible (*personality*) ways. As we morally mature, not only do we choose and set (new) ends of our own – act on maxims – but we can make sure that the ends we set are respectful of all other beings who are also capable of rational end setting. (More on this later.)

Kant argues that though the second predisposition (to humanity) necessarily involves comparative uses of reason and rational end setting, it does not necessarily involve acting as motivated by practical reason. Correspondingly, Kant argues that such susceptibility or to recognize the moral ought – what ultimately enables me to do something *just because* doing so is the right thing to do (to act from duty) – must be seen as a third predisposition to good in human nature, a predisposition to "*personality*," since it enables each of us not only to be a rational (end-setting) being but "at the same time [a] *responsible* being" (*RGV* 6: 26). The predisposition to personality is revealed in our capacity for "moral feeling," which is a basic susceptibility to act as our practical reason demands (*RGV* 6: 27).

The predisposition to personality, Kant further clarifies, is not "physical." Rather, it is a susceptibility to morality that manifests as *moral* feeling, a moral responsiveness to a particular situation. As Kant says in the *Metaphysics of Morals*, moral feeling is a "subjective condition [. . .] of receptiveness to the concept of duty"; it is the "natural predisposition of the mind [. . .] for being affected by the concepts of duty, antecedent predispositions on the side of *feeling*"; it is something without which we would be "morally dead" (*MS* 6: 399–400). In being moved to do something merely because it is the right thing to do. In so doing, we use "the free power of choice" to incorporate "moral feeling into [our] maxim" by making duty the incentive upon which we act (*RGV* 6: 28; cf. 6: 26n). Moreover, to act in this way (on universalizable maxims from the motive of duty) is to have realized personality, meaning our capacity to act in morally responsible and, so, in truly free ways.

Because we are able to set ends of our own and because we have a sensible and self-recognitional nature, we will also, unsurprisingly, act in destructive ways in relation to each other and ourselves. Kant's critique of our ineradicable liability to do bad things is outlined in his account of the propensity to evil in the *Religion* (6: 29–32). Why everyone will not only do bad things, but we will also develop various pathologies is explained by a combination of factors, including the following: how the predispositions to animality and humanity involve non-moralizable (and so corruptible) aspects of ourselves; how these predispositions in their raw forms are stronger than our capacity to act out of duty; and how, finally, in our early lives we are subject to other people's often bad behaviors and choices and at the same time we are not able to assume responsibility for our actions. This is not the place for a detailed analysis.[16] Instead, let me simply note that trailing the predispositions to animality and humanity are temptations to develop pathological inclinations. For example, instead of taking joy in others' accomplishments and feeling sadness about their failures, we sometimes experience envy or we take pleasure in others' misfortunes (*Schadenfreude*). Both kinds of temptations concern how the predisposition to humanity involves comparative uses of reason, of comparing ourselves to others. Not having been instilled with an adequate sense of worth in virtue of having been affirmed by others (perhaps a parent), one is inherently tempted to want to be better than others (to be unequal) (*RGV* 6: 27). Likewise, it is tempting, when others are unsuccessful or fail, to feel empowered due to feeling comparatively superior (by not having failed). The degree to which these self- and other-damaging behaviors have a subjective hold on us differs, but we are all liable to these feelings to some extent, and it is a lifelong project to learn to assume responsibility for transforming our pathologies such that we develop healthy emotional orientations to ourselves and others. Kant's account of evil is therefore both a happy and a sad one: Although the predispositions to animality and humanity can be used "inappropriately" (*RGV* 6: 28) or be "corrupted" (*RGV* 6: 30) in that we develop pathologies, they cannot be destroyed or "eradicate[d]" (*RGV* 6: 30). Moreover, and fortunately, although motivationally weak, the third predisposition (to personality) cannot be corrupted. Hence, attitudes and behaviors stemming from pathologies due to the corruption of our first two predispositions to good can be (but not necessarily always are) managed in morally responsible ways by the third and because they cannot be destroyed, they can be relied on as we seek to heal wounds and deal with pathological behavior in constructive ways.

Notice that, for Kant, leading good lives involves many non-moralized ways of being: We eat, drink, affectionately love, compete, and challenge ourselves joyously (and not from the motivation of duty). Here, we do as we do because we are pursuing a happy, good life. Our highest good, as we saw earlier, is to bring "happiness" and "morality" into union, not to eliminate happiness. Moreover, because we don't act as motivated by our practical reason here, we don't add "moral worth" to our actions, as Kant says in the *Groundwork* (*GMS* 4: 401). And there is nothing wrong with that, not even upon reflection. Rather, Kant's claim is that we should always be ready to adopt the reflective stance in regard to these ways of being, and we should do so as necessary – when something seems problematic, puzzling, or difficult to handle. Perhaps we often feel ourselves wanting to act out of envy or *Schadenfreude*. Maturing involves not only realizing the first two predispositions well – developing as emotionally healthy, embodied, social and rational beings – but also the third one, the one that makes it possible for us, ultimately, to respond to moral feeling and to assume moral responsibility for what we're doing, including our pathologies.[17] Hence, Kant argues in the Doctrine of Virtue, "conscience is not something that can be acquired [. . .] rather, every human being, as a moral being, *has* a conscience within him originally"; growing up or morally maturing is not about acquiring a conscience, but rather learning to pay "heed to" it, and so also to the verdict of our practical reason (*MS* 6: 400).

Relatedly, in the second *Critique*, Kant clarifies that rational self-love "merely *infringes upon* [animalistic] self-love, inasmuch as it only restricts it, as natural and active in us even prior to the moral law" (*KpV* 5: 73). The preceding interpretation can make sense of this: the predisposition to animality in human beings enables basic emotional orientations in the world that involve inherently unreflective, non-moralizable elements and so can and does operate in important ways before a human being has developed the ability to act rationally *and* morally responsibly on her own. But because humans have a capacity for reflective self-consciousness (the "I") and abstract conceptual reasoning powers, our project from the start is to reflectively develop, transform, and integrate in good ways, those unreflective non-moralizable elements. For example, our animalistic sex drive is not simply driven by instinct and then developed associatively, as it is for other animals, because it is something we transform into an aspect of our lives that has important creative, aesthetic, social, and morally responsible aspects to it.[18] Now, Kant only talks about the relationship between "rational" and "animalistic" self-love in this passage, since he is after how rational self-love (as enabled by the capacity for humanity) can restrict animalistic self-love. But we can expand on his point by arguing similarly that the aim of *moral* self-love (acting out of duty) is not to replace animalistic and rational self-love by striving to act only as motivated by moral duty; indeed, trying to do so is impossible and damaging rather than healing. Rather, moral self-love enables us to restrict these other two kinds of self-love when we are not realizing them in ways that are truly good for us. Someone who has developed an emotionally healthy, morally good (virtuous) character moves easily between unreflective and reflective (non-moralizable and moralizable) normative ways of being.

Kant's position, then, is not, as the critics worry, one according to which the human self is simply a rational, immaterial self that relates to everything (material) as distinct from itself and that always aims to relate to everything in a self-reflective, moralized way. Whether we develop Kant's view of the role of non-moralizable aspects of ourselves using the contemporary philosophical language of relational selves, reactive attitudes, second-personal address, or affectionate love, Kant does think that an emotionally healthy human being will realize and live much of her life within the sphere of what I've called non-moralizable, yet normative emotions that reveal the importance of the particular individuals who enable us to flourish as who we are. The aim is never to replace these affectionate, particular ways of being with hyper-reflective, moralized ways of being only. Instead, the highest aim is always to make sure that our ways of realizing these non-moralizable forms of self-love (as enabled by the predispositions to animality and humanity and based in our individual conceptions of happiness) are in "close union" with moral love ("moral" self-love as ultimately enabled by the predisposition to personality). Practical reason helps us develop (by assuming responsibility for developing) the capacities for animality and humanity in ways that are truly good for us as the particular embodied and social, yet free beings we are.

3. Difference and Kant's Universal Theories of Freedom

In the introduction to the *Metaphysics of Morals*, Kant emphasizes that a complete practical philosophy contains a counterpart to a metaphysics of morals, namely a moral – or what we often today call a philosophical – anthropology. He continues by emphasizing that such a moral anthropology should only deal

> with the subjective conditions in human nature that hinder people or help them in *fulfilling* the laws of a metaphysics of morals [. . .]. It cannot be dispensed with, but it must not precede a metaphysics of morals or be mixed with it; for one would then run the risk of bringing forth false or at least indulgent moral laws, which would misrepresent as unattainable what has only not been attained just because the law has not been seen and presented in its purity [. . .] or because spurious or impure incentives were used for what is itself in conformity with duty and good. This would leave no certain moral principles, either to guide judgment or to discipline the mind in observance of duty, the precepts of which must be given a priori by pure reason alone.
>
> (*MS* 6: 217)

Moral or philosophical anthropology deals with social phenomena such as religious, gendered and cultural differences. Kant's proposal is that in order to critique gender or cultures, we need an account of human nature that can then be fleshed out with regard to a particular moral anthropological phenomenon. We also need an account of human nature to spell out aspects of what we commonly call moral psychology, including affective love, grief, and forgiveness. Sometimes we also want to critique an issue that concerns both moral (philosophical) anthropology and moral psychology, such as sexuality. Moreover, although Kant restricts his reflections in the preceding quote to moral anthropology, his more general point seems to be that although a complete practical philosophy requires such normative accounts (of moral anthropology and moral psychology) to complete the full practical account of the human being, these accounts must nevertheless not take the place of freedom. The main problem with letting accounts of the non-moralized aspects of moral psychology and moral anthropology take the place of human freedom in philosophical accounts of our practical being is that they do not capture something that can be seen as unconditionally, universally, or objectively true, something all human beings merely by virtue of being capable of moral responsibility (positive freedom, or autonomy) can recognize and accept as true (morally justified).[19] From the point of view of freedom, accounts of these normative, yet partially unreflective aspects of our human nature deal with subjective conditions that make it either easier or harder for us to be moral (to do the right thing). That is, they concern inherently contingent (not universal), subjective (not objective), and conditional (not unconditional) aspects of our practical lives. We must, in other words, not present these normative, yet non-moralizable aspects of ourselves as what they are not. Indeed, it is because they concern what is inherently subjective and contingent that we cannot have universal objective moral knowledge (as enabled by the critique of practical reason) or universal objective scientific knowledge (as enabled by the critique of pure reason) about them, and why Kant thinks that critiquing them requires us to use the philosophical tools of the third *Critique*. Moreover, if this is not our approach, we also run the danger of mistaking what is possible for what we only contingently experience, what is often simply a result of our own prejudices.[20] And, of course, the history of extreme violence and oppression of various social groups, including Kant's own failure to see these phenomena well – his own liability to think and say racist, sexist, and homophobic things – could not be a better illustration of this danger. The preceding claim is rather that the recognition of this danger and of mistakes made (even if not some of his own) were reasons why Kant ensured that his theory of freedom set the framework within which concerns of non-moralizable aspects of human nature were given space.[21]

In the *Anthropology*, Kant makes a related point, this time regarding the danger and mistake of letting culture – even good aspects of our inherited or historical culture – set the framework of justification for our moral reflections rather than letting moral reflections on freedom set the framework within which inherited culture is given its proper justification:

> In a civil constitution, which is the highest degree of artificial improvement of the human species' good predisposition to the final end of its destiny, animality still manifests itself earlier and, at bottom, more powerfully than pure humanity [. . .]. The human being's self is always ready to break out in aversion toward his neighbor, and he always presses his claim to unconditional freedom; freedom not merely to be independent of others, but even to be master over other beings who by nature are equal to him [. . .]. This is because nature within the human being strives to lead him from culture to morality, and not (as reason prescribes) beginning with morality and its law, to lead him to a culture designed to be appropriate to morality. This inevitably establishes a perverted, inappropriate tendency: for example, when religious instruction, which necessarily should be a moral culture, begins with historical culture, which is merely the culture of memory, and tries in vain to deduce morality from it.
>
> (*Anth* 7: 327–8)

Kant emphasizes here that our animality and self-recognitional sociality are both realized developmentally earlier and are emotionally stronger (more powerful) than our humanity in its pure form. Moreover, by "pure humanity" I presume Kant here, as in the *Religion*, means the idea of humanity considered "wholly intellectually" (*RGV* 6: 28), and so includes the predisposition to humanity's idea of rational (universalizable) end setting as well as the predisposition to personality (acting as motivated by practical reason). The possible emotional tension created by the nature of the predisposition to animality and our social sense of self is made inherently tenuous by the fact that we are also, at heart, "unsocial," meaning we want to live our *own* lives and set our *own* ends. Hence, it is subjectively very hard for us – and this is one reason why we will all sometimes fail – to make sure that we actually live in a way that is oriented towards others as having equal worth, a way that is also justifiable upon moral reflection. These are also reasons why it is so psychologically tempting for us to start with culture and then strive for morality (starting with shared cultural notions and then try to get each other to respect one another's difference) rather than letting morality (reciprocal, respectful freedom) set the framework within which culture is developed and, so, morally justified.

Kant's example here is religious instruction, or the way in which many religious people, leaders, and institutions are so easily drawn towards thinking that the justification of their religious beliefs-as-inherited-in-memory (tradition or "culture of memory") is the source of morality, rather than considering religion something that has an existential grounding function in one's emotional life. They do not consider that this (or any) historical culture is unfit for the purpose of deducing morality, or for determining the normative framework that is objectively true and recognizable as such for all human beings, regardless of historical and cultural, including religious, background.

The argument works similarly with regard to reforming our legal-political cultures and institutions: though there is a place for love of country and for making space for the need to adjust our legal-political institutions to our states' particular histories and circumstances, it would be equally wrong to infer from this – as some virtue, communitarian, and legal positivist theories do – that the source of political obligations and legitimacy in these states is this affectionate love of country, culture, or the sheer fact that some legal rules are recognized by many or enforced. Our moral duty to obey and the legal right to coercively enforce the law must always be sought in universal principles of freedom, in what is universally true for all, which can be discovered philosophically only by critiquing our capacity for practical reason, namely our capacity for interacting respectfully with one another as free beings. The proper spheres for difference (religious, cultural, ethnic, sexual, gendered, and so on) and for morality are therefore distinct; they deal with different, though complementary, aspects of our lives. And, of course, just as our expression of our personal emotional selves should be consistent with the expression of our moral selves, so should a national or a religious culture in that they should be consistent with respect for each person as free and equal. No sound interpretation of one's religion, culture, history, sexuality, or nation can justifiably be inconsistent with the demands of morality.

Notes

1 Thanks to Lucy Allais, Sorin Baiasu, Barbara Herman, Krupa Patel, Sally Sedgwick, Mark Timmons, and Shelley Weinberg for invaluable help with this chapter. Note that early drafts of parts of the chapter were published in Varden (2020a).

2 These discussions are sometimes framed in so-called analytic terms and sometimes in more continental terms.

3 For a Kantian example, see Allais (2008).

4 See also Albrecht (2015).

5 Butler (1990, 1993, 1997, 2004, 2004, 2005).

6 For Kantian examples, see, for example, the works of Marcia Baron, Carol Hay, Barbara Herman, Thomas E. Hill Jr., Onora O'Neill, Arthur Ripstein, and Helga Varden.

7 In the analytical feminist tradition, I'm here thinking of philosophers such as Claudia Card, Ann Cudd, Carol Hay, Barbara Herman, Rae Langton, Martha Nussbaum, Jennifer Nedelsky, Onora O'Neill, Susanne Sreedhar, and Anita Superson.

8 I'm especially thinking of French thinkers like Hélène Cixous, Michel Foucault, Luce Irigiray, and Julia Kristeva, who in turn were often influenced not only by other French thinkers like Jacques Derrida and Jacques Lacan, but also, of course, by Sigmund Freud and the psychoanalytic tradition.

9 In the English speaking tradition, many thinkers writing on these themes are profoundly inspired by the French tradition, such as Susan Brison, Ann Cahill, Penelope Deutscher, Cressida Heyes, Jacob Hale, Laurie Shrage, and Chloê Taylor.

10 For related discussions on Kant on race, see, for example Allais (2016), Hill and Boxill (2001), Kleingeld (2007), Mills (1999, 2014).

11 This is a frequently used line of argument among legal positivists. For communitarian versions of this argument see Alasdair MacIntyre, Charles Taylor, and Michael Sandel. For more, see Varden (2016).

12 See (*RGV* 6: 28).

13 For fuller development, see Varden (2014, 2016, 2020a).

14 I'm grateful to Andrew Cutrofello for suggesting to me that given Kant's systematicity it is likely that there is an intimate connection between these three drives (self-preservation, sex drive and propagation, and basic sociality) and the three relational categories (substance, causality, and community).

15 For more on my account of our non-human animals, see Varden (2020b).

16 For more on all of this, see (Varden 2020a).

17 See also (*RGV* 6: 26n, 75n).

18 See Varden (2020a) for more.

19 I'm indebted to Katerina Deligiorgi (2012, 2017, 2020) for much of my thinking on this point.

20 It is not hard to see that this account can be brought into fruitful dialogue with much of the existing literature found predominantly in the feminist and continental philosophical traditions on various kinds of (say, racial or sexual) violence against historically oppressed identities.

21 In Varden (2020a) I argue that Kant from the start was uncomfortable and uncertain about his belief that women couldn't be scholars or partake in public reasoning; in "Kant's Racism," Allais agrees with Kleingeld that Kant became more consistent in relation to his moral philosophy by condemning slavery and colonialism, and in Varden (2020a) I argue that Kant never managed to relate well to his own homophobia. The point here – like in Allais' "Kant's Racism" – is that Kant was aware of the dangers of dehumanizing others by means of sophisticated rationalization and self-deception. The contingency of claims about human nature makes them particularly apt for such dangerous and oppressive purposes. In addition, here and in Varden (2020b), I argue that Kant constructed his practical philosophy with these dangers explicitly in mind, namely by making sure that principles of freedom set the framework within which unreflective aspects of human nature are given their due place.

References

Albrecht, I. (2015) "How We Hurt the Ones We Love," *Pacific Philosophical Quarterly* 98(2), Electronic copy.

Allais, L. (2008) "Dissolving Reactive Attitudes: Forgiving and Understanding," *The South African Journal of Philosophy* 27: 1–23.

Allais, L. (2016) "Kant's Racism," *Philosophical Papers* 45(1–2): 1–36.

Butler, J. (1990) *Gender Trouble: Feminism and the Subversion of Identity*, New York: Routledge.

Butler, J. (1993) *Bodies that Matter: On the Discursive Limits of "Sex"*, New York: Routledge.

Butler, J. (1997) *The Psychic Life of Power: Theories in Subjection*, Stanford: Stanford University Press.

Butler, J. (2004) *Precarious Life: Powers of Violence and Mourning*, London: Verso.

Butler, J. (2005) *Giving an Account of Oneself*, New York: Fordham University Press.

Darwall, S. (2006) *The Second-Person Standpoint: Morality, Respect, and Accountability*, Cambridge, MA: Harvard University Press.

De Beauvoir, S. (2011) *The Second Sex*, C. Borde and S. Malovany-Chevallier (trans.), New York: Vintage Books.

Deligiorgi, K. (2012) *The Scope of Autonomy: Kant and the Morality of Freedom*, Oxford: Oxford University Press.

Deligiorgi, K. (2017) "Interest and Agency," in M. Gabriel and A.M. Rasmussen (eds.), *German Idealism Today*, Germany: De Guyter Verlag.

Deligiorgi, K. (2020) "Kant, Schiller, and the Idea of a Moral Self," *Kant-Studien* 111(2): 303–22.

Hill, Jr., T.E. and Boxill, B. (2001) "Kant and Race," in B. Boxill (ed.), *Race and Racism*, Oxford: Oxford University Press, pp. 448–71.

Kleingeld, P. (2007) "Kant's Second Thoughts on Race," *Philosophical Quarterly* 57: 573–92.

Mills, C. (1999) *The Racial Contract*, Ithaca: Cornell University Press.

Mills, C. (2014) "Kant and Race, Redux," *Graduate Faculty Philosophy Journal* 35: 1–33.

Varden, H. (2014) "The Terrorist Attacks in Norway, July 22nd 2011 – Some Kantian Reflections," *Norsk Filosofisk Tidsskrift/Norwegian Journal of Philosophy* 49(3–4): 236–59.

Varden, H. (2016) "Self-Governance and Reform in Kant's Liberal Republicanism: Ideal and Non-Ideal Theory in Kant's Doctrine of Right," *DoisPontos* 13(2): 39–70.

Varden, H. (2020a) *Sex, Love, and Gender: A Kantian Theory*, Oxford: Oxford University Press.

Varden, H. (2020b) "Kant and Moral Responsibility for Animals," in L. Allais and J. Callanan (eds.), *Kant on Animals*, Oxford: Oxford University Press, pp. 157–75.

Further Reading

A. Cohen, *Kant and the Human Sciences: Biology, Anthropology and History* (London: Palgrave Macmillan, 2009) – this an examination of the role of biology for Kant's account of huma sciences. P. Frierson, *Kant's Questions: What Is the Human Being?* (London: Routledge, 2013): an introduction to Kant's philosophy of human nature; further development of Kant's philosophy of human nature can also be found here: R. Louden, *Kant's Human Being* (New York: Oxford University Press, 2011). The following are some useful texts on Kant's thoughts on gender difference, race and women: U.P. Jauch, *Immanuel Kant zur Geschlechterdifferenz: Aufklärerische Vorurteilskritik und bürgerliche Geschlechtsvormundschaft* (Wien: Passagen Verlag, 1988); P. Kleingeld, "Kant's Second Thoughts on Race," *The Philosophical Quarterly* 57(229) (2007): 573–92; M. Mikkola, "Kant on Moral Agency and Women's Nature," *Kantian Review* 16(1) (2011): 89–111; S.M. Shell, *Kant and the Limits of Autonomy* (Cambridge: Harvard University Press, 2009) – an examination of Kant's idea of autonomy, its limits and their political implications today. J.H. Zammito, *Kant, Herder, and the Birth of Anthropology* (Chicago: University of Chicago Press, 2002): defending the interesting thought that the pre-Critical Kant might have become more influential than the Critical Kant without the Critical turn.

V. EDUCATION

33

MORAL EDUCATION

G. Felicitas Munzel

★★★

Two things fulfill the mind [*Gemüt*] with ever new and increasing admiration and reverence, the oftener and the more steadily we reflect on them: the starry heavens above me and the moral law within me.

(KpV *5: 161*)

These familiar poetic lines from the Conclusion of Kant's *Critique of Practical Reason*, words his friends and followers immediately identified with both the man and his work, are upon further reflection more than an autobiographical statement. They are a succinct expression of Kant's overarching anthropological and moral vision of human nature in which he captures the crucial role of aesthetic responsiveness in human life and moral judgment. In its broadest terms, the question for education entails how one brings about this moral/anthropological vision. As Kant cryptically states in the *Groundwork*, "morality requires anthropology for its application to human beings" (*GMS* 4: 412). The focus of this essay is on two anthropological features at the core of the subjective side of moral judgment and so of central importance for an account of moral education: the notion of aesthetic responsiveness and its seat in mind [*Gemüt*].[1]

The aim of his doctrine of method in the second *Critique*, Kant writes, is to comprehend

how we can secure access to the human mind [*Gemüt*] and an influence on its maxims by the laws of pure practical reason; that is, how objectively practical reason can also be made subjectively practical.

(*KpV* 5: 151)

Earlier in the same text Kant observes that the moral law in its subjectively practical form as the "true motivation" that has its source in pure practical reason, "allows us to perceive [*spüren*, literally 'sense,' 'feel,' or 'get a taste of'] the sublimity of our own supersensible existence" and "effects" [*wirkt*] within us, subjectively speaking, "respect for our higher vocation" (*KpV* 5: 88). In the *Critique of Judgment* we read that the "sublime in nature" is misplaced. Truly speaking, the "sublime

DOI: 10.4324/9781003406617-44

must always have reference to our *Denkungsart*; that is, to maxims which secure supremacy over sensibility for the intellectual and for the ideas of reason"; "the feeling of the sublime in nature" is actually "respect for our own vocation" (*KU* 5: 274, 257; see also 5: 245, 246, 264, 265). Such affirmations are ubiquitous in Kant's writings, from his early lectures on anthropology, to the later essays. Coming to understand the integral role of the human aesthetic capacities allows us to appreciate such exclamations as, "Duty! Thou sublime and mighty name," as more than rhetorical flourishes (*KpV* 5: 86).[2] The issue of gaining access to the mind for the moral law is a development in Kant's own thinking from the point to which he takes the discussion in the *Groundwork*. Near the end of this work he writes that

> in order for a sensibly affected [*sinnlich affizierten*] rational being to will that which reason alone prescribes as the ought, of course requires a capacity of reason *to instill a feeling of pleasure* or of being pleased in the fulfillment of duty.
>
> (*GMS* 4: 460; Kant's emphasis)[3]

To explicate Kant's subsequent development of this requirement entails articulating the sense of "mind" expressed by the concept of *Gemüt* and comprehending its relation to reason (as the author of the moral ought). The next step is to expand the account of the resulting feeling of pleasure beyond the familiar notion of moral feeling, to the meaning, role, and significance of Kant's fourfold delineation summarized in his *Metaphysical Principles of Virtue*, the four specific "aesthetic preliminary concepts of the mind's responsiveness to concepts of duty in general": moral feeling (as respect for the law), conscience, love of humanity, and respect for oneself (self-esteem) (*TL* 6: 399). Inherent to our human nature as moral beings, we have an obligation, writes Kant in his 1797 text, to cultivate these natural endowments. In this chapter I conclude these two analyses with an exploration of the correlation of these four aesthetically felt responses with (1) Kant's fourfold articulation of the categorical imperative, (2) his fourfold logical structure of judgment per se, and (3) the categories of freedom. The correlation allows one to achieve a more complete account of moral consciousness in its subjective and objective dimensions, both of which must be taken into consideration in moral education.

1. Mind (*Gemüt*) and Human Aesthetic Capacity

In order to better appreciate their moral *philosophical* significance (and so beyond either an exegetical or philological exercise), both terms, aesthetic and mind [*Gemüt*], benefit from some clarification as to the sense in which Kant uses them and as they are used in this essay. As he notes in the *Critique of Pure Reason*, his use of the term "aesthetic" refers to our capacity of sensibility [*Sinnlichkeit*] and its use in this sense is "more in line with the ancient sensible/intelligible distinction" (*KrV* A21/B36fn). Moral judging also involves two sides, broadly speaking intelligible and sensible, but the sides differ in their origin and function from theoretical reason. Granted, purely formally (objectively) considered, the moral law is sufficient onto itself, issuing its imperative to human choice-making and serving as the motive power for such choice-making and willing (both being intelligible powers of setting ends, but also subject to the influence of sensuousness – the inclinations and passions – as distinct from sensibility). However, as we saw in the preceding passage from the *Critique of Practical Reason*, the question must be addressed as to how the laws of pure practical reason gain access to the human mind [*Gemüt*] and an influence on its maxims. The two sides here are pure practical reason and "mind" in its sense as *Gemüt*. In the operation of reason on mind (distinct from, albeit in connection with, reason's determination of choice-making and willing), no constitutive judgment takes place (as it does in the first *Critique*); rather an aesthetic response to reason's command is evoked. This aesthetic response is already expressed by Kant in terms of the beautiful and the sublime in his early lectures on anthropology and in the *Critique of Practical Reason*. In the latter text he initially treats aesthetic pleasure in the beautiful as a propaedeutic stage to moral judgment proper which is accompanied by the feeling of the sublime. In the two-stage process of arousing consciousness of the moral law in his students' minds, Kant speaks of an "employment of judgment" which is "not yet an interest in actions and their morality"; it does, however, "give to virtue or *Denkungsart* in accordance with moral laws a form of beauty" which gives rise to "admiration," without yet therefore inspiring an effort "to seek it" (*KpV* 5: 160).

Kant considerably develops his discussion of aesthetic feeling in relation to morality in the *Critique of Judgment*. For example, "the attunement of the mind [*Gemüt*] to the feeling of the sublime requires a receptivity [or responsiveness, *Empfänglichkeit*] on its part for ideas" (*KU* 5: 265). The "attunement of mind [*Gemüt*]" in the case of the "sublime in nature" is "similar" to its attunement in its "moral" use (*KU* 5: 268). The sublime involves a double movement, one that Kant retains in the moral context (see *KpV* 5: 160–1). In the feeling of the sublime we find that which "repels sensibility" to be something that "at once attracts" us, because reason here "exercises its dominance solely in order to enlarge" the domain of sensibility "commensurate with its own practical domain" (*KU* 5: 265). Hence, one can see the aesthetic capacity as literally a partner in reason's efforts to bring about this enlargement of sensibility, for the sake of producing within the latter the counterimage of the moral law (character as the resolute *Denkungart* in accordance with the moral law).

This aesthetic responsiveness, then, is the attunement of mind [*Gemüt*] as a capacity of sensibility [*Sinnlichkeit*]. Put into Kant's critical terminology, this attunement of mind is the condition for the possibility of having a felt pleasurable experience of the motive force of reason's moral imperative. It is not itself the source of moral motivation and so from reason's standpoint it plays a supporting role. As the condition for the possibility of a pleasurable response to reason's command, this supporting role is nonetheless essential. It facilitates the human appreciation of the moral so that the undeniable effort required for good moral judgment, good moral character, and a good moral complete life is not an onerous imposition on human nature and empirical human life, but rather is revered as precisely that which fulfills our highest human purpose. Kant explicitly says as much in the *Critique of Judgment*: through "the agreement of taste with reason, that is of the beautiful with the good, the former may be used as an instrument" on behalf of our "aims in regard to the good"; such use is achieved through the attunement of mind [*Gemüt*], which preserves itself and is subjectively universally valid, providing support for [literally, being laid under] that *Denkungsart* which can only be preserved [or sustained] through arduous resolve, but which is objectively universally valid (*KU* 5: 230–1).[4]

The operative sense of mind in all these passages is that of *Gemüt* as the seat of the exercise of the aesthetic sensibilities. The term *Gemüt* is often (with good reason) translated as "heart," "soul," or "feeling soul" and in this sense it remains a prevalent concept in German language and culture. The English term "mind" is also used in a wide range of meanings, but its most prevalent use in contemporary, analytical epistemological discussion takes its cue from the modern mind/body distinction and so it connotes logical, cognitive processes. In this sense "mind" does not render the meaning of *Gemüt*, either in the ordinary language sense, or in Kant's use of it. In the *Friedländer Anthropology Lectures*, in his discussion of the human sense of self, Kant distinguishes two aspects of the "soul": *Geist* (intellect) and *Gemüt* (*V-Anth/Fried* 25: 474).

> *Gemüt* is the way in which the soul is affected [*afficirt*] by things. It is the power to reflect upon one's state and to relate one's state to oneself and one's personality. [. . .] *Gemüt* is thus a power of being sensitive to [*empfinden*] that of which one has a sensation [*empfinden*]. [. . .]

Thus in the soul, *Gemüt* is something different from what we otherwise call heart [*Gemüt*] or feeling [*Gefühl*].

(*V-Anth/Fried* 25: 474)

So already in this early text Kant's anthropology includes an account of the soul as a principle of life that is a consciousness of being affected, as well as a reflective power in relation to this consciousness. It is further the power that allows us to identify ourselves with this conscious state. Several pages later in the text Kant makes a statement that fairly resonates with his later critical moral philosophy:

The greatest perfection of the powers of the mind [*Gemüt*] is based on our subordinating them to our power of choice [*Willkür*], and the more they are subjugated to the free power of choice, all the greater perfection of the powers of the mind do we possess. If we do not have them under the control of the free power of choice, all provisions for such perfection are thus in vain, if we cannot do what we want with the powers of the mind.

(*V-Anth/Fried* 25: 488)

In his discussion in the *Critique of Practical Reason* of making objective principles subjective, of making objectively practical reason, subjectively practical, Kant invokes the sense of mind we see in his anthropology lectures. He writes that if "human nature were not so constituted" that "even subjectively, the exhibition of pure virtue can have more power over the human mind [*Gemüt*] and can provide far greater motivation" not only to effectuate the "legality of actions," but "to produce firmer resolve to prefer the law to everything else purely out of respect for it," than could ever be generated by appeals to the "attractions [. . .] of all that may be counted as happiness or even by all threats of pain and harm," if this were not so, then there would be no means of "ever bringing about the morality of the *Gesinnung*" (of one's moral mindedness) (*KpV* 5: 151–2). Here one has a clear statement of the role of the sense of mind being invoked as effectively a middle term between the moral and empirical human self. It is in mind as the seat of sensibility that the consciousness of reason's imperative reigns over the awareness of our feelings originating in the entire realm of human life that falls under happiness and self-interest. It is a higher sensibility that we find aesthetically so pleasing that the pain of subjugating our empirically based feelings is mitigated. Indeed a preference for that of which we are aesthetically sensible is aroused. Thus too, in the cultivation of moral judgment, the first stage in Kant's account is to "occupy the power of judgment" with exercises that allow the students to "feel their own cognitive powers" (*KpV* 5: 160); that is, they become aware of and learn to enjoy the expansion of their rational faculty beyond natural instincts, thus beginning to be cognizant and appreciative of their own inherent ground of freedom, initially realized in judgments that are purposive (*KpV* 5: 159–60).

Kant's remarks in his critique of aesthetic judgment continue this line of distinctions.[5] The object of a pure and unconditioned intellectual being pleased is the moral law in its might, [a might] that it exerts in us over any and all of those incentives of the mind [*Gemüt*] that precede it; [. . .] this might actually reveals itself aesthetically only through sacrifice (which is a deprivation, though one that serves our inner freedom, in return for which it reveals in us an unfathomable depth of this supersensible power, whose consequences extend beyond what we can foresee).

(*KU* 5: 271)

This service on behalf of inner freedom is noted by Kant in the *Critique of Practical Reason*: well established respect for the moral law is the best, even sole guard against ignoble and corrupting impulses entering the mind (*KpV* 5: 161). Earlier in the text he also states that the greatness of soul for which human beings, as a result of the moral motivational grounds, recognize they are destined, provides "abundant compensation" for the sacrifices that the independence from inclinations entails (*KpV* 5: 152). The line that Kant is seeking to walk is to articulate an aesthetically felt response that plays a beneficial role in moral life and judgment while not agitating the mind to the extent of destroying its composure (and thus impeding inner freedom).[6]

From even just these selected passages, one might extrapolate some of the specific differences in the characteristics of the aesthetic attunement of mind [*Gemüt*] from its other states and other impulses as follows. First and foremost, the aesthetic attunement promotes inner freedom, while other states impede it. Passions and inclinations are temptations for the power of choice to be swayed by them; in the aesthetic attunement of mind its powers are governed by the free power of choice. The aesthetic attunement enables us to feel, not only understand, our vocation [*Bestimmung*] as moral beings and hence as capable of being free from subjugation to the passions and inclinations. There is also a difference in the endurance of the state of mind. To be agitated can come on very suddenly, it can easily fluctuate in its intensity, but it can also be fleeting. So, for example, it is a commonplace to say that time heals. An aesthetic attunement such as one informed by conscience, for example, may not only endure for a long time, it may even become more intense over time, especially when it is a case of being troubled by a bad conscience, by the consciousness of having failed in one's moral judgment. It is time, then, to turn to the specific four states of mind which Kant identifies.

2. Aesthetic Preliminary Concepts of the Mind's Responsiveness to Concepts of Duty in General[7]

The opening paragraph of this short section of the *Metaphysical Principles of Virtue* is effectively a summary in Kant's own words of our discussion to this point of the sense of mind and its aesthetic attunement that plays an essential role in moral life. This conception of mind is central for understanding how motivation that has its origin in the moral self can be efficacious in human nature as a whole; it bridges the moral and the empirical and so is the essential component of how and why human nature is capable of rising up to the moral, or the sphere of true infinity (as Kant calls it in the *Critique of Practical Reason*). Kant's own succinct statement of our capacities that make us capable, from the human, subjective side of our nature, of fulfilling our moral vocation reads as follows:

> There are such moral properties, that, if one does not possess them, there can also not be any duty to acquire them. These are moral feeling, conscience, love of neighbor, and respect for oneself (self-esteem). There is no obligation to have these, because they are subjective conditions of responsiveness to the concept of duty [and] do not serve as the basis of the objective conditions of morality. All told, they are aesthetic and preliminary, but natural aptitudes of mind [*Gemütsanlagen*] (*praedispositio*) to be affected [*afficirt*] by concepts of duty. It cannot be regarded as a duty to have these aptitudes; rather every human being has them and by means of them [every person] can be obligated. The consciousness of them is not empirical in origin, but can only follow upon [the consciousness] of a moral law, upon its effect on the mind.
>
> (*TL* 6: 399)[8]

Kant's identification of these aesthetic moral properties as preliminary concepts [*Vorbegriffe*] invites a comparison with his discussion in the *Critique of Pure Reason* where space and time are described as concepts of outer and inner sense. Anthropology, in Kant's conception of this science, is the knowledge of human beings as the object of inner sense (*V-Anthro/Fried* 25: 473). So from this standpoint we have here properties of inner sense which, further, as concepts are formative principles. In this case they are not formative of an object; rather they are formative of the mind's moral attunement. Kant expresses just this reservation in his discussion of moral feeling in his ensuing discussion of the aesthetic preliminary concepts in his *Metaphysical Principles of Virtue*. Even though in the opening paragraph he has himself referred to the aesthetic state of mind in terms of "inner sense," he notes that it is not fitting to call moral feeling a "moral sense" precisely because "by the word sense one usually means a theoretical faculty of perception directed to an object," while in this case the moral feeling is only "subjective" and "yields no cognition" (*TL* 6: 400). Presumably Kant's concern is that the introduction of terminology from his critical theoretical cognitive account will confuse the clear critical moral hierarchical order which places moral motivation squarely with reason's imperative. The cognitive terminology could tempt one to fall back into conventional usage in which empirically based sense experience is the focus and one attempts to make cognitive claims about it. Nonetheless, the fact that Kant himself raises the issue in this short account of moral feeling in the text indicates that he is thinking about the comparison.

The claim in our discussion here is that Kant is employing his critical standpoint even as he examines the subjective side of human moral life and so, another way to put the fine line he is walking, is to say that the critical insights (formal principles and how they work) are informing his account of the subjective side, while he seeks to be clear about the difference it makes to regard the various matters from the subjective (and not the objective) side. Again, the notion that concepts give rise to feeling is found in Kant's early anthropology lectures:

> concepts are to become incentives in us, they are to rouse feeling, and to motivate us to act in accordance with such concepts, and thus according to principles. Human beings who do not have such a feeling which can be roused through a concept, have no moral feeling. This is the sensitiveness, sensitivity, or the feeling through all concepts of the understanding.
>
> (*V-Anthro/Fried* 25: 649–50)

The interpretation I am offering here is to say that while reason's moral concepts are the source of moral motivation, in order for the mind to be formed, to achieve a moral attunement and responsiveness to the moral imperative and thereby raise human nature to the concrete fulfillment of its moral vocation, Kant's anthropology fills in an account of the subjective condition of the possibility of this fulfillment. As we read in the passage cited earlier, this subjective condition consists in the aesthetic and preliminary, but natural aptitudes of mind [*Gemütsanlagen*] [*praedispositio*)] to be affected [*afficirt*] by concepts of duty.

These aptitudes turn out to be exactly four in number which hence further invites the correlation with the four formulations of the categorical imperative, the four logical functions of judging per se, and with the categories of freedom. For the remainder of the discussion here, I will highlight what Kant says about these four aesthetic preliminary concepts in his *Metaphysical Principles of Virtue* and explore what insight the mentioned correlations might yield.[9]

Moral feeling as respect for the moral law is of course the one best known to Kant's readers. In his opening line, Kant expresses it in the familiar terms of the "receptivity for pleasure or displeasure" arising "solely from the consciousness of the agreement or disagreement of our action with the law of duty" (*TL* 6: 399). He goes on to make a distinction that is not as well recognized. He describes the "aesthetic state [*Zustand*]," the "rousing of inner sense" [*Afficirung des inneren Sinnes*] as being either a "pathological or a moral feeling," where the first precedes the representation of the law, while the second can only follow upon this representation (*TL* 4: 399). The implied caveat here may be that in the moral context it is not enough to take the mind's state of pleasure or displeasure into consideration; it must always be done in connection with the sequential order of its state in relation to the representation of the moral law. Otherwise one might again fall into a temptation of treating the aesthetic state as a basis for adhering to the law, instead of recognizing it as the response to how well the agent did or did not adhere to the law. In the *Critique of Practical Reason* Kant had made the point as follows:

> and so respect for the law is not the incentive to morality; rather *it is morality itself, subjectively regarded as incentive*, inasmuch as pure practical reason, by rejecting all the rival claims of self-love, procures a high repute for the law which now solely has influence.
>
> (*KpV* 5: 76; emphasis added)

In his 1797 text Kant goes on to make the familiar point that as moral beings we are originally endowed with this moral feeling and so any obligation in regard to it can only consist in "cultivating" it and "even strengthening it through admiration for its inscrutable origin" (*TL* 6: 399–400). In this light, Kant's poetic statement in the conclusion of the *Critique of Practical Reason*, following his account of how teachers should go about cultivating moral judgment in their students, summarizes the nature and extent of our pedagogical duties with respect to this human aptitude.

In his section "concerning conscience," Kant begins with the statement that it likewise is not acquired and that there is no duty to do so; "rather insofar as every human being is a moral being, he has it originally within him" (*TL* 6: 400). To say that someone has no conscience means that such an individual does not heed its dictum, for to be actually devoid of conscience would entail not ascribing anything to oneself as having been done in accordance with duty, or conversely not reproaching oneself for having done something contrary to duty (*TL* 6: 400–1). Kant then states the point even more strongly: namely that there "is no such thing as an erring conscience" (*TL* 6: 401). As Kant puts it in a later section of the *Metaphysics of Morals*, conscience is an "innate judge" of humans over themselves, a "court" before which they stand for sentencing (*TL* 6: 437ff; *RGV* 6: 77, 146n). As such a "presentation of duty," conscience is an "original intellectual moral aptitude," whose "business" is one of "human beings with themselves" (*TL* 6: 438). Most pertinent for our discussion here is the exercise of reason, in its function as conscience, of an on-going self-assessment to ensure that its guiding activity, the bringing of all contemplated and executed actions before it for moral judgment, is not allowed to lapse. It is a role of conscience that Kant defines in his *Religion*: one "could define conscience as the 'power of moral judgment passing judgment on itself.'" That is to say, "conscience does not judge actions as cases that fall under the law"; this is the work of

> reason insofar as it is subjectively practical. Rather, here *reason judges itself*, as to whether it has really undertaken in all diligence such judgment of actions (as to whether they are just or unjust), and it calls upon individuals to be witnesses for or against themselves as to whether or not

such judgment has been exercised (*RGV* 6: 186, emphasis added). It is just in this "subjective judgment, as to whether or not I have compared" a given case with "my practical (here judging) reason, for the purpose" of making the objective judgment as to whether or not the thing considered is a matter of duty, "that I cannot be mistaken," writes Kant in his *Metaphysics of Morals* (*TL* 6: 401). For, to be mistaken in that is "not to have exercised practical judgment at all" and so too, "unscrupulousness is not a lack of conscience, but the propensity to ignore such judgment" (*TL* 6: 401). Conscience is thus intimately bound up with our moral self-consciousness and ensuring that its activity would not lapse. Once again, insofar as there is a duty with regard to conscience, it is a duty to "cultivate it, to sharpen our attentiveness to the voice of the inner judge and to employ every means of securing it a hearing" (*TL* 6: 401).[10]

One can begin to see here that these aesthetic preliminary concepts seem to be connected with one another. That the requisite judgment has taken place or not evokes the response of conscience; its conformity or not to duty evokes moral feeling. Kant refers to the third concept in three different ways, as love of neighbor in his opening paragraph, as love of humanity [*Menschenliebe*, also translated as philanthropy] in the sub-heading, and as benevolence [*Wohlwollen, amor benevolentiae*] in his discussion. He begins by taking issue with the common usage of "love" in this context because "love is a matter of sensation" and so there cannot be anything like a "duty to love" (*TL* 6: 401). The duty that we can and do have toward other human beings is beneficence (within our means and abilities); we have this duty irrespective of whether we love an individual or not, and irrespective of the sad observation that the better we know them, we do not find human beings to be particularly worthy of love (*TL* 6: 402). Even where we observe vice or misanthropy, the duty of beneficence remains and, where it is frequently exercised, especially when it succeeds, one gradually gets to the point of actually loving the other individual. On this basis Kant interprets the dictum to love one's neighbor as oneself as follows:

> this does not mean you should immediately (at first) love and through this love (subsequently) be beneficent, but rather, do good to your neighbor, and this beneficence will bring about love of humanity in you (as a proficiency of the inclination to be beneficent in general).
>
> (*TL* 6: 402)

In his early anthropology lectures, in his discussion of educating the child, Kant is specific that the "child must be kept [on the course] to humanity," that it be reared so that it is "prepared to exercise humanity" (or humaneness [*Menschlichkeit*]) "toward others," and that "the respect for the dignity of humanity in his person is the final level of education and already borders on the age of youth" (*V-Anth*/Fried 25: 727). So once again, in his overall account it is central to moral education that these aesthetic capacities be cultivated (not unlike the cultivation of talents with which human beings are endowed).

In his discussion of respect [*reverentia*, reverence] Kant essentially repeats the same distinctions he has made for the other three. It is incorrect to say one has a duty of self-esteem; rather one should say that

> the law within oneself inevitably exacts respect for one's own being, and this feeling (which is of a special kind) is the ground of certain duties, that is, of certain actions consistent with one's duty to oneself. It is not that one has a duty of self-respect, for one must have respect for the law within oneself, in order to be able to conceive of a duty at all.
>
> (*TL* 6: 402–3)

The first two aesthetic preliminary concepts thus deal, broadly speaking, with the form of the judgments one makes – namely that the practical judgment has been done out of respect for the law and that the judgment in fact has taken place as it should. The second two deal with what one might call the referents of such judgments, the beings in relation to which they are made, others and oneself. All may be seen as formative principles for the attunement of mind that is accomplished in its aesthetic response to reason's moral law.

3. Correlation of Aesthetic Preliminary Concepts With Categorical Imperative, Logical Functions of Judgment, and Categories of Freedom

Do these four concepts pair up with the four formulations of the categorical imperative? In Kant's summary in the *Groundwork* of the first three formulas of the "same law," he writes that one of them unites the other two in itself; the difference among them, is "more subjective than objectively practical, namely *in order to bring an idea of reason nearer to intuition* (according to a certain analogy) and thereby nearer to feeling" (*GMS* 4: 436, emphasis added). All maxims, Kant goes on, have three aspects: "a form which consists in universality," a "matter, namely an end," and a "complete determination of all maxims", which entails that "all maxims from one's own legislation ought to harmonize with a possible realm of ends, as a realm of nature" (*GMS* 4: 436). Kant continues that there is a progression here as there is in the "categories of the unity of the form of the will (its universality), the plurality of its matter (its objects, i.e. its ends), and the allness or totality of its system" of ends. While Kant then comments that one does better in moral judging to proceed in accordance with the strict method and so from the universal formula, he ends with the following statement:

> If one however wants at the same time to obtain *access* for the moral law, then it is very useful to take one and the same act [*Handlung*] through the three named concepts and thus, as far as may be done, to bring it nearer to intuition.
>
> (*GMS* 4: 436–7)

The latter statement (in which the emphasis on "access" is Kant's own), in light of our previous citations, indicates that already here in the articulation of the objective formal principle of the moral law, Kant is taking into account the issue of access to the mind. This gives further warrant for inquiring as to how one might pair up the four aesthetic preliminary concepts with the four formulations of the categorical imperative.

These four formulations may be seen in terms of the preceding groupings, with two dealing with the form of legislation and two dealing with the ends, the beings in relation to which the legislation is being exercised. So while Kant himself does not explicitly spell out the correlation, arguably the division into form and matter (ends) which he does specify serves as a reliable guide. That moral feeling is the aesthetic subjective counterpart to the objective universal formulation of the moral law seems the most straightforward, given Kant's own frequent reference to the moral feeling of respect for the law in his critical moral philosophy. The third formulation in which the law is understood as "the supreme limiting condition of all subjective ends" and so is expressed as the "idea of the will of every rational being as a will giving universal law," has to do with the consistency of the rational will, of its own autonomous rule with the universal law that applies to all rational beings in general (*GMS* 4: 431). So there is here a kind of formal, internal check that brings to mind the definition of conscience as the "power of moral judgment passing judgment on itself." The second formula of the categorical imperative that calls upon us to treat the humanity in ourselves and others always as an end and never merely as a means correlates with the feeling of respect for oneself as a moral being, the self-esteem we feel when we recognize the plane of existence that is true infinity as our very vocation. This leads directly to the idea of a universal realm of ends and the call to act accordingly: as a legislative member in such a universal realm of ends (*GMS* 4: 438). Kant's discussion of the duty of beneficence, whose repeated exercise will give rise to the feeling of benevolence seems to correlate well with this fourth formulation of the law. To seek to make these correlations serves two purposes. We see that Kant refers to the subjective side of morality within the course of his discussion of its objective principles. Correlating the four aesthetic attunements of mind that, taken individually and all together, yield a sensation of being pleased with the moral duty to which we are called and indeed to prefer it (subjectively speaking) to the empirically based impulses, completes the account of the subjective and objective sides of morality to which Kant refers throughout his writings. Second, the correlation affords an explanation as to why Kant selects four such aesthetic preliminary concepts and why these four in particular.

Both the facts that Kant speaks of bringing the idea of reason, its objective practical law nearer to intuition, and that a moral judgment (while not a cognitive act that constitutes an object) does take the form of the logical functions (for which in this case, the corresponding categories will be those of freedom) invite considering a further correlation with the fourfold division of the table of judgments. The examination of our judgments, as to whether they are well made or not, entails being clear about their logical coherence and it is through making these judgments that we comprehend ourselves as moral beings, as well as such relevant ideas as the moral good, humanity as an end in itself, realm of ends, and so forth. Conversely, would we truly comprehend what is meant by respect, conscience, self-esteem, and benevolence, if we did not have the felt sensations? In short, the logical elements are the same. The crucial difference is that now the exercise of reason, its determination of willing, *precedes* the felt perceptions (as opposed to unifying sensible intuitions into a cognizable object). When Kant says that the fully articulated moral law brings it closer to intuition and that doing so is useful to gain access to the mind, in light of the discussion here he is positing two aims. The second of these, gaining access to the mind, has been our focus and we have examined the role of the aesthetic preliminary concepts in this process. The first aim may be seen as having been realized in this very process; that is, we come to realize the meaning (comprehend the law in its different formulations) precisely in and through the relation of reason and mind.

If then one adds these logical elements, the divisions of the table of judgments, to the foregoing correlation, it may look as follows. Here again the first universal formulation of the law (with its attendant moral feeling of respect) is the most straightforward; it identifies the range (quantity) for which the law holds. The inner assessment of the autonomous agent as to the consistency of its willing with the universal law that applies to all rational beings in general, connected with practical reason's assessment as to whether the called for judgment has been exercised (conscience), fulfills the logical aspect of judgment that Kant designates as quality. The inner assessment calls for a judgment that is in the affirmative or negative. In treating humanity in myself and in others as an end (with its attendant self-esteem), I am specifying the categorical relation of the law to the essence of humanity (with relation being of course the third division of the table of judgments). Finally, in Kant's discussion of the totality of a realm of ends, Kant notes that it is possible only through the legislation of all rational beings as members, and hence it is necessary that they act precisely as such members of a universal realm of ends (*GMS* 4: 438). The fourth formulation then (with its attendant benevolent attunement of mind) connects with apodictic modality.

This same fourfold division constitutes the structure of the table of the categories of freedom. Kant ends his discussion of this table by claiming that the table gives one an overview "of the entire plan of what one must accomplish, indeed of every question of practical philosophy which has to be answered, and at the same time of the order which is to be followed" (*KpV* 5: 67). It is beyond the scope of the discussion here to attempt to even begin the articulation of such an "entire plan," or even to take into account "the concepts of good and evil, as consequences of the a priori determination of the will" (*KpV* 5: 65). The focus here is Kant's stated aim of subordinating a priori the "manifold of desires to the unity of the consciousness of a practical reason that commands [in the name of] the moral law," which is to say to subordinate the manifold to "a pure will" (*KpV* 5: 65).

For the human will is, of course, not pure; it is pathological and the resulting actions of willing also belong to two spheres: under the law of freedom they belong to the conduct of an intelligible being and, at the same time, as occurrences in the sensible world, they belong to the realm of appearance (*KpV* 5: 65). Through the table, writes Kant, freedom is manifest as a causality that makes actions possible as appearances in the sensible world and so freedom's causality does refer to the categories of the possibility of actions in nature; in other words it refers to categories of the understanding under the fourfold logical functions of quantity, quality, relation, and modality (*KpV* 5: 67). To put it still otherwise, the causality of freedom makes possible the appearance of morally well ordered results of the determination a priori of a will that is subject to the inclinations and passions. As categories of freedom, while organized in the same logical functions, they are however concerned with the "determination of a free power of choice [*Willkür*]" and are based on "a pure practical law a priori" (*KpV* 5: 65). Since it is a matter of such an internal determination of the activity of willing and choosing, and since the categories therefore directly refer to the actuality – to the moral minded-ness of the will [*Willensgesinnung*] – which they themselves bring about, these practical concepts (or categories) are also at once cognitions (*KpV* 5: 66). In other words, in their determination of our willing and choosing we at once comprehend their meaning. Kant does not say it here, but in light of our interpretation, such a comprehension of their meaning would be facilitated by a felt aesthetic response.

Under the heading of quantity Kant identifies the range of individual, collective and universal maxims and precepts subject to the command of the moral law and so, once again, this division of the table can be correlated with the aesthetic responsiveness of moral feeling or respect. Under quality he identifies the rules of commission, omission, and exceptions. Such affirmative and nega-tive assessments correlate with the kind of assessment that evokes the response of conscience. The categories of relation deal with the state of a person and a person's interaction with others and thus may be correlated with the aesthetic response of self-esteem that attends treating oneself and others as ends. The categories of modality are the only ones for which Kant himself offers some explica-tion. He notes that they "initiate the transition from practical principles as such to those of lived morality [*Sittlichkeit*]," which subsequently can be presented in a dogmatic form through the moral law (or, in other words, can be comprehended as necessary). Recognizing our duties to ourselves and others, and ultimately as members of a realm of ends correlates (as it did earlier) with the aes-thetic response of beneficence.

Where the discussion of the table of the categories of freedom goes further than our foregoing correlations is that here we have formative principles of human willing with explicit attention to the dual intelligible and sensible realms that are involved. The goal is to achieve a unified moral consciousness of the pathologically affected human will determined by a pure will (that is, by prac-tical reason and its moral law). Although Kant does not in these passages employ the language of *Gemüt* or the aesthetic concepts, he does refer to them elsewhere in the *Critique of Practical Reason*. A complete account of a unified moral consciousness requires the account of the felt perception of the motivating influence of practical reason's law giving. What emerges from laying the tables of the activities of judging, willing, and felt perceiving alongside one another is a picture of human moral self-consciousness in which these activities are connected. Kant's anthropological understanding of humanity goes beyond the classical definition of the human as a rational animal. In his hierarchy of the human aptitudes for the good, the responsiveness of respect for the moral law is the third and highest level that he calls personality (with animality and the human rational nature being the other two) (*RGV* 6: 26). The complete picture of moral self-consciousness certainly has personality at its core, but the tables help us to see how it fits into the full context of a lived human moral life. Thus they can serve as a valuable pedagogical tool for the task of education which is to cultivate all these aptitudes of mind in order to facilitate the achievement of a morally well ordered human life, both individually and collectively. Such a life, for Kant, is imbued with the vision which he expresses in the famous words that became his legacy.

Notes

1 Contemporary Anglo-American scholarship on Kant's moral philosophy has primarily focused on the relation of reason to the empirical, sensuous realm of inclinations and passions and the analytical, ethical discussions tend to take place in terms of the perceived issue of the connection between "pure" and "applied" ethics. Left out of this discussion is the role of aesthetic responsiveness, a role central also to my elucidation of Kant's conception of moral character. See Munzel (1999) especially "Character and the Aesthetic Capacities of Feeling," 126–132, as well as 296–313. Also see Munzel (2012) especially 269–273.
2 In his essay on theory and praxis, Kant repeats his avowal of the animating and elevating power of the idea of duty for the human mind [*Gemüt*]; consciousness of our capacity for a pure moral comportment of mind "discloses in us a depth of divine aptitudes" and we "feel, as it were, a solemn thrill [*heiligen Schauer*]" as we reflect "on the greatness and sublimity of our true vocation and determination [*Bestimmung*]" (*TP* 8: 287–88).
3 The translations are my own and follow the glossary in the Cambridge volume of Kant's *Lectures on Anthropology*.
4 In his discussion of beauty as the symbol of the morally good, Kant develops the sense of analogy that first provides the intuition whereby we may establish the reality of the objects of our concepts of reason. To thus be able to have an image of the morally good before the mind is another way aesthetic sensibility serves the operations of reason in the moral sphere. See Munzel (1995).
5 See *KU* 5: 204, 330–1, 207, 271.
6 See *V-Anth/Fried* (25: 589–90).
7 This is the title of section XII of the second part of Kant's *Metaphysical Principles of Virtue*.
8 The translation of *Anlagen* as "aptitudes," emphasizes these as active, formative and structuring principles (not as passive dispositions). See the "Note on Translation" at the beginning of *Kant's Conception of Moral Character* (Munzel 1999).
9 All four of these concepts are found numerous times throughout Kant's writings, but there is not space here to give something approaching a complete account of how he treats them in his works as a whole. Likewise the passages cited throughout the chapter highlight points that Kant repeats many times, also in other texts not cited here.
10 For a fuller account of Kant's conception of conscience, see Munzel (2014).

References

Munzel, G.F. (1995) " 'The Beautiful Is the Symbol of the Morally-Good': Kant's Philosophical Basis of Proof for the Idea of the Morally-Good," *Journal of the History of Philosophy* 33: 301–30.
Munzel, G.F. (1999) *Kant's Conception of Moral Character: The "Critical" Link of Morality, Anthropology, and Reflective Judgment*, Chicago: The University of Chicago Press.
Munzel, G.F. (2012) *Kant's Conception of Pedagogy: Toward Education for Freedom*, Evanston: Northwestern University Press.
Munzel, G.F. (2014) "What Does His *Religion* Contribute to Kant's Conception of Practical Reason?" in G.E. Michalson (ed.), *Kant's Religion Within the Boundaries of Mere Reason: A Critical Guide*, Cambridge: Cambridge University Press.

Further reading

K. Roth and C. Surprenant (eds.), *Kant and Education: Interpretations and Commentary* (London: Routledge, 2012) brings together a number of relevant texts for the issues discussed in this chapter. For a general evaluation of Kant's thought for the topics, see C. Surprenant's "Kant's Contribution to Moral Education"; a general account of the links in Kant between ethics, education and anthropology is offered by M. Kuehn's "Kant on Education, Anthropology and Ethics"; R. Velkley's "Educating Through Perplexity: Kant and the German Enlightenment" places Kant's ideas on education in the broader cultural context of Germany at the time; the significant relation between Kant's philosophy of human nature and his account of moral education is discussed in R. Dean's "Moral Education and the Ideal of Humanity" and A. Cohen's "Enabling the Realization of Humanity: The Anthropological Dimension of Education"; see also S.M. Shell on Kant's broader account of humanities, in "Kant on the Humanities".

VI. LOGIC, MATHEMATICS, AND NATURAL SCIENCES

34

LOGIC

Huaping Lu-Adler

***

Logic is undoubtedly an important part of Kant's Critical philosophy. Curiously, though, he published very little on the subject and mostly in the form of fragments that are scattered in a handful of texts. He did have a sizable logic corpus comprising these materials: his handwritten notes (*Reflexionen*) on logic, transcripts of his logic lectures, and the *Logik* compiled by G. B. Jäsche. These materials are indispensable to a full grasp of Kant's theory of logic, but are affected by various philological problems and so cannot be directly treated as conclusive records of Kant's views on logic.[1]

A theory of logic can be reconstructed from the aforementioned materials that not only synthesizes Kant's remarks about logic but also illuminates its relation to his Critical philosophy on the one hand and to the history of logic on the other. Such a reconstruction must reflect Kant's avowed philosophical rigor, his keen attention to philosophical problems, and his knowledge of and critical relation with previous treatments of such problems. It is with these constraints in mind that I shall consider two branches of Kant's so-called general logic, namely pure (or formal) and applied logics. I focus on the most basic philosophical issues involving these logics, issues that Kant the Critical philosopher can be expected to address but neglected to do so explicitly.

My first goal in this chapter (section 1) is to warn against simplistic portrayals of Kant's work on logic and to carve out space for fruitful philosophical engagements with it. My second goal is to find, in section 2, a meaningful way to connect Kant's work on logic with his broader commitments and with his philosophical system as a whole.

1. Pure Logic – Its Alleged Completeness and Its Possibility as Proper Science

The common impression of Kant's theory of logic is more or less shaped by his following claims in the *Critique of Pure Reason*:

(i)   Logic seems "finished and complete" since Aristotle (Bviii; "completeness claim").
(ii) There are general and transcendental logics. Transcendental logic investigates laws of the understanding and reason "insofar as they are related to objects *a priori*", while general logic

   DOI: 10.4324/9781003406617-46

presents the rules of thinking in general without regard to any relation of the cognition to objects (A55–7/B79–82).

(iii) General logic divides into pure and applied logics. Applied logic studies "the rules of the use of the understanding under the subjective empirical conditions that psychology teaches us", whereas pure logic is a "proven doctrine" that is thoroughly *a priori* and "draws nothing from psychology" (A53–4/B77–8).

The completeness claim is often the first to occur to scholars when they connect Kant with traditional logic and, because of the perceived connection, he is sometimes held partly responsible for the (alleged) lack of innovations in logic during the few decades after him. For a historian who wishes to show that there were in fact innovative logical developments during those decades, then, it is natural first to distance the supposed innovations from Kant's work on logic. Consider the following statement with which Stephan Käufer opens his discussion of the 19th-century logic.

> Canonical histories of logic, such as that of I. Bochenski or William and Martha Kneale, ignore the work of nineteenth-century philosophers working on traditional logic. This disregard is somewhat justified. Mainstream philosophers working on logic in the nineteenth century make no enduring or significant changes to the old scholastic syllogistic logic; and their concerns do not seem to be properly logical at all, [. . .] Kant's work illustrates this approach to logic. [. . .] Kant adheres to the Aristotelian syllogistic and [. . .] [claims] that logic is correct and complete, and further improvements are neither necessary nor possible (1781: Bviii).
>
> (Käufer 2010: 809)

With this depiction of Kant's view on logic, Käufer is quick to draw a sharp line between it and the developments in logic during the early decades of the 19th century by uncovering the "logical radicalism" that characterized the period and that aimed at "a complete overthrow of logic". If this radical movement arose *"because* of Kant's work", it was a conscious revolt against his declaration that the traditional logic was complete. Kant's work on logic was thereby virtually swept into the dustbin of traditional logic – with the exception of his "astoundingly complex and innovative" transcendental logic, the title of which however "seems misleading from the point of view of modern logic" (Käufer 2010: 809).

These remarks suggest how, when assessing Kant's position in the history of logic, scholars tend to focus on the completeness claim and to view past developments through the lens of modern logic – and thereby beg a question that was crucial to Kant and many post-Kantian philosophers alike, namely what counts as *proper logic*. The same remarks also indicate how little the *philosophical* meaning of the completeness claim is understood or even noticed nowadays, independently of whether or how, as a historical fact, it might have delayed or otherwise provoked logical innovations during the decades after its announcement. It is precisely this philosophical meaning that we must decipher, though, before we can determine what responses to the completeness claim are appropriate, illuminating, and so on, or whether the claim is as implausible as it has been depicted. Let us take a closer look, then, at how *Kant* presented the claim in its original context.

The completeness claim pertains only to pure general logic – or "formal logic" as it is often called – defined by preceding (ii) and (iii). This focus on formal logic is evident from Kant's appeal to "the peculiar nature of this science":

> the boundaries of logic, however, are determined quite precisely by the fact that logic is the science that exhaustively presents and strictly proves nothing but the formal rules of all

thinking (whether this thinking be empirical or *a priori*, whatever origin or object it may have, and whatever contingent or natural obstacles it may meet with in our minds).

(Bviii–ix)

If the completeness claim expresses "Kant's disbelief in the possibilities of logic to develop any further from its alleged Aristotelian perfection" (Vilkko 2009: 203), what he denied was more precisely the possibility of logic admitting more *content* than what belongs to pure general logic, that is, all the formal rules of thinking in general. An existing logical theory, such as the Aristotelian one, is complete only insofar as it contains the said content. Meanwhile, this theory may still be imperfect in non-trivial ways. From Kant's standpoint, especially, the logic presented by Aristotle was not yet built upon a firm foundation, without which it still lacked the proper *form* of a strict science and so could not withstand the attacks from its modern critics.[2]

By this analysis, the completeness claim is primarily a philosophical one about logic as such and only derivatively a historical one about the Aristotelian logic in particular. Philosophical rigor demands that Kant be able to establish the possibility of a complete construction of formal logic and explain how the rules of thinking to be included therein can be "demonstrated" from principles *a priori*.[3] After all, "the fact that since the time of Aristotle it has not had to go a single step backwards, [. . .] [and] has also been unable to take a single step forward" (Bviii) would at best indicate – but should not be confused as a genuine argument for – the completeness of formal logic. Nor does Kant appear guilty of any such confusion. The claim is worded carefully: logic since Aristotle "seems to all appearance to be finished and complete [*allem Ansehen nach geschlossen und vollendet zu sein scheint*]" (Bviii). The expression 'scheinen' is appropriate for its context, conveying not a sense of uncertainty about whether logic since Aristotle is actually complete, but an acknowledgement of the need yet to explain this perception of the historical situation of logic – as Kant subsequently does in reference to the unique nature of logic *qua* science.

This approach to the history of logic clearly reflects Kant's conception of "history of philosophy" in general.

A history of philosophy is of such a special kind, that nothing can be told therein of what has happened, without knowing beforehand what should have happened, and also what can happen. Whether this has been investigated beforehand or whether it has been reasoned out haphazardly. For it is the history, not of the opinions which have chanced to arise here or there, but of reason developing itself from concepts.

(*FM* 20: 343)

On this view, a history of philosophy is always constructed and the construction boils down to an inquiry about the possibility "to bring a history into a system of reason, which requires the derivation of the happenings from a principle [*ableitung des Zufälligen aus einem Princip*]" (*FM* 20: 342). Accordingly, to warrant his claim that the history of logic has not exceeded Aristotle's work, Kant needs to find the "principle" in accordance with which the Aristotelian logic – although Aristotle himself might have discovered its content only haphazardly – can be reconstructed and thereby brought into a "system of reason".[4]

We can now separate two kinds of reaction to the completeness claim. One may dispute it as a mere factual claim about the historical happenings involving formal logic, like De Morgan did when he wrote in 1860 that innovations in logic had nudged people toward recognizing that "Kant's dictum about the perfection of the Aristotelian logic may possibly be false" (De Morgan 1966: 247). Alternatively, one may target the notion of formal logic that underlies the claim, a notion that pertains directly to the nature of this purported science and that determines what *can count* as genuine innovations of logic. This kind of response exemplifies an appropriate philosophical engagement with Kant's work on logic. It also captures what is distinctive about the most influential reactions to Kant's theory of logic during the period following the publication of the 1787 edition of the *Critique*, in which text alone was the completeness claim explicitly made and argued.

Such reactions can be traced to one basic concern: given Kant's emphasis on the sheer formality of pure logic and hence on its absolute autonomy in relation to all other sciences, could he ever *prove* it as complete?[5] This concern is essentially about the foundation of formal logic as "science" – in Kant's strict sense of the term, as an apodictically certain and systematically ordered whole of cognition in accordance with *a priori* principles (*MAN* 4: 467–8). That is, to prove a formal logic as complete Kant must identify the grounding *principium* or *principia* from which its content can be systematically derived. As K. L. Reinhold (an early advocate of Kant's Critical philosophy) put it, one can never be certain about the completeness of a logic without deducing it as a system from fundamental principles (*Grundsätze*). In fact, the Critical philosophy as a whole must be grounded in an absolutely first principle, which for Reinhold cannot be a rule of logic but rather a representation of the most basic fact of consciousness. Without being founded ultimately on this principle, Reinhold argued, neither logic nor any other purported science would achieve the status of strict science (Reinhold 1791: 118–21, 137–8).

Reinhold's work made it clear that, if Kant's critique of metaphysics presupposed formal logic, the latter needed a critique as much as metaphysics did, namely an examination of its possibility as proper science. Among the philosophers who promptly followed upon this call for the critique of formal logic, J. G. Fichte would arguably exert the greatest impact with his *Wissenschaftslehre* – to the extent that Jäsche, as we shall see, would feel compelled to address its challenges directly while defending Kant's treatment of formal logic in the *Critique*.

On Fichte's account, "every logical proposition and logic in its entirety must be deduced from the *Wissenschaftslehre*", the latter being a science of the foundation of all knowledge. Without such a deduction, logic would be "no more than a castle in the air" (Fichte 1794a, SW I: 68).[6] In particular, the most basic logical proposition "A = A" must be deduced from the absolute "I am" or self-positing act of the pure I that is the first principle of all knowledge (Fichte 1794a, SW I: 69–70, 1794b, SW I: 98–9). As to why the entire logic must be grounded in the said act, Fichte's argument begins with a general question about the source of the feeling of *necessity* that accompanies certain representations: how can we know whether "postulated laws of thought are really laws of thought"? By Fichte's analysis, neither the empiricist nor the dogmatist could explain why "the intellect must act precisely thus", that is, in accordance with postulated laws. The empiricist would have to abstract the laws from experience, which however could not ground representations of true necessity. The dogmatist would reduce all necessary laws to universal properties of objects, but such reduction would amount to trading one unproven assertion for another and therefore explain nothing. As the only plausible alternative, all necessary laws of thought must be deduced from the intellect construed as pure *act*. The deduction would accord with the Kantian Critical method: it starts with "one and only rationally determined and genuinely explanatory assumption" of the intellect as a law-governed act and, through reflection and abstraction, arrives at representations of the laws of thought as what make the said act possible. The intellect would thereby be shown to stand in a self-legislative relation to those laws: it "gives its laws to itself in the course of its operation" (Fichte 1797, SW I: 440–3).

Although Kant would denounce the *Wissenschaftslehre* as "nothing more or less than mere logic" (*Br* 12: 370), he was in no position to ignore the philosophical issues it was intended to address. By asserting that formal logic presents "the absolutely necessary rules of thinking, without which no use of the understanding takes place" (A52/B76), Kant invited questions similar to the ones raised by Fichte: on what basis can we know any putative logical rules *as necessary laws* of thought? How do we know that the understanding must be used *precisely* in accordance with those laws? Kant could not leave such questions unanswered if he were to make good of his statement that pure general logic is "properly science" (A54/B78), implying that its content – all formal rules of thinking – can be systematically deduced *a priori* from certain grounding principles.

Absent any explicit answer to those questions in the *Critique*, it remains to be seen whether an answer may be found elsewhere or whether Kant at least left enough clues for it to be constructed on his behalf. After all, the early critics of his work on logic only targeted his expressed views in the *Critique* and so might be under-informed in their perception of the work. One may hope, then, to find out more about what Kant had to say about the foundation of logic *qua* science by tapping into the remainder of his logic corpus.

Recall that the *Logik* edited by Jäsche belongs to this logic corpus. It is now commonly treated as the default reference for Kant's theory of logic outside the *Critique*.[7] We must be mindful of the historical backdrop against which the text was compiled, however. It appeared in 1800. By that time, thanks to Reinhold and Fichte among others, it had presumably become a received view that Kant omitted to establish the scientific status of formal logic. Unsurprisingly, then, in the preface to the *Logik* Jäsche gave an apology for Kant regarding the perceived omission and did so with explicit reference to Fichte's attempt at deducing logic from the highest principle of all knowledge. The apology was conciliatory, going roughly as follows. Kant's chief mission (in the *Critique*) was to counter dogmatism and *restrict the valid use* of logical rules. It would indeed be meaningful to ask whether those rules themselves need further deduction from an absolutely first principle – a "highly significant question" that Fichte made a worthwhile effort to address with his *Wissenschaftslehre*. However, a division of labor must be made for "Kant the logician" versus "Kant the transcendental philosopher". If the latter Kant must tackle the transcendental question of *how pure logic is possible as science*, Kant the logician could "continue confidently and certainly to explain and to prove, without permitting himself to worry about the transcendental question", a question to be deferred to its proper place – somewhere other than in the *Critique* (*Log* 9: 6–9).

This one-thing-at-a-time strategy is worth trying. For that purpose, we need to find materials in places besides the *Critique* for expounding a Kantian answer to the question about the possibility of pure logic as science. We cannot know what materials to look for without an antecedently outlined plan, though. Here we may have to proceed under the general assumption that, as Jäsche put it, if Kant was too "occup[ied] with a scientific grounding of the whole system of philosophy proper" to carry out a transcendental critique of formal logic *qua* science, he nevertheless left clues here and there as to how the critique might go generally speaking. The natural place to begin in search of such clues is still the *Critique*, where we may hope to find the "architectonic ideas for a truly purposeful and well-order arrangement and treatment of this science" (*Log* 9: 5). Jäsche saw the *Logik* as the product of a deliberate application of such a procedure, selecting materials from Kant's unpublished notes and lectures on logic in light of how he "would have worked on logic according to *his* architectonic plan" (*Log* 9: 5).

In an experimental spirit and for the sake of initiating an effort to rethink Kant's relation with formal logic, I now follow Jäsche's methodology and sketch how Kant's critique of this logic might proceed – in a way that would address the Fichtean challenges and at the same time further clarify the philosophical underpinnings of his completeness claim.

This critique may begin with an analysis of the nature of logical laws (whatever they may turn out to be). On Kant's account, such laws are universal and necessary, as laws "without which no use of the understanding or of reason takes place at all" (*Log* 9: 13).[8] As such, they must be deduced from *principia a priori* (*V-Lo/Wiener* 24: 791–3). There must then be "a special source of cognition" for them (as there must be one for any strictly universal and necessary laws), the source being "a faculty of *a priori* cognition" (B4). Since logic as science must exhibit systematic unity, the requisite faculty of cognition can only be reason, which alone is "the faculty of the unity of the rules of understanding under principles" (A302/B359). Reason together with the understanding – or the act of thinking that is characteristic of both – is also the object of this cognition. To that extent, logic is the "self-cognition" of reason as regards the laws of its own activity (*Log* 9: 14).[9]

Whence could specific logical laws be cognized as the necessary laws of thought? If, as we saw earlier, to answer this question is partly to account for the consciousness of necessity that accompanies the representations of those laws, Kant would rule out two answers – the empiricist one that tries to derive all cognitions from experience and the nativist one that traces necessary cognitions to inborn representations. Kant would find the former position inconsistent and the latter explanatorily vacuous. In his own view, certain cognitions must be originally acquired *a priori* through as it were the epigenesis of pure reason, an absolutely spontaneous activity of generation (B166–8; *ÜE*-8: 221–2). Although Kant used this notion of "original acquisition" explicitly to account only for the source of pure concepts and pure intuitions, he had reasons to extend it to the pure cognition of logical laws (insofar as they are *represented as* necessary laws of thought). Briefly, the representations of these laws must originate *a priori* through a creative act of reason, because otherwise experience could not ground the consciousness of necessity that accompanies them and reducing them to innate representations would only amount to trading one question for another.[10]

This original creative act of reason presumably consists in reflecting on the mere capacity of thinking, in abstraction from all content of thought, and thereby articulating the laws that constitute the capacity and make the act of thinking possible. Logic *qua* science would be the product of this articulation. By Kant's final analysis, this science can have "no other grounds or sources than the nature of human understanding" (*V-Lo/Blomberg* 24: 25). Thus, if there must be a "principle" from which formal logic must be derived *a priori* as a system, this principle can only be an idea of the nature of human understanding. The derivation would begin with a pure analysis of that idea. The analysis would include, among other things, (i) the specification of thinking as the law-governed act [*Handlung*] or capacity [*Vermögen*] or power [*Kraft*] of the understanding and reason,[11] and (ii) the distinction of three kinds of cognition – concept, judgment, and inference – that must originate, as to form, through such a power.[12] From this analysis specific logical rules are to be deduced as what constitute the necessary, merely formal conditions of the genesis of all possible concepts, judgments and inferences.[13]

Suppose Kant is thus shown to *have* an answer to the question regarding the possibility of formal logic as science, which answer also doubles as the philosophical footing of his claim that the history of logic cannot exceed Aristotle's discovery (insofar as the content of logic is concerned). (Recall his view that a history of logic is only constructed with reference to the idea of what *ought* to be included in it as a possible science.) Moving forward, however, we need to ask: how plausible is the answer? How does it compare with Fichte's account of the foundation and genesis of logic *qua* science? In particular, if Kant was committed to the view that logical laws – represented as the necessary formal conditions of thinking – must be somehow obtained through the epigenetic power of pure reason, would he agree with Fichte that reason is self-legislative in relation to those laws? It is not that Kant's theory of formal logic, once filled out, must be measured against Fichte's. It is rather that, provided Fichte's was a direct, serious, and highly influential *philosophical* engagement with Kant's theory, comparing the two helps to keep us focused on the aspects of the latter that cannot be simply falsified by subsequent historical happenings involving formal logic.

2. Applied Logic – Its Status as "Logic"

On Kant's official account, only pure logic is "properly science" (A54/B78) and hence it alone is logic strictly so called, for the latter must consist in "dogmatic instruction from principles *a priori*, in which one has insight into everything through the understanding without instruction from other quarters attained from experience" (*Log* 9: 14–15).[14] If logic is to be science, applied logic cannot be a part thereof, as it concerns the "contingent and natural laws" regarding "how we think under various hindrances" and so draws on empirical psychology (*V-Lo/Wiener* 24: 791–2).[15] Nonetheless, overall Kant's logic corpus contains more invested treatments of topics in applied logic – viz., prejudice, error, doxastic attitude – than typical formal-logical topics like syllogism.

This appearance is puzzling. Kant's considered view seems to be that topics like prejudice belong more to anthropology and psychology than to logic. Among the things to be expulsed from logic proper, he insists in the *Critique*, are "*psychological* chapters about our different cognitive powers" and "*anthropological* chapters about our prejudice" besides the metaphysical chapters (Bviii). Why, then, should Kant treat topics like prejudice under the title "logic"? Might it not be more appropriate to delegate them to anthropology and psychology, while limiting logic strictly to pure logic? Certainly, Kant based his logic lectures on Meier's *Auszug aus der Vernunftlehre*, where topics like prejudice were discussed in depth.[16] Kant's practice of including similar topics in logic cannot be explained *simply* by that observation, though. Instead, we want to know: might there be some *philosophical* significance to Kant's regarding pure and applied logics as two "part[s]" of logic broadly construed to be "the science of the rules of understanding in general" (A52–3/B76–8), when "science" is taken in a less stringent sense?

In the search for an answer to this question, it is instructive to consider Kant's remarks on logic in his announcement of the program of his lectures for the winter semester 1765–66 ("Announcement"). There Kant characterizes logic in general as a "critique and canon" of the understanding. Assuming the common understanding borders on "crude concepts and ignorance" in one direction and "science and learning" in the other, Kant distinguishes two kinds of logic. The first provides the "quarantine" that one must undergo to "migrate from the land of prejudice and error, and enter the realm of a more enlightened reason and the sciences". Afterwards one can take up the second kind of logic or "the critique and canon of *real learning*", to become reflectively acquainted with the rules governing all forms of sciences in which the understanding is used.[17] This logic, which amounts to the "critique and the canon of the whole of philosophy in its entirety", should be postponed until after one has developed the ability to "draw up a precise ground-plan, on the basis of which an edifice of reason, which is permanent in duration and regular in structure, can be erected". Kant therefore decides to lecture on the first kind of logic and to base the lecture on Meier's *Auszug* for its attention to the cultivation of common understanding as well as that of learned reason, which cultivations serve to prepare one for "the life of action and society" and "the life of contemplation", respectively (*NEV* 2: 310–11).

Note that when he made the "Announcement" (1765) Kant had undertaken an all-important Rousseauian turn, which he described as follows.

> There was a time when I believed that this [acquisition of knowledge] alone could constitute the honor of mankind, and I had contempt for the rabble who know nothing. *Rousseau* brought me around. [. . .] I learned to honor human beings, and I would find myself far more useless than the common laborer if I did not believe that this consideration could impart to all others a value in establishing the rights of humanity.
>
> (*Bem* 20: 44)

In other words, by 1765 Kant had come around to recognize the need for reexamining the ends of reason and to locate the true value of an inquiry in its contribution to humanity – an insight he would reaffirm two decades later in terms of the Baconian call for laying "the foundation of human utility and empowerment" (Bii).

In these terms the two kinds of logic mentioned in the "Announcement", as different as they seem to be, may still be deeply connected: they jointly contribute to "human utility and empower-ment" as the ultimate *end*. This teleological orientation would not be taken away from either kind of logic, of course, if one were to stop calling it "logic". The shared title "logic" is nevertheless sug-gestive: logic in its most general sense may be seen as a two-part "critique and canon" that examines the workings of the human understanding in two ways – one *in abstracto* and the other *in concreto* – with respect to the contingent empirical conditions of the thinking subject. If Kant emphasizes the mutual independence of these two studies, it is because in general he finds it necessary "to *isolate* cognitions that differ from one another in their species and origin" in order to "securely determine the proper value and influence of the advantage that a special kind of cognition has over the aim-less use of the understanding" (A842/B870; see Bviii). Now, pure and applied logics do differ as to origin, being cognition *a priori* versus cognition from experience. Eventually, however, they may be reconnected within the overall system of philosophy in which "the relation of all cognition to the essential ends of human reason" is exhibited (A839/B867).

If there is one *telos* that can connect applied and pure logics in a meaningful way, it is presumably that of ending "infinite errors" (Bii). Error, by Kant's definition, consists in judging to be true what is false.[18] It deviates from how the faculty of judgment ought to be excised and we are fully "culpa-ble" for it, our fault lying in "not [being] cautious enough in venturing a judgment, for which we do not have enough cognition" (*V-Lo/Wiener* 24: 832). It is within our capacity to avoid error, so long as we correctly use our faculty of judgment. A key task of logical inquiry is then to explain the mechanism and catalog the sources of error and to identify norms for the correct use of the faculty of judgment – all in a way that "claims nothing infinite, and nothing beyond what is mortal" (Bii).

Such a task serves to bridge the theory of human understanding *in abstracto* (pure logic) and its study *in concreto* (applied logic).[19] The former tells how the understanding necessarily operates on its own independently of its relation to any other faculty. It expounds the laws that are constitutive of all possible acts of the understanding. Error is impossible when the understanding acts alone: it would be against the nature of the understanding for it to deviate in its act of judging from its own laws. The cause of error must then involve some other force or faculty that can interact with the understanding in such a way as to distract the latter from its proper destination.[20] The job of locating this other force and specifying its role in the genesis of error belongs to applied logic. Combining the two logics, we get a rich picture of *human* understanding that shows, on the one hand, what it is essentially capable of doing and, on the other, how it may nevertheless deviate from its destined path under contingent empirical conditions. If the former sets the normative standard for all uses of the understanding, the latter reminds us that meeting the standard involves conscious efforts to pass judgments only in proportion to our cognition.

On this reading, both pure and applied logics may be organically integrated into Kant's philo-sophical system in a way that speaks to his deepest commitments. To fully flesh out this interpreta-tion, one may have to turn to Kant's notes and lectures on logic. Earlier I pointed out that one could hardly vouch for a reading of Kant's theory of logic simply by citing materials from those texts, and that a methodical selection of such materials would already presuppose an antecedently and independ-ently formed interpretative hypothesis. My conjecture about the final connection between pure and applied logics respected this methodological constraint. It was not derived from an immediate analysis of Kant's notes or lectures on logic, but recommended itself first as a hypothesis informed by his published works. Suppose I have sufficiently motivated the hypothesis by considering Kant's remarks about logic in the "Announcement" and his Rousseauian-Baconian commitment, coupled with the call for a philosophical explanation of his practice of treating both pure and applied logics under "logic". Now it can be put to test: it will advance as a worthy hypothesis if, say, it offers a perspective from which to organize the contents of Kant's notes and lectures on logic in a way that is coherent, thorough, and illuminating.[21]

In sum, this chapter began by clearing the way for a proper philosophical assessment of Kant's work on logic. I rejected a stereotypical portrayal of his relation to the traditional logic that was based on a simplistic reading of his completeness claim about the history of logic. I distinguish two types of reaction to this claim, depending on whether it is treated as a mere factual claim about contingent historical events or as primarily a philosophical claim about the nature of (formal) logic. The latter alone should be the target of any serious philosophical engagement with Kant's theory of logic.

Meanwhile, my discussions were also meant to encourage a total reexamination of Kant's work on logic – partly by connecting it organically with other parts of his philosophy. This call for reexamination follows upon a recent trend among Kant scholars to take his applied logic more seriously than ever before – and justifiably so. My reflection on the status of "applied logic" in a way supplements those scholars' work, by asking how it might fit in Kant's overall philosophical system in the first place. But it also serves as a reminder that, as tempting as it is to reap all the potential riches from the applied portion of Kant's logic corpus without hesitation, we should still mind the philological problems affecting much of the corpus and approach it in a methodologically disciplined and philosophically savvy way.

Notes

1 See Lu-Adler (2015).
2 See Capozzi and Roncaglia (2009).
3 *V-Lo/Wiener* (24: 793); *V-Lo/Dohna* (24: 694); *V-Lo/Pölitz* (24: 505–6); *Log* (9: 14–15).
4 Kant regards Aristotle's categories similarly: while Aristotle merely "stumbled on" the categories, Kant's catalogue of them "is systematically generated from a common principle [. . .] and has not arisen rhapsodically from a haphazard search for pure concepts, of the completeness of which one could never be certain" (A80–1/B106–7).
5 On Kant's theory of logical formality, its originality, and its reception during the 19th century, see McFarlane (2000) and Heis (2012).
6 In citing Fichte, I follow the standard practice of using the pagination from the relevant volume of *Johann Gottlieb Fichtes sämmtliche Werke* (SW) (edited by I. H. Fichte, Berlin: Veit, 1845–46).
7 In a letter dated May 29, 1801, Kant rejected the suggestion that the *Logik* was issued without his authorization (*Br* 12: 372). The tone of the letter was noticeably reactionary, though. To my knowledge, there is no evidence that Kant read the *Logik* closely if at all. There is no record of him commenting on any specific part of the text.
8 Also: A52/B76; *Refl* (1628 16: 44); *V-Lo/Dohna* (24: 694); *V-Lo/Pölitz* (24: 503); *V-Lo/Hechsel* (LV 2: 273).
9 Also: *V-Lo/Wiener* (24: 792); *V-Lo/Dohna* (24: 697); *V-Lo/Blomberg* (24: 24–5).
10 See Lu-Adler (2018).
11 *Log* (9: 11); *V-Lo/Philippi* (24: 311); *V-Lo/Pölitz* (24: 502); *V-Lo/Busolt* (24: 608); *V-Lo/Dohna* (24: 693); *V-Lo/Wiener* (24: 790); *V-Lo/Bauch* (LV 1: 3–6); *V-Lo/Hechsel* (LV 2: 271–72); *V-Lo/Warschauer* (LV 2: 505).
12 *V-Lo/Wiener* (24: 904); *V-Lo/Pölitz* (24: 565); *V-Lo/Busolt* (24: 653); *V-Lo/Hechsel* (LV 2: 389).
13 See Lu-Adler (2015).
14 Also: *V-Lo/Wiener* (24: 793); *V-Lo/Blomberg* (24: 13, 25); *V-Lo/Dohna* (24: 694); *V-Lo/Pölitz* (24: 505–6). On "dogmatic" (versus "historical" and "mathematical") cognition, see *V-Lo/Dohna* (24: 697, 724); *V-Lo/*

Wiener (24: 797–98, 830–31). Generally, Kant argues, "science must always be dogmatic" in that "it must prove its conclusions strictly *a priori* from secure principles" (Bxxxv).

15 On necessary versus contingent laws of thinking, see *V-Lo/Dohna* (24: 693); *Log* (9: 12–3); *Refl* (1620 16: 40; 1628 16: 44; 1603 16: 33). Relatedly, Kant argues that only *logica artificialis* (not *logica naturalis*) can be properly called "logic" (*V-Lo/Wiener* 24: 791; *Refl* 1579 16: 18).

16 See Pozzo (2005).

17 Kant will continue to distinguish "a *logica* of the common understanding and of healthy reason and a *logica* of learnedness" (*V-Lo/Blomberg* 24: 17–8). The first logic becomes "applied logic" in the *Critique*, described at one point as "merely a cathartic of the common understanding". The second logic bifurcates into "organon[s] of this or that science", which pertain to the particular use of the understanding, and the "canon of the understanding in general" (pure logic) serving as the "propaedeutic" to all particular sciences (A52–3/B76–8).

18 *V-Lo/Wiener* (24: 832); *V-Lo/Blomberg* (24: 105); *V-Lo/Dohna* (24: 720); *Log* (9: 53).

19 "Understanding" is here taken in the broad sense as "the faculty of cognition of rules [. . .] in general", which contrasts with sensibility and includes three powers – reason, the understanding narrowly construed (A51–2/B75–6), and the power of judgment (*Anth* 7: 196–97).

20 *V-Lo/Blomberg* (24: 102); *V-Lo/Wiener* (24: 824–25); *V-Lo/Dohna* (24: 720); *Log* (9: 53–4).

21 As a programmatic suggestion, one may try to structure Kant's applied logic around the topic of error. If the basic mechanism of error can be described in terms of a general account of different cognitive faculties (viz., sensibility besides the understanding), the identification of specific causes of error – for the sake of finding effective remedies – hinges on a thorough analysis of various kinds of prejudice, degrees of certainty, and so on.

References

Capozzi, M. and Roncaglia, G. (2009) "Logic and Philosophy of Logic from Humanism to Kant," in L. Haaparanta (ed.), *The Development of Modern Logic*, Oxford: Oxford University Press, pp. 78–158.

De Morgan, A. (1966 [1860]) "Logic," in P. Heath (trans. and ed.), *On the Syllogism and Other Logical Writings*, New Haven: Yale University Press, pp. 247–70.

Fichte, J.G. (1988 [1794a]) *Über den Begriff der Wissenschaftslehre*. Translated as "Concerning the Concept of the *Wissenschaftslehre*," in D. Breazeale (trans.), *Fichte: Early Philosophical Writings*, Ithaca: Cornell University Press, pp. 94–135.

Fichte, J.G. (1982 [1794b]) *Grundlage der Gesamten Wissenschaftslehre*. Translated as "Foundations of the Entire Science of Knowledge," in P. Heath (trans.), *J.G. Fichte: Science of Knowledge*, Cambridge: Cambridge University Press, pp. 87–286.

Fichte, J.G. (1797) *Erste Einleitung in die Wissenschaftslehre*. Translated as "First Introduction to the Science of Knowledge," in P. Heath (trans.), *J.G. Fichte: Science of Knowledge*, Cambridge: Cambridge University Press, pp. 3–28.

Heis, J. (2012) "Attempts to Rethink Logic," in A. Wood and S. Hahn (eds.), *The Cambridge History of Philosophy in the Nineteenth Century (1790–1870)*, Cambridge: Cambridge University Press, pp. 95–132.

Käufer, S. (2010) "Post-Kantian Logical Radicalism," in D. Moyar (ed.), *The Routledge Companion to Nineteenth Century Philosophy*, London: Routledge, pp. 809–36.

Lu-Adler, H. (2015) "Constructing a Demonstration of Logical Rules, or How to Use Kant's Logic Corpus," in R. Clewis (ed.), *Reading Kant's Lectures*, Berlin: Walter de Gruyter, pp. 136–58.

Lu-Adler, H. (2018) "Epigenesis of Pure Reason and the Source of Pure Cognitions: How Kant Is No Nativist About Logical Cognition," in P. Muchnik and O. Thorndike (eds.), *Rethinking Kant*, vol. 5, Newcatsle: Cambridge Scholarly Publishing, pp. 35–70.

McFarlane, J. (2000) *What Does It Mean to Say That Logic Is Formal?* PhD dissertation, Pittsburgh: University of Pittsburgh.

Pozzo, R. (2005) "Prejudices and Horizons: G.F. Meier's Vernunftlehre and Its Relation to Kant," *Journal of History of Philosophy* 43(2): 185–202.

Reinhold, K.L. (1791) *Über das Fundament des philosophischen Wissens*, Jena: Johann Michael Mauke.

Vilkko, R. (2009) "The Logic Question During the First Half of the Nineteenth Century," in *The Development of Modern Logic*, Oxford: Oxford University Press, pp. 203–21.

Further reading

H. Lu-Adler, *Kant and the Science of Logic* (Oxford: Oxford University Press, 2018), chs. 1, 5, further develop the main interpretative claims of this chapter. T. Nunez, "Logical Mistakes, Logical Aliens, and the Laws of Kant's Pure General Logic," *Mind* 128 (2018): 1149–80; C. Tolley, "Kant and the Nature of Logical Laws," *Philosophical Topics* 34 (2006): 371–407 offer accounts of Kant's logic that contrast well with the account presented in this chapter.

35

MATHEMATICS

Frode Kjosavik

★★★

None of Kant's works is devoted to philosophy of mathematics in its own right, but his conception of mathematics forms an integral part of his philosophy. Mathematics was a rational science already in antiquity and could perhaps serve as a model for what is achievable by reason (cf. B-Introduction).[1] Furthermore, if mathematics is not analytic, as the rationalists would have it, but synthetic, then its procedure of establishing connections between concepts by extra-conceptual yet non-empirical means might be a clue as to how metaphysics – being concerned with the fundamental principles of cognition – can be set on "the secure course of a science" as well. Still, mathematics and philosophy differ over the status of definitions, propositions, method and evidence,[2] as is clear from the section of the Doctrine of Method in CPR entitled "The discipline of pure reason in dogmatic use" (B740–66). Kant there presents the core of his mature position, that is, that mathematics is based on construction of concepts in pure intuition. The importance ascribed to intuition has been subject to much discussion among commentators. The present account is an attempt to bring the various roles of intuition together with other aspects of Kant's position – and with a view to subsequent developments in mathematics. It is organized in accordance with the tripartite division of the Method section into (1) real definitions, (2) axioms and (3) demonstrations.

1. Concepts and the Link to Intuition

Diagrams in Euclid's *Elements* are sometimes dismissed as a mere aid to the proofs, called for only because of its incomplete axiomatization of geometry. More careful historical studies have suggested an essential role for diagrams as constitutive parts of the proofs.[3] Either way, it will here be argued that Kant does not merely take ancient tradition or contemporary mathematical practice for granted. There are deep reasons why intuition is indispensable. Indeed, both geometry and arithmetic depend on intuition for the very representation of their subject matter, as we shall see.

It is only in mathematics that there are real definitions (cf. B757).[4] That is so because mathematical objects are given through their definitions and not independently of these. The definition of a circle is that it is a curve in the plane which contains all points that are equidistant from a given point. Through this definition, a concept is generated, and an object, in the sense of what falls under

DOI: 10.4324/9781003406617-47

428

a mathematical concept, or a class thereof, is given (cf. B287). One thinks the object through the concept only by exhibiting it a priori in intuition. There is thus a procedure for generating *images* for the concept. The representation of this procedure is the *schema* (cf. B179). The concept cannot be divorced from its schema, which brings an image to mind:

> We cannot think of a line without *drawing* it in thought, we cannot think of a circle without *describing* it, we cannot represent the three dimensions of space at all without *placing* three lines perpendicular to each other at the same point.
>
> (B154)

Due to the intimacy between concept and image, roundness can be *intuited* in the geometrical *concept* of a circle (cf. B176). There can be no real definition of a circle that does not also introduce a schema for its concept. The definition is a genetic one, that is, it "contains" the "figurative synthesis," or *original* construction, that consists in rotating a line segment around a fixed point. However, even though a schema is "contained in" the concept of a circle, it is not analytically contained in it like a discursive mark. Rather, the schema represents a procedure of imagination which underlies a synthetic extension of what is thought through the discursive marks of the concept.

What emerges from this simple case of cognizing a circle, then, is a *triad* of concept – schema – image, rather than a dichotomy between concept and intuition. Each member of the triad has functional roles. Thus, concepts enter into judgments, whereas schemata and images do not. Concepts and schemata can represent a complexity that images cannot, like that of an n-sided figure for a large n. Hence, in the *Streitschrift* (1790) against the neo-Leibnizan Johann Eberhard, Kant maintains that he has more resources at his disposal than the rationalists will grant him. A geometrical object is given in intuition and for the use in imagination thanks to conceptual and schematic construction rules rather than images (cf. *ÜE* 8: 211–12). In a letter to K. L. Reinhold (May 19, 1789, *Br* 11: 40–8), Kant emphasizes "the possibility of exhibiting the concept of a chiliagon in intuition" independently of the "degree" – "the power of the imagination to grasp the manifold" (*Br* 11: 46). The conceptual rule for construction here also has the distinct functional role of mixing constructions that are schematically different in kind, that is, the arithmetical one for n and the geometrical one for a straight line, in the concept of an n-sided figure.

While geometrical concepts can represent complexity of a high degree, those of a straight line and of a circle remain fundamental. The first three *postulates* of Euclid's *Elements* are precisely about these fundamental concepts, or their construction through idealized straightedge and compass operations. The real definition of a circle becomes itself the means of construction, and Euclid's Postulate 3 follows from it as a practical corollary:

> The proposition "to describe a circle" is a practical corollary of the definition (or so-called postulate), which could not be demanded at all if the possibility – yes, the very sort of possibility of the figure – were not already given in the definition.
>
> (Letter to Herz, May 26, 1789, *Br* 11: 53)[5]

A postulate is thus "a principle that determines a possible action, in the case of which it is presupposed that the way of executing it is immediately certain" (*Log* 9: 112).

Kant is of course aware of more abstract ways of conceiving of a circle, for example, as a "limit" to a sequence of regular polygons with 2^n sides, $n \to \infty$ (cf. *Refl* 2, 14: 6). But a real definition has to come with a recipe for the construction of the object, that is, with a schema, whereas definition through a limit process does not. As Bolzano – and later Weierstrass – discovered, there are "curves" which are only available through limit processes – they cannot be constructed through a figurative synthesis. They would therefore not be genuine geometrical figures according to Kant's account. But the fact that a sequence of intuitable curves can be without an intuitable limit need not lead to a "crisis of intuition."[6] We learn nothing from mere images, anyway, independently of concepts and schemata that underlie the images. Furthermore, Kant certainly acknowledges that the "analytic method" in geometry, which relies on abstract equations, is "rich in inventions" (*ÜE* 8: 192), though he also sees an essential role for "synthetic geometry," including Apollonius's theory of conic sections, in securing intuitive foundations for it.

Still, even Euclidean concepts have geometrical content that relies on metaphysical concepts, like that of space itself, which is not constructible. Indeed, according to Kant's critical thought, the "real essence of space and time and the reason why the former has three dimensions, the latter only one, are unknowable" (Letter to Reinhold, May 12, 1789, *Br* 11: 37). Limitations of definitions are anticipated in *Inquiry*, the Prize Essay of 1764, which contains an elaborate comparison between mathematics and metaphysics. There, Kant mentions examples of basic concepts that are at least not analyzable within mathematics: that of "magnitude in general ['Grösse'], of unity, of plurality ['Menge'], of space, and so on" (*UD* 2: 279–80).

A *definable* concept, by contrast, "contains" an *arbitrary* synthesis, that is, it comes with an invented schema for producing pure images. The arbitrariness is not that of a mere contradiction-free conjoining of discursive marks. If so, there could be a *mathematical* definition even of a biangle, that is, of a two-sided plane figure. After all, there is nothing contradictory in its concept (cf. B268), as there would be for Leibniz. For there to be a representation of a possible figurative synthesis, something has to be wholly thought through the concept, and not just partially, mark by mark. Only in that way can there be a construction that can in principle be fully executed and exhibited. This is an extra check that is put on a concept that is to be mathematically, and not just "logically," possible. The concept of a biangle contradicts the axiom 'two straight lines do not enclose a space' (cf. B204), as well as the uniqueness claim built into Euclid's Postulate 1 (cf. Section 2), so it is mathematically impossible.

There could of course be a spherical "biangle." A special geometry of figures on the surface of a sphere in no way challenges the status Kant ascribed to Euclidean geometry. He even makes a reference to spherical figures, including triangular ones, in *Prolegomena* (*Prol* 4: 285). The defense of the logical consistency of the concept of a biangle is not related to this. If there were a curved space that could not be "fitted into" a Euclidean 3-space, on the other hand, that would indeed pose a challenge, that is, a geometrical space that could not be generated and contained within metaphysical space as it is given to us. A possible Kantian way out arguably lies in mere symbolization of alternative geometries as well as in Euclidean modelling thereof. I shall go into "ostensive" and "symbolic" forms of construction in Section 3.

The claim that concepts come with schemata and definitions with constructions is not limited to synthetic geometry but applies to more abstract mathematical disciplines as well. Thus, arithmetic deals with "the synthesis of that which is homogeneous (of units)" (B205). As a synthesis of *units*, it is discrete. Number is *identified with* the schema of magnitude [*quantitatis*], which "summarizes the successive addition of one (homogeneous) unit to another" (B182). There is a schema for number in general (cf. B179), and it must be this which turns each particular number *n* into a schema for counting over finitely many steps. Since numbers are *identified with* schemata, the numerical concepts would seem to be entirely parasitic on their schemata, which deliver real genetic definitions of the objects in question. As in geometry, there is a distinct domain of objects, then. After all, arithmetic is concerned not only with quantity as such but with determinate quantities, or "quanta" that are more abstract than those of geometry. It is just that the quantities of arithmetic are not identical to numbers, in the genuine, schematic sense of "number," even if numbers may be the canonical route to them.

Furthermore, just as there are images for geometrical concepts, there are images for arithmetical ones. "Thus, if I place five points in a row, • • • • •, this is an image of the number five" (B179). The image should not be construed as merely spatial but rather as a sequence of temporal steps, each of which consists in the placement of a spatial mark. In addition to the counting synthesis, unit by unit, of which time is the form, there are other syntheses corresponding to arithmetical operations, including syntheses of addition and multiplication. Such syntheses are also built into any position system, like the decadic or tetradic one (cf. B104; *KU* 5: 254). There must be a general schema for, for example, adding numbers as well as images of additions of particular numbers. Kant's account of adding 5 to 7 (B15–16) is precisely of an *image* for the concept of 7, itself already formed, to which "I now add the units," that is, 5 units. With an image for the concept of this operation, an image for the concept of 12 is also formed in the process: I "see the number 12 arise" (B16). Segner, to whom Kant makes a reference, uses dots to create images for arithmetic in a similar way. Properties can be grasped, then, only on the basis of how these images have been generated in accordance with discursive rules. A position system makes it easy to keep track of how the complex symbols are composed, but a unary and more image-like notation would work well for small operational steps on small quantities.

Since there are real genetic definitions, one should expect there to be postulates as practical corollaries thereof in arithmetic as well. Kant does not bring up this topic in *KrV*, but in his correspondence with Schultz arithmetic is said to have postulates, or immediately certain practical judgments. '3 + 4 = 7' is given as an example, when taken as a prescription, or "subjectively," that is, 'to add 4 to 3 so as to find 7' (cf. Letter to Schultz, November 25, 1788, *Br* 10: 556). However, it is a theoretical judgment when taken "objectively," in terms of two equivalent ways of determining the same quantity.

> Thus I can arrive at a single determination of a quantity by means of $3 + 5$, or $12 - 4$, or 2×4, or 2^3, namely 8. But my thought '$3 + 5$' did not include the thought '2×4.' Just as little did it include the concept '8,' which is equal in value to any of these.
>
> (*Br* 10: 555)

What is "thought" in these cases is actually a synthesis of productive imagination – be it of addition, of subtraction, of multiplication, and so on, or the primary one of mere counting that is represented through a particular number schema. The concept '8' is no more contained in the concept '$3 + 5$' than is the concept '2^3.' "Objectively" they are all determinations of the same quantity, whereas "subjectively," what is prescribed in each case relies on the form of the synthesis, for example, that of counting, of addition, of exponentiation and so on.

The postulates for arithmetic that Kant has in mind could also be general principles rather than specific judgments. After all, it is practical corollaries of the *fundamental* concepts of a straight line and a circle that are considered to be postulates in Euclidean geometry. Taking only the schemata for arithmetical operations in general as fundamental, one might put forth general postulates, as does Schultz for "quanta" of the appropriate kind, in his *Prüfung*: "From several given homogenous quanta, to generate the concept of one quantum *through their successive connection* i.e., to transform them into *one whole*" (1789: 221).

Concepts of negative quantities and of rational quantities generally can similarly be formed from determinate syntheses. That is not so with irrational quantities, however, like $\sqrt{2}$, which cannot be conceived of as a determinate ratio to a unit but only by way of a potentially infinite sequence of rational approximations. (Cf. Kant's letter to Rehberg, dated some time before September 25, 1790, *Br* 11: 207–10; cf. also *Refl* 13–14, 14: 53–9.) There is therefore no "complete numerical concept" of it. Within geometry, a circle can be thought both through its real genetic definition and as a "limit" to a sequence of polygons, as noted earlier. In arithmetic, there can in effect only be a "limit" notion of an irrational quantity. Kant does remark, however, that the concept of $\sqrt{2}$ can be constructed by way of the diagonal of a square, which does suggest that there is indeed an alternative to the limit notion – albeit for Kant notably only by means of geometrization.

2. Axioms and Intuitive Evidence

In addition to real definitions, geometry also has axioms. These are not self-evident to thought, like analytic principles, but they are still cognized with apodictic certainty, insofar as Kantian non-rational, sensible intuition is invoked to exhibit spatial objects and operations. Axioms are said to be principles [*Grundsätze*] which are synthetic a priori and immediately certain (B760). As such, they "can be exhibited in intuition" (*Log* 9: 110), unlike discursive principles. As synthetic, they also contrast with analytic principles, like "the whole is greater than its [proper] part" (cf. B16–17) or "equals added to or subtracted from equals give an equal" (cf. B204–5). Such analytic principles may play an important role in mathematics, but only in so far as they can be represented by symbols, for example, "(a+b) > a" (B17). Symbolization is not essential to them, though. Moreover, there is symbolization even in formal logic, which remains analytic, that is, the logical forms are fixed by rational thought rather than constrained by constructibility conditions.[7]

The analytic principles mentioned here are among the five "common notions" in Euclid, which are self-evident and indemonstrable, and which were taken as "axioms" in the Aristotelian sense. In so far as they are concerned with equivalence and with the part-whole relation generally, they came to be regarded as valid for all the mathematical sciences. An "axiom" for Kant, on the other hand, is a synthetic principle that can be established through a construction in pure intuition, or through variation over such constructions, without additional inferential steps. It is immediately certain, but it could be a mathematical theorem and available mediately, through other synthetic principles. The triangle inequality – that two sides together are greater than the third – seems to be a case in point, in so far as it is accorded the same status as an axiom (cf. B39; B205). This is a theorem within Euclidean geometry, but it can also be established more directly in intuition by appropriate variation, say, over the generic cases of acute, right and obtuse triangles.

The five "postulates" in Euclid, P1-P5, arguably correspond to both postulates and axioms in Kant's sense. In their original formulation, P1 and P2 concern the possibility of drawing straight line segments and extending them indefinitely, respectively, whereas P3 concerns the possibility of drawing circles. P1-P3 are thus prescriptions for how to construct by way of translations and rotations. As such, they are postulates. But one can also turn them into theoretical propositions about properties of space, or of geometrical objects contained in space. As such, they become axioms. Thus, for example, P1, the postulate 'to draw a straight line from any point to any other,' becomes the axiom 'there can be one and only one straight line between two given points.' P4 and P5, stating the equality of right angles and the existence of unique parallels, respectively, involve relations between geometrical figures, that is, between line segments or their indefinite extensions. In the way they are formulated by Euclid, they are not prescriptions for constructions. Unlike the axioms in Euclid – the "common notions" – they do relate to geometrical constructs specifically, though, and not to magnitudes in general. Taken as axioms in Kant's sense, P4 and P5 can be understood as stating the strict homogeneity of Euclidean space, both with regard to position, direction and scale.

By subscribing to an axiomatic conception of geometry, Kant distanced himself from the view that it is analytic, as Leibniz, Wolff and Eberhard maintained. If it were analytic, a *reductio ad absurdum* proof could be given for it, that is, it would be contradictory to reject one or more of the axioms. Kant would not have objected to this method of proof as such. In mathematics, such "apagogic" proofs come with evidence of their own and are accepted as an alternative to "ostensive" proofs (B817–20). However, in searching for apagogic proofs of Euclidean geometry, the great mathematician Lambert, with whom Kant corresponded, hit upon "models," and thereby "ostensive" evidence of sorts, for alternative geometries. Still, this possibility is remote to Kant.[8] After all, he does not consider axioms as *foundational*, that is, as a mere base for inferring theorems, nor as *formal*, that is, as robbed of all intuitive content. Rather, their content is self-justifying within mathematics – their truth is established through a construction in pure intuition alone.

For this to be the case, Kant holds that we ultimately have to be acquainted with metaphysical space through pure intuition, even if we lack insight into why space is the way it is. In the Fourth Argument of the Metaphysical Exposition, space is said to be represented as an infinite given magnitude. Similarly, in his notes for Schultz's Kästner review, which was part of the dispute with Eberhard, a distinction is drawn between an infinite metaphysical space that is "given" and finite geometrical spaces that are "made."[9] It is metaphysical space which grounds the construction of geometrical concepts (cf. *ZREM* 20: 420–1), in particular that of a line segment that is successively extended, and not axioms as foundational principles. This accords well with the claims of the Transcendental Exposition to the effect that forms of intuition, or metaphysical concepts thereof, are themselves "principles" to which we have epistemic access and which make mathematics possible as a science.

This also brings together two roles for pure intuition in mathematics. Firstly, it is a *source of properties* which are thereby *given* to us, and not just abstractly conceived. That includes properties of metaphysical space, or of geometrical objects contained therein. It also includes properties of metaphysical time that space cannot possess as such, like that of being a linear order, which can only be arbitrarily introduced in some determinate direction or other in space. Secondly, pure intuition is also *a medium for construction*, enabling and constraining what we generate in mathematics. The scene that is thereby set for construction can be space in geometry, space and time in kinematics, but it could also be time alone, as in arithmetic and algebra – even if the signs are themselves spatial, just as the constructions in geometry are themselves temporal. To be sure, algebra as such is more abstract than arithmetic, but with quantitative determinations substituted for the letters, it can turn into "general arithmetic," as Kant dubs it in the letter to Schultz (quoted in Section 1), ranging over all quantities, be they rational or irrational. In his reply to Rehberg's objections, Kant claims that even in the latter case a temporal scene of construction is required. I shall go into this second role for pure intuition in geometry and arithmetic in the next section.

Kant sees no room for axioms in arithmetic (cf. B205; cf. again the letter to Schultz). Superficially, geometry contrasts with arithmetic because there are universal principles in the former and only singular ones, that is, "numerical formulae," in the latter. There are theorems in higher arithmetic which are general and concern properties of integers, but these are not expressible within ordinary arithmetic dealing in counting and calculations. Schultz, Kant's most trusted expositor, took the laws of commutativity and associativity for addition as the two axioms of arithmetic in his own work (cf. Schultz 1789: 219). But while Schultz accepts equations with letter symbols as part of ordinary [*gemeine*] arithmetic, these laws are not expressible in arithmetic as Kant conceives of it – only their instances are – and there is no evidence that Kant envisaged an axiomatic basis for arithmetic, contrary to Gottfried Martin's famous thesis.[10] Additionally, as Frege also observed, a particular integer cannot be a representative of all integers in the manner in which, say, a particular triangle can play a generic role and represent all triangles in a geometrical proof.[11] There is no generality to the individuals in arithmetic, except for their universal use, as Kant points out (cf. again B205).

At a deeper level, the main difference is that arithmetic is not about time, in the way geometry is about space. Arithmetic does not rely on an axiomatic characterization of an extra-conceptual given. In Brouwer's intuitionism, temporal intuition of "two-oneness" was still the source of natural numbers.[12] In Kant, it is not even that, but merely the source of the linear order property and the medium for construction of numerical concepts. Time has no beginning or discrete units as such, which are both required in representing an initial element and successive repetition, or a sequence of rational approximations, as in ordinary and "general" arithmetic, respectively. Apparently, such a progression is already contained in number as a schema for quantity, which gives rise to a potentially infinite sequence of particular numbers. There is no geometrical schema that similarly contains the structure of space. For each number, there are temporal images which can serve as templates for determining the size of multiplicities. Even numbers as thus conceived are not objects in their own right, unlike geometrical figures. Rather, theoretical judgments of arithmetic are singular formulae that identify determinations, or forms of synthesis, of one and the same quantity, as we saw in Section 1. A particular "number," in the sense of a schema, only represents one such determination.

3. Proofs in the Medium of Pure Intuition

Kant distinguishes between two forms of construction in mathematics – *ostensive* or *geometrical* vs. *symbolic* or *characteristic*. An ostensive construction of a geometrical figure, or of its concept, presents an object of that kind, or under that concept, for example, a circle with a determinate radius. A symbolic construction of a concept within arithmetic or algebra, by contrast, does not. However, all constructions are arguably ostensive in the sense that they *exhibit operations* in intuition.[13] With regard to Euclidean geometry, the operations are ultimately those of translation and rotation. With regard to arithmetic and algebra, a symbolic construction "exhibits all the procedures through which magnitude is generated and altered in accordance with certain rules in intuition" (B745). Furthermore,

> the mathematician cannot make the smallest assertion about any object whatsoever without exhibiting it (or, if we are considering only quantities without qualities, as in algebra, exhibiting quantitative relationships for which the symbols stand) in intuition.
>
> (Letter to Reinhold, May 19, 1789, *Br* 11: 42)

The difference in properly ostensive constructions is that *objects* falling under constructible concepts are also exhibited in intuition, that is, quanta with qualities. In arithmetic, it is at most numerals that are exhibited as objects, not quantities. Even with later developments – like the famous Hilbert strokes in finitary mathematics, which are numerals that model themselves – abstract quantities are not made quasi-geometrical, or amenable to exhibition in spatial or temporal intuition as such.

The central passage on ostensive construction of geometrical concepts is the following.

> I construct a triangle by exhibiting an object [*Gegenstand*] corresponding to this concept, either through mere imagination, in pure intuition, or, in accordance with that one [*derselben*], also on paper, in empirical intuition, but in both cases completely *a priori*, without having had to borrow the pattern for it from any experience.
>
> (B741, my translation)[14]

An ostensive construction always takes place in *pure* intuition. After all, it is a construction in space, which is given through pure intuition. Thus, the construction in empirical intuition is said to be in accordance with *mere* imagination or *pure* intuition, since it is itself a construction in pure space as well. A pure intuition need not occur in isolation from empirical intuition but can be reached from an empirical spatial cognition by removing any contributions from the understanding and from sensation (cf. B35).

In such ostensive constructions, an *object* [*Gegenstand*] is exhibited. Kant's general characterization of construction is "to *construct* a concept means to exhibit *a priori* the intuition corresponding to it" (B741). He thus speaks both of exhibition *in* and *of* intuition. A way to reconcile these two statements is to take the exhibition *of* a "corresponding intuition" to be itself a pure (partial or complete) spatial image of a geometrical figure, or a pure (partial or complete) image of temporal steps – in ordinary and "general" arithmetic. The construction is still *in* pure intuition, then, since pure images can only be *in* pure space or time, as scenes for construction.

The distinction between two *modes* of constructing a concept a priori – in mere pure intuition or also in empirical intuition – must not be confused with the distinction in the *Streitschrift* between two *kinds* of construction, namely, those that are pure or "schematic" and those that are empirical, or "technical" (Cf. *ÜE* 8: 191–2). The latter – which are called "mechanical" in *KrV* (B749) – are carried out on some material with actual instruments, for example, with a straightedge and a compass in applications of elementary geometry, or with more complex machines in applications of higher geometry. Measurements of lengths, angles and so on, can then be made on the technical construct. These activities belong to "art," or practical technique, not to a theoretical science concerned with insight into principles.

In the First Introduction to *KU*, Kant emphasizes that what is utilized in geometrical construction a priori are

> not the actual tools (*circinus et regula*), which can never give those shapes with mathematical precision. Rather, they are to signify only the simplest kinds of exhibition of the imagination *a priori*, which cannot be matched by any instrument.
>
> (*EEKU* 20: 198)

A technical construction, on the other hand, is a posteriori, and exactness is a major concern (cf. B746). To be sure, a technical construction may be intertwined with a schematic one that is guiding it, but as long as the focus is not on ideal operations, like those of translation and rotation as such, it does not belong to geometry as a pure science.

This leads us to two forms of "abstraction" that may be contained in an ostensive construction of a geometrical concept. Firstly, there may be idealization from a vague, inexact shape to a sharp, exact shape. Kant speaks explicitly of figures which are "empirical" (B741–2). These cannot be identified with "pure shapes in space" (B180). The token-type distinction is thereby effectively drawn. While this contrast is highlighted through the difference between technical and schematic construction, in that even carefully crafted tokens cannot replace exact types, it is certainly implied also in core passages in *KrV* on the method in mathematics. In the *Streitschrift* (*ÜE* 8: 191n), in playing down the significance that Eberhard ascribes to the senses in a Kantian conception of mathematics, Kant speaks of how propositions can be proved by the geometer on an irregular circle drawn in the sand. Similarly, in the letter to Herz quoted in Section 1, it is said that all properties can be demonstrated on a circle drawn "free hand" just as well as on one that is "drawn by rotating a straight line attached to a point" (*Br* 11: 53).

Secondly, there may be generalization from a determinate figure, like a circle with a particular radius, to a class of figures of which the former is merely a representative, like the class of all circles.

What is taken into account – to turn to the example in *KrV* of constructing a triangle – is not merely a particular instance but

> the action of constructing the concept, to which many determinations, e.g., those of the magnitude of the sides and the angles, are entirely indifferent, and thus we have abstracted from these differences.
>
> (B742)

The two-fold abstraction can advance beyond this minimum, however, in that ostensive construction can involve geometrical properties which are not exemplified as such and of which it is therefore merely *symbolic*. Admittedly, this idea is not much developed, but there are very suggestive remarks in *Inquiry*. The infinite divisibility of space can be demonstrated "[b]y means of this symbol [. . .]," that is, a construction with a "straight line standing vertically between two parallel lines [. . .]," where lines are drawn from one of the two parallels "to intersect the other two lines," and so on (*UD* 2: 279). In the proof, which is given more completely and with a concrete illustration in the *Physical Monadology*, finite line segments are arguably themselves symbolic of lines that are "indefinitely extended" (*MoPh* 1: 478). Even properties that can be instantiated, like circularity or triangularity, are only exhibited through a finite selection of instances. Hence, a geometrical construction is in that sense always "symbolic" of properties, albeit of course in an ideographical rather than strictly conventional manner. Although Kant is not explicit on this, an ostensive construction could not be a construction *of a general concept* if this were not the case.[15]

In addition to constructibility in pure intuition, Kant is very much concerned with the applicability of geometry, and of mathematics generally, to portions of matter. In that respect, "even the possibility of mathematics must be shown in transcendental philosophy" (B761). The metaphysical concept of space requires a "transcendental deduction" (cf. B119–21), as does the principle of the axioms of intuition, namely, in the Analytic of *KrV*, where space is brought together with the three categories of quantity, and thereby with measurement of extensive magnitudes. It is ideal shapes, then, and ultimately axioms of intuition, that underlie shape determinations of physical things, like a round plate, and the measurement of their extension. A plate that appears to be circular will under closer inspection turn out not to be exactly so. A formula from geometry can be true only of a pure figure that is schematically constructible. Circles as pure figures are not to be eliminated by turning them into contours of round things that are given to us in empirical intuition.

Accordingly, geometry has its own distinct domain of objects.[16] In the present account, even arithmetic is taken to be about quantities which are given as *objects* through true identity statements that assign the same value to two symbolic expressions, as we saw in Section 1.[17] However, these quantities are more abstract than geometrical quanta and are not to be construed as quasi-geometrical and intuitable as such.[18] A triangle, on the other hand, can be exhibited in pure intuition, and Kant states explicitly that the geometer *gives* himself an *object* through the concept of such a figure. To be sure, the statement is then qualified, in that the "object" is said to be the mere *form of an object* (cf. B271). The real possibility of form *cum* matter – the tokening of the type – cannot be proved within mathematics itself but only formal possibility, that is, that an objective form or formal object is schematically constructible and thus conforms to space and time. Space and time are in turn identified as forms of *empirical* intuition, or "*data* for possible experience" (B298), only within transcendental philosophy. Without the applicability to "an appearance present to the senses" (B299), the concepts and principles of mathematics would be "a mere play" with representations, without "objective validity" (B298).

The gap between pure and empirical intuition, or between constructibility in mere imagination and real applicability, implies that the geometer cannot read off properties from what is given to the senses, not even from a physical diagram (cf. Bxi–ii). It is rather the other way around – which mathematical properties that are to be assigned to a concrete model depends on schematic constructions, and thus also on conceptualization. Acts of a priori imagination remain crucial, then, that is, pure figurative syntheses, which are both rule-bound and exhibited through being executed. Sensible configurations help the mathematician to keep track of the constructions, but there is no sensory input to be considered because of its properties – just an output from pure imagination, or from the forms of sensibility as determined by rules of the understanding. The construction of a geometrical figure is an act of spontaneity through which a determinate geometrical space, a pure figure, is generated or "cut" from all-inclusive, metaphysical space.

Kant's assimilation of symbolic constructions to ostensive ones makes sense only if symbols are also manipulated in the medium of pure intuition, without ambiguities of poor inscription, and without physical or practical length constraints as to which numerals it is possible to inscribe. To be sure, concepts of symbols are not themselves constructed, as if the signs were geometrical figures. However, temporal steps are marked by signs, and arithmetic and algebra have their own combinatorial, or permutational, rules that make a pure symbolism possible. Only in that manner can the symbol manipulation come with "intuitive certainty, i.e., self-evidence" (B762). Thus, in algebra one "displays by signs in intuition the concepts" and "secures all inferences against mistakes by placing each of them before one's eyes" (B762). This Kantian notion of intuitive evidence had a distinct influence on Hilbert's idea of securing mathematics through manipulation of signs and a formal approach.[19]

The background to the brief remarks in *KrV* is no doubt the more extensive account of this issue in *Inquiry*. There, Kant states that the meanings of the signs are not relevant to their manipulation as such.[20] Patterns of signs are transformed step by step, and "when the conclusion is drawn, the meaning of the symbolic conclusion is deciphered [entziffert]" (UD 2: 278). There can be no change in meaning that subreptitiously brings about fallacious inferences. In mere discursive discourse, by contrast, the signs are word shapes that belong to a natural language, not the symbols of an artificial notation. Transparency is lacking as to how words are composed and as to how they combine to relate thoughts to each other. The same word shape can even stand for different concepts, and there can be a mix-up of meanings in a line of reasoning, so "one must still pay careful attention to whether it is really the same concept which is connected here with the same sign" (UD 2: 284–5). The importance of this warning is of course famously brought out in the Paralogisms of *KrV*.

4. Concluding Remark

We see, then, that concepts, principles and proofs within mathematics require ostension or symbolization in pure intuition. The intuitability condition Kant puts on all mathematical disciplines can be construed as a demand for structural transparency.[21] Mere discursive discourse does not exhibit objects and operations in the way that a mathematical construction does. This is ultimately also the reason why mathematics is synthetic a priori. It relies by necessity on intuition as a source of structures that can be grasped definitionally or axiomatically as well as on intuition as the medium for demonstrations of the properties of these structures. Moreover, the fact that not only ostensive but also symbolic constructions yield intuitive evidence is the key to a Kantian conception of even the most abstract fields of mathematics.

Notes

1 References to *KrV* are to the B-pagination.
2 For a discussion of Kant's view of the contrast between metaphysics and mathematics, both in his pre-critical and critical writings, see Kjosavik (2020).
3 Cf. Shabel (2003). For criticism of the "diagrammatic" approach for not being sensitive enough to the role of construction in Kant, see Friedman (2012).
4 Cf. Heis (2014) for the historical context of real definitions.
5 Zweig's translation has been slightly modified.
6 Cf. Hahn (1980/1933), which severely underestimates the role of thought, and thereby construction: "He [Kant] believed that mathematics is founded on pure intuition, not on thought. Geometry [. . .] deals with the properties of the space that is fully and exactly presented to us by pure intuition" (P. 74).
7 But cf. Kjosavik (2019), which argues that reflection on constructibility conditions in mathematics might lead to a broadly Kantian critique of classical logic.
8 For an account of why even Lambert thought of Euclidean geometry as privileged for constructive reasons, see Dunlop (2009).
9 Cf. Friedman (2000) on this distinction, as well as Onof and Schulting (2014).
10 Cf. Parsons (1983: 119–23); Parsons (2012: 97–8).
11 Cf. Frege (1950: §13).
12 Cf. Brouwer (1913: 85).
13 For criticism of the neglect of this in Shabel (2003), see Smit (2003).
14 The phrase "*in accordance with* [*nach derselben*]" is missing from the translation by Guyer and Wood but not from Pluhar's translation, which is close to mine.
15 Sandmel (2001) – a very comprehensive and broadly Kantian work – introduces instructive notions of "ideographical symbols" and "symbolic substrates" for ostensive constructions.
16 These are "defective objects" in Parsons, coming under the categories of quantity but not those of quality and relation (2012: 107).
17 For an explicit rejection of the claim that arithmetic and algebra have domains of their own, see Friedman (1992: 113).
18 However, Sutherland suggests what seems to be a quasi-geometrical notion of a "pure unit" to account for particular number concepts in Kant (2008: 162–3).
19 Cf. Hilbert (1967/1926: 376) on this.
20 Notably, in Parsons (1983: 138) Kant's view in *Inquiry* is taken to suggest a position that is *incompatible* with that of *KrV*, in so far as "operation with signs according to the rules, without attention to what they signify, is in itself a sufficient guarantee of correctness."
21 Cf. Kjosavik (2009) for more on this structural transparency, conceived of as an "isomorphic," or map-like, way of representing through pure intuition.

References

Brouwer, L.E.J. (1913) "Intuitionism and Formalism," *Bulletin of the American Mathematical Society* 20: 81–96.
Dunlop, K. (2009) "Why Euclid's Geometry Brooked No Doubt: J.H. Lambert on Certainty and the Existence of Models," *Synthese* 167: 33–65.
Frege, G. (1950) *The Foundations of Arithmetic*, J.L. Austin (trans.), Oxford: Blackwell.
Friedman, M. (1992) *Kant and the Exact Sciences*, Cambridge, MA: Harvard University Press.
Friedman, M. (2000) "Geometry, Construction, and Intuition in Kant and His Successors," in G. Sher and R. Tieszen (eds.), *Between Logic and Intuition: Essays in Honor of Charles Parsons*, Cambridge: Cambridge University Press, pp. 186–218.
Friedman, M. (2012) "Kant on Geometry and Spatial Intuition," *Synthese* 186: 231–55.
Hahn, H. (1980/1933) "The Crisis in Intuition," in B. McGuinness (ed.), *Empiricism, Logic, and Mathematics*, Dordrecht: D. Reidel, pp. 73–102.
Heis, J. (2014) "Kant (vs. Leibniz, Wolff and Lambert) on Real Definitions in Geometry," *Canadian Journal of Philosophy* 44: 605–30.
Hilbert, D. (1967/1926) "On the Infinite," in J. van Heijenoort (ed.), *From Frege to Gödel: A Source Book in Mathematical Logic 1879–1931*, Cambridge, MA: Harvard University Press, pp. 367–92.

Kjosavik, F. (2009) "Kant on Geometrical Intuition and the Foundations of Mathematics," *Kant-Studien* 100: 1–27.

Kjosavik, F. (2019) "Kant on the Possibilities of Mathematics and the Scope and Limits of Logic," *Inquiry.* doi: 10.1080/0020174X.2019.1651087

Kjosavik, F. (2020) "Kant on Method and Evidence in Metaphysics," in F. Kjosavik and C. Serck-Hanssen (eds.), *Metametaphysics and the Sciences: Historical and Philosophical Perspectives*, New York: Routledge, pp. 19–37.

Onof, C. and Schulting, D. (2014) "Kant, Kästner and the Distinction Between Metaphysical and Geometric Space," *Kantian Review* 19: 285–304.

Parsons, C. (1983) "Kant's Philosophy of Arithmetic," in *Mathematics in Philosophy*, Ithaca: Cornell University Press, pp. 110–49.

Parsons, C. (2012) *From Kant to Husserl*, Cambridge, MA: Harvard University Press.

Sandmel, T. (2001) *Matematisk erkjennelse: Grunnriss av en transcendentalfilosofisk fundert matematikkfilosofi*, PhD thesis, Oslo: Unipub.

Schultz, J. (1789) *Prüfung der Kantischen Critik der reinen Vernunft*, vol. 1, Königsberg: Hartung.

Shabel, L. (2003) *Mathematics in Kant's Critical Philosophy: Reflections on Mathematical Practice*, New York: Routledge.

Smit, H. (2003) "Lisa Shabel: Mathematics in Kant's Critical Philosophy," *Notre Dame Philosophical Reviews*, https://ndpr.nd.edu/news/mathematics-in-kant-s-critical-philosophy/ (last accessed: 7/11/2003).

Sutherland, D. (2008) "Arithmetic from Kant to Frege: Numbers, Pure Units, and the Limits of Conceptual Representation," *Royal Institute of Philosophy Supplement* 63: 135–64.

Further reading

On the importance of Euclid for Kant's philosophy of mathematics, see J. Hintikka, "Kant on the Mathematical Method [1967]," in *Knowledge and the Known* (Dordrecht: D. Reidel, 1974), ch. 8. For an influential account of arithmetical construction in Kant, see J. Michael Young, "Kant on the Construction of Arithmetical Concepts," *Kant-Studien* 73 (1982): 17–46. A careful discussion of developments in Kant's thought on arithmetical symbolism is offered by O. Rechter, "The View from 1763: Kant on the Arithmetical Method Before Intuition," in E. Carson and R. Huber (eds.), *Intuition and the Axiomatic Method* (Dordrecht: Springer, 2006), pp. 21–46. For a recent analysis of Kant's views of numbers, see D. Sutherland, "Kant's Conception of Number," *Philosophical Review* 126 (2017): 147–90. On Kant's influence on Brouwer and Hilbert, see C. Parsons, "The Kantian Legacy in Twentieth-Century Foundations of Mathematics," in *Philosophy of Mathematics in the Twentieth Century* (Cambridge, MA: Harvard University Press, 2014), ch. 1.

36

PHYSICS

Katherine Dunlop

★★★

Metaphysical Foundations of Natural Science (*MAN*) stands as Kant's most important Critical-period work on physics,[1] and raises many puzzles for students of Kant's Critical philosophy. Several of these arise already in the Preface explaining the aim of the book, which is to lay the foundation for a science of body or "extended nature" (4: 467). Kant places stringent conditions on such a discipline: a science, "properly so-called", is a system of cognitions connected as grounds and consequences, in which all explanations ultimately derive from a "pure part" containing only *a priori* principles, which are cognized as necessary (*MAN* 4: 468). This deductive structure confers apodictic certainty on the system as a whole. Natural science (in this exacting sense of "science") presupposes, in particular, metaphysics of the nature of its subject matter; if the science concerns "a particular nature of this or that kind of thing", such as matter, the basis from which it seeks metaphysical principles is the empirical concept of such a thing (*MAN* 4: 469–70). A question that arises here is what the "pure part" of a natural science, such as the doctrine of body (corporeal nature), contributes to generalizations about how specific kinds of things behave in various circumstances, which would seem to derive their warrant entirely from experience.[2] Another, perhaps more urgent, question is how the contents of *MAN* themselves can satisfy this description. A main claim of *MAN* is that an essential property of matter is an attractive force which is exerted, immediately and at a distance (Theorem 7, Dynamics), by every part of matter on every other part (Theorem 8, Dynamics).[3] From context, it is clear that Kant thinks the attribution of such a force to matter is required for the correctness of Newton's theory of gravitation. But it is hard to see how reason could arrive *a priori* at these claims about gravitational force, when Newton ventures them only on the basis of extensive empirical argumentation.[4]

Kant claims in the Preface that considering the concept of matter under the four headings of the Table of Categories (quantity, quality, relation, and modality) will yield principles that are indispensable not only for the doctrine of body that they found, but also for transcendental philosophy. One question this raises is what lack or gap in transcendental philosophy is filled by thus exemplifying its concepts and propositions *in concreto*. A closely related question is how exactly these principles are to be derived. Since the first *Critique* already asserts the applicability of the Categories to all objects

DOI: 10.4324/9781003406617-48

of experience, it would seem that *MAN*'s methodology must be to instantiate the first *Critique*'s universally quantified claims to the particular case of matter; but then its argument would be trivial.

The contents of *MAN* raise a further large-scale puzzle. As noted, *MAN* incorporates central results of Newton's physics, and it cites Newton's *Principia* far more than any other work. But *MAN* also features some views in sympathy with Leibniz's, such as that all mechanical laws presuppose dynamical laws (4: 537) and that "absolutely hard" bodies are impossible on account of the continuity of change (4: 552). Moreover, as recent scholarship has documented, Kant's own Laws of Motion are of Leibnizian, not Newtonian, provenance. This leads us to wonder how Kant's project is situated with respect to the two competing worldviews.

Perhaps more than any other area of Kant studies, contemporary (Anglophone) understanding of *MAN* has been shaped by a single scholar, Michael Friedman. In work going back over three decades, culminating in *Kant's Construction of Nature* (2013), Friedman has powerfully illuminated the arguments of *MAN* by situating them within the contexts of Kant's own philosophical development and the confrontation between Newton's and Leibniz's views. In §1 of this chapter, I outline how Friedman's account answers the questions about *MAN* raised earlier. §2 considers the place of Kant's arguments that matter essentially has attractive and repulsive force within his overall project, as Friedman understands it. In §§3–4, I give some reasons for questioning Friedman's reading of one key passage, which constitutes part of Kant's argument that attractive and repulsive forces are essential to matter. I argue in §5 that this passage can be taken to allude to Euler's views rather than exclusively to Newton's (as Friedman supposes). While my discussion is thus confined to a short portion of Kant's text, I hope to give some sense of its importance for the whole, as well as illustrate the sort of contribution for which Friedman's work has opened up room.

1.   Explaining the Possibility of a Quantitative Treatment of Matter

I cannot here discuss Friedman's view of the relationship between *MAN* and the first *Critique*, except to say that Friedman sustains a case that *MAN* is crucially important for understanding the role of *a priori* cognition of space and motion in constituting experience, and thus for understanding transcendental idealism. Friedman's approach to other issues we have raised – the methodology of *MAN*, the epistemological status of its claims, and the importance of Newton's theory for Kant's project – can be briefly explained with reference to a central passage from the Preface, which characterizes the project of *MAN*:

> [P]rinciples for the *construction* of the concepts that belong to the possibility of matter in general must first be introduced. Therefore, a complete analysis of the concept of matter in general will have to be taken as the basis, and this is a task for pure philosophy [. . .] and is therefore a genuine metaphysics of corporeal nature.
>
> (4: 472)

Friedman takes Kant to provide principles for constructing, specifically, the partial concepts [*Teilbegriffe*] into which the concept of matter is thus analyzed, such as the properties of movability, inertia, and filling space.

Friedman's understanding of Kant's "principles for constructing" these concepts represents his solution to another interpretive puzzle arising from Kant's claim to base *a priori* metaphysical cognition on an empirical concept. If the concepts that "belong to the possibility of matter in general" are empirical (as we may reasonably suppose), like the concept of matter itself, they cannot literally be capable of construction. For to construct a concept is to exhibit an object corresponding to the concept completely *a priori*, as Kant maintains in the first *Critique* (A713/B741). But no object can be put forth *a priori* as an instantiation of an empirical concept, since objects are recognized to correspond to empirical concepts only in virtue of experientially given features.[5] Friedman takes it that to "construct" such concepts is to explain how their quantitative structure becomes possible (Friedman 2013: 32). Construction in this broader sense, to which empirical concepts are clearly amenable, fulfills the purpose of securing mathematics' application to the doctrine of body (*cf.* *MAN* 4: 470).

As it turns out, the construction (in this sense) of the concept of mass essentially involves Newton's theory of universal gravitation. Central to Kant's account of how the concept of mass is mathematized, by means of Newton's theory, are applications of the relational categories (substance, causality, and interaction), and this is one respect in which Kant's foundations are recognizably "metaphysical" (Friedman 2013: 529). His foundations are also "metaphysical" in that they remedy the ontological excess of Newton's own foundation, by providing an alternative conception of "absolute space" (Friedman 2013: 20). Newton's argument for universal gravitation provides a means to determine the center of gravity of the solar system, and Kant understands this argument as the basis for a procedure for referring all motion and rest to "absolute space", understood as a reference frame determined by "the common center of gravity of all matter" (*MAN* 4: 563).[6]

Friedman's account of how quantitative structure is conferred on the constituent elements of the concept of matter satisfactorily explains the epistemological status of *MAN*'s claims. Facts such as the immediacy and universality of attraction "acquire a transcendental dimension" (2013: 527) insofar as they are presupposed by procedures for determining quantities by means of Newton's theory. These procedures are part of the "successive", "step by step" empirical realization of "both mathematical concepts and pure concepts of the understanding" (Friedman 2013: 130). The category of substance, to take a prime example, is first schematized in accordance with our forms of intuition as the temporally extended "real" (A144/B183); then realized as an object of empirical intuition, specifically outer sense-perception; and ultimately realized as the empirical concept (of matter) whose quantity is determined by the Newtonian procedures. But the "transcendental dimension" acquired by the presuppositions of the procedures does not amount to apriority in any strong sense. The presuppositions remain empirical insofar as they make possible only more specific, "lower-level", realizations of the pure concepts, to which we can envisage alternatives.

Friedman argues specifically that "our" empirical concept of matter (2013: 528) – which incorporates the "universal applicability of the mechanical laws of motion" as well as the "universally penetrating character of gravitational force" – is contingent (2013: 569),[7] because it is opposed to a "mechanical" concept which Kant's predecessors favored. Friedman's account of why we must adopt a concept of matter characterized "dynamically" (in terms of force) will be a main focus of the following discussion.

2. The Attribution of Fundamental Forces to Matter

The second chapter of *MAN*, "Dynamics", is the longest and is widely recognized for its importance as the locus of Kant's "dynamical" theory of matter. Friedman acknowledges that his interpretive schema fits the other chapters better than "Dynamics", which does not culminate in a construction of the property it treats.[8] But Friedman maintains that in "Dynamics" the concept of quantity of matter is, while not "mathematized", yet "extensively discussed", yielding a "profound reconsideration of the Newtonian concept of quantity of matter" in the light of a (similarly reconsidered) metaphysical concept of substance. In this way, Kant "develops a metaphysical foundation for a general concept of matter or material substance that is most appropriate, in his view, for the Newtonian mathematical theory of motion" (2013: 104).

Each chapter of *MAN* begins by stating a determination of the concept of matter. The property adduced at the beginning of "Dynamics" is that of filling space. Kant defines "filling" a space as "resist[ing] every movable that strives through its motion to penetrate into a certain space", in contrast to merely being present at all points of the space without offering resistance (*MAN* 4: 496–7). A main conclusion of "Dynamics" is that matter must have both attractive force and repulsive force in order to take up any determinate volume of space. Since the forces are in this way required for the possibility of matter, they are essential to it (Theorem 6, Note) and called "original" (*MAN* 4: 503; 4: 509) and "fundamental" (*MAN* 4: 513).

For the goal of securing mathematics' application to the doctrine of body, the attribution of fundamental forces to matter appears particularly important. The penultimate paragraph of the chapter claims that

> all that metaphysics can ever achieve toward the construction of the concept of matter and [promoting] the application of mathematics to natural science, with respect to those properties whereby matter fills a space in a determinate measure[, is] to view these properties as dynamical, and not as unconditioned original positings.
>
> (*MAN* 4: 534)

To regard the properties as "dynamical" is to explain them in terms of "fundamental forces". The intended contrast is with "a merely mathematical treatment" (*MAN* 4: 534), and earlier in the chapter Kant objected to the "mathematical-mechanical" mode of explanation that, in contrast to the "metaphysical-dynamical mode", it allows too much "freedom to the imagination" (*MAN* 4: 525). So Kant appears to reject the "mechanical" concept of matter in favor of the "dynamical" one because despite its name, the mechanical or "mathematical" concept is less suitable for the application of mathematics.

Friedman's distinctive contribution is his detailed account of how the attribution of fundamental forces to matter conduces to this end. Friedman initially explains the connection between fundamental forces and mathematics' application in reference to the Remark to Theorem 5 of "Dynamics". Theorem 5 asserts that "the possibility of matter requires an attractive force". The necessity that attractive force is thus shown to have raises the question, which the Remark then addresses, of why attractive force is "only adjoined to [the concept of matter] through inferences", while impenetrability features as "the first distinguishing mark" of matter and is "immediately given with [this] concept" (*MAN* 4: 509). Kant maintains (for reasons we will soon give) that only "the resistance and repulsion of impenetrability" can give rise to "the magnitude and figure of something extended, and thus [. . .] the concept of a determinate object in space, which forms the basis of everything else one can say about this thing" (*MAN* 4: 510). Friedman's way of putting this point is that the fundamental force of repulsion is uniquely necessary for "our first application of mathematics to the objects of outer experience",[9] whereby we conceptualize the objects as having geometrical properties such as "determinate volumes, figures, and relative spatial positions" (Friedman 2013: 175). Friedman understands this application of geometrical concepts as the starting point of "an empirical constructive procedure of progressively rationalizing or objectifying our sensory experience under the concept of a determinate object in space" (2013: 176).

Kant's concern with specifically Newtonian procedures for estimating quantity becomes apparent, on Friedman's reading, in the continuation of this "empirical constructive procedure". At the procedure's first stage, "we are still quite limited in our ability to apply [. . .] mathematical concepts to bodies"; most notably, we cannot yet apply "the Newtonian concept of quantity of matter". But "by further observation of [the bodies'] volumes, figures, and changing (relative) spatial positions", we can "establish the laws of the fundamental force of attraction" by following the argument of Book 3 of [Newton's] *Principia* (Friedman 2013: 177). Crucially for Friedman's reading, these laws are established mainly on the basis of empirical data (concerning the orbits of the primary planets and their satellites). So when Kant rejects the mechanical mode of explanation because it is "severely limited in its ability to follow Newton's argument in Book 3" (Friedman 2013: 180), his espousal of the rival dynamical approach rests on "the empirical success of Newton's theory in comparison with the opposing mechanical philosophy" (Friedman 2013: 569).

The most important of the laws governing attraction, in this context, is that the force of universal gravitation is proportional to the quantity of matter of a body exerting the force (Proposition 7, Corollary 2 in *Principia*'s Book 3). The immediately following Proposition 8 shows that "the weights of bodies towards different planets", such as terrestrial bodies falling towards Earth or satellites orbiting the primary planets, "are given in terms of the inverse-square gravitational force acting between the center of the planet and that of the body" (Friedman 2013: 173). One can then determine the weights of equal bodies at equal distances from primary bodies in the solar system (the Sun, Jupiter, Saturn, and the Earth), in accordance with the distances and times of orbit of these bodies' satellites (Proposition 8, Corollary 1, Book 3). The proportionality of attraction to the attracting body's quantity of matter is then used to determine the quantity of matter of the primary bodies (Proposition 8, Corollary 2, Book 3). Then the density of the primary bodies is found by dividing quantity of matter by volume (Proposition 8, Corollary 3, Book 3). Thus "geometrical/kinematical information" afforded by the "first application" of mathematical concepts (volume, figure, and spatial situation) makes possible the application of further mathematical concepts. Friedman emphasizes that this second stage of the "empirical constructive procedure" is mediated by the fundamental force of attraction.

In this manner, attributing attraction, as a fundamental force, to matter makes it possible to "articulate a generally applicable concept of quantity of matter". Specifically, the quantity of celestial bodies can now be determined in relation to the traditional statical concept of weight (heretofore applicable only to bodies near the Earth's surface), which ultimately allows us to specify "a privileged frame of reference relative to which both celestial and terrestrial motions may be described within a single unified system of the world" (Friedman 2013: 178). The need for such a frame of a reference in reducing all rest and motion to absolute space ensures the "transcendental" status of those applications of concepts which this specification presupposes (see Friedman's Chapter 35). At the same time, the important role played by empirical data in establishing the applicability of the mathematical concepts (see Friedman's Chapter 24) keeps these presuppositions from being *a priori* in any strong sense.

The separation into two stages of the application of mathematical concepts to matter corresponds to the two halves of Kant's "balancing argument" (Theorems 5 and 6 of "Dynamics"), each of which argues that "space would be empty" if matter were subject to only one of the fundamental forces, without its action being "balanced" by the other force. In Theorem 5, Kant argues explicitly that matter would "by its repulsive force alone, if no other force counteracted it, be confined within no limit of extension; that is, it would disperse itself to infinity, and no specified quantity of matter would be found within any specified space", so that if matter did not have attractive force "all spaces would be empty" (*MAN* 4: 508). Since there is no further talk of matter's having quantity in the proofs of Theorems 5 and 6, we might well wonder if the "balancing" of forces is required specifically for the application of mathematical concepts to matter, rather than for the mere possibility of matter (as Theorems 5 and 6 assert). But as we have seen, in the Remark to Theorem 5 Kant claims that matter must have repulsive force in order for concepts of "magnitude and figure" to apply to it (*MAN* 4: 510). (Kant's point is specifically to explain why repulsive force, as the "ground of impenetrability", has a particularly tight connection with the concept of matter, when, according to the argument he has just given, attractive force is required for matter's possibility just as much as repulsive force.) The question I will press is whether Kant is here concerned with the Newtonian concept of quantity of matter, or only with geometrical and kinematical concepts.

3. Questioning Friedman's Reading of the Remark to Proposition 5

I begin with some preliminary grounds for questioning whether the Remark to Theorem 5 of "Dynamics" already concerns Newton's procedure for determining the quantity of matter of celestial bodies.

The first of these is that Kant does not use the term "*Quantität*" in the Remark (he does refer in the Proof to a "specified quantity of matter" – *MAN* 4: 508). He instead speaks of the "*Grösse*" of an object (*MAN* 4: 509) and the "first application of our concepts" of "*Grösse*" to matter (*MAN* 4: 510). To be sure, "*Quantität*" and "*Grösse*" do not differ sharply in meaning. At most, "*Quantität*" might be said to have a narrower meaning, since it designates the abstract property that is possessed by concrete instances,[10] for which German has no other term than "*Grössen*" (they are called "*quanta*" in Latin). But in the first *Critique* and *MAN*, Kant tends to reserve the use of "*Quantität*" for certain specific contexts.

In the *Critique of Pure Reason*, Kant uses "*Quantität*" in parallel with "*Qualität*" (A70–80/B95–106, A264–81/B319–38, A714–15/B742–3); to designate the abstract property possessed by *quanta* (A143/B182–3, A717/B745); or in reference to matter, to designate that which "natural philosophers" seek to empirically measure (B17, B21*n*., A173/B215). Kant's usage of "*Grösse*" and "*Quantität*" in *MAN* does not follow such a clear pattern, but there are some striking trends. "*Quantität*" occurs only three times (at 4: 495, 4: 505, and 4: 508) before what Friedman calls the "Newtonian" concept of quantity of matter, as proportional to "universal attraction", is officially introduced (in Remark 2 to Theorem 7 and the Note to Explication 7 of the Dynamics – *MAN* 4: 514–16). Accordingly, in the first chapter ("Phoronomy") Kant claims to determine motions and the construction of motions in general as "*Grössen*" (*MAN* 4: 487), not as "*Quantitäten*".[11] (We may note here that Kant aims thereby to give an *a priori* basis for the application of mathematics to natural science – *MAN* 4: 487.) In the "Mechanics" chapter, Kant continues to speak of the amount of motion as "*Grösse*" as long as its estimation is either phoronomical (merely in terms of speed) or mechanical (in terms of speed and quantity of matter), but when he uses this amount to determine the quantity of matter, he calls it "*Quantität*" (*MAN* 4: 538–41).[12] So Kant seems to reserve "*Quantität*" for those properties which natural philosophers seek to empirically determine (as when they estimate the quantity of matter in relation to that of motion); he does not use "*Quantität*" for that property of motion which is constructed in giving an *a priori* basis for the application of mathematics.[13]

These considerations may lead us to suspect that when Kant does *not* use "*Quantität*", he is not concerned with quantity of matter in the Newtonian sense (as proportional to attraction), or indeed with any property that becomes measurable only empirically, in natural science. Closer examination of the text of the Remark to Theorem 5 of "Dynamics" deepens the suspicion that it does not concern quantity of matter in the Newtonian sense. To support his claim that if matter had only attractive force, we could not obtain any "determinate concept of any object in space, since neither figure, nor magnitude, nor even the place where it would be found could strike our senses", Kant argues that attraction alone would "never disclose to us a matter of determinate *volume* and *figure*" (*MAN* 4: 509–10). The most straightforward reading of this passage is that matter's having repulsive force is a necessary condition on our attributing a determinate quantity, in the sense of *volume*, to it, because this is a necessary condition on our perceiving the body as having a determinate *shape*. Relating repulsive force to volumetric considerations in this way would support the claim that repulsive force is necessary for matter, defined as "resist[ing] every movable that strives through its motion to penetrate into a *certain* space" (*MAN* 4: 496, emphasis added).

A further reason to read Kant as arguing that matter's having a certain force is a necessary condition on its having a determinate volume is that he argues in precisely this fashion in his *Physical Monadology* of 1756. Proposition X of *Physical Monadology* asserts that "Bodies would not have a determinate volume [*definite volumine*] in virtue of the force of impenetrability alone"; thus "there must be another force, which is likewise inherent in them, the force of attraction" (*MoPh* 1: 483).[14]

On the basis of this evidence, we might conclude that both Theorem 5 (including its Proof) and the accompanying Remark in fact concern the possibility of matter's having (determinate) volume, rather than quantity of matter in the Newtonian sense. The overall thrust of the passage would then be that matter must have both attractive and repulsive force in order to have volume, which is also what Kant asserts in *Physical Monadology*'s Proposition X: "The two forces together define the limit of the extension of bodies" (*MoPh* 1: 483).

Such a reading of Theorem 5 would put in doubt Friedman's claim that "the main point of Kant's balancing argument" is "to articulate a distinctive concept of matter (Kant's own dynamical concept) possessing just those structural features that are necessary to explain Newton's successful mathematization" of the concept of quantity of matter (Friedman 2013: 509–10). Since quantity of matter, in the Newtonian sense, is not at issue in any other Theorem or Proof of the "Dynamics" chapter,[15] but "Dynamics" wholly contains Kant's grounds for privileging the dynamical concept of matter over the mechanical one, we might further question Friedman's contention that Kant rejects the mechanical conception because it is not adequate to Newton's argument in Book 3 (and thus does not provide for a generally applicable concept of quantity of matter). On a larger scale, Friedman's interpretation would face the problem that the attribution of attraction to matter (as a fundamental force) is presupposed by the first, rather than the second, stage of the constructive procedure by which pure concepts are empirically realized. But since empirical data become crucial only in the procedure's second stage, we lose our explanation of how this presupposition is transcendental without being *a priori* (in a strong sense).

4. The Moon Test in the Argument for Universal Gravitation

Now Friedman is well aware of the correspondence between the arguments of *Physical Monadology* and those of *MAN*. Friedman is also cognizant that Theorem 5 and its Proof are subject to the weaker reading that I just proposed. For Friedman himself claims that when Kant later appeals to the Proof of Theorem 5 (specifically, in the Proof of Theorem 7 of "Dynamics"), "the role of the fundamental force of attraction is precisely to insure that the quantity of matter in question possesses a boundary [*Grenze*] or limiting surface" (2013: 209).

Friedman's strongest ground for taking the Remark to Theorem 5 to instead concern quantity of matter in the Newtonian sense is the highly significant allusion he finds there to Proposition 8 of *Principia*'s Book 3. Kant argues in the Remark that attraction could "disclose to us" only "the striving of our organ [toward] a point outside us (the center of the attracting body)", but never "a matter of determinate *volume* and *figure*", because "the attractive force of all parts of the earth can affect us no more, and in no other way, than as if it were wholly united at the earth's center" (*MAN* 4: 509). According to Friedman, Kant asserts this property of gravitational force with deliberate regard to how it figures in Newton's argument. Kant is specifically concerned with the "moon test" explained in Proposition 4 of *Principia*'s Book 3, which establishes that the acceleration the moon would have towards Earth, if it were deprived of all (inertial) motion and allowed to fall, is the same as the acceleration g of gravity, as measured by pendulums. Proposition 8, in Friedman's words, "adds support for this argument by showing that" the attraction of any body towards Earth "may be treated as if it were solely directed towards [Earth's] center", although it is "actually compounded out of infinitely many attractive forces, most of which are not directed towards the center" (2013: 173). Friedman claims Kant "underscores the importance" of the moon test "by mentioning 'the attraction of a mountain, or any stone, etc.' after discussing the attraction of the earth" (Friedman 2013: 178). Now the Scholium following Proposition 4 asks us to imagine that Earth is orbited by several moons, the lowest of which is small and nearly touches the tops of Earth's smallest mountains, so that its attraction towards Earth can be straightforwardly compared with the weights of terrestrial bodies. There is no mention of a particular terrestrial body (such as a stone). Friedman suggests, however, that Kant is alluding to the "inverse moon test" described in Newton's *Treatise of the System of the World* (1728), a more "popular" presentation of *Principia*'s Book III, in which a stone is "projected from the top of a high mountain" with increasing velocity until it finally comes to orbit Earth.

Friedman also identifies fundamental differences between *Physical Monadology* and *MAN*, such that the former's arguments could not work in the latter context. In *MoPh* quantity of matter, in the sense of mass, is "a *third* fundamental force", on par with the attractive and repulsive forces, namely the "*vis inertiae* by which a body strives to conserve its state of motion or rest" (2013: 182). But Friedman finds in *MAN* two "distinguishable concepts of quantity of matter", each linked to one of the fundamental forces, and takes the "balancing" argument to link the two concepts with a third, "mechanical", concept of quantity of matter, through the intermediary concept of the "aggregate of the movable in a given space" (Friedman 2013: 191).[16] Now the allusion Friedman finds in the Remark to Theorem 5, to Newton's procedure for determining the quantity of matter of celestial bodies, gives rise to the idea "that we could generate a notion of the quantity of matter in a given space through attractive force alone", specifically by "suppos[ing] that the space in question is occupied by a distribution of attracting points" (Friedman 2013: 185). The possibility of determining the quantity of matter in such a configuration is important for the view of *Phyiscal Monadology*, on which the indivisible "monads" that exercise attractive and repulsive force are separated from one another by determinate volumes of space. But, according to Friedman, the proof of Theorem 6 "is intended to undermine" the idea that the quantity of matter so configured could be determined by Newton's procedure (Friedman 2013: 185).[17] So the second half of the "balancing" argument links repulsive force with (a concept of) quantity of matter in a way that forecloses the approach of *MoPh*.[18]

The differences Friedman identifies between *MAN* and *Physical Monadology* are clearly important. But it remains open to question whether they explain the balancing argument, or for that matter any material in "Dynamics" prior to the introduction of the notion of quantity of matter (following Theorem 7). As I remarked earlier, matter's quantitative properties are not referred to anywhere (either as "*Quantität*" or as "*Grösse*") in Theorem 6 or its proof. Absent any textual cue, it would seem question-begging to assert that the balancing argument must function differently in *MAN* than in *Physical Monadology because* the earlier version of the argument is not adequate to ground the linkage between the mechanical and the dynamical concepts of quantity of matter.

The allusion Friedman finds, in the Remark to Theorem 5, to Newton's procedure for determining the quantity of matter seems to be just such a cue. The sentence in question reads:

> the attractive force of all parts of the earth can affect us no more, and in no other way, than as if it were wholly united in the earth's center, and this alone influenced our sense, and the same holds for the attraction of a mountain, or any stone, etc.
>
> (*MAN* 4: 509)

I submit that while this can be taken to refer to Newton's *procedure*, it does not fit Newton's *texts* so closely. As remarked earlier, "a stone" is mentioned in connection with the "moon test" only in Newton (1728), not in *Principia*. But it is only in *Principia* that the property of gravitational force referred to in the first part of the sentence – that it can be considered to be directed solely toward a body's center, despite being compounded of forces directed toward all the body's parts – is, as Friedman says, invoked to support the moon-test argument.

In *Principia*, Newton comments that he applied certain results from Book I to "discern the truth of" Proposition 8 of Book III and thereby resolve the following worry:

> [Having] found that the gravity toward a whole planet arises from and is compounded of the gravities toward the parts and that toward each of the individual parts it is inversely proportional to the squares of the distances from the parts, I was still not certain whether that proportion of the inverse square [calculated in terms of distance from the body's center] obtained exactly in a total force compounded of a number of forces, or only very nearly so. For it could happen that a proportion which holds exactly enough at very great distances might be markedly in error near the surface of the planet, because there the distances of the particles may be unequal and their situations dissimilar.
>
> (Quoted in Friedman 2013: 173–4 n. 113)

The problem of unequal distance and diverging direction near the surface of the planet is clearly important to resolve for the project of extending the statical concept of weight, in terms of which we reckon the quantity of matter of bodies near the surface of the earth, into a universally applicable concept of quantity of matter. Having addressed the worry, Newton shows (in the Corollaries to Proposition 8) how to find the weights of bodies toward the planets, and then find the planets' masses and densities; the following Proposition 9 asserts that within the surface of a planet, gravity is proportional to distance from its center.

But in the corresponding sections of (Newton 1728), no such worry appears. First, in a passage corresponding to Proposition 6 of *Principia*'s Book III, Newton asserts, and gives experimental evidence for, the proportionality of centripetal force to the quantity of matter of attrac*ted* bodies. Newton then claims that "reason requires" that the force "should be also proportional to the quantity of matter in the attracting body. For all action is mutual, and makes the bodies mutually to approach one another, and therefore must be the same in both bodies" (1728: 38). This corresponds to the application of the Third Law of Motion to prove Proposition 7 ("Gravity exists in all bodies universally and is proportional to the quantity of matter in each") in Book III. In the following discussion, Newton states an analogue of Proposition 8 (that "the motive force by which every globe is attracted to another, and which, in terrestrial bodies, we commonly call their weight" varies as the inverse square of the distance between their centers) only after first introducing the content of Proposition 9 (that within the surface of a body, gravity varies as distance from the center) (1728: 45). He then asserts, without further ado, that "from these principles well understood, it will now be easy to determine the motions of the celestial bodies among themselves" (1728: 46). The accuracy of the inverse-square proportion near a body's surface is not discussed in the course of this reasoning, or discussed at all (as far as I can see) in Newton (1728).[19]

In defense of Friedman's interpretation, it might be suggested, rather plausibly, that Kant became familiar with Newton's argument through both *Principia* and Newton (1728), and constructed his allusion without troubling over which details came from which text. So the difficulty just raised is not grave. But I think it opens up room to consider other interpretations of the passage. One merit of Friedman's reading is that "eagerness to make the reference to the moon test explicit" would explain why Kant misleadingly suggests that "the attractions of non-spherical and non-uniform bodies (such as a mountain and perhaps a stone) have the same properties as those of spherical uniform bodies" (2013: 178 n123). I believe this advantage can be preserved, without attributing to Kant a concern with the accuracy of the inverse-square proportion.

5. The Moon Test in Euler's *Letters to a German Princess*

As I will now explain, Kant can instead be taken to allude to Euler's *Letters to a German Princess* (which he is known to have read). In the end, I will argue, it matters less which text was Kant's source than whether Kant was specifically concerned with Newton's procedure for determining the quantity of matter.

In the *Letters*, Euler first establishes the properties of terrestrial gravity, and then observes that Newton attributes gravitational force to all heavenly bodies. With respect to terrestrial gravity, Euler explains that (as with any force) there are two things to be considered: its direction, and its quantity [*grandeur*]. Euler argues, first, that gravity is directed toward the center of the earth. In particular, he maintains in Letter XLIX that a body placed inside a channel passing through the earth's center would be attracted to the center (1833: 178–9). In the following Letter L, he argues that inside this channel gravity will be proportional to distance from the center. As we have seen, Newton also holds that inside a planet gravity is proportional to distance from the center. In *Principia* and in Newton (1728), Newton argues specifically that this proportionality would hold inside a channel in the earth (but in contrast to Euler, he separates this reasoning from his exposition of the basic properties of gravity).[20] Euler thus raises the issue, at least implicitly, of how the attractive force of the whole earth is composed out of attractions toward its parts.

"Having traveled in idea to the center of the earth", Euler writes in Letter L, "let us now return to its surface and ascend to the top of the highest mountains", and then imagine a body "gradually removing from our globe, until it reached the sun, or one of the fixed stars" (1833: 181). To illustrate how gravity would be diminished by such a removal, Euler asserts that "a terrestrial body placed at the distance of the moon would [. . .] be forced towards the center of the earth with a power 3600 times less than at the surface of the globe", which would, however, be sufficient to make the body descend to the earth if it were not supported. He anticipates the objection that there is a body at that height, namely the moon, which "must therefore be subject to this effect of gravity, and yet [. . .] does not fall to the earth" (1833: 182). The solution to this difficulty is that such a fall is prevented by the rapidity of the moon's motion, and to illustrate it Euler gives two examples:

> A stone dropped from the hand, without having any motion impressed upon it, falls immediately in the direction of a straight vertical line; but if you throw this stone, impressing on it a sideways motion, it no longer falls immediately downward, but moves in a curved line before it reaches the earth. . . .
>
> A cannonball [,] fired from the top of a high mountain [,] might perhaps fly several miles before it reached the ground. If the direction of the cannon is farther elevated, and the strength of the powder increased, the ball will be carried much farther [, so that] the ball should not light till it had reached the antipodes; nay, farther still, till it should not fall at all, but return to the place where it was shot off; and thus perform a little tour around the globe. It would thus be like a little moon, making its revolutions round the earth.
>
> (1833: 182–3)

Euler concludes that the height of the moon and the "prodigious velocity with which it is carried" are sufficient to explain its continuing to orbit the earth. So here a stone and a mountain are discussed in connection with the earth's attraction of bodies under, at, and above its surface.

To be sure, Euler's account of the projectiles' behavior is very similar to (and probably modeled after) the "inverse moon test" discussed in Newton (1728). So it might not seem to matter which of these texts Kant has in mind. But as we have just seen, Euler puts forward this thought-experiment in order to defend the thesis that gravity extends as far as the moon, not to vindicate a general procedure for determining quantity of matter. In fact, Euler does not explain how the mass of attracting bodies can be found (namely, from the distances and times of their satellites' orbits) until Letter LVI. Euler's project here is rather to give a qualitative account of the properties by which gravity makes itself known, as it first did to Newton.[21]

It would be natural for Kant to allude to such observations in the Remark to Theorem 5, since he is primarily concerned there with the epistemological issue of how we are led to ascribe attractive force to matter, when attractive force "can give us in itself either no sensation at all, or at least no determinate object of sensation" (4: 510). But it is less important to identify the exact target of Kant's allusion than to see that the moon test was discussed not only outside the context of *Principia's* Book III (and its recapitulation in Newton 1728), but even without regard to Newton's procedure for determining the quantity of matter of celestial bodies. Whether or not Kant had Euler's text in mind, he could have put the moon test to the same use as Euler. So we can grant that Kant was alluding to Newton's comparison between the moon and a stone, without having to conclude that Kant was concerned with the universal applicability of the Newtonian concept of quantity of matter.

6. Conclusion

I have questioned whether Kant is concerned with Newton's procedure for determining the quantity of matter of celestial bodies in the "balancing" argument of the "Dynamics" chapter. (I do not dispute that Kant may be concerned with this procedure elsewhere in *MAN*.) The balancing argument is supposed to show that attractive and repulsive forces are essential to matter, and thereby establish the superiority of Kant's "dynamical" concept of matter over a "mechanical" concept. If Kant is not claiming that the attribution of attractive force to matter is a condition on determining the quantity of matter of bodies in general (terrestrial and celestial), we need another way to understand his view that privileging the dynamical concept over the mechanical one "promotes the applicability of mathematics to natural science" (*MAN* 4: 534). I will conclude by marking this as an area for future work.

Notes

1 Kant's *Opus Postumum* is also important for his view of physics. But since it was begun only after the third *Critique* was completed, it can justifiably be regarded as coming after Kant's Critical period. Its doctrinal relationship to the rest of his work cannot be considered here.

2 Peter Plaass raises the question with respect to how a "pure part" can "lend apodictic certainty to the whole that [. . .] also contains something empirical" (Plaass 1994: 238).

3 "*Lehrsatz*" in *MAN* is standardly translated "Proposition", but I will translate it by "Theorem" here to avoid confusion with the "Propositions" of Newton's *Principia*.

4 I am glossing over some subtleties here. First, Newton resists ascribing attractive force to matter as an *essential* property; Kant claims this puts Newton "at variance with himself" (*MAN* 4:515). Second, only one result in the *Principia* depends on the assumption that *every part* of matter attracts every other part, in contrast

to the weaker assumption of "macroscopic inverse-square gravity between celestial bodies" (Smith 2014: 275). See Smith 2014 for discussion.

5 See Dunlop (2012: 94–5) and McNulty (2014: 398–9).

6 It may well seem strange that Newton's theory of universal gravitation could supply the means to replace his own notion of absolute space with a different concept. For Newton's presentation of the absolute/relative distinction, in a "Definitions" section preceding the arguments of the *Principia*, leads us to expect that his theory of universal gravitation presupposes his notion of absolute space. But it is widely recognized that Newton's methods for determining states of motion, in accordance with his Laws of Motion, cannot give empirical content to the distinction between motion and rest (in absolute space) that his notion of absolute space entails (for discussion, see DiSalle 2006). Put roughly, Newton gives us the means to determine "the situation of the planets to one another", but not whether the entire solar system is at rest or moves uniformly in absolute space. Newton appears to acknowledge this limitation in *Treatise of the System of the World*, which Friedman cites as a source for Kant (see §4 below). In the *Treatise* the "hypothesis" that the whole system moves uniformly (1728: 50) is rejected, as undetectable by means of "sensible effects" (1728: 19; *cf.* DiSalle 2006: 49). In this sense, Newton's notion of space carries extra commitments beyond what is required for the argument that establishes universal gravitation and determines the solar system's center of mass.

7 What Friedman claims to be contingent is, more precisely, the *analysis* of our concept of matter that shows it to have the features "in virtue of which Newton has successfully mathematized its quantity" (2013: 569).

8 As Friedman puts it, the argument of the "Dynamics" chapter "does not directly issue in the application of mathematics to any further central concepts of the mathematical theory of motion": "following the discussion of the mathematical structure of the concept of speed or velocity in the [first chapter], the next concept whose precise mathematical structure is articulated by Kant is that of mass or quantity of matter [in the third chapter]" (Friedman 2013: 104). See also Dunlop (2022).

9 Friedman's wording is closer to Kant's claim, in the same passage, that "the first application of our concepts of magnitude [*Grössen*] to matter, through which it first becomes possible for us to transform our outer perceptions into the empirical concept of a matter, as object in general, is grounded only on that property whereby it fills a space" (*MAN* 4: 510).

10 See Sutherland (2004).

11 Kant also claims that the "Phoronomy" is a pure "doctrine of the magnitude" (*Grössenlehre*) of motion (*MAN* 4: 489, 495). One might think that in this context he had to use "*Grössen*" rather than "*Quantität*", but "*Quantitätlehre*" is an allowable combination and occurs as early as 1821 (in *Vorschule der mathematischen Geographie, ein Lehrbuch ihrer nöthigen Vorkenntnisse von Dr. Klein*, Chemnitz: bei C. G. Kretschmar).

12 Thus the procedure that was described in "Phoronomy" as a construction of motion as a "*Grösse*" (*MAN* 4: 487), specifically constructing one magnitude as a composition of others (*MAN* 4: 493–5), is described as construction of the "*Quantität*" of a motion in "Mechanics", where it is applied to determine the quantity of matter (*MAN* 4: 538).

13 Along the same lines, Kant starts to use "*Grösse*" alongside "*Quantität*" to refer to amount of matter when he embeds his account in a more general philosophical context, first contrasting it to the way matter is understood in a monadological physics (*MAN* 4: 539–40) and then subsuming it under a more general account of the magnitude of substance (*MAN* 4: 541–3).

14 To be sure, the claim here is that *attractive*, rather than *repulsive*, force is necessary for having a certain volume. But the argument for this Proposition is strikingly similar to the Proof of Theorem 5 (which asserts the necessity of attractive force, in contrast to the Remark, which explains the special epistemological status of repulsive force). Kant argues in *Physical Monadology* that if only the "force of impenetrability" existed, then "bodies would have no cohesive structure at all, for the particles would only repel each other, and no body would have a volume which was circumscribed by a determinate limit" (*MoPh* 1: 484). The Proof of Theorem 5 similarly maintains that matter would "by its repulsive force alone, if no other force counteracted it, be confined within no limit of extension; that is, it would disperse itself to infinity, and no specified quantity of matter would be found within any specified space" (4: 508). In both contexts, Kant concludes that the force by which matter repels must exist together with a force that acts in the opposite direction.

15 Quantity of matter in the Newtonian sense is explicitly discussed in Remark 2 to Theorem 7 and Note 1 to Theorem 8. Kant makes clear that the latter discussion, at least, is not essential to the aims of the chapter as a whole (4: 517–8; *cf.* 4: 522–3).

16 This linkage lays the groundwork for Kant's definition of "quantity of matter" as "the aggregate of the movable in a determinate space" (Explication 2, "Mechanics", 4: 537). See Ch. 23 of Friedman (2013).

17 Friedman takes the argument to proceed as follows: "according to Kant, since all the attracting points in such a distribution must also attract one another, the only stable configuration would be one in which they all coalesced into a single point (and therefore had no actual distances from one another). But this configuration, on Kant's view, would be one in which there is no quantity of matter in the space in question after all" (2013: 185).

18 Friedman maintains that the Proof of Theorem 6 in fact amounts to a "definitive rejection" of the possibility of "isolated point-masses" (Friedman 2013: 186). Their impossibility renders the arguments of *MoPh* inapplicable in *MAN*, where matter is conceived as a "true continuum" (see Friedman 2013: 138–9).

19 The property stated in Proposition 9 of *Principia*'s Book III (the proportionality of gravity inside a body to distance from the center) is a case of the determination of the attractive force of a whole body, by composition of forces toward its parts. That Newton asserts this property before stating the analogue of Proposition 8 in Newton (1728) might suggest that in Newton (1728), just as in *Principia*, the issue of how attraction toward a whole is compounded from attraction toward the parts is raised in order to vindicate the extrapolation (of the notion of weight toward the earth) involved in the moon test. But considering the behavior of gravity within the surface of the earth is, at best, an indirect and obscure way of dealing with the accuracy of the inverse-square proportion just above the earth's surface.

20 In *Principia*, the result is Proposition 19 of Book III, which is shown by applying Corollary 3 of Proposition 91, Book I. In Newton (1728), the example of the channel is discussed on p. 82, after the book's halfway point, while the analogues of Propositions 6 through 10 of Book III are in the first half of the book.

21 Thus in the following Letter LII, Euler claims that when an apple fell on Newton's head, Newton considered whether "this force would have always acted upon the apple, had the tree been a good deal higher", even as high as the moon; Newton then "conjectured that motion might be the cause of this, just as a bomb frequently flies over us without falling vertically". On this account, Newton's "first reasonings" on this subject were "very simple, and scarcely differed from those of the rustic [*paysan*]", until "aided by the most sublime geometry, he discovered that the moon in its motion was subject to the same laws which regulate that of a bomb" (1833: 185–6).

References

DiSalle, R. (2006) *Understanding Space-Time*, Cambridge: Cambridge University Press.

Dunlop, K. (2012) "Kant and Strawson on the Content of Geometrical Concepts," *Nous* 46: 86–126.

Dunlop, K. (2022) "The Applicability of Mathematics as a Metaphysical Problem," in M.B. McNulty (ed.), *Kant's Metaphysical Foundations of Natural Science: A Critical Guide*, Cambridge: Cambridge University Press, pp. 54–79.

Euler, L. (1833) *Letters of Euler on Different Subjects in Natural Philosophy Addressed to a German Princess. With Notes, and a Life of Euler, by David Brewster, LL.D.*, vol. 1–2. New York: J. & J. Harper.

Friedman, M. (2013) *Kant's Construction of Nature*, Cambridge: Cambridge University Press.

McNulty, M.B. (2014) "Kant on Chemistry and the Application of Mathematics in Natural Science," *Kantian Review* 19: 393–418.

Newton, I. (1728) *A Treatise of the System of the World*, London: F. Fayram.

Plaass, P. (1994) *Kant's Theory of Natural Science*, Dordrecht: Springer.

Smith, G.E. (2014) "Closing the Loop," in E. Schliesser and Z. Biener (eds.), *Newton and Empiricism*, Oxford: Oxford University Press, pp. 262–352.

Sutherland, D. (2004) "The Role of Magnitude in Kant's Critical Philosophy," *Canadian Journal of Philosophy* 34: 411–41.

Further Reading

M. Bennett McNulty (ed.), *Cambridge Critical Guide to Kant's Metaphysical Foundations of Natural Science* (Cambridge: Cambridge University Press, 2022) is an up-to-date collective commentary on *MAN*. K. Pollok, *Kants "Metaphysische Anfangsgründe" der Naturwissenschaft* (Hamburg: Felix Meiner Verlag, 2001) is an invaluable resource for readers of German. E. Watkins, *Kant on Laws* (Cambridge: Cambridge University Press, 2019); M. Stan, "Kant's Third Law of Mechanics: The Long Shadow of Leibniz," *Studies in History and Philosophy of Science Part A* 44 (2013): 493–504, situate Kant's laws of mechanics in a tradition stemming from Leibniz.

37

BIOLOGY[1]

Alix Cohen

★★★

According to Kant, that there is a special part of natural science solely dedicated to the study of liv-ing beings (i.e. biology) is due to the fact that they display peculiar features that make them stand out in our experience of the natural world.[2] As exhibited by "the structure of a bird, the hollow-ness of its bones, the placement of its wings for movement and of its tail for steering, etc." (*KU* 5: 360), the organization of living beings seems to require explanation in a way that is not shared by inorganic nature. "[N]ature, considered as a mere mechanism, could have formed itself in a thousand different ways without hitting precisely upon the unity" (*KU* 5: 360), and yet we are dissatisfied with the claim that organisms are the product of this kind of contingency. It is thus that the maxim of teleology "is suggested by particular experiences" (*KU* 5: 386). While Kant's account seems relatively straightforward, this chapter will suggest that the reasons behind his defense of the use of teleology in biology are in fact a lot more complex, which is why they remain the object of heated interpretative debates.

I will begin by focusing on the special character of organisms, and show that for Kant, it consists in their unique capacity to self-organize. In section 2, I will show that the problem they present takes the form of an antinomy that opposes mechanical and teleological modes of explanation. After examining a number of interpretations of the antinomy, I will turn to its resolution and question whether it is satisfactory. In the final section, I will use Kant's endorsement of epigenetic accounts of organic generation as an illustration of his view of the legitimate use of teleology in biology. In con-clusion, I will suggest that interpretative disagreements about Kant's account of biology ultimately come down to different conceptions of the analogy (or lack thereof) between organisms and artefacts.

1. The "Special Character" of Organisms

What does the "special character" of organisms consist in according to Kant (*KU* 5: 369)? He initially describes their distinctive features through the example of a tree. These features, which all have to do with the fact that organisms in some sense produce themselves, can be grouped into three categories: conservation, generation and reproduction. First, "conservation" means that the tree grows, regenerates and repairs itself: "one part of this creature also generates itself in such a way

    DOI: 10.4324/9781003406617-49

that the preservation of the one is reciprocally dependent on the preservation of the others." Thus, an organism produces itself at the level of its parts. Second, "generation" means that the tree's leaves protect the branches that nourish them:

> This plant first prepares the matter that it adds to itself with a quality peculiar to its species, which could not be provided by the mechanism of nature outside of it, and develops itself further by means of material which, as far as its composition is concerned, is its own product.
>
> (*KU* 5: 369)

In this sense, an organism produces itself as an individual. Finally, "reproduction" means that a tree can produce other trees:

> [A] tree generates another tree in accordance with a known natural law. However, the tree that it generates is of the same species; and so it generates itself as far as the species is concerned.
>
> (*KU* 5: 371)

Organisms produce offspring of the same kind and thus secure the survival of their species; that is, an organism produces itself at the level of the species.

These characteristics call for two remarks. First, the self-productive feature of organisms operates at three levels: the species, the individual and the parts. And rather than being merely juxtaposed, these functions are intrinsically coordinated. It is because the parts of the organism work together towards the survival of the whole that it can produce offspring and secure the survival of the species. Second, not only are the parts organized, the organization of the whole affects the organization of each part since the parts have the ability to adapt for the sake of the whole.

> [I]ts parts reciprocally produce each other, as far as both their form and their combination is concerned, and thus produce a whole out of their own causality, the concept of which, conversely, is in turn the cause [. . .] of it in accordance with a principle.
>
> (*KU* 5: 373)

This is the reason why organisms have often been thought of by analogy with artefacts: they both seem to be products of some form of design. As Kant acknowledges, living beings are in some sense an "*analogue of art*" (*KU* 5: 374), which has led some commentators to interpret him as grounding his notion of organisms on this analogy.[3] Yet while it is tempting to focus on Kant's discussion of the resemblance between artefacts and organisms, as it is often done, I believe that Kant actually goes out of his way to emphasize their contrast. As he notes, "An organized being is thus not a mere machine [. . .]. One says far too little about nature and its capacity in organized products if one calls this an *analogue of art*" (*KU* 5: 374). The analogy between organisms and artefacts omits the fact that nature "organizes itself" (*KU* 5: 374), and yet this is the crucial respect in which organisms fundamentally differ from artefacts. Whereas the parts of an organism exist for and through the whole, the parts of a machine do not produce each other and, more importantly, they do not contain the cause of their production.

> [T]he producing cause of the watch and its form is not contained in the nature (of this matter), but outside of it, in a being that can act in accordance with an idea of a whole that is possible through its causality.
>
> (*KU* 5: 374)

Machines owe their organization to an external intention whereas organisms do not: they self-organize. Whereas the former are intentional purposes, the latter are natural purposes.

> [Organisms] first provide objective reality for the concept of an end that is not a practical end but an end of nature, and thereby provide natural science with the basis for a teleology.
>
> (*KU* 5: 376)

The shortcomings of the analogy between organisms and artefacts have led some commentators to focus their attention on another analogy Kant discusses, namely "a remote analogy with our own causality in accordance with ends" (*KU* 5: 375). It is not only that organisms and rational beings share self-producing and self-organizing features, but more importantly that we can only think of organisms by analogy with our own free purposiveness.[4] While this analogy may be more promising, it remains that whether we think of organisms by analogy with artefacts or human rationality, as Kant concludes, "[s]trictly speaking, the organization of nature is therefore not analogous with any causality that we know" (*KU* 5: 375).[5] For although purposive causality and natural causality both have objective reality, their combination, the concept of 'natural purpose' (*Naturzweck*), cannot be derived directly from experience: "The concept of a thing as a natural end [. . .] is still not a concept that can be abstracted from experience", which entails that "it cannot be treated dogmatically for the determining power of judgment" (*KU* 5: 396). Organisms differ from the rest of the natural world, they are beings without compare, and their uniqueness makes them uniquely troubling. As I will show in the following section, the problem they present takes the form of an antinomy that opposes mechanical and teleological modes of explanation.

2. The Antinomy of the Power of Judgment

Just as all the antinomies of the Kantian corpus, the antinomy of the power of judgment consists in two propositions that are in conflict with each other. Its thesis expresses the necessity of judging things according to mechanical principles alone, whereas the antithesis argues for the restriction of the thesis and the resort to teleological principles in order to account for specific objects, namely organisms. By contrast with all the other antinomies however, the antinomy of the power of judgment has two formulations:

[Antinomy 1]

The first maxim of judgement is this *thesis*: All production of material things and their forms must be judged to be possible in terms of merely mechanical laws.

The second maxim is this *antithesis*: Some products of material nature cannot be judged to be possible in terms of merely mechanical laws. (Judging them requires a quite different causal law − viz., that of final causes) (*KU* 5: 387).

[Antinomy 2]

Thesis: All production of material things is possible in terms of merely mechanical laws.

Antithesis: Some production of material things is not possible in terms of merely mechanical laws (*KU* 5: 387).

The difference between the two formulations is that whilst antinomy 2 makes claims about the nature of the world, antinomy 1 is composed of heuristic maxims for our judgment. Antinomy 2 expresses a contradiction about the world (i.e. an ontological conflict), whereas antinomy 1 expresses a conflict within judgement (i.e. an epistemic-methodological conflict).

On this basis, a number of commentators have argued that antinomy 2 is genuinely contradictory but that antinomy 1 is the resolution of this contradiction. In other words, they believe that the contradiction is unravelled once the thesis and the antithesis are in the form of reflective judgement (antinomy 1) as opposed to determinant judgement (antinomy 2).[6] As heuristic methods of inquiry, these principles cannot in fact conflict; we just have to choose to follow one method or the other for the appropriate objects. Thus if these commentators were right, the contradiction would simply lie in a slip from the logical (i.e. judgement) to the ontological (i.e. the world) and, in this sense, it could be quickly addressed. There would be a genuine contradiction at the level of determinant principles (antinomy 2), but its resolution would consist in reaffirming the reflective nature of the principles (antinomy 1).

> Hence all semblance of an antinomy between the maxims of strictly physical (mechanical) and teleological (technical) explanation rests on our confusing the *autonomy* of reflective judgment (which holds merely subjectively for our use of reason regarding the particular empirical laws) with the *heteronomy* of determinative judgment, which must conform to the laws (universal or particular) that are given by understanding.
>
> (*KU* 5: 389)

From the point of view of reflective judgement, the thesis would simply cohabit with the antithesis, both of them being subjective maxims. Yet I believe that the conflict cannot be so easily resolved and that antinomy 1, far from resolving the contradiction, is intrinsically conflicting if not contradictory.[7]

To support this claim, we should begin by noting that a reconciliation between the propositions of antinomy 1 would have been straightforward if Kant had opposed the following claims:

[Antinomy 3]

Thesis: All production of material things must be judged to be possible in terms of mechanical laws.
Antithesis: Some production of material things cannot be judged to be possible merely in terms of mechanical laws.

What antinomy 3 suggests is that the central questioning of the thesis is not carried out by the remark in brackets in antithesis 1. For when the 'merely' is taken out of the thesis, as in antinomy 3, no conflict remains but a simple restriction of the applicability of the thesis. The antinomy then amounts to stating the insufficiency of mechanism for the explanation of organisms and requiring teleology as a necessary complement to mechanism.[8] But the point is precisely that antinomy 2 consists in a genuine contradiction: it opposes a universal proposition and a particular one which denies the universality of the first. There is thus a direct contradiction between the propositions of antinomy 2, and converting them into reflective judgements, as per antinomy 1, does not remove the conflict between them. It simply amounts to displacing it from the world (antinomy 2, which is an ontological contradiction) to the mind (antinomy 1, which is an epistemological conflict); or from a description to a prescription, with the thesis recommending to proceed as if everything could be explained mechanically and the antithesis recommending to proceed as if organisms could only be explained teleologically. Only a schizophrenic scientist could follow both maxims without facing a methodological conflict. In this sense, underlying the fact that the propositions of the antinomy are reflective judgements as opposed to determinant ones does not solve their opposition. The epistemological conflict between mechanism and teleology remains and it is radical. It opposes a universal methodological principle and a proposition that denies the possibility of its application to all objects. Or to put this claim slightly differently, thesis 1 claims that the only possible model of understanding is mechanical, and antithesis 1 not only denies the possibility of its application to all objects (first clause), but also puts forward a "quite different" understanding (*KU* 5: 387), namely a teleological one (second clause).

While commentators now largely agree that antinomy 2 consists in a genuine contradiction, there is disagreement as to the nature of the conflict that opposes mechanism and teleology. Two main interpretative options can be found in the literature. According to the most popular one, first put forward by Peter McLaughlin, mechanism "means the reduction of a whole to the properties (faculties and forces) which the parts have 'on their own', that is independently of the whole" (McLaughlin 1990: 153). Mechanical explanations explain the functioning of a whole by the behavior of its parts. On this interpretation, organisms resist this form of explanation because of their self-organizing character, which distinguishes them from artefacts but more importantly from other, non-organic natural wholes. It is this particular feature that entails that their parts cannot be accounted for independently of the whole, and thus that they need to be accounted for teleologically.[9] A second interpretative option, defended by Hannah Ginsborg, argues that organisms question the mechanical model of explanation because they cannot be accounted for merely in virtue of "the mere forces of matter as such" (Ginsborg 2004: 37). On her account, organisms are so complex that they cannot be explained by attraction, repulsion, and the laws of mechanics. Ginsborg thus puts forward a different interpretation of the notion of mechanism, or mechanical explanation. On her account, "we explain something mechanically when we explain its production as a result of the unaided powers of matter as such." In this sense, contrary to McLaughlin, she does not think of mechanism as a type of causality (Ginsborg 2004: 40, 42).[10]

Whilst it falls well beyond the scope of this chapter to settle these debates, I would like to note that there is a sense in which they ultimately bring us back to our starting point, namely how we should think about the analogy between organisms and artefacts. For McLaughlin, organisms are importantly unlike artefacts, and it is this dissimilarity that entails that the former, and not the latter, call for teleological explanations (McLaughlin 1990: 152–3). For Ginsborg however, organisms and artefacts both call for teleological explanations since we cannot help but think of them both as products of design. On her reading of Kant, it is a different feature of organic products, namely the unique complex arrangement of matter they exhibit, that calls for teleology (Ginsborg 2004: 37). While each conception of the analogy between organisms and artefacts leads to a different interpretation of the antinomy between teleology and mechanism, the next section will show that no matter which one we adopt, we face further interpretative difficulties.

3. The Resolution of the Antinomy and Its Implications for Biology

Since "[w]hat is at issue is . . . a special character of *our* (human) understanding with regard to the power of judgment in its reflection upon things in nature" (*KU* 5: 406), the contrast between our understanding and an intuitive understanding is often seen as the key to the resolution of the antinomy.[11] For it enables Kant to identify the distinctive features of our cognitive powers and the characteristics of our way of representing the world. We, endowed with a discursive understanding, cannot conceive the possibility of reconciling teleological and mechanical accounts within one single theory since for us, they conflict. But by contrast with our discursive mode of cognition, an intuitive understanding does not resort to either the distinction between mechanism and teleology, or the concept of natural purpose, to grasp the distinctive feature of organisms.

> [I]t is not at all necessary here to prove that such an *intellectus archetypus* is possible, but only that in the contrast of it with our discursive, image-dependent understanding (*intellectus ectypus*) and the contingency of such a constitution we are led to that idea (of an *intellectus archetypus*), and that this does not contain any contradiction.
>
> (*KU* 5: 408)

Thus somehow paradoxically, it is the subjective nature of the conflict between mechanism and teleology, the fact that it is the result of our distinctive cognitive apparatus, that enables us to ascertain that mechanism and teleology are in fact compatible, albeit in the supersensible. The role of the appeal to the supersensible is to assure us, or at least reassure us, that mechanism and teleology are not only compatible with each other, they can be united in a single principle – despite the fact that we have no access to it. Thereby, "[t]he possibility that both may be objectively unifiable in one principle (since they concern appearances that presuppose a supersensible ground) is secured" (*KU* 5: 413).

Yet one may worry that Kant's solution to the antinomy is not fully satisfactory with regard to the methodology we should follow in investigating nature and organisms in particular. Even though its resolution is meant to allow us to proceed "confidently", "without being troubled by the apparent conflict between the two principles for judging this product" (*KU* 5: 413), the conflict remains. It is resolved in the supersensible, but in the empirical world, we are left with "two heterogeneous principles" (*KU* 5: 412). For when we study organisms, we must choose between one and the other: "one kind of explanation excludes the other, even on the supposition that objectively both grounds of the possibility rest on a single one" (*KU* 5: 412). Thus, there is a sense in which the conflicting nature of mechanism and teleology remains. By arguing that the conflict between mechanism and teleology is natural to our cognitive powers, Kant has in effect legitimated it for us.

> [T]here can be drawn no explanation, i.e., a distinct and determinate derivation of the possibility of a natural product that is possible in accordance with those two heterogeneous principles.
>
> (*KU* 5: 412)

Despite these caveats, Kant proceeds to draw the implications of the resolution of the antinomy for our use of mechanical and teleological principles. Insofar as teleological explanations refer to the possibility of our judgments, they lack objective explanatory power:

> [Teleology] does not pertain to the possibility of such things themselves (even considered as phenomena) in accordance with this sort of generation, but pertains only to the judging of them that is possible for our understanding.
>
> (KU 5: 408)[12]

Because of their reflective nature, teleological judgments are hypothetical modes of explanation that cannot attain the level of objectivity required by physical science. That is why Kant continually repeats that teleological explanations are not informative:

[P]ositing ends of nature in its products provides no information at all about the origination and the inner possibility of these forms, although it is that with which theoretical natural science is properly concerned.

(*KU* 5: 417)

However, the fundamental point is that teleology, although not self-sufficient, is not illegitimate as such; it is illegitimate only if used outside the limits of human knowledge.[13] Doing away with it would lead to the loss of a precious heuristic principle.

[T]eleological judging is rightly drawn into our research into nature, at least problematically, but only in order to bring it under principles of observation and research in *analogy* with causality according to ends, without presuming thereby to *explain* it.

(*KU* 5: 360)[14]

Consequently, first, we should hold on to teleology as a principle for reflective judgment whatever turns out to be the case constitutively.[15] Second, we should always think of organisms as being mechanically possible and go as far we can in our mechanical explanation of them.

It is thus rational, indeed meritorious, to pursue the mechanism of nature, for the sake of an explanation of the products of nature, as far as can plausibly be done, and indeed not to give up this effort because it is impossible in itself to find the purposiveness of nature by this route, but only because it is impossible for us as humans.

(*KU* 5: 418)

Thus on my reading, and in agreement with a number of recent interpretations put forward in the literature, Kant is and remains committed to the claim that all objects of experience, including organisms, can be accounted for in mechanical terms.[16] This point is sometimes misunderstood when read in light of Kant's infamous comment on the possibility of a Newton of a blade of grass:

It would be absurd for humans even to make such an attempt or to hope that there may yet arise a Newton who could make comprehensible even the generation of a blade of grass according to natural laws that no intention has ordered; rather, we must absolutely deny this insight to human beings.

(*KU* 5: 400)

It is tempting to read this passage as denying the possibility of mechanical explanations of organisms.[17] However, I believe that it should be interpreted as supporting a very different and more complex claim, which I can spell out in two parts. On the one hand, an authentic Newton of a blade of grass would in effect be a physicist rather than a biologist in the sense that he would dissolve biology into a branch of physics. He would account for organic phenomena entirely mechanically, and would provide a scientific account of the functioning of an organism *qua* natural object, just as he would of any other physical object.[18] Yet on the other hand, there can never be a Newton of a blade of grass *qua* living being unless he becomes a biologist and adopts teleology as an epistemic principle. For biology, as the science of organisms properly called, can never be reduced to physics since the very concept of organism defines them in teleological terms as natural purposes.[19] However, if he relies on teleological principles, even reflectively or heuristically, he cannot be an authentic Newton. Thus strictly speaking, there can never be a Newton of a blade of grass.[20]

To provide further support for this claim, the following section examines the reasons behind Kant's approval of epigenesis, and Blumenbach's account of it in particular, as the only viable theory of life. As I will show, it provides a useful illustration of Kant's view of the interaction and the coordination of teleology and mechanism in biology.

4. The Origin of Life

Two essential features of epigenesis are particularly attractive for Kant.[21] First, it does not try to account for the possibility of an original form of organization. By leaving aside the question of life's beginnings, it limits itself to the claim that an organism can only be conceived as the product of another organism: it "begins all physical explanation of these formations with organized matter" (*KU* 5: 424).[22] By contrast, what Kant calls a "daring adventure of reason" is the thought that an organism could be generated mechanically by "crude, unorganized matter" (*KU* 5: 419). Any theory that takes as its starting point an organic form of life, no matter how outlandish, will fare better than those starting from inert matter. What is not absurd however, although it is often misunderstood as such, is the thought that mother nature, "the maternal womb of the earth", could bear simple organisms, which would then bear organisms that are better suited to their environment.

Second, epigenesis rightly characterizes nature not only as something that develops mechanically, but as something that is productive and has a teleological element. The conception of nature as producing is conveyed by the concept of *Bildungstrieb*, or "formative impulse", that Kant borrows from Blumenbach.

> [Blumenbach] calls the faculty in the matter in an organized body (in distinction from the merely mechanical formative power that is present in all matter) a formative drive [*Bildungstrieb*] (standing, as it were, under the guidance and direction of that former principle).
>
> (*KU* 5: 424)

Kant approves of Blumenbach's use of the *Bildungstrieb* because it accounts for the original organization of matter without resorting to a mechanistic explanation of the origin of life. In this sense, the decisive contribution of epigenesis to the debates on organic generation is to acknowledge a primitive organization and, accordingly, subordinate mechanical principles to teleological principles: "our judging of them [organisms] must always be subordinated to a teleological principle as well" (*KU* 5: 417).[23]

Furthermore, Kant's official support for epigenesis as the only viable theory of organic generation is supplemented with a strong preformationist component.[24] In this sense, his endorsement of epigenesis is limited by the role assigned to natural predispositions, which are ordering principles or predispositions inherent in the organism's stock.[25] These natural predispositions, which are dynamic and purposive, play the role of limiting structures that prevent the mutation of species. As such, they account for the fact that species cannot transform and their characteristics are predetermined.

> I myself derive all organization from organic beings (through generation) and all later forms (of this kind of natural things) from laws of the gradual development of original predispositions [*ursprünglichen Anlagen*], which were to be found in the organization of its phylum.
>
> (*ÜGTP* 8: 179)

According to Kant, some structuring powers or predispositions, acting upon specific pre-existent "germs" (*Anlagen*), underlie the development of organisms. The role played by these predispositions is crucial: they predetermine the evolution of organisms by providing intrinsic purposive structures that guide their development – so much so that an organism "incorporate[s] nothing into its generative power that does not belong to one of the undeveloped original predispositions of such a system of ends" (*KU* 5: 420).[26] As a result, Kant's theory of organic generation, which I have also called an "epigenesis of natural predispositions", provides a useful illustration of what I take to be the basic tenant of his account of biology, namely the subordination of mechanical explanations to teleological principles.[27] The direction is provided by the latter but the bulk of the work is achieved by the former.

5.   Conclusion

This chapter began with Kant's claim that a special part of natural science is solely dedicated to organisms because they exhibit peculiar features that make them stand out in our experience of the natural world. To conclude, I would like to suggest that the interpretative disagreements that pertain to the "special character" of organisms are ultimately based on different conceptions of the analogy between organisms and artefacts (*KU* 5: 369). Depending on how this analogy is formulated, a different account of the distinctive feature of organism ensues, from which a particular notion of purposiveness follows.

As shown in this chapter, a number of commentators defend that organisms are importantly unlike artefacts, although this claim leads them to different conclusions. For McLaughlin, it is the uniqueness of organisms that should be emphasized: it consists in a part/whole relationship that differs in fundamental ways from the part/whole relationship found in artefacts.[28] For Breitenbach, organisms are also unlike artefacts, but rather than following McLaughlin in emphasizing their uniqueness, she focuses on their resemblance to something else, namely our own form of rationality.[29] By contrast to both McLaughlin and Breitenbach, according to Ginsborg, organisms are very much like artefacts, so much so that this resemblance does not tell us anything particularly interesting about them. This leads her to search for another special feature of organisms, a feature she locates in the complex arrangement of matter they exhibit. Thus, Ginsborg's interpretation of the analogy between organisms and artefacts determines her understanding of the purposiveness uniquely found in organisms.

What I take this to suggest is that looking at interpretative debates on Kant's account of biology through the lens of the analogy between organisms and artefacts enables us to think about them in a new way. These debates are usually presented as disagreements about the notion of purposiveness at play in Kant's account of organisms; i.e. Ginsborg relies on a weak notion of primitive purposiveness as a means-ends activity while Breitenbach uses a stronger notion of practical activity and McLaughlin puts forward a model based on technical-practical causes.[30] However, my discussion points to the fact that these disagreements ultimately stem from different conceptions of the analogy between organisms and artefacts; i.e. for Ginsborg, organisms are unlike artefacts, whereas for Breitenbach and McLaughlin, they are alike. Reformulating the debate in this way is valuable for it prompts us to return to the original motivation behind Kant's project. To understand why a special part of natural science is solely dedicated to organisms, we must identify what sets them apart from all other beings. As I have argued, the only way of doing so is to compare and contrast them with other beings, and thus explore the possibility of thinking about them analogically while remaining aware of the limitations of this exercise. In this sense, analogical thinking is central to the Kantian conception of living beings because they are and ultimately remain beings without compare.

Notes

1 I would like to thank Angela Breitenbach, Ido Geiger and Cain Todd for their helpful comments on earlier drafts of this chapter.

2 Dedicating a chapter to Kant's theory of biology may seem like a non-starter since he does not actually use the term 'biology'. The concept was first used to refer to a single coherent discipline in the nineteenth century. Yet the application of this concept to 'pre-biological' theories of life, and to Kant's theory in particular, is now acknowledged as unproblematic (see, for instance, Zumbach 1984 and Zuckert 2007). For, although Kant's model of biological science is somewhat different from what we now call biology, there is no doubt that they are equally concerned with the scientific study of living beings.

3 See for instance McFarland (1970: 111), McLaughlin (1990: 39), Guyer (2005: 95, 329) and Ginsborg (2015: 337). As Ginsborg writes, "one of the intuitions motivating my approach is that our ascription of functions to biological entities reflects a conception of them as analogous to artefacts" (Ginsborg 2015: 337). However, she does acknowledge that for Kant, this analogy has serious limitations (Ginsborg 2015: 250).

4 As Breitenbach has argued, "the purposive organization and end-directedness of our rational capacities themselves [. . .] can provide the ground for an analogy with the particular character of living nature" (Breitenbach 2014: 136). See also Neiman (1994: 81ff).

5 Breitenbach addresses this problem by arguing further that the analogy between our own purposiveness and the natural purposiveness of organisms provides us with a symbolic representation of life in nature (Breitenbach 2014: 140–2).

6 E.g., Cassirer (1938), Ernst (1909) and Butts (1984). For critical discussions, see McFarland (1970: 122), McLaughlin (1990: 137) and Cohen (2004).

7 For the further claim that it is the only antinomy of the Kantian corpus to be genuinely conflicting due to its unique structure, see Cohen 2004.

8 This change to the antinomy, as per antinomy 3, entails that strictly speaking, it is not an antinomy in the Kantian sense of the term. However, my point here is to use the contrast between antinomy 1 and 3 to highlight the genuine conflicting nature of antinomy 1, and thus the sense in which it is an antinomy in the Kantian sense of the term.

9 Along similar lines, see Guyer (2005: 354), Zammito (2006: 759) and Zuckert (2007: 101).

10 For an interpretation that combines the accounts of Ginsborg and McLaughlin, see Breitenbach: "mechanistic explanations in Kant's *Critique of Judgment* thus refer to empirical laws about the causal interactions between the forces of the material parts of natural objects" (Breitenbach 2006: 708). For alternative interpretations of the antinomy, see Quarfood (2004: 160–208).

11 E.g., Quarfood (2004: 207–8).

12 This is the reason why Kant refutes all the philosophical systems that account for the phenomenon of organic purposiveness in a dogmatic, unreflective fashion (see *KU* 5: 390–5). For an account of Kant's refutation of the idealism and the realism of purposiveness, see Zumbach (1984: Chapter 3) and McLaughlin (1990: 158–61). What is important for my analysis is that these models "absolutely cannot justify any objective assertion" (*KU* 5: 395).

13 "I do not find it advisable to use a theological language in matters that concern the mere cognitions of nature and their reach (where it is quite appropriate to express oneself in teleological terms) – in order to indicate quite diligently to each mode of cognition its boundaries" (*ÜGTP* 8: 178).

14 See also Kant's claim that it is "allowed to use the teleological principle where sources of theoretical cognition are not sufficient" (*ÜGTP* 8: 160). For an account of the role of teleology that goes beyond the heuristic model, see Breitenbach (2008).

15 For a slightly different version of this claim, see Watkins (2009: 202).

16 Teufel (2014) is particularly enlightening on this point.

17 For a discussion of this claim, see for instance Zammito (2006: 765–6).

18 Cornell succinctly formulates the point: To reject Kant's argument we would have to "explain away" the organism (Cornell 1986: 408). See also: McLaughlin (1990: 178) and Geiger (2009: 542–3).

19 Recall the starting point of this chapter. According to Kant, organisms have a "special character" (*KU* 5: 369) – they stand out in the natural world because they self-organize.

20 I have presented a lengthier defense of this claim in Cohen 2020.

21 For an account of the scientific context of the time and the debates on generation, see Sloan 2002; Zammito 1992, 2003.

22 As Kant notes, Blumenbach "rightly declares it to be contrary to reason that raw matter should originally have formed itself in accordance with mechanical laws" (*KU* 5: 424). Kant's relationship with Blumenbach has been the subject of numerous divergent interpretations. See for instance Lenoir (1982), Sloan (2002: Section 3) and Zammito (2003).

23 See also the title of §80: "On the necessary subordination of the principle of mechanism to the teleological principle in the explanation of a thing as a natural end" (*KU* 5: 417). For a discussion of the epistemic status of the *Bildungstrieb* for Blumenbach and Kant, see the conflicting interpretations of Lenoir (1980: 84–5) and Richards (2000: Section 2.4).

24 This appears most clearly in Kant's definition of epigenesis as "the system of generic preformation, since the productive capacity of the progenitor is still preformed in accordance with the internally purposive predispositions that were imparted to its stock, and thus the specific form was preformed virtualiter" (*KU* 5:423). See also *RezHerder* (8: 62–3).

25 Both Sloan and Zammito importantly remark that Kant's resort to natural predispositions makes his theory diverge radically from Blumenbach's version of epigenesis (Sloan 2002: 246–7; Zammito 2003: 93). In this sense, as Zammito writes, Kant believed that "epigenesis implied preformation: at the origin, there had to be some inexplicable (transcendent) endowment, and with it, in his view, some determinate restriction in species variation. Thereafter, the organized principles within the natural world could proceed on adaptive lines. This made epigenesis over into Kant's variant of preformation" (Zammito 2003: 88).

26 Despite the fact that Kant brings these natural predispositions into play in his account of organic generation in the *Critique of the Power of Judgment*, he does not expound their nature in any detail there, but does so instead in the context of his earlier discussions of human races. See for instance Cohen (2009: 25–9).

27 Contrast with Quarfood (2004: 102–14).

28 See McLaughlin (1990: 50) for the emphasis on the limits of the analogy, and McLaughlin (1990: 153) for a discussion of the part/whole relationship that is specific to organisms: "we cannot understand, conceive, or even 'become acquainted with' a causal relation in which a whole acts upon the properties of its parts, as seems to be the case in the organism" (McLaughlin 1989: 179–80). This interpretation is based on a close reading of *KU* (5: 407–408).

29 See for instance "it is the goal-directed and self-organizing features of human reason, that is, our capacity to set ourselves ends and to try to realize them by a coherent and unified employment of our rational faculties, that provides the analogon for living nature" (Breitenbach 2014: 136).

30 See in particular Ginsborg (2015: 243), Breitenbach (2014: 138) and McLaughlin (1990: 38–9).

References

Breitenbach, A. (2006) "Mechanical Explanation of Nature and Its Limits in Kant's Critique of Judgment," *Studies in History and Philosophy of Science (Part C)* 37(4): 694–711.

Breitenbach, A. (2008) "Two Views on Nature: A Solution to Kant's Antinomy of Mechanism and Teleology," *British Journal for the History of Philosophy* 16(2): 351–69.

Breitenbach, A. (2014) "Biological Purposiveness and Analogical Reflection," in I. Goy and E. Watkins (eds.), *Kant's Theory of Biology*, Berlin and New York: Walter de Gruyter, pp. 131–48.

Butts, R. (1984) *Kant and the Double Government Methodology*, Dordrecht, Boston and Lancaster: D. Reidel Publishing.

Cassirer, H.W. (1938) *A Commentary on Kant's Critique of Judgment*, New York: Barnes & Noble.

Cohen, A. (2004) "Kant's Antinomy of Reflective Judgment: A Re-Evaluation," *Teorema* 23(1–3): 183–97.

Cohen, A. (2009) *Kant and the Human Science: Biology, Anthropology and History*, London: Palgrave Macmillan.

Cohen, A. (2020) "Kant on Evolution: A Re-Evaluation," in J. Callanan and L. Allais (eds.), *Kant and Animals*, Oxford: Oxford University Press, pp. 124–34.

Cornell, J.F. (1986) "Newton of the Grassblade? Darwin and the Problem of Organic Teleology," *Isis* 77: 405–21.

Ernst, W. (1909) *Der Zweckbegriff bei Kant und sein Verhältnis zu den Kategorien*, Berlin: Reuther & Reichard.

Geiger, I. (2009) "Is Teleological Judgement (Still) Necessary? Kant's Arguments in the Analytic and in the Dialectic of Teleological Judgement," *British Journal for the History of Philosophy* 17(3): 533–66.

Ginsborg, H. (2004) "Two Kinds of Mechanical Inexplicability in Kant and Aristotle," *Journal of History of Philosophy* 42(1): 33–65.

Ginsborg, H. (2015) *The Normativity of Nature: Essays on Kant's Critique of Judgement*, Oxford: Oxford University Press.

Guyer, P. (2005) *Kant's System of Nature and Freedom: Selected Essays*, Oxford: Oxford University Press.

Lenoir, T. (1980) "Kant, Blumenbach, and Vital Materialism in German Biology," *Isis* 71: 77–108.

Lenoir, T. (1982) *The Strategy of Life: Teleology and Mechanics in Nineteenth Century German Biology*, Dordrecht and Boston: D. Reidel.

McFarland, J.D. (1970) *Kant's Concept of Teleology*, Edinburgh: Edinburgh University Press.

McLaughlin, P. (1989) "What Is an Antinomy of Judgment," *Proceedings of the Sixth International Kant Congress* 2(2): 357–67.

McLaughlin, P. (1990) *Kant's Critique of Teleology in Biological Explanation*, Lewiston, NY: The Edwin Mellen Press.

Neiman, S. (1994) *The Unity of Reason: Rereading Kant*, New York: Oxford University Press.

Quarfood, M. (2004) *Transcendental Idealism and the Organism*, Stockholm: Almqvist & Wiksell International.

Richards, R.J. (2000) "Kant and Blumenbach on the *Bildungstrieb*: A Historical Misunderstanding," *Studies in History and Philosophy of Biological and Biomedical Sciences* 31(1): 11–32.

Sloan, P. (2002) "Preforming the Categories: Eighteenth Century Generation Theory and the Biological Roots of Kant's A Priori," *Journal of the History of Philosophy* 40(2): 229–53.

Teufel, T. (2014) "The Impossibility of a Newton of the Blade of Grass in Kant's Teleology," in O. Nachtomy and J.H. Smith (eds.), *The Life Sciences in Early Modern Philosophy*, Oxford: Oxford University Press.

Watkins, E. (2009) "The Antinomy of Teleological Judgment," *Kant Yearbook* 1: 197–221.

Zammito, J.H. (1992) *The Genesis of Kant's Critique of Judgment*, Chicago: Chicago University Press.

Zammito, J.H. (2003) "'This Inscrutable *Principle* of an Original *Organization*': Epigenesis and 'Looseness of Fit' in Kant's Philosophy of Science," *Studies in History and Philosophy of Science (Part C)* 37(4): 73–109.

Zammito, J.H. (2006) "Teleology Then and Now: The Question of Kant's Relevance for Contemporary Controversies Over Function in Biology," in J. Steigerwald (ed.), *Studies in History and Philosophy of Biological and Biomedical Sciences* 37(4): 748–70.

Zuckert, R. (2007) *Kant on Beauty and Biology: An Interpretation of the Critique of Judgment*, Cambridge: Cambridge University Press.

Zumbach, C. (1984) *The Transcendent Science: Kant's Conception of Biological Methodology*, The Hague, Boston and Lancaster: Nijhoff.

Further reading

H. Ginsborg, "Kant on Understanding Organisms as Natural Purposes," in E. Watkins (ed.), *Kant and the Sciences* (Oxford: Oxford University Press, 2001, pp. 231–58) is an influential interpretation of the concept of purposiveness. I. Goy and E. Watkins (eds.), *Kant's Theory of Biology* (Berlin and New York: Walter de Gruyter, 2014) is a collection of papers by leading scholars, it is a useful overview of some recent debates. P. McLaughlin, *Kant's Critique of Teleology in Biological Explanation* (Lewiston, NY: The Edwin Mellen Press, 1990) – one of the first extensive treatments of teleology in biology, it has become a reference in the field. E. Watkins, "The Antinomy of Teleological Judgment," *Kant Yearbook* 1 (2009): 197–221 is a helpful presentation and critical discussion of debates surrounding the antinomy of the power of judgment.

PART 3

Posthumous Writings and Lectures

38

OPUS POSTUMUM

Giovanni Pietro Basile

★★★

Although *OP* has been in print, if only in an incomplete form, eighty years after the death of Kant, it has never ceased to arouse considerable interest in Kantian studies. Over the decades, research on these writings has given rise to a considerable body of literature that covers all the varied range of issues treated in it.[1]

Certainly research has given much attention to the later Kant's relationship to the sciences. A first area of interest concerns the relationship of *OP* to Newtonian physics. While Burkhard Tuschling (1971) has tried to show a progressive divergence of Kant's *OP* from Newtonian mechanics, more recent studies (Friedman 1992; Massimi 2008) point out, however, the affinity of *OP* to Newton's physics. An additional research topic is Kant's interest in chemistry and, in particular, in the chemistry of Lavoisier (Friedman 1992; Vasconi 1998) and in crystallography (Fritscher 2009). A very comprehensive study concerning mathematics in *OP* has been published by Gregor Büchel (1987). Finally, biology and the notion of organism in *OP* are the subject of a number of studies. In addition to the pioneering work of Heinz Heimsoeth (1940) we must at least mention the studies of Klaus Düsing (1986: 143–205) and of Hein van den Berg (2014: 149–259), which highlight the substantial continuity of *OP* with the third *Critique*. In particular, van den Berg points out that in *OP* Kant continues to consider biology as a science based on the teleological principle, in contrast to a mere mechanical explanation of organisms (2014: 187–220), and that he rejects materialism and hylozoism (2014: 221–59).

More specifically epistemological and theoretical problems that are recurrent in studies on *OP* are the genesis of the main problem of *OP*, that is, the transition from *MAN* to physics as an answer to a deficiency in critical thought; the notion of ether and, more specifically, its transcendental deduction; self-affection and the self-positing of the subject; the idea of God and the system of ideas in the highest standpoint of transcendental philosophy. They will be examined in this chapter. Every comprehensive interpretation of *OP* is committed to the task of explaining the mutual relationship among the preceding topics.

Among the main Kantian scholars that have offered an interpretation of the whole *OP* in the last decades, the following must be mentioned: Gerhard Lehmann (1969), Vittorio Mathieu (1989), Tuschling (1971, 2001), Michael Friedman (1992), Eckart Förster (2000). Lehmann considers *OP*

 DOI: 10.4324/9781003406617-51

as a "critique of technical reason" (1969: 289) in continuity with the third *Critique*, but breaking with the first *Critique*. According to Mathieu, Kant's reflections in *OP* follow a coherent systematic thread, which he tries to reconstruct, by highlighting the substantial correlation with the first *Critique*. Tuschling argues that Kant, in *OP*, radically modifies his previous conception of matter, aiming at a metaphysical dynamics as a transcendental doctrine, and progressively departs from his own critical philosophy towards a form of Spinozism. According to Friedman, *OP* aims at extending the metaphysical foundation of the natural sciences through a general system of inductive and deductive principles, although Kant's attempt was doomed to failure. Förster claims that Kant finds, thanks to the ether deduction and the notion of self-positing of the subject, the solution of the transition-problem and, thanks to a new idea of God, the solution of a central problem of Critical philosophy, that is, the synthesis of theoretical and practical philosophy in a unique system of transcendental philosophy.

Finally, the historical-philological questions and the problem of the method of interpretation should not be forgotten, given the special nature of the texts of *OP*. The current critical edition (AA 21 and 22) is deficient in many respects. A new critical edition of *OP* edited by Eckart Förster together with Jacqueline Karl is in preparation. In this new edition, all the resources related to Kant's last project will be presented in chronological order. Moreover, the transcript of the original manuscripts will also be thoroughly revised, corrected and supplemented. This new edition is therefore expected to provide an important instrument for furthering research on *OP*.

This chapter will present four main areas of ongoing research related to Kant's last project: 1) the problem of the method for its interpretation; 2) the initial problem of the Kantian project; 3) the notion of ether in *Uebergang 1–14* as the main turning point in the whole *OP*; 4) the idea of God and the system of transcendental philosophy as the final topic of *OP*. This chapter will devote a special emphasis on the second area of research just highlighted.

1. Interpreting the *OP*

According to the most reliable dating, Kant's notes related to *OP* were distributed from 1795 up to February 1803 and include, in addition to the early leaves, fourteen drafts in chronological order (Basile 2013: 502). The initial title of the work was: "Transition from the metaphysical foundations of natural science to physics [*Übergang von den Metaphysischen Anfangsgründen der Naturwissenschaft zur Physik*]." Over time, a thematic evolution can be noted. Initially, Kant's reflections deal with the physical properties of matter and the attempt to develop a system of the forces of matter. In later drafts – *Uebergang 1–14* (May–August 1799) and *Conv. X/XI* (August 1799April 1800) – wider epistemological and natural philosophical issues emerge. The last two drafts – *Conv. VII* (April–December 1800) and *Conv. I* (December 1800–February 1803) – deal predominantly with issues relating to the transcendental dialectic of the first *Critique*.

It is clear that no investigation of *OP* is possible without a deep historical-critical analysis of the texts. The question is whether and under which conditions a systematic interpretation of *OP* is possible. Some interpreters have dealt with this question from quite different perspectives (Lehmann 1969: 89–116; Tuschling 1971: 3–14; Mathieu 1989: 9–14, 57–85; see also Basile 2013: 361–7). If the reconstruction of the implicit system of *OP* is not to remain simply arbitrary, it needs a "rule" or a "canon". Such a rule can be provided by the historical-critical procedure, but can also be found in the works of the Critical period. Lehmann considers for instance the third *Critique* to be such a rule, Mathieu by contrast gives preference to the first one. Lehmann affirms further that in *OP* there exist a "superficial [*superfizielle*]" and an "inner [*innere*]" system (Lehmann 1969: 98) that are in contradiction to each other. Interpreting Kant means therefore to set the deep system of his texts free

468

from its historical form. Interpretation is, in this sense, reconstruction of a thought and hence also destruction of the reference to the historical framework. Against Lehmann, Tuschling defends the principle that the interpretation of *OP* should not go beyond the descriptive reconstruction of what he considers "a scientific journal" (1971: 13) of the elderly philosopher. Mathieu claims that the reconstruction of the implicit system of *OP* presupposes the constant reference to the chronological order of the materials: the implicit system has to match (at least asymptotically) with the historical development of Kant's notes.

It is an undeniable fact that, within *OP*, there are "turning points" in Kant's thought. How to interpret them leads to two fundamental questions that set the interpretative horizon of any investigation of *OP*. The first question deals with the possibility of reconstructing a systematic internal consistency of the texts of *OP*, given their incompleteness, or if it is more appropriate to admit one or more breaking points, as signs of unsolvable aporias faced by Kant in his investigation. The second fundamental question concerns the relationship of *OP* to the corpus of Kant's Critical works, above all *KrV*, *MAN* and *KU*. The resumption and further development in *OP* of themes already treated in the "Critical period" authorize one to speak of a "post-Critical" Kant. It is, however, an open question, whether the post-Critical developments are in substantial continuity with the Critical thinking or if they exceed it, progressing towards a form of absolute idealism.

2. The Initial Problem of the Transition–Project

The fact that Kant began working on *OP* as a new project presupposes his dissatisfaction with his current philosophical system and his wish to correct or retract its deficiencies. The open question is the identification of these deficiencies and the works in which they emerge. Since the original title of the Transition-project referred explicitly to *MAN* and both writings deal with the matter and its properties, a direct link between *MAN* and the Transition-project is undeniable. Nevertheless one may wonder if the issue of a "transition" from metaphysics to physics at its origin should not be linked with an analogous problem of "transition" concerning the reflecting judgment in the third *Critique*.

MAN and the Transition-project: Some scholars hold the view that, with *OP*, Kant was aiming at extending the exposition of the metaphysics of nature in *MAN*. The Transition-project would then constitute the treatise of rational psychology foreseen by the Architectonic, (A846f./B874f.) but still missing in the Kantian system (Drivet 2002), or an extension of the metaphysical foundation of the science of nature, required after the scientific revolution in chemistry with Lavoisier (Friedman 1992; Vasconi 1999). The elementary chemistry introduced by the latter marked, in fact, the transition from the phlogistic theory to quantitative chemistry based on the notion of imponderable caloric fluid or ether. Kant would have seen in this very notion of ether a concept constructible in the intuition and, therefore, the condition to apply mathematics to chemistry, which is the criterion for genuine science given in *MAN* (4: 470f.). Other scholars differ in that they consider that the Transition-project cannot be understood as a mere complement to the metaphysical foundation of Newtonian physics provided in *MAN*. It would originate from the necessity of a substantial revision of the *Metaphysical Foundations of Dynamics* and the *Metaphysical Foundations of Mechanics* or even of the complete work of 1786 (Tuschling 1971; Hoppe 1969).

More recently it has been proposed that, in his Transition-project, Kant was aiming not at the revision of the dynamics and mechanics of *MAN*, but at a revision of the transition from dynamics to mechanics contained in the *General Remark to Dynamics* in *MAN* (Emundts 2004). Dynamics has to explain why matter, thanks to the interaction of the fundamental forces of attraction and repulsion, fills up a certain space. Mechanics deals instead with the principles of the interaction between moving bodies. In the *Dynamics-Remark* Kant aims at deducing the general properties of matter – density, cohesion, elasticity and mechanical or chemical processes – from the two fundamental forces (*MAN* 4: 523–35). Cohesion is especially crucial for explaining the constitution of the bodies as presupposed by mechanics. With the Transition-project, Kant revised his position because he noted a circularity in his previous conception of matter in *MAN* concerning cohesion.[2] He tries to overcome this problem by distinguishing between the two fundamental forces of attraction and repulsion expounded in the dynamics and the system of the intermediate moving forces – including a derivative repulsive force (elasticity) and a derivative attractive force (cohesion)– which he explains as properties of ether. Ether is now added to the two fundamental forces of attraction and repulsion as "the third [*das dritte*]" (*OP* 22: 211.25) necessary (and no longer just hypothetical) principle, on which is based the *a priori* treatment of the properties of matter. The doctrine of the transition in *OP* would therefore revise only the *Dynamics-Remark* of *MAN*. The system of the moving forces of matter, moreover, takes as well a new position in the system of natural philosophy. It is no longer an appendix of the metaphysical principles of dynamics, but it takes on an intermediate position between the metaphysical principles of natural philosophy (now corresponding to the four main sections of *MAN*) and physics as an experimental science, with the function of transition from one to another.

Reflecting judgment and the initial problem of *OP*: The question can be asked whether or not the genesis of the Transition-project can be exhaustively explained exclusively in the context of the specific problems of *MAN*. More specifically, one may ask if the work on the transition from metaphysics to physics, which Kant perhaps already conceives in 1790 (Förster 2000: 51–3), is to be linked with the issue of the transition from the sensible to the supersensible, from the concept of nature to the concept of freedom, that is, from physics to metaphysics brought about by the reflecting judgment, which is dealt with in the *Introduction* to the third *Critique* (*EEKU* 20: 246; *KU* 5: 175f., 179, 185, 196).

The first to suggest the possibility of a correlation, at least implicitly, between the problem of the "*Übergang*" in *KU* and the problem of the "*Übergang*" in *OP* was Lehmann (1969: 295–302), according to whom Kant, with the Transition-project, tried to extend to physics the principle of reflecting judgement already applied in *KU* to the doctrines of taste and of the purposes of nature. According to Mathieu, on the contrary, Kant with *OP* gives up the regulative finalism of the third *Critique* and returns to the transcendental perspective of the first *Critique*, aiming now to anticipate experience not only formally but also materially (1989: 238–46). A third interpretation has been elaborated by Friedman (1992: 242–64). According to this interpretation, Kant provided with *MAN* the *a priori* foundation of Newtonian mechanics, performing a transition from principles to the empirical ("from the top down"), whereas the reflecting judgement of *KU* supplies a transcendental principle for investigating further fields of experimental physics – heat, light, electricity, magnetism, chemistry and so on – performing a transition from the empirical to principles ("from the bottom to the top"). The unification of the theory of gravitation with the fields of empirical physics in a universal system of nature would have been accomplished in the doctrine of the Transition-project, whose principles have to be therefore at the same time both constitutive (transition "from the top down") and regulative (transition "from the bottom up").

According to Förster (2000: 7–11), however, the project of the transition from metaphysics to physics follows upon the discovery of the reflecting judgement expounded in the third *Critique*. Thanks to this new principle, the concept of nature evolves from one of a blind mechanism, like in the first *Critique* and in *MAN*, to the concept of nature, that is in itself systematic. Only by elaborating an *a priori* justification that nature is to be thought of as in itself systematic, can one assume that physics is likewise systematic. Hence Kant faces the task of developing a new system from *a priori* principles.

In relation to the thesis of Förster, Dina Emundts observes (2004: 71f.) that the possibility of developing a full system of natural science is not necessarily dependent on the introduction of the principle of the finality of nature in *KU*, for two reasons. The first is that the elementary system of the Transition-project holds entirely *a priori* concepts that determine relationships between moving forces, whereas *KU* deals with statements on the compliance with laws of particular materials, that can be known only through the inquiry of nature. The second reason is that the possibility, at least in principle, of a complete presentation of the moments of the specific diversities of matter had already been established in the *Dynamics-Remark* of *MAN*. Emundts, therefore, affirms the independence of the Transition-project from the specific task of *KU* (2004: 24f.).

The problem of a possible correlation between the concept of the transition in *KU* and that discussed in *OP* can be perhaps developed further, on the basis of the following considerations.

Transition in *KU* and the genesis of the Transition-project: In the *Appendix to Transcendental Dialectic*, Kant notices that the dynamic principles of the understanding are "merely regulative principles of *intuition*", but they are also

> constitutive in respect of *experience*, since they render the *concepts*, without which there can be no experience, possible *a priori*. But principles of pure reason can never be constitutive in respect of empirical *concepts*; for since no schema of sensibility corresponding to them can ever be given, they can never have an object *in concreto*.
>
> (A664/B692)

Principles of pure reason can find however a regulative employment, since reason aims at rendering systematic the unity of all possible empirical acts of the understanding (A664/B692). In this sense, "the idea of reason is an analogon of a schema of sensibility", although "the application of the concepts of the understanding to the schema of reason does not yield knowledge of the object itself [. . .] but only a rule or principle for the systematic unity of all employment of the understanding" (A665/B693). Nevertheless, the principles of pure reason must also have – *although only indirectly* – objective reality in respect to the object of experience, because they indicate "the procedure whereby the empirical and determinate employment of the understanding can be brought into complete harmony with itself" (A665f./B693f.). It is to be noticed that Kant affirms here the contiguity of understanding and reason: "The understanding is an object for reason, just as sensibility is for the understanding" (A664/B692). That means that ideas of reason can be applied to the empirical laws of the understanding as the concepts of the understanding can be applied directly to the phenomena. It is precisely this continuity between understanding and reason that is denied in *KU*.

In the *Dynamics-Remark* of *MAN*, Kant refers to the regulative employment of reason applied to the philosophy of nature: "[A]ll natural philosophy consists [. . .] in the reduction of given, apparently different forces to a smaller number of forces and powers that explain the actions of the former" (*MAN* 4: 534). This reduction proceeds however only up to the two fundamental forces of attraction and repulsion. By contrast, it is impossible not only to deduce the various empirical forces and properties of matter (that are knowable only from experience) from these two fundamental forces, but also to demonstrate *a priori* that the only possible concept of matter is the dynamic one (*MAN* 4: 525 and 534). All that metaphysics can achieve concerning the concept of matter is to allow the consideration of the properties of matter as dynamic – an explanation which Kant prefers to the mathematical and mechanical construction of matter, which presupposes the position of original and unconditional elementary particles (*MAN* 4: 534). From the two fundamental forces can be deduced, instead, a system (that Kant hopes to be complete) of all "moments" [*Momente*] – density, cohesion, elasticity and chemical properties – under which the various properties of matter can be brought. This system undertakes the function of a transition from the metaphysical dynamics to physics. Its elements can be considered as regulative principles with respect to empirical forces. But they are also to be acknowledged, at least indirectly, as objectively valid, to the extent that they assure *a priori* the systematic unity of the employment of understanding. Such "moments" of matter are, in a way, already "mediating concepts [*Mittelbegriffe*]", although they still belong to dynamics.

In the *Introduction* to *KU* Kant explicitly acknowledges the existence of a "great gulf [*unübersehbare Kluft*]" (*KU* 5: 175)[3] between the realm of the natural concepts, as the sensible, and the realm of the concept of freedom, as the supersensible, so that no transition from the one to the other is possible by means of the theoretical employment of reason. Yet this transition is possible by means of the reflecting judgment, that is "a middle term [*Mittelglied*] between understanding and reason" (*KU* 5: 177). Therefore the judgement needs a principle to ascend from the particular in nature to the universal (*KU* 5: 180). This principle is the concept of a finality of nature of the faculty of judgment, so that it provides a "mediating concept [*vermittelnden Begriff*]" between the concepts of nature and the concept of freedom, bringing about, in this way, the transition from pure theoretical to pure practical reason (*KU* 5: 196).

Shortly after the publication of the third *Critique*, the essay *Baco and Kant* by the Jewish philosopher Salomon Maimon, for whom Kant had high regard, appeared. Maimon himself sent a copy of his work to Kant.[4] In this essay, that he wrote without reading *KU*, he compares the Baconian inductive method with the *a priori* Kantian one (Maimon 1965: 519–21). According to him, the inductive method allows the expansion of the knowledge of nature, but can never build a complete system of all forms and principles of knowledge. Such a system remains, in the Baconian view, an idea that we approach asymptotically, without ever being able to reach it. Kantian philosophy, in contrast, offers such a complete system but cannot anticipate specific empirical knowledge. Maimon notes, therefore, that Kant's theory of knowledge fails to provide the transition from the universal transcendental concepts and principles of experience in general to those of the special experiences, so that there is a gap between these two sorts of concepts and principles.[5] Maimon calls into question the ability of Kantian philosophy to bridge that gap. He identifies clearly the problematic which Kant deals with in his Transition-project.

From his point of view, Kant can certainly argue against Maimon that the transition from particular to general concepts according to the Baconian inductive method is ensured by the transition from the sensible to the supersensible achieved by the reflecting judgment. However, in *KU* he had established that: 1) there is a gap between metaphysical and sensitive nature; 2) the bridging of this gap lies in the province of the faculty of judgment as the middle term between understanding and reason; and 3) the transition from physics to metaphysics is brought about by the reflecting judgement. Maimon's observations may have drawn Kant's attention to the failure of a correlative transition from metaphysics to physics, that somehow would be, at least indirectly, also up to the determining judgment to provide. If the transition from metaphysics to physics is to be supplied by the system of the moments of the properties of matter, this system can no longer be part of the metaphysical principles of dynamics (see Basile 2013: 376–80).

3. The Notion of Ether in *Uebergang 1–14* as the Main Turning Point in *OP*

As already mentioned, until May 1799, Kant's efforts focus in *OP* on the formulation of the problem of the transition from *MAN* to physics (with which the introduction should have dealt) and on the development of a system of forces of matter. Already at this stage, the concept of ether in *OP* shows a certain ambivalence. It is predominantly conceived as a material, for example, as the "caloric [*Wärmestoff*]" (see *OP* 22: 215.24f.) or as a "matter of light [*Lichtstoff*]" (see *OP* 21: 469.4–6), or also as the basic element of the physical-chemical processes (see *OP* 21: 467.12–15). But already in the draft *Elem. System 1–6* (February–May 1799) it is considered as a substance that is neither hypothetical nor derivable from experience (*OP* 21: 192.27–30). A turning point occurs with the draft *Uebergang 1–14*, where several attempts to prove the existence of ether appear, where ether is defined on the one hand as a material and as something real, and on the other hand as a principle *a priori*, that can be demonstrated according to the principle of identity.

Referring to a draft of the ether proof near the end of *Uebergang 1–14* (*OP* 22: 550f.), it is clear that ether is not merely empirical, because it is not an object of a possible experience. Therefore its reality cannot be inferred from experience. The notion of ether cannot, however, be reduced to a mere regulative concept. The sentence: "Now the concept of the whole of outer experience also presupposes all possible moving forces of matter as combined in collective unity" (*OP* 22: 550.27–9) surely affirms that the concept of ether has only the collective unity of a transcendental ideal and, in this sense, it assumes the character of a regulative principle of reason. Nevertheless, ether exists as the origin of the movement of all materials and moving forces of bodies. It acts, therefore, indirectly but really on our sensory organs. It has the nature of a phenomenon, but of an indirect one. It is a particular material in space and yet it fills up space. It is "the hypostatized space itself" (*OP* 21: 224), "a material [. . .] which is given *a priori*" (*OP* 22: 551.14).

Ether is therefore now, at the same time, matter and form, given and thought, of physical and metaphysical nature. It is precisely this duality of the concept of ether that is at the origin of the difficulty faced by the very idea of a transcendental deduction of this concept, since it seems not possible to demonstrate *a priori* the existence of a material entity, without leaving the ground of Critical philosophy.

Three fundamental interpretations of the ether proof in *Uebergang 1–14* have been proposed. According to the first interpretation, such a deduction could at the most be valid only for the ether as a principle, not for the ether as a material. A second line of interpretation asserts that Kant with the proof of ether as principle and as substance abandoned his former Critical positions. A third line of interpretation defends the substantial compatibility of the ontological ether proof with Critical philosophy. From the interpretation of the ether proof the consequence is the comprehension of the doctrine of self-affection in *Conv. X/XI* either as a new start after a failure or as a further development on the basis of that proof. The interpretation of the ontological ether proof turns out therefore to be crucial not only for the understanding of the whole *OP*, but also for the evaluation of the Critical system from a post–Critical perspective.

According to the first line of interpretation just introduced, Kant was actually forced to admit that the problem of an ontological ether proof is insurmountable. For Lehmann (1969: 254–6, 278) the ether proof fails in demonstrating its material existence. It demonstrates only that ether is the idea of the whole of the moving forces. That is why Kant gives up the "ether deduction" and tries in *Conv. X/XI* a new deduction based on the self-affection of the subject. Friedman (1992: 290–341) affirms that Kant wants to deduce ether both as a regulative and as a constitutive principle, as both collective and distributive unity, because only this would resolve the problem of unifying the system of the natural sciences (mechanics and chemistry). But as there is no way to establish *a priori* the existence of an object corresponding to such a representation of ether, its concept cannot be considered more than an idea or ideal of reason and, in this sense, the ether deduction must be considered a failure (Friedman 1992: 328).

The main representative of the second line of interpretation is Tuschling (2001; see also Edwards 2000: 147–92), who believes that, with the ontological proof of ether, Kant wanted to abandon intentionally the Critical perspective, which does not allow an ontological proof even for the supersensible being par excellence (*schlechthin*), namely God. Kant, in other words, by demonstrating the reality of ether as a substance, accomplished (or at least prepared) the abolition of the distance between object and subject, that would anticipate the turning point to a form of Spinozism, that is, of speculative idealism, in the following drafts.

Other scholars defend instead the coherence of the concept of ether in *Uebergang 1–14*, the soundness of its proof and their substantial compatibility with the Critical philosophy. According to them the doctrine of self-affection provides a step forward in continuity with *Uebergang 1–14*. What follows is a short account of the three most representative versions of this position: the ones of Vittorio Mathieu, Eckart Förster and Bryan Hall.[6]

Mathieu is the first Kant scholar who emphasized the fundamental meaning of the ether proof for the systematic interpretation of *OP*. He sees in the ether proof a further development of the doctrine of schematism of the first *Critique* (Mathieu 1989: 111–85). According to Mathieu, Kant conceives with ether the possibility of a physical reality, which can be constructed *a priori* (1989: 282–6). It would correspond to what the epistemologist and Nobel Prize laureate in physics Percy Williams Bridgman (1927) called a physical "construct". According to Bridgman, physical "objects" like elementary particles or fields constitute theoretical constructs that are nevertheless real for the physicist and are presupposed in the investigation of nature (Mathieu 1989: 283). In the same way other scholars compare the concept of ether in *OP* with the notion of physical field (Wong 1995) and the relationship of ether to mechanical matter with the relationship between energy and mass or between the four fundamental forces of nature and the elementary particles (Waibel 2001: 155f.). In this sense, the notion of ether in *Uebergang 1–14* can be understood as a particular case of "phenomenon of phenomenon" or "indirect phenomenon", a concept which the draft *Conv. X/XI* deals with. "Phenomena" are the "*Data*" of sensible representations, "phenomena of phenomena" are "the thing in itself [*Sache an sich selbst*]" (*OP* 22: 329.14–21) which the physicist deals with. In other words, the physicist "sees" the usual sensation of a color or of a sound, for instance, as light and sound waves that he can explain as effects of particular forces and can construct through mathematical functions.

In contrast to Friedman, Förster claims that Kant instead successfully performs his ether deduction precisely because he represents ether as an ideal of reason (2000: 75–116). According to Förster, in fact, the principle of formal purposiveness of nature, introduced in the third *Critique*, allows Kant for the first time to think of nature in itself systematic. The systematicity of nature implies that its empirical laws must be therefore as well systematic and that the collective whole of moving forces must precede the distributive unity of them in experience. This collective whole of moving forces is therefore the regulative principle on which the system of the transition is based. In turn, the systematic of the transition must provide physics with a sketch of a system. The principle on which the transition is based must be therefore both regulative and constitutive. Kant identifies it with ether, the existence of which must be now demonstrated *a priori* in order to solve the transition-problem. The three constitutive elements of the ether proof are the following statements: 1) perceptions of outer objects are the effect of moving forces of matter onto our senses; 2) space itself must be an object of sense as a condition for experience of outer objects; 3) the possibility of experience as the systematic unity of a distributive whole of perceptions presupposes the systematic collective unity of the corresponding forces, and this is the concept of ether as hypostasized space. This last step allows thinking of ether as a transcendental ideal in the Critical sense, that is, as "the idea of an individual thing thoroughly determined or determinable by the idea alone" (Förster 2000: 92). This makes it possible now to deduce the properties of ether from its mere concept, that is, analytically, and indirectly its actuality from the conditions of possible experience. Thanks to the demonstration of ether, the elementary system of the moving forces of matter can be now developed from the concept of this ether, and in turn provides a topic for classification of forces *a priori*. This elementary system of moving forces would however remain useless for knowledge, in a stronger Kantian sense, of the actual forces, if it were not possible to "insert" into the manifold of sense what is expected to be extracted from experience. Now we are capable of such insertion because perception implies not only passivity, but also an active use of our own moving forces, that is, of our body: every affection is therefore to be understood also as a self-affection. The possibility of experience thus implies our position as corporeal subjects, which gives the concepts of the elementary system their objective validity.

According to Brian Hall (2015), Kant started to work on *OP* in order to fill a gap in the first *Critique*. The first *Critique* provided in fact only formal transcendental conditions of experience – space, time, categories, apperception. Later on Kant realized that a material transcendental principle for the unity of experience fails in this system of transcendental principles. The ether deduction in *OP*, proving *a priori* the existence of a substance that is also a principle, gives a partial solution to this problem. The ether deduction fails however to demonstrate that the formal transcendental conditions together with the material transcendental condition are sufficient for the unity of experience. It is *Conv. X/XI* that deals successfully with this further problem. Hall emphasizes not only the systematic continuity between *Uebergang 1–14* and *Conv. X/XI* but also that Kant's post-Critical conception of substance lies within the Critical horizon.

4. The Idea of God and the System of Transcendental Philosophy: The Final Issue of *OP*

The last drafts – *Conv. VII* and *Conv. I* – mark once more a turning point with respect to the previous ones. Their main topics – self-positing of the subject, the idea of God, the system of the ideas of the transcendental philosophy – refer to questions treated in the *Transcendental Dialectic* of the first *Critique*. A current question for studies on *OP* is whether the new developments of Kantian thought are substantially in line with the Critical philosophy or, rather, attest a break and an evolution towards speculative idealism. A similar question can be asked about the connection of the last two drafts with the previous investigations of *OP*. On the one hand, the reduction of the thing in itself to a mere *ens rationis* (see for instance *OP* 22: 32.27), the self-positing of the subject (see for instance *OP* 22: 25.2–10) the identification between *I think* and *I am* (see for instance *OP* 22: 102.20–5) seem to aim at the self-determining of I as subject of knowledge and as existing subject, thus exceeding the positions of the *Paralogisms*.

On the other hand, the self-positing of the subject can be considered as the original spontaneity, correlative of the constitutive receptivity of the subject with respect to the physical world as highlighted by the conception of ether and the notion of self-affection in the previous drafts. After dealing with nature so to speak "as the sum total of all appearances (*materialiter spectata*)" (B 163) through the notion of ether, Kant examines the correlative concept, that is the sensible subject of self-affection. But the sensible subject, in turn, presupposes the intelligible subject, that is, the *I think* as the transcendental subject of knowledge. The correlative notion of the intelligible subject, not as subject of knowledge but of action, is the idea of God as the absolutely supersensible reality and, as such, corresponding to ether as the principle of absolutely sensible nature. (See Förster 2000: 141.) As is the case of ether, God can be given a proof, although only indirectly not on the theoretical, but on the practical level, in view of our duties as divine commandments (*OP* 22: 121.9–22).

The claim of a "practical-ontological" proof of God and statements like "[t]he concept of God is the concept of a *compelling* subject outside of me" (*OP* 21: 15.26f.) seem *prima facie* to contradict the autonomy of reason which requires thinking of God as an idea *of* man and *in* man, which is also repeatedly stated in *OP*.[7] Several scholars have nevertheless shown that it is at least possible to understand the doctrine of God in *OP* as being in agreement with the one of Kant's published works (Förster 2000: 117–47; Guyer 2005: 281–93, 305–13; Marty 2004). Guyer for instance illustrates this thesis by means of three examples: 1) God as the subject of categorical imperative is not necessarily in contradiction with the notion of the "highest good" in the *Critiques*; 2) there is an essential convergence between God as idea, stated in *OP*, and as postulate in *KpV*; 3) Kant transforms Spinozism into his own moral-practical transcendental idealism. Hence, statements where Kant seems to express acceptance of Spinozism do not refer to the historical Spinoza.

Each one of the four main drafts of *OP* deals predominantly with one of the ideas of the transcendental system: *Uebergang 1–14* with the notion of ether, *Conv. X/XI* with the sensible subject, *Conv. VII* with the intelligible subject and *Conv. I* with the idea of God. This chronological development finds its systematic expression in the system of ideas in the highest standpoint of transcendental philosophy, that contains three ideas: the world, God and man that connects both. (See for instance *OP* 21: 38.27–32.) It is man, as a sensible and intelligible subject, that performs the transition between God, as the supersensible idea *schlechthin*, and the world, as the sensible idea *schlechthin*. The subject that poses itself as the subject of knowledge has not yet fulfilled its purpose. It has to pose itself also as a moral subject, namely as a person. It has to rise, therefore, from the realm of nature to the realm of freedom and think of God as the subject of the categorical imperative (*OP* 21: 22.30f.). The system of ideas in the highest standpoint of transcendental philosophy shows the possibility of a systematic unity of *OP* that puts man at the center of Kant's last inquiry. Dealing once more with the questions "What can I know?" and "what may I hope?" (as the question concerning religion), Kant's ultimate project answers also the last question of the Kantian philosophy: "What is man?" (*Log* 9: 25; *Br* 11: 429).

Notes

1 For a complete account of the history of interpretation of *OP*, see *Kants Opus postumum und seine Rezeption* (Basile 2013).
2 Chapter 2 of Emundts' monograph provides a complete account of the debate on this circularity-problem by Kant (2004: 74–117).
3 In the last chapter of the same *Introduction*, Kant insists on the existence of a "broad gulf [*große Kluft*]" dividing the supersensible from the phenomena (*KU* 5:195).
4 Maimon's essay came out in May 1790 in the *Berliner Journal für Aufklärung*. On May 9th, Maimon sent a copy of it to Kant (Cfr. *Br* 11: 171).
5 "[S]o fehlt doch hier augenscheinlich der Uebergang von den allgemeinen transscendentalen Begriffen und Sätzen, die sich auf Erfahrung überhaupt beziehen, zu denjenigen, die sich auf besondere Erfahrungen beziehen [. . .][.] Es ist hier eine Lücke zwischen den transscendentalen Begriffen und Sätzen und den besonderen Begriffen und Sätzen der Erfahrung" (Maimon 1965: 519–21). ["The transition from the general transcendental concepts and principles, which refer to experience in general, to those, which refer to particular experiences, is evidently still missing [. . .][.] There is a gap here between the transcendental concepts and propositions and the particular concepts and principles of experience" (translated by myself).]
6 Paul Guyer (Guyer 1991) and Hubertus Busche (Busche 2010) also maintain the soundness of the ether proof from the point of view of Critical philosophy.
7 Reiner Wimmer's studies have provided by far the most complete account of the statements about God in *OP*. (See for instance Wimmer 1992.)

References

Basile, G.P. (2013) *Kants Opus postumum und seine Rezeption*, Berlin and Boston: Walter de Gruyter.
Bridgman, P.W. (1927) *The Logic of Modern Physics*, New York: Palgrave Macmillan.

Büchel, G. (1987) *Geometrie und Philosophie*, Berlin and New York: Walter de Gruyter.

Busche, H. (2010) "Der Äther als materiales Apriori der Erfahrung. Kants Vollendung der Transzendentalphilosophie im *Opus postumum*," in H. Busche and A. Schmitt (eds.), *Kant als Bezugspunkt philosophischen Denkens. Festschrift für Peter Baumanns zum 75. Geburtstag*, Würzburg: Königshausen & Neumann, pp. 53–83.

Drivet, D. (2002) "La genesi dell'Opus postumum in Kant: Un dato filologico importante," *Studi Kantiani* 15: 127–63.

Düsing, K. (1986) *Die Teleologie in Kants Weltbegriff*, Bonn: Bouvier.

Edwards, J. (2000) *Substance, Force, and the Possibility of Knowledge: On Kant's Philosophy of Material Nature*, Berkeley, Los Angeles and London: University of California Press.

Emundts, D. (2004) *Kants Übergangskonzeption im Opus postumum: Zur Rolle des Nachlaßwerkes für die Grundlegung der empirischen Physik*, Berlin and New York: Walter de Gruyter.

Förster, E. (2000) *Kant's Final Synthesis: An Essay on the Opus Postumum*, Cambridge, MA and London: Harvard University Press.

Friedman, M. (1992) *Kant and the Exact Sciences*, Cambridge, MA and London: Harvard University Press.

Fritscher, B. (2009) "'Kritik der naturhistorischen Vernunft': Umrisse einer historischen Epistemologie der kantischen 'Archäologie der Natur'," in V. Gerhardt, R.-P. Horstmann and R. Schumacher (eds.), *Kant und die Berliner Aufklärung. Akten des IX. Internationalen Kant-Kongresses*, vol. 4–5, Berlin and New York: Walter de Gruyter, pp. 513–20.

Guyer, P. (1991) "Kant's Ether Deduction and the Possibility of Experience," in G. Funke (ed.), *Akten des siebenten Internationalen Kant-Kongresses*, vol. 1–2, Bonn and Berlin: Bouvier, pp. 119–32.

Guyer, P. (2005) *Kant's System of Nature and Freedom: Selected Essays*, Oxford: Clarendon.

Hall, B. (2015) *The Post-Critical Kant: Understanding the Critical Philosophy Through the Opus Postumum*, New York and London: Routledge.

Heimsoeth, H. (1940) "Kants Philosophie des Organischen in den letzten Systementwürfen. Untersuchungen aus Anlaß der vollendeten Herausgabe des *Opus postumum*," *Blätter für Deutsche Philosophie* 14: 81–108.

Hoppe, H. (1969) *Kants Theorie der Physik. Eine Untersuchung über das Opus postumum von Kant*, Frankfurt a. M.: Klostermann.

Lehmann, G. (1969) *Beiträge zur Geschichte und Interpretation der Philosophie Kants*, Berlin: Walter de Gruyter.

Maimon, S. (1965/1790) "Baco und Kant. Schreiben des H.S. Maimon an den Herausgeber dieses Journals," *Berlinisches Journal für Aufklärung* 7(2): 99–122; in V. Verra (ed.) (1965–1976) *Salomon Maimon, Gesammelte Werke*, vol. 2, Hildesheim: Olms, pp. 519–21.

Marty, F. (2004) "La loi morale comme commandement divin dans l'*Opus postumum*," in M. Castillo (ed.), *Criticisme et Religion*, Paris: L'Harmattan, pp. 29–48.

Massimi, M. (2008) "Why There Are No Ready-Made Phenomena: What Philosophers of Science Should Learn from Kant," in M. Massimi (ed.), *Kant and Philosophy of Science Today*, Cambridge: Cambridge University Press, pp. 1–35.

Mathieu, V. (1989) *Kants Opus Postumum*, G. Held (ed.), Frankfurt a. M.: Klostermann.

Tuschling, B. (1971) *Metaphysische und transzendentale Dynamik in Kants opus postumum*, Berlin and New York: Walter de Gruyter.

Tuschling, B. (2001) "Übergang: Von der Revision zur Revolutionierung und Selbst-Aufhebung des Systems des transzendentalen Idealismus in Kants *Opus postumum*," in H.F. Fulda and F. Stolzenberg (eds.), *Architektonik und System in der Philosophie Kants*, Hamburg: Meiner, pp. 128–70.

Van den Berg, H. (2014) *Kant on Proper Science: Biology in the Critical Philosophy*, Dordrecht: Springer Science+Business Media.

Vasconi, P. (1999) *Sistema delle scienze naturali e unità della conoscenza nell'ultimo Kant*, Firenze: Olschki.

Waibel, V. (2001) "'Des principes régulateurs qui sont en même temps constitutifs'," in C. Erismann (ed.), *Années 1796–1803. Kant. Opus postumum. Philosophie, Science, Ethique et Théologie. Actes du 4e Congrès international de la Société d'études kantiennes de langue française. Lausanne: 21–23 octobre 1999. Sous la direction de Ingeborg Schüßler*, Paris: Vrin, pp. 147–57.

Wimmer, R. (1992) "Die Religionsphilosophie in 'Opus Postumum'," in F. Marty and F. Ricken (eds.), *Kant über Religion*, Stuttgart, Berlin and Köln: Kohlhammer, pp. 195–229.

Wong, W.-C. (1995) "Kant's Conception of Ether as a Field in the *Opus postumum*," in H. Robinson (ed.), *Proceedings of the Eighth International Kant Congress*, vol. 1–2, Memphis: Milwaukee Marquette University Press, pp. 405–11.

Further readings

E. Adickes, *Kants Opus postumum dargestellt und beurteilt* (Berlin: Reuther & Reichard, 1920) is a classic and the work of one of the most competent experts on *OP*. S. Blasche, *et al.* (eds.), *Übergang: Untersuchungen zum Spätwerk Immanuel Kants*. Beiträge der Tagung des Forums für Philosophie Bad Homburg vom 13. bis 15. Oktober 1989 zu Kants *Opus postumum* (Frankfurt am Main: Klostermann, 1991), collects the proceedings of the first congress on *OP*. C. Erismann (ed.), *Années 1796–1803. Kant. Opus postumum. Philosophie, Science, Ethique et Théologie. Actes du 4e Congrès international de la Société d'études kantiennes de langue française. Lausanne: 21–23 octobre 1999. Sous la direction de Ingeborg Schüßler* (Paris: Vrin, 2001) provides numerous contributions on all main topics of *OP*. E.-O. Onnasch (ed.), *Kants Philosophie der Natur. Ihre Entwicklung im* Opus postumum *und ihre Wirkung* (Berlin and New York: Walter de Gruyter, 2009) contains several papers dealing with the philosophy of nature of the post-critical Kant. G.P. Basile and A. Lyssy (eds.), *Perspectives on Kant's Opus Postumum* (New York: Routledge, 2022) brings together several recent contributions that cover a wide spectrum of topics in *OP*. S. Howard's recent monograph *Kant's late philosophy of nature. The Opus postumum* (Cambridge: Cambridge University Press, 2023) represents a valuable contribution on the philosophy of nature in the *Opus postumum*.

39

LECTURES

Steve Naragon

★★★

Immanuel Kant's forty-one years of academic lectures have come down to us primarily in the form of a great quantity of student notes. They span eleven different academic subjects and over thirty years of Kant's teaching career, from the Herder notes of 1762–64 to the Vigilantius notes of the mid-1790s. These notes have value to the extent they reflect what Kant actually said in his lectures. If this is granted then their value lies in several directions: they clarify and develop points made in his published writings, they consider topics not discussed in any of the published writings, they provide much of the philosophical context against which these writings were to be understood, they offer new perspectives into Kant's intellectual development, and they round out our understanding of Kant's life and personality.

Before we can properly use these notes, however, we need to consider a set of three nested questions: (1) How reliable are the Academy edition transcriptions of the various sets of notes? (2) Assuming reliable transcriptions, how reliable are these notes in conveying what Kant said in the lectures? (3) Assuming reliable notes, when did Kant say these things? That is, for any given set of notes (or with compiled notes: for any given passage in a set of notes) when was the source-lecture?

If we cannot trust the Academy edition transcription of the notes, for instance, or if we are not sure how accurately these notes reflect what Kant said in the classroom or in what semester he said them, then we are hard pressed to make much use of the notes at all. Addressing these three questions is therefore a principal task of this chapter.

Before turning to that, however, we should first consider a possible alternative source of information on Kant's lectures, namely, Kant's own notes. These would certainly be more reliable than the written records of students and, as it happens, we have something like this in the form of some of Kant's "reflections" collected in AA 14–19. Many of these were written in the particular textbook over which Kant was lecturing, and occasionally they make an appearance in the student notes as well. Similarly, Kant's *Anthropology* (1798) could be viewed as a reworked set of his notes for those lectures,[1] and the *Holstein-Beck* notes on physical geography are actually an early copy of Kant's own notes upon which his lectures were based (this is a unique situation among the student lecture notes). These two popular disciplines enjoy a strong grounding in these two texts that stem directly from Kant, but each gains from the supplementary material from the notes. The *Diktattext*, of

 DOI: 10.4324/9781003406617-52

which Holstein-Beck is a copy supervised by Kant, was composed quite early in Kant's career, and the later notes on physical geography provide us with new material, while the many anthropology notes, all of which pre-date the published version, offer additional material as well as insight into Kant's intellectual development. As for the other frequently taught subjects – metaphysics, logic, and moral philosophy – there is simply no comparison between the continuity of discussion found in the notes and the fragmentary nature of the various reflections in the *Nachlass*. The textbooks with Kant's many marginalia served as points of reference for the lectures, but the student notes provide our best window into those lectures.

1. Kant's Lectures

Kant taught at the university in Königsberg – the *Academia Albertina* – for fifteen years as an unsalaried instructor (*Privatdozent*) followed by twenty-six years as the salaried full professor of logic and metaphysics, to which he was appointed in the summer of 1770.

Kant was a popular lecturer although his courses were considered difficult. He was free to offer private lectures on whatever he chose (within the context of the philosophy faculty), but his promotion to full professor required that he offer one public course each semester: metaphysics in winter and logic in summer. He continued teaching his usual assortment of private lectures, offering anthropology in the winter, physical geography in the summer, and for a number of years lecturing on philosophical encyclopedia, natural law, moral philosophy, and physics on a two-year rotation.

Kant's teaching load was normal for the university of his day, and it dropped steadily over the years from an average of five courses per semester during the 1750s down to three in the 1780s and two in the 1790s. Nearly all courses met four hours each week on the usual lecture days of Monday, Tuesday, Thursday, and Friday. The few courses taught on a Wednesday-Saturday schedule met for two hours each day, except for the mandated pedagogy course, which appears to have met just two hours per week.

While the records are incomplete, the information we have shows that Kant taught logic most often (fifty-six times), followed by metaphysics (fifty-three) and physical geography (forty-nine). He taught these three courses nearly every semester until he became a full professor, after which he taught each of them once a year. His first course on anthropology was given in 1772/73, and every winter semester thereafter (for a total of twenty-four semesters). These four courses formed the core of his teaching as a full professor, with metaphysics and anthropology offered each winter, and logic and physical geography each summer. Kant also offered private lectures in mathematics nearly every semester at the beginning of his career, abruptly stopping after 1763/64 (fifteen semesters total). Theoretical physics (twenty-one) and moral philosophy (twenty-eight) were alternated during much of his career, along with natural law (twelve), which he first taught in 1767, and philosophical encyclopedia (ten), which he first taught in 1767/68. Occasional courses were given on natural theology (four) and pedagogy (four), as well as mechanics (two), mineralogy (one), and Latin style (one). Student notes are unavailable from these last four subjects.

2. The Textbooks

The government in Berlin took an interest in the textbooks used at the university. Professors were required to base their lectures on a published text and were chastised by the cultural minister if they did not; students were similarly expected to own the textbooks used in the courses they attended.[2] Occasionally certain texts were discouraged (such as those by Crusius),[3] but for the most part instructors appeared to have had a free hand.

One should consult the relevant textbook when using the student notes. Of the three potential sources of content in the notes – Kant, the student taking the notes, and the textbook – the last is at times ubiquitous, especially in the early Herder notes, providing the outline of the lectures and serving as a direct source of much of the content. It is sometimes quoted but more often paraphrased, sometimes with Kant's agreement but more often with a silent emendation or correction.

We have evidence of eighteen different textbooks that Kant used, and six of Kant's personal copies have been located. Three of these were destroyed or lost during World War II (Achenwall on natural law, Eberhard on natural theology, and Baumgarten's introduction to practical philosophy), although fortunately Kant's annotations had already been transcribed and printed in the Academy edition (AA 18–19). The three textbooks still extant are Baumgarten on metaphysics (the third and fourth editions, although only the fourth edition was used in the lectures) and Meier on logic (with annotations of the 4th edition of Baumgarten and of Meier in AA 15–18). Some of these books were interleaved to provide extra room for writing notes.

3.   Publication of the Notes

Some notes were published in Kant's day, beginning with his own *Anthropology* (1798) which, while not student notes, was indicative of the content of the lectures, as were Jäsche's *Logic* (1800), Rink's *Physical Geography* (1802), and (possibly) *Pedagogy* (1803). Even before these, various fragments had appeared in print in Hippel (1778–81; various subjects), Coing (1788; natural theology), Forberg (1796; anthropology), Mellin (1797–1804; anthropology), and then Vollmer's four-volume physical geography (1801–5) that elicited a public censure from Kant (AA 12: 372). A handful of publications appeared a few decades later: Pölitz's volumes on natural religion (1817) and metaphysics (1821); Bergk's (under the pseudonyms 'Heinichen' and 'Starke') volumes on anthropology (1826, 1831a, 1831b) and one with a fragment on physical geography (1833); Mrongovius's translations into Polish of his own notes on moral philosophy and natural theology (1854) – and that was it, until scholars began publishing selections alongside their analysis: Erdmann (1880, 1883, 1884), Arnoldt (1890a, 1890b, 1892) and Heinze (1894) in the late eighteenth century; and Schlapp (1901), Adickes (1911, 1913), Menzer (1911, 1924), Kowalewski (1924), Krauß (1926), Horn (1936), and Beyer (1937) in the early decades of the twentieth century.

After various delays, the Academy began publishing the lecture notes in 1966 under the editorship of Gerhard Lehmann, with his last volume appearing in 1983. The final two volumes to complete the initial plan, and under new editors, are the notes on anthropology (AA 25; 1997) and physical geography (AA 26; pt. 1: 2009, pt. 2.1 and 2.2: 2020).[4] So far 100 of the notes (some complete, but many as fragments) have been published, and the last twenty years have seen a greater availability of these notes in English, with thirty translated so far. All of this has resulted in much more scholarly attention and integration of the notes into Kant studies, and with that a heightened need to understand their status and to address our initial set of three questions.

4.   How Reliable Is the Academy Transcription in Conveying the Notes?

The Academy edition and translations based on it are generally one's only access to these notes – although some have been published elsewhere and others not at all.[5] Reliability of the transcriptions varies widely between those prepared by the late editor Gerhard Lehmann (vols. 24, 27, 28, and 29) and the more recent work by Reinhard Brandt and Werner Stark (vol. 25: Anthropology) and Stark (vol. 26: Physical Geography). The Lehmann volumes suffer from many transcriptional errors and problematic editing, and considerable caution is required when using them.[6]

5. How Reliable Are the Notes in Conveying the Lectures?

Anyone using these lecture notes should pause to reflect on who wrote them. Even Kant questioned their reliability:

> Those of my students most capable of grasping everything are just the ones who bother least to take detailed and verbatim notes; instead they write down just the main points for reflecting on later. Those who are most thorough in note-taking are seldom capable of distinguishing the important from the unimportant. They pile a mass of misunderstood stuff alongside what they may possibly have grasped correctly.
>
> (Letter to Herz, 20 October 1778, *Br* 10: 242)

Similarly, we hear from Borowski that Kant "was not keen on students taking notes. It bothered him when he noticed that more important material was overlooked, while the less important was noted down" (1804: 187).

Nearly all of the note takers were teenagers, and some quite young (sixteen was the average age at matriculation). They arrived in Kant's classroom with such widely varying levels of intelligence and academic preparedness that it is quite right to question their ability to provide reliable guidance – what could such efforts possibly add to Kant's own writings? It would seem they were just as likely to misunderstand Kant as not, whose lectures were known to be quite challenging. A former student of Kant's wrote that:

> Whoever did not understand this way of his [viz., where he would present a deficient position, followed by criticisms and progressively improved positions] would take his first explanation as the correct and fully exhaustive one, and so would not follow him very closely after that, thus collecting mere half-truths – just as several sets of student notes have convinced me.
>
> (Jachmann 1804: 29–30)

As Kant aged, the difficulty of the lectures, and thus of taking good notes, was a result not just of the subject matter but also of his delivery – something to consider when using the notes from the 1790s:

> When I came to the university at Michaelmas 1793, Kant was already in his 70th year, his voice was weak, and he would get himself tangled up in his lectures and become unclear. [. . .] To a young man of 15–16 years under those circumstances, not much of his philosophical lectures could be put into a context that made them understandable; what I grasped was an occasional illuminating point or spark in the soul. I don't believe that it went any better at that time with the older students.
>
> (Reusch 1848: 6)

This is why Rosenkranz and Schubert chose to omit the student lecture notes from their 1838–42 edition of Kant's writings (1838: vol. 1, pp. x–xi).

On top of this worry is the fact that many of the notes were the product of a "flourishing branch of industry in Königsberg" (Adickes 1913: 8), with "professional" copyists – professional only in the sense that they worked for money – churning out notes for sale to students, almost certainly without ever having stepped foot into Kant's lecture hall and otherwise untutored in the subject-matter of what they were copying, thus opening their work to the most egregious errors.

And yet despite Kant's reservations about the value of these notes, he took considerable pains procuring them for his acquaintances: metaphysics, philosophical encyclopedia, anthropology, and possibly logic, for his former student Marcus Herz (*Br*, 10: 235–6, 244–5, 245–6, 247), and physical geography for the Minister of Culture Karl von Zedlitz (*Br*, 10: 222–3, 224–5, 235–6), both in Berlin. This surely counts as an endorsement of their worth.

Wilhelm Dilthey broke rank with past editors of Kant's writings (Hartenstein 1838–39, 1867–68; Rosenkranz and Schubert 1838–42), arguing to include the lectures as the fourth part of the newly conceived critical edition of Kant's writings undertaken by the Royal Prussian Academy of Sciences (i.e., the Academy edition). Dilthey viewed the lecture notes as an important part of Kant's "intellectual legacy." While recognizing the uncertainty of their transmission, he found they provided context for the published writings, enhanced our understanding of Kant's intellectual development, and offered us a picture of Kant's teaching activity and his influence on his students (Dilthey 1902; AA 1: viii–xiv). The discussion since then has favored Dilthey. The notes are always secondary to Kant's published writings and should be used only alongside those publications and Kant's reflections and correspondence, but there is otherwise much that they have to offer us that can be found nowhere else.[7]

6.   How Reliable Are the Lectures in Conveying Kant's Thought?

A question preliminary to the third question (of dating) has also been raised in the past: Even if the notes accurately reflect Kant's spoken words, did Kant actually believe what he said?

Rosenkranz suggested that Kant lived a "double life," expressing traditional beliefs in the classroom and censoring certain actual beliefs that eventually made their way into his writings (1838: vol. 3, vii–viii). This worry received attention near the end of the nineteenth century,[8] but Rudolf Malter has more recently argued that the notes themselves speak clearly against such "intellectual schizophrenia" on Kant's part (1974: 217–18), and since then the steady growth in their use to chart Kant's intellectual development should put this worry entirely to rest.[9] Kant himself offers testimony against any "double life" in his 1797 public notice regarding Hippel's authorship:

[These verbatim passages from the *Critique of Pure Reason*] gradually flowed as fragments into the notebooks of my students, from my side with respect to a system that I was carrying around in my head, but only in the period from 1770 to 1780 could be brought about.[10]

(AA 12: 361)

Kant elaborates on this relationship between his teaching and his published writings in an earlier draft of that notice:

For the university teacher has that advantage over the unaffiliated scholar in his scientific work: that – since with every new course on a subject he must prepare for each lesson (as, to be fair, must always be done) – new views and perspectives always open up to him, partly while preparing, partly – which happens even more often – while in the middle of the presentation, which helps him to correct and expand his sketch from time to time.

(AA 13: 539)

7.   When Were the Source Lectures for the Notes?

We must be able to date the source lecture of the notes within a fairly narrow approximation, without which the notes are of little use, but doing this is rarely straightforward. For instance, a student might buy a set of notes and then add the date he attended the lectures; here the date corresponds to any marginalia, but not to the body of the notes (cf. the *Euchel* anthropology notes). Or a student might borrow a set of notes and copy them out himself, adding the current date (which is now in the same hand as the notes), as we find with the *Puttlich* anthropology notes. Or a student might copy material from an earlier set of notes into his own notes, such as the *Dohna-Wundlacken* anthropology notes, which mingle notes from 1772/73 with his own from 1791/92.

Equally misleading, a former student might purchase notes after finishing the course (or even after leaving the university) as a record of what he learned or might have learned. Hermann Blomberg, for example, attended the university in the early 1760s, left his name (but not a date) on what are now the *Blomberg* logic notes – good circumstantial evidence that the source lecture of the notes was in the early 1760s, although other evidence indicates the source lecture was actually a decade later.

These possibilities – and there are many more like them – should inspire caution when assigning a source lecture to a set of notes.[11]

8. What Is the Provenance of the Notes?

It is helpful to distinguish different types of manuscripts.[12] Let a *Nachschrift* be any manuscript where the writer of the text is not the source of the text and the *original* source is the spoken word (e.g., Kant's actual lecture). Three sorts of *Nachschriften* concern us: a *Mitschrift* (notes written down in the classroom), a *Reinschrift* (a clean copy of these notes prepared at home),[13] and an *Abschrift* (copies made from a second set of notes, sometimes assembled from multiple sets). Most of the student notes are *Abschriften*, followed by *Reinschriften* and a very few *Mitschriften* (most of the 8° *Herder* notes and perhaps the last two pages of the *Vienna* logic notes).

9. Single Source Versus Multiple Source

A set of notes might have a single source prepared by a single student attending a single course of lectures (which in turn might be copied various times). Or there might be multiple sources from different semesters – either a student acquiring a set of notes from a previous semester and adding text to those notes, or else someone compiling a set of notes from various sets.

We know too little of about one-fifth of the notes to sort them into any of these types, but of the remainder, about 60% are single-source and 40% composite in some way. What matters in the end is knowing the (approximate) date of the source-lecture for any particular passage in the notes, but this is more straightforward when the notes have a single source.

About half of the single source notes were written by a single known author attending the lectures from which the notes arose, which is how most readers initially think of the notes. Examples include the notes by Herder (physical geography, logic, mathematics, metaphysics, moral philosophy, physics), Philippi (anthropology, physical geography, logic), Mrongovius (logic, metaphysics, moral philosophy, physics, natural theology, anthropology), Volckmann (physical geography, logic, metaphysics, natural theology), Dohna-Wundlacken (anthropology, physical geography, logic, metaphysics), and Vigilantius (physical geography, logic, metaphysics, moral philosophy).

Other single source notes are copies from an ancestral set of notes, which itself appears to have stemmed from a single semester, for instance, the *Korff*, *Pölitz 1*, and *Rosenhagen* metaphysics notes, all of which appear to stem from a common (and now lost) ancestor, as do the thirteen sets belonging to the *Kaehler* group of moral philosophy notes.

Multiple-source notes are of two kinds. The first are bought or copied notes that then have material added from a later semester (e.g., the *Collins* moral philosophy, the *Matuszewski* anthropology), or parts of which are incorporated into a newly written set of notes (e.g., the *Mrongovius* moral philosophy). About 5% of the notes are of this kind.

The second kind of multiple-source notes were compiled from multiple textual-sources (about one-fourth are like this). Here we have material from (normally) different source-lectures, but now the composition is a result of someone (most likely a professional copyist who never attended the lectures) compiling a new set of notes from two or more other sets. Here the *Pillau* physical geography takes the prize for compositional diversity, having made use of nine different sets, according to Adickes (1911: 279–80).

10. Overview of the Available Notes

From Kant's early years as a lecturer we have only the Herder notes, with the supply increasing dramatically once Kant became a full professor in 1770. We currently know of 164 sets of student notes, with 126 of these available in some form – although once duplicates are eliminated the count drops to fifty-one available. In terms of distinct sets of notes, the most are on physical geography (eleven),[14] followed by anthropology (nine), logic (nine), metaphysics (nine), moral philosophy (five), physics (three), and a single set each from natural theology, philosophical encyclopedia, natural law, mathematics, and pedagogy, although these last two are problematic: the mathematics notes clearly come from a mathematics course but possibly not Kant's, while the pedagogy text is clearly Kant's but may have little to do with his lectures on pedagogy. I will close with summary remarks on each group of notes.

Metaphysics. Kant used the Baumeister (1736) textbook for a few semesters early in his career before settling on Baumgarten (1757). Both follow a general four-part outline of Wolffian metaphysics: ontology, cosmology, psychology (empirical and rational), and natural theology. His lectures appear to have extended over all four parts, although less systematically over natural theology, and he may have been rushed at the end, as the notes are not as full here. Kant also used Baumgarten's *Metaphysica* as the textbook for his lectures on anthropology (the empirical psychology section) and on natural theology (the fourth part), and there is a considerable overlap of content worth exploring.

We know of seventeen sets of notes, with thirteen available at least in part. Of these thirteen, three (*Pölitz 1*, *Korff*, *Rosenhagen*) appear to be copies of a common set of notes, *von Schön 3* (unpublished) is a near-verbatim fragment of *von Schön 2*, and *Willudovius* (unpublished) exists only as forty scattered lines of text copied out by Adickes in the early twentieth century, thus bringing the effective number of distinct sets of notes down to nine. Of the nine, three have been preserved almost in their entirety (*Herder*, *Mrongovius*, *Dohna-Wundlacken*) and the other six as large fragments. The notes, with their likely date of source-lecture, are *Herder* (1762–4; AA 28: 5–55, 137–8, 143–58, 843–946), the *Pölitz 1* group (c.1777–80; AA 28: 185–350), *Mrongovius* (1782/83; AA 29: 747–940), *Volckmann* (1784/85; AA 28: 355–459), *von Schön* (c.1789–91; AA 28: 463–524), *Pölitz 3.2* (1790/91?; AA 28: 531–610), *Königsberg* (c.1791/92; AA 28: 709–816), *Dohna-Wundlacken* (1792/93; AA 28: 615–702), and *Vigilantius* (1794/95; AA 28: 821–38, 29: 945–1040).

Logic. Kant lectured on logic more than on any other subject, with notes spanning from the fragmentary *Herder* (1762–64) to *Bauch* (1794); his textbook was G. F. Meier's *Auszug aus der Vernunftlehre*. There is some superficial overlap with the introductory sections of the metaphysics notes, where we find summary histories of the disciplines and a discussion on the nature of concepts and judgments. In the metaphysics notes this is normally followed by equally brief accounts on the use of philosophy, and of metaphysics in particular. This similarity between the notes offers some explanation for why a section from the *Pölitz 3.1* logic notes was published with the metaphysics notes (in Pölitz 1821; cf. AA 28: 531–40).

We know of twenty-six sets of notes with nineteen available at least in part. Nine of the manuscripts appear to be complete, and a tenth (*Volckmann*) is a very large fragment. Three sets (*Warsaw, Bauch, Hechsel*) are published in Pinder (1998), a five-page fragment (*Grünheide*) is published in Kowalewski (2000), and *Volckmann*, having been recovered only in 2000, remains unpublished, as are a few fragments from *Herder*. Jäsche claimed his 1800 *Logic* was based solely on Kant's annotations in his copy of Meier's *Auszüge* (1752), but it soon became clear (Erdmann 1880; Heinze 1894; Schlapp 1901) that one or more sets of student notes also entered into the text: these lost notes we designate as *Jäsche*.

Five (or six) sets of notes (*Hechsel, Pölitz, Warsaw, Vienna, Hoffmann, Jäsche?*) are related in a complicated and yet to be fully explicated fashion, with at least one source lecture from 1780–82. Four other sets of notes (*Blomberg, Bauch, Grünheide, Philippi*) are closely related with their source lecture in the early 1770s.

This leaves us with the following nine available sets of notes: *Herder* (1762–64; AA 24: 3–6, 1099–1100), the *Blomberg* group (early 1770s; AA 24: 9–301), *Hintz* (1775; AA 24: 943–4), the *Hechsel* group (1780–82; Pinder 1998: 271–499), *Volckmann* (early 1780s), *Mrongovius* (1784?; AA 24: 1043–7), *Busolt* (1789; AA 24: 605–86), *Dohna-Wundlacken* (1792; AA 24: 689–784), and a fragment from *Vigilantius* (1793; Hinske 1991: 150).

Physical Geography. Kant lectured on physical geography nearly every semester during his years as a lecturer, and then every summer semester thereafter, lecturing from his own notes since there was no standard textbook available. These notes – prepared between 1757 and early 1759 and dubbed the *Diktattext* by Adickes (1911: 10) – have been lost, but were preserved in a copy, the *Holstein-Beck* notes, which has corrections and additions (amounting to some 1100 words) in Kant's own hand. The presence of this *Diktattext* makes the lecture notes on physical geography unlike those from any of the other lectures, since copies of the *Diktattext* circulated and found their way into thirteen of the sets of notes currently available to us (and as Adickes discovered, not by way of an oral lecture, but through copying written texts).

We know of thirty-six sets of notes with thirty-two available at least in part. Stark (2020) divides these notes into eleven groups representing the temporal span of the lectures – from *Holstein-Beck* (1757–59; AA 26: 7–320) and *Herder* (1763–64) to *Vigilantius* (1793), along with two groups of compilations. Six sets are single source: *Holstein-Beck* (1757–59), *Herder* (1763–64), *Hesse* (1770), *Dönhoff* (1782), *Reicke* (1787), and *Vigilantius* (1793) – although we have only scattered fragments of the latter two. Several of the compilations are predominantly grounded in one semester, with discernible additions from another.

Anthropology. Kant began lecturing on anthropology with 1772/73 and continued every winter semester up to his retirement in 1796. Roughly the first half of this course was based on the empirical psychology section (§§504–739) of Baumgarten's *Metaphysica* (1757). Rather surprisingly, Kant continued to lecture on empirical psychology in his metaphysics lectures. He claimed in an October 1778 letter to Markus Herz that he shortened this discussion (*Br*, 10: 242), and a content comparison of the extant metaphysics notes bears this out somewhat: empirical psychology comprises a large percentage of *Herder* (1762–64), less so of *Pölitz 1* (late 70s), and considerably less of notes from the 1780's, but then increases in two of the sets from the 1790s (*Königsberg* and *Vigilantius*). Yet it is odd that Kant did not drop empirical psychology from the metaphysics lectures altogether, given his many comments that it does not belong there – "empirical psychology must thus be entirely banned from metaphysics" (A848/B876; see also *V-Anth/Collins*, 25: 8; *V-Met/L1/ Pölitz* 28: 175; *V-Met/Volckmann*, 28: 358, 366–7; *V-Met/Schön*, 28: 470; *V-Met/L2/Pölitz*, 28: 541; *V-Met/Dohna*, 28: 670; *V-Met/Mron*, 29: 757). And yet in the last set of metaphysics notes from 1794/95, about 18% of the original notes still concern empirical psychology.

Kant also migrated material from the physical geography lectures (viz., the ethnographical remarks on Europeans in Part III of the physical geography) into the "anthropological characteristic" section of the anthropology lectures, and an essential feature of geography notes stemming from after 1772/73 is the absence of this discussion (Stark 2011: 79; cf. Wilson 2006: 8–20). There is also a detailed exposition of the relationship of these two courses in the opening pages of both the *Kaehler* and the *Messina* physical geography notes (AA 26.2: 299–300, 621–22).

We know of forty-seven sets of notes with thirty-six available at least in part. One of these (*Naumburg*) was located only in 1999 and has not been published. Many of the notes are copies, some are compilations, and they fall into nine distinct groups, with two of these (A and B) stemming from 1772/73, the first semester the course was offered. The most reliable set of notes serves as the representative of each group: the *Collins* group (1772/73; *V-Anth/Collins* 25: 7–238), the *Parow* group (1772/73; *V-Anth/Parow* 25: 243–463), the *Friedländer* group (1775/76; *V-Anth/Fried* 25: 469–728), *Pillau* (1777/78; *V-Anth/Pillau* 25: 733–847), the *Starke* group (1781/82; AA 25: 853–1203), the *Mrongovius* group (1784/85 *V-Anth/Mron*), the *Busolt* group (1788/89? *V-Anth/Busolt*), *Dohna-Wundlacken* (1791/92; Kowalewski 1924: 71–373), and *Reichel* (1793/94; AA 25: 1553–7). The *Dohna-Wundlacken* notes were written down during the semester he attended the lectures (1791/92), but also include passages copied from a set of notes originating in 1772/73. Similarly, the *Mrongovius* notes from 1784/85 include marginalia copied from a 1772/73 set of notes.

Moral Philosophy. Kant lectured on moral philosophy twenty-eight times throughout his career, from his third semester up until 1793/94, normally making use of two Latin textbooks by Baumgarten: the *Initia philosophia* (1760) and the *Ethica philosophica* (1763).[15] The former concerns the general principles of ethics, and the latter discusses substantive questions of ethics: a section on religion followed by discussions of our general and special duties. The lecture notes have two parts that mirror this structure. Of particular interest are the *Mrongovius* notes of 1784/85 that foreshadow themes in the *Groundwork of the Metaphysics of Morals* (1785), and the *Vigilantius* notes of 1793/94 that anticipate aspects of the *Metaphysics of Morals* (1797), and which Kant lectured on instead of his normal course of metaphysics that winter.

We know of twenty-three sets of notes with fourteen available at least in part. Thirteen of the twenty-three (eight of the fourteen available) have been found to share a common ancestor stemming from 1774–77, in effect leaving us with five sets of notes spanning most of Kant's lecturing career (setting aside the *Bering* and *Hippel* fragments): *Herder* (1763/64; AA 27: 3–89), the *Kaehler* group (1774–77; Stark 2004), *Powalski* (1782/83, possibly a compilation; AA 27: 93–235), *Mrongovius* (1784/85; AA 27: 597–642) and *Vigilantius* (1793/94; AA 27: 479–732) – this last is a copy prepared in the late 1800s, the original having since been lost.

Brauer and *Collins* are the most widely used of the notes on moral philosophy; the former was published in Menzer (1924) and translated into English by Infield (1930), the latter was published by Lehmann (*V-Mo/Collins*, 27: 243–471) and translated into English by Heath (Heath and Schneewind 1997). Both sets belong to the *Kaehler* group, and Stark (2004) argues that *Kaehler* itself, discovered only in 1997, is closest to the source notes and lecture. Krauß (1926, 66) found *Brauer* the least reliable of the notes in this group.

Natural Law. Kant lectured on natural law twelve times (between 1767 and 1788) and appears to have always used the two-volume Latin text by Achenwall (1763). Although Kant lectured on both volumes, only his copy of the second volume was found, with the marginalia transcribed by Adickes and Berger (*Refl* 19: 325–613) before it too was lost during World War II.

Of the two known sets of notes only the *Feyerabend* (*V-NR/Feyerabend* 27: 1319–94) is available. The source lecture is dated to 1784 and the notes consist of an introduction (about 20% of the notes) that discusses the relationship between the philosophy of right and moral philosophy and which bears strong affinities with the *Groundwork* (1785). The middle section (about 60% of the notes) concerns the first Achenwall volume, and the remainder is a rather rushed discussion of the second volume. An English translation of these notes and related materials was recently published (Rauscher and Westphal 2016).

Natural Theology. Kant lectured on natural theology only four times: once in 1774 and the rest in the mid-1780s. Kant never announced this course in the catalog and it appears to have been a fall back course for when another course failed to attract enough students (e.g., moral philosophy in 1783/84, encyclopedia in 1787). Jachmann wrote that Kant was quite interested in the course when theology students were enrolled, however, as he saw it as a means to further enlighten the Prussian pulpits (1804: 31–2).

Five sets of notes are available, but all appear to stem from Kant's lectures of 1783/84, save for a brief additional set of notes (eight manuscript pages) appended to *Mrongovius 3* that comes from a later semester. Kreimendahl (1988: 326–8) is persuaded that *Coing* and *Mrongovius 3* are both copies of a common set of notes (originating in the 1783/84 lectures), and agrees with Beyer that *Pölitz 2* and *Volckmann 4* stem from a different set of notes, although from the same lectures. Baumgarten's *Metaphysica* is listed as a textbook for this course as well; part four concerns *theologia naturalis* (§§800–1000), and Wood finds that, as a whole, the notes read as a running commentary on §§815–982 (Wood and di Giovanni 1996: 337).

Kant presumably also lectured on natural theology in all of his metaphysics lectures, although it is understandable that he might often have run out of time at the end of the semester. There is some discussion of natural theology in *Herder* (1762–4; *V-Met/Herder* 28: 137–8, 150–1, 907–23), *Volckmann* (1784/85; *V-Met/Volckmann* 28: 450–9), *Pölitz 3.2* (c.1790–91; *V-Met/L2/Pölitz* 28: 595–609), *Dohna* (1792/93; *V-Met/Dohna* 28: 690–702), and *Vigilantius* (1794/95; *V-Met/Arnoldt* 29: 1040) with relatively extensive notes in *Pölitz 1* (c.1777–80; *V-Met-L1/Pölitz* 28: 301–50) and *Königsberg* (c.1791/92; *V-Met/K2/Heinze* 28: 775–812). These notes discuss transcendental theology, physico-theology, moral-theology, God's attributes, and the divine actions.

Physics. Kant lectured on physics twenty-one times, beginning with the very first semester and every semester the first three years, then about once every two years, the last in 1787/88. It occasionally failed for lack of students; for instance, Kant taught his Anthropology course for the first time in 1772/73 to replace a failed physics offering.

We know of three sets of notes, of which one is complete (*Mrongovius*, dated 1785; AA 29: 97–169), one is a large fragment (*Friedländer*, dated 1776; AA 28: 75–91), and one several small fragments (*Herder*, dated 1763; AA 28: 158–66, 29: 69–71), although the *Herder* fragments might stem from someone else's lectures.

Mathematics. Kant appears to have lectured on mathematics at least fifteen of his first seventeen semesters at the university. He may have taught this course normally as a two-semester sequence with arithmetic, geometry, and trigonometry (the first three parts of Wolff's German *Auszug* 1717) normally taught during the winter semester, and mechanics, hydrostatics, aerometry, and hydraulics (the next four parts of Wolff's textbook) normally taught during the summer semester. It is remarkable that Kant taught a course on mathematics nearly every semester for the first eight years of his teaching career, and then (as far as we know) never so much as announced another course, much less taught one.

The only candidates for student notes from these lectures are two four-sheet manuscripts from Herder (1762–63; AA 29: 49–66) and several pages (unpublished) from one of Herder's student notebooks. The evidence that they come from Kant's lectures is only circumstantial: Kant was lecturing on mathematics at the time and Herder was attending his courses free of charge (Herder

1846: 133–4), but we are also told that Herder attended the mathematics lectures of F. J. Buck "with great diligence" (Böttiger 1998: 125). A recent discussion of these notes is found in Moretto (2015).

Encyclopedia. Kant lectured on philosophical encyclopedia ten semesters, from 1767/68 to 1781/82. The German-language textbook (Feder 1767) consists of three parts: an introduction to the history of philosophy, a sketch of the central areas of philosophy (logic, metaphysics, physics, practical philosophy), and a bibliography of important books in the different areas of philosophy. Much of this content overlaps with introductory parts of the logic and metaphysics lectures.

We know of three sets of notes, of which only one is available, the *Friedländer* (AA 29: 5–45), which dates from either 1777/78, 1779/80, or 1781/82.

Pedagogy. Kant lectured on pedagogy just four semesters (from 1776/77 to 1786/87). This was a course mandated by government decree (June 13, 1774) with the hope of improving the level of teaching in the Prussian public schools. It was to be offered publicly (free of charge) each semester by the philosophy faculty, which they did on a rotating basis.

Apart from some brief published remarks on pedagogy – *Announcement* (AA 2: 305–13), *Philanthropinum* (AA 2: 447–52) – there is an extended discussion at the end of the *Friedländer* anthropology notes (*V-Anth/Fried*, 25: 722–28) dated to 1775/76, a year prior to Kant's first course of lectures on pedagogy. Remarks on education are scattered throughout the anthropology notes, but nowhere else in a stand-alone section like in *Friedländer*, nor does this material appear in the pedagogy lectures as edited by Rink.

We know nothing of the manuscript(s) that Rink used in preparing his publication (Rink 1803; AA 9: 439–99), and it is entirely possible that this text does not stem, in any direct sense, from Kant's pedagogy lectures at all. Weisskopf (1970) is the most thorough study of this work, but see also Stark (2000, 2012).

Notes

1 The other books published during the last years of Kant's life and that are outwardly similar to the *Anthropology* (1798) do not at all share its status, since the *Logic* (published by Jäsche in 1800) and the *Physical Geography* and *On Pedagogy* (published by Rink in 1802 and 1803) were prepared independently of Kant, whose only participation was to give the editors his blessing. Jäsche's *Logic* is a blend of Kant's notes written in his textbook by Meier and one or more sets of student notes. Rink's two-volume *Physical Geography* is a blend of the *Diktattext* (Kant's notes composed in 1757–59 from which he lectured) and a now-lost set of notes from 1774; its failings were well documented over a century ago by Adickes (1911, 1913). The *Pedagogy* remains a mystery, but is not in any direct sense related to Kant's lectures.
2 As decreed on March 31, 1781 (quoted in Bornhak 1900: 132).
3 An edict from Minister von Zedlitz (dated December 25, 1775) forbade Weymann and Wlochatius from teaching Crusius' philosophy, "the lack of value of which has been long agreed upon by the more enlightened scholars" (quoted in Arnoldt 1908–9: v.248).
4 An additional volume that collects together all of Herder's student notes from Kant's lectures into a single volume is currently in preparation. This will replace the notes already published on metaphysics (in AA 28), moral philosophy (in AA 27), logic (in AA 24), and mathematics and physics (both in AA 29), and will include the first publication of his notes on physical geography.
5 Pinder (1998; three sets of logic notes), Stark (2004; one set of notes on moral philosophy) – and the various volumes edited by Hinske's working group in Trier that offer improved texts of the published notes on logic (1986, 1989–90, 1995, 1999) and natural law (Delfosse *et al.* 2010, 2014). For those still unpublished, see Naragon (2014).
6 For assessments of AA 24 (logic), see Hinske (1989–90: xxx–xxxvii) and Oberhausen (2000); of AA 27 (moral philosophy), see Schwaiger (2000); of AA 28–29 (metaphysics), see Naragon (2000); of AA 29.1, see Stark (1984, 1985).
7 For a useful history of how these notes were understood and their inclusion in the academy edition, see Sala (1982).

8 Cf. Arnoldt (1892: 402, 428), Heinze (1894: 658), and Vaihinger (1895: 428–9). Stark also discusses this (1987: 139–40).
9 Consider Ameriks (1982) on the paralogisms, Klemme (1996) on the Kantian subject and, most recently, Dyck on Kant's rational psychology (2014).
10 This receives support from Ludwig Borowski, a former student and later dinner guest and friend of Kant's, who in his 1804 biography of Kant considered the puzzle of how he managed to write and publish so much, given his lecturing duties, his long afternoons of socializing and walks, and his many visitors. His answer was that "in part much that he presented to the public in his writings was first worked out in his lectures" (Borowski 1804: 174).
11 Adickes was one of the first to call attention to these difficulties (1911: 2–3).
12 In this I am following Stark (1991).
13 We have one instance of multiple drafts – a *Mitschrift* and the later *Reinschrift* – among the *Herder* metaphysics notes. A four-page manuscript in pencil (V-Met/Herder AA 28:843–49) is clearly a *Mitschrift* that was the basis of about six pages of a *Reinschrift* written in ink (V-Met/Herder AA 28:22–30).
14 With the physical geography notes, this refers to *types* as opposed to distinct sets.
15 We do not know which edition Kant used of the *Ethica philosophica*, and none of his copies are extant. A passage from the first edition (1740) appears in the *Herder* notes, but this might be Herder's own access to that edition. Both the second (1757) and third (1760) editions are reprinted at AA 27: 737–869, 873–1028. As for the *Initia philosophiae*, however, Kant's copy was available to Adickes and so his annotations were published (AA 19: 7–269, 282–309) before the book itself was lost during the destruction of World War II.

References

Achenwall, G. (1763) *Jus naturae inusum auditorium*, 2 parts, 5th ed., Göttingen: Bossiegel.
Adickes, E. (1911) *Untersuchungen zu Kant's physischer Geographie*, Tübingen: Mohr.
Adickes, E. (1913) *Ein neu aufgefundenes Kollegheft nach Kants Vorlesungen über physische Geographie*, Tübingen: Mohr.
Ameriks, K. (1982) *Kant's Theory of Mind: An Analysis of the Paralogisms of Pure Reason*, Oxford: Clarendon Press.
Arnoldt, E. (1890a) "Zur Beurtheilung von Kants *Kritik der reinen Vernunft* und Kants *Prolegomena*. No. 2. Kants Vorlesungen über Anthropologie," *Altpreußische Monatsschrift* 27: 97–107.
Arnoldt, E. (1890b) "Zur Beurtheilung von Kants *Kritik der reinen Vernunft* und Kants *Prolegomena*. No. 3. Kant's Vorlesungen über physische Geographie und ihr Verhältniss zu seinen anthropologischen Vorlesungen," *Altpreußische Monatsschrift* 27: 228–314.
Arnoldt, E. (1892) "Zur Beurtheilung von Kant's Kritik der reinen Vernunft und Kant's Prolegomena. No. 4 und No. 5. Characteristik von Kant's Vorlesungen über Metaphysik und möglichst vollständiges Verzeichniss aller von ihm gehaltener oder auch nur angekündigter Vorlesungen," *Altpreußische Monatsschrift* 29: 400–46, 465–564.
Arnoldt, E. (1908–9) *Kritische Exkurse im Gebiete der Kant-Forschung*, vol. 4–5 of Emil Arnoldt, *Gesammelte Schriften*, O. Schöndörffer (ed.), 10 vols., Berlin: Cassirer.
Baumeister, F.C. (1736) *Institutiones metaphysicae*, Wittenberg: Zimmermann.
Baumgarten, A.G. (1757) *Metaphysica*, 4th ed., Halle: Hemmerde.
Baumgarten, A.G. (1763) *Ethica philosophica*, 3rd ed., Halle: Hemmerde.
Baumgarten, A.G. (1760) *Initia philosophiae practicae primae acroamatice*, Halle: Hemmerde.
Bergk, J.A. [pseudonym: Dr. Heinichen], ed. (1826) *Taschenbuch für Menschenkenntnis und Menschenbesserung nach Hippel, Wieland, Sterne, Helvetius, Shakespeare und Kant. Mit einer Abhandlung über Menschenkenntniß*, Quedlinburg and Leipzig: Ernst.
Bergk, J.A. [pseudonym: Friedrich Christian Starke], ed. (1831a) *Immanuel Kant's Menschenkunde oder philosophische Anthropologie: Nach handschriftlichen Vorlesungen*, Leipzig: Expedition des europäischen Aufsehers.
Bergk, J.A. [pseudonym: Friedrich Christian Starke], ed. (1831b) *Anweisung zur Menschen- und Weltkenntniss: Nach dessen Vorlesungen im Winterhalbjähre von 1790–1791*, Leipzig: Expedition des europäischen Aufsehers.
Bergk, J.A. [pseudonym: Friedrich Christian Starke], ed. (1833) *Immanuel Kant's vorzügliche kleine Schriften und Aufsätze: Mit Anmerkungen herausgegeben von Fr. Ch. Starke. Nebst Betrachtungen über die Erde und den Menschen aus ungedruckten Vorlesungen von Imm. Kant*, 2 vols., Leipzig: Expedition des europäischen Aufsehers.
Beyer, K. (1937) *Kants Vorlesungen über die philosophische Religionslehre*, Halle: Akademischer Verlag.
Bornhak, C. (1900) *Geschichte der preussischen Universitätsverwaltung bis 1810*, Berlin: Reimer.

Borowski, L.E. (1804) *Darstellung des Lebens und Charakters Immanuel Kants, Von Kant selbst genau revidirt und berichtigt*, Königsberg: Nicolovius.

Böttiger, K.A. (1998) *Literarische Zustände und Zeitgenossen. Begegnungen und Gespräche in klassischen Weimar*, K. Gerlach and R. Sternke (eds.), 2nd ed., Berlin: Aufbau Verlag.

Coing, J.F. (anon.) (1788) *Die vornehmsten Wahrheiten der natürlichen Religion vorgetragen und gegen die neueren Einwürfe verteidigt von E.n.d.E.r.W*, Leipzig: Weidmann.

Delfosse, H., Hinske, N. and Bordoni, G.S. (eds.) (2010) *Stellenindex und Konkordanz zum "Naturrecht Feyerabend," Teilband 1: Einleitung des Naturrechts Feyerabend*, Stuttgart-Bad Cannstatt: Frommann-Holzboog.

Delfosse, H., Hinske, N. and Bordoni, G.S. (eds.) (2014) *Stellenindex und Konkordanz zum "Naturrecht Feyerabend," Teilband 2: Abhandlung des Naturrechts Feyerabend (Text und Hauptindex)*, Stuttgart-Bad Cannstatt: Frommann-Holzboog.

Dilthey, W. (1902) "Vorwort," in *Kant's gesammelte Schriften*, W. Dilthey (ed.), Berlin: Georg Reimer, pp. v–xv.

Dyck, C.W. (2014) *Kant and Rational Psychology*, Oxford and New York: Oxford University Press.

Erdmann, B. (1880) "Review of *Die formale Logik Kants in ihren Beziehungen zur transcendentalen*, by Moritz Steckelmacher (1879)," *Göttingische gelehrte Anzeigen* 20: 609–34.

Erdmann, B. (1883) "Eine unbeachtet gebliebene Quelle zur Entwicklungsgeschichte Kants," *Philosophische Monatshefte* 19: 129–44.

Erdmann, B. (1884) "Mittheilungen über Kant's metaphysischen Standpunkt in der Zeit um 1774," *Philosophische Monatshefte* 20: 65–97.

Feder, J.G.H. (1767) *Grundriß der Philosophischen Wissenschaften nebst der nöthigen Geschichte, zum Gebrauch seiner Zuhörer*, Coburg: Findeisen.

Forberg, F.C. (anon.) (1796) *Der Mensch, oder Compendiöse Bibliothek des Wissenswürdigsten von der Natur und Bestimmung des Menschen, und von der Geschichte der Menschheit, Heft II: Seelenlehre*, Eisenach and Halle: Gebauer.

Hartenstein, G. (ed.) (1838–39) *Immanuel Kant's Werke*, 10 vols., Leipzig: Modes und Baumann.

Hartenstein, G. (ed.) (1867–68) *Immanuel Kant's sämmtliche Werke*, 8 vols., Leipzig: Leopold Voss.

Heath, P. and Schneewind, J.B. (eds.) (1997) *Immanuel Kant, Lectures on Ethics*, P. Heath (trans.), J.B. Schneewind (intro.), Cambridge: Cambridge University Press.

Heinze, M. (1894) *Vorlesungen Kants über Metaphysik aus drei Semestern*, Leipzig: Hirzel.

Herder, E. (ed.) (1846) *Johann Gottfried von Herders Lebensbild*, 6 vols., Erlangen: Blaesing.

Hinske, N. (1986) *Stellenindex und Konkordanz zu "Immanuel Kant's Logik" (Jäsche Logik), vol. 2 of the Kant-Index*, Stuttgart-Bad Cannstatt: Frommann-Holzboog.

Hinske, N. (1989–90) *Stellenindex und Konkordanz zur "Logik Blomberg," vol. 3 (parts 1–3) of the Kant-Index*, Stuttgart-Bad Cannstatt: Frommann-Holzboog.

Hinske, N. (1991) *Personenindex zum Logikcorpus, vol. 14 of the Kant-Index*, Stuttgart-Bad Cannstatt: Frommann-Holzboog.

Hinske, N. (1995) *Stellenindex und Konkordanz zur "Logik Pölitz," vol. 6 (parts 1–2) of the Kant-Index*, Stuttgart-Bad Cannstatt: Frommann-Holzboog.

Hinske, N. (1999) *Stellenindex und Konkordanz zur "Wiener Logik," vol. 5 (parts 1–2) of the Kant-Index*, Stuttgart-Bad Cannstatt: Frommann-Holzboog.

Hippel, T.G. von (1778–81) *Lebensläufe nach aufsteigender Linie, nebst Beilagen A, B, C*, 3 vols., Berlin: Voß.

Horn, A. (1936) *Immanuel Kants ethisch-rechtliche Eheauffassung: Eine Rechtfertigung seines Eherechts*, dissertation, Reprint: Würzburg.

Infield, L. (trans.) (1930) *Immanuel Kant, Lectures on Ethics*, J. MacMurray (intro.), London: Methuen and Co.

Jachmann, R.B. (1804) *Immanuel Kant geschildert in Briefen an einen Freund*, Königsberg: Nicolovius.

Jäsche, G.B. (ed.) (1800) *Immanuel Kants Logik, ein Handbuch zu Vorlesungen*, Königsberg: Nicolovius.

Klemme, H. (1996) *Kants Philosophie des Subjekts*, Hamburg: Meiner.

Kowalewski, A. (ed.) (1924) *Die philosophischen Hauptvorlesungen Immanuel Kants: Nach den aufgefundenen Kolleghaften des Grafen Heinrich zu Dohna-Wundlacken*, München and Leipzig: Rösl.

Kowalewski, A. (ed.) (2000) *Kant-Volksausgabe*, S.L. Kowalewski and W. Stark (eds.), Bd. 1, Hamburg: Meiner.

Krauß, W. (1926) *Untersuchungen zu Kants moralphilosophischen Vorlesungen*, doctoral dissertation, Tübingen: Typescript.

Kreimendahl, L. (1988) "Kants Kolleg über Rationaltheologie. Fragmente einer bislang unbekannten Vorlesungsnachschrift," *Kant-Studien* 79: 318–28.

Malter, R. (1974) "Rev. of *Kant's gesammelte Schriften*, vol. 28, G. Lehmann (ed.) (1968, 1970, 1972)," *Kant-Studien* 65: 214–18.

Meier, G.F. (1752) *Auszug aus der Vernunftlehre*, Halle: Gebauer.

Mellin, G.S.A. (1797–1804) *Encyclopädisches Wörterburch der kritischen Philosophie, oder Versuch einer fasslichen und vollständigen Erklärung der in Kants kritischen und dogmatischen Schriften enthaltenen Begriffe und Sätz*, 11 vols., Züllichau, Jena and Leipzig: F. Frommann.

Menzer, P. (1911) *Kants Lehre von der Entwicklung in Natur und Geschichte*, Berlin: Reimer.

Menzer, P. (ed.) (1924) *Eine Vorlesung Kants über Ethik*, Berlin and Charlottenburg: Pan Verlag Rolf Heise.

Moretto, A. (2015) "Herder's Notes on Kant's Mathematics Course," in R.R. Clewis (ed.), *Reading Kant's Lecture*, Berlin: Walter de Gruyter.

Mrongovius, K.C. (1854) *Rozprawa filozoficzna o religii I moralnosci miana przez Imanuela Kanta a na jezyk polski przelozona przez Mrongoviusa*, Danzig: Szrota.

Naragon, S. (2000) "The Metaphysics Lectures in the Academy Edition of Kants Gesammelte Schriften," in R. Brandt and W. Stark (eds.), *Zustand und Zukunft der Akademie-Ausgabe von Kants Gesammelten Schriften*, Berlin: Walter de Gruyter, pp. 189–215.

Naragon, S. (2014) "Unpublished Notes," *Kant in the Classroom*, https://users.manchester.edu/facstaff/ssnaragon/kant/Notes/notesListUnpublished.htm.

Oberhausen, M. (2000) "Die *Vorlesungen über Logik*. Zu Band XXIV der AA," in R. Brandt and W. Stark (eds.), *Zustand und Zukunft der Akademie-Ausgabe von Kants Gesammelten Schriften*, Berlin: Walter de Gruyter, pp. 160–71.

Pinder, T. (ed.) (1998) *Immanuel Kant, Logik-Vorlesung, Unveröffentlichte Nachschriften*, 2 vols., Hamburg: Meiner.

Pölitz, K.H.L. (ed. and anon.) (1817) *Immanuel Kant, Vorlesungen über die philosophische Religionslehre*, Leipzig: Franz.

Pölitz, K.H.L. (ed.) (1821) *Immanuel Kant, Vorlesungen über Metaphysik*, Erfurt: Kayser.

Rauscher, F. (ed. and trans.) and Westphal, K. (trans.) (2016) *Immanuel Kant, Lectures and Drafts on Political Philosophy*, Cambridge: Cambridge University Press.

Reusch, C.F. (1848) *Kant und seine Tischgenosse*, Königsberg: Tag & Koch.

Rink, F.T. (ed.) (1802) *Immanuel Kant's physische Geographie: Auf Verlangen des Verfassers, aus seiner Handschrift herausgegeben und zum Theil bearbeitet von D. Friedrich Theodor Rink*, Königsberg: Göbbels and Unzer.

Rink, F.T. (ed.) (1803) *Immanuel Kant über Pädagogik*, Königsberg: Nicolovius.

Rosenkranz, K. (1838) "Vorrede," in K. Rosenkranz and F.W. Schubert (eds.), *Immanuel Kant's sämmtliche Werke*, vol. 3, Leipzig: Voss, pp. v–xi.

Rosenkranz, K. and Schubert, F.W. (eds.) (1838–42) *Immanuel Kant's sämmtliche Werke*, 12 vols., Leipzig: Voss.

Sala, G. (1982) "Die Veröffentlichung der Vorlesungsnachschriften Kants in der Akademie-Ausgabe," *Theologie und Philosophie* 57: 72–80.

Schlapp, O. (1901) *Kants Lehre vom Genie und die Entstehung der "Kritik der Urteilskraft"*, Göttingen: Vandenhoeck & Ruprecht.

Schwaiger, C. (2000) "Die Vorlesungsnachschriften zu Kants praktischer Philosophie in der Akademie-Ausgabe," in R. Brandt and W. Stark (eds.), *Zustand und Zukunft der Akademie-Ausgabe von Kants Gesammelten Schriften*, Berlin: Walter de Gruyter, pp. 178–88.

Stark, W. (1984) "Kritische Fragen und Anmerkungen zu einem neuen Band der Akademie-Ausgabe von Kant's Vorlesungen," *Zeitschrift für philosophische Forschung* 38: 292–310.

Stark, W. (1985) "Antwort auf die Erwiderung 'Zum Streit um die Akademie-Ausgabe Kants' von G. Lehmann," *Zeitschrift für philosophisches Forschung* 39: 630–3.

Stark, W. (1987) "Neue Kant-Logiken. Zu gedruckten und ungedruckten Kolleghesten nach Kants Vorlesungen über Logik," in R. Brandt and W. Stark (eds.), *Neue Autographen und Dokumente zu Kants Leben, Schriften und Vorlesungen*, Hamburg: Meiner, pp. 123–64.

Stark, W. (1991) "*Quaestiones in terminis*. Überlegungen und Fakten zum Nachschreibewesen im universitären Lehrbetrieb des 18. Jahrhunderts. Aus den Präliminarien einer Untersuchung zu Kants Vorlesungen," in M. Stern (ed.), *Textkonstitution bei mündlicher und bei schriftlicher Überlieferung*, Tübingen: Max Niemeyer, pp. 90–9.

Stark, W. (2000) "Vorlesung – Nachlass – Druckschrift? Bemerkungen zu *Kant über Pädagogik*," in R. Brandt and W. Stark (eds.), *Zustand und Zukunft der Akademie-Ausgabe von Kants Gesammelten Schriften*, Berlin: Walter de Gruyter, pp. 94–105.

Stark, W. (ed.) (2004) *Immanuel Kant: Vorlesung zur Moralphilosophie*, M. Kuehn (intro.), Berlin: Walter de Gruyter.

Stark, W. (2011) "Kant's Lectures on 'Physical Geography': A Brief Outline of Its Origins, Transmission, and Development: 1754–1805," in S. Elden and E. Mendieta (eds.), O. Reinhardt (trans.), *Reading Kant's Geography*, Albany: SUNY Press, pp. 69–85.

Stark, W. (2012) "Immanuel Kant *Ueber Pädagogik*: Eine Vorlesung wie jede andere?" *Jahrbuch für historische Bildungsforschung* 18: 147–68.

Stark, W. (2020) "Typologie," *Immanuel Kant: Vorlesungen über Physische Geographie*, https://telota-webpublic. bbaw.de/kant/base.htm/geo_typ.htm

Vaihinger, H. (1895) "Bericht über die Kantiana für die Jahre 1892 bis 1894," *Archiv für Geschichte der Philosophie* 8: 419–40, 513–64.

Vollmer, J.J.W. (ed.) (1801–5) *Physische Geographie*, vol. 4 in 7 parts, Mainz and Hamburg: Gottfried Vollmer.

Weisskopf, T. (1970) *Immanuel Kant und die Pädagogik. Beiträge zu einer Monographie*, Zürich: Editio Academic.

Wilson, H. (2006) *Kant's Pragmatic Anthropology. Its Origin, Meaning, and Critical Significance*, Albany: SUNY Press.

Wolff, C. (1717) *Auszug aus den Anfangsgründe aller mathematischen Wissenschaften*, Halle: Rengerischen Buchhandlung.

Wood, A., and di Giovanni, G. (eds. and trans.) (1996) *Immanuel Kant, Religion and Rational Theology*, Cambridge: Cambridge University Press.

Further readings

R. Brandt and W. Stark (eds.), *Zustand und Zukunft der Akademie-Ausgabe von Kants Gesammelten Schriften* (Berlin: Walter de Gruyter, 2000) reviews the state of the Academy edition, including essays on the lecture notes on logic (Hinske, Oberhausen, Pinder), pedagogy (Stark), ethics (Schwaiger), and metaphysics (Naragon). Two early collections devoted to notes recently made available on anthropology and physical geography are B. Jacobs and P. Kain (eds.), *Essays on Kant's Anthropology* (Cambridge: Cambridge University Press, 2003); S. Elden and E. Mendieta, *Reading Kant's Geography* (Albany: SUNY Press, 2011). A growing and excellent body of *Critical Guides* (Cambridge: Cambridge University Press) includes collections by A. Cohen (ed.), *Kant's Lectures on Anthropology* (Cambridge: Cambridge University Press, 2014); L. Denis and O. Sensen, *Kant's Lectures on Ethics* (Cambridge: Cambridge University Press, 2015); and C. Fugate, *Kant's Lectures on Metaphysics* (Cambridge: Cambridge University Press, 2019). R. Clewis (ed.), *Reading Kant's Lectures* (Berlin: Walter de Gruyter, 2015) offers a comprehensive array of essays on each of the disciplines on which Kant lectured, with a similar offering by B. Dörflinger, C. La Rocca, R. Louden and U. Marques (eds.), *Kant's Lectures/Kants Vorlesung* (Berlin: Walter de Gruyter, 2015). Finally, S. Naragon, *Kant in the Classroom* (https://users.manchester.edu/facstaff/ssnaragon/kant/Home/index.htm), is an online website focussing on Kant's lecturing activity, the student notes, and their historical and institutional context.

PART 4

Kant and Contemporary Kantians

A. Theoretical Philosophy

40

THE 'CONTINENTAL' TRADITION

Marguerite La Caze

★★★

1. Introduction

What is distinctive about readings of Kant's theoretical philosophy in the continental tradition? To answer this question, I centre on Martin Heidegger's reading of Kant's *Critique of Pure Reason*. His dispute with Ernst Cassirer over how to interpret Kant appears to mark a turning point or split into two broad schools of thought concerning Kant's work. More specifically I explore Heidegger's views on the role of the imagination in the two Transcendental Deductions, and his claim that Kant turned away from the imagination in the B edition of the *Critique*. I then consider continental interpretations of Heidegger's work, the influences it has had on continental readings of Kant, and deviations from that reading.

2. The Shibboleth and Heidegger's Reading of the First *Critique*

Do the differences between the Transcendental Deductions A and B in the first *Critique* constitute a shibboleth that separates continental and analytic philosophy? Howard Caygill states that although the general conclusion of the two transcendental deductions is the same,

> expressing a preference for one of the other of the deductions has become a shibboleth in Kant studies, with Heidegger and the continental tradition preferring the first, and the more Cartesian Anglo-American tradition opting for the second version.
>
> (Caygill 1995: 153)

To address the question concerning whether the versions of the Transcendental Deduction constitute a shibboleth of this kind, we need to take a closer look at Heidegger's reading of Kant's *Critique* and consider why he would prefer Transcendental Deduction A and why the continental tradition

DOI: 10.4324/9781003406617-55

may have followed him in this preference. In summing up the significance of Heidegger's interpretation of Kant's first *Critique* in continental philosophy, Daniel Dahlstrom concludes that Heidegger's

> *KPM* [*Kant and the Problem of Metaphysics*] has become something of a canonical reading of the *Critique of Pure Reason*, perhaps explaining the relative dearth . . . of comparable studies of the *Critique*.
>
> (2010: 400)

His point is that although Kant's first *Critique* has been influential on numerous continental philosophers, there has been no study apart from Heidegger's that focuses on the whole work, hence its central status.[1] Heidegger's interpretation is so significant because of its "impact on others" and "its controversial interpretation of the transcendental analytic" (2010: 383). Dieter Heinrich, likewise, says that Heidegger's reading "[f]or more than a quarter of a century, determined the method as well as the interpretive goal of almost all publications in the field" (1994: 17).[2] These statements indicate the importance that Heidegger's reading of Kant's metaphysics is taken to have in the tradition of continental philosophy.

So let's turn to Heidegger's interpretation in *Kant and the Problem of Metaphysics*, also known as his Kant-book.[3] His reading of Kant's first *Critique* is a reaction against the readings of the neo-Kantians, such as Hermann Cohen and Cassirer, which stressed the epistemological aspect of Kant's project as a foundation of science.[4] Heidegger notes that his interpretation is a "thoughtful dialogue between thinkers" (1997a: xx) and his overall approach is to examine Kant's project as a whole, stressing the new grounding for metaphysics, and its relevance for human existence, looking beyond the literal meaning to what Kant really meant. Many of his analyses use etymological tracings of terms to uncover connections that are not obvious in the text. Heidegger reads the Transcendental Aesthetic and Analytic as Kant's ontology, and interprets Kant's project as centred on the question of Being or fundamental ontology (1997b: 13–18).[5] He takes up Kant's idea of a "common root" for sensibility and understanding. Kant says in the introduction that "there are two stems of human knowledge, namely *sensibility* and *understanding*, which perhaps spring from a common, but to us unknown, root" (1986: A15/B29). Heidegger adopts this as a key to understanding the *Critique*. According to Heidegger, that common root is imagination: "the origin of pure intuition and pure thinking as transcendental faculties is shown to be based on the transcendental power of imagination as a faculty" (Heidegger 1997b: 138).[6] He also takes this idea further, arguing that imagination connects theoretical and practical reason (1997b: 159); however, I will focus on the question of imagination as the source for our receptive and spontaneous faculties.

In the Kant-book, Heidegger argues that Kant's first *Critique* shows that the transcendental condition of the experience of objects is the imagination, which itself is based in time (1997b: 173–6). Imagination is described by Kant in the Metaphysical Deduction as "a blind but indispensable function of the soul, without which we would have no knowledge whatsoever, but of which we are scarcely ever conscious" (1986: A78/B103), a description that does not appear to imply such a pivotal or complex role in his project. To understand Heidegger's view, we need to examine the details of his argument. He begins by arguing that synthesis is the effect of the power of imagination, as imagination links representations, taking his cue from the first part of the previous quotation: "Synthesis in general [. . .] is the mere result of the power of imagination" (1997b: 63; 1986: A78/B103). In Kant, the syntheses are apprehension in intuition, reproduction in imagination, and recognition in a concept (1986: A99–104). These *a priori* syntheses enable us to perceive singular objects, recall them, and recognize them as belonging to categories. The syntheses themselves presuppose an *a priori* unity of consciousness, or transcendental unity of apperception, according to

Kant. In interpreting these arguments, Heidegger expands on imagination's role, contending that the centrality of the imaginative synthesis shows it is structurally central to the syntheses essential to knowledge.

Most generally, Heidegger contends that since temporality is at the basis of experience and the possibility of knowledge, Kant has inaugurated an ontology of *human* finitude, rather than that of finite knowing in general. "Transcendence" is what he calls knowing or "the experiencing of what is experienced as such" (1997b: 118), which is elucidated in the Transcendental Deduction. His view concerning the importance of human finitude to the *Critique* is based on the idea that Kant introduces a profound concept of time in the Transcendental Deduction, in the first edition at any rate, which binds the receptivity of intuition and the activity of synthesis. The focus of his discussion is section 3, and Kant's account of the interconnectedness of the three syntheses, from understanding to intuition and from intuition to understanding (1997b: 76–84). In this section, Heidegger seizes on the following sentence:

> Thus the principle of the necessary unity of pure (productive) synthesis of the imagination, prior to [*vor*] apperception, is the ground of the possibility of all knowledge, especially of experience.
>
> (1986: A118)

His interpretation that imagination and Transcendental Apperception thus form a structural unity is contested.[7] Nevertheless he then argues that pure synthesis has to unify something given to it *a priori*, which must be time, and so imagination is mediator between time and pure apperception (1997b: 82; 84). Heidegger concludes that the essence of the Transcendental Deduction is that it is based in the pure synthesis of the imagination.

For Heidegger, the transcendental Schematism is more important than the Transcendental Deduction, since the Schematism brings together intuition and understanding, making concepts spatio-temporal through the imagination.[8] The Schematism was also unchanged through the two editions, and so imagination was not downgraded in that chapter. His idea here is that in order to intuit something, we have to turn towards it, so to speak, and in doing so we prepare for what might be offered to us. And what might be offered is what he calls a "pure look" [*Anblick*] (1997b: 90). The imagination forms this look and also provides an image [*Bild*], such as the image or look of the landscape. Heidegger distinguishes between the immediate look of something, a look that is an imitation such as a photograph, and a look of something in general, a schema-image. To his way of thinking, a rule or schema must be "relative to possible schema-images, of which no uniqueness can be demanded" (1997b: 99).[9] The idea of the schema-image is that of a general image that can be brought to bear in perceptions of a particular object, such as a house. Then, as Kant notes, a schema is a product of imagination that "concerns the determination of inner sense in general according to conditions of its form (time)" (A142/B181). From Kant's characterization of the schemata, Heidegger finds that it is time that enables us to experience the world as offered to us, and provides the pure horizon within which we experience any specific horizon.

The first two parts of the book, discussed so far, stay relatively close to Kant's text; to continue, as Heidegger advises us, he needs "a more original appropriation" of Kant's contribution to ontology (1997b: 125). Thus, to support and develop his interpretation, Heidegger turns to Kant's discussion of imagination in his *Anthropology from a Pragmatic Point of View*, where he defines imagination as "a faculty of intuition without the presence of an object" (*Anth* 7: 167; Heidegger 1997b: 128). It should be noted that Kant first provides the explicit definition of imagination, as given in the *Anthropology*, and central to Heidegger's development of his views, in the second edition Transcendental

Deduction of the *Critique*, as "*Imagination* is the faculty of representing in intuition an object that is *not itself present*" (1986: B151; 1997b: 131).[10] Thus Heidegger analyzes imagination as a feature of intuition that differs from perception in not intuiting something present. This reading of imagination is crucial for his stress on the notion of self-affection and for his connection of receptivity and spontaneity. Central to Heidegger's argument that imagination is the "common root" or foundation for the syntheses of understanding and intuition is his claim that imagination "is the original unity of receptivity and spontaneity" (1997b: 153). The thought is that imagination can give itself an image, it both creates and receives an image, it is active and yet included in sensibility. Its spontaneous features are seen in that "it is for Kant a faculty of comparing, shaping, combining, distinguishing, and in general of binding-together (synthesis)" (1997b: 130). The receptivity comes from its alliance with sensibility.

To elaborate the power of imagination, Heidegger turns to an account of its specifically transcendental power. He observes how Kant sometimes refers to imagination as an original capacity, along with sense and apperception (A94), yet does not allocate imagination a section of its own and also refers to two stems of knowledge, namely sensibility and understanding, in the Transcendental Logic and Dialectic (1997b: 135–7; 1986: A50/B74; A294/B350). So perhaps the confusion could be resolved by understanding imagination as the common root of the two stems, Heidegger suggests. By this proposal he means that both pure intuition and pure thought grow out of transcendental imagination. Heidegger contends that imagination is at the base of intuition because pure intuitions can only present intuitable things through the pure power of imagination:

> Pure intuition, therefore, can only be 'original' because according to its essence it is the pure power of imagination itself which formatively gives looks (images) from out of itself.
>
> (1997b: 142)

To provide more support in Kant for this point, he quotes Kant as saying that space and time "As forms to be intuited, these are indeed Something, but they are not in themselves objects which can be intuited (*ens imaginarium*)" (A291/B347). As Heidegger's translator notes, the reference to the imaginary occurs after the previous sentence; nonetheless, he concludes that, "on the grounds of its essence, pure intuiting is pure imagination" (1997b: 143). On his account, understanding pure intuition in terms of pure imagination enables a positive explanation of the intuited.

Next, imagination is argued to be the basis of thought and understanding. Heidegger's argument is that understanding works through the schemata, or that Kant refers to the schematism of our understanding, and yet pure schemata are "a transcendental product of the power of imagination" (A142–1/B181, Heidegger's translation; 1997b: 150). This view is based on the idea that the thinking of the understanding in the Schematism is not working as judgment but as the forming or conceiving, and so is really pure imagination. Furthermore, the unity of understanding, Heidegger maintains, must be made through some kind of representing. Understanding is then linked to reason, through the claim that this representative character that makes the entire unity is the forming of ideas, and the thought of understanding in its essence must have the same character as reason. There is no important distinction between understanding and reason, since Heidegger believes Kant has inappropriately borrowed this distinction from formal logic (1997b: 152). The decisive further move that he makes is to argue that transcendental imagination is both spontaneous and receptive:

> the power of the imagination is also and precisely a faculty of intuition, i.e. of receptivity. And it is receptive, moreover, not just apart from its spontaneity. Rather, it is the original unity of receptivity and spontaneity, and not a unity which was composite from the first.
>
> (1997b: 152–3)

Likewise, Heidegger suggests that pure intuition is also spontaneous, and in having the dual character of receptivity and spontaneity he ascribes to imagination, its essence also lies in imagination. Similarly, understanding is receptive because it is receptive as letting the rules of linking things together occur. For him, it is transcendental imagination as receptive imagination that underlies the freedom of understanding and reason.[11]

In his reading, Heidegger connects the syntheses to time by considering the apprehensive synthesis or the capacity for forming representations as present or concerned with what is present, as a mode of imagination's power (1997b: 179–81). The capacity to reproduce representations is past, in that imagination links what was experienced earlier with what is current (1997b: 181–4). Finally, the synthesis of recognition is interpreted as the capacity to anticipate future representations, in that the other two syntheses have to be linked to the conceptual unity of understanding, and it is in that sense a future mode. Moreover, Heidegger argues that the futural aspect of time has priority over the other two aspects of past and present (1997b: 187–8).[12] Imagination is therefore rooted in time, or as he states: "the transcendental power of imagination is original time" (1997b: 197). What he is suggesting is that imagination has the synthetic character required to make sense of each of the syntheses, each of these reveal a temporal character, and so we should understand imagination as fundamentally temporal.

Heidegger goes beyond Kant in constructing a link between imagination and time.[13] Returning to his discussion of the Schematism, he maintains that it goes further than the *Anthropology* in showing the power of the imagination "as a free forming of images", indeed, of "the pure image of time" (1997b: 131). He reminds us that productive imagination, which is *a priori* in Kant, concerns the unity of the synthesis of the manifold or multiplicity of appearances, and enables the affinity of appearances or their correspondence to the rules of apperception, their association, and their reproduction according to laws. Heidegger sees pure imagination, concerning objectivity in general, as "necessarily productive" (1997b: 133). He takes himself to have proven that transcendental imagination is the origin of *a priori* intuition, and "[t]hus, it has been proven in principle that time, as a pure intuition, springs forth from the transcendental power of imagination" (1997b: 173). However, Heidegger wishes to demonstrate more explicitly how time is grounded in the imagination.

Reproductive or empirical imagination concerns our ability to reproduce a representation in the synthesis of reproduction, the only synthesis that Kant explicitly connects to time, in that the synthesis, which involves recall of former representations, can enable us to think of a period of time (A101). However, turning to Kant's *Lectures on Metaphysics*, where in a section on psychology, Kant discusses the relations between the "forming faculty" [*bildende Kraft*] and time, Heidegger takes Kant to be saying that the forming [*bilden*] aspect of the imagination [*Einbildung*] "is in *itself* relative to time" (*V-Met-L1/Pölitz* 28: 235; Heidegger 1997b: 175). For this idea, Heidegger proposes that pure imagining must form time, because pure intuition needs the power of imagination to form a likeness, (connected to the present), reproduce (related to the past) and prefigure (related to the future).[14] His contention is that time taken as a sequence of nows can only occur on the basis of a more profound experience of time. Thus he concludes that

> If the transcendental power of imagination, as the pure, forming faculty, in itself forms time – i.e., allows time to spring forth – then [. . .] the transcendental power of imagination is original time.
>
> (1997b: 187, 196)

Imagination connects perceptions in time so determines inner sense in relation to time.

Heidegger also reads time as self-affection or self-activating and structuring the self (1997b: 188–95, 1997a: 386–99). His view is that a finite subject must be able to be self-activated, and so time forms "the essential structure of subjectivity" (1997b: 189). For this claim, he turns to the Aesthetic, with regard to the form of intuition:

> Since this form does not represent anything save in so far as something is posited in the mind, it can be nothing but the mode in which the mind is affected through its own activity (namely, through this positing of its representation), and so is affected by itself; in other words, it is nothing but an inner sense in respect of the form of that sense.
>
> (B 68)

One can see the connection between imagination as enabling an experience of time and a construction of the self through connecting future, past, and present, and the idea of time as ecstatic temporality that differs from Kant's linear conception of time. Heidegger takes this idea further to connect the I with time and assert that this explains the I's ungraspability as temporal. He sums up his argument overall as "[o]riginal time makes possible the transcendental character of imagination, which in itself is essentially spontaneous receptivity and receptive spontaneity" (1997b: 197). This seemingly paradoxical formulation is one of the most controversial aspects of his interpretation, as we shall see.

Clearly, Heidegger prefers Transcendental Deduction A as providing a key to the central role of transcendental imagination and its temporal character, and claims that Kant turns away from the imagination in the second edition deduction, and promotes the understanding. He writes dramatically that "Kant shrank back from the unknown root" (1997b: 160). His evidence provided for this "shrinking back" includes Kant's deletion of two passages referring to imagination as one of the three basic sources of knowledge (A94, A115), and his revision of the Transcendental Deduction. Imagination is demoted and made dependent on understanding, instead of remaining as a separate faculty, and is there "in name only" (1997b: 164).[15] The reason Heidegger supplies for Kant's change of mind is his fear that imagination, perceived as a lower faculty linked to sensibility by the traditional disciplines of anthropology and psychology, could undermine the primacy of reason, and that "in between [the two editions] pure reason as reason drew him increasingly under its spell" (1997b: 168). The preference for one version of the Transcendental Deduction over the other, or one edition of the first *Critique* over the other is made a question of the role of the imagination and time, which for him are essential to examine ontological knowledge. As Charles Sherover, a sympathetic reader of Heidegger, says,

> the fact is that Heidegger justifiably focuses on the A edition just because of his interest in the priority of temporality as pervasive in human experience; this priority is far more clearly unmitigated in the A edition.
>
> (1971: 180)

In considering the impact of Heidegger's Kant-interpretation on the continental tradition in Kant studies, I wish to show the diversity of that tradition, and begin by considering an early criticism of Heidegger's approach.

3.   Cassirer's Criticisms of Heidegger's Kant Interpretation

One of the first critics of Heidegger's reading of Kant is neo-Kantian Ernst Cassirer, in "Kant and the problem of metaphysics: Remarks on Heidegger's interpretation of Kant" (1967). His criticisms of the Kant-book, along with Rudolf Carnap's criticisms of Heidegger's view of nothing, part of discussions between the three at Davos, Switzerland, in 1929 are taken by Michael Friedman (2003), Peter Gordon (2010) and others to be a turning point in the analytic/continental divide, one that sharpened and deepened that divide, with Carnap and Heidegger representing two opposing approaches to philosophy, one focused on formal logic and the other on subjective human thought.[16] Stephan Käufer remarks that Cassirer's appraisal is "the first and to date perhaps still the best examination of Heidegger's work as a Kant scholar" (2011: 178). Certainly, Cassirer's piece is an admirably clear, fair, and rigorous assessment of Heidegger's interpretation. He agrees with Heidegger's emphasis on the importance of the Schematism, praising him for the "extraordinary power" and "the greatest sharpness and clarity" of his analysis of the productive imagination (1967: 139). However, he finds that Heidegger's arguments that intuition is primary in a way that understanding is not are unfounded in Kant's text, and the spontaneity of the understanding is at least crucial to our experience and knowledge (1967: 141–2).

More broadly, Cassirer contends that in Heidegger's reading "[t]he distinction between phenomenon and noumenon is effaced: for all existence belongs now to the dimension of time and thus to finitude" (1967: 47). By taking away that fundamental distinction, Kant's position must break down, or no longer be his position, because for Kant our finitude is only one aspect of our existence, as freedom and reason go beyond finitude.[17] Furthermore, to understand Kant's system one must deal with all three *Critiques* (1967: 149). In sum, as Cassirer noted, "Heidegger has attempted to transfer Kant's analysis from the foundation of the objective deduction purely and exclusively to that of the subjective deduction" (1967: 151). Even more crucially, Cassirer disputes Heidegger's central claim that Kant drew away from the imagination in the second Transcendental Deduction: "did he not retain the core of his doctrine of transcendental imagination even in the second edition and permit it to remain in its decisive systematic intermediary position?" (1967: 153). This is an important claim that needs to be examined, so I will consider that view in the following sections as part of a discussion of continental responses to Heidegger's interpretation.

4. Criticisms of Heidegger's Reading in the Continental Tradition

In a significant paper, "Heidegger's Kantian turn," Dahlstrom argues that Heidegger's reading of Kant constitutes an important part

> of the argument for his basic contention that knowledge or the possibility of experience, even as Kant explains it, is based upon understanding being in terms of temporality, conceived as an original, yet finite, transcending.
>
> (1991: 331)

This reading, Dahlstrom maintains, is not an attempt to understand Kant as such, but to correct his mistakes and make the critique "adequate" (1991: 332). Nevertheless, Heidegger's interpretation must be evaluated in terms of its use of textual evidence that reads Kant by the text's own lights. Dahlstrom considers his reading as carried out in *Kant and the Problem of Metaphysics* and in his lectures on Kant's *Critique*, seeing Heidegger as finding Kant to be on the right track in seeing the importance of time as a condition of possibility for experience. Furthermore, Heidegger sees his own distinction between original time as ecstatic temporality and a vulgar conception of time as a series of "nows" in Kant's work. Finally, the unity of the original sense of time is "the way of being most basic to the human subject and the ground for understanding other modes of being and, indeed, for experiencing other beings" (1991: 337).

Self-affection is the crucial concept in Heidegger's interpretation of the Transcendental Deduction. Dahlstrom summarizes Heidegger's theses as

> (1) the original (ecstatic) sense of time is (identical to) self-affection, (2) Self-consciousness is dependent upon self-affection, and (3) self-affection provides the underlying structure to the transcendental schemata.
>
> (1991: 338)

Heidegger's argument, as we have seen, is that because time is not given to us by experience, it must be the effect of the mind on itself. Moreover, there is no further self-consciousness beyond this way of affecting itself. Time then makes it possible to be a self and to recognize something distinct from the self, that is, apperception or self-consciousness and knowledge of objects. However, Dahlstrom contends that "there can be little doubt that he [Heidegger] is transposing his own account of an original, ecstatic sense of temporality onto Kant's transcendental conception of time" (1991: 339). This ecstatic sense of time is one that focuses on past, present, and future as aspects of temporal experience, and has a fundamental futural focus. Furthermore, he notes that Heidegger makes a shift from the neo-Kantian focus on judgment, intellect, and apperception, to imagination, sentience, and self-affection (1991: 340).

In regard to the question of the imagination, Dahlstrom notes:

> What Heidegger interprets as pure sentience in this connection is not some blind sensibility, but the *a priori* synthesis of the manifold of pure intuition by a transcendental faculty attributed by Kant himself – at least in the second edition of the *KrV* – to sentience, namely, the transcendental imagination.
>
> (1991: 351)

In this sense, Dahlstrom is acknowledging that the definition of imagination provided in the second version of the Transcendental Deduction is crucial for Heidegger's argument.

After providing a detailed account of Heidegger's interpretation of Kant, Dahlstrom turns to criticism of Heidegger's claim that Kant identifies time and self-affection. The quotation from Kant, apropos of time, that Heidegger uses is:

> Since this form does not represent anything save in so far as something is posited in the mind, it can be nothing but the mode in which the mind is affected through its own activity (namely, through this positing of its representation), and so is affected by itself.
>
> (1986: B68)

However, Dahlstrom argues that "[p]lainly, Kant does not identify time here as self-affection, but rather as the way or manner, or simply as that through which, the mind affects itself" (1991: 353). Thus, Heidegger's interpretation "is simply unacceptable" (1991: 353). Rather, time is the fundamental form of our self-intuition, and Kant explains that we affect our inner sense, for example, the understanding affects inner sense whenever we attend to something (B157n). Furthermore, Kant himself explains self-affection through the idea of the unity of the passive and active subject, or the thinking subject knowing itself as an object of thought (B155). The problem with Heidegger's claim is the attribution of identity to time and self-affection. So Dahlstrom concludes that "Kant's account of self-affection is thus diametrically opposed to the interpretation given it by Heidegger" (1991: 355). The spontaneity of the understanding is what constitutes the unity of self-consciousness, not time as self-affection, and so the interpretation of the Kant-book is not one that Kant could agree with. Heidegger himself notes in his preface to *Kant and the Problem of Metaphysics'* second edition, that the book's interpretation is "violent" and that it has "shortcomings" but that thinkers learn from these (1997b: xx) and in the fourth preface he refers to an "overinterpretation" (1997b: xviii).[18] Yet Heidegger had already said in the book itself that "Certainly, in order to wring from what the words say, what it is they want to say, every interpretation must necessarily use violence" (1997b: 202). Thus, to reiterate the point in the preface is not to acknowledge a change of mind or to self-criticize.

In a later article, Dahlstrom provides a more supportive reading, showing how Heidegger takes a phenomenological approach to understanding the Transcendental Deduction A, in that he looks for the lived experience of the syntheses of cognition. Furthermore, he finds Heidegger's argument for the necessity for pure imagination to the intellectual and intuitive syntheses grounded in Kant's text. Moreover, the discussion of the Schematism is consistent in linking schemata, images and imagination. Ultimately, he concludes that

> Heidegger's interpretation makes a powerful case that it [Kant's project] succeeds – by Kant's own lights, at least in the *Critique's* first edition – only by according pure imagination a foundational role.
>
> (2010: 399)

Thus, Dahlstrom's construal lends credence to the view that it is the role of the imagination in the first edition deduction that forms the core of Heidegger's Kant-interpretation. However, he does fault Heidegger for neglecting the significance of synthetic *a priori* principles in determining objects in nature. While many continental thinkers fault Heidegger's interpretation in a range of ways, it is found compelling and influential, as Dahlstrom notes. Nevertheless, that influence does not necessarily revolve around a preference for the Transcendental Deduction A, as I will explain.

5. The Continental Tradition's Rejection of the Shibboleth

Many scholars are in agreement that Heidegger's reading of Kant says more about his philosophical development than about Kant, and that his work *Being and Time* (1962) is very Kantian, since Heidegger was working on Kant before and during the writing of *Being and Time*, as Käufer observes (2011: 180).[19] Heinrich, who examines the pre-history of the interpretation, argues that Kant had no belief in the genuine possibility of a common root for intuition and understanding, that the idea of the imagination as a common root can be found in Hegel and other German idealists, and that

> Surely Heidegger did not realize the extent to which his results diverge from the explicit position of the Kantian text. Those who do not know that position from their own studies will be led astray by Heidegger's interpretation, since the detailed textual references imply that it is a historical exegesis.
>
> (1994: 54)

In spite of the agreement about the close relationship between Heidegger's thinking and his interpretation of Kant, both the sharp distinction between the two versions of the Transcendental Deduction, and the view that Heidegger "preferred" the first to the second, have been questioned.

There exists a consistency between the A and B deductions, which even Heidegger himself is aware of. Käufer concedes this point, while defending Heidegger's concept of "receptive spontaneity" from Cassirer's criticisms, arguing that Heidegger does not impose his own views on Kant, but rather incorporates Kant's views into his own, in terms of original temporality and the temporal ecstasies (2011: 185). The receptive spontaneity is taken from the idea of attunement and competence in which we are affected by objects and disclose them as well. He further defends this concept by quoting Kant: "receptivity can make knowledge possible only when combined with spontaneity" (A97). However, Käufer admits that "the overall scheme of the argument" is similar in the A and B editions (2011: 187), and concludes that "Heidegger, guided by his existentialism, unduly expands on what is at stake in Kant's analysis of the transcendental subject" (2011, 196). The expansion is to the idea of a concrete, existing self, whereas Kant is concerned to delimit the conditions of cognition.

The tradition goes further in demonstrating how even Heidegger's reading comprehends the importance of developments in the second Transcendental Deduction. For instance, Emilia Angelova, following Heinrich's reading that imagination still plays a role as an idea of an independent cognitive faculty, argues for the continuity of A and B deductions. She contends that

> Kant's notion of intellectual intuition (act, spontaneity, freedom, radical faculty) corresponds with imagination, not with apperceptive self-consciousness, and this notion carries on from the A into the B deduction without changing its essence.
>
> (2009: 66)

There is a parallel between imagination and intellectual intuition, although Kant argues that intellectual intuition is impossible for a finite being, unlike for a god. Imagination brings into mind or makes present what is absent. The thinking of this interpretation is that while Kant does not use the same language, his conceptualization of imagination is continuous between the two deductions, and Kant did not "shrink back" from the imagination, as Heinrich notes (1994: 40).

Furthermore, in continental readings of Kant's first *Critique*, there are not clear preferences for Transcendental Deduction A. For example, Gilles Deleuze does not mention Heidegger's reading in his book covering Kant's three *Critiques*, *Kant's Critical Philosophy*.[20] Taking yet another perspective, he simply accepts that understanding is more determining of cognition than imagination. Deleuze states that in the first *Critique*

> understanding was dominant because it determined inner sense through the intermediary of a synthesis of the imagination, and even reason submitted to the role which was assigned to it by the understanding.
>
> (2008: x)

Similarly, in explaining the transcendental method of the first *Critique*, he writes: "When understanding legislates in the interest of knowledge, imagination and reason still retain an entirely *original* role, but in conformity with tasks determined by the understanding" (2008: 8). Thus, he is clear that understanding is more significant than the imagination.

In his outline of the Transcendental Deduction, Deleuze describes imagination as an activity of synthesis, and one of the active faculties, in contrast to sensibility: "Taken in its activity, synthesis refers back to *imagination*; in its unity, to *understanding*; and in its totality, to *reason*" (2008: 7). In considering the role of the imagination, he notes that "the synthesis of the imagination, taken in itself, is not at all self-conscious" (A78/B103; 2008: 13). Here he is quoting from both A and B editions; however, as he continues to explain how Kant argues that synthetic knowledge is possible, he shifts to the B edition, arguing "all use of the understanding is developed from the 'I think'; moreover, the unity of the 'I think' is understanding itself" (2008: 14; B134fn). The understanding and its categories provide unity for imagination's synthesis, and the imagination "relates phenomena to the understanding" (2008: 14–15). Furthermore, the imagination schematizes or determines things as spatio-temporal, an operation which is itself subject to the categories of the understanding. Hence Deleuze takes the B Transcendental Deduction as definitive, comparative to that of the A version.

While the specific point about the shibboleth of the Transcendental Deduction cannot be conclusively supported, this is not to say that continental readings of Kant's theoretical philosophy do not have a range of shared features. Most broadly, one could say that the continental tradition of Kant scholarship is one that, whether following Heidegger or not, questions the prominent place that Kant gives to understanding and reason in the first *Critique*, in favour of the imagination, the emotions, sensibility, the irrational, the unthought, or the precognitive. Some of that tradition has also sought to articulate a concrete and embodied human self conceived as a development of the perceived abstraction and disembodiment of Kant's notion of the self. In terms of influence, the question of time and its role in our experience, and the historicist and finite slant of Heidegger's reading of Kant, is a crucial guide in continental thought in all areas.

The notion of time as self-affection has been one of the more influential concepts from Heidegger's interpretation of Kant. Maurice Merleau-Ponty takes up the notion of time as self-affection in *Phenomenology of Perception*, writing:

> Time is 'self-affection of itself': time, as a thrust and a passage towards a future, is the one who affects; time, as a spread-out series of presents, is the one affected; the affecting and the affected are identical because the thrust of time is nothing other than the transition from one present to another.
>
> (2012, 449)

He sees this idea of temporality as clarifying subjectivity in a way that Kant's transcendental "I" does not.[21]

Giorgio Agamben, in *Remnants of Auschwitz*, likewise takes up time as self-affection, reading Heidegger's interpretation as continuous with Kant's text. He writes that

> A perfect equivalent of shame can be found precisely in the originary structure of subjectivity that modern philosophy calls *auto-affection* and that, from Kant onward, is generally identified as time.
>
> (1999: 109)

Indeed, Agamben's phrasing makes clear he takes this way of thinking to be both obvious and widely shared. Thus, the influence of Heidegger's interpretation of Kant appears in unexpected places and an interest is shown in some of the more surprising features of it.[22]

6. Conclusion

This chapter shows how the continental tradition of Kant scholarship is diverse, in spite of its traceability to Heidegger's Kant-book, and that the Transcendental Deduction is not the shibboleth it may appear to be. Perhaps more compelling than the specific features of his interpretation, the very idea of a violent reading, that teases out what the text wanted to say or ought to have said, is one that has influenced continental Kant scholarship and continental scholarship in the twentieth and twenty-first century more generally.[23] To consider further how Kant has influenced continental theoretical philosophy, how continental philosophers have explored other aspects of Kant's theoretical philosophy could be examined, and to understand the continental tradition in general further, we would need to take a more syncretic look at the tradition and examine the influence of Kant's *oeuvre*.

Notes

1 Adorno's lectures on the first *Critique*, given in 1959, can be counted among the full studies; however, they were not published in German until 1995 and in English until 2001. He distinguishes his method of interpretation from Heidegger's thus: "*I* think it wholly impermissible simply to twist what is *said* in a text like the *Critique of Pure Reason*, and to turn it upside down. But even more important is the question of how to justify the claim that *more* is said in such an interpretation than can be found on the page" (2001: 79).

2 It should be noted that Heinrich first published this essay in 1955, so the years of influence he is describing are soon after its publication.

3 I will focus on this book, as it is the book most relevant to the question of a tradition, since Heidegger's earlier lectures were not published in German until 1977 (1997a). Page references are to the original pagination.

4 Claude Piché observes that "Heidegger nowhere enters into a detailed discussion of the Marburg School's, or at least not of Cohen's and Natorp's, interpretation of Kant" although his approach is comparable (Rockmore 2000: 180, 201). Cassirer also makes this point regarding Cohen's Kant interpretation (1967: 135).

5 Pierre Kerszberg argues that Kant would reject Heidegger's reading, which "amounts to transforming this unconditioned [Being] into an Idea of Reason. [. . .] What shall we gain by admitting Being among the Ideas of Reason?" (Rockmore 2000: 37). In contrast, Serck-Hanssen provides a strong defence of this aspect of Heidegger's interpretation (2015).

6 Heinrich criticises Heidegger's interpretation here, arguing that a careful analysis of Kant's writings demonstrates he did not accept there could be such a root (1994: 19–27).

7 Weatherston argues convincingly that "*vor*" here should be understood as "before" as one might stand before a judge, rather than as "prior to" (2002: 158–60).

8 Käufer suggests that what is most important about Heidegger's reading is its insistence on the importance of the Transcendental Deduction and Schematism to the unity of Kant's project (2011: 177).

9 See Jean-Luc Nancy's discussion of this part of the Kant-book (2005: 80–99).

10 Arendt cites both in her seminar on imagination (1982: 79).

11 Moreover, productive imagination is linked by Heidegger to the spontaneity of practical freedom; however, that link need not be discussed here (1997b: §30).

12 Schalow defends Heidegger's interpretation on this point by arguing that "futurity is integral to transcendental apperception and thereby suggests the source of affinity between it and imagination" (1992: 199).

13 As Weatherston notes, Heidegger generally neglects the importance of space to the first *Critique* throughout his interpretation (2002, 147). This neglect is due to the view Heidegger finds in Kant that "time has a pre-eminence over space" (1997b: 49). He discusses space as a pure intuition (1997b: 44–7) and as equally rooted in transcendental imagination (1997b: 140–5, 200–1).

14 See Heidegger (1997a: 415) for a more detailed discussion of the forming character of imagination.

15 In *Being and Time,* Heidegger maintains that Kant "shrinks back" from an understanding of time and of Being (1962: 23).

16 As Friedman notes, all three philosophers were educated in the neo-Kantian tradition, Cassirer in the Marburg School, Heidegger in the Southwest School, and Carnap was familiar with both (2003: 16). He suggests that Cassirer's work is a valuable resource for bringing the two traditions together (2003: 29). Hanna disputes this account of consequences of Davos, arguing the divide did not occur until after 1945 (2008: 174–6).

17 Heidegger contests Cassirer's reading, maintaining that he has completely misunderstood his interpretation, and the centrality of finitude to understanding human faculties (1997b: Appendices IV and V).

18 Gordon takes these comments by Heidegger to indicate a belated acceptance of Cassirer's criticisms (2010: 281); however, his comments only concede that Kant was not primarily concerned with ontology.

19 For instance, Veronica Vasterling reads Heidegger's account of time in Kant as solving some of the problems in his own account of time (Rockmore 2000: 85–102), as does Heinrich (1994: 54), and others. Heidegger suggests the same himself in the Kant-book (1997b: 203).

20 Deleuze also discusses Kant's first *Critique* in his book with Guattari, *What is Philosophy?* (1994: 31–2), and extensively in *Difference and Repetition* (2004).
21 Jacques Derrida refers to Heidegger's reading and cites passages from it in the context of his discussion of *Being and Time* (1982: 31–2, 45, 50).
22 See also Luce Irigaray's discussion of Kant in *Speculum of the Other Woman* (1985: 203–13).
23 Ann Murphy discusses the proliferation of rhetoric of violence in continental philosophy in *Violence and the Philosophical Imaginary* (2012).

References

Adorno, T.W. (2001) *Kant's Critique of Pure Reason*, R. Tiedemann (ed.) and R. Livingstone (trans.), Cambridge: Polity.

Agamben, G. (1999) *Remnants of Auschwitz: The Witness and the Archive*, D. Heller-Roazen (trans.), New York: Zone Books.

Angelova, E. (2009) "A Continuity Between the A and B Deductions of the *Critique*: Revisiting Heidegger's Critique of Kant," *Idealistic Studies* 39(1–3): 53–71.

Arendt, H. (1982) *Lectures on Kant's Political Philosophy*, R. Beiner (ed.), Chicago: University of Chicago Press.

Cassirer, E. (1967) "Kant and the Problem of Metaphysics: Remarks on Martin Heidegger's Interpretation of Kant," in M.S. Gram (ed.), *Kant: Disputed Questions*, Chicago: Quadrangle Books, pp. 131–57.

Caygill, H. (1995) *A Kant Dictionary*, Oxford: Blackwell.

Dahlstrom, D.O. (1991) "Heidegger's Kantian Turn: Notes to His Commentary on the *Kritik der Reinen Vernunft*," *The Review of Metaphysics* 45(2): 329–61.

Dahlstrom, D.O. (2010) "The Critique of Pure Reason and Continental Philosophy: Heidegger's Interpretation of Transcendental Imagination," in P. Guyer (ed.), *The Cambridge Companion to Kant's Critique of Pure Reason*, Cambridge: Cambridge University Press, pp. 380–400.

Deleuze, G. (2004) *Difference and Repetition*, P. Patton (trans.), London: Acumen.

Deleuze, G. (2008) *Kant's Critical Philosophy: The Doctrine of the Faculties*, H. Tomlinson and B. Habberjam (trans.), London: Continuum.

Deleuze, G. and Guattari, F. (1994) *What Is Philosophy?* H. Tomlinson and G. Burchell (trans.), New York: Columbia University Press.

Derrida, J. (1982) *Margins of Philosophy*, A. Bass (trans.), Chicago: The University of Chicago Press.

Friedman, M. (2003) "A Turning Point in Philosophy: Carnap-Cassirer-Heidegger," in P. Parrini, W.C. Salmon and M.H. Salmon (eds.), *Logical Empiricism: Historical and Contemporary Perspectives*, Pittsburgh: University of Pittsburgh Press, pp. 13–29.

Gordon, P.E. (2010) *Continental Divide: Heidegger, Cassirer, Davos*, Cambridge: Harvard University Press.

Hanna, R. (2008) "Kant in the Twentieth Century," in D. Moran (ed.), *The Routledge Companion to the Twentieth Century*, London: Routledge.

Heidegger, M. (1962) *Being and Time*, J. Macquarrie and E. Robinson (trans.), New York: Harper.

Heidegger, M. (1997a) *Phenomenological Interpretation of Kant's Critique of Pure Reason*, P. Emad and K. Maly (trans.), Bloomington: Indiana University Press.

Heidegger, M. (1997b) *Kant and the Problem of Metaphysics*, R. Taft (trans.), 5th ed., Bloomington: Indiana University Press.

Heidegger, M. (2010) *Logic: The Question of Truth*, T. Sheehan (trans.), Bloomington: Indiana University Press.

Heinrich, D. (1994) *The Unity of Reason: Essays on Kant's Philosophy*, R.L. Velkley (ed.), J. Edwards (trans.), Cambridge: Harvard University Press.

Irigaray, L. (1985) *Speculum of the Other Woman*, G.C. Gill (trans.), Ithaca: Cornell University Press.

Kant, I. (1986) *Critique of Pure Reason*, N.K. Smith (trans.), Houndmills: Macmillan.

Käufer, S. (2011) "Heidegger's Interpretation of Kant," in D.O. Dahlstrom (ed.), *Interpreting Heidegger: Critical Essays*, Cambridge: Cambridge University Press, pp. 175–96.

Merleau-Ponty, M.-P. (2012) *The Phenomenology of Perception*, D.A. Landes (trans.), London: Routledge.

Murphy, A. (2012) *Violence and the Philosophical Imaginary*, Albany: SUNY Press.

Nancy, J.-L. (2005) *The Ground of the Image*, J. Fort (trans.), New York: Fordham University Press.

Rockmore, T. (ed.) (2000) *Heidegger, German Idealism, and Neo-Kantianism*, Amherst: Humanity Books.

Schalow, F. (1992) *The Renewal of the Heidegger-Kant Dialogue: Action, Thought, and Responsibility*, New York: SUNY Press.

Serck-Hanssen, C. (2015) "Towards Fundamental Ontology: Heidegger's Phenomenological Reading of Kant," *Continental Philosophy Review* 48: 217–35.

Sherover, C. (1971) *Heidegger, Kant and Time*, Bloomington: Indiana University Press.

Weatherston, M. (2002) *Heidegger's Interpretation of Kant: Categories, Imagination and Temporality*, Houndmills: Palgrave Macmillan.

Further reading

S. Baiasu and A. Vanzo (eds.), *Kant and the Continental Tradition* (London: Routledge, 2020) has chapters on the relation between Kant and major continental philosophers. G. Banham, "The Continental Tradition: Kant, Hegel, Nietzsche," in J. Mullarkey and B. Lord (eds.), *The Continuum Companion to Continental Philosophy* (London: Bloomsbury, 2021) explores Kant's legacy for the future of continental philosophy. C.H. Hamburg, "A Cassirer-Heidegger Seminar," *Philosophy and Phenomenological Research* 25(2) (1964): 208–22, provides an account of their meeting in Davos. J. Kneller, *Kant and the Power of Imagination* (Cambridge: Cambridge University Press, 2007), ch. 5, examines the role of imagination in the breadth of Kant's work. S. Luft (ed.), *The Neo-Kantian Reader* (London: Routledge, 2015) has a large collection of original works by neo-Kantians, and a section on "The Davos Dispute." T. Nenon (ed.), *Kant, Kantianism, and Idealism: The Origins of Continental Philosophy* (Durham: Acumen, 2010) contains essays on late-eighteenth- and nineteenth-century idealism. F. Raffoul, *Heidegger and the Subject* (New York: Humanity Books, 1998) considers in detail in Chapter 4 the relationship between Kant's and Heidegger's views of the subject.

41

THE 'ANALYTIC' TRADITION

James O'Shea

★★★

Kant's complex relationship to what came to be known as the twentieth-century 'analytic' tradition in philosophy might usefully be divided into three phases. (1) First, spanning roughly the first two-thirds of the twentieth century, there was predominantly, though not entirely, a rejection of Kant's theoretical philosophy, beginning with the Cambridge analysts Russell and Moore, followed also by the logical positivists, and then by the so-called ordinary language philosophers at mid-century. (2) Second, during the 1960s several influential books on Kant by such Anglo-American philosophers as P.F. Strawson, Graham Bird (1962), and Jonathan Bennett (1966) defended certain key arguments in Kant's *Critique of Pure Reason* and thereby helped to stimulate a marked improvement in many analytic philosophers' estimation of the merits of Kant's theoretical philosophy. John Rawls' work on justice and the history of ethics at Harvard stimulated a similar revival of Kant's practical philosophy (see Chapter 39). (3) Finally, the subsequent decades from the mid-1960s to the present have witnessed a wide variety of striking uses made of broadly 'analytic Kantian' ideas in theoretical philosophy by such prominent analytically trained philosophers as Wilfrid Sellars, Gareth Evans, Hilary Putnam, Donald Davidson, Michael Dummett, John McDowell, Rae Langton, and Robert Brandom, among others. In many cases these analytic-Kantian ideas have drawn upon the mid-century work of the later Wittgenstein; and also in many cases these Kant-influenced philosophers have encouraged the downplaying of any sharp or hostile distinction between the so-called 'analytic' and 'continental' streams in contemporary philosophy.

In a previous piece (O'Shea 2006) I have attempted to provide a concise overview of the reception of Kant's philosophy among analytic philosophers during the periods covered by (1) and (2): from the 'early analytic' reactions to Kant in Frege, Russell, Carnap and others, to the systematic Kant-inspired works in epistemology and metaphysics of C. I. Lewis (1929; cf. O'Shea 2015) and Strawson (1959, 1966), in particular, and ending with a very brief discussion of more recent figures. Kant's influence on the history of analytic philosophy across these periods has also been given helpful treatments by Coffa 1991; Friedman 2001; Hanna 2001; Macbeth 2014; Sluga 1980; Westphal 2010. However, rather than directly presenting once again the influential analytic Kantian lines of argument in Strawson's work (for this see also Glock 2003; Cassam 2017), or their important further development by Gareth Evans (1980, 1982; cf. Cassam 1997; Kitcher 2011; McDowell 1996), this

DOI: 10.4324/9781003406617-56

chapter will use the recently reinvigorated work of Wilfrid Sellars (1912–1989) in the second half of the twentieth century as the basis for presenting some of the most familiar analytic Kantian themes that continue to animate current debates. Since as it happens the relationships between Sellars' philosophy and Kant are often misunderstood, in my view, this chapter also aims to clarify certain topics in current philosophical debates. In what follows I will consider just three such topic-areas among many: (1) conceptual analysis and the structure of human knowledge; (2) laws of nature, the causal modalities, and the pragmatic or relative a priori; and (3) the disputes concerning Kant and nonconceptual content.

1. Conceptual Analysis and the Structure of Human Knowledge

In his 1973 "Autobiographical Reflections" Sellars wrote that during his Rhodes scholarship at Oriel College, Oxford from 1934 to 1936, he studied Kant's *Critique of Pure Reason* with H. H. Price as his tutor. Kant convinced him, Sellars tells us, that

> a skeptic who grants knowledge of even the simplest fact about an event occurring in Time is, in effect, granting knowledge of the existence of nature as a whole. I was sure he was right.
>
> (Sellars 1975: 285)

Kant would subsequently figure centrally in Sellars' thinking throughout the rest of his career. From 1947 to 1967 the influence was often more implicit than explicit, as for example in his most famous article "Empiricism and the Philosophy of Mind" (Sellars 1956), in which he argued against the "myth of the given." But it then became more explicit in *Science and Metaphysics: Variations on Kantian Themes* (1968) and in a series of penetrating articles on Kant from 1967 to 1978, collected posthumously in *Kant's Transcendental Metaphysics* (2002). But let us begin with the theme of that earliest conviction at Oxford, and consider what Sellars' subsequent works suggest about this insight of Kant's into the structure of human knowledge. For generally speaking these turn out to be the sorts of views shared by many other analytic Kantians from Strawson to today.

Unlike Kant, though reflecting Kant's revolutionary focus on *logical form* as the key to the nature of human understanding, it has been distinctive of Strawson, Sellars and subsequent analytic Kantians to attempt to clarify Kant's accounts of the understanding's necessary conceptual connections through a primary focus on our *linguistic* practices. This is not surprising given the key focus on language throughout much of twentieth-century philosophy. This was certainly the case for Sellars, who developed a novel inferential role semantics during roughly the period when the later Wittgenstein was completing his *Philosophical Investigations* (1953) (cf. Sellars' 1954 "Some Reflections on Language Games," in Sellars 1963). Sellars defended a holistic 'language game' conception of the meaning of linguistic expressions, and hence also, by extension, of human conceptual thinking in general.

On this view meaning and conceptual content are understood in terms of the norm-governed 'use' or functioning of linguistic expressions in accordance with the normative "ought-to-be" rules of criticism and "ought to do" rules of action that are implicit in a given community's social-linguistic behavior. In the transcendental deduction Kant had characterized the understanding as "the **faculty of rules**" (A126; A132/B171), with the twelve a priori categories and corresponding principles of pure understanding providing a conceptual "legislation for nature." Such conceptual connections are necessary, Kant famously argued, if any potentially self-conscious experience is to be possible at all. Sellars sought to explicate and to update Kant's conception of the understanding and its necessary relation to our faculty of sensibility in terms of his own twentieth-century analytic conceptions of meaning, knowledge, and experience. As Sellars in one place put the relationship between his philosophy and Kant's:

> Implicit in the above conception of language as a rule governed system are a number of important implications for a linguistically oriented epistemology. Instead, however, of developing these implications directly, I shall explore certain features of Kant's epistemology which will turn out to be their counterparts. For once it is appreciated that Kant's account of the conceptual structures involved in experience can be given a linguistic turn and, purged of the commitment to innateness to which, given his historical setting he was inevitably led, his theory can be seen to add essential elements to an analytic account of the resources a language must have to be the bearer of empirical meaning, empirical truth, and, to bring things to their proper focus, empirical knowledge.
>
> (Sellars 2002: 268, OAPK §31)[1]

Methodologically, this passage sums up well the spirit of analytic Kantianism in the ways to be explored in this chapter.[2]

On Sellars' analytic reading,

> the core of Kant's 'epistemological turn' is the claim that [. . .] all so-called ontological categories are in fact epistemic. They are 'unified' by the concept of empirical knowledge because they are simply constituent moments of this one complex concept.
>
> (2002: 270, KTE II §9)

In particular, Kant's categories are *meta*-concepts that serve to classify the epistemic powers or functions of the first-order concepts that exhibit the given logical form. For example, in the judgment that 'snow is white', *snow* is functioning as a *substance* concept, which is to say that it satisfies or exhibits the epistemic powers distinctive of the substance-attribute form of a judgment when applied to objects of possible experience. (The latter epistemic functions are spelled out in Kant's arguments for the Analogies and the other principles of understanding.) To so judge, Sellars explains, is "to be committed to the idea that the representable *snow* and the representable *white* belong together regardless of what anyone happens to think," and thus to be committed "to the idea that representing that snow is white are (epistemically) correct" (2002: 274, KTE III §21). Objective nature, accordingly, is "the system of those representable spatial and/or temporal states of affairs which *did*, *do*, or *will obtain*, whether or not they *were*, *are*, or *will be* actually represented" (2002: 270, KTE I §6).

On Sellars' interpretation of the aims and method of Kant's first *Critique*, it turns out to "be an *analytic* truth that objects of empirical knowledge conform to logically synthetic universal principles," such as the synthetic a priori principle that every event has a cause, or that substance persists through all change, or that all such changes take place within a single coherent system of spatial and temporal relations. According to Sellars, rather than attempting "to *prove* that there is empirical knowledge," Kant's analysis

> is such as to rule out the possibility that there could be empirical knowledge not implicitly of the form "such and such a state of affairs belongs to a coherent *system* of states of affairs of which my perceptual experiences are a part."
>
> (2002: 271, KTE II §§10–11, italics added)[3]

515

Kant's transcendental analytic thereby "undercuts both the skeptic and the 'problematic idealist'" or indeed *any* epistemological view that raises "the illegitimate question of how one can justifiably move from" certain (alleged) items of experience "that seem to involve no intrinsic commitment to such a larger context" – such as the sense-datum appearances of an atomistic empiricist, for example – to "the larger context to which we *believe* them to belong" (2002: 271, KTE II §11), that is, to the objective nature of which they are a part. It is this systematic and holistic conceptual analysis that convinced Sellars during his Oxford days that Kant must be right: that is, that "a skeptic who grants knowledge of even the simplest fact about an event occurring in Time" – even if it were simply the 'immediate' or 'given' experience of one's own subjective state – "is, in effect, granting knowledge of the existence of nature as a whole."

Chapter 1 of P. F. Strawson's 1959 groundbreaking book, *Individuals: An Essay in Descriptive Metaphysics*, had in a broadly similar spirit attempted to show that the complex concept of a single spatio-temporal system of persisting material bodies forms the indispensable core or structure of our most basic and permanent conceptual scheme. Roughly put, Strawson argued that the possibility of even coherently raising a skeptical doubt about the existence of objective, reidentifiable particulars already presupposes the general idea that particulars are related within one spatiotemporal framework (as opposed to each stretch of experience constituting an isolated world, as it were); and he argued furthermore that our conception of the latter spatiotemporal framework itself already requires the concept of persisting, reidentifiable particulars (material bodies), given that – as Kant himself had stressed – space and time are not *themselves* objects of perception. In effect, then, as Strawson put it, the skeptic "pretends to accept a conceptual scheme, but at the same time quietly rejects one of the conditions of its employment" (1959: 35).[4]

Both Strawson and Sellars, in their different ways, attempted to make good on these general systematic claims by providing more specific accounts of why something like Kant's account of our objectively valid, self-aware knowledge of one unified spatiotemporal nature, and of principles of causal lawfulness and material persistence in general (not to mention principles of moral freedom and rational agency), could be reformulated and defended using the insights of "modern analytical philosophy" (Strawson 1997: 232).

2. Laws of Nature, the Causal Modalities, and the Pragmatic or Relative A Priori

One core component of Sellars' Kantian analysis lies in his various arguments since the early 1950s that Kant was essentially right in his contention that any possible empirical knowledge must be such as to represent the objective world as governed by necessary *laws of nature*. The following is an illustrative passage, in this case from Sellars' 1967 article "Some Remarks on Kant's Theory of Experience":

> To conceive of an event as occurring at a time is to commit oneself to the idea that the *concept* of that event and the *concept* of that time belong together regardless of what one happens to think. But there is nothing about the sheer concept of a particular time which requires that it be occupied by a certain event. The belonging must, Kant concludes, be a matter of the temporal location of the event relative to other events and, *as belonging*, be the inferability (in principle) of its occurrence at that location from the occurrence of the events to which it is thus related.

> (Sellars 2002: 279, KTE VI §36)

Thus, what

> Kant takes himself to have proved is that the concept of empirical knowledge involves the concept of inferability in accordance with laws of nature. To grant that there is knowledge of the *here* and *now* is [. . .] to grant that there are general truths of the sort captured by lawlike statements.
>
> (2002: 338, TTC §54)

The deeper grounds for Sellars' semantically updated defense of Kant on causal connections and other principles of objective lawfulness in nature were originally explored in detail in Sellars' long 1957 article "Counterfactuals, Dispositions, and the Causal Modalities."[5] In section §26 of the B-Deduction, Kant states that the "[c]ategories are concepts that prescribe laws *a priori* to appearances, thus to nature as the sum total of all appearances" (B163). Without the conception of laws governing "everything (that can even come before us as an object) [. . .], appearances could never amount to cognition of an object corresponding to them" (A158–9/B197–8). The analogies of experience, for example, prescribe laws of material persistence, causal necessitation and mutual interaction that govern the existence of appearances in nature in their necessary temporal relations to one another. The result in Kant is that no empirical object of our cognition – in fact, no ostensible reality-directed intentionality or representational purport at all, however minimal, and whether 'inner' or 'outer' – is possible except within the "larger context" (to repeat Sellars' phrase) of an objectively valid conception of nature's general law-governed intelligibility.

In Sellars' updated "*transcendental linguistics*" (2002: 281, KTE IX §40) version of Kant's claim that our concepts of objects prescribe laws or rules governing their behavior, the idea is that the very possibility of a linguistic item having any empirically significant *conceptual content* at all requires that such terms are governed by counterfactual-sustaining, material-inferential norms of use (i.e., "extra-logical" inferences the validity of which depends on the *content* of the relevant terms, rather than on formal-logical relations alone). In his 1953 article "Is There a Synthetic '*A Priori*'?" Sellars put it this way:

> Let me now put my thesis by saying that the conceptual meaning of a descriptive term is constituted by what can be inferred from it in accordance with the logical and extra-logical rules of inference of the language (conceptual frame) to which it belongs. [. . .] [W]here 'x is B' can be validly inferred from 'x is A,' the proposition 'All A is B' is unconditionally assertable on the basis of the rules of the language. Our thesis, then, implies that every primitive descriptive predicate occurs in one or more logically synthetic propositions which are unconditionally assertable – in short, true *ex vi terminorum* [. . .], true by implicit definition. But a logically synthetic proposition which is true *ex vi terminorum* is, by the conventions adopted at the opening of the chapter, a synthetic a priori proposition.
>
> (Sellars 1963: 317, ITSA §9 ¶61)

Or as Sellars had put the claim in 1957, it

> is only because the expressions in terms of which we describe objects [. . .] locate these objects in a space of implications, that they *describe* at all, rather than merely label.
>
> (Sellars 1957: 306–7, §108; cf. Brandom 2015: Chs. 1, 3; O'Shea 2015: §III)

In the spirit of C. I. Lewis's (1929) *pragmatic conception of the a priori*, however, and in light of pressing issues of systematic conceptual change in science and mathematics that had become ever more evident since Kant's time, Sellars argued that "while every conceptual frame involves propositions which, though synthetic, are true *ex vi terminorum*," as just explained, "every conceptual frame is also but one among many which compete for adoption in the marketplace of experience" (Sellars 1963: 320, ITSA §10 ¶68). In many ways Sellars' resulting framework-relativized conception of Kant's synthetic a priori can be compared with Michael Friedman's more recent (2001) relativized conception of the "constitutive a priori," in which Friedman fruitfully explores the legacy of Kant's thought in relation to the logical empiricist and positivist traditions.

Returning to the fundamental Kantian idea of concepts of objects as involving the prescription of laws of nature, Robert Brandom has in recent years offered detailed pragmatic analyses and defenses of Sellars' material inference-license or "space of implications" conception of the causal modalities. Defending what he calls the (modal) Kant-Sellars thesis, Brandom's contention, drawing on his Sellarsian inferentialist semantics, is that the practice of "deploying any ordinary empirical vocabulary," however simple (e.g., "this is red"), already presupposes

> *counterfactually robust inferential* practices-or-abilities – more specifically, the practical capacity to associate with materially good inferences *ranges of counterfactual robustness*.
> (Brandom 2015: 160, italics in original)

Put crudely, the wider upshot of Sellars' and Brandom's analytic reflections on inference and causal necessity is that empiricists in the Humean tradition have been wrong to suppose that there is any alleged stratum of *modally uncommitted* or necessity-free empirical discourse, whether in a sense-datum or a physicalist language. To the contrary, Kant was basically right on target: the very possibility of any empirically significant concepts or terms presupposes that such terms are already embedded within a framework of lawful inferences governed by natural necessities or other modal constraints. The empiricist-leaning skeptic about causal necessity and other modalities, if this Kantian view is correct, has no place to stand.

One finds the preceding characteristically holistic, empirically realist, and modally rich views about the necessary conceptual structure of human knowledge not only in such analytic Kantians as Strawson, Sellars, and Brandom (2009), but also in the robustly Kantian and Hegelian themes defended in John McDowell's rightly influential book, *Mind and World* (1996). The following Sellarsian reflections by McDowell on the conceptual prerequisites of even the most simple human cognitions (here, for example, of color qualities) will provide a convenient transition to the next section:

> [N]o one could count as making even a directly observational judgment of colour except against a background sufficient to ensure that she understands colours as potential properties of things. The ability to produce 'correct' colour words in response to inputs to the visual system (an ability possessed, I believe, by some parrots) does not display possession of the relevant concepts if the subject has no comprehension of, for instance, the idea that these responses reflect a sensitivity to a kind of state of affairs in the world, something that can obtain anyway, independently of these perturbations in her stream of consciousness. The necessary background understanding includes, for instance, the concept of visible surfaces of objects and the concept of suitable conditions for telling what colour something is by looking at it.
> (McDowell 1996: 12)

McDowell argues that Kant's account of the necessary interconnections in human knowledge between sensory intuition and conceptual understanding, as reflected, for instance, in Kant's famous dictum that "thoughts without content are empty, intuitions without concepts are blind" (A51/B75), should convince us that "even though [sensory] experience is passive, it draws into operation [conceptual] capacities that genuinely belong to spontaneity" (McDowell 1996: 12, 2016). However, McDowell's particular way of defending the Kantian view that conceptual capacities are necessarily drawn into operation in sense experience has become a focal point of heated debates in its own right, both in the interpretation of Kant's philosophy and in the philosophy of perception and theory of knowledge more generally. It turns out that on this important topic, too, Sellars has been a crucial, if controversial and often misunderstood figure within the broadly 'analytic Kantian' tradition, as we shall now see.

3. Perception, Intuitions, and Concepts: Nonconceptualism and Conceptualism

Kant holds that "intuition and concepts constitute the elements of all our cognition" (A50/B74). Concepts have their origin in our active understanding and are representations of *general* properties, relations, and rules that can pertain to more than one object. Intuition has its source in our passive sensibility and is that by means of which *singular* (roughly, particular) objects are "immediately" or directly "given" to our cognition. The latter is possible for finite beings like ourselves only insofar as we are affected by such objects through the "receptivity of impressions" of those objects by means of sensation (A19/B33; A50/B74). Sensible intuition "contains only the way in which we are affected by objects," while concepts pertain to the various ways in which we think and make judgments about objects. Kant of course famously argued that the experience of any objects at all is possible for us only if such objects are structured, a priori, by the two pure forms of sensible intuition, space and time, and by the twelve pure forms of conceptual understanding, the categories.

What has led to interpretive controversies, at least on one crude way of setting up the issue, is that Kant appears both to hold that we *cannot* have sensible intuitions of particular objects in space and time *without* concepts, but also to hold the opposite, that is, that nonconceptual sensible intuition in its own right either *does* or could give us and other animals sensible intuitions of particular objects.

In support of the former "conceptualist"-leaning readings, Kant holds, as noted earlier, that "intuitions without concepts are blind" (A51/B75). Similarly, among the conclusions of his transcendental deduction are that "the manifold in a given intuition [. . .] necessarily stands under categories" (B143), and that "everything that may ever come before our senses must stand under the laws that arise a priori from the understanding alone" (B160), since an "**object**" of our cognition is precisely "that in the *concept* of which the manifold of a given intuition is **united**" (B137, italics added; cf. A109, A112, etc.). Such passages certainly seem to suggest that concepts *are* necessary for any sensible intuition of an object.

On the other hand, Kant also holds that "objects are given to us by means of sensibility" (A19/B33), not understanding. In the case of sensibility and intuition (as opposed to what he indicates needs to be shown in the transcendental deduction in relation to the categories of understanding), Kant writes that "objects can indeed appear to us without necessarily having to be related to functions of the understanding"; for in such a case "[a]ppearances would nonetheless offer *objects* to our intuition, for intuition by no means requires the functions of thinking" (A89–90/B122–3, italics added). These passages certainly seem to suggest that concepts are *not* necessary in order to have sensible intuitions of objects per se, though perhaps they are necessary for the sort of full-blown, self-aware perceptual experience of objects at play in the transcendental deduction (cf. Allais 2015, 2016). The issue is a fundamental one because it concerns how to understand the crucial relationship between our sensory and intellectual faculties in Kant's philosophy.

Not surprisingly commentators have sought to reconcile the ostensible inconsistencies or tensions in Kant's text on this matter by means of a wide variety distinctions: for example between different senses of 'intuition', or between cognition, or experience, or perception, and the mere sensory-intuitive presentation of particulars; or between different textual contexts and purposes, and so on (for comprehensive recent discussions, see the articles in Schulting 2016).[6] Here I can only summarily sketch how Sellars grappled with (and in part, originated) this complex interpretive issue in Kant in ways that have in retrospect turned out to be groundbreaking if controversial in their own right, though I think their significance has often been misunderstood in the subsequent literature.

It must be admitted that the issue is complicated by the fact that in Chapter 1 of his *Science and Metaphysics: Variations on Kantian Themes* (1968), Sellars argues that Kant is pulled in two different but insightful directions on this topic, and that Kant unfortunately fails to harmonize his view satisfactorily without further distinctions being drawn, some of which are peculiar to Sellars (and controversial). The interesting fact is that Sellars anticipated and defended central contentions of *both* sides in the current dispute between conceptualists and nonconceptualist interpreters.

In the literature Sellars is almost universally, but misleadingly classified in this debate as a *conceptualist*, usually cited along with the well-known Sellars-influenced and more straightforwardly conceptualist Kantian-Hegelian philosophers, John McDowell and Robert Brandom. This is partly for good reason, since all three philosophers build on Sellars' "logical space of reasons" passage to argue that our conceptual capacities must be operative in any state that is to constitute an instance not only of perceptual *knowledge* (as in this famous passage) but of any object-directed human intentionality whatsoever:

> The essential point is that in characterizing an episode or a state as that of *knowing*, we are not giving an empirical description of that episode or state; we are placing it in the logical space of reasons, of justifying and being able to justify what one says.
>
> (Sellars 1956: VIII, §36)

These three analytic Kantians all agree with Kant that, for beings like us, the possibility of our representing any empirically mind-independent object of experience at all requires the sorts of conceptual syntheses that Kant articulates throughout the transcendental analytic, though of course they differ from Kant and from each other on important details. McDowell (1996, 2009, 2016) in particular argues quite strongly that while passive sensibility (sensible intuition) is indeed ultimately required in order for any empirical object to be given to us as thinkable or knowable by us, the *representational content* of any such cognition for a rational animal is necessarily *conceptual* content. McDowell (1996: Ch. 3) argued in particular against the coherence of Gareth Evans' (1982) conception of "non-conceptual" representational content, and his idea, for example, that the sensory information that is systematically generated in response to objects typically constitutes a dimension of nonconceptual representation of those objects that is independent of, though essential to, their rational integration into our higher-level conceptual cognition of empirical objects in our perceptual experiences. It is primarily due to the fact that McDowell's conceptualism, as it came to be known, highlighted genuine affinities with Sellars' "space of reasons" conception of the role of our conceptual capacities in human perceptual knowledge and intentionality that Sellars is almost invariably cited as a conceptualist on this issue.

In fact, however, Sellars' own complex conception of perceptual experience, reflected in his reading of what he thinks Kant *almost* got entirely right (Sellars 1968: Ch. 1), was a hybrid or mixed view that sought to defend the essential roles in human perceptual cognition of both conceptual representation *and* a substantive, integrated form of object-directed nonconceptual sensory representational content. Sellars argued that Kant tends to use terms such as "intuition" and "sensible intuition" in two different ways in different contexts. Paradigmatically in the transcendental aesthetic, Kant seeks to characterize the role of sensory intuition in abstraction or "isolation" from (A22/B36), but anticipating, the necessarily combined role of sensibility and understanding in our actual perceptual cognitions of empirical objects as articulated throughout the *Critique of Pure Reason* (cf. Rosenberg 2005: Ch. 3; Conant 2017). Sellars takes the primary uses of "intuition" and "sensible intuition" to occur in the latter contexts, and thus models our *singular intuitions* of objects on such indexical perceptual subject-terms as *this red apple*. I will consider this "conceptualist" aspect of Sellars' view first.

Intuitions in this primary sense, for Sellars and for Sellars' Kant, are thus our directly object-evoked (i.e., non-inferential) but conceptualized sense-perceptual responses to being affected by objects through sensation, as for example in the singular perceptual thought, *this red apple (here-now)* is such and such. On this reading Kant's key insight into our empirical cognition was to see that concepts figure in our perceptual experience not only as explicitly general representations in the predicate position of our judgments, as it were, but also in the very subject-terms that *give* us any objects of thought and judgment in the first place. This is roughly the way in which Sellars and McDowell[7] interpret such pivotal passages as the following from the so-called metaphysical deduction of the categories in the first *Critique* ("The Clue to the Discovery of all Pure Concepts of the Understanding"), with the "same function" in this passage referring to *conceptual* synthesis, a synthesis which also governs what Kant later in the *Critique* will call the "productive imagination":

> The same function that gives unity to the different representations **in a judgment** also gives unity to the mere synthesis of different representations **in an intuition**, which expressed generally, is called the pure concept of understanding.
>
> (A79/B104–5)

For Sellars and Sellars' Kant, then, singular and immediate sensible intuitions of objects, in this primary sense, are a certain kind of passively and sensorily evoked singular *thought* arising in direct response to, and directly *about*, the given object of the kind thus classified in the conceptual response (e.g. *this red apple*). Note that this singular conceptualized intuiting, as the subject-term of a perceptual thinking or judging, is "to be distinguished from the conceptual synthesis of recognition in a concept, in which the concept occupies a predicative position" in a judgment (Sellars 1968: Ch. 1, SM §40).

Unlike McDowell and other conceptualists, however, Sellars *also* thinks that Kant was right to regard sensibility as providing, in its own right, and as an essential part of the explanation of why our full-blown sensible intuitions of objects in the preceding primary sense have the character that they do, a qualitatively rich and spatially (or quasi-spatially) structured form of "nonconceptual representation" of objects. For Sellars, it was a crucial insight of Kant's distinction between sensibility and understanding to break the sensory-cognitive continuum that had characterized both Locke's sensualizing of the understanding and Leibniz's intellectualizing of the appearances (cf. A271/B327), and thereby to distinguish between nonconceptual sensory representations of objects and conceptual representations of objects.[8]

Suppose that one sees (visually perceives) two physical objects on the table, a red ball next to a green cube. In normal adult human perception, for both Kant and Sellars, to sensibly intuit these physical objects *as* a red ball next to a green cube requires that one's direct, non-inferential sensible intuition or perceptual response be structured *inter alia* by the *conceptual* rules or representations *red*, *ball*, *cube*, *square*, *next to*, at a minimum, and these empirical concepts will themselves be structured instances (involving the productive imagination) of the a priori forms and laws of space, time, and the categories. But Sellars argues, and he finds this in Kant, too, that this explanation in terms of intuitions as object-evoked singular conceptualized thoughts is *insufficient* to explain both the qualitative and the systematic character of our perceptual responses. The latter requires that such intuitions are systematically generated and informed also by *nonconceptual* sensory representations of the objects, both qualitative and relational, which will involve structured forms and qualities of sensing that systematically reflect the subject's or animal's sensory faculties rather than its intellectual abilities (e.g., Sellars 1968: SM I, §§43–7; cf. Rosenberg 2005: Ch. 3; Landy 2015: Ch. 3).[9] Sellars argues that to make this distinction clearly, however, one has to distinguish, as Kant almost did but did not, the sense in which *the manifold of sense or receptivity in the subject is itself (analogously) 'spatial'*, for instance, from the literal sense in which *the outer physical objects thereby intuitively and conceptually represented are spatial*. Our sensings must in some systematic nonconceptual manner encode the geometrical spatial information about the outer objects thereby represented, for example, the physical cube next to the ball (as opposed to on top of a pyramid, etc.), without such sensory states of the perceiver being themselves literally square and spherical, and so on. Sellars sums up this key aspect of his reading of Kant on sensibility this way:

> Kant's failure to distinguish clearly between the "forms" of receptivity proper and the "forms" of that which is represented by the intuitive conceptual representations which are "guided" by receptivity – a distinction which is demanded both by the thrust of his argument, and by sound philosophy – had as its consequence that no sooner had he left the scene than these particular waters were muddied by Hegel and the Mills, and philosophy had to begin the slow climb "back to Kant" which is still underway.
>
> (Sellars 1968: I, §75)

That is, with the post-Kantian philosophers Hegel and J. S. Mill *et al.*, we were unfortunately subsequently back to the ill-fated sensory/cognitive continuum in either the rationalist Leibnizian intellectualizing direction (Hegel) or the empiricist Lockean sensualizing direction (the Mills). Sellars takes his way of embedding a nonconceptualism within conceptualism to be crucial to reinstating this central Kantian distinction.

For reasons of space I can only take us to this beginning of Sellars' story about the role of nonconceptual forms of sensory representation and its role in Kant's critical philosophy. But I hope this is sufficient nonetheless to encourage the detailed reassessment of Sellars' originating contribution to this current debate among analytic Kantians and contemporary philosophers of perception. In particular it should give pause to the unqualified designation of Sellars as a conceptualist, while nonconceptualism is standardly traced back to its first origin in the similarly robust nonconceptual/conceptual combined view of Gareth Evans (1982) some years later. Sellars himself ultimately took his defense of nonconceptual sensory representations, and in particular certain problems pertaining to the place of color qualities in the natural world, in rather radical directions that need not be swallowed whole in order to preserve key aspects of all of the insights that I have hoped to bring out in this chapter, including his attempt to embed a substantive Kantian nonconceptualism within the strongly conceptualist aspects of his view (cf. O'Shea 2016; Landy 2015, "Postscript on Transcendental Idealism").

The main point I wish to stress in closing, however, is that here in the case of the philosophy of perception, just as we saw earlier in the case of questions concerning knowledge and scepticism, conceptual analysis, a priori knowledge, and causal laws, as well as a host of other topics in ontology, epistemology, action theory, and philosophy of mind not mentioned here, philosophers such as Sellars, Strawson, and a long list of others have continued to make important contributions not only to the understanding of Kant's theoretical philosophy and its lasting significance, but also to the development of distinctively "analytic Kantian" approaches to some of the most hotly contested philosophical disputes of our own time.[10]

Notes

1 In references to Sellars' works, I will also in some instances include the article abbreviations and section or paragraph references that are now standardly used for his works. In this case 'OAPK' refers to Sellars' "Ontology, the A Priori and Kant," collected in Sellars (2002) by Jeffrey Sicha. Sicha explains (p. 261) that this was an unpublished typescript from the mid-1960's (apparently revised by Sellars in 1970) which was to be "Part One" of a longer piece, "Part Two" of which was published as "Kant's Theory of Experience" in 1967 (KTE, also in Sellars 2002).

2 Note that there are important alternative or perhaps supplementary analytic appropriations of Kant that see him as a precursor of key insights in contemporary cognitive science: see in particular Brooks (1994). Note also that Sellars was quite happy to cast Kantian insights not only in terms of conceptual and pragmatic analyses but also as phenomenology, which he saw as complementary tasks (or in fact, when done well, as virtually the same projects).

3 See also Sellars (2002: 338), "Toward a Theory of the Categories" (TTC § 53): "A transcendental argument does not prove that there *is* empirical knowledge – what premises could such an argument have? – nor that there are *objects* of empirical knowledge. It simply explicates the concepts of *empirical knowledge* and *object of empirical knowledge*." Sellars argues, however, that Kant's explication of the concept of empirical knowledge will thereby undermine any skeptical or classical empiricist attempt to restrict the objects of knowledge to something that falls short of a knowledge of external, physical objects in space.

4 Parts of this paragraph are adapted from O'Shea (2006).

5 See O'Shea 2015 for a more detailed account of the following Kantian idea of *concepts as prescribing laws*, as that conception developed from Kant to C. I. Lewis, and Sellars, and most recently as defended in Brandom's "modal Kant-Sellars thesis" (cf. Brandom 2015).

6 The contributions by the various authors in the Schulting (2016) volume on *Kantian Nonconceptualism* provide an excellent resource for those interested in the most recent and best work on this topic. Two other helpful recent contributions to the debates concerning Kant and conceptualism vs. nonconceptualism are Golob (2016) and Allais (2015: Ch. 7). These and the Schulting volume will provide more extensive background than I can provide here to the general interpretive and philosophical disputes concerning Kant on this particular topic, and each also offers a detailed take on the matter based on careful analyses of a variety of key passages from Kant's works. See also Ginsborg (2008), Hanna (2011), and from a Sellarsian-Kantian perspective, Rosenberg (1986/2008: Ch. 4), O'Shea (2012), and Landy (2015: Ch. 3).

7 See, for example, Sellars (1968: Ch. 1, §10), and McDowell (2009: 29ff., 70, 94, 109, 148, 260–1, 265–6, 271). See also Conant (2017).

8 For Sellars it is crucial to distinguish (a) the *intentionality* of conceptual representation – for example, in the singular conceptualized intuition *of* a red apple (intuition in the primary sense), which is at bottom based on concepts as rules or law-prescribing functions, from (b) the *intensionality* but *non*-intentionality of the nonconceptual sensible intuition or sensory representation ('sense impression') *of a red bulgy-shaped expanse*, which explains the occurrence and the character (relational and qualitative) of that same overall perceptual response (cf. Sellars 1956: IV, §24, and 1968: I, §58). Both contexts are, as it were, *de dicto* non-extensional, i.e. one can't infer either from "Jones is conceptually representing (i.e., thinking *of*) O," or from "Jones (or some other animal) is having a visual sense impression *of* O," that the empirical object O exists. On Sellars' adverbial account, one can sense *in-the-of-an-O-manner* (e.g., sensing-red-square-ly, i.e. in the way *normally* caused by red square objects), without there actually being a red, square empirical object in one's environment. Space does not permit further details here on Sellars's views on sense perception.

9 See in particular Landy (2015) for more detail and a sympathetic analysis of Kant's views on sensibility as inspired by Sellars' reading of Kant. For my own part I suspect that Sellars, Rosenberg, and Landy might in the end read a bit too much of Sellars' own views about sense impressions (and counterpart sense-impression manifolds in the scientific image, etc.) back into Kant's own actual views about sensations and "impressions," though Sellars himself was highly circumspect and qualified in this particular regard (see O'Shea 2016).

10 One other major contribution made to contemporary philosophy by analytic Kantians that I must at least mention has to do with the nature of *the thinking self* and focuses on the insights contained in Kant's views

on this topic in the transcendental deduction and the paralogisms of pure reason. See for a start: Strawson (1966), Sellars (2002: 403–18), Evans (1982: Ch. 7), Rosenberg 2008/1986: Chs. 2–3, 2005: Ch. 12), Brooks (1994), Cassam (1997), Kitcher (2011), and Longuenesse (2017).

In the last few decades there have also been an increasing number of works on Kant making notable use of the tools and distinctions characteristic of contemporary analytic metaphysics and ontology. One influential example of this was Rae Langton's *Kantian Humility* (1998), which ably defended an interpretation of Kant's central distinction between appearances and (Leibnizian) things in themselves in terms of a conception of intrinsic vs. relational properties that she had adapted and developed from David Lewis at Princeton.

References

Allais, L. (2015) *Manifest Reality: Kant's Idealism and His Realism*, Oxford: Oxford University Press.

Allais, L. (2016) "Conceptualism and Nonconceptualism in Kant: A Survey of the Recent Debate," in D. Schulting (ed.), *Kantian Nonconceptualism*, London: Palgrave Macmillan.

Bennett, J. (1966) *Kant's Analytic*, Cambridge: Cambridge University Press.

Bird, G. (1962) *Kant's Theory of Knowledge*, London: Routledge & Kegan Paul.

Brandom, R.B. (2009) "Norms, Selves, and Concepts," in *Reason in Philosophy: Animating Ideas*, Cambridge, MA: Harvard University Press.

Brandom, R.B. (2015) *From Empiricism to Expressivism: Brandom Reads Sellars*, Cambridge, MA and London: Harvard University Press.

Brooks, A. (1994) *Kant and the Mind*, Cambridge: Cambridge University Press.

Cassam, Q. (1997) *Self and World*, Oxford: Oxford University Press.

Cassam, Q. (2017) "Knowledge and Its Objects: Revisiting the Bounds of Sense," *European Journal of Philosophy* 24(4): 907–19.

Coffa, J.A. (1991) *The Semantic Tradition from Kant to Carnap*, L. Wessels (ed.), Cambridge: Cambridge University Press.

Conant, J.B. (ed.) (2017) "Kant's Critique of the Layer-Cake Conception of Human Mindedness in the B-Deduction," in J.O'Shea (ed.), *Sellars and His Legacy*, Oxford: Oxford University Press.

Evans, G. (1982) *The Varieties of Reference*, J. McDowell (ed.), Oxford: Oxford University Press.

Evans, G. (1985/1980) "Things Without the Mind – A Commentary Upon Chapter Two of Strawson's *Individuals*," in *Collected Papers*, Oxford: Oxford University Press.

Friedman, M. (2001) *The Dynamics of Reason*, Stanford, CA: CLSI Publications.

Ginsborg, H. (2008) "Was Kant a Nonconceptualist?" *Philosophical Studies* 137(1): 65–77.

Glock, H.-J. (2003) "Strawson and Analytic Kantianism," in *Kant and Strawson*, Oxford: Oxford University Press, pp. 15–42.

Golob, S. (2016) "Kant as Both Conceptualist and Nonconceptualist," *Kantian Review* 21(3): 367–91.

Hanna, R. (2001) *Kant and the Foundations of Analytic Philosophy*, Oxford: Oxford University Press.

Hanna, R. (2011) "Beyond the Myth of the Myth: A Kantian Theory of Non-Conceptual Content," *International Journal of Philosophical Studies* 19(3): 323–98.

Kitcher, P. (2011) *Kant's Thinker*, Oxford: Oxford University Press.

Landy, D. (2015) *Kant's Inferentialism: The Case Against Hume*, New York: Routledge.

Langton, R. (1998) *Kantian Humility: Our Ignorance of Things in Themselves*, Oxford: Clarendon.

Lewis, C.I. (1929) *Mind and the World Order: Outline of a Theory of Knowledge*, New York: Dover.

Longuenesse, B. (2017) *I, Me, Mine: Back to Kant, and Back Again*, Oxford: Oxford University Press.

Macbeth, D. (2014) *Realizing Reason: A Narrative of Truth and Knowing*, Oxford: Oxford University Press.

McDowell, J. (1996) *Mind and World*, 2nd ed., Cambridge, MA: Harvard University Press.

McDowell, J. (2009) *Having the World in View: Essays on Kant, Hegel, and Sellars*, Cambridge, MA: Harvard University Press.

McDowell, J. (2016) "A Sellarsian Blind Spot," in J. O'Shea (ed.), *Sellars and His Legacy*, Oxford: Oxford University Press, pp. 100–16.

O'Shea, J.R. (2006) "Conceptual Connections: Kant and the Twentieth-Century Analytic Tradition," in G. Bird (ed.), *The Blackwell Companion to Kant*, Oxford: Blackwell, pp. 513–27.

O'Shea, J.R. (2012) *Kant's Critique of Pure Reason: An Introduction and Interpretation*, London: Routledge.

O'Shea, J.R. (2015) "Concepts of Objects as Prescribing Laws: A Kantian and Pragmatist Line of Thought," in R. Stern and G. Gava (eds.), *Pragmatism, Kant, and Transcendental Philosophy*, London: Routledge, pp. 196–216.

O'Shea, J.R. (2016) "What to Take Away from Sellars' Kantian Naturalism," in J. O'Shea (ed.), *Sellars and His Legacy*, Oxford: Oxford University Press, pp. 130–48.

Rosenberg, J.F. (2005) *Accessing Kant: A Relaxed Introduction to the Critique of Pure Reason*, Oxford: Clarendon Press.

Rosenberg, J.F. (2008/1986) *The Thinking Self*, Atascadero, CA: Ridgeview Publishing.

Schulting, D. (ed.) (2016) *Kantian Nonconceptualism*, London: Palgrave Macmillan.

Sellars, W. (1956) "Empiricism and the Philosophy of Mind," in *Sellars* (1963), pp. 127–98.

Sellars, W. (1957) "Counterfactuals, Dispositions, and the Causal Modalities," in H. Feigl, M. Scriven and G. Maxwell (eds.), *Minnesota Studies in the Philosophy of Science*, vol. II, Minneapolis, MN: University of Minnesota Press, pp. 225–308.

Sellars, W. (1963) *Science, Perception and Reality*, Atascadero, CA: Ridgeview Publishing Company.

Sellars, W. (1968) *Science and Metaphysics: Variations on Kantian Themes*, London: Routledge; re-issued by Atascadero, CA: Ridgeview Publishing Company.

Sellars, W. (1975) "Autobiographical Remarks (Feb 1973)," in H.-N. Castañeda (ed.), *Action, Knowledge and Reality*, New York: Bobbs-Merrill, pp. 144–50.

Sellars, W. (2002) *Kant's Transcendental Metaphysics. Sellars' Cassirer Lectures Notes and Other Essays*, J.F. Sicha (ed. and intro.), Atascadero, CA: Ridgeview Publishing Company.

Sluga, H. (1980) *Gottlob Frege*, London: Routledge.

Strawson, P.F. (1959) *Individuals: An Essay in Descriptive Metaphysics*, London: Methuen.

Strawson, P.F. (1966) *The Bounds of Sense: An Essay on Kant's Critique of Pure Reason*, London: Methuen.

Strawson, P.F. (1997) "Kant's New Foundations of Metaphysics," in *Entity and Identity and Other Essays*, Oxford: Oxford University Press.

Westphal, K.R. (2010) "Kant's *Critique of Pure Reason* and Analytic Philosophy," in P. Guyer (ed.), *The Cambridge Companion to Kant's Critique of Pure Reason*, Cambridge: Cambridge University Press, pp. 401–30.

Wittgenstein, L. (1953) *Philosophical Investigations*, G.E.M. Anscombe, P.M.S. Hacker and J. Schulte (trans.), Oxford: Basil Blackwell; revised 4th ed., 2009.

Further Reading

There is a fascinating exchange between J. Haugeland and J. McDowell, who formed part of a reading group on Kant at Pittsburgh with James Conant (see Conant 2017) on how to interpret and derive insights from Kant's first *Critique*, in Part IV of *Giving a Damn: Essays in Dialogue with John Haugeland*, Z. Adams and J. Browning (eds.) (Cambridge, MA: MIT Press, 2017). Debates about Kant's transcendental proofs or modes of argumentation are further discussed in R. Stern's (1999) *Transcendental Arguments: Answering the Question of Justification* (Oxford: Oxford University Press, 2000); B. Stroud, *Understanding Human Knowledge: Philosophical Essays* (Oxford: Oxford University Press, 2000); K.R. Westphal's *Kant's Critical Epistemology: Why Epistemology Must Consider Judgment First* (London: Routledge, 2020) contains historically rich and analytically probing defenses of preservable insights in Kant's account of our knowledge, and L. Stevenson's *Inspirations from Kant: Essays* (Oxford: Oxford University Press, 2011) examines Kantian analytic themes in a similar spirit. G. Bird and M. Friedman usefully debate "Kantian Themes in Contemporary Philosophy," *Proceedings of the Aristotelian Society: Supplementary Volume* 72 (1998): 111–51, while a good example of Kant's contemporary relevance from a logical point of view is J. MacFarlane's "Frege, Kant, and the Logic in Logicism," *Philosophical Review* 111 (2002): 25–65. Two recent Special Issues of journals guest edited by G. Gava are relevant to these issues: one in the *British Journal for the History of Philosophy* (27(2) 2019) on the theme, *Kant's Philosophical Method: Receptions and Transformations*, and the other in *Synthese* (vol. 198 Supplement, 2021) on *The Current Relevance of Kant's Method in Philosophy*. Also relating Kant's transcendental philosophical approach to contemporary debates are the contributions to J. Smith and P. Sullivan (eds.), *Transcendental Philosophy and Naturalism* (Oxford: Oxford University Press, 2011).

B. Practical Philosophy

42

KANTIAN PHILOSOPHIES OF HOPE, HISTORY, AND THE ANTHROPOCENE

Andrew Chignell

***

1. Kant's Third Question

No casual reader of Kant will be surprised to learn, upon arriving at the Canon of Pure Reason at the end of the first *Critique*, that "What can I know?" and "What should I do?" are two of the three questions driving his philosophical enterprise.[1] It *is* surprising to learn, however, that the third and in some sense central question for Kant is "What may I hope (*Was darf ich hoffen*)?" (A806/B833). Kant wrote no *Critique* or *Metaphysical Foundations* of hope, and he makes little explicit effort even to say what hope is.[2] Compared to stalwarts like "*Erkenntnis*," "*Urteil*," and "*Vernunft*," the word "*Hoffnung*" barely shows up at all in the critical philosophy – and many of those uses are by-the-by ("I hope to have shown [. . .]").

What Kant does say in this passage is that "What may I hope?" is a distinct question that also *unites* the other two: it acts as a bridge between their domains. The question about hope is "simultaneously practical and theoretical" – it "concerns happiness" and "finally comes down to the inference that something **is [. . .] because something ought to happen**" (A805–6/B833–4, original emphasis).

Here is one way to interpret this: For the Kantian mind, any correct answer to the question, "What ought I do?" will take the form: *Act from subjective principles ("maxims") that you can reasonably will to be universal laws.*[3] But although adherence to the form is what makes the action right, the action will also have an *end* – we are trying to produce, obtain, or further some outcome. So when we perform the action, we also naturally *hope* that the end will be achieved – through our own efforts, or with the help of others. Such hope, in turn, implicitly commits us to the "real practical possibility"[4] of the end, and thus to the actual existence of the means to the end.

By way of example: when someone (or at least someone of a Kantian mind) sends money to a charity in order to improve the lot of the poor, she is acting from duty: she thinks she *ought* to do this, no matter what, and that the maxim of her will could reasonably be universalized. But if she is like most of us, she also naturally hopes that the money *actually helps someone*. The rightness of the act is not tied to the accomplishment of the end, but the end is intended and hoped-for all the same. Such hope clearly presupposes that the end *can* be attained: that it is really, practically possible.

DOI: 10.4324/9781003406617-58

And that in turn presupposes that other things actually *exist*. For instance, it presupposes the *actual existence* of (a) the needy, (b) the charity, and (c) a causal path between the two such that the gift financially improves someone's lot. But such existence-claims, according to Kant, are in the domain of the theoretical.

This is how the third question operates as a bridge between the practical and the theoretical: we start by acting as we ought, we then hope for certain outcomes of those acts, and we ultimately affirm propositions about what *is*. If the hope in question is practically rational (remember, the question is about what we *dürfen*[5]), then the theoretical "is"-claim inherits a *prima facie* kind of moral justification. It is *prima facie* justification because it can be defeated in a number of ways. In the case of the charitable gift, the presuppositions are about empirical matters, and so the justification can be defeated by *evidence* that, say, the causal pathway does not in fact exist. *Prima facie* moral justification can also be defeated by showing that forming the hope or theoretical commitment in question tends to lead to bad moral behavior.

That's a complicated piece of reasoning, obviously. My goal is not to reconstruct it in detail here,[6] but rather to note that the steps involving hope turn out to be inessential, at least if you are inclined (as the Kantian mind clearly is) to some version of the idea that believing you ought to do something requires believing that it is practically possible. For if our subject acts from what she takes to be her duty in order to bring about a certain end (helping the needy via giving to that charity) then she *already* – just by taking herself to be bound to do this – presupposes that her end is really, practically possible. This means that she *already* presupposes the existence of what is required to make it really, practically possible: the needy, the charity, the causal path, and so on. There's no need to appeal to any hopes she has in the matter.

As though to confirm this, after stating his three questions in the Canon, Kant proceeds to focus on Belief or faith (*Glaube*) – a shift that leads many commentators to ignore the distinction between the concepts of hope and Belief when discussing the third question.[7] Even more strikingly, the canonical presentation of the moral theistic "proof" in the second *Critique* almost entirely marginalizes hope. There are a few uses of the word, but the proof itself goes directly from *ought* to *can* to *is*. In this context the end that we set is a bit more abstract, and not entirely empirical: we aim at a perfectly just situation in which happiness is exactly apportioned to virtue (Kant calls this state the "Highest Good"). When we will the Highest Good, so the argument goes, we also presuppose that it is really, practically possible. This in turn underwrites defeasible rational Belief (*Vernunftglaube*) in the *actuality* of whatever is required for the Highest Good to be really, practically possible – namely, the existence of God and the immortality of the soul (5: 124–5). Again, hope has dropped out; reflection on our moral duty directly grounds Belief.

Kant is not the first to slip like this between thinking of some of our key moral, historical, and religious commitments in terms of what we would now call hope, and thinking of them as warranting more robust states like Belief (faith). A number of pre-Kantian authors also do this – perhaps because the relevant Greek and Latin terms simply had wider denotations (see section 2). In section 3, I'll consider the way Kant's views seem to evolve on this issue – he starts off more optimistic but tends, especially in the "End of All Things" essay of 1794, towards a kind of *hopeful pessimism* at best. I then examine (in section 4) a different version of Kant's moral proof that does, I think, succeed in locating a role for hope that is distinct from that of Belief, expectation, optimism, and so on. It is this "moral-psychological" version of Kant's argument that finally shows how hope – for the Kantian mind at its best – can be an *essential* bridge between a practical ought and a theoretical is.

In section 5 I turn to some contemporary writing in ecology in order to look at how the concepts of hope, expectation, despair, and pessimism are used in those contexts. Although some recent discussions of the "good Anthropocene" slip beyond hope into full-blown optimism, most authors working on ecological and environmental topics are careful to keep the attitudes distinct. This is for good reason, since there is not much rational room for optimism on ecological matters. (By contrast, there is still a tendency among contemporary theologians to follow earlier Christian authors in slipping beyond hope to optimistic Belief or even certainty with respect to their eschatologies, even if they continue to use the language of hope.[8])

The main point is this: although Kant himself does at times slip from talk of hope to talk of something more robust (i.e. expectation in the mode of Belief), and although various figures before and after him do the same, the Kantian mind at its best identifies an important role for unslipping hope to play in the philosophies of history and religion. Sober, critical reason is careful to avoid self-deception or pollyannaish naïveté in circumstances where there is little to justify positive expectation in either a doxastic or a non-doxastic mode. Within those bounds, however, the Kantian mind *may* (*darf*) still tenaciously hope, and may also employ various psychological techniques to support that hope. The result is an attractive kind of *hopeful pessimism* that can still provide *prima facie* moral justification for certain theoretical affirmations.

2. Expectation Versus Hope

The Greek word "*elpis*" can be translated into English as "hope," "expectation," "optimism," or even "confidence" – depending on context. Because "*elpis*" (like the Latin "*spes*") is ambiguous in this way, it is often difficult to tell which concept a classical author has in mind. To say that the tradition "slips" between the two concepts is not meant pejoratively, since some of these authors clearly did not have the contemporary distinction in mind (see Cairns 2020). But some did, and in any case *hope* and *expectation* do seem to be distinct concepts (whereas *optimism* is just a species of expectation – the expectation of something positive).

Philosophers and theologians in the Christian tradition, in particular, fluctuate between construing *elpis/spes* as directed towards a good outcome that is taken to be *at least possible* (i.e. what *we* would call hope) and a good outcome that seems *very likely* or *secure* (what *we* would call positive expectation or optimism). The latter application of the term typically occurs when authors are thinking of it as a theological virtue directed towards the afterlife: consider here Augustine's "man of good hope" (Augustine 420: ch. 31). Thomas Aquinas, however, is characteristically clear-eyed about the conceptual distinction and simply distinguishes two different kinds of "*spes*." The first kind is the infused theological virtue – this is a habitual, confident expectation whose traditional object is the afterlife. But the second kind of hope is a passion that can take many different objects. Aquinas calls it a "movement of appetite," and his analysis sounds quite contemporary:

> Hope is a movement of appetite aroused by the perception of what is agreeable, future, arduous, and *possible of attainment*. It is the tendency of an appetite towards this sort of object.
> (Aquinas 1265–1274: *ST* 1a2ae. 40–4, my emphasis)[9]

Here the cognitive element involved in the passion of hope is the "perception" that its object is at least *possible*.[10] Elsewhere we're told that "hoping would be out of the question if the good that is hoped for did not appear possible."[11]

Thomistic clarity on this distinction notwithstanding, subsequent authors slip into the conflation again by using the relevant term ("*elpis*," "*spes*," "hope," "*Hoffnung*" etc.) to refer to positive expectation or optimism. I cannot go through all the texts here, but it is easy to find passages in Bonaventure, Calvin, Hobbes, Descartes, Locke, and Hume that use "hope" to refer to an attitude involving (in Locke's words) "the thought of a probably future enjoyment of a thing" (Locke 1975

[1690]: II.xx.9). Influenced by some of these classical authors, no doubt, the *Oxford English Dictionary* somewhat bafflingly cites the following as the two primary meanings of "hope":

1. Expectation of something desired; desire combined with expectation.
2. Feeling of trust or confidence.

Contemporary psychologists also tend to slip between two notions here: the leading "Hope Scales" theory articulated by C.R. Snyder, for instance, takes hope to be "the perception that one can reach desired goals" (see Gallagher *et al.* 2020: 192ff). The "can" there sounds like a belief in mere possibility. But Snyder and colleagues go on to develop measures that characterize this "perception" in terms of the ability to find "pathways" to the hoped-for outcome, as well as the "agency" to take those pathways when they open up. That sort of "pathway" and "agency" thinking sounds more like expectation/optimism than mere hope.

It is unusual for contemporary Anglophone philosophers to side with Thomas Aquinas over John Locke, the *OED*, and contemporary psychologists, but a quick survey of the (small but growing) literature on hope suggests that most philosophical authors now clearly distinguish hope from expectation, as well as from trust and confidence.[12] Hope is importantly different from expectation in that it can be directed towards outcomes that the subject regards as *merely* possible, and thus be accompanied by fear of disappointment. *Expectation*, by contrast, always involves the estimation that the state is more probable than not; it may even be certain, and so there is less room for fear.

3. Kant's Shifting Emphasis: From Expectation to Hope

For Kant, as we have seen, the primary object of hope is happiness, and if the hope is rationally *permissible* (hope that we "may" have) then the happiness must be apportioned to our moral worthiness. In such contexts, Kant suggests that such hope can underwrite Beliefs regarding the direction of history, its supersensible basis, and our individual destinies. However, we also saw that the canonical version of the moral proof in the second *Critique* seems to render hope otiose: it moves from the fact that we ought to *will* the Highest Good to Belief in the existence of *whatever is required* for the real, practical possibility of the Highest Good. While it is perhaps unfair to say that Kant conflates the two concepts in that context, it is clear that he hasn't zeroed in on the distinctive role that hope plays in his system, and is more interested in the Belief that it presupposes.

Interestingly, as Kant witnesses various political disappointments (in particular concerning the accession of Friedrich Wilhelm II and the French Revolution), he becomes less willing to express optimistic expectations of progress regarding this-worldly history, and also grows cagey regarding what to say about justice in the world to come. Whereas his pre-critical 1759 essay on "Optimism" stoutly defends the full-dress Leibnizean best-possible-world theory, the 1791 essay "On the Failure of all Philosophical Trials in Theodicy" recommends skepticism about whether evils contribute to a greater good – in this world or the next.

By that time, Kant was also clearly distinguishing hope from expectation. In the "Failure" essay he *dismisses* theological efforts to show that we can reasonably "expect (*erwarten*)" that "in a future world a different order of things will obtain, and each will receive that which his deeds here below are worthy of according to moral judgment" (*MpVT* 8: 262). Instead, Kant follows what he takes to be the biblical example of Job, and says that apart from the natural laws we simply have no basis for conjecture regarding how an afterlife might be arranged. Thus although reason might "allow itself an appeal to patience, and the *hope* of a future improvement, how can it *expect* (*erwarten*)" any such thing? Kant concludes that, given what we know of the laws, "the agreement of human fate with divine justices, according to the concepts that we construe of the latter, is *just as little to be expected* there as here" (*MpVT* 8: 262, my emphasis). But even in the absence of any warrant for expectation, Kant thinks that we may still *hope* for the Highest Good and form Beliefs about what it presupposes.

A similar evolution occurs in his essays in the philosophy of history and politics. Well into the 1780's, Kant's efforts in this domain are largely optimistic in tone.[13] But by the early 1790s, Friedrich Wilhelm II (and his reign of censorship) had come to the throne in Prussia, while Robespierre (and his Reign of Terror) had taken hold in France. In a 1794 piece called "The End of All Things," Kant seems open to the idea that the final end of history could be a "perverted" one in which evil has the last word, and that Christianity might be responsible:

> If Christianity should ever come to the point where it ceased to be worthy of love (which could very well transpire if instead of its gentle spirit it were armed with commanding author-ity), then, because there is no neutrality in moral things[. . .], a disinclination and resistance to [Christianity] would become the ruling mode of thought among people; and the **Anti-Christ**, who is taken to be the forerunner of the last day, would begin his – albeit short – regime (presumably based on fear and self- interest); but then, because Christianity, though once allegedly destined to be the world religion, would not after all be favored by fate to become it, and **the (perverse) end of all things**, in a moral respect, would arrive.
>
> (*EaD* 8: 339, original bold)

Admittedly, there are passages from the mid- to late-1790s that suggest that Kant, if pressed, would still endorse expectation (in the mode of Belief) about the trajectory of history and our ultimate moral end. But these late-career reflections, especially in "The End of All Things," also show him sympathetically entertaining the idea that hope is the most that's warranted. In any case, his final position was much weaker than that of his contemporaries who viewed the *expectation* of dramatic moral progress as both justified and politically essential. In the 19th-century this expectation even took the form of *epistemic* certainty (rather than mere Belief) regarding the machinations of reason, Spirit, and capital to bring about positive change. In this respect, then, it is Hegel and Marx, rather than Kant, who are the true heirs of Paul, Augustine, Bonaventure, and Calvin.

I now want to turn to another version of Kant's moral argument – one that comes to prominence at this same time in the 1790s, and one that (unlike the canonical version in the second *Critique*) preserves a distinct and essential role for unslipping hope that is not expectation.

4. The Moral–Psychological Argument Against Despair

The goal of Kant's moral proof is to ground practical Belief in the existence of God, freedom, and the future life of the soul. As noted earlier, the canonical version of the argument (found most prominently in the second *Critique*) says that we ought to will the Highest Good, and that only then may we hope for its attainment. If the hope is rational, it provides moral justification for Belief in what it presupposes – the existence of God and the future life. We also saw, however, that this ver-sion can be articulated so as to make the hope component otiose.

The version of the moral proof that makes hope *essential* is harder to piece together from the texts, but significant gestures can be found in writings from the 1790s – especially the third *Critique*, *Religion*, and the "Theory and Practice" essay of 1793. I have reconstructed it in detail elsewhere (Chignell 2023); here I will just provide a sketch.[14] The main idea is that, for most of us anyway, sustaining what Kant calls "moral resolve" [*moralische Entschliessung*] in the face of apparent inefficacy and widespread injustice *psychologically* requires that we be able to hope that the ends we are striving for will be fulfilled – that the justice we are trying to promote will be achieved (*Rel* 6: 5). The fact that such hope is required (at least for some of us) to sustain resolve provides it with a defeasible kind of moral justification (for those same some of us).

But, as noted at the outset, a deep, life-structuring hope like that presupposes a firm commitment to the possibility of its object: in this case the real, practical possibility of the Highest Good. And that commitment only makes sense if we postulate the existence of the entities or states that are required to make it really, practically possible – that is, God and the afterlife of genuinely free agents. The commitment to these items cannot take the form of ordinary conviction [*Überzeugung*] – which for Kant requires sufficient theoretical evidence – so it must take the form of Belief [*Glaube*]. In short, if it is rational to seek to shore up our moral resolve, and if this involves implementing strategies to preserve our hope for certain outcomes, then we are defeasibly morally justified in adopting Belief in the *existence* of various supersensibles. It is because we *may* hope for the Highest Good that we *may* defeasibly Believe in what is required for the object of hope to *be* practically possible. Thus the argument goes from *we ought* to *we may hope* to *it is*.[15]

I think this moral-psychological argument is intriguing in its own right, but also because its structure can be applied in certain naturalistic, this-worldly contexts too. We saw in the charity case that the hope to "make a difference" as an activist, philanthropist, or consumer might require for its sustenance the Belief that there is a mechanism in the world that can bring about the real-world difference in question. If Kant's moral-psychological argument is valid, then there are defeasible moral grounds for such Belief, even in the absence of sufficient empirical evidence regarding such a mechanism. In the same way, analogues of Kant's argument might be able to support theoretical commitments regarding individual or collective impacts over time, or even about the direction of history.[16]

In the next section, I consider one such analogue according to which the demoralizing effects of pessimistic expectation in the Anthropocene can be offset by participation in hope-sustaining "reenchanting" efforts – even at a very local level where one's actions are very unlikely to make a difference. The goal is not to get rid of the realism or the pessimistic expectations – after all, they are based in overwhelming empirical evidence. Rather, the goal, is to see how we might supplement them with resolve-sustaining hope.

5. Sustaining Hope in the Anthropocene

By comparison to most 18th- and 19th-century figures, philosophers, and social scientists nowadays are reluctant to speak of historical or moral progress. There are still optimists who contend – on empirical grounds rather than armchair reflection – that the technological achievements and apparent moral progress of the last century provide reason to expect that both will continue.[17] But most people seem to be inductive pessimists regarding our economic and especially our ecological trajectory.

Those who feel rationally compelled to such pessimism about our predicament still have a choice about whether to accompany it with, for example, (a) a handwringing sort of despair, (b) a Stoic sort of inward-looking apathy, (c) a Montaignian-Nietzschean sort of cheerful acceptance, or (d) a resolute Kantian search for what we may still be able to hope, in an effort to sustain our resolve. Even if the crooked timber of humanity cannot be straightened to the point where optimism is reasonable, the Kantian mind at its best still asks: what *may* we hope, and what sorts of postures and activities can we take up, while staying within the bounds of reason, in order to *sustain* moral action? In his works from the early 1790s, Kant offers the moral-psychological argument in answer to these questions. In our own context, the massive literature on the "Anthropocene" is a good place to look for other suggestions.[18] Here I have space for just a quick glance at a couple of authors.

"Anthropocene" refers to the period in natural history when human beings and their effects on the rest of nature become as potent as a geologic force. The term offers, among other things, a new and more evocative way of talking about the Weberian idea that our natural environment can become so rationalized, misshapen, and "disenchanted" that the line between technocratic reason and "Nature" itself is blurred. In the dystopian narratives of the Anthropocene, *homo sapiens* has been replaced (in the words of sociologist Bronislaw Szerszynski) by "*homo consumens*, that other-than-human assemblage of humans, technology, fossil fuels, and capitalist relations" (2012: 175).

The German theologian Jürgen Moltmann sketched an apocalyptic vision like this back at the turn of the millennium, just as "Anthropocene" was first starting to be used in print by geochemists, biologists, anthropologists, and geographers to characterize our new geological home (*Heimat*). Moltmann claimed that

[i]t is impossible to make oneself 'the master and possessor of nature' if one is still part of nature and dependent on it. The modern culture of mastery has produced its own downside, which reveals its catastrophic effects in the disappearance of natural living spaces.

(2004a: 4)

And the related disappearance, he might have added, of natural living *species* – faster than in previous mass extinction events, by most estimates (see DeVos *et al.* 2015).

Some theorists of the Anthropocene (especially some of the more Marxian and "deep ecology" authors) expect and even welcome the ultimate economic collapse that would, after a period of inevitable disruption, make room for a kind of human life that is in harmony with non-human nature. But that eschaton is very hard to conceive, and not just from an environmental point of view: here consider Frederick Jameson's famous suggestion that it is easier to imagine the end of the world than it is to imagine the end of capitalism.

Other theorists argue that we can expect deliverance from such ecological disasters, even within the current economic system, as a result of individual and collective action. One of the most radical individual actions involves *refusing* to conceive (or "expect") in the biological way: in progressive pockets across North America (e.g. Ithaca, NY), it is not unusual to come across the anti-natalist bumper sticker: "Save the Earth, Don't Give Birth."[19] For those who do decide to give birth, optimism about our species' future is encouraged by reflection on our collective powers of ingenuity. Stewart Brand (long-time editor of the *Whole Earth Catalog*) is now an unyielding technologist-optimist who writes in the expectation of a "Good Anthropocene" – that is, a time when our environmental plight is viewed as a series of what former Secretary of State Rex Tillerson once called "engineering problems" that will be overcome by innovation (two guys in a garage in Palo Alto . . .).[20]

So there are expectations on both sides. But, somewhat orthogonally, there are also discussions about the role and power of hope in the *absence* of optimism. This is the characteristically Kantian approach. Soon after Moltmann wrote his millennial reflections on "Progress and Abyss" and what he calls, following Bill McKibben, "the end of nature," there were the 9/11 attacks and other man-made miseries that followed. But even as the human world was gathering for another set of wars, Moltmann turned away from the abyss and instead wrote messianic reflections on "The Promise of the Child."[21] Similarly, some ecology-focused geographers and sociologists find it necessary to ignore their long-term pessimistic expectations and do things to cultivate hope, if only in order to sustain moral resolve.

Holly Jean Buck is one of the latter: while resisting the slip into Brand's sort of optimism, Buck calls for more hopeful visions of "the charming Anthropocene" – where "charming" refers to the kind of "reenchanting" that we actively perform rather than seek outside ourselves in "nature." She asks: "If the Anthropocene were not an anthology of scary tales, drawn from an awkward bricolage of science and preternatural fears, what else could it be?" (Buck 2015: 2).

This is in effect the Kantian question about hope applied to our current ecological predicament. It directs our focus away from reasonable but mostly pessimistic expectations regarding the rapacious denizens of the Anthropocene, and invites us to focus in hope on a less likely but perhaps still *just* possible future in which "human traits like tending, altruism, creativity, art and craftsmanship, and cooperation reclaim their status as basic human nature" (2015: 2).[22]

Millenials in the global north are apparently the first generation most of whose members expect to live *less prosperously* than their parents. Overall, their attitude is the reverse of the old "middle-class" assumption that (in Moltmann's words) "the all-important thing was social [i.e. financial] advancement from one generation to the next" (Moltmann 2004a: 7). There are some downsides to this, to be sure, but one of the positive effects of recognizing our situation in the Anthropocene is that it reduces expectations regarding the self and instead refocuses our minds (in hope) on crucial, large-scale collective ends. This is clearly reminiscent of Kant's claim that we must – each of us – hope for happiness, but only as *part* of the collective accomplishment of the Highest Good.

In keeping with the moral-psychological reflections in the last section, the Kantian millennial mind will also look for ways in which local, individual and communal "enchanting practices" might help *sustain* those hopes, and our moral resolve in general. Buck puts this point nicely:

> We know about sea level rise and ocean acidification and the changing nitrogen cycle, about planetary boundaries and potential tipping points. Enchanting practices are no stand-in for large-scale political change, but as companion to proactive critique they can help create the critical mass of engagement and care to give humans and nonhumans a habitable Anthropocene.
>
> (Buck 2015: 8)

Again, the contemporary Kantian mind is not interested in self-deceptive pollyannism, but it does seek out – and regard as morally justifiable – reasonable psychological strategies for sustaining moral hope and resolve. As opposed to the "effective altruist" impulse always to identify and do what is most likely to make the largest difference, some of these reenchanting strategies will involve hyper-local efforts that do not – or at least not obviously – connect to the larger concern. Still, Kant's moral-psychological argument (as I have interpreted it in the previous section, anyway) allows us to combine those hopes with the Belief that these efforts can somehow "help create the critical mass of engagement" required to make the Anthropocene more habitable, or even "charming." At the very least, cultivating such hope in the local context can galvanize us to re-enter the global or collective struggle, even if we have no real expectations for ultimate success.

6. Conclusion: *Homo Religiosus* and *Homo Sperans*

Kant says in his lectures on the philosophy of religion, as well as in the published *Religion* itself, that the "minimum of theology" or "minimum of cognition in religion" is the Belief that God's existence is really possible (*Lectures* 28: 998; *Religion* 6: 153–4n). It is important for Kant that such a commitment is all that is required as part of our duty, but it also seems like a fairly low bar for counting as religious. It is supposed to be accompanied, however, by a sophisticated complex of other attitudes, desires, and affections – including (on my reading) deep moral *hope* for the existence of God, the consummation of creation, and even extramundane assistance – that would not fit well within a baldly atheistic framework.[23] It might also involve hope for the advent of a new kind of human being at the end of all things. This would not be mere *homo consumens* but rather *homo sperans*: a being that engages in short-term reenchanting strategies for sustaining resolve – the kind of resolve that in turn supports long-term collective efforts that might make a real difference. The hope for the advent of *homo sperans* is the hope that we can become the sorts of beings whose ecological and geological legacy is less devastating than the one that we now reasonably expect.

One of the reasons for resisting the way previous thinkers have slipped between hope and expectation, then, is just for the sake of conceptual tidiness – clearly there are two different concepts here and it's good to keep them distinct. A more important reason, however, is that doing so makes conceptual room for the Kantian idea that an authentic moral-religious life can be based entirely in pessimistic, non-expectant but still tenaciously lived hope. This is the sort of hope that Kant describes in the "Theory and Practice" essay of 1793:

> It is quite irrelevant whether any empirical evidence suggests that these plans, which *are founded only on hope*, may be unsuccessful. For the idea that something which has hitherto been unsuccessful will therefore never be successful does not justify anyone in abandoning even a pragmatic or technical aim [. . .]. This applies even more to moral aims, which, so long as it is not demonstrably impossible to fulfil them, amount to duties.
>
> (8: 309–10, my emphasis)

As long as our apparently futile efforts – which are "founded only on hope" – are not *demonstrably impossible* – we can, and in many cases ought, to keep performing them. For Kant himself, as we know, this hope presupposes Belief in the actual existence of God and the future life of the soul. But in the passages on the "minimum of theology," he seems willing to set aside such Belief in order to leave room for mere hope (combined with Belief in real possibility).

Such a low bar approach would make it easier for people to train themselves (liturgically,[24] perhaps, or through Buck's "tending" and "enchanting" practices) to focus on the real possibility of good but unlikely outcomes (including even the Highest Good). That's the propositional side of deep, activism-sustaining hope. There is also a yearning, passionate, affective side that makes it seem like a genuinely religious stance, even if it is in no way certain or expectant. In this way, Kantian hope is compatible with the pessimistic expectation that the end of all things will indeed turn out to be disastrous and "perverse." For the Kantian mind in the Anthropocene, then, the "minimum of theology" might be just the right amount.[25]

Notes

1 This chapter is an abbreviated and revised version of Chignell (2022b), which is published under Creative Commons Attribution 4.0 International License [http://creativecommons.org/licenses/by/4.0/].

2 Although see (Chignell 2021b) for a gesture at an argument according to which hope is in fact the primary topic of the third *Critique*, and (Sweet 2022) for a sustained albeit somewhat different argument to that effect.

3 This is the "Universal Law" formulation of the Categorical Imperative. Allen Wood (Wood 1999) has argued that what is really action-guiding for Kant is not this but the much less formal "Formula of Humanity."

4 Kant's term is "real possibility." I include "practical" here to indicate that it's not merely what contemporary philosophers call "metaphysical" possibility; rather, the outcome is supposed to be accomplishable by the beings and powers in the actual world. Compare (Wood 1999) for the argument that "realizability" is a key part of the argument and (Willaschek 2016) for more on "practical possibility" and realizability (Chignell 2023).

5 Günther Zöller (2013) appeals to Grimm's Dictionary to argue that "*dürfen*" was used not only in the sense of "permission" but also in the sense of "need" (*bedürfen*), or may even "having grounds for" (*Grund haben*). So the third question may well be "What do I *need* to hope for?" or even "What do I have grounds to hope for?" Thanks to Claudia Blöser for discussion here.

6 See my (2020) and (2022a) for an effort to do that.

7 I use "Belief" to translate "*Glaube*": the latter's meaning, for Kant, is different in important ways from both "belief" and "faith" in English. See (Chignell 2007).

8 I discuss a few examples of this in (2022b). It is tempting to think that some theological authors are thinking of "hope" along the lines of "trust." We already have expectations (or even certainty) regarding the ultimate providential outcome, but we sometimes have trouble "living into" what we can expect, especially when faced with personal challenges and collective injustices. So "hope" becomes the virtue of "arduous" living into what one already expects. On that account of hope, it would not only be compatible with expectation but a kind of affective complement to it. Thanks to Olualuwatoni Alimi for discussion of this point.

9 Although he gets the claim about mere possibility right, from a contemporary point of view we might wonder about Aquinas's further claims that hope is only properly directed to what is "arduous" and "future." Aquinas follows the classical tradition (e.g. Cicero) in viewing desire as a movement of appetite towards what is agreeable and not-yet-obtained. He also incorporates the Platonic distinction between passions of the concupiscible and irascible parts of the sensitive soul. This concept of hope takes it to be a passion of the irascible part – the part that "resists the attacks that hinder what is suitable" for us (1265–1274: *ST* I.81.2). This is presumably why he says that hope's object must be "arduous" to obtain. This part of the concept has fallen out of the contemporary conception, however: it seems clear that hope can be directed at something relatively easy to acquire (I hope we'll have ice cream after dinner!). It also seem clear that hope can take the present or past as an object ("I hope my horse won yesterday!"). For a helpful study of Aquinas on hope, see Hause (Draft). For a criticism, see Wolterstorff (2004). Thanks to Ryan Darr for discussion of Aquinas's position here.

10 Kierkegaard is Thomistic on this score. He says that "hope is a passion for the possible" (2009: 106ff), but like Aquinas he clearly delineates this "natural" or "pre-moral" hope – which involves a great deal of uncertainty – from "Christian hope," which is secure. See Fremstedal (2012).

11 Aquinas (1265–1274: *ST* 2a2ae.17,7). To fill this out, it would be worth inquiring further into the notion of "possibility" that Aquinas is using here. Again, see Hause (Draft).

12 One exception to this is Wheatley (1958). Compare McGeer (2008).

13 See for example the 1784 essay, "Idea for a Universal History with a Cosmopolitan Purpose."

14 Robert M. Adams (1979) was one of the first contemporary scholars to sketch this broadly psychological version of a moral argument – an argument from the need to avoid despair and "demoralization" in the ethical life. For other efforts in a similar direction see Fugate (2014), Ebels-Duggan (2016) and Chance and Pasternack (2018).

15 Kant's view differs here from that of the author of the epistle to the *Hebrews*. Kant thinks that the hope and the faith (Belief) have different objects, whereas the biblical author takes them to have the same object and different epistemic standings ("faith shows the reality of things hoped for" *Heb.* 11:1).

16 For a more elaborate discussion, see (Chignell 2022a).

17 See Steven Pinker's list of recent books, most of which repeat the argument that from the perspective of human health and well-being, things have been getting quite a bit better, and so we can continue to expect more of the same.

18 Compare here the entire collection of essays on *Ecology, Ethics, and Hope* edited by Brei (2016).

19 Another slightly less memorable phrase is Donna Haraway's: "Make Kin, Not Babies!" in Haraway (2015). For the most famous recent anti-natalist argument, see Benatar (2008).

20 Brand's notorious line in the *Last Whole Earth Catalog* (1971) is effectively his response to people who question whether we ought to be interfering with the climate in such dramatic ways: "We are as gods and might as well get good at it." Compare Hamilton (2015), the title of which is "The Theodicy of the 'Good Anthropocene.'"

21 This is the first chapter of his 2003 book which was translated into English as *In the End – The Beginning* (2004b).

22 For another vision of the Anthropocene that also includes both dystopian realism and hope (as well as sex, romantic love, and fly-fishing) see Nadzam and Jamieson (2015).

23 For more on the "minimum of theology" see Allen Wood (1991). On the rationality of hope for extramundane assistance see Chignell (2013).

24 For more on this theme, see (Chignell 2021a).

25 For helpful discussions of earlier drafts of this chapter, I am grateful to Holly Jean Buck and Tess Pendergrast, to participants in the "Expectation and Joy" workshop at Yale University (especially John Hare, Jennifer Herdt, Jürgen Moltmann, and Miroslav Volf), to participants in the "Religion, Ethics, and Politics" workshop at Princeton University, and to an audience in the Institute for Philosophy and Religion at Boston University. I'm also grateful to Toni Alimi, Claudia Blöser, Ryan Darr, Sean Duggan, Kyla Ebels-Duggan, Alexander Englert, Judah Isseroff, Brendan Kolb, and Allen Wood for written comments.

References

Adams, R.M. (1979) "Moral Arguments for Theistic Belief," in C.F. Delaney (ed.), *Rationality and Religious Belief*, Notre Dame, IN: University of Notre Dame Press.

Aquinas, T. (1265–1274/1920) *Summa Theologiæ of St. Thomas Aquinas*. Fathers of the English Dominican Province (ed. and trans.), 2nd and revised ed., Chicago: English Dominicans/Brittanica (Abbreviated as *ST* in references).

Augustine (1961[420]) *Enchiridion (Handbook) on Faith, Hope, and Love*, H. Paolucci (ed. and trans.), New York: Henry Regnery.

Benatar, D. (2008) *Better Never to Have Been: The Harm Of Coming Into Existence*, New York: Oxford University Press.

Brand, S. (1971) *The Last Whole Earth Catalog: Access to Tools*, New York: Random House.

Brei, A. (ed.) (2016) *Ecology, Ethics, and Hope*, New York: Rowman and Littlefield.

Buck, H.J. (2015) "On the Possibilities of a Charming Anthropocene," *Annals of the Association of American Geographers* 105(2): 369–77.

Cairns, D. (2020) "Hope in Archaic and Classical Greek," in C. Blöser and T. Stahl (eds.), *The Moral Psychology of Hope*, Lanham, MD: Rowman and Littlefield, pp. 15–36.

Chance, B. and Pasternack, L. (2018) "Rational Faith and the Pantheism Controversy: Kant's 'Orientation Essay' and the Evolution of His Moral Argument," in D. Dahlstrom (ed.), *Kant and His German Contemporaries*, vol. 2, New York: Cambridge University Press, pp. 195–214.

Chignell, A. (2007) "Belief in Kant," *Philosophical Review* 116(3): 323–60.

Chignell, A. (2013) "Rational Hope, Moral Order, and the Revolution of the Will," in E. Watkins (ed.), *The Divine Order, the Human Order, and the Order of Nature*, New York: Oxford University Press.

Chignell, A. (2020) "Hope and Despair at the Kantian Chicken Factory: Moral Arguments About Making a Difference," in L. Allais and J. Callanan (eds.), *Kant on Animals*, Oxford: Oxford University Press.

Chignell, A. (2021a) "Liturgical Philosophy of Religion: An Untimely Manifesto About Sincerity, Acceptance, and Hope," in M.D. Eckel, T. Jardin and A. Speight (eds.), *The Future of the Philosophy of Religion*, Boston: Springer.

Chignell, A. (2021b) "Knowledge, Anxiety, Hope: How Kant's First and Third Questions Relate," in B. Himmelmann and C. Serck-Hanssen (eds.), *The Court of Reason: Proceedings of the 13th International Kant Congress*, Berlin: DeGruyter.

Chignell, A. (2022a) "Inefficacy, Despair, and Difference-Making: A Secular Application of Kant's Moral Argument," in L. Caranti and A. Pinzani (eds.), *Kant and the Contemporary World*, London: Routledge.

Chignell, A. (2022b) "Hopeful Pessimism: The Kantian Mind at the End of All Things," in M.D. Eckel, T. Jardin and A. Speight (eds.), *Faith, Hope, Love: The Theological Virtues and Their Opposites*, Boston: Springer. http://creativecommons.org/licenses/by/4.0/.

Chignell, A. (2023) "Demoralization and Hope: A Psychological Reading of Kant's Moral Argument," *The Monist* 105.

DeVos, J.M., Joppa, L.N., Gittleman, J.L., Stephens, P.R. and Pimm, S.L. (2015) "Estimating the Normal Background Rate of Species Extinction," *Conservation Biology* 29: 452–62.

Ebels-Duggan, K. (2016) "The Right, the Good, and the Threat of Despair: (Kantian) Ethics and the Need for Hope in God," *Oxford Studies in Philosophy of Religion* 7: 81–108.

Fremstedal, R. (2012) "Kierkegaard on the Metaphysics of Hope," *Heythrop Journal* 58: 51–60.

Fugate, C. (2014) "The Highest Good and Kant's Proof(s) of God's Existence," *History of Philosophy Quarterly* 31(2): 137–58.

Gallagher, M., D'Souza, J.M. and Richardson, A. (2020) "Hope in Contemporary Psychology," in C. Blöser and T. Stahl (eds.), *The Moral Psychology of Hope*, Lanham, MA: Rowman and Littlefield, pp. 189–208.

Hamilton, C. (2015) "The Theodicy of the 'Good Anthropocene'," *Environmental Humanities* 7: 233–8.

Haraway, D. (2015) "Anthropocene, Capitalocene, Plantationocene, Chthulucene: Making Kin," *Environmental Humanities* 6: 159–65.

Hause, J. (Draft) *Misconceiving Hope.*

Kierkegaard, S. (2009) *Christian Discourses*, H. Hong and E. Hong (ed. and trans.), Princeton, NJ: Princeton University Press.

Locke, J. (1975 [1690]) *An Essay Concerning Human Understanding*, P. Nidditch (ed.), Oxford: Clarendon Press.

McGeer, V. (2008). "Trust, Hope, and Empowerment," *Australasian Journal of Philosophy* 86(2): 237–54.

Moltmann, J. (2004a) "Progress and Abyss: Remembrances of the Future of the Modern World," in M. Volf and W. Katerburg (eds.), *The Future of Hope*, Grand Rapids, MI: Eerdmans, pp. 3–26.

Moltmann, J. (2004b) *In the End – The Beginning*, London: SCM Press.

Nadzam, B. and Jamieson, D. (2015) *Love in the Anthropocene*, New York: OR Books.

Szerszynski, B. (2012) "The End of the End of Nature: The Anthropocene and the Fate of the Human," *The Oxford Literary Review* 34(2): 165–84.

Sweet, K. (2022) *Kant on Freedom, Nature and Judgment: The Territory of the Third Critique*, New York: Cambridge University Press.

Wheatley, J.M.O. (1958) "Wishing and Hoping," *Analysis* 18(6): 121–31.

Willaschek, M. (2016) "Must We Believe in the Realizability of Our Ends? On a Premise of Kant's Argument for the Postulates of Pure Practical Reason," in T. Höwing (ed.), *The Highest Good in Kant's Philosophy*, Berlin: Walter de Gruyter.

Wolterstorff, N. (2004) "Seeking Justice in Hope," in M. Volf and W. Katerberg (eds.), *The Future of Hope: Christian Tradition Amid Modernity and Postmodernity*, Grand Rapids, MI: Eerdmans.

Wood, A. (1991) "Kant's Deism," in P. Rossi (ed.), *Kant's Philosophy of Religion Reconsidered*, Bloomington, IN: Indiana University Press.

Wood, A. (1999) *Kant's Ethical Thought*, New York: Cambridge University Press.

Zöller, G. (2013) "Hoffen – Dürfen. Kants kritische Begründung des moralischen Glaubens," in D. Heidemann and R. Weicker (eds.), *Glaube und Vernunft in der Philosophie der Neuzeit*, Hildesheim and New York: Olms, pp. 245–57.

Further Reading

K. Moran, *Community and Progress in Kant's Moral Philosophy* (Washington, DC: Catholic University Press of America, 2012) – a text that argues for the significant role community plays in several respects in Kant's philosophy.

P. Wilford and S. Stoner (eds.), *Kant and the Possibility of Progress: From Modern Hopes to Postmodern Anxieties* (Philadelphia: University of Pennsylvania Press, 2021) – a valuable source for contributions on hope and progress in Kant.

43

RAWLSIANS AND OTHER KANTIANS

Alyssa R. Bernstein

★★★

1. Introduction

Assessing the influence of Kant's moral and political philosophy since World War II, William Arthur Galston wrote in 1993:

[E]vidence of Kant-inspired practical philosophy [has become] pervasive. From Robert Nozick on the libertarian right to Jürgen Habermas on the participatory left come appeals to Kantian concepts and premises, variously interpreted. John Rawls is of course the chief representative of this tendency within liberal thought.

(Galston 1993: 207)

According to Galston, this upsurge of interest was due to post-WWII developments not only in philosophy but also in social reality: in Europe, observers noticed that "Kant's followers were far less open to Nazi appeals than were either existentialists or legal positivists," and in the United States, many professional philosophers who were concerned to "take rights seriously"[1] came to doubt that utilitarianism could yield "determinate and plausible answers to the key questions of practical philosophy" (Galston 1993: 207). Some of these philosophers, inspired by Kant's conception of the virtuous person and by his idea that morality requires us always to treat the humanity in every person as an end in itself and never merely a means, turned to his practical philosophy for guidance in formulating principles of rational social organization and legitimate authority (Galston 1993: 208).

Looking ahead from the year 1992, Howard Lloyd Williams wrote:

As the end of the twentieth century approaches events appear to have gone markedly in Kant's direction [. . .]. In recent years we have seen decisive and peaceful change occur in Europe along the lines Kant would have recommended [through] public and enlightened debate towards a society of free, equal and independent individuals.

(Williams 1992: xiii)

  DOI: 10.4324/9781003406617-59

At present, given recent political developments in many countries such as the rise of autocratic governments and upsurges of ethnic nationalism and religious intolerance, it no longer seems that events overall have gone markedly in Kant's direction. However, progress according to Kantian moral and political values remains possible. It may be assisted by clarifying Kant's concepts and arguments, developing them, and using them to address current issues, as done in recent decades by several philosophers including John Rawls.

Rawls is widely regarded as the greatest moral and political philosopher since John Stuart Mill. Rawls's philosophy is inspired and informed by Kant's, and Rawls is often credited for Kant's influence in current political philosophy. In the second section of this chapter, I focus on affinities between these two philosophers' conceptions of political legitimacy and justice, both domestic and international. In the third section, I explain Rawls's political constructivism and his view of its relation to Kant's philosophy of practical reason. Section 4 briefly surveys certain disagreements about whether Rawlsians can be Kantians and whether Kantians can be Rawlsians. Section 5 concludes.

2. Political Legitimacy and Justice in Kant and Rawls

In this section, I discuss first Kant's and then Rawls's conceptions of political legitimacy and justice, domestic and international. Accurately interpreting each conception requires paying due attention to the technical meanings assigned to the words "a state," "a nation," and "a people." It is important to note that although Kant and Rawls use these same words, they do not assign to them precisely the same technical meanings.

Kant's terms, "a state", "a nation", and "a people" can all be used to refer to the same society, but "a nation" carries connotations of a state's external political relations, while "a people" carries connotations of a state's internal political relations, that is, the relations among its individual members, thought of as the source of the government's authority and the ultimate ground of the state's moral status. Kant's term "a state" is normative. The idea of the state as a moral person, which is "still the central structural feature of contemporary international law," was developed by both Kant and Emmeric de Vattel, both of whom criticized defenders of "enlightened absolutism" who saw other states as possessions that could be acquired by military conquest or by inheritance, exchange, purchase or gift (Cavallar 1999: 57).

Kant makes clear that the term "a nation," as he uses it, does not imply that its members share ethnicity or ancestry:

> As natives of a country, those who constitute a nation can be looked upon analogously to descendants of the same *ancestors* (*congeniti*) even though they are not. Yet in an intellectual sense and from the perspective of rights, since they are born of the same mother (the republic) they constitute as it were one family (*gens, natio*), whose members (citizens of the state) are of equally high birth [since there are no ranks among citizens in a republic, in contrast to other forms of state].
>
> (*RL* 6: 343)

Similarly, the term "a people," as Kant uses it, does not by itself imply that the individuals constituting it share ethnicity or ancestry (although in at least two instances Kant says that different peoples will have different histories and may well have different languages and religions) (*ZeF* 8: 344, 367). Kant's main arguments about rights, whether rights of individuals or of states, do not depend on any assumptions that the members of a people share ancestry, ethnicity, language, or religion. Only his claims about whether and when, historically, peoples can become capable of self-government and of cooperating with other states in accordance with a right of nations depend on any such assumptions.

According to Kant, "no right over a people can be thought" apart from "the idea of the original contract" (*ZeF* 8: 344). Kant links governmental authority to the possibility of consent; he does not regard it as dependent on any actual, implied, or presumed act of consent (Pippin 2006: 417). Properly speaking, says Kant, the original contract, that is, "the act by which a people forms itself into a state," is "only the idea of this act, in terms of which alone we can think of the legitimacy of a state" (*RL* 6: 315). This idea limits the authority of the ruler: "what a people may never decide upon for itself, a monarch may still less decide upon for a people; for his legislative authority rests precisely on this, that he unites in his will the collective will of the people" (*WA* 8: 39–40). More generally: "*What a people cannot decree for itself, a legislator also cannot decree for a people*" (*TP* 8: 304). A civil constitution can be based only on the idea of an original contract which, although only an idea of reason,

> has its undoubted practical reality, namely to bind every legislator to give his laws in such a way that they *could* have arisen from the united will of a whole people and to regard each subject, insofar as he wants to be a citizen, as if he has joined in voting for such a will. For this is the touchstone of any public law's conformity with right. In other words, if a public law is so constituted that a whole people *could not possibly* give its consent to it (as, e.g., that a certain class of *subjects* should have the hereditary privilege of *ruling rank*), it is unjust [*nicht gerecht*]; but if it is *only possible* that a people could agree to it, it is a duty to consider the law just, even if the people is at present in such a situation or frame of mind that, if consulted about it, it would probably refuse its consent.
>
> (*TP* 8: 297)

Actual constitutions may be better or worse, says Kant; each of them is a kind of social contract which may or may not "well be reconciled with the idea of the original contract" (*RL* 6: 340). According to Kant, the "only constitution that accords with right [is] that of a pure republic;" thus "the constituting authority" is obligated to bring about replacement of "the old (empirical) statutory forms, which served merely to bring about the *submission* of the people," by "the original (rational) form" (*RL* 6: 340). Such reform "will finally lead to what is literally a state," which is "the final end of all public right" (*RL* 6: 341).

There is some disagreement among Kant scholars about how to interpret Kant's idea of a republic. According to Pauline Kleingeld, by "republic" Kant means "a political system that is based on the principles of the freedom and equality of the citizens, and, depending on which text one reads, their independence as co-legislators [. . .] or their dependence on a common legislation" (Kleingeld 2006: 481). A republic is governed by the rule of law, not a despot's caprice; its laws are enacted by the citizens through their representatives; the legislative, executive, and judicial branches of government are separate; and "neither the territory of a republic nor the offices associated with its government are the personal property of the officers in function" (Kleingeld 2006: 481). According to Fernando Tesón, "[b]y *republican* Kant means what we would call today a liberal democracy, that is, a form of political organization that provides for full respect for human rights" (Tesón 1998: 3). However, as Allen Wood rightly points out:

> Kant accepted existing occupational and property qualifications for voting and officeholding that held in his day wherever such institutions existed at all. Only those who are not economically dependent on others, he argued, are in a position to give their independent voice, and

participate in the state as 'active citizens', by voting and holding office. The rest (including servants, wage-laborers, peasants working land owned by others, and of course all women) are 'passive citizens': the state protects their rights, but they have no claim to participate in making decisions for it.

(Wood 2005: 175)

In *Toward Perpetual Peace*, Kant offers to "the legislative authority of a state [. . .] instructions about the principles of its conduct toward other states," specifically "universal maxims of waging war and establishing peace" (*ZeF* 8: 368–9). By "peace" Kant refers to a condition of right. Arguing in favor of a treaty-like international agreement, he proposes six "preliminary articles" stating prohibitions, and three "definitive articles" stating requirements. The preliminary articles mark out the beginning of the road to perpetual peace, and the definitive articles specify the destination. At the end of the road, all states would have republican civil constitutions and would securely enjoy a condition of freedom "conformably with the idea of the right of nations," and all foreigners would have the right to visit (to be treated without hostility and not to be turned away if this would destroy them) (*ZeF* 8: 356, 358).[2] Securing such a condition of peace requires establishing a federation of free states (*ZeF* 8: 385). As Kant acknowledges, this destination is an ideal which may never be attained and may not even be attainable, but is to guide efforts to establish perpetual peace through constant reform of legal and political structures.

Rawls uses the terms "a state," "a people," and "a nation" primarily when discussing the law of peoples (LP), his conception of principles of right and justice for international law and practice; in the rest of his philosophy, these three terms play no fundamental roles. Rawls's term "a state," unlike Kant's, is not normative; as Rawls uses it, an entity can be literally or fully a state despite satisfying only few, if any, requirements of justice or right. Contrastingly, as Rawls uses the term "a people," any entity classifiable as a people is a political society that satisfies to at least some degree certain essential requirements of right and justice (Rawls 1999: 4, 17, 25–7, 34–7, 44–5, 62). In this respect Rawls's normative term "a people" is similar to Kant's normative term "a state." Further similarities between Rawls and Kant are that Rawls's term "a people" implies nothing about shared ethnicity or ancestry, and that Rawls's main arguments about rights (of individuals and of states) do not assume that the members of a people share ancestry, ethnicity, language, or religion. Rawls's term "a nation" (which refers to "a pattern of cultural values") is not synonymous with Kant's term, nor with Rawls's terms "a state" or "a people" (Rawls 1999: 25, note 20). Moreover, the term "a nation" plays no role in any of Rawls's arguments about human rights or international justice.

In *A Theory of Justice* (TJ) Rawls inquires about the most appropriate conception of justice, or "moral basis," for a democratic society (TJ, p. viii/xviii rev.). Aiming to develop an alternative to the predominant philosophical conception of justice, utilitarianism, Rawls develops a conception that draws from the social contract tradition and is, he says, "highly Kantian in nature" (TJ, p. viii/xviii rev.). Rawls initially proposes a "vague" general conception of justice, according to which justice requires an equal distribution of basic social goods (liberty and opportunity, income and wealth, and the social bases of self-respect) unless an unequal distribution of any or all of them would be to everyone's advantage (TJ, p. 62/54 rev.). He then develops it into a more specific conception, "justice as fairness" (JF), which applies in favorable social conditions and requires giving priority to certain liberties and opportunities by means of the institutions of a liberal constitutional democracy. The principles of justice as fairness require equal provision, for all, of certain "basic" liberties, which have priority over the values of perfectionist conceptions as well as over aggregate social welfare; they also require equal provision, for all, of "fair" (not merely formal) opportunities; further, the principles hold that a just democratic society's basic institutions and policies may allow differences in income, wealth, and social positions only if they function so as to maximally benefit the worst-off.

As Rawls explains in his second book, *Political Liberalism*, he came to realize that the moral values underlying the social ideal developed in TJ required him to revise his argument for justice as fairness, and to work out a conception of political justice for a constitutional democratic regime that a plurality of reasonable doctrines could have good reasons to endorse (Rawls 2005, xxxix). To this end, he developed a "political conception" of how the core democratic values of freedom and equality for all citizens could feasibly be realized in a society's basic institutional structure. Rawls was led to develop his "political liberalism" (PL) by his concern about whether justice as fairness would be stable once realized in institutions. It would be stable only if it would foster in the society's members a steady disposition to uphold their just institutions.

Rawls sought to ensure that his conception of a just society would provide an ideal that was realistic, in the sense that actual human psychological tendencies and limitations would not prevent its achievement under normal conditions, that is, the "circumstances of justice" discussed in TJ (restricted altruism and moderate scarcity), to which Rawls later, in his second book, added "the fact of reasonable pluralism." Rawls took these conditions, limitations, and tendencies into consideration when developing his conception of justice, instead of attempting to ground principles in pure practical reason alone; however, he sought, as did Kant, principles implicit in widely familiar moral judgments. Specifically, Rawls analyzed the considered judgments about justice made by citizens of constitutional democracies and found in the public political cultures of such societies (Kant, *Groundwork*, 4: 392; Rawls, *Collected Papers*, p. 393).

When Rawls addresses, in TJ, the question of the most appropriate conception of justice for a democratic society, he considers it in the context of the broader question of whether social justice is compatible with human nature; he also argues, broadly, that anyone who has the capacity for moral personality to the minimum degree requisite for functioning as a citizen is entitled to the equal rights of citizenship (Rawls 1999: 441–9). Similarly (although not identically), according to Rawls's political liberalism persons are to be thought of as having certain features "implicit in their taking part in a fair system of social cooperation and seeking and presenting public justifications for their judgments on fundamental political questions"; specifically, they are to be thought of

> as reasonable and rational, as free and equal citizens, with the two moral powers (capacities for a conception of justice and a conception of the good) and having, at any given moment, a determinate conception of the good, which may change over time.
>
> (Rawls 2005: 481–2)

Rawls explains in his second book that as he conceives a liberal conception of justice, it endorses the idea of society as a fair system of cooperation over time among free and equal citizens, and determines fairness by applying the criterion of reciprocity; however, "since these ideas can be interpreted in various ways, we get different formulations of the principles of justice" (Rawls 2005: 450–1).

In both JF and LP, fair terms of cooperation are expressed by the principles of a public political conception; the principles specify basic rights and duties within the main institutions (Rawls 1993: 16). Rawls develops his conception of domestic justice, meaning a just political society, by using "the original position," a theoretical device that resembles in certain respects Kant's theoretical device of the original (rational) contract[3] (*RL* 6: 340). Both devices are to be used to guide establishment and reform of domestic political and legal institutions. Rawls develops his conception of international justice, or a just society of peoples, by using a version of the original position. His ideal of a society of peoples significantly resembles Kant's ideal of a federation of free states; both ideals are to be used to guide establishment and reform of international political and legal institutions.

In developing LP, Rawls uses three related yet distinct ideas of justice. In characterizing liberal and nonliberal societies, he uses two ideas of justice which "stand at opposite poles": a liberal conception of justice and a nonliberal but decent conception, which is "a minimal idea" (Rawls 1999: 68). The third idea of justice is "based on the familiar idea of the social contract," but is more general than the idea Rawls calls "justice as fairness" (JF), which he introduced and developed in his first book, *A Theory of Justice* (Rawls 1999: 3–4). Rawls starts with "the social contract idea of the liberal political conception of a constitutionally democratic regime," and then extends it by introducing an original position in which the parties represent peoples (Rawls 1999: 10, 17). In this case the original position is again a "model of representation," but models different agents (Rawls 1999: 33). Thus, in LP Rawls raises the idea of the social contract to yet a higher level of abstraction than that to which he had raised it in JF (Rawls 1971/1999: 11).

Rawls's LP, like Kant's philosophy of international right, is mainly concerned with the problem of how to minimize war while at the same time securing basic rights for individual human persons through law and protecting and promoting representative government. Rawls, like Kant, regards international law as essential to all of these aims. Both philosophers focus on questions about the permissibility of international uses of force or pressure by state governments.

When addressed to Kant's philosophy of international right, the three following questions, which are of pressing interest in our own historical period, reveal respects in which his view is unclear or otherwise unsatisfactory: (1) What are the basic human rights that may permissibly be secured by international uses of coercive force or economic or diplomatic pressure? (2) Is humanitarian military intervention ever morally permissible? (3) Given the fact of reasonable pluralism, what principles can form the basis of a peaceful and just global order? Rawls's LP, when read in light of these questions, can be seen to provide valuable clarifications, revisions, and developments of Kant's philosophy.

In LP, Rawls formulates principles that can help to realize and fulfill Kant's second definitive article for perpetual peace ("The right of nations shall be based on a federalism of free states." [*ZeF* 8: 354]). Rawls also develops a justification for these principles that satisfies the requirements of public reason (as he construes this), and offers an account of human rights and criteria for governmental legitimacy appropriate for a law of peoples, from the point of view of his political liberalism (explained next in section 3). In addition, Rawls provides accounts of when a state's conduct makes it an outlaw state and of measures that may permissibly be taken against outlaw states. Thus LP supplies some of what is lacking from Kant's work at these points, from the point of view of political liberalism.

3. Rawls's Political Constructivism

Although Rawls's philosophy diverges from Kant's in important respects, it is Kantian in other important respects. Rawls characterizes his own theoretical work as "political, not metaphysical" (Rawls 1985). Yet it is philosophy: Rawls's political constructivism systematically addresses important and currently relevant questions, both practical and philosophical. The philosophical questions concern a certain possibility and its necessary conditions; the practical questions concern how these conditions could in principle be fulfilled. Rawls structures his theoretical inquiry so that the practical questions are subordinate to the philosophical ones, and his method of reasoning is disciplined, careful, and clear. When discussing Rawls's philosophy, one must keep track of the significant differences between his earlier and later writings; here I present the final form of his view.

Rawls wrote that the previous two centuries of debate in the tradition of democratic thought had displayed deep disagreements about "how basic institutions are to be arranged so as to be most appropriate to the freedom and equality of democratic citizenship" (Rawls 2001: 2). The roots of these disagreements are non-philosophical as well as philosophical, Rawls writes, but since the competing claims of liberty and equality are understood, ordered, weighted, and justified differently by different philosophical and moral doctrines, a central task of political philosophy is to seek "reasoned common ground for political agreement" and, if none can be found, then to narrow "the divergence of philosophical and moral opinion" so as to permit "social cooperation on a footing of mutual respect among citizens" (Rawls 2001: 1–2). Assuming that value pluralism is a permanent condition of free democratic societies, Rawls argues that citizens "need to consider what kinds of reasons they may reasonably give one another when fundamental political questions are at stake" (Rawls 1999: 131, 2001: 4).

Three kinds of conflict divide the citizens of a democratic society: (1) conflicts deriving from differences in status, class position, or occupation, or from differences in ethnicity, gender, or race; (2) conflicts deriving from irreconcilable comprehensive doctrines; and (3) conflicts deriving from the burdens of judgment (Rawls 1993: 54–8, 100, 1999: 177). Rawls aimed to address primarily conflicts of the first kind in his first book, *A Theory of Justice*, which presented his conception of social justice "as a comprehensive liberal doctrine in which all the members of its well-ordered society affirm that same doctrine" (Rawls 1999: 179). Rawls's second book, *Political Liberalism*, "regards that society as impossible," and aims to address primarily the problem of conflicts deriving from irreconcilable comprehensive doctrines; for this purpose, he develops the idea of political liberalism with its idea of public reason (Rawls 1999: 179).

Rawls confronts the "torturing question" of whether democracy and comprehensive doctrines can be compatible (Rawls 1999: 175). Concerned both about "fundamentalist religions" and about "nonreligious (secular) doctrines, such as those of autocracy and dictatorship, of which our century offers hideous examples," Rawls emphasizes that all "[u]nreasonable doctrines are a threat to democratic institutions, since it is impossible for them to abide by a constitutional regime except as a *modus vivendi*"[4] (Rawls 1999: 178–9, 1993: 126, 146–50.) He argues that "a plurality of conflicting reasonable comprehensive doctrines, religious, philosophical, and moral" is "the normal result" of the "culture of free institutions" in any democratic society securing for all of its citizens the freedoms of religion, conscience, speech, and assembly, and that such a society may become unstable unless both the non-religious and the religious acknowledge that their own basic liberties can be ensured only in a reasonably just constitutional democracy, and endorse such a regime even though their own comprehensive doctrines may not prosper under it (Rawls 1999: 131, 151).

In order to show how democracy and comprehensive doctrines can be compatible, Rawls develops the idea of a freestanding political conception of justice. Such a conception would presuppose neither the truth nor the falsity of any particular reasonable comprehensive doctrine, thus minimizing conflict between political values and other values (Rawls 1993: 140). Ideally it would be an adequate framework of thought for discussion of fundamental political questions.

Political philosophy, as Rawls views it in light of his aims, comprises conceptions of justice that work entirely within the category or domain of the political. A conception of justice, whether liberal or not, is what Rawls calls "a political conception" if it has the following three features. (1) It applies primarily to the basic structure of society (its main political, economic, and social institutions). (2) Although it may be derived from, or supported by, one or more comprehensive doctrines, it "presents itself in its own terms as freestanding," instead of "as depending upon, or as presupposing" the truth of any particular comprehensive doctrine, whether religious or secular. (3) All of its fundamental ideas belong to the category of the political. The main fundamental ideas of political liberalism include the idea of political society as a fair system of cooperation and the idea of citizens as reasonable, rational, free and equal (Rawls 1993: 374–6, 389).

A political conception of justice "is worked out first as a freestanding view that can be justified *pro tanto* without looking to, or trying to fit, or even knowing what are, the existing comprehensive doctrines" (Rawls 1993: 389). However, it may, although freestanding, "be embedded in various ways – or mapped, or inserted as a module – into the different doctrines" that different citizens may affirm, and may be or become an essential component of each of them (Rawls 1993: 12, 387). If the same political conception of justice is embedded in several reasonable comprehensive views, then their adherents can justify it publicly; if they do so, then there is "a reasonable overlapping consensus" among them on the conception of justice (Rawls 1993: 134, 387). Furthermore, if the political conception is also "complete," then it may have "the capacity to shape those doctrines toward itself" (Rawls 1993: 389).

Rawls's political liberalism is animated by the hope that its political values alone can, "in working political practice," ground a democratic society's basic institutional structure (Rawls 1993: 140). These values "govern the basic framework of social life – the very groundwork of our existence – and specify the fundamental terms of political and social cooperation" (Rawls 1993: 138–9). They express the idea that

> since political power is the coercive power of free and equal citizens as a corporate body, this power should be exercised, when constitutional essentials and basic questions of justice are at stake, only in ways that all citizens can reasonably be expected to endorse, in the light of their common human reason.
>
> (Rawls 1993: 139–40)

Rawls argues both that it would be unreasonable to use state power to compel allegiance to any comprehensive doctrine, and that one can acknowledge this consistently with affirming one's own.

In *Justice as Fairness: A Restatement*, published in 2001, Rawls emphasizes that he still has confidence in the main ideas of the conception of justice presented three decades earlier, in *A Theory of Justice*, which he now revises (Rawls 2001: xv). Those main ideas are the two principles of justice (which he reformulates and explicates in Part II of the book), the argument for them using the heuristic device of the original position (which he reorganizes and presents in Part III of the book), and six "fundamental ideas" (presented in Part I of the book). Five of these fundamental ideas are "closely related," as Rawls makes clear by introducing them in a particular sequence:

> [W]e start with the organizing idea of society as a fair system of cooperation and then make it more determinate by spelling out what results when this idea is fully realized (a well-ordered society), and what this idea applies to (the basic structure). We then say how the fair terms of cooperation are specified (by the parties in the original position) and explain how the persons engaged in cooperation are to be regarded (as free and equal citizens).
>
> (Rawls 2001: 25)

The sixth fundamental idea is that of public justification, which encompasses the ideas of public reason, reflective equilibrium, and overlapping consensus (Rawls 2001: 26). Rawls argues that if we share his aim, namely, to develop "a workable political conception of justice" for a democratic society, then we should start with the idea of society as a fair system of cooperation (Rawls 2001: 25).

The idea that a just democratic society is a fair system of cooperation among the citizens remains vague and of little practical value unless fair terms of cooperation can be specified. As a way to specify fair terms, Rawls proposes imagining that the principles of justice for the basic structure of the society are to be settled by an agreement among its citizens (all of whom have the two moral powers [Rawls 2001: 18–19, 24]) under conditions that are fair to all. Fair conditions are such that not only are coercion, threats, deception, and fraud ruled out, but also none of the citizens can exercise any unfair bargaining advantages. Such conditions would be ensured if the citizens were behind a "veil of ignorance" which, while allowing them relevant general information, prevented them from knowing their own or each other's distinguishing features and circumstances (such as sex, gender, race, ethnic group, comprehensive doctrine, economic class or social position).

This imaginary situation is the heuristic device called "the original position." Rawls claims that

> the agreement that would be reached can be worked out deductively by reasoning from how the parties are situated and described, the alternatives open to them, and [. . .] what the parties count as reasons and the information available to them.
>
> (Rawls 2001: 17)

If the original position suitably models reasonable citizens' considered convictions about fair conditions of agreement and about appropriate restrictions on reasons for favoring or rejecting principles of justice, then it can make clear to them the reasons for regarding the resulting principles (those to which the parties in the original position would agree) as specifying fair terms of cooperation. If so, then the original position can serve as a public point of view from which the citizens of a well-ordered society can adjudicate their claims. Rawls uses the original position to argue for his own proposed set of principles and against utilitarian conceptions of justice (Rawls 2001: 80–134). He also argues that the original position, his set of principles of justice, and their justification together constitute "a public framework of thought," which provides "a basis of objectivity" that is appropriate for the limited purposes of political liberalism (Rawls 1993: 110).

Rawls characterizes his own view as constructivist because it represents certain practical principles as the outcome of a procedure of construction that "embodies all the relevant requirements of practical reason" (Rawls 1993: 90). It is a form of political constructivism because it develops principles of political justice for a democratic society; it develops these principles from an idea of society as a fair system of social cooperation together with an idea of citizens as free and equal;[5] and it develops the principles by way of citizens' "common practical reason" (Rawls 1993: 90). Rawls argues that the procedure of construction, which uses the theoretical device of the original position, "models [. . .] the appropriate conceptions of society and person" as well as the relevant requirements of practical reason, by showing that rational agents representing and trying to advance the interests of citizens would, "under reasonable, or fair, conditions" select certain principles of political justice (Rawls 1993: 95–6). If the procedure is "correctly formulated," then actual citizens "should be able to accept its principles and conceptions along with their reasonable comprehensive doctrine" (Rawls 1993: 97).

Rawls contrasts his own political constructivism with (what he takes to be) Kant's moral constructivism.[6] He argues that although both types "are objective," only political constructivism's "conception of objectivity" is "appropriate" for political liberalism, in view of "the need for a democratic society to secure the possibility of an overlapping consensus on its fundamental political values" and given the purpose of developing principles of political justice that can be the focus of such a consensus (Rawls 1993: 89–90). However, Rawls claims, "Kant's view could grant that political constructivism provides an appropriate basis of objectivity for its limited political purposes" (Rawls 1993: 110).

Rawls argues that both his own political constructivism and Kant's moral constructivism have six aspects widely recognized as necessary and sufficient for any conception of objectivity, although each explains them differently (Rawls 1993: 115–16). These six "essentials of objectivity are [. . .] the features required of a framework of thought and judgment if it is to be an open and public basis of justification for citizens as free and equal" (Rawls 1993: 115). Rawls explains that both Kant's moral constructivism and his own political constructivism conceive the objective point of view as "calling upon practical reason," and express "the point of view of persons [. . .] suitably characterized as reasonable and rational" (Rawls 1993: 116).

Rawls says he follows Kant's way of distinguishing theoretical reason, which "is concerned with the knowledge of given objects," from practical reason, which "is concerned with the production of objects" according to a conception of them, "for example, the conception of a just constitutional regime taken as the aim of political endeavor" (Rawls 1993: 93). He emphasizes that although he uses certain ideas about reason of which Kant is the historical source, these are distinct and separable from other views of Kant's, and justice as fairness is distinct from Kant's moral constructivism (Rawls 1993: 100–1). Its aim is different, and this difference entails others.

According to Rawls, a conception of objectivity may conceive of correct judgments either as true, "in the familiar way," or else as reasonable, as in political constructivism (Rawls 1993: 92, 111). Although he does not explicitly define his term "reasonable," one can infer its meaning from the ways he uses it in justice as fairness (applying it to persons, institutions, and comprehensive doctrines, as well as to principles, judgments, decisions, and their grounds); his comments about this term are to be interpreted in that light (Rawls 1993: 94, 1999: 136–7, 2001: 82). According to Rawls, to judge a political conception as morally true or false would be to give it "a metaphysical foundation as part of [one's] own comprehensive doctrine" (Rawls 1993: 126). Since he aims only "to work out a political conception of justice that citizens as reasonable and rational can endorse on due reflection," which will enable them to reach "free and informed agreement on questions of constitutional essentials and basic matters of justice," he "leave[s] the concept of a true moral judgment to comprehensive doctrines" (Rawls 1993: 116, 127–8). However, he points out that if any of the reasonable doctrines in an overlapping consensus is true, then the political conception is endorsed by a true doctrine and is therefore "correct, or close thereto," and in such a case all of those reasonable doctrines "yield the right conception of political justice" (Rawls 1993: 128).

4. Rawlsians and Kantians

Among scholars of both Kant and Rawls, some emphasize differences between their philosophies, while others emphasize commonalities. As regards Rawls's political constructivism, both Allen W. Wood and Onora O'Neill contend that Rawls misunderstands Kant. However, Wood and O'Neill themselves differ on how to interpret Kant. Wood contends that Rawls errs both in regarding Kant's practical philosophy as constructivist and in himself embracing constructivism (Wood 2008: 282–5). Although O'Neill agrees with Rawls that Kant's practical philosophy is constructivist, she contends that Rawls misunderstands the relation between Kant's philosophy of right and the rest of his practical philosophy (O'Neill 2003: 350, 2015: 76, note 15). However, on this latter point some interpreters of both Kant and Rawls (such as myself) disagree with O'Neill. Moreover, interpreters of Kant take conflicting positions on how duties of right are related to duties of virtue; participants in this debate include O'Neill, Wood, Jürgen Habermas, Arthur Ripstein, Paul Guyer, Marcus Willaschek, and Sorin Baiasu (Baiasu 2016).

Among scholars of Kant's philosophy of right, some deny while others assert that Rawls's political philosophy is Kantian. Howard Williams distinguishes "between those political philosophers who are concerned to carry the original Kantian project further, like Wolfgang Kersting, Otfried Höffe, Ernest Weinrib and Fernando Tesón, and those contemporary political philosophers who have given up the original project," although they "seek to draw inspiration from Kant's thinking;" Williams argues that both Rawls and Habermas belong to the latter category, because they both have abandoned metaphysics (Williams 1999: 1). However, questions about how arguments developed by Rawls and Habermas relate to Kant's arguments remain open as long as scholars disagree about how to interpret these three philosophers' conceptions of moral justification. As indicated earlier, Kant scholars disagree about whether Kant's practical philosophy is constructivist and about whether Rawls interprets it correctly. Furthermore, Habermas does not make clear what sort of justification he offers, if any, for the principles of his discourse ethics (Kelly 2000: 248).

According to Arthur Ripstein, Rawls is standardly interpreted as providing "a broadly Kantian perspective on a set of questions that have their roots less in Kant than in the empiricist and utilitarian tradition of Bentham and Mill" (Ripstein 2009: 3). Ripstein suggests that this interpretation may be incorrect, expressing his belief that "there is a more Kantian way of understanding the entire Rawlsian enterprise, focused on his conception of persons as free and equal, and on his emphasis on the coercive structure of society" (Ripstein 2009: 4 note 9). Yet Ripstein does not himself develop such an interpretation.

Paul Guyer contends that principles of distributive justice like those found in Rawls's political philosophy can be grounded in Kant's philosophy of right (Guyer 2000). According to the critical analysis of Guyer's argument offered by Michael Nance and Jeppe von Platz, Guyer argues that "Kant's theory of property implies a contractualist theory of distributive justice; in turn, this implies that the distribution of property rights must be fair, and that fairness is secured only by something like Rawls's second principle of justice" (Nance and von Platz 2018: 250). Nance and von Platz argue instead that Kant's philosophy of right does not imply a single theory of distributive justice; it "is compatible with, but does not require, a number of principles of distributive justice – including those principles we find in Rawls's justice as fairness" (Nance and von Platz 2018: 251).

5. Conclusion

Rawls makes clear that he sees important affinities between his own philosophy and Kant's. Interpreting Kant as a moral constructivist, Rawls calls himself a political constructivist. He also emphasizes that he agrees with Kant that the objective point of view on the answers to the moral and political questions they respectively pose is "the point of view of persons [. . .] suitably characterized as reasonable and rational" (Rawls 1993: 116). However, when arguing that political liberalism's conception of justice can be the focus of an overlapping consensus, Rawls highlights the differences between his own philosophy and Kant's, for the reasons explained earlier.

It is important to address the disputed questions about the relations between the philosophies of Kant and Rawls, for many reasons additional to the value of accurate intellectual history and sound philosophical education. The philosophies of Kant and Rawls provide the best available theoretical justifications for constitutional democracy and social and international justice. In view of the recent deterioration of such institutions and practices and their supporting cultural and material conditions, and in view of the need to develop effective and just international and domestic policies and institutions for coping with the climate crisis, there are strong moral reasons to study, write, and teach about the philosophical works of Kant and Rawls.[7]

Notes

1 By using the phrase, "taking rights seriously," Galston here refers to a book with this title, by Ronald Dworkin, a legal philosopher advancing a broadly Kantian conception of dignity (Dworkin 1977).
2 For further discussion of Kant's cosmopolitanism, see Bernstein (2009).
3 For detailed discussion of their differences, see my chapter "Rawls as Reader of Kant's Political and Moral Philosophy," in *Rawls* (Buenos Aires: Katz Editores, forthcoming in 2023).
4 A *modus vivendi* (a way of getting along) is such that "social unity is only apparent, as its stability is contingent on circumstances remaining such as not to upset the fortunate convergence of interests" (Rawls 1993: 147).
5 "The moral agent here is the free and equal citizen as a member of society, not the moral agent in general" (Rawls: 1993: 107–10).
6 For an explanation of Rawls's interpretation of Kant's moral philosophy as a form of constructivism, see my article "Autonomy and Objective Moral Constructivism: Rawls versus Kleingeld & Willaschek," in *Philosophia* (forthcoming in 2023).
7 For very helpful comments on an early draft I am grateful to Allen W. Wood.

References

Baiasu, S. (2016) "Right's Complex Relation to Ethics in Kant: The Limits of Independentism," *Kant-Studien* 107(1): 2–33.

Bernstein, A.R. (2009) "Kant, Rawls, and Cosmopolitanism: *Toward Perpetual Peace* and *The Law of Peoples*," *Jarbuch für Recht und Ethik* 17: 3–52.

Bernstein, A.R. (forthcoming in 2023) "Autonomy and Objective Moral Constructivism: Rawls versus Kleingeld & Willaschek," *Philosophia*.

Bernstein, A.R. (forthcoming in 2023) "Rawls as Reader of Kant's Political and Moral Philosophy," in Joan Vergés Gifra and Hugo Omar Seleme (eds.), *Rawls*, Buenos Aires: Katz Editores.

Cavallar, G. (1999) *Kant and the Theory and Practice of International Right*, Cardiff: University of Wales Press.

Dworkin, R. (1977) *Taking Rights Seriously*, Cambridge, MA: Harvard University Press.

Galston, W. (1993) "What Is Living and What Is Dead in Kant's Practical Philosophy?" in R. Beiner and W.J. Booth (eds.), *Kant & Political Philosophy*, New Haven: Yale University Press.

Guyer, P. (2000) *Kant on Freedom, Law, and Happiness*, Cambridge: Cambridge University Press.

Kelly, E. (2000) "Habermas on Moral Justification," *Social Theory and Practice* 26: 223–49.

Kleingeld, P. (2006) "Kant's Theory of Peace," in P. Guyer (ed.), *The Cambridge Companion to Kant and Modern Philosophy*, Cambridge: Cambridge University Press.

Nance, M. and von Platz, J. (2018) "From Justice to Fairness: Does Kant's Doctrine of Right Imply a Theory of Distributive Justice?" in K.A. Moran (ed.), *Kant on Freedom and Spontaneity*, Cambridge: Cambridge University Press.

O'Neill, O. (2003) "Constructivism in Rawls and Kant," in S. Freeman (ed.), *The Cambridge Companion to Rawls*, Cambridge: Cambridge University Press.

O'Neill, O. (2015) *Constructing Authorities: Reason, Politics and Interpretation in Kant's Philosophy*, Cambridge: Cambridge University Press.

Pippin, R. (2006) "Mine and Thine? The Kantian State," in P. Guyer (ed.), *The Cambridge Companion to Kant and Modern Philosophy*, Cambridge: Cambridge University Press.

Rawls, J. (1971/1999) *A Theory of Justice*, Cambridge, MA: Harvard University Press.

Rawls, J. (1980) "Kantian Constructivism in Moral Theory," in S. Freeman (ed.), *John Rawls: Collected Papers*, Cambridge, MA: Harvard University Press.

Rawls, J. (1985) "Justice as Fairness: Political Not Metaphysical," *Philosophy and Public Affairs* 14: 223–52.

Rawls, J. (1993/1996/2005) *Political Liberalism*, New York: Columbia University Press.

Rawls, J. (1999) *The Law of Peoples*, Cambridge, MA: Harvard University Press.

Rawls, J. (2001) *Justice as Fairness: A Restatement*, E. Kelly (ed.), Cambridge, MA: Harvard University Press.

Ripstein, A. (2009) *Force and Freedom*, Cambridge, MA: Harvard University Press.

Tesón, F.R. (1998) *A Philosophy of International Law*, Boulder: Westview Press.

Williams, H.L. (1992) "Introduction," in H.L. Williams (ed.), *Essays on Kant's Political Philosophy*, Chicago: University of Chicago Press.

Williams, H.L. (1999) "Kant, Rawls, Habermas and the Metaphysics of Justice," *Kantian Review* 3: 1–17.
Wood, A.W. (2005) *Kant*, Oxford: Blackwell Publishing.
Wood, A.W. (2008) *Kantian Ethics*, Cambridge: Cambridge University Press.

Further Reading

Kantian Review 23(4) (Special journal issue on Kant & Rawls, edited by Huw Williams and Katrin Flikschuh and published in December 2018; includes articles by Sorin Baiasu, Katrin Flikschuh, Paul Guyer, Peter Niesen, Onora O'Neill, and Peri Roberts.) A.R. Bernstein, "Political, not Metaphysical, yet Kantian? A Defence of Rawls," in S. Baiasu, S. Pihlström and H. Williams (eds.), *Politics and Metaphysics in Kant* (Cardiff: University of Wales Press, 2011). (Explains Rawls's conception of political philosophy, rebutting criticisms of it presented in Katrin Flikschuh's book, *Kant and Modern Political Philosophy*.) A.R. Bernstein, "'Original Position', 'Law of Peoples', and 'Second Original Position'," in D. Chatterjee (ed.), *Encyclopedia of Global Justice* (Cham, Switzerland: Springer, 2012). (Three 3,000-word expository articles in open-access publication; available in print or at https://link.springer.com/referencework/10.1007/978-1-4020-9160-5.) S. Freeman, *Rawls* (New York: Routledge, 2011) (Provides an authoritative, thorough, and accessible exposition and analysis of all of Rawls's major works). L. Krasnoff, "Kantian Constructivism," in J. Mandle and D.A. Reidy (eds.), *A Companion to Rawls* (Oxford: Wiley Blackwell, 2014) (A careful study of Rawls's 1980 Dewey Lectures on Kantian constructivism and their place in Rawls's intellectual trajectory.) J. von Platz, *Theories of Distributive Justice: Who Gets What and Why* (New York: Routledge, 2020). (One chapter provides an excellent introduction to Rawls's theory of distributive justice; the other chapters expound and compare Robert Nozick's libertarianism, Friedrich A. von Hayek's right-liberalism, and G.A. Cohen's socialism.)

C. Teleological Philosophy

Geophysical Philosophy

44

CONTEMPORARY KANTIAN PHILOSOPHY OF ART

Kenneth F. Rogerson

★★★

In this chapter I want to take a look at the influence Kant's position on Aesthetics has had on contemporary discussions in the field. To do this I will start with a brief overview of Kant's account of Beauty as presented in the "Critique of Aesthetic Judgment," which is the first half of the *Critique of the Power of Judgment* (often referred to as the Third *Critique*). Following this overview, I will identify a small number of themes running through Kant's aesthetics, themes which have influenced the direction of the contemporary debate on aesthetics and the philosophy of art. More specifically, I will compare current discussions of Kantian themes with how Kant saw these issues and how these issues fit with his larger theory.

1. Sketch of Kant's Position

The Kant's goal in the "Critique of Aesthetic Judgment" is to ground a kind of 'objectivity' concerning aesthetic judgments – what Kant calls judgments of Beauty. That is to say, Kant holds that under the proper circumstances, we can be justified in claiming, across the board, that a certain object is aesthetically good (i.e. "Beautiful"). However, to say that Kant was looking to justify the 'objectivity' of aesthetic judgment is not quite right. Instead, in the "Critique of Aesthetic Judgment," as elsewhere in the Critical Philosophy, Kant is trying to find a satisfactory position between the two dominant philosophical schools of his day: Rationalism and Empiricism. As Kant saw it, the Rationalists (Baumgarten [2007], for example) held that aesthetic judgments were simply special cases of ordinary empirical, cognitive judgments. Specifically aesthetic judgments were thought to be a kind of judgment of perfection. For instance, we could judge how 'perfectly' a painting portrayed its subject. While such a position had the advantage, Kant thought, that aesthetic judgments could be as objective as cognitive judgments he also thought that this account left out something very important, namely, that aesthetic judgments are fundamentally subjective. They are judgments about a pleasing aesthetic experience. In this regard the empiricist's account has a certain advantage. Empiricists, like Hume, held that aesthetic judgments were not cognitive, objective judgments, but instead an expression of one's purely subjective tastes (Hume 1965). The problem with Hume's purely subjective account, Kant held, is that there could be no claim to objectivity of our aesthetic

 DOI: 10.4324/9781003406617-61

judgments. On this account, apparently, everyone can have their own tastes. Kant also found this unacceptable.

Kant wants to hold a middle ground between the rationalists and the empiricists. Kant agrees with the empiricists that aesthetic judgments are subjectively based upon pleasure but believes that such judgments make a claim to universal validity something like a cognitive judgments. Kant holds that aesthetic judgments claim a kind of 'subjective universality.' On this account when I make an aesthetic judgment I claim that the object not only pleases me but should also be pleasing to all others who properly appreciates the object. To say that an object is aesthetically good is to say that it is universally pleasing. To hold such a position it is incumbent upon Kant to explain what is it about some objects that they are capable of giving us a universal, shared feeling of pleasure.

One of the first substantive claims Kant makes in the "Critique of Aesthetic Judgment" is that proper aesthetic judgments must be "disinterested." What this means for Kant at first blush (and we shall get into more detail in the next section) is that aesthetic judgments are not judgments that an object satisfies certain interests that we might have. For example to say that a painting is aesthetically good is not to say that it does a good job of covering a whole in the wall. Kant casts about to find some source of pleasure which does not depend upon our various subjective interests or peculiar tastes. What Kant hits upon is a unique kind of intellectual pleasure. It is the presumed pleasure in engaging our cognitive faculties of the imagination and understanding but not in a usual cognitive fashion. When we properly attend to an aesthetic object, we hope that our faculties of imagination and understanding engage in a "free play" or "free harmony."

The notion of a free harmony of the imagination and understanding is pivotal to Kant's account of aesthetic judgment; however this notion is also one of the most difficult to grasp. To get a basic understanding of free harmony we must briefly consider how Kant, in the *Critique of Pure Reason*, explains how ordinary cognition works. For Kant cognition is a matter of applying concepts (using the faculty of the "understanding") to the manifold of sense data (using the faculty of the "imagination"). Further, for Kant, concepts are rules of organization of a manifold of sense. For example, to cognize an object as a dog is to use the 'dog rule' (dog concept) to organize the sense data that is provided to us. Hopefully, we see that all of the leg, head, tail perceptions follow the organizational rule (concept) dog – tail in back, head in front, and so on. For Kant cognition is an activity of two mental faculties – imagination to gather up the sense data and the understanding to recognize the orderliness of that manifold.

Kant wants to hold that what makes an aesthetic experience valuable is that aesthetic judging works a bit like cognitive judging – but with some important differences. When we appreciate a good aesthetic object Kant claims that like cognition we engage our faculties of imagination and understanding. We take in a manifold of sense data and we attempt to see organization in this manifold by using our faculty of understanding, which normally applies a rule (concept) to the manifold. However, Kant holds that in aesthetic judging we use the faculty of the understanding in an indeterminate or free manner. We see an orderliness in the manifold but not an orderliness that is pinned down by a specific concept. Importantly, Kant wants to argue that objects that engage our faculties of imagination and understanding are a source of universal, shared pleasure. This is a central claim for Kant since it will ground the supposed subjective universality of aesthetic judgments.

The argument for free harmony as a universal pleasure shows up in various spots in the "Critique of Aesthetic Judgment," notably paragraphs 9, 21, and 38. I shall here paint the argument in broad strokes since other chapters in the present anthology will address the specifics. Kant wants to argue that experiencing the mental state of the free harmony of the imagination and the understanding is pleasing since "harmonizing" these faculties satisfies the very purpose or goal of the cognitive faculties and does so in a way we did not expect. In ordinary cases of cognition when we apply the 'dog' rule to a manifold of sense this is altogether expected and predictable. However, Kant seems to hold, when a manifold of sense complies with our cognitive purpose of finding order in a manifold without the use of an antecedent concept, we find this pleasing since, in general, we take satisfaction in achieving our cognitive goals. But further Kant argues that pleasure in free harmony is universal since everyone capable of cognizing the world in the way I do must work with the same purpose of finding manifolds of sense orderly. And, presumably, everyone will also take pleasure when an object suits our cognitive purposes when we did not expect that it would – which is what happens with a "free harmony of the imagination and the understanding."

For the balance of this chapter I want to focus on four features of Kant's aesthetics that seem to follow from the brief sketch provided earlier. In the next sections I will discuss how these features have been taken up and modified in contemporary discussions of aesthetics. Literally the first topic (the first "moment") of Kant's "Critique of Aesthetic Judgment" is the claim that proper aesthetic appreciation is "disinterested." Largely as a result of Kant's talk about disinterestedness in aesthetics there came to be a significant debate in the 20th century about the content and role of disinterestedness in aesthetics. Similarly, Kant's making the free harmony of the imagination and the understanding the centerpiece of his theory of aesthetic value seems to imply a kind of formalist position in aesthetics. For Kant to say that the pleasure of aesthetic taste rests upon a certain relationship between the imagination and the understanding is to say we find pleasure in a certain kind of ordering of elements provided by sense. But this sounds like some version of formalism – we are aesthetically interested only in the way elements in an aesthetic object are organized, not in any further content. And, it must be admitted Kant himself seems to encourage seeing his aesthetic theory as formalistic (*KU* 5: 225). Unfortunately, this understanding of Kant is complicated by the fact that in the latter sections of the *Critique* he stresses the importance of Beauty as the expression of aesthetic ideas. Kant seems to go so far as to make expression of idea a requirement for proper aesthetic objects (*KU* 5: 356). In what follows I will consider the effect that Kant's dual notions of formalism and expression of ideas has had on the contemporary discussion of aesthetics.

Finally, I want to take look at contemporary positions on the grounding of aesthetic value judgments. Are such judgments objective, subjective or some other alternatives, and compare these position to Kant claim that aesthetic judgments are subjectively universal in the sense described earlier.

2. Disinterestedness

Although Kant did not invent the notion of disinterestedness in aesthetics, most of the contemporary debate about disinterestedness comes out of Kant's treatment of the matter. In this section I want to take a look at the contemporary discussion of disinterestedness and compare this to Kant's original treatment. The contemporary discussion of disinterestedness begins in the mid-twentieth century by such figures as Edward Bullough (Bullough 1995 [1912]), Jerome Stolnitz (Stolnitz 1960), and Roger Scruton (Scruton 1974). Stolnitz and Scruton see themselves as quite self-consciously extending the work of Kant. The goal of each of these authors was to develop an account of disinterestedness within a larger framework of what is called and Aesthetic Attitude theory. Although there are important differences between people who have held Aesthetic Attitude theories the central idea is that there is a distinct way in which to attend to an aesthetic object. To simplify here, we should attend to an object 'for its own sake.' This is to be contrasted with an interested attitude toward an object. Such interested attitudes will typically be practical ones. So, to take a disinterested, aesthetic attitude toward a piece of sculpture would be to consider how it looks irrespective of what practical purpose we might put the sculpture to – for example, we should not be thinking about whether the sculpture would make a good door stop. Or, we should not be thinking about how much the sculpture might fetch at auction. Such practical attitudes are anti-thetical to proper aesthetic appreciation.

The thesis of disinterestedness within these Aesthetic Attitude theories was supposed to answer a number of questions in aesthetic theory. Having the proper aesthetic attitude, presumably, would help to define what are proper aesthetic properties. If we attend to weight, the market value, or the durability of a sculpture, we are likely doing so out of some practical interest. And, accordingly, we are attending to the wrong features for aesthetic appreciation. Alternatively, if we are attending to the shape, color, or texture of a sculpture for no practical reasons, then we are likely attending to proper features. The upshot of this is that we may now start to define relevant and irrelevant aesthetic properties for a genre of art. For sculpture, shape, color and texture are relevant aesthetic properties while weight, market value and durability are not. It may even be the case that a disinterested Aesthetic Attitude can define what can count as an aesthetic object. For example one might hold that a proper aesthetic object is one that we can take a distinterested aesthetic attitude toward. Stolnitz takes such a position and draws the controversial conclusion that any object can be viewed with disinterested attention. And, as such, any object (either art or nature) can be regarded as an aesthetic object. Of course it's likely going to be the case that most objects will not be very good aesthetic objects, but that is not the point.

For Bullough and Stolnitz, Aesthetic Attitude theory is psychological. To adopt an aesthetic attitude is to adopt a certain way of attending to an object. It is to be in a certain frame of mind.[1] Such an Aesthetic Attitude theory came under attack by George Dickie in an influential paper entitled "The Myth of the Aesthetic Attitude" (Dickie 1964).[2] Dickie simply denies that there is a distinct, psychological (disinterested) way in which we attend aesthetically versus when we attend in an interested fashion. Dickie claims that what is often pointed to as wrong-headed interested attention will turn out to be cases where we are simply not attending to artwork. When we consider the sculpture's monetary value, Dickie would say, we are not, in fact, attending to the work at all. Alternatively, if we actually are attending to the work, then our motives (interested or not) don't make any difference. In the end Dickie simply denies that there is some special psychological state that will define the proper way to engage in aesthetic appreciation. And as such, disinterestedness cannot be used, for example, to pick out aesthetically relevant properties.

Since this 20th century discussion of disinterestedness comes out from an understanding of Kant's aesthetic, it will be worthwhile to take a look at Kant's actual position and see, for example, whether it suffers from the same sort of problems that people like Dickie find with the 20th century version. Kant's discussion of disinterestedness occurs in the first "moment" of the "Analytic of the Beautiful," which is the first part of the "Critique of Aesthetic Judgment." The stated purpose of the "Analytic" is to analyze the nature of aesthetic judgment, that is, what kind of judgments are aesthetic judgments of taste. In what could be considered a basic, first premise of Kantian Aesthetics is the claim that aesthetic judgments are fundamentally judgments of pleasure. They are a claim that an object gives us pleasure. But Kant is at pains, in the first moment, to distinguish proper aesthetic pleasure from other kinds of pleasure we might derive from objects. In fact, the conclusion of the first Moment is the following: "Taste is the faculty for judging an object or kind of representation through a satisfaction or dissatisfaction without any interest. The object of such a delight is called beautiful" (KU 5: 211).

Kant holds that a proper aesthetic judgment is founded upon a pleasure that is other than an interested pleasure where, oddly enough, Kant defines an interested pleasure as one connected to the "existence of the thing" (KU 5: 204). Further, for Kant, interested pleasures come in two varieties: either pleasure in the agreeable or pleasure in the good. Pleasures in the agreeable are simple, immediate, purely subjective pleasures in things and activities: skiing, eating ice cream cones, and so on. Pleasures in the good are those of a practical nature. A sharp knife pleases me because it is good at performing a function that is useful to me. It is perhaps difficult to see how the agreeable and the good are both cases of interests in the sense of having a connection with the "existence of the object." What Kant has in mind is that for the agreeable we are concerned with the real existence of, say, an ice cream cone since we need the real, causal properties to be present if we are to get ice-cream-eating pleasure. Similarly we need the knife to be a real object if we are to be able to cut our steak.

While it is clear that Kant holds that an aesthetic experience of an object ought to be disinterested, it can be argued that Kant does not hold an aesthetic attitude theory of disinterestedness. Traditional aesthetic attitude theories (e.g. Bullough and Stolnitz) hold by adopting a certain psychological attitude we could identify aesthetically relevant properties. Kant's position appears to work rather the other way around. Kant starts with what might be called aesthetically irrelevant properties and looks for the relevant properties – with no mention of a special psychological state. Specifically, Kant wants to argue that pleasure derived from some kinds of "interests" (in the good or in the agreeable) are not aesthetically relevant. We must look for something in the object that gives us pleasure but is not based upon these interests. Kant's notion of "attending disinterestedly" means something like not attending to aesthetically irrelevant features. It is a position on what features we should attend to, not how we should attend. In this respect Scruton's account might come closer to the original Kant.

Assuming I have given a correct interpretation of Kant's account of disinterestedness, it seems to avoid Dickie's criticisms. Dickie's main criticism of disinterestedness theories is that they assume there to be a unique, psychological attitude in aesthetic experience. If Kant's account of disinterestedness is not psychological, then Dickie's criticisms do not apply. However, there is some potential disadvantage toward Kant's account versus that of someone like Stolnitz. Stolnitz attempts to discover aesthetically relevant properties via the account of disinterestedness. That is to say, aesthetically relevant properties will be those properties we attend to when we ignore the interested properties. Kant's position, to be coherent, has to begin with an account of aesthetically irrelevant properties (the agreeable and the good) and, then hopefully argue for what properties are relevant. This means that Kant has to have an argument for relevant and irrelevant aesthetic properties which is independent of his account of disinterestedness.

3. Formalism

As sketched earlier, Kant argues that the proper basis of a universal pleasure that is the foundation of an aesthetic judgment of taste is the quasi-cognitive mental state of the free harmony of the imagination and the understanding. This position presumably leads to a kind of aesthetic formalism – or so Kant has typically been understood. The move from free harmony to formalism is thought to go as follows. For Kant the faculty of imagination is the faculty for receiving sense input (sense data). It is the job of the faculty of understanding to discern the organizational structure of a manifold of sense data. To use the dog example from earlier we receive various snapshot perceptions of legs, tail, head, and so on by the senses and the understanding seeks to find the appropriate concept (rule) that describes the organization of this manifold of the sense. In this case it is the concept 'dog' (the dog rule of organizing the manifold of sense). In the dog example the relationship between the imagination and the understanding is similar to mental activity that lies at the basis of aesthetic judging. Aesthetic contemplation will also be a matter of judging a manifold of sense to display some kind of orderliness. Although a proper interpretation of a free, non-conceptual orderliness of a manifold of sense is highly controversial, nonetheless, it is clear that Kant holds that the key feature of an object that is relevant to aesthetic judgment is the orderliness of the manifold of sense presented by the object.[3] It is the way in which elements of an object are arranged. In one of the most formalistic passages in the third moment of the *Critique* Kant announces that "(i)n painting and sculpture, indeed in all the pictorial arts, in architecture and horticulture, insofar as they are fine arts, the *drawing* is what is essential" (*KU* 5: 225). And by the context, it is clear that by "drawing" Kant means an object's form.

For Kant aesthetic judgments of taste must be founded upon a universally shareable pleasure. Kant believes that such a pleasure is to be found when certain objects engage our cognitive faculties in a free harmony. But to say that an object engages our faculties in a free harmony is to say something about the *way* in which its elements are organized. As such, Kant has been understood as a kind of formalist concerning aesthetic value. When judging an object aesthetically all that matters is how the elements of the work are organized.

Kant's perceived formalism is taken up in the 20th century by the likes of Clive Bell (1913) and Roger Fry (1920). Seemingly much like Kant, Bell stress that the only relevant aesthetic properties when it comes to the perceptual arts are line and color. To be a formalist, like Bell, it is not only important to give some sense of what one means by aesthetic formal properties, but also define what form is to be contrasted with – presumably the contrast is with content. Bell has a collection of different kinds of properties that are inappropriate focus on "content." But, we may divide them up into two large categories: properties that lie outside the immediate attention to the work itself and inappropriate (non-formal) properties that are in some sense in the work. Non-formal (contentful) properties lying outside the aesthetic object itself will be things like the intentions of the artist, the sociocultural setting of the work, the work's political significance, and so on. Irrelevant properties inside an aesthetic object will include representational content (formalists of this period very much favored abstract art), or thematic content (Picasso's Guernica is a favorite example of Bell's). All of these "content" items will be aesthetically irrelevant for a formalist of Bell's stripe.

One might well question the extent to which this 20th-century formalist movement matches up to Kant's original project. The simple answer here is that there is much more going on in Kantian aesthetics than this rather simple claim that the aesthetic is only concerned with the spatial and temporal configuration of some simple elements. To complicate matter, I will introduce three concepts which seem to take Kant in a direction away from the pure formalism of his 20th-century successors: free and dependent beauty, representationalism, and expression of aesthetic ideas.

In paragraph 16 of the *Critique* Kant makes what has become a controversial distinction between free and dependent beauty. One of Kant's basic theses as we saw earlier is that aesthetic judgments are not judgments which involve concepts or purposes – instead, we have a "free" (non-conceptual) harmony of the faculties. Examples of free beauties in paragraph 16 are flowers and:

> designs a la grecque, foliage for borders or on wall-papers, etc., signify nothing by themselves; they do not represent anything – no object under a determinate concept, and are free beauties.
>
> (*KU* 5: 229)

Alternatively, dependent (or adherent) beauties are objects that do fall under a concept or purpose. Some of Kant's examples of dependent beauties are various kinds of buildings with specific purposes (e.g. a church, palace, arsenal, or summer-house). The basic point here seems to be that certain objects (flowers, designs a la grecque) can be aesthetically appreciated with no concept of what the object should be, but for other objects (church, palace, etc.) we may also appreciate their beauty, but must recognize that they are intended to serve some purpose.

There are several interpretative problems that arise with the free/dependent distinction. While this is not the place to settle these interpretative issues, some of them need to be mentioned. First, it seems as though for Kant dependent beauty is (always?) inferior to free beauty. It also seems that for Kant natural beauty is often or always a matter of free beauty; whereas, art is typically dependent. This leads to an unfortunate conclusion that natural beauty is superior to artistic beauty.[4] All of this to one side, it appears to be the case that Kant allows some non-formal properties to be part of proper aesthetic objects.

Recently, Nick Zangwill (Zangwill 2001) has embraced the Kantian distinction between free and dependent beauty to support his notion of a "moderate" formalism.[5] According to Zangwill's moderate formalism some non-formal properties of an object can contribute to the aesthetic value of an object. That is to say, according to Zangwill objects of pure beauty are ones where we only consider formal properties as counting aesthetically. Dependent beauties are ones where we consider both formal and non-formal properties as counting aesthetically. It is far from clear that this is what Kant is doing with the free/dependent distinction. Specifically, it is unlikely that Kant wants to say that in addition to the formal properties that a church has, we should also see the *aesthetic* worth of a church insofar as it functions well as a church – which seems to be the position that Zangwill advocates.

Sometimes it is thought that all representational art fits in Kant's category of dependent beauty. Kant surely encourages such a view when he claim that free beauties (and not dependent beauties) "signify nothing by themselves; they do not represent anything" (*KU* 5: 229). And, further, later on in the *Critique* Kant makes the bold claim that all artistic beauty is representational, "a beauty of nature is a beautiful thing, a beauty of art is a beautiful representation of a thing" (*KU* 5: 311). Likely Kant did not mean to include representational art as dependent beauty since the examples of dependent beauty in paragraph 16 are examples of purpose-built objects not objects (like paintings and sculptures) that represent some other object. Nonetheless, contrary to Zangwill's position, there is no indication that Kant would count good representation as an aesthetic quality, that is, a quality that can count in our aesthetic evaluation of an object.[6]

So far, there is little reason to think that Kantss formalism is anything other than the extreme formalism of someone like Clive Bell. However, after making seemingly strong formalist remarks in the early parts of the *Critique* in the latter parts Kant seems to change his tune considerably with the introduction of the doctrine of beauty as the expression of "aesthetic ideas." Kant goes so far as to say in paragraph 51 that "(b)eauty (whether in nature or art) may in general be termed the *expression of aesthetic ideas*" (5: 320). This position seems very anti-formalist. Kant now seems to hold that an important aesthetic property is some kind of content that an object has. Aesthetic objects need to be about something – have something to say. In the next section we will take a look at Kant's notion of beauty as the expression of aesthetic ideas and see how it relates both to his supposed formalism and to contemporary versions of beauty as expressive.

4. Expression

In the latter sections of the *Critique* (starting at paragraph 42) Kant introduces the claim that aesthetic objects (both art and nature) should be seen as expressing "aesthetic ideas." In this section I want to spell out what Kant takes aesthetic ideas to be, how such ideas are expressed in works of art or nature, and how this doctrine of aesthetic ideas relates to his formalism. In addition I will make some remarks about how Kant's discussion of expression relates to more recent positions of expression in aesthetics.

The introduction of the notion of an aesthetic idea refers back to a basic distinction in the *Critique of Pure Reason* between concepts and ideas. For Kant concepts (whether empirical or a priori) are to be used to describe our empirical, knowable world. Alternatively, ideas refer to things and states of affairs that lie beyond our knowable empirical world. The favorite examples of Ideas of Reason from the first *Critique* are God, freedom, and immortality. Kant is quite clear that since these notions refer to something beyond possible experience, the content of the ideas will be rather sketchy. For example, the idea of God would be very abstract – the notion of a being that is not limited by space and time, not finite in power, knowledge, or goodness and so on.

When Kant talks specifically about aesthetic ideas he retains the notion that ideas, as opposed to concepts, refer to things and states of affairs that lie beyond possible experience, but now Kant thinks that aesthetic objects are able somehow suggest or give us a sense of things and states of affairs which we cannot actually experience. Further, Kant holds that the way that aesthetic objects are able to refer that which lies beyond experience is to employ symbols which operate analogically. So, for example, an artwork may represent "Jupiter's eagle, with the lightning in its claws" but suggest by way of analogy the "splendid queen of heaven" (5: 315).

In sum, aesthetic ideas are supposed to give us a sensible, though symbolic, representation of objects and states of affairs which are literally beyond our sensible experience. As indicated earlier, the doctrine of aesthetic ideas seems a considerable departure from Kant's alleged formalism. However, there is a general consensus among scholars that Kant's doctrine of aesthetic ideas is at least consistent with his formalism.[7] In Kant's description of the way a "genius" creates an artwork that expresses an aesthetic idea, he holds that the artist must arrange the elements of the work in such a way that it engages our faculties in a free harmony and in doing so is able to express an idea. Aesthetic ideas are expressed by the formal arrangement of elements in a work. In this way, appreciating art (or nature) as expressing aesthetic ideas is consistent with Kant's claim that we should appreciate aesthetic objects as they engage the free harmony of the imagination and understanding. There is, however, disagreement between Kant scholars as to whether expression of idea is a necessary feature of aesthetic objects or merely contingent. I happen to believe Kant holds that expression of aesthetic ideas is necessary if for no other reason than to take seriously the quote from paragraph 51 that beauty should be defined as the expression of aesthetic ideas.

On the face of it, Kant's doctrine of beauty as expressive differs significantly of the popular 20th-century Expression Theory of Art. The more recent version of Expression theory deals almost exclusively with the notion that art expresses emotions. For example one might say that Edvard Munch's "The Scream" expresses the emotion of anxiety. Alternatively, Kant talks about a variety of objects or states of affairs about which we could have aesthetic ideas (God, despotic states, and so on). Nonetheless, there is room in Kant's account for emotions or at least character traits: We can see buildings as "majestic and stately" or "plains laughing and gay" (*KU* 5: 354). To claim that art (and nature) express emotions is at least compatible with Kant's account of beauty as the expression of ideas. Emotions, it may seem odd to say, would count as something beyond ordinary empirical inspection. This would be particularly true for Kant concerning other people's emotional states. While Kant seems to be able to count emotions as "ideas" able to be expressed by aesthetic objects, it is clear that the category of what can be "expressed" for Kant is much wider than the 20th-century doctrine of Expression Theory.

Another difference between Kant and the 20th-century doctrine of Expression is that on the more contemporary account it is thought that an artwork expresses an emotion of the artist.[8] For example, on this account "The Scream" expresses the emotion of angst that Munch has felt. Art expresses an artist's emotions. Expression Theory has been much criticized for this view. It does not seem necessary that an artist put his or her emotions into a work in order to express an emotion. Nor, does it seem required that when we appreciate an object like the "The Scream" that we should imagine the angst that the artist may have felt. On this score Kant seems on stronger ground. There is no requirement in Kant that in order to express any the idea of an emotion that the artist literally have the emotion. Instead, Kant gives an admittedly obscure account of how an artist comes to express an idea in an artwork. This is his account of "genius." Recall from earlier that in order to express any idea in Kant an object must be constructed in such a way that when properly appreciated it engages our cognitive faculties in a free harmony which is able to conjure to mind some idea. In the case of "The Scream" Munch is able to arrange the representation of a man on a bridge and choose specific colors and wavey lines all coming together to give us a sense of what angst is like. How Munch is able to do this, Kant would say, it is a bit of a mystery – such is the nature of genius. But again, it is quite clear that for Kant, it need not be the case that Munch is somehow getting his emotion into the painting or that we only properly appreciate the painting if we think we are sensing Munch's angst.

5.   Subjective Universal Validity

As we have already seen, Kant takes a unique position for the time concerning the evaluative status of aesthetic judgments of taste. For Kant aesthetic judgments are not merely subjective as judgments of the "agreeable" are. We say of the agreeable that they give us pleasure but with no further claim that our pleasure is anything but idiosyncratic to us. But neither are judgments of beauty objective judgments as are simple cognitive judgments like "this cat is yellow." Judgments of beauty are "aesthetic" in the sense that they are founded on pleasure. However, Kant is looking for some way to claim that an object gives me aesthetic pleasure and will (or ought to) give everyone else pleasure as well. Kant is looking for the source of a universal or necessary pleasure. Kant believes that he finds this with the quasi-cognitive mental state of the free harmony of the imagination and the understanding. So far as I know no contemporary has tried to justify the universality of a pleasure based upon our cognitive faculties. But this is not to say that Kant's general program of finding something universally pleasing in aesthetic experience is not of interest to contemporaries. There seems to be a fair amount of agreement that judgments of beauty are technically aesthetic judgments, that is to say they are judgments that the appreciation of an object gives the viewer a positive experience. But if we grant this and are opposed to any sort of subjectivism or relativism, then Kant's broad position has contemporary appeal.[9] And there are independent reasons why we would not want to be mere subjectivists or relativists. When we say that a certain object is aesthetically good (or bad) it seems that we are not merely expressing our personal preference or, for that matter, the preferences of a certain group or culture. The upshot here is that if we think that the basis of an aesthetic judgment of taste is a positive (pleasurable) experience and yet also believe that our aesthetic judgments are normative for others (i.e. we think that there are correct and incorrect aesthetic judgments), then Kant's general position that aesthetic judgments claim to be subjectively universal seems to be on solid ground. Of course, we can grant all of this while being skeptical of whether the source of the universal pleasure at the basis of an aesthetic judgment is a certain harmony of our cognitive faculties.

But Kant might want even more than the position that beauty is the source of a universal pleasure. Towards the very end of the *Critique* Kant makes a bold claim about the connection between beauty and morality.

> Now, I say, the beautiful is the symbol of the morally good, and also only in this respect (that of a relation that is natural to everyone, and that is also expected for everyone else as a duty) does it please with claim to the assent of everyone else.
>
> (*KU* 5: 353)

It is far from settled as to what exactly what Kant wants to do with the claim that beauty is the symbol of morality, or for that matter how he wishes to defend such a claim. However, the following is a plausible explanation. Kant seems to hold that it is not enough that aesthetic experience rests upon a pleasure, even a universal pleasure. It seems to be Kant's position that the foundation of beauty be a universal, *non-trivial*, pleasure. That is to say, it would be more than slightly embarrassing if Kant were to discover a universal pleasure at the foundation of our experience of beauty, but it was a pleasure that was simply less satisfying and less important to people than some, mere subjective pleasures. I believe that Kant's attempted link between aesthetic experience and morality is a way of solving a problem like this. Kant believes that he can say that aesthetic experience is a source of universal pleasure that is, in some way, important to our moral like.

Notes

1 As we shall see, Scruton puts forward a non-psychological version of disinterestedness.
2 See my paper "Dickie's Disinterest" (Rogerson 1987).
3 See my Rogerson (2008).
4 This interpretation of Kant is disputed by the likes of Crawford (1974), Guyer (1997) and Rogerson (2008).
5 See Zangwill (2001: 59–62).
6 See Zangwill (2001: 62–7).
7 See Guyer (1977: 63f.).
8 See Beardsley (1981: section 6).
9 See Zangwill (2014: section 1).

References

Baumgarten, A.G. (2007) *Aesthetica/Ästhetik*, D. Mirbach (ed.), vol. 2, Hamburg: Felix Meiner Verlag.
Beardsley, M. (1958/1981) *Aesthetics: Problems in the Philosophy of Criticism*, New York: Harcourt, Brace.
Bell, C. (1913) *Art*, London: Chatto and Windus.
Bullough, E. (1995 [1912]) "'Psychical Distance' as a Factor in Art and as an Aesthetic Principle," in A. Neill and A. Ridley (eds.), *The Philosophy of Art: Readings Ancient and Modern*, New York: McGraw-Hill.
Crawford, D. (1974) *Kant's Aesthetic Theory*, Madison: Wisconsin University Press.
Dickie, G. (1964) "The Myth of the Aesthetic Attitude," *American Philosophical Quarterly* 1: 56–65.
Fry, R. (1920) *Vision and Design*, London: Chatto and Windus.
Guyer, P. (1977) "Formalism and the Theory of Expression in Kant's Aesthetics," *Kant-Studien* 68(1): 46–70.
Guyer, P. (1997) *Kant and the Claims of Taste*, 2nd ed., Cambridge: Cambridge University Press.
Hume, D. (1965) *Of the Standard of Taste and Other Essays*, J.W. Lenz (ed.), New York and Indianapolis: Bobbs-Merrill.
Rogerson, K. (1987) "Dickie's Disinterest," *Philosophia* 17: 149–60.
Rogerson, K. (2008) *The Problem of Free Harmony in Kant's Aesthetics*, Albany: SUNY Press.
Scruton, R. (1974) *Art and Imagination*, London: Methuen.
Stolnitz, J. (1960) *Aesthetics and Philosophy of Art Criticism*, New York: Houghton Mifflin.

Zangwill, N. (2001) *The Metaphysics of Beauty*, Ithaca, NY: Cornell University Press.
Zangwill, N. (2014) "Aesthetic Judgment," in E.N. Zalta (ed.), *The Stanford Encyclopedia of Philosophy*, http://plato.stanford.edu/archives/fall2014/entries/aesthetic-judgment/.

Further Reading

H.E. Allison, *Kant Theory of Taste* (Cambridge: Cambridge University Press, 2001); P. Guyer, *Kant and the Claims of Taste* (Cambridge and London: Harvard University Press, 1979) are must reads for any serious scholar of Kant's aesthetic theory. Immodestly, I also recommend my own two monographs: *Kant's Aesthetics: The Roles of Form and Expression* (Lanham, MD, New York and London: University Press of America, 1986) and *The Problem of Free Harmony in Kant's Aesthetics* (Albany, NY: SUNY Press, 2008); J.H. Zammito, *The Genesis of Kant's Critique of Judgment* (Chicago and London: The University of Chicago Press, 1992) is a very useful historical guide to the third *Critique*. Finally, R. Wicks, *Kant on Judgment* (London and New York: Routledge, 2007) offers a rare section-by-section commentary on the third *Critique*.

45

CONTEMPORARY KANTIAN PHILOSOPHY OF SCIENCE

Katharina T. Kraus

★★★

1. Introduction

Deeply fascinated by the scientific developments of his own time, Kant is famous for his appraisal of Newtonian physics, which for him serves as a paradigm case for all sciences *properly* so-called.[1] Newtonian science is the exemplar upon which Kant models his own natural philosophy.[2] Some commentators even claim that Newtonian physics must be thought of as necessarily complementing Kant's Critical philosophy in general.[3] Yet the progress of science, such as the development of non-Euclidean mathematics, relativity theory, and quantum mechanics, has often been viewed as a challenge to some of Kant's core claims or even as a threat to the whole of his Critical philosophy. Despite these allegations, however, numerous philosophers have attempted to develop Kant's philosophy of science so as to reconcile it with the revolutionary findings of newly emerging research programmes in physics, biology, and psychology.[4]

This chapter explores the extent to which a Kantian approach to philosophy of science enables philosophical insights that are still relevant today. It will not defend Kant's specific theories of physics or of proper science against attacks launched on the basis of certain results of modern research programmes. Rather, it focuses on certain cognitive constraints that a Kantian approach places on science *in general*: namely the demand of systematicity, according to which nature is regarded as systematically unified and from which emerge regulative principles that guide our scientific endeavours. It will be suggested that a Kantian philosophy of science is a serious alternative to naturalistic theories of science, broadly construed as those theories that naturalise the relation between the cogniser and nature by fully reducing it to natural or scientific terms. As a result, the chapter outlines how a Kantian theory of science is able to acknowledge the diversity and autonomy of *particular* sciences.

Section 1 introduces Kant's account of systematicity, based on the Appendix to the Dialectic in the *Critique of Pure Reason* and on the two Introductions to the *Critique of the Power of Judgment*, and identifies the philosophical issue that it addresses, namely the underdetermination of our scientific view of the world. Section 2 reviews two main lines of interpretations. Against the prevailing methodological or heuristic reading, it is argued that the demand of systematicity – despite being

DOI: 10.4324/9781003406617-62

merely *regulative* (as opposed to being constitutive) – is for Kant a *transcendental* condition of *empirical* cognition *in general*, since it is a necessary condition of the very intelligibility of nature. Section 3 then discusses – in light of this reconstruction of Kant's view – its philosophical significance for a contemporary Kantian approach to philosophy of science. This discussion suggests that a Kantian approach is not only compatible with the modern sciences, but that it advances the debate about the foundational principles of the sciences by refusing to construe those principles in a naturalistic way.

2. The Principle of Systematicity and the Problem of Scientific Underdetermination

In his Critical philosophy, Kant draws a close connection between science and systematicity: science is a body of cognitions that are ordered in a systematic way. The clearest articulation of this view can be found in the following two passages – one from the Doctrine of Method in the *Critique of Pure Reason* and the other from the Preface of the *Metaphysical Foundations of Natural Science*:

> systematic unity is that which first makes ordinary cognition into science, i.e., makes a system out of a mere aggregate of it, [. . .] I understand by a system, however, the unity of the manifold cognitions under one idea.
>
> (A832/B861)

> Every doctrine that is supposed to be a system, that is, a whole of cognition ordered according to principles, is called a science.
>
> (*MAN* 4: 467)

A body of cognitions constitutes a system if it is ordered in accordance with principles. More precisely, for a body of cognitions to be a *rational* system, it is required that cognitions be ordered according to *rational* principles (see *MAN* 4: 467). Such rational principles fall within the scope of reason (*Vernunft*) or, more generally, of those faculties that deal with the deliverances of the understanding (*Verstand*), viz. cognitions.[5] Reason, according to one of its definitions, is specified as "the faculty of the unity of the rules of understanding under principles" (A302/B359). That is, reason does not directly relate to (or even determine) objects of experience, but "applies to the understanding": Reason defines the rules by which the understanding works so that our cognition reaches or approaches systematic unity (A302/B359). Kant claims further that it must – in some sense – be "presupposed" that the systematic completeness of all cognitions prescribed by reason "conforms to nature itself" (A653/B681) and hence "we simply have to presuppose the systematic unity of nature as objectively valid and necessary" (A651/B679). Kant thus moves from an *epistemic* claim about the systematic relations among our cognitions to a *metaphysical* claim about the unity of nature itself.

Two questions arise. Why should science pursue systematicity at all? And why should nature as such be assumed to be systematically unified? We find two strands of replies in Kant's Critical writings. On the one hand, the demand of systematicity is understood to be an integral part of Kant's Critical conception of reason, which first makes possible his distinctive conceptions of science and nature. On the other hand, the demand of systematicity is understood to be a useful or perhaps even necessary tool for the actual pursuit of the sciences to *get things right* with regard to nature itself. As will become clear in Section 3, much of the understanding of the principle of systematicity depends on which of the two strands is emphasised.

With regard to Kant's Critical philosophy in general, it can be seen from the very definition of nature why certain epistemic claims about cognition are closely – indeed conceptually and in this sense necessarily – related to metaphysical claims about nature. Nature is defined as the "sum total" of all possible objects of *our* experience, and the transcendental conditions of experience are shown to be at the same time the necessary conditions of possible objects of experience (see, e.g., B161–3). The understanding provides the "source of the laws of nature", insofar as it defines the rules according to which our sensible representations are to be combined in order to yield cognition of objects (A127). These rules are given through the categories, the pure concepts of the understanding, which define the conceptual forms of all experience through which we grasp objects in nature. In particular, the category of causality prescribes *a priori* to nature the principle that every change in nature must have a cause upon which it follows in accordance with a necessary rule or law (see A189/B232ff.). In order for us to be able to cognise an objective sequence of states in nature we must assume *a priori* that every (state of an) empirical object observable in time and space must have a lawful, causal connection to *some* other (state of an) empirical object. This transcendental principle of causality gives "formal unity" to nature; it serves as the "original ground of [nature's] necessary conformity to law" (B165). In other words, in cognising nature we must think of it as containing lawfully connected objects, giving rise to objective sequences of their states; for, otherwise, no experience of causal sequences would be possible. Kant's transcendental conception of nature thus implies the *formal* or *transcendental lawlikeness* of nature itself.[6]

Although this formal lawlikeness is a necessary condition of any causal experience and thus of any particular empirical law that we may find operative in nature, it is a rather weak kind of lawlikeness. It tells us neither (i) the *actual cause* of a particular effect we observe, nor (ii) which *particular empirical law* governs an observed causal sequence.[7] Moreover, it does not tell us whether (iii) nature – in its material sense as the sum total of empirically real phenomena – can *in fact* be represented through a *complete system of empirical laws*.[8] The formal lawlikeness determines *a priori* only *that* nature must display lawful connections, if the experience of causal relations in nature is to be possible at all. Yet, in turn, this means that there is an *underdetermination* (at least at the level of the categories) with respect to (i) the *actual cause* that determines a particular effect, (ii) the *particular empirical law of nature* (or *necessary* rule) according to which all similar effects must have similar causes, and (iii) the *complete system* of laws of nature. In the third *Critique*, Kant explicitly alerts us to the problem of underdetermination for (ii) empirical laws as follows:

> many modifications of the universal transcendental concepts of nature [. . .] are left undetermined by those laws that the pure understanding gives *a priori*, since these pertain only to the possibility of a nature (as object of the senses) in general, [. . .]. [T]here must nevertheless also be laws for [nature], which, as empirical, may seem to be contingent, in accordance with the insight of *our* understanding, but which, if they are to be called laws [. . .] must be regarded as necessary on a principle of the unity of the manifold, even if that principle is unknown to us.
> (*KU* 5: 179–80)[9]

The understanding's transcendental-formal principle of causality alone cannot guarantee that a particular natural law obtains or – a fortiori – that nature in its material meaning is really a unity that can be represented through a complete system of empirical laws. Even if Kant provides an argument for a formal principle of causality in the Second Analogy, this argument does not settle how to draw an *actual inductive* inference to an empirical law of nature, nor how to arrive at a complete system of empirical laws. Rather, Kant requires further arguments for the *empirical lawlikeness* of nature.[10] Neither the understanding nor the senses nor the combination of both, it seems, can deliver a complete account of nature and its laws, as we will see in Section 3.[11]

Kant is aware of the problem of underdetermination also in the context of scientific practice. First, scientists simply do not have a full description of nature through empirical laws at their disposal. Rather, every scientific field that deals with empirical reality lacks some knowledge of causes, laws, and full explanatory grounds.[12] Therefore, scientists require some guidance in how to derive further laws of nature. Secondly, every empirical law that scientists postulate remains under scrutiny and may be refuted by future empirical research.[13] The observed regularities may not be instances of the presumed necessary, lawful connection, but require some revision of the scientific concepts or of the laws assumed to be involved. Thirdly, the relationship between different scientific disciplines or between the domains governed by different, at times even opposing, empirical laws often remains unclear or even disputable.[14] It is often controversial whether a set of empirical laws (or even an entire discipline) can be reduced to a more general set of laws (or a more foundational discipline). For example, it is still a matter of debate today to what extent human psychology can be explained by appealing only to the physical-chemical processes observed in the human brain, rather than to laws of ethology or to genuine laws of psychology.

Kant acknowledges that in the worst case our observations of nature would not display the kind of uniformity that we need to grasp nature according to a well-defined set of laws. Rather, nature could remain "a raw chaotic aggregate" (*EEKU* 20: 209) such that we would have to discover infinitely many special empirical laws:

> one need only consider the magnitude of the task of making an interconnected experience out of given perceptions of a nature that in the worst case contains an infinite multiplicity of empirical laws.
>
> (*KU* 5: 184)

The need for addressing this problem of underdetermination can be seen as one of the reasons for Kant to supplement the cognition-constitutive principles of the understanding by introducing regulative principles of reason based on the idea of systematicity, according to which nature is merely regarded as a systematic whole such that our experience of nature can form a systematic unity of cognitions.[15] This idea is supposed to provide rules for finding particular empirical laws that are left undetermined by the understanding.

This demand for systematicity seems *prima facie* imposed upon nature "for the sake of *our* faculty of cognition, in order to make possible a system of experience in accordance with particular laws of nature" (*KU* 5: 184), yet without necessarily having an objective realisation in nature itself. Kant also calls it a subjective "interest of reason" (A648/B676). In its most general articulation, the idea of systematicity is specified as the "idea of the *maximum* of division and unification of the understanding's cognition in one principle" (A665/B693).[16] This idea is then explicated in terms of the principles of homogeneity, specification, and affinity, which are required to find relations among concepts (and subsequently among cognitions that correspond to certain objects in nature) in terms of genera and species and by assuming continuity between them. These principles also guide us in looking for higher, ever more general levels of description (e.g., unifying the description of electric and magnetic effects in a common theory of electromagnetism) and in distinguishing particulars in smaller degrees at ever more specific levels of description (e.g., finding more subspecies of plants).[17]

Central for the current discussion is the epistemic and the metaphysical status of these regulative principles of systematicity. On the one hand, Kant construes them as merely subjectively valid *maxims* of reason that guide the employment of the understanding without directly determining objects in nature. They only instruct our epistemic enquiries in searching for further pieces of experience and acquiring a more comprehensive insight into nature and may thus be understood as *principles of discovery*. On the other hand, Kant attributes "objective, but indeterminate validity" (A663/B691) to the idea of systematicity: only if systematicity is assumed to "pertain to nature itself" can the regulative principles of reason be used to supply a "mark of empirical truth" (A651/ B679) or the "touchstone of truth" (A647/B675) for our cognitions and thus serve as *principles of justification*. These two characterisations produce an interpretative conflict: If systematicity is viewed as a merely subjective maxim that is heuristically conducive, but not strictly necessary for cognition, then reason could not be an indispensably necessary arbiter of the "empirical truth" of a cognition. But if systematicity is viewed as an objectively valid principle to which, however, nothing in nature corresponds, then reason might introduce an idealistic moment into our cognition of nature that contradicts Kant's empirical realism (and which may lead precisely to the rationalist conception of nature that Kant criticises in the Antinomies).[18] In what follows, I explore how each of the two major lines of interpretation attempts to resolve this interpretive difficulty.

3. Systematicity: Regulative Principle *and* Transcendental Condition?

With his seminal contribution (Buchdahl 1969) to the study of Kant's philosophy of science, Gerd Buchdahl highlighted the central role of systematicity for acquiring scientific insight. Since then, two major lines of interpretation have developed: a *methodological interpretation* that stresses the heuristic, hypothetical and subjective character of systematicity, and a *transcendental interpretation* that emphasises its (indeterminately) objective, necessary and truth-relevant character.

According to the methodological interpretation, the demand of systematicity is considered as a "heuristic" tool guiding us in looking for further cognition.[19] Considering all cognitions as systematically connected aids us in discovering and articulating further cognitions and empirical laws within a systematic taxonomy of concepts and cognitions (e.g., Kepler's laws of celestial motions can be subsumed under Newton's laws of motion). For Grier, reason must avail itself of the idea of systematicity, in order to "consider a disparate set of phenomena as ideally unified", rather than really unified (Grier 2001: 298). This interpretation sees the primary role of systematicity in the context of scientific "discovery and articulation of empirical laws" (Grier 1997: 22). The unity of nature is "projected" by reason to fulfil its subjective "demand for the systematic unity of thought" (Grier 1997: 20). The unity itself is only "hypothetical in character" and remains a subjective *illusion* or *fiction* without corresponding to anything real (Grier 1997: 22, see also Grier 2001: 300). In this sense, the principle of systematicity provides a subjectively useful method for ordering cognitions, but does not have any objective bearing upon their contents.

Kitcher also pursues a methodological reading. For him, systematicity is a methodological principle that defines the "ideal limit of inquiry", which is conducive to achieve scientific progress (Kitcher 1986: 214). What counts as a causal law can be understood only against the background of a system that would emerge from an ideally extended inquiry, the outcome of which finally defines truth.[20] The demand of systematicity thus provides only a framing condition for our minds to recognise explanatory patterns and dependencies between different real phenomena.[21] Similarly, Sturm (2009: 153–62) argues that in order for scientists to be able to find and corroborate empirical laws, these laws must be understood within a structured order of concepts and cognitions, even though such an order is only projected and subject to further revisions.

The methodological reading is supported by passages in which Kant characterises reason as supplying

> only a heuristic [. . .] concept, as it shows not how a concept is constituted but how, under the guidance of that concept, we ought to seek after the constitution and connection of objects of experience.

> (A671/B699, also A663/B691)

In the *third* Critique, the principle of systematicity is characterised as "a subjectively necessary transcendental *presupposition*" (*EEKU* 20: 209, see also *KU* 5: 181) and associated with the reflective power of judgment. It is, therefore, often understood as defining the way in which subjects like us must reflect upon nature, without asserting that nature is *in fact* a unity.[22]

Hence, the methodological reading can elegantly make sense of systematicity as a merely regulative principle, rather than a constitutive claim about nature itself. It resolves the interpretive difficulty mentioned earlier by downplaying the role of reason as the objectively valid arbiter of empirical truth for cognition in general. The truth-promoting function of reason is understood only in terms of a meta-principle that facilitates higher-order scientific theorising and progress towards a more comprehensive scientific picture of the world.

Yet the methodological reading struggles with accommodating those passages in which Kant emphasises the principle's "indispensably necessary" use (A644/B672) and its "objective, but indeterminate validity" (A663/B691), as well as those passages in which he even rejects viewing it "merely as a methodological device" (A661/B689). Although this reading is the prevailing interpretation, there is an alternative line of interpretation available, paying particular attention to the principle's being a "transcendental presupposition" (A651/B679, A678/B706; *EEKU* 20: 209) or a "transcendental principle" (A650/B678, A663/B691; *KU* 5: 181).

The main idea of a transcendental reading is that the demand of systematicity is a *necessary condition* of *empirical* cognition *in general*, namely insofar as the objects of our experience only become *intelligible* to us if we can make sense of them as parts of a systematisable whole, viz. nature. Only then can these objects be conceptualisable (and hence cognisable) according to a system of concepts (and, respectively, of cognitions). So understood, the principle of systematicity not only implies that, at the higher-order level of science, empirical laws and scientific theories ought to be put into a systematic order, but also implies that, at the more basic levels, nature as such must be assumed to fit our efforts for empirical conceptualisation and hence cognition. Systematicity is thus a transcendental, though regulative, condition of empirical cognition in general: it must be presupposed, if we are to be able to find adequate empirical concepts for *all* objects we encounter in nature (see *KU* 5: 211).[23]

Although Buchdahl is often viewed as a proponent of the methodological reading, having first highlighted the central role of regulative principles for Kant's philosophy of science, this classification might be short-sighted.[24] Buchdahl (1969) does put most of his emphasis on the methodological import of systematicity for the discovery of scientific theories, but he also develops a substantial interpretation of the interaction between reason and the understanding, which shows marks of a transcendental reading. He argues that reason's idea of systematicity must supplement the understanding's principle of causality in order to account for the "empirical lawlikeness" of nature (Buchdahl 1967: 214). He conceives of reason as contributing to the procedural realisation of the *a priori* principles of the understanding, thereby providing rules for specifying those aspects of cognition that are left contingent or undetermined from the perspective of the understanding (Buchdahl 1992). A full employment of the understanding, and thus a full exploration of empirical reality, can only be accomplished through the involvement of reason.[25] Reason's regulative principles are thus necessary ingredients for Kant's empirical realism (esp. Buchdahl 1992: 245–87).

Further versions of the transcendental interpretation have been advocated more recently. Geiger (2003, 2009) frames it in terms of a meaning-enabling function of reason in the acquisition of empirical concepts: the idea of systematicity is a "necessary condition of the very meaningfulness of empirical concepts" (Geiger 2003: 285). Only by finding its place within a systematic network of concepts can a newly acquired empirical concept be used to refer to an object given in experience. The idea is transcendental because it first enables the formation of empirical concepts whose contents are determined through their "conceptual relations within a systematic whole of concepts" (Geiger 2003: 290). Nonetheless, it is also only regulative, since such a system can never be completed, but must be assumed as a guideline for all empirical enquiries.[26]

Abela (2006) emphasises the justificatory role that the demand of systematicity plays in the acquisition of empirical knowledge, insofar as it "suppl[ies] an empirical criterion for truth-conditional judgments" (Abela 2006: 409). While the understanding provides formal conditions that any truth-apt judgment must fulfil, reason offers "discriminating-conditions" according to which empirical criteria of truth can be found on the basis of considerations of coherence and systematicity (Abela 2006: 421–2).[27] Sturm's account shows signs of the transcendental reading insofar as, for him, the demand of systematicity also provides *criteria* or *standards* for the acceptability of scientific explanations (Sturm 2009: 156, 160–1, 176–9).

More recently, perspectivalist and contextualist readings have been proposed that combine the meaning-enabling and justificatory roles of reason. According to Massimi's (2017) perspectivalist reading, reason "makes possible a perspectival systematic space of reason for the correct use of the understanding" (Massimi 2017: 76). Such a space is necessary to confer "universality and unanimity" to *our* scientific knowledge claims, which nonetheless remain confined to the distinctive human perspective (Massimi 2017: 78–9).[28] Kraus (2020) has developed a reading of reason as "generating contexts of intelligibility" (Kraus 2020: 194ff.), within which the understanding can properly operate, generate truth-apt judgments of objects, and approximate the goal of scientific inquiry, which for Kant is the pursuit of truth as the "agreement with the object" (A821/B849). The details of this view will become relevant in the last section.

Without being able to settle this debate within the limited space of this chapter, I would like to point out what I take to be the crucial advantage of the transcendental reading over the methodological one. And this brings us back to the issue of underdetermination discussed earlier. On the methodological reading, reason offers a helpful heuristic maxim to deal with the underdetermination of empirical laws and empirical concepts that the employment of the understanding leaves us with. Nonetheless, on this reading, it is possible to acquire single instances of empirical cognition without employing the principle of systematicity. In consequence, we could have experience of a single object subsumed under an empirical concept, without being able to infer other empirical cognitions from it or to further analyse it in conceptual terms. Suppose we have the experience of a tree, without being able to relate it to any other concepts, such as "leaves", "branches", "stem", or "roots". The determination of this experience would then have to be sufficiently accomplished by sensibility (in combination with the formal principles of the understanding). Yet this account of experience involves an empiricist assumption, since it implies that it is possible to read off the defining marks of an empirical concept directly from the representations yielded by our senses. Similarly, suppose that in a single cognition we discovered the cause C of some particular effect E that we have observed, which, however, bears no systematic relation to any other cause we have observed so far. In order for the discovery of a single cause C to be possible, it must be possible for us to read off the empirical fact that C is the actual cause of E directly from our sensation. The gap between transcendental principles and empirical cognitions left by the understanding would have to be filled by sensibility.[29]

The methodological reading could accept this empiricist leaning, but then would have to assume – in order to avoid scepticism about empirical lawlikeness – that sensibility yields direct insight into particular empirical causes and hence into particular governing empirical laws of nature. This, however, implies that nature, as it exists out there and independently of the mind, must be assumed – in a strong, constitutive sense – to display the systematic connections that are graspable by our cognitive faculties. But this would turn Kant's account of nature into a sort of transcendental realism. Hence, the methodological reading of systematicity does not find an adequate answer to the problem of underdetermination.

By contrast, the transcendental reading reflects Kant's basic insight that *our* concept of nature crucially depends on *our* cognitive faculties (regardless of nature's mind-independent features). The principle that we must view nature as a unified system is a demand of our reason, but at the same time it necessarily completes the account of empirical cognition and answers a need that is left unanswered by the understanding.[30] The principle defines an additional *transcendental* condition of cognition in general, namely a necessary condition of the *intelligibility* of experience. The principle of systematicity imposes a condition on nature as a whole, understood as the totality of objects of possible experience, rather than on single objects: only if we live in such a nature that conforms to this condition can it be intelligible for our faculties of cognition at all; only then can all the objects that we possibly experience be conceptualisable and cognisiable in truth-apt judgments. Only then can we develop "marks" or "touchstones" for *empirical* truth in an ongoing process of scientific research: we accept as true only those empirical cognitions or laws of nature that can be made sense of within a system of cognitions or laws, whose *empirical* aspects remain under scrutiny. Hence, even though the principle of systematicity is *subjectively* demanded by *our* reason, it can now also be seen as an *objectively* but indeterminately valid presupposition with regard to nature itself: only under this presupposition, which remains theoretically unprovable and therefore without determative force with respect to nature as a whole, does it make sense for us to proceed with our scientific investigations of objects in nature. It might be best understood as a *practical* presupposition that is indispensably necessary for the practice of science to be an intelligible endeavour, even though we can never definitely *know* whether nature is actually intelligible. In the final section, I outline a Kantian philosophy of science based on this transcendental conception of nature that could serve as an important alternative to naturalistic philosophies of science.

4. A Kantian Philosophy of Science: The Diversity and Autonomy of the Sciences

Much of today's philosophy of science is underwritten by a naturalistic presumption according to which the relationship between the cogniser and the cognised object can be explained in purely scientific (or, more broadly, natural) terms. Depending on the scientific discipline one takes to be most fundamental with respect to this relationship, one adopts different views.[31] For example, evolutionary theory takes the epistemic relationship to be the outcome of a historical process of natural selection vis-à-vis our cognitive capacities, while neuroscience accounts for it in terms of the physiological processes of the brain and the peripheral nervous system in interaction with the environment. It is common to all these naturalistic approaches that they must presuppose the explanatory priority of a specific scientific theory over a general theory about the mind's representational capacities. That is, they must view the entities postulated by a specific scientific theory as more fundamental than our basic capacity for thought and cognition.[32] Yet these naturalistic explanatory frameworks cannot justify our fundamental entitlement to think of nature as being intelligible at all, since none of their explanations can do without the presupposition of nature's intelligibility.

Unlike naturalistic philosophies of science, a Kantian approach does not presuppose the primacy of a specific scientific theory, such as evolutionary theory or neuroscience, but rather takes our basic capacity for representation to be fundamental.[33] It carves out the basic conditions that must obtain between nature and our cognitive faculties in order for us to be able to examine nature at all, one condition being that nature is assumed to be lawful and systematic. The unity of nature is not a fact that can be discovered from empirical observations or derived from the laws of logic. Rather, it is a necessary and regulative principle that scientists must assume in order to be able to make sense of the diversity of empirical reality in a lawful way. The basic question as to why we are entitled to make the assumption that nature fits our cognitive faculties is primarily a question about the *very concept* of nature and as such defies naturalisation. This question cannot be sufficiently answered in scientific terms or by empirical inquiry, but this very concept must already be presupposed in the acquisition of any specific scientific terms and theories.

A Kantian approach to philosophy of science, I finally propose, offers an attractive account of the diversity of the sciences and their relative but irreducible autonomy. Following the transcendental interpretation, my preceding considerations suggest that the demand for systematicity is by no means confined to the so-called improper sciences, such as biology and psychology, that is, those sciences that are less amenable to a strictly scientific methodology including mathematisation, nomological description, and experimental reproducibility. Even the "proper" sciences, such as physics, require principles of systematicity in order for their empirical concepts and laws to have sense and meaning.[34] By defining a science in general as "a system, [i.e., . . .] the unity of the manifold cognitions *under one idea*" (A832/B861, emphasis added), Kant provides a goal-directed account of science, according to which each science is based on a distinctive guiding idea of reason.

According to Kraus's (2020) contextualist reading of reason, the guiding idea of a science can be understood to "generate[] a context of intelligibility" within which we can first make sense of an experience as a "certain *kind of cognition*" and determine through it objects that are available in the corresponding "domain of nature" and that hence belong to the subject matter of the corresponding science (Kraus 2020: 206).[35] By generating such a context of intelligibility, we acquire not only an outline of the whole domain, but also a specific set of procedural rules that normatively guide us in achieving, or at least approximating, the goal of scientific inquiry: that is, *getting things right* within that particular domain. For each specific science, reason's general demand for systematicity is thus exemplified through discipline-specific rules that guide the more basic conceptualising and cognising activities in empirical research within the discipline-specific domain of nature.

If this account is correct, then even the mathematical and physical sciences are based on domain-defining ideas that normatively guide research in these sciences. Newtonian physics is, for example, based on the idea of absolute physical space (see *MAN* 4: 558), which outlines the domain within which the laws of Newtonian mechanics can be applied to determine physico-material objects. In biology the idea of natural purposiveness (see *KU*, §§73–4) delineates the domain of organic-living nature and is, moreover, needed to make sense of a "heap" of matter as a living being, the parts of which can then be described in terms of physico-chemical processes.[36] In psychology the idea of the soul delineates the domain of psychological reality and is, moreover, needed to make sense of a "bundle" of mental states (and corresponding behavioural states) as belonging to a trans-temporally unified person.[37]

Hence, each science requires a specific idea that outlines its distinctive domain of nature as an *irreducible whole* that must be assumed to be *intelligible* in order for scientists to determine discipline-specific objects within that domain at all (e.g., physico-material objects, organisms, persons). In those sciences in which mathematisation and nomological description have further progressed, the domain and its objects can be exclusively described by domain-specific efficient-causal laws (e.g., Newtonian physics). In less developed sciences the discipline-specific principles of systematicity are particularly important in first making out the proper objects of scientific inquiry (e.g., biology, psychology).[38] While scientists still aim to find mechanical, efficient-causal explanations for all natural phenomena, they can first begin with this task once they have contextualised the phenomenon to be explained within an adequate context of intelligibility, as generated by a discipline-specific idea (e.g., by adopting the corresponding system of scientific concepts).[39]

One important merit of the Kantian approach to philosophy of science developed in this chapter is the way that it allows for acknowledging the continuity between the "proper" sciences, such as physics, and the "improper" sciences, such as biology and psychology, without succumbing to the route of mechanistic reduction. Both require principles of systematicity in order to confer meaning to a conceptual description of nature. In addition to the ubiquitous principle of efficient causality, the Kantian approach justifies the use of goal-directed (or teleological) descriptions, which today is often called top-down (or downward) causation, as a legitimate method that is necessary to proceed further towards an objective grasp of nature – a grasp that is both increasingly unified and increasingly specified, despite always remaining confined to our distinctive human perspective.[40] Understanding the demand of systematicity as a necessary condition of the intelligibility of nature *within the human perspective*, as sketched here, highlights the fundamental relationship between the *human* scientists and their distinctive objects of scientific inquiry.[41] The Kantian approach thus presents a serious alternative to naturalistic and reductionist theories of science.[42]

Notes

1 See *MAN* (4: 469).
2 Falkenburg (2020).
3 Friedman (1992, 2013).
4 The Neo-Kantian philosophers further developed Kant's philosophy of science, trying to reconcile it with the scientific findings in mathematics (Cohen 1883), physics (Cassirer 1923), and experimental psychology (Natorp 1912). For a survey on Kant's relevance for science in the nineteenth century, see Friedman & Nordman (2006).
5 In the third *Critique*, Kant introduces the reflective power of judgment to complete the task of systematization, initially attributed to reason in the first *Critique*. On the relationship between reason (in its regulative use) and reflective judgment, see Guyer 1990a. While the chapter focuses mainly on the first *Critique*, it indicates further developments of Kant's view in the third *Critique*.
6 Buchdahl (1967: 214, 1971: 24–5) introduces the notion of "transcendental lawlikeness" [*Gesetzmäßigkeit*] to denote the sort of "lawlikeness" that is already conceptually contained in Kant's notion of nature based on the transcendental principles of the understanding, especially that of causality.
7 For example: "empirical laws as such, can by no means derive their origin from the pure understanding" (A127); "Particular laws, because they concern empirically determined appearances, cannot be completely derived from the categories" (B165).
8 Kant distinguishes between "*natura formaliter spectata*" – nature viewed with respect to the formal principles that make nature and our experience thereof possible – and "*natura materialiter spectata*" – nature viewed as "the sum total of all appearances, insofar as those are in thoroughgoing connection through an inner principle of causality", i.e., the real "things of nature" (B163, A418–419/B446, see also *MAN* 4: 467).
9 See also: "The actions of the understanding, however, apart from the schemata of sensibility, are *undetermined*" (A664–5/B692–3), as well as O'Shea (1997) and Abela (2006). On the problem of underdetermination in the third *Critique*, see Zuckert (2007: 31–61).
10 Buchdahl (1967: 214, 1971, 25) distinguishes between "transcendental lawlikeness", which determines the formal notion of nature ("*natura formaliter spectata*") based on the principles of the understanding, and "empirical lawlikeness" of nature, which determines the material notion of nature ("*natura materialiter spectata*") based on additional principles of systematicity demanded by reason (see fn. 8).
11 There is an on-going debate regarding Kant's account of empirical laws (see Massimi and Breitenbach 2017, Watkins 2019). The main positions are (1) the *Derivation account*, according to which necessity can only be "injected" into or conferred by the transcendental principles of the understanding (Friedman 1992: 2013); on this account, the laws of physics, in particular mechanics, are the only laws that can be deductively derived; (2) the *Best-system account*, according to which the necessity of empirical laws is the result of an ideal unlimited process of inquiry (Kitcher 1986); (3) the *Necessitarian account*, according to which necessity is "built into the nature of things" in terms of their natural causal powers (Messina 2017); and (4) the *Reason-based account,* according to which reason provides – with its principles of systematicity – an additional *transcendental* conditions of "empirical lawlikeness" (Buchdahl 1969: 651ff., Buchdahl 1971, O'Shea 1997).

12 See Kant's discussion of incomplete theories held by scientists and philosophers in *Thoughts on the true estimation of living forces* (GSK), and *What real progress has metaphysics made in Germany since the time of Leibniz and Wolff?* (*FM* 20: 326–7).

13 See Kant's discussion of various errors committed by scientists and philosophers in *GSK* and *FM* (20: 326–7).

14 See Kant's discussion of the development of a science (A832/B860–A835/B863) and of the proper "place" of empirical psychology within the system of the sciences (A848/B876).

15 *A priori* concepts of reason are called "ideas" (see A310/B366ff.). On the distinction between constitutive and regulative principles, see A647/B675. In the third *Critique*, Kant focuses on the principle of purposiveness, see Ch. 37 (Biology), Ginsborg (2006, 2017), Zuckert (2007), and Breitenbach (2014, 2017).

16 Like a category of the understanding, an idea of reason is explicated by a corresponding "schema of reason" (A665/B693), which "contains the outline (*monogramma*) and the division of the whole into members in conformity with the idea, i.e. *a priori*" (A833/B861). See Kraus (2020: 202–6).

17 See A652/B680–A668/B696; *KU* (5: 185–186). See Watkins (2019: 212–23).

18 On the antonomies, see Falkenburg (2020).

19 E.g., Vaihinger (1911), Kitcher (1986, 1994), Guyer (1990b), Grier (1997, 2001).

20 Kitcher assumes that Kant holds a coherence, rather than a correspondence, theory of (scientific) truth. But note that for Kant truth is the "correspondence of cognition with its object" (A58/B82).

21 Kitcher's interpretation of Kant here reminds us of his own view of scientific progress (cf. Kitcher 1994).

22 E.g., Guyer (1990a), Zuckert (2007: esp. 41–52) takes the principle to be subjectively necessary for empirical concept formation.

23 Ginsborg (2006: 466) and Zuckert (2007: esp. 41–61) articulate this idea most clearly with regard to the principle of purposiveness.

24 Abela (2006) sees Buchdahl as a major proponent of the methodological reading; see also O'Shea (1997).

25 Allison (2004: 423–48), too, reads the idea of systematicity as a "transcendental condition" of experience insofar as it is "indispensable for the proper functioning of the understanding" (Allison 2004: 432).

26 Ginsborg offers a weaker version, construing the principle of systematicity as a "thin" normative constraint of the "activity of empirical conceptualization *überhaupt*" (Ginsborg 2017: 72). Based on her account of reflective judgment, she argues that conceptualization must be guided by the presupposition of a "normative fit between nature and our judging of it" (Ginsborg 2017: 77).

27 Similarly, O'Shea (1997).

28 See also Zuckert (2020).

29 In a similar vein, Geiger (2003: 287–91) and Abela (2006: 416–17) detect an empiricist bias with the methodological reading.

30 See O'Shea (1997) on the harmonic relation between reason's interests and the understanding's needs.

31 See also current attempts to naturalize epistemology and our mental capacities, e.g., Dretske (1995), Kornblith (2014).

32 Ginsborg (2006: 467) points out this prioritization in her discussion of teleosemantic accounts of cognition.

33 For a comparison of Kantian approaches with contemporary naturalistic approaches to the principle of teleology, see Ginsborg (2006), Breitenbach (2009, 2017) and Ch. 23.

34 On "proper" science, see Van den Berg (2014).

35 Sturm (2009: 127–82) offers a detailed account of how ideas delineate scientific domains. See also Zuckert (2017).

36 Breitenbach (2009, 2014) has pioneered a transcendental reading of Kant's conception of living nature and of biology based on the idea of purposiveness. See also Ch. 37 in this volume.

37 See Kraus (2018); on the conceptualization of psychological phenomena, see also Kraus (2020: 231–40).

38 On the use of regulative ideas in chemistry, see McNulty (2015).

39 On the plurality of the sciences see Breitenbach and Choi (2017). For Breitenbach (2017: 250–4), the principle of purposiveness first makes possible a conception of scientific research as a goal-directed activity. On Kant's anti-naturalism and the importance of teleology for science in general, see Falkenburg (2020: 231–42).

40 The epistemic status of top-down causation is a recurring issue in contemporary philosophy of science, which is also central to discussions about the possibility of reduction and emergence within and across scientific disciplines. For a contemporary discussion see Ellis *et al.* (2012). For a contemporary argument against intertheoretic reductionism in neuroscience, see Craver (2005). Craver and Bechtel (2007) offer an argument for the assumption of top-down (or final) causation in neuroscience, without accepting top-down (or final) causes as explanatory causes. Scientific explanations must still appeal to mechanic or efficient causes.

41 Massimi (2018) develops a Kantian perspectivist account of science, highlighting its potential to explain (and ultimately resolve) cases of scientific disagreement.

42 For helpful comments on earlier drafts of the chapter, I thank Alix Cohen, Ido Geiger, Nick Jardine, Sasha Mudd, and Aaron Wells, as well as audience members at the Annual Conference of the UK Kant Society in Southampton in 2016 and at the Colloquium of the History and Philosophy of Science Program at the University of Notre Dame in 2017.

References

Abela, P. (2006) "The Demands of Systematicity: Rational Judgment and the Structure of Nature," in G. Bird (ed.), *A Companion to Kant*, Oxford: Blackwell, pp. 408–22.

Allison, H. (2004) *Kant's Transcendental Idealism*, 2nd ed., New Haven: Yale University Press.

Breitenbach, A. (2009) "Teleology in Biology: A Kantian Approach," *Kant Yearbook* 1: 31–56.

Breitenbach, A. (2014) "Biological Purposiveness and Analogical Reflection," in I. Goy and E. Watkins (eds.), *Kant's Theory of Biology*, Berlin and New York: Walter de Gruyter, pp. 131–48.

Breitenbach, A. (2017) "Laws in Biology and the Unity of Nature," in M. Massimi and A. Breitenbach (eds.), *Kant and the Laws of Nature*, Cambridge: Cambridge University Press, pp. 237–55.

Breitenbach, A. and Choi, Y. (2017) "Pluralism and the Unity of Science," *The Monist* 100(3): 391–405.

Buchdahl, G. (1967) "The Relation Between 'Understanding' and 'Reason'," *Proceedings of the Aristotelian Society* 67: 209–26.

Buchdahl, G. (1969) *Metaphysics and the Philosophy of Science: The Classical Origins – Descartes to Kant*, Oxford: Blackwell.

Buchdahl, G. (1971) "The Conception of Lawlikeness in Kant's Philosophy of Science," *Synthese* 23: 24–46.

Buchdahl, G. (1992) *Kant and the Dynamics of Reason: Essays on the Structure of Kant's Philosophy*, Oxford: Blackwell.

Cassirer, E. (1923) *Substance and Function, and Einstein's Theory of Relativity*, Chicago and London: Open Court.

Cohen, H. (1883) *Das Prinzip der Infinitesimalmethode und seine Geschichte: Ein Kapitel zur Grundlegung der Erkenntnisskritik*, Berlin: Dümmler.

Craver, C. (2005) "Beyond Reduction: Mechanism, Multifield Integration and the Unity of Neuroscience," *Studies in History and Philosophy of Science* 36: 373–95.

Craver, C. and Bechtel, W. (2007) "Top-Down Causation Without Top-Down Causes," *Biology and Philosophy* 22: 547–63.

Dretske, F. (1995) *Naturalizing the Mind*, Cambridge, MA: MIT Press.

Ellis, G., Noble, D. and O'Connor, T. (2012) "Top-Down Causation," *Interface Focus* 2: 1–140.

Falkenburg, B. (2020) *Kant's Cosmology. From the Pre-Critical System to the Antinomy of Pure Reason*, Berlin: Springer.

Friedman, M. (1992) *Kant and the Exact Sciences*, Cambridge, MA: Harvard University Press.

Friedman, M. (2013) *Kant's Construction of Nature: A Reading of the Metaphysical Foundations of Natural Science*, Cambridge: Cambridge University Press.

Friedman, M. and Nordmann, A. (2006) *The Kantian Legacy in Nineteenth-century Science*, Cambridge, MA: MIT Press.

Geiger, I. (2003) "Is the Assumption of a Systematic Whole of Empirical Concepts a Necessary Condition of Knowledge?" *Kant-Studien* 94: 273–98.

Geiger, I. (2009) "Is Teleological Judgment (Still) Necessary? Kant's Arguments in the Analytic and in the Dialectic of Teleological Judgment," *British Journal for the History of Philosophy* 17: 533–66.

Ginsborg, H. (2006) "Kant's Biological Teleology and Its Philosophical Significance," in G. Bird (ed.), *A Companion to Kant*, Oxford: Blackwell, pp. 455–69.

Ginsborg, H. (2017) "Why Must We Presuppose the Systematicity of Nature?" in M. Massimi and A. Breitenbach (eds.), *Kant and the Laws of Nature*, Cambridge: Cambridge University Press, pp. 71–88.

Grier, M. (1997) "Kant on the Illusion of a Systematic Unity of Knowledge," *History of Philosophy Quarterly* 14: 1–28.

Grier, M. (2001) *Kant's Doctrine of Transcendental Illusion*, Cambridge: Cambridge University Press.

Guyer, P. (1990a) "Reason and Reflective Judgment: Kant on the Significance of Systematicity," *Noûs* 24: 17–43.

Guyer, P. (1990b) "Kant's Conception of Empirical Law," *Aristotelian Society Supplementary Volume* 64: 221–42.

Kitcher, P. (1986) "Projecting the Order of Nature," in R. Butts (ed.), *Kant's Philosophy of Science*, Dordrecht: Reidel, pp. 201–33.

Kitcher, P. (1994) "The Unity of Science and Nature," in P. Parrini (ed.), *Kant and Contemporary Epistemology*, Dordrecht: Kluwer Academic, pp. 253–72.

Kornblith, H. (2014) *A Naturalistic Epistemology: Selected Papers*, Oxford: Oxford University Press.

Kraus, K. (2018) "The Soul as the 'Guiding Idea' of Psychology: Kant on Scientific Psychology, Systematicity, and the Idea of the Soul," *Studies in History and Philosophy of Science* 71: 77–88.

Kraus, K. (2020) *Kant on Self-Knowledge and Self-Formation: The Nature of Inner Experience*, Cambridge: Cambridge University Press.

Massimi, M. (2017) "What Is This Thing Called 'Scientific Knowledge'? Kant on Imaginary Standpoints and the Regulative Role of Reason," *Kant Yearbook* 9: 63–83.

Massimi, M. (2018) "Points of View: Kant on Perspectival Knowledge," *Synthese* Special Issue on *The Current Relevance of Kant's Method in Philosophy*. doi: 10.1007/s11229-018-1876-7.

Massimi, M. and Breitenbach, A. (eds.) (2017) *Kant and the Laws of Nature*, Cambridge: Cambridge University Press.

McNulty, M.B. (2015) "Rehabilitating the Regulative Use of Reason: Kant on Empirical and Chemical Laws," *Studies in History and Philosophy of Science (Part A)* 54: 1–10.

Messina, J. (2017) "Kant's Necessitation Account of Laws and the Nature of Natures," in M. Massimi and A. Breitenbach (eds.), *Kant and the Laws of Nature*, Cambridge: Cambridge University Press, pp. 131–49.

Natorp, P. (1912) *Die allgemeine Psychologie nach kritischer Methode*, Tübingen: Siebeck.

O'Shea, J. (1997) "The Needs of the Understanding: Kant on Empirical Laws and Regulative Ideals," *International Journal of Philosophical Studies* 5: 216–54.

Sturm, T. (2009) *Kant und die Wissenschaften vom Menschen*, Paderborn: Mentis.

Vaihinger, H. (1911) *Die Philosophie des Als Ob. System der theoretischen, praktischen und religiösen Fiktionen der Menschheit auf Grund eines idealistischen Positivismus. Mit einem Anhang über Kant und Nietzsche*, Berlin: Reuther & Reichard.

Van den Berg, H. (2014) *Kant on Proper Science*, Dordrecht: Springer.

Watkins, E. (2019) *Kant on Laws*, Cambridge: Cambridge University Press.

Zuckert, R. (2007) *Kant on Beauty and Biology: An Interpretation of the* 'Critique of Judgment', Cambridge: Cambridge University Press.

Zuckert, R. (2017) "Empirical Scientific Investigation and the Ideas of Reason," in M. Massimi and A. Breitenbach (eds.), *Kant and the Laws of Nature*, Cambridge: Cambridge University Press, pp. 89–107.

Zuckert, R. (2020) "Attempting to Exit the Human Perspective: A Priori Experimentation in Kant's *Critique of Pure Reason*," in A.-M. Crețu and M. Massimi (eds.), *Knowledge from a Human Point of View*, Berlin: Springer.

Further reading

G. Buchdahl, *Metaphysics and the Philosophy of Science: The Classical Origins – Descartes to Kant* (Oxford: Basil Blackwell, 1969) is a classic introduction to philosophy of science in the early modern period, offering a detailed interpretation of Kant's philosophy of science. B. Falkenburg, *Kant's Cosmology. From the Pre-Critical System to the Antinomy of Pure Reason* (Berlin: Springer, 2020) provides a comprehensive account of Kant's metaphysics of nature, as it develops from the 1750's to the Critical turn in 1781. M. Friedman, *Kant's Construction of Nature: A Reading of the Metaphysical Foundations of Natural Science* (Cambridge: Cambridge University Press, 2013) offers a detailed interpretation of Kant's *Metaphysical Foundations of Natural Science*. M. Massimi and A. Breitenbach (eds.), *Kant and the Laws of Nature* (Cambridge: Cambridge University Press, 2017) assembles a set of articles on Kant's account of laws of nature in different scientific disciplines. H. Van den Berg, *Kant on Proper Science* (Dordrecht: Springer, 2014) provides an illuminating account of Kant's conception of proper science. E. Watkins (ed.), *Kant and the Sciences* (Oxford: Oxford University Press, 2001) assembles a set of articles on Kant's accounts of various scientific disciplines. E. Watkins, *Kant on Laws* (Cambridge: Cambridge University Press, 2019) offers a comprehensive study of the notion of law as it is employed in Kant's theoretical and practical philosophy, concerning both science and morality.

INDEX

Waismann, F. 64
Waxman, Wayne 4, 44–54
Weinrib, Ernest 551
Weisskopf, T. 489
Weltkenntnis 376–7, 379, 383
Westphal, Kenneth 4, 94–105
Westphal, Merold 345n5
Willaschek, Marcus 4, 130–9
Wille 10, 18, 152, 290; *see also* will, the
Williams, Bernard 388
Williams, Howard Lloyd 360, 541, 551; on Doctrine of Right 4, 298–307
will, the: arbitrary 306; causality by means of 62; determination of 226; moral-mindedness of 411; noumenal 17; regulation of 12; see also good will
Williamson, T. 103
Wittgenstein, L. 64, 103, 513
Wolff, Christian 15, 26, 34–8, 139n1, 433; *Auszug* 488; on content of morality being grasped through reason 168; doctrine of right and virtue of 293; focus on the will in general 147; Halle, dismissal from post at 39; Kant's attack on 295, 344; metaphysics 485; on metaphysics, Kant's citation of 59–60; perfectionism of 170; "*Philosophia practica universalis*" 293
Wolffian Academy 11
Wolffianism 11
Wolterstorff, Nicholas 345n11
Wood, Allen 152, 176n3, 488; on Formula of Humanity 537n3; on Idea of History 5, 349–58, 360, 378; on "minimum of theology" 538n23; on Pasternack's attempt to 'dismantle to conundrum' 326, 332n9; on Rawls 550; on republicanism 543–4; on theory of religion 324, 325, 326, 327, 328; on understanding of evil 328; *verzeichnen*, translation of 221n21

Zangwill, Nick 563
Zoeller, W. 360